The Hague Peace Conferences

---

and Other International Conferences
Concerning the Laws and Usages of
War - Texts of Conventions
with Commentaries

ALEXANDER PEARCE HIGGINS

COSIMOCLASSICS

NEW YORK

Soldiers, and other persons officially attached to armies, shall be respected and taken care of when wounded or sick, by the belligerent in whose power they may be, without distinction of nationality.

(Cp. G. C. 1864, Art. 6.)

Nevertheless, a belligerent who is compelled to abandon sick or wounded to the enemy shall, as far as military exigencies permit, leave with them a portion of his medical personnel and material to contribute to the care of them.

from C hapter I, Article I

PREFACE

IN 1904 I published translations of the Declarations of Paris and St Petersburg, the Convention of Geneva, 1864, the draft Brussels Declaration, 1874, and the Conventions signed at the First Peace Conference, together with a short introduction and a few notes. I did so chiefly for the sake of students attending my lectures in Cambridge, as, at that time, there was not to my knowledge any one book in which the English texts of these important international documents could be found. The present work contains in addition to the French texts of the foregoing (except the Brussels Declaration) the French and English versions of the Geneva Convention of 1906, the Final Act and Conventions of the Second Peace Conference, 1907, and the London Naval Conference of 1909. I have also included in my commentary on Convention No. 10 of the Hague Conference, 1907 (10 H. C. 1907), a translation of the Convention signed at the Hague on the 21st Dec. 1904, exempting hospital ships from state port dues and taxes in the ports of the signatory Powers. Great Britain is not a party to this Convention. The Conventions of the First Conference as amended by the Second are printed in parallel columns, the changes being shown in italics, and cross-references occur throughout. The French texts have been taken from the official sources, and in the case of the Hague Conventions of 1907 they have throughout been carefully compared with the texts contained in *La Deuxième Conférence Internationale de la Paix* published by the Dutch Government. As regards the translations, I have made the British official translations the basis of my work[1]: I have however in nearly all cases compared them with those contained either in Mr E. A. Whittuck's *International Documents*, Professor James Brown Scott's *Texts of the Peace Conferences at the Hague*, 1899 *and* 1907 (which contains the official United States translations), Professor T. E. Holland's *Laws of war on land*, Dr Westlake's *International Law, War*, or General G. B. Davis's *Elements of International Law*. In the case of the Declaration of London, I have adhered to the official translation with a few exceptions. To each of the Conventions I have appended a commentary

---

[1] In the case of the Conventions of 1899 which were revised in 1907 the translations of the portions common to both Conventions as given in *Parl. Papers*, Misc. No. 1 (1899), Misc. Nos. 1 and 6 (1908) show considerable variations; similarly the translations of all the Hague Conventions of 1907, contained in the last two Parliamentary Papers, differ considerably.

in which I have given an account of its origin, and its relation to the general rules of law on the subject with which it deals. In the case of the Hague Conventions, which form the greater portion of this volume, I have endeavoured from the official records, and more particularly from the Reports presented to the Conferences by the various Committees, to ascertain the meaning which their framers intended them to have. In the case of the Conventions of 1899 I have generally limited myself to the changes made by the Conference of 1907, as those Conventions have already been fully dealt with by various writers. In the case of the Geneva Convention of 1906 I have confined myself to calling attention to the chief changes made in that of 1864, referring students for a fuller explanation of the Convention to the work of Professor Holland cited above. In the case of the Declaration of London the commentary is supplied by the official translation of the General Report presented to the Naval Conference prepared by M. Renault on behalf of the drafting Committee, to which I have added a few footnotes. I have in each case appended a list of books and articles dealing with the subject under discussion: the lists are in no case exhaustive, but are intended to assist students, for whom this work is primarily intended, in following up their examination of the questions dealt with.

The two final volumes of the official account of the Second Peace Conference, *La Deuxième Conférence Internationale de la Paix* (cited throughout this work as *La Deux. Confér.*), were not published until a large part of this book was in the press; I therefore relied chiefly in the early portions on the excellent Reports to the Conference contained in the first volume, and in *Parliamentary Papers*, Miscellaneous, No. 4 (1908) [Cd. 4081]. I also derived considerable assistance from the valuable work of M. Ernest Lémonon, *La seconde Conférence de la Paix*, and the reports of the proceedings of the Conference in *The Times*. Professor J. B. Scott's lectures on *The Hague Peace Conferences of* 1899 *and* 1907 were published too late to be of any use to me except in regard to the last two Conventions. Sir Thomas Barclay's *Problems of International Practice and Diplomacy* (cited as *Problems, etc.*) has afforded me assistance on nearly all the subjects dealt with. I have endeavoured to acknowledge the sources of my information in all cases.

In the Chapter on the Hague Conferences of 1899 and 1907 (pp. 39–59) I have traced the working of the Conventions of 1899 and given an account of the cases which have come before the Permanent Arbitration

Court; in the commentary on the Final Acts of the Conferences I have discussed the *Vœux* adopted and in the Chapter on the Results of the Second Peace Conference (pp. 518-526) I have summarised the work of the Second Peace Conference.

I have appended a list of the signatory States at the conclusion of the commentary on each Convention as well as Tables of signatory States of the Conventions of both Conferences. It is important to remember that none of the Conventions of the Second Peace Conference have up to the present been ratified, the United States of America and San Salvador being the only Powers which have notified the Netherland Government that they are ready to ratify the Conventions: the Declaration of London also has not at present been ratified by any of the signatory Powers.

The delay in publication has been due largely to personal causes, but also to the desire to include the results of the London Naval Conference, which complete in many important points work which the Hague Conference of 1907 found itself unable to bring to a conclusion.

I have to thank His Majesty's Controller of the Stationery Department and the British Foreign Office for allowing me to make use of their translations, and to make quotations from the various Government publications referred to in the notes, particularly for permission to reproduce the Instructions to the British Delegates at the Second Peace Conference and the translations of the Declaration of London and M. Renault's Report, and for affording me other assistance. I have also to thank the Foreign Offices of the Netherlands and Switzerland, and the Secretary-General of the Permanent Court of Arbitration at the Hague for courteously furnishing me with information and official lists of signatory Powers, and in the case of the last-named for copies of the Minutes of the cases heard before the Permanent Court. To my friend Mr A. H. Charteris, M.A., LL.B., Lecturer in International Law in the University of Glasgow, I am under special obligation, as not only has he kindly read the whole of the proof sheets, but he has also made many valuable suggestions both as regards the translations and commentary. I have to thank the staff, readers and printers of the University Press for their careful and courteous co-operation.

A. PEARCE HIGGINS.

CAMBRIDGE,
September, 1909.

TABLE OF CONTENTS

		PAGE
Preface		v
Table of Contents		viii
List of Cases cited		x
Introduction		xi
Declaration of Paris		1
Commentary		3
Declaration of St Petersburg		5
Commentary		7
Geneva Convention 1864		8
Commentary		12
Draft of Additional Articles (Geneva) 1868		14
Geneva Convention 1906		18
Commentary		35
The Peace Conference of 1899		39
The Second Peace Conference of 1907		51
Final Acts of the International Peace Conferences		60
Commentary		72
I. Conventions for the pacific settlement of international disputes 1899 and 1907		95
Commentary		164
II. Convention respecting the limitation of the employment of force for the recovery of contract debts		180
Commentary		184
III. Convention relative to the commencement of hostilities		198
Commentary		202
IV. Conventions concerning the laws and customs of war on land (1899 and 1907)		206
Commentary		256
The Brussels Draft Declaration 1874		273
V. Convention respecting the rights and duties of neutral Powers and persons in war on land		281
Commentary		290
VI. Convention relative to the status of enemy merchant-ships at the outbreak of hostilities		295
Commentary		300

VII. Convention relative to the conversion of merchant-ships into war-ships . 308
    Commentary 312

VIII. Convention relative to the laying of automatic submarine contact mines 322
    Commentary 328

IX. Convention respecting bombardment by naval forces in time of war . 346
    Commentary 352

X. Conventions for the adaptation of the principles of the Geneva Convention to maritime war (1899 and 1907) 358
    Commentary 382
    Convention relating to hospital ships of 21 December, 1904 . . 392

XI. Convention relative to certain restrictions on the exercise of the right of capture in maritime war 395
    Commentary 401

XII. Convention relative to the establishment of an International Prize Court 407
    Commentary 431

XIII. Convention respecting the rights and duties of neutral Powers in maritime war 445
    Commentary 457

XIV. Declarations (1899 and 1907) prohibiting discharge of projectiles, etc. from balloons 484
    Commentary 488

    Declaration II (1899) prohibiting the use of asphyxiating gases . . 491
    Commentary 493

    Declaration III (1899) prohibiting the use of bullets with a hard envelope 494
    Commentary 495

    Draft Convention relative to the creation of a Judicial Arbitration Court 498
    Commentary 509

    The Results of the Second Peace Conference 518

    List of signatory Powers of the Conventions of the First Peace Conference 527

    List of signatory Powers of the Conventions of the Second Peace Conference 530

    Final Protocol of the London Naval Conference 538

    Declaration of London 540

    General Report presented to the Naval Conference on behalf of the Drafting Committee 567

    Appendix. Instructions of British Delegates to the Second Peace Conference 614

    Addenda and Errata 626

    Index 627

LIST OF CASES CITED

	PAGE			PAGE
Actaeon.	90	Lola		403
Alabama	387	Malacca		315
Amy Warwick	431	Manjur.		471
Anna	461	Muscat Dhows Arbitration.		48
Anne	461	Nashville		473
Aryol	385	Novara.		405
Askold.	474	Oldhamia		91
Aurora.	474	Oleg		474
Boedes Lust.	300	Orel		385
Buena Ventura	301	Panama		401
Czarewitch	474	Paquette Habana		403, 404
Diana	474	Peterburg		315
Dogger Bank Inquiry.	167	Pious Fund of the Californias		
Eliza Ann	461	Arbitration		44
Felicity.	90	Ryeshitelni		463
Florida.	437, 461, 463	St Kilda		91
General Armstrong	462	Santissima Trinidad		317
Gran Para	317	Sir William Wallace		437
Grosovoi	474	Smolensk		315
Hip-sang	91	Terek		474
Ikhoma	91	Thea		91
Japanese Leases Arbitration	48	Tuscarora		473
Johanna Emilie	300	Variag		390
Knight-Commander	91	Venezuelan Arbitration		46
Korietz.	390	Young Jacob and Joanna		403
Lena	471	Zamtchug		474
Leucade	90			

INTRODUCTION

DURING the past fifty years attempts have been made by means of international Conferences to arrive at a definite understanding with reference to various rules of international law, and more particularly those relating to war, for notwithstanding nearly twenty centuries of Christian teaching, war still remains the final arbiter of nations. Arbitration treaties have, however, been increasing rapidly, and the peoples of the world are looking with growing favour on a pacific settlement of international disputes. The various Peace Societies, the Federations of Parliamentary Delegates, the Unions of workers of all classes and the great International Bureaux for posts, telegraphs, money, etc. are all assisting to bring about a greater freedom of inter-communication of ideas, and a larger conception of the oneness of humanity. Such organisations may, in the course of time, succeed in breaking down rooted national prejudices, and removing ambitious aspirations; meantime, however, these two forces are potent, and the era of perpetual peace is still far distant. The development of international law has been in the past and is still following in a striking manner the order of evolution of national laws, and progress is undoubtedly marked by the endeavours, increasingly successful, to regularise the methods to be adopted when peaceful methods of solving international disputes have failed, and the lists are set and "princes and states that acknowledge no superior on earth put themselves on the justice of God for the deciding of their controversies by such success as it shall please Him to give to either side." Bacon's idea of war bears a strong resemblance to that which underlay the judicial combat in England: "it was no appeal to brute force; it was an appeal to the God of battles[1]." Litigants in civil cases have, however, moved a long way from the position in which states still find themselves; self-help, even regulated self-help, has nearly, if not quite, ceased to exist in civilised communities

[1] F. W. Maitland, *Social England*, Vol. i. p. 414.

which live under the rule of law; but in the domain of international differences, forcible self-redress and the peaceful settlement of disputed questions still exist side by side. The attempt at the Second Peace Conference to formulate a Convention for the compulsory submission to arbitration of even the simplest questions failed of achievement. The Society of Nations, as such, was not yet ready for the interposition of the International Praetor with his "Mittite ambo hominem," though it readily acknowledged the value of the principle.

The results of the various Conferences which are set forth in the following pages all tend in one direction. They are attempts, for the most part only partially successful and characterised by all the defects inherent to compromises wherein the political aspirations of the various states of the world have been sought to be adjusted, to bring into existence a code of rules which shall be universally recognised as binding on belligerents and neutrals, failing a peaceful settlement of their quarrels. Self-help is recognised, but it is gradually being regulated, and alongside this regulated self-help there has been provided a method for peaceful settlement by the creation of the Hague Tribunal. These international Acts also register the desire that should war break out, peaceful intercourse between belligerents and neutrals shall be disturbed as little as possible, and the sufferings of those involved minimised.

Many of these Conventions represent the first attempt at an international agreement on the subjects with which they deal, in other cases they are the results of more mature deliberation, and their practical value has been tested by time and the trying ordeal of war.

The question is often put as to the value of Conventions regulating the conduct of war—Will they stand the test of a life and death struggle of nations? Will not the written laws of war be set aside and the necessities of war excuse acts which the laws of war condemn? It is recognised in several of the following Conventions that the rules they enunciate are to be observed "so far as military necessities permit"; the rules themselves represent the standard of conduct at which commanders are to aim, but, as practical men, the delegates have recognised that there must be some cases when the observance in the strict letter of the provisions will be impossible[1]. It is with the view of diminishing the evils of war "so far as military necessities permit" that the signatory Powers have adopted the Regulations on the laws and customs of war on land. No legislation can specify beforehand the precise circumstances which would justify a commander

---

[1] See G. C. 1906, Arts. 1, 15; 4 H. C. 1907, preamble, Art. 54; 9 H. C. 1907, Arts. 2, 6; Declaration of London, Art. 49.

in failing to act on the rules laid down, but no circumstances can justify the violation of the fundamental principle of these rules, which prohibit the infliction of needless suffering to individuals and mere wanton destruction of property[1]. The laws of war set forth in the following pages are binding on the parties to the Conventions; they were made to be observed and good faith is predicated of all international agreements. The practice of states in recent wars bears striking witness to the power of law under severe trial. There were some complaints of breaches of the laws of war, and in the Russo-Japanese war neutrals had occasion to enter strong protests against some of the Russian practices; but the latter had reference to the unwritten laws of naval warfare. The breaches of universally accepted rules of war which have been definitely and conclusively proved to have been committed during recent years have been few. International law works, notwithstanding the absence of the Austinian sanction. The rule of right operates apart from the terrors of punishment, and the more highly civilised states become, the more complete their acceptance of the "perfect law of liberty," the more will they act the law they live by without fear. The moral force of the solemn promise of a nation should be enough to secure the observance of its international obligations, but besides this, there is another factor no state can afford to neglect which has become of increasing importance during the past half century, namely the public opinion of the world. International law is based on the practice of civilised states in their dealings with each other, and such practice is the embodiment in action of the moral consciousness of communities. Public opinion is one of the great formative influences of the law of nations, and an educated public opinion in each state is at the same time one of the safeguards for the due observance of international law and the best guarantee for an equitable solution of the difficulties which international Conventions have failed to solve. International law-breakers are in the long run arraigned at the bar of humanity, and history records their sentences. It is said that when Germany was asked by Thiers after the fall of the Second Empire "A qui donc faites-vous la guerre?" von Ranke, calling to mind the horrors of the ravages of the Palatinate, replied "A Louis XIV!"[2] Might is not necessarily Right in international or national law; the generation that witnesses a gross violation of the law of nations will not often see the punishment which follows, "Raro antecedentem scelestum Deseruit pede Pœna claudo."

[1] See T. E. Holland, *The Laws of War on Land*, p. 13; L. Oppenheim, *International Law*, Vol. II. § 69; J. Westlake, *War*, p. 115.

[2] See F. Despagnet, *Droit international public* (5th ed.), § 89 (on the sanction of International Law).

Law, be it national or international, must always wait on and fall short of the highest standards of morality current among those governed by it. The record of the growth of the conventional law of nations as evidenced by the international treaties contained in the following pages is far from satisfying the aspirations of the idealist, but it shows a steady, if slow progress towards a more clearly defined system of the rules regulating the intercourse of nations whether as belligerents or neutrals; it also shows the beginnings of an international judicature for the peaceful settlement of disputes, and affords reasonable ground for the hope that the Court established at the Hague in 1899 may ere long become permanent both in fact and in name. States have at last begun to take in hand the work of clearing up difficulties, settling disputed points and preparing the way for a systematic statement of the rules of international law.

The political antagonisms and unconcealed jealousies of states are factors of supreme importance in considering the future of international law, but the record of the past shows an increasing sense of the solidarity of the human race and the gradual elevation of the ideal of international justice. A study of what has been achieved may be of assistance in stimulating those moral aims which shall in the future make war increasingly difficult, and reduce to a minimum the sufferings of those involved.

DECLARATION OF PARIS, 1856[1]

Déclaration de Paris, 1856.

Les Plénipotentiaires qui ont signé le Traité de Paris du trente Mars, mil huit cent cinquante-six, réunis en Conférence,—

Considérant :

Que le droit maritime, en temps de guerre, a été pendant longtemps l'objet de contestations regrettables :

Que l'incertitude du droit et des devoirs en pareille matière, donne lieu, entre les neutres et les belligérants, à des divergences d'opinion qui peuvent faire naître des difficultés sérieuses et même des conflits :

Qu'il y a avantage, par conséquent, à établir une doctrine uniforme sur un point aussi important :

Que les Plénipotentiaires assemblés au Congrès de Paris ne sauraient mieux répondre aux intentions dont leurs Gouvernements sont animés, qu'en cherchant à introduire dans les

The Declaration of Paris, 1856.

The Plenipotentiaries who signed the Treaty of Paris of the 30th March, 1856, assembled in conference,—

Considering :

That maritime law, in time of war, has long been the subject of deplorable disputes :

That the uncertainty of the law and of the duties [of states] in such a matter gives rise to differences of opinion between neutrals and belligerents which may occasion serious difficulties and even conflicts :

That it is consequently advantageous to establish a uniform doctrine on so important a point :

That the Plenipotentiaries assembled in Congress at Paris cannot better respond to the intentions by which their Governments are animated than by seeking to introduce into inter-

---

[1] *British State Papers*, 1856, Vol. LXI. p. 155 ; De Martens, *Nouveau Recueil de Traités*, Vol. XV. p. 731 ; Hertslet, *Map of Europe by Treaty*, Vol. II. p. 1282 ; Twiss, *International Law*, Vol. II. p. 512 ; Phillimore, *International Law*, Vol. III. pp. 11, 302, 359 ; Halleck, *International Law*, Vol. II. pp. 81, 117, 118 ; Maine, *International Law*, Chap. VI. ; J. Westlake, *War*, pp. 128, 154, 228, 304 ; Wheaton (Atlay's edition), *International Law*, pp. 491, 503, 648, 691 ; Hall (5th ed.), *International Law*, pp. 526, 691, 713, 718 ; T. J. Lawrence, *International Law*, pp. 386, 408, 431-5, 567-571 ; J. B. Scott, *Leading Cases in International Law*, pp. 898-901 (notes) ; H. Taylor, *International Law*, pp. 440, 513, 516, 722 ; N. Bentwich, *Private property in War*, pp. 15, 50, 79, 105 ; T. Gibson Bowles, *The Declaration of Paris* (1900) ; L. Oppenheim, *International Law*, Vol. II. pp. 93, 183-6, 339, 406 ; E. Nys, *Le droit international*, Vol. III. pp. 189-197, 234 ; J. B. Moore, *Digest of International Law*, Vol. V. p. 195 ; Vol. VII. pp. 561-583 ; Sir T. Barclay, *Problems of International Practice and Diplomacy*, pp. 102, 206.

rapports internationaux des principes fixes à cet égard :

Dûment autorisés, les susdits Pléni-potentiaires sont convenus de se concerter sur les moyens d'atteindre ce but ; et étant tombés d'accord ont arrêté la Déclaration solennelle ci-après :—

1. La course est et demeure abolie :

2. Le pavillon neutre couvre la marchandise ennemie, à l'exception de la contrebande de guerre :

3. La marchandise neutre, à l'exception de la contrebande de guerre, n'est pas saisissable sous pavillon ennemi :

4. Les blocus, pour être obligatoires, doivent être effectifs, c'est-à-dire, maintenus par une force suffisante pour interdire réellement l'accès du littoral de l'ennemi.

Les Gouvernements des Plénipotentiaires soussignés s'engagent à porter cette Déclaration à la connaissance des États qui n'ont pas été appelés à participer au Congrès de Paris, et à les inviter à y accéder.

Convaincus que les maximes qu'ils viennent de proclamer ne sauraient être accueillies qu'avec gratitude par le monde entier, les Plénipotentiaires soussignés ne doutent pas que les efforts de leurs Gouvernements pour en généraliser l'adoption ne soient couronnés d'un plein succès.

La présente Déclaration n'est et ne sera obligatoire qu'entre les Puissances, qui y ont, ou qui y auront accédé.

Fait à Paris, le seize Avril, mil huit cent cinquante-six.

national relations fixed principles in this respect:

The above-mentioned Plenipotentiaries, being duly authorised, resolved to concert among themselves as to the means of attaining this object ; and, having come to an agreement, have adopted the following solemn Declaration :—

1. Privateering is and remains abolished :

2. The neutral flag covers enemy's goods, with the exception of contraband of war :

3. Neutral goods, with the exception of contraband of war, are not liable to capture under enemy's flag :

4. Blockades, in order to be binding, must be effective ; that is to say maintained by a force sufficient really to prevent access to the enemy's coastline.

The Governments of the undersigned Plenipotentiaries engage to bring the present Declaration to the knowledge of the States which have not been called upon to take part in the Congress of Paris, and invite them to accede to it.

Convinced that the maxims which they now proclaim cannot but be received with gratitude by the whole world, the undersigned Plenipotentiaries doubt not that the efforts of their Governments to obtain the general adoption thereof will be crowned with full success.

The present Declaration is not and shall not be binding except between those powers who have acceded or shall accede to it.

Done at Paris, April 16th, 1856.

The signatory Powers to the Treaty of Paris were Great Britain, Austria, France, Russia, Sardinia, and Turkey.

At the same time the following Protocol recorded that "on the "proposition of Count Walewski [the senior French Plenipotentiary], and "recognising that it is for the general interest to maintain the indivisi-"bility of the four principles mentioned in the Declaration signed this "day, the Plenipotentiaries agree that the Powers which shall have signed "it or which shall have acceded to it, cannot hereafter enter into any "arrangement in regard to the application of the right of neutrals in time "of war which does not at the same time rest on the four principles which "are the object of the said Declaration. Upon an observation made by "the Plenipotentiaries of Russia, the Congress recognises that as the "present resolution cannot have a retroactive effect it cannot invalidate "antecedent Conventions[1]."

The outbreak of the Crimean War in 1854 found the two Allied Powers, Great Britain and France, with different principles as to the maritime law of capture. Great Britain adhered to the rule of the *Consolato del Mare* which rendered enemy property, ship or cargo capturable, neutral property, ship or cargo being free. France, except where otherwise bound by treaty, was free to act on the maxim "robe d'ennemi confisque robe d'ami," by which neutral goods on board enemy ships and neutral ships carrying enemy goods were liable to capture[2]. The Allied Powers notified that throughout the war they would not capture enemy goods on neutral ships, or neutral goods on enemy ships: they further intimated that they would not issue Letters of Marque. These practices, which at first were only intended to apply to the war then in progress, were embodied in this famous Declaration.

The only maritime Powers which, up to the assembling of the Hague Conference of 1907, had withheld their formal acceptance of this Declaration were the United States, Spain, Mexico, Venezuela, Bolivia and Uruguay. The United States during the Civil War of 1861, and Spain and the United States during the war of 1898, adhered to its principles. The refusal of the United States to formally adhere was due to the rejection of the "Marcy Amendment" exempting private property from capture at sea[3]. At the Seventh Plenary Meeting of the Hague Conference on the 27th Sept. 1907, the delegates of Spain and Mexico, in voting on the Convention (No. 7) relative to the conversion of merchant ships into war ships[4], declared that

[1] *British State Papers* (1856), Vol. LXI. p. 150.
[2] See J. Westlake, *War*, pp. 120–8.
[3] J. B. Moore, *Digest of International Law*, Vol. VII. p. 563.
[4] See *post*, p. 808.

their governments adhered to the Declaration of Paris in its entirety[1]. The first paragraph of the Declaration will be dealt with in relation to this Convention. The absence of a definition of contraband of war and the divergence in the practice of maritime states in regard to blockade have caused the Declaration to have had only a modified application[2], while the adoption of the contention that the sinking of neutral prizes is lawful if the captor cannot spare men for a prize crew would result in a practical abrogation of the freedom accorded to neutrals by the third paragraph.

The Fourth Committee of the Hague Conference of 1907 considered the questions of contraband and blockade. On the former subject, five different proposals were brought before the Committee, the most noteworthy being the British for the complete abolition of contraband of war. This proposal received 26 votes, 5 states voted against, and 4 abstained from voting. The question was then submitted to a special Sub-Committee: but as there appeared to be no prospect of a unanimous vote, the Fourth Committee reported to the 7th Plenary Meeting of the Conference that the whole question should be submitted to a fresh examination by the states interested[3].

The discussion on the subject of blockade shewed so great a divergence between the extreme Continental view as embodied in a proposal of the Italian delegate, and the Anglo-American view as embodied in a proposal of the British and United States delegates, that on the proposition of Sir Edward Fry the further consideration of the matter was suspended[4].

The subject of the destruction of neutral prizes was discussed at the Hague Conference in 1907, and is dealt with subsequently[5].

A Conference of certain Powers interested in questions affecting maritime warfare on the invitation of the British Government met in London in December, 1908, for a further discussion of questions left unsolved by the Hague Conference[6].

---

[1] *Parl. Papers*, Misc. No. 4 (1908), p. 48. *La Deuxième Conférence Internationale de la Paix*, T. 1. (*Actes et Documents*), p. 234.

[2] J. Westlake, *War*, pp. 228–232.

[3] *Parl. Papers*, pp. 194–6. *La Deux. Confér.* T. 1. pp. 256–260.

[4] *Parl. Papers*, pp. 197–8. *La Deux. Confér.* T. 1. p. 262.

[5] See *post*, p. 89; also pp. 557, 597.

[6] See *post*, p. 540.

DECLARATION OF ST PETERSBURG, 1868[1]

Sur la proposition du Cabinet Impérial de Russie, une Commission Militaire Internationale ayant été réunie à Saint-Pétersbourg, afin d'examiner la convenance d'interdire l'usage de certains projectiles en temps de guerre entre les nations civilisées, et cette Commission ayant fixé d'un commun accord les limites techniques où les nécessités de la guerre doivent s'arrêter devant les exigences de l'humanité, les Soussignés sont autorisés par les ordres de leurs Gouvernements à déclarer ce qui suit :

Considérant que les progrès de la civilisation doivent avoir pour effet d'atténuer autant que possible les calamités de la guerre ;

Que le seul but légitime que les Etats doivent se proposer durant la guerre est l'affaiblissement des forces militaires de l'ennemi ;

Qu'à cet effet, il suffit de mettre hors de combat le plus grand nombre d'hommes possible ;

Que ce but serait dépassé par l'emploi

On the proposition of the Imperial Cabinet of Russia, an International Military Commission having assembled at St Petersburg in order to examine into the expediency of forbidding the use of certain projectiles in time of war between civilized nations, and that Commission, having by common agreement fixed the technical limits at which the necessities of war ought to yield to the requirements of humanity, the Undersigned are authorized by the orders of their Governments to declare as follows:

Considering that the progress of civilization should have the effect of alleviating as much as possible the calamities of war;

That the only legitimate object which States should endeavour to accomplish during war is to weaken the military forces of the enemy;

That for this purpose it is sufficient to disable the greatest possible number of men;

That this object would be exceeded

---

[1] *Parliamentary Papers* (1869), Vol. LXIV. p. 659 ; De Martens, *Nouveau Recueil de Traités*, Vol. XVIII. pp. 450–474 ; T. E. Holland, *The Laws of War on Land*, pp. 3, 4, 12, 41, 77, 141 ; Idem, *Studies, etc.* p. 66 ; F. Despagnet, *Cours de droit inter.* p. 567 ; W. E. Hall, *Int. Law*, p. 532 ; Halleck, *Int. Law*, Vol. I. p. 563 ; T. J. Lawrence, *Int. Law*, pp. 438–9 ; A. Mérignhac, *Lois et coutumes de la guerre*, p. 150 ; E. Nys, *Le droit inter.* Vol. III. p. 162 ; L. Oppenheim, *Int. Law*, Vol. II. p. 118 ; A. Rivier, *Droit inter.* Vol. II. p. 261 ; T. A. Walker, *Principles of Int. Law*, p. 330 ; J. Westlake, *War*, pp. 53, 72.

d'armes qui aggraveraient inutilement les souffrances des hommes mis hors de combat, ou rendraient leur mort inévitable ;

Que l'emploi de pareilles armes serait dès lors contraire aux lois de l'humanité ;

Les Parties Contractantes s'engagent à renoncer mutuellement, en cas de guerre entre elles, à l'emploi par leurs troupes de terre ou de mer, de tout projectile d'un poids inférieur à 400 grammes qui serait ou explosible ou chargé de matières fulminantes ou inflammables.

Elles inviteront tous les Etats, qui n'ont pas participé par l'envoi de Délégués aux délibérations de la Commission Militaire Internationale réunie à Saint-Pétersbourg, à accéder au présent engagement.

Cet engagement n'est obligatoire que pour les Parties Contractantes ou Accédantes en cas de guerre entre deux ou plusieurs d'entre elles : il n'est pas applicable vis-à-vis de Parties non-Contractantes ou qui n'auraient pas accédé.

Il cesserait également d'être obligatoire du moment où, dans une guerre entre Parties Contractantes ou Accédantes, une partie non-Contractante, ou qui n'aurait pas accédé, se joindrait à l'un des belligérants.

Les Parties Contractantes ou Accédantes se réservent de s'entendre ultérieurement toutes les fois qu'une proposition précise serait formulée en vue des perfectionnements à venir que la science pourrait apporter dans l'armement des troupes, afin de maintenir les principes qu'elles ont posés et de

by the employment of arms which uselessly aggravate the sufferings of disabled men, or render their death inevitable;

That the employment of such arms would, therefore, be contrary to the laws of humanity;

The Contracting Parties engage mutually to renounce, in case of war among themselves, the employment by their military or naval troops of any projectile of a weight below 400 grammes[1], which is either explosive or charged with fulminating or inflammable substances.

They will invite all the States which have not taken part in the deliberations of the International Military Commission assembled at St Petersburg, by sending Delegates thereto, to accede to the present engagement.

This engagement is obligatory only upon the Contracting or Acceding Parties thereto, in case of war between two or more of themselves; it is not applicable with regard to non-Contracting Parties or Parties who shall not have acceded to it.

It will also cease to be obligatory from the moment when, in a war between Contracting or Acceding Parties, a non-Contracting Party or a non-Acceding Party shall join one of the belligerents.

The Contracting or Acceding Parties reserve to themselves to come hereafter to an understanding whenever a precise proposition shall be drawn up in view of future improvements which science may effect in the armament of troops, in order to maintain the principles which they have established, and

[1] About 14 ounces avoirdupois.

concilier les nécessités de la guerre
avec les lois de l'humanité.

    Fait à Saint - Pétersbourg, le vingt-neuf Novembre onze Décembre, mil huit cent soixante-huit.

to conciliate the necessities of war with the laws of humanity.

    Done at St Petersburg, the 29 Nov. 11 Dec. 1868.

    The Conference at St Petersburg which was summoned by the Emperor Alexander II. was composed of military delegates from the following Powers who signed the Convention:—Great Britain, Austria and Hungary, Bavaria, Belgium, Denmark, France, Greece, Italy, The Netherlands, Persia, Portugal, Prussia and the North German Confederation, Russia, Sweden and Norway, Switzerland, Turkey, and Würtemberg. Baden and Brazil subsequently acceded to the Declaration.

    The reasons for the summoning of the Conference at St Petersburg are set forth in a Memorandum which the military delegates took into consideration. From this it appears that in 1863 a bullet had been introduced with a cap which exploded on contact with a hard substance. The object of the-bullet was to blow up military and ammunition wagons when the bullet was fired from a short distance. In 1867 a modification was introduced which enabled the bullet to explode on contact with a soft substance. General Milutine the Russian War Minister induced his government to summon a conference of military delegates to see if an agreement could be arrived at in reference to the use of such explosive bullets. The Prussian delegate was prepared to discuss the wider question of weapons, but the other delegates were opposed to this, and ultimately the Declaration was agreed to as set forth above[1].

    The Declaration of St Petersburg is the first formal agreement restricting the use of weapons of war, both in land and maritime warfare. The statement of the reasons for this restriction is marked by a high feeling of humanity. War is necessarily productive of great pain to the combatants, and the civilised world has agreed that it is inhuman to "uselessly aggravate the sufferings of disabled men." This Declaration is by reference incorporated into the Regulations respecting the laws and customs of war on land annexed to the Conventions on this subject adopted by both the Hague Conferences (Art. 23), and similar humane principles prompted the Three Declarations of the Conference of 1899. Although general principles are enunciated in the preamble to the Declaration the application made at the time was a limited one, and appears to be practically obsolete; but the fact of the adoption of these principles is of great importance; a standard has been set, which it is to be hoped no civilised state will in the future fail to reach.

---

[1] For Protocols see De Martens, *Recueil, etc.* Vol. xviii. pp. 450–474.

GENEVA CONVENTION, 1864[1]

Convention pour l'amélioration du sort des militaires blessés dans les armées en campagne.

Convention for the amelioration of the condition of soldiers wounded in armies in the field.

La Confédération suisse, S.A.R. le Grand-Duc de Bade, S.M. le Roi des Belges, S.M. le Roi de Danemark, S.M. la Reine d'Espagne, S.M. l'Empereur des Français, S.A.R. le Grand-Duc de Hesse, S.M. le Roi d'Italie, S.M. le Roi des Pays-Bas, S.M. le Roi de Portugal et des Algarves, S.M. le Roi de Prusse, S.M. le Roi de Wurtemberg—également animés du désir d'adoucir, autant qu'il dépend d'eux, les maux inséparables de la guerre, de supprimer les rigueurs inutiles, et d'améliorer le sort des militaires blessés sur les champs de bataille, ont résolu de conclure une Convention à cet effet et ont nommé pour leurs Plénipotentiaires, savoir :

The Swiss Confederation, His Royal Highness the Grand Duke of Baden, His Majesty the King of the Belgians, His Majesty the King of Denmark, Her Majesty the Queen of Spain, His Majesty the Emperor of the French, His Royal Highness the Grand Duke of Hesse, His Majesty the King of Italy, His Majesty the King of the Netherlands, His Majesty the King of Portugal and the Algarves, His Majesty the King of Prussia, His Majesty the King of Wurtemberg, being equally animated by the desire to mitigate, as far as depends upon them, the evils inseparable from war, to suppress useless severities, and to ameliorate the condition of soldiers wounded on the field of battle, have resolved to conclude a Convention for that purpose, and have named as their Plenipotentiaries, that is to say :

(Suivent les noms des Plénipotentiaires.)

(Here follow the names of the Plenipotentiaries.)

---

[1] *British State Papers,* 1865, Vol. LVII. p. 471 ; G. F. de Martens, *Nouveau Recueil de Traités,* Vol. XVIII. p. 607 ; Vol. XX. pp. 375–399 ; Holtzendorff, *Handbuch des Völkerrechts,* Vol. IV. §§ 74–77 ; Bluntschli, *Das Völkerrecht,* pp. 329 *et seq.* § 586 ; Despagnet, pp. 585–8 ; Mérignhac, *Les lois et coutumes de la guerre sur terre,* pp. 114–139 ; Hall, pp. 401–6 ; Lawrence, pp. 338, 339, 491–3 ; T. E. Holland, *Studies in International Law,* pp. 61–65 ; Idem, *The Laws and Customs of War on Land,* pp. 18–27 (containing commentary on this Convention) ; Halleck, Vol. II. p. 36 ; Wheaton, p. 474 ; Maine, p. 156 ; T. A. Walker, *Science of International Law,* pp. 357–362 ; H. Taylor, § 528 ; J. Westlake, *War,* pp. 60–72 ; L. Oppenheim, Vol. II. pp. 123–8 ; J. B. Moore, *Digest of International Law,* Vol. II. p. 474 ; Vol. VII. p. 235.

Lesquels, après avoir échangé leurs pouvoirs, trouvés en bonne et due forme, sont convenus des articles suivants :

1. Les ambulances et les hôpitaux militaires seront reconnus neutres, et, comme tels, protégés et respectés par les belligérants, aussi longtemps qu'il s'y trouvera des malades ou des blessés.

La neutralité cesserait si ces ambulances ou ces hôpitaux étaient gardés par une force militaire.

2. Le personnel des hôpitaux et des ambulances, comprenant l'intendance, les services de santé, d'administration, de transport des blessés, ainsi que les aumôniers, participera au bénéfice de la neutralité lorsqu'il fonctionnera, et tant qu'il restera des blessés à relever ou à secourir.

3. Les personnes désignées dans l'article précédent pourront, même après l'occupation par l'ennemi, continuer à remplir leurs fonctions dans l'hôpital ou l'ambulance qu'elles desservent, ou se retirer pour rejoindre le corps auquel elles appartiennent.

Dans ces circonstances, lorsque ces personnes cesseront leurs fonctions, elles seront remises aux avant-postes ennemis par les soins de l'armée occupante.

4. Le matériel des hôpitaux militaires demeurant soumis aux lois de la guerre, les personnes attachées à ces hôpitaux ne pourront, en se retirant,

Who, after having exchanged their powers, found in good and due form, have agreed upon the following articles:

1. Ambulances and military hospitals shall be recognised as neutral, and, as such, shall be protected and respected by the belligerents, so long as any sick or wounded may be therein.

Such neutrality shall cease if these ambulances or hospitals shall be held by a military force.

(*Cp. G. C.* 1906, *Arts.* 6–8.)

2. Persons employed in hospitals and ambulances, including the staff for superintendence, medical service, administration, transport of wounded, as well as chaplains, shall participate in the benefit of neutrality whilst so employed, and so long as there remain any wounded to bring in or to succour.

(*Cp. Add. Art.* 1868, *Art.* 1. 3 *H. C.* 1899, *Art.* 7. *G. C.* 1906, *Art.* 9. 10 *H. C.* 1907, *Art.* 10.)

3. The persons designated in the preceding article may, even after occupation by the enemy, continue to fulfil their duties in the hospital or ambulance which they serve, or may withdraw in order to rejoin the corps to which they belong.

Under such circumstances, when those persons shall cease from their functions, they shall be delivered, by the occupying army, to the outposts of the enemy.

(*Cp. Add. Art.* 1868, *Art.* 1. 3 *H. C.* 1899, *Art.* 7. *G. C.* 1906, *Art.* 12. 10 *H. C.* 1907, *Art.* 10.)

4. As the equipment of military hospitals remains subject to the laws of war, persons attached to such hospitals cannot, in withdrawing, carry

emporter que les objets qui sont leur propriété particulière.

Dans les mêmes circonstances, au contraire, l'ambulance conservera son matériel.

5. Les habitants du pays qui porteront secours aux blessés seront respectés et demeureront libres. Les généraux des puissances belligérantes auront pour mission de prévenir les habitants de l'appel fait à leur humanité, et de la neutralité qui en sera la conséquence.

Tout blessé recueilli et soigné dans une maison y servira de sauvegarde. L'habitant qui aura recueilli chez lui des blessés sera dispensé du logement des troupes, ainsi que d'une partie des contributions de guerre qui seraient imposées.

6. Les militaires blessés ou malades seront recueillis et soignés, à quelque nation qu'ils appartiendront.

Les commandants en chef auront la faculté de remettre immédiatement aux avant-postes ennemis, les militaires blessés pendant le combat, lorsque les circonstances le permettront, et du consentement des deux partis.

Seront renvoyés dans leurs pays ceux qui, après guérison, seront reconnus incapables de servir.

Les autres pourront être également renvoyés, à la condition de ne pas reprendre les armes pendant la durée de la guerre.

away any articles but such as are their private property.

Under the same circumstances an ambulance shall, on the contrary, retain its equipment.

(*Cp. G. C.* 1906, *Arts.* 12 *and* 14.)

5. Inhabitants of the country who may bring help to the wounded shall be respected, and shall remain free. The generals of the belligerent powers shall make it their care to inform the inhabitants of the appeal addressed to their humanity, and of the neutrality which will be the consequence of it.

Any wounded man entertained and taken care of in a house shall be considered as a protection thereto. Any inhabitant who shall have received wounded men into his house shall be exempted from the quartering of troops, as well as from a part of the contributions of war which may be imposed.

(*Cp. Add. Art.* 1868, *Art.* 4.

G. C. 1906, *Art.* 5.)

6. Wounded or sick soldiers shall be brought in and taken care of, to whatever nation they may belong.

Commanders-in-chief shall have the power to deliver immediately to the outposts of the enemy soldiers who have been wounded in an engagement, when circumstances permit this to be done, and with the consent of both parties.

Those who are recognised, after their wounds are healed, as incapable of serving, shall be sent back to their country.

The others may also be sent back, on condition of not bearing arms again during the continuance of the war.

(*Cp. Add. Art.* 1868, *Art.* 5.

G. C. 1906, *Art.* 2.)

Les évacuations, avec le personnel qui les dirige, seront couvertes par une neutralité absolue.

Evacuations [i.e. convoys of sick and wounded], together with the persons under whose directions they take place, shall be protected by an absolute neutrality.

(*Cp. G. C.* 1906, *Art.* 17.)

7. Un drapeau distinctif et uniforme sera adopté pour les hôpitaux, les ambulances, et les évacuations. Il devra être, en toute circonstance, accompagné du drapeau national.

Un brassard sera également admis pour le personnel neutralisé, mais la délivrance en sera laissée à l'autorité militaire.

Le drapeau et le brassard porteront croix rouge sur fond blanc.

7. A distinctive and uniform flag shall be adopted for hospitals, ambulances, and evacuations. It must on every occasion be accompanied by the national flag.

An arm-badge (*brassard*) shall also be allowed for individuals neutralised, but the delivery thereof shall be left to military authority.

The flag and arm-badge shall bear a red cross on a white ground.

(*Cp. G. C.* 1906, *Arts.* 18, 19, 20.)

8. Les détails d'exécution de la présente Convention seront réglés par les commandants-en-chef des armées belligérantes, d'après les instructions de leurs Gouvernements respectifs, et conformément aux principes généraux énoncés dans cette Convention.

8. The details of execution of the present Convention shall be regulated by the Commanders-in-chief of the belligerent armies, according to the instructions of their respective Governments, and in conformity with the general principles laid down in this Convention.

(*Cp. G. C.* 1906, *Art.* 25.)

9. Les Hautes Puissances Contractantes sont convenues de communiquer la présente Convention aux Gouvernements qui n'ont pu envoyer les Plénipotentiaires à la Conférence internationale de Genève, en les invitant à y accéder ; le Protocole est à cet effet laissé ouvert.

9. The High Contracting Powers have agreed to communicate the present Convention to the Governments which have been unable to send Plenipotentiaries to the International Conference of Geneva, with an invitation to accede thereto ; the Protocol is for that purpose left open.

(*Cp. G. C.* 1906, *Art.* 32 (2, 3).)

10. La présente Convention sera ratifiée, et les ratifications en seront échangées à Berne, dans l'espace de quatre mois, ou plus tôt si faire se peut.

En foi de quoi les Plénipotentiaires respectifs l'ont signée, et y ont apposé le cachet de leurs armes.

10. The present Convention shall be ratified, and the ratifications shall be exchanged at Berne, in four months, or sooner if possible.

In witness whereof the respective Plenipotentiaries have signed the same, and affixed the seal of their arms.

Fait à Genève, le vingt-deuxième jour du mois d'août, de l'an mil huit cent soixante-quatre.

Done at Geneva, the twenty-second day of August, one thousand eight hundred and sixty-four.

(*Suivent les signatures des Plénipotentiaires.*)

(*Here follow the signatures.*)

A Conference of representatives of Switzerland, Baden, Belgium, Denmark, Spain, France, Hesse, Italy, Holland, Portugal, Prussia, and Würtemberg met at Geneva in August, 1864. This Conference was to a large extent due to the philanthropic efforts of MM. Gustav Moynier and Henri Dunant, both citizens of Switzerland. Having been eye-witnesses of the sufferings of the wounded at Magenta and Solferino, and the disease incident to the campaign, and the want of the needful medical and surgical appliances, M. Dunant in 1862 published a book entitled *Le Souvenir de Solferino*, which gave a terribly graphic description of the misery and suffering of the sick and wounded in war[1]. A Swiss Society called *La Société Genevoise d'Utilité Publique* took up the ideas of M. Dunant with enthusiasm, and the Swiss Government was induced to summon a Conference to consider the subject of the treatment of the sick and wounded in war. The foregoing Convention was the result.

The following is a list of the states who have signed or adhered to this Convention (under the provisions of Article 9) with the dates of their signature or adherence:—The Argentine Republic (1879), Austria-Hungary (1866), Belgium (1864), Brazil (1906), Bolivia (1879), Bulgaria (1884), Chili (1879), China (1904), Colombia (1906), Congo (1888), Cuba (1907), Denmark (1864), Dominica (1907), Ecuador (1907), France (1864), Germany (1906), Great Britain (1865), Greece (1865), Guatemala (1903), Holland (1864), Honduras (1898), Hayti (1907), Italy (1864), Japan and Corea (1886 and 1903), Luxemburg (1888), Mexico (1905), Montenegro (1875), Nicaragua (1898), Norway (1864), Peru (1880), Persia (1874), Portugal (1866), Paraguay (1907), Panama (1907), Roumania (1874), Russia (1867), Salvador (1874), Servia (1876), Siam (1895), Spain (1864), Sweden (1864), Switzerland (1864), Turkey (1865), the United States of America (1882), Uruguay (1900), Venezuela (1894). In many cases the adherence of Powers was due to their ratification of the Convention with respect to the laws and customs of war on land signed at the Hague Conference of 1899, which by Article 21 incorporated the Geneva Convention of 1864.

[1] In 1901, M. Dunant was awarded the Nobel Prize for his efforts to mitigate the severity of war. A new edition of his work was published at Amsterdam in 1902.

This Convention was the first step towards the codification of rules of war applicable to land warfare. It represented the best existing practice on the subject, and the immunities which states were in the habit of according to those engaged in tending the sick and wounded. The lapse of nearly 35 years had rendered the terminology out of harmony with the existing arrangements of Army Medical Corps, and the use of the terms *neutre* and *neutralité* to describe the inviolability of persons and things covered by it was inexact. The Convention has no application to voluntary Aid Societies either of the belligerents or neutral Powers unless forming part of the belligerent armies. There was a growing desire for its revision[1], and among the "Wishes" (*Vœux*) expressed by the Hague Conference of 1899 was one to the effect that the Swiss Federal Government would take steps to call a Conference for the revision of the Convention. This Conference, which was attended by representatives of 37 Powers, met at Geneva in June, 1906, and adopted the Convention set forth on pages 18–35 which as between the contracting Powers now takes the place of that of 1864. As several important states, parties to the Convention of 1864, have not up to the present ratified the Convention of 1906, the former Convention will still regulate their relations in case of war between such of the parties who signed it but who have not ratified the latter Convention (Art. 31 of Geneva Convention, 1906).

The Geneva Conference of 1868. In 1868 the Swiss Government, at the request of a Conference of Red Cross Societies held at Paris during the Exhibition of 1867, summoned another Conference of the Powers to consider the subject of the treatment of sick and wounded in war. The following 14 Powers were represented at a Conference which met at Geneva in October, 1868: Austria-Hungary, Baden, Bavaria, Belgium, Denmark, France, the North German Confederation, Great Britain, Italy, Holland, Sweden and Norway, Switzerland, Turkey and Würtemberg. They agreed to a Convention of 15 Articles, the first five being explanations and additions to the Convention of 1864. The subsequent Articles are an application to naval warfare of the same principles. Owing to various causes the Convention was never ratified, but with some modi-

---

[1] See Lueder, *La Convention de Genève*; Mérignhac, *La Conférence de la Paix*, § 76; also list of works cited by the same author on p. 127 of *Les Lois et Coutumes de Guerre*; see also references given in note 1, p. 8 *ante*, and note 1, p. 18 *post*. A valuable sketch of the legislation in various countries for enforcing the Geneva Convention will be found in two Articles of Prof. Gustave de Roszkowski in *La Revue de Droit International* (2nd series), Vol. VI. [1904] pp. 76, 188. See *British Parliamentary Papers* relating to the Geneva Convention of 1906 [1908, Cd. 3933] for a translation of the various enactments and regulations (pp. 64–73).

fications its provisions have been acted on by belligerents since 1868[1]. The principles of Articles 6–15 were embodied in the Convention adopted by the Hague Convention (1899) for the adaptation to maritime warfare of the principles of the Geneva Convention of 1864[2]. The following is a translation of the *Projet d'articles additionels à la Convention du 22 Août*, 1864[3].

ART. 1. The personnel designated in Article 2 of the Convention shall continue after occupation by the enemy to give their services, according to the measure of the necessities, to the sick and the wounded of the ambulance or hospital which they serve.

When they shall make a request to withdraw, the commander of the occupying forces shall fix the moment of their departure, which he cannot under any circumstances defer, except for a short period in case of military necessities.

(Cp. G. C. 1864, Arts. 2, 3. G. C. 1906, Art. 12.)

ART. 2. Provision ought to be made by the belligerent powers to assure to the persons neutralized, who have fallen into the hands of the enemy's army, the complete enjoyment of their pay (*la jouissance intégrale de son traitement*).

(Cp. G. C. 1906, Art. 13.)

ART. 3. In the conditions provided for by Articles 1 and 4 of the Convention, the term ambulance applies to field hospitals and other temporary establishments, which follow the troops on the field of battle to receive there the sick and wounded.

(Cp. G. C. 1906, Art. 6.)

ART. 4. In accordance with the spirit of Article 5 of the Convention, and under the reserves mentioned in the Protocol of 1864, it is explained that, as regards the division of the charges relative to the billeting of troops and the contributions of war, account will only be taken of the charitable spirit shown by the inhabitants in so far as equitable considerations may be applicable.

(Cp. G. C. 1906, Art. 5.)

ART. 5. In extension of Article 6 of the Convention, it is stipulated that with the reservation of officers, the detention of whom may be important to the success of the war, and within the limits fixed by the second paragraph of this Article, the wounded who have fallen into the hands of the enemy, although they may not have been recognized as incapable of service, ought to be sent back

---

[1] It served as a *modus vivendi* during the Franco-German War of 1870 (L. Renault, *Les deux Conférences de la Paix*, p. 173).

[2] M. G. de Lapradelle is of opinion that the Convention of 1899 is inferior to that of 1868 (*La Conférence de la Paix*).

[3] De Martens, *Nouveau Recueil Général de Traités*, Vol. XVIII. pp. 612–9; Vol. XX. pp. 400–435; Sir T. Twiss, *International Law*, Vol. II. p. 534.

to their country after their wounds are healed, or sooner if it be possible, on condition always of not resuming arms during the continuance of the war.

(Cp. G. C. 1906, Art. 2.)

Articles concerning Naval Warfare (*la marine*).

ART. 6.   Boats which, at their risk and peril, during and after the engagement, pick up, or which, having picked up the shipwrecked or the wounded, convey them on board a neutral or hospital ship, shall enjoy, until the completion of their mission, such a degree of neutrality as the circumstances of the engagement and the situation of the vessels in conflict will allow to be applied to them.

The appreciation of these circumstances is left to the humanity of all the combatants.

The shipwrecked and wounded so picked up and saved cannot serve during the continuance of the war.

(Cp. 3 H. C. 1899, Art. 6.   10 H. C. 1907, Art. 9.)

ART. 7.   Every person employed in the religious, medical or hospital service of any captured vessel is declared inviolable (*neutre*).   On leaving the vessel, he carries away the articles and instruments of surgery which are his own private property.

(Cp. 3 H. C. 1899, Art. 7.   10 H. C. 1907, Arts. 9, 10.)

ART. 8.   The persons designated in the preceding Article ought to continue to fulfil their functions on board the captured vessel, to assist in the evacuations of the wounded made by the victorious side, after which they should be free to return to their own country, in accordance with the second paragraph of the first additional Article above mentioned.

The stipulations of the second additional Article above mentioned are applicable to the pay of these persons.

(Cp. 3 H. C. 1899, Art. 7.   10 H. C. 1907, Art. 10.)

ART. 9.   Military hospital ships remain subject to the laws of war, as regards their equipment; they become the property of the captor, but the latter cannot divert them from their special purpose during the continuance of the war.

ART. 10.   Every merchant ship, to whatever nation it may belong, laden exclusively with wounded or sick, whose removal it is effecting, has the protection of neutrality; but the mere fact of a visit, notified in her log-book, by an enemy cruiser, renders the wounded and sick incapable of serving during the continuance of the war.

(Cp. 3 H. C. 1899, Arts. 6, 9.)

The cruiser shall even have the right of putting on board a commissioner to accompany the convoy to verify in this manner the good faith of the operation.

If the merchant ship carries a cargo in addition, the neutral character shall still protect it, provided that the cargo be not of a nature to be confiscated by the belligerent.

Belligerents retain the right of prohibiting neutralised vessels from having any communication and taking any direction which they consider prejudicial to the secrecy of their operations. In urgent cases special conventions may be made between the commanders-in-chief to neutralise temporarily in a special manner ships intended for the transport of the wounded or sick.

(*Cp.* 3 *H. C.* 1899, *Art.* 4.)

ART. 11. Wounded or sick sailors and soldiers on board ship, to whatever nation they may belong, shall be protected and taken care' of by the captors. Their restoration to their country is made subject to the provisions of the sixth Article of the Convention and the fifth additional Article.

(*Cp.* 3 *H. C.* 1899, *Art.* 8.   10 *H. C.* 1907, *Art.* 11.)

ART. 12. The distinctive flag to be added to the national flag to denote a ship or boat of any kind which claims the benefit of neutrality in virtue of the principles of this Convention is the white flag with a red cross. Belligerents exercise in this respect all such verification as they judge necessary.

Military hospital ships shall be distinguished by white external painting, with a green broad band.

(*Cp.* 3 *H. C.* 1899, *Art.* 5.   10 *H. C.* 1907, *Art.* 5.)

ART. 13. Hospital ships, equipped at the expense of associations for the aid of the wounded recognized by the Governments which have signed this Convention, being provided with a commission issued by the sovereign, who shall have expressly authorized their fitting out, and with a document from a competent maritime authority, certifying that they have been submitted to its control during their fitting out and at their final departure, and that they were then appropriated exclusively to the object of their mission, shall be considered as neutral as well as all the persons employed in them.

They shall be respected and protected by the belligerents.

They shall make themselves known by hoisting with their national flag the white flag with a red cross. The distinctive mark of the persons employed on them during the exercise of their functions shall be an arm-badge of the same colours ; their external painting shall be white with a red broad band.

These ships shall bring aid and assistance to the wounded and shipwrecked belligerents, without distinction of nationality.

They ought not in any way to embarrass the movements of the combatants.

During and after an engagement they shall act at their own risk and peril.

The belligerents shall have over them the right of control and visit; they may refuse their assistance, may enjoin them to remove to a distance and may detain them, if the gravity of the circumstances require it.

The wounded and shipwrecked picked up by these vessels cannot be claimed by any of the combatants, but they are under an obligation not to serve again during the continuance of the war.

(*Cp. 3 H. C.* 1899, *Arts.* 3, 4.   10 *H. C.* 1907, *Arts.* 3, 4.)

ART. 14.   In naval wars, any strong presumption, that one of the belligerents profits from the benefit of neutrality in any interest other than that of the wounded and sick, allows the other belligerent, until proof of the contrary, to suspend the Convention as regards him.

If this presumption becomes a certainty, the Convention may be denounced as regards him during the continuance of the war.

ART. 15.   The present Act shall be drawn up in a single original Act, which shall be deposited in the archives of the Swiss Confederation.

An authentic copy of this Act shall be delivered, with an invitation to accede thereto, to each of the powers who have signed the Convention of 22 August, 1864, as likewise to those who have successively acceded to it.

In faith whereof the undersigned Commissioners have drawn up the proposed additional articles and affixed the seals of their arms.

Done at Geneva, the 20th day of October, 1868.

GENEVA CONVENTION, 1906[1]

CONVENTION POUR L'AMÉLIORATION DU SORT DES BLESSÉS ET MALADES DANS LES ARMÉES EN CAMPAGNE.

CONVENTION FOR THE AMELIORATION OF THE CONDITION OF THE WOUNDED AND SICK IN ARMIES IN THE FIELD.

Sa Majesté le Roi du Royaume-Uni de la Grande-Bretagne et d'Irlande, Empereur des Indes; Sa Majesté l'Empereur d'Allemagne, Roi de Prusse; Son Excellence le Président de la République Argentine; Sa Majesté l'Empereur d'Autriche, Roi de Bohême, &c., et Roi Apostolique de Hongrie; Sa Majesté le Roi des Belges; Son Altesse Royale le Prince de Bulgarie; Son Excellence le Président de la République du Chili; Sa Majesté l'Empereur de Chine; Sa Majesté le Roi des Belges, Souverain de l'État indépendant du Congo; Sa Majesté l'Empereur de Corée[2]; Sa Majesté le Roi de Danemark; Sa Majesté le Roi d'Espagne; le Président des États-Unis d'Amérique; le Président des États-Unis du Brésil; le Président des États-Unis Mexicains; le Président de la République Française; Sa Majesté

His Majesty the King of the United Kingdom of Great Britain and Ireland, Emperor of India; His Majesty the German Emperor, King of Prussia; His Excellency the President of the Argentine Republic; His Majesty the Emperor of Austria, King of Bohemia, &c., and Apostolic King of Hungary; His Majesty the King of the Belgians; His Royal Highness the Prince of Bulgaria; His Excellency the President of the Republic of Chile; His Majesty the Emperor of China; His Majesty the King of the Belgians, Sovereign of the Independent State of the Congo; His Majesty the Emperor of Corea; His Majesty the King of Denmark; His Majesty the King of Spain; the President of the United States of America; the President of the United States of Brazil; the President of the United States of Mexico; the President

[1] *British State Papers*, Treaty Series, 1907, No. 15 [Cd. 3502]; Papers relating to the Geneva Convention, 1906 [1908, Cd. 3933]; G. B. Davis, *The Geneva Convention of 1906, American Journal of International Law*, Vol. I. p. 400; T. E. Holland, *The New Geneva Convention, Fortnightly Review*, August, 1907; Idem, *The Laws of War on Land*, Section VI., contains a concise commentary on the articles of this Convention; J. Delpech, *La Conférence de la revision de la Convention de Genève, Rev. gén. de droit int. pub.* Vol. XIII. p. 629; L. Vannutelli, *La revisione della Convenzione di Ginevra, Rivista di diritto internazionale*, Vol. I. p. 421; *Actes de la Conférence de Genève*, 1906; Sir T. Barclay, *Problems, etc.* pp. 52, 261; Chr. Meurer, *Die neue Genfer Konvention, Zeitschrift für Völkerrecht und Bundesstaatsrecht*, Vol. I. (1906), p. 521.

[2] See post, p. 35.

le Roi des Hellènes; le Président de la République de Guatémala; le Président de la République de Honduras; Sa Majesté le Roi d'Italie; Sa Majesté l'Empereur du Japon; Son Altesse Royale le Grand-Duc de Luxembourg, Duc de Nassau; Son Altesse Royale le Prince de Monténégro; Sa Majesté le Roi de Norvège; Sa Majesté la Reine des Pays-Bas; le Président de la République du Pérou; Sa Majesté Impériale le Schah de Perse; Sa Majesté le Roi de Portugal et des Algarves, &c.; Sa Majesté le Roi de Roumanie; Sa Majesté l'Empereur de Toutes les Russies; Sa Majesté le Roi de Serbie; Sa Majesté le Roi de Siam; Sa Majesté le Roi de Suède; le Conseil Fédéral Suisse; le Président de la République Orientale de l'Uruguay,

Également animés du désir de diminuer, autant qu'il dépend d'eux, les maux inséparables de la guerre, et voulant, dans ce but, perfectionner et compléter les dispositions convenues à Genève, le 22 août, 1864, pour l'amélioration du sort des militaires blessés ou malades dans les armées en campagne;

Ont résolu de conclure une nouvelle Convention à cet effet, et ont nommé pour leurs Plénipotentiaires, savoir:

(*Suivent les noms des Plénipotentiaires.*)

Lesquels, après s'être communiqué leurs pleins pouvoirs, trouvés en bonne et due forme, sont convenus de ce qui suit:

of the French Republic; His Majesty the King of the Hellenes; the President of the Republic of Guatemala; the President of the Republic of Honduras; His Majesty the King of Italy; His Majesty the Emperor of Japan; His Royal Highness the Grand Duke of Luxemburg, Duke of Nassau; His Royal Highness the Prince of Montenegro; His Majesty the King of Norway; Her Majesty the Queen of the Netherlands; the President of the Republic of Peru; His Imperial Majesty the Shah of Persia; His Majesty the King of Portugal and the Algarves, &c.; His Majesty the King of Roumania; His Majesty the Emperor of All the Russias; His Majesty the King of Servia; His Majesty the King of Siam; His Majesty the King of Sweden; the Swiss Federal Council; the President of the Oriental Republic of the Uruguay,

Being equally animated by the desire of mitigating, as far as possible, the evils inseparable from war, and desiring, with this end in view, to improve and to complete the arrangements agreed upon at Geneva on the 22nd August, 1864, for the amelioration of the condition of wounded or sick soldiers in armies in the field;

Have resolved to conclude for this purpose a new Convention, and have named as their Plenipotentiaries, that is to say:

(*Here follow the names of the Plenipotentiaries.*)

Who, after having communicated to each other their full powers, found in good and due form, have agreed as follows:

CHAPITRE PREMIER.—*Des Blessés et Malades.*

ARTICLE PREMIER.

Les militaires et les autres personnes officiellement attachées aux armées, qui seront blessés ou malades, devront être respectés et soignés, sans distinction de nationalité, par le belligérant qui les aura en son pouvoir.

Toutefois, le belligérant, obligé d'abandonner des malades ou des blessés à son adversaire, laissera avec eux, autant que les circonstances militaires le permettront, une partie de son personnel et de son matériel sanitaires pour contribuer à les soigner.

ART. 2.

Sous réserve des soins à leur fournir en vertu de l'article précédent, les blessés ou malades d'une armée tombés au pouvoir de l'autre belligérant sont prisonniers de guerre et les règles générales du droit des gens concernant les prisonniers leur sont applicables.

Cependant, les belligérants restent libres de stipuler entre eux, à l'égard des prisonniers blessés ou malades, telles clauses d'exception ou de faveur qu'ils jugeront utiles ; ils auront, notamment, la faculté de convenir :

De se remettre réciproquement, après un combat, les blessés laissés sur le champ de bataille ;

De renvoyer dans leur pays, après les avoir mis en état d'être transportés

CHAPTER I.—*The Wounded and Sick.*

ARTICLE 1.

Soldiers, and other persons officially attached to armies, shall be respected and taken care of when wounded or sick, by the belligerent in whose power they may be, without distinction of nationality.

(*Cp. G. C.* 1864, *Art.* 6.)

Nevertheless, a belligerent who is compelled to abandon sick or wounded to the enemy shall, as far as military exigencies permit, leave with them a portion of his medical personnel and material to contribute to the care of them.

(*New.*)

ART. 2.

Except as regards the treatment to be provided for them in virtue of the preceding Article, the wounded and sick of an army who fall into the hands of the enemy are prisoners of war, and the general provisions of international law concerning prisoners are applicable to them.

(*New.*)

Belligerents are, however, free to arrange with one another such exceptions and mitigations with reference to sick and wounded prisoners as they may judge expedient; in particular they will be at liberty to agree—

To restore to one another the wounded left on the field after a battle ;

To repatriate any wounded and sick whom they do not wish to retain as

ou après guérison, les blessés ou malades qu'ils ne voudront pas garder prisonniers ;

De remettre à un État neutre, du consentement de celui-ci, des blessés ou malades de la partie adverse, à la charge par l'État neutre de les interner jusqu'à la fin des hostilités.

prisoners, after rendering them fit for removal or after recovery ;

To hand over to a neutral State, with the latter's consent, the enemy's wounded and sick to be interned by the neutral State until the end of hostilities.

(*Cp. G. C.* 1864, *Art.* 6.
Add. Art. 1868, *Art.* 5.)

ART. 3.

Après chaque combat, l'occupant du champ de bataille prendra des mesures pour rechercher les blessés et pour les faire protéger, ainsi que les morts, contre le pillage et les mauvais traitements.

Il veillera à ce que l'inhumation ou l'incinération des morts soit précédée d'un examen attentif de leurs cadavres.

ART. 3.

After each engagement the Commander in possession of the field shall take measures to search for the wounded, and to insure protection against pillage and maltreatment both for the wounded and for the dead.

He shall arrange that a careful examination of the bodies is made before the dead are buried or cremated.

(*New.*)
(*Cp.* 10 *H. C.* 1907, *Art.* 16.)

ART. 4.

Chaque belligérant enverra, dès qu'il sera possible, aux autorités de leur pays ou de leur armée les marques ou pièces militaires d'identité trouvées sur les morts et l'état nominatif des blessés ou malades recueillis par lui.

Les belligérants se tiendront réciproquement au courant des internements et des mutations, ainsi que des entrées dans les hôpitaux et des décès survenus parmi les blessés et malades en leur pouvoir. Ils recueilleront tous les objets d'un usage personnel, valeurs, lettres, etc., qui seront trouvés sur les champs de bataille ou délaissés par les blessés ou malades décédés dans les

ART. 4.

Each belligerent shall send as soon as possible to the authorities of the country or army to which they belong the military identification marks or tokens found on the dead, and a nominal roll of the wounded or sick who have been collected by him.

The belligerents shall keep each other mutually informed of any internments and changes, as well as of admissions into hospital and deaths among the wounded and sick in their hands. They shall collect all the articles of personal use, valuables, letters, &c., which are found on the field of battle or left by the wounded or sick who have died in the medical

établissements et formations sanitaires, pour les faire transmettre aux intéressés par les autorités de leur pays.

establishments or units, in order that such objects may be transmitted to the persons interested by the authorities of their own country.

(*New.*)

(*Cp.* 10 *H. C.* 1907, *Art.* 17.)

ART. 5.

L'autorité militaire pourra faire appel au zèle charitable des habitants pour recueillir et soigner, sous son contrôle, des blessés ou malades des armées, en accordant aux personnes ayant répondu à cet appel une protection spéciale et certaines immunités.

ART. 5.

The military authority may appeal to the charitable zeal of the inhabitants to collect and take care of, under his direction, the wounded or sick of armies, granting to those who have responded to this appeal special protection and certain immunities.

(*Cp. G. C.* 1864, *Art.* 5. *Add. Art.* 1868, *Art.* 4. 10 *H. C.* 1907, *Art.* 9.)

CHAPITRE II.—*Des Formations et Établissements Sanitaires.*

CHAPTER II.—*Medical Units and Establishments.*

ART. 6.

Les formations sanitaires mobiles (c'est-à-dire celles qui sont destinées à accompagner les armées en campagne) et les établissements fixes du service de santé seront respectés et protégés par les belligérants.

ART. 6.

Mobile medical units (that is to say, those which are intended to accompany armies into the field) and the fixed establishments of the medical service shall be respected and protected by the belligerents.

(*New nomenclature.*)

(*Cp. G. C.* 1864, *Art.* 1. *Add. Art.* 1868, *Art.* 3. 10 *H. C.* 1907, *Art.* 1.)

ART. 7.

La protection due aux formations et établissements sanitaires cesse si l'on en use pour commettre des actes nuisibles à l'ennemi.

ART. 7.

The protection to which medical units and establishments are entitled ceases if they are made use of to commit acts harmful to the enemy.

(*Cp. G. C.* 1864, *Art.* 1. 10 *H. C.* 1907, *Art.* 8 (1).)

ART. 8.

Ne sont pas considérés comme étant de nature à priver une formation ou un établissement sanitaire de la protection assurée par l'article 6 :

1°. Le fait que le personnel de la formation ou de l'établissement est armé et qu'il use de ses armes pour sa propre défense ou celle de ses malades et blessés ;

2°. Le fait qu'à défaut d'infirmiers armés, la formation ou l'établissement est gardé par un piquet ou des sentinelles munis d'un mandat régulier ;

3°. Le fait qu'il est trouvé dans la formation ou l'établissement des armes et cartouches retirées aux blessés et n'ayant pas encore été versées au service compétent.

ART. 8.

The following facts are not considered to be of a nature to deprive a medical unit or establishment of the protection guaranteed by Article 6 :—

1. That the personnel of the unit or of the establishment is armed, and that it uses its arms for its own defence or for that of the sick and wounded under its charge.

2. That in default of armed orderlies the unit or establishment is guarded by a piquet or by sentinels furnished with an authority in due form.

3. That weapons and cartridges taken from the wounded and not yet handed over to the proper department are found in the unit or establishment.

(*New.*)

(*Cp.* 10 *H. C.* 1907, *Art.* 8 (2).)

CHAPITRE III.—*Du Personnel.*

ART. 9.

Le personnel exclusivement affecté à l'enlèvement, au transport et au traitement des blessés et des malades, ainsi qu'à l'administration des formations et établissements sanitaires, les aumôniers attachés aux armées, seront respectés et protégés en toute circonstance ; s'ils tombent entre les mains de l'ennemi, ils ne seront pas traités comme prisonniers de guerre.

Ces dispositions s'appliquent au personnel de garde des formations et établissements sanitaires dans le cas prévu à l'article 8, n° 2.

CHAPTER III.—*Personnel.*

ART. 9.

The personnel engaged exclusively in the collection, transport, and treatment of the wounded and the sick, as well as in the administration of medical units and establishments, and the Chaplains attached to armies, shall be respected and protected under all circumstances. If they fall into the hands of the enemy they shall not be treated as prisoners of war.

These provisions apply to the guard of medical units and establishments under the circumstances indicated in Article 8 (2).

(*Cp. G. C.* 1864, *Art.* 2. *Add. Art.* 1868, *Art.* 1. 3 *H. C.* 1899, *Art.* 7. 10 *H. C.* 1907, *Art.* 10.)

ART. 10.

Est assimilé au personnel visé à l'article précédent le personnel des Sociétés de secours volontaires dûment reconnues et autorisées par leur Gouvernement, qui sera employé dans les formations et établissements sanitaires des armées, sous la réserve que ledit personnel sera soumis aux lois et règlements militaires.

Chaque État doit notifier à l'autre soit dès le temps de paix, soit à l'ouverture ou au cours des hostilités, en tout cas avant tout emploi effectif, les noms des Sociétés qu'il a autorisées à prêter leur concours, sous sa responsabilité, au service sanitaire officiel de ses armées.

ART. 11.

Une Société reconnue d'un pays neutre ne peut prêter le concours de ses personnels et formations sanitaires à un belligérant qu'avec l'assentiment préalable de son propre Gouvernement et l'autorisation du belligérant lui-même.

Le belligérant qui a accepté le secours est tenu, avant tout emploi, d'en faire la notification à son ennemi.

ART. 12.

Les personnes désignées dans les articles 9, 10 et 11 continueront, après qu'elles seront tombées au pouvoir de

ART. 10.

The personnel of Voluntary Aid Societies, duly recognized and authorized by their Government, who may be employed in the medical units and establishments of armies, is placed on the same footing as the personnel referred to in the preceding Article, provided always that the first-mentioned personnel shall be subject to military law and regulations.
(*New.*)
Each State shall notify to the other, either in time of peace or at the commencement of or during the course of hostilities, but in every case before actually employing them, the names of the Societies which it has authorized, under its responsibility, to render assistance to the regular medical service of its armies.
(*Cp.* 3 *H. C.* 1899, *Art.* 2.
10 *H. C.* 1907, *Art.* 2.)

ART. 11.

A recognized Society of a neutral country can only afford the assistance of its medical personnel and units to a belligerent with the previous consent of its own Government and the authorization of the belligerent concerned.

A belligerent who accepts such assistance is bound before making any use of it to notify the fact to his adversary.
(*New.*)
(*Cp.* 3 *H. C.* 1899, *Art.* 3.
10 *H. C.* 1907, *Art.* 3.)

ART. 12.

The persons designated in Articles 9, 10, and 11, after they have fallen into the hands of the enemy, shall

l'ennemi, à remplir leurs fonctions sous sa direction.

Lorsque leur concours ne sera plus indispensable, elles seront renvoyées à leur armée ou à leur pays dans les délais et suivant l'itinéraire compatibles avec les nécessités militaires.

Elles emporteront, alors, les effets, les instruments, les armes et les chevaux qui sont leur propriété particulière.

continue to carry on their duties under his direction.

When their assistance is no longer indispensable, they shall be sent back to their army or to their country at such time and by such route as may be compatible with military exigencies.

They shall then take with them such effects, instruments, arms, and horses as are their private property.
(*Cp. G. C.* 1864, *Art.* 3, 4. *Add. Art.* 1868, *Art.* 1. 3 *H. C.* 1899, *Art.* 7. 10 *H. C.* 1907, *Art.* 10.)

Art. 13.

L'ennemi assurera au personnel visé par l'article 9, pendant qu'il sera en son pouvoir, les mêmes allocations et la même solde qu'au personnel des mêmes grades de son armée.

Art. 13.

The enemy shall secure to the persons mentioned in Article 9, while in his hands, the same allowances and the same pay as are granted to the persons holding the same rank in his own army.
(*Cp. Add. Art.* 1868, *Art.* 2. 3 *H. C.* 1899, *Art.* 7. 4 *H. C.* 1907, *Art.* 17. 10 *H. C.* 1907, *Art.* 10.)

Chapitre IV.—*Du Matériel.*

Art. 14.

Les formations sanitaires mobiles conserveront, si elles tombent au pouvoir de l'ennemi, leur matériel, y compris les attelages, quels que soient les moyens de transport et le personnel conducteur.

Toutefois, l'autorité militaire compétente aura la faculté de s'en servir pour les soins des blessés et malades ; la restitution du matériel aura lieu dans les conditions prévues pour le personnel sanitaire, et, autant que possible, en même temps.

Chapter IV.—*Material.*

Art. 14.

If mobile medical units fall into the hands of the enemy they shall retain their material, including their teams, whatever may be the means of transport and whoever may be the drivers employed.
(*Cp. G. C.* 1864, *Art.* 4 (2).)

Nevertheless, the competent military authority shall be free to use the material for the treatment of the wounded and sick. It shall be restored under the conditions laid down for the medical personnel, and so far as possible at the same time.
(*New.*)

ART. 15.

Les bâtiments et le matériel des établissements fixes demeurent soumis aux lois de la guerre, mais ne pourront être détournés de leur emploi, tant qu'ils seront nécessaires aux blessés et aux malades.

Toutefois, les commandants des troupes d'opérations pourront en disposer, en cas de nécessités militaires importantes, en assurant au préalable le sort des blessés et malades qui s'y trouvent.

ART. 15.

The buildings and material of fixed establishments remain subject to the laws of war, but may not be diverted from their purpose so long as they are necessary for the wounded and the sick.

(*New.*)
(*Cp. G. C.* 1864, *Art.* 4 (1).)

Nevertheless, the Commanders of troops in the field may dispose of them, in case of urgent military necessity, provided they make previous arrangements for the welfare of the wounded and sick who are found there.

(*Cp.* 10 *H. C.* 1907, *Art.* 7.)

ART. 16.

Le matériel des Sociétés de secours, admises au bénéfice de la Convention conformément aux conditions déterminées par celle-ci, est considéré comme propriété privée et, comme tel, respecté en toute circonstance, sauf le droit de réquisition reconnu aux belligérants selon les lois et usages de la guerre.

ART. 16.

The material of Voluntary Aid Societies which are admitted to the privileges of the Convention under the conditions laid down therein is considered private property, and, as such, to be respected under all circumstances, saving only the right of requisition recognized for belligerents in accordance with the laws and customs of war.

(*New.*)

CHAPITRE V.—*Des Convois d'Évacuation.*

CHAPTER V.—*Convoys of Evacuation.*

ART. 17.

Les convois d'évacuation seront traités comme les formations sanitaires mobiles, sauf les dispositions spéciales suivantes :

1°. Le belligérant interceptant un convoi pourra, si les nécessités militaires l'exigent, le disloquer en se

ART. 17.

Convoys of evacuation shall be treated like mobile medical units, subject to the following special provisions :—

(*Cp. G. C.* 1864, *Art.* 6 (5).)

1. A belligerent intercepting a convoy may, if military exigencies demand, break it up, provided he takes

chargeant des malades et blessés qu'il contient.

(*New.*)

2°. Dans ce cas, l'obligation de renvoyer le personnel sanitaire, prévue à l'article 12, sera étendue à tout le personnel militaire préposé au transport ou à la garde du convoi et muni à cet effet d'un mandat régulier.

L'obligation de rendre le matériel sanitaire, prévue à l'article 14, s'appliquera aux trains de chemins de fer et bateaux de la navigation intérieure spécialement organisés pour les évacuations, ainsi qu'au matériel d'aménagement des voitures, trains et bateaux ordinaires appartenant au service de santé.

Les voitures militaires, autres que celles du service de santé, pourront être capturées avec leurs attelages.

Le personnel civil et les divers moyens de transport provenant de la réquisition, y compris le matériel de chemin de fer et les bateaux utilisés pour les convois, seront soumis aux règles générales du droit des gens.

CHAPITRE VI.—*Du Signe Distinctif.*

ART. 18.

Par hommage pour la Suisse, le signe héraldique de la croix rouge sur fond blanc, formé par interversion des couleurs fédérales, est maintenu comme emblème et signe distinctif du service sanitaire des armées.

---

charge of the sick and wounded who are in it.

(*New.*)

2. In this case, the obligation to send back the medical personnel, provided for in Article 12, shall be extended to the whole of the military personnel detailed for the transport or the protection of the convoy and furnished with an authority in due form to that effect.

(*New.*)

The obligation to restore the medical material, provided for in Article 14, shall apply to railway trains, and boats used in internal navigation, which are specially arranged for evacuations, as well as to the material belonging to the medical service for fitting up ordinary vehicles, trains, and boats.

(*New.*)

Military vehicles, other than those of the medical service, may be captured with their teams.

(*New.*)

The civilian personnel and the various means of transport obtained by requisition, including railway material and boats used for convoys, shall be subject to the general rules of international law.

(*New.*)

CHAPTER VI.—*The Distinctive Emblem.*

ART. 18.

As a compliment to Switzerland, the heraldic device of the red cross on a white ground, formed by reversing the Federal colours, is retained as the emblem and distinctive sign of the medical service of armies.

(*Cp. G. C.* 1864, *Art.* 7.)

ART. 19.

Cet emblème figure sur les drapeaux, les brassards, ainsi que sur tout le matériel se rattachant au service sanitaire, avec la permission de l'autorité militaire compétente.

ART. 19.

With the permission of the competent military authority this emblem shall be shown on the flags and armlets (*brassards*), as well as on all the material belonging to the Medical Service.

(*New.*)

ART. 20.

Le personnel protégé en vertu des articles 9, alinéa 1ᵉʳ, 10 et 11 porte, fixé au bras gauche, un brassard avec croix rouge sur fond blanc, délivré et timbré par l'autorité militaire compétente, accompagné d'un certificat d'identité pour les personnes rattachées au service de santé des armées et qui n'auraient pas d'uniforme militaire.

ART. 20.

The personnel protected in pursuance of Articles 9 (paragraph 1), 10, and 11 shall wear, fixed to the left arm, an armlet (*brassard*) with a red cross on a white ground, delivered and stamped by the competent military authority, and accompanied by a certificate of identity in the case of persons who are attached to the medical service of armies, but who have not a military uniform.

(*Cp. G. C.* 1864, *Art.* 7.)

ART. 21.

Le drapeau distinctif de la Convention ne peut être arboré que sur les formations et établissements sanitaires qu'elle ordonne de respecter et avec le consentement de l'autorité militaire. Il devra être accompagné du drapeau national du belligérant dont relève la formation ou l'établissement.

ART. 21.

The distinctive flag of the Convention shall only be hoisted over those medical units and establishments which are entitled to be respected under the Convention, and with the consent of the military authorities. It must be accompanied by the national flag of the belligerent to whom the unit or establishment belongs.

(*New.*)

Toutefois, les formations sanitaires tombées au pouvoir de l'ennemi n'arboreront pas d'autre drapeau que celui de la Croix-Rouge, aussi longtemps qu'elles se trouveront dans cette situation.

Nevertheless, medical units which have fallen into the hands of the enemy, so long as they are in that situation, shall not fly any other flag than that of the Red Cross.

(*New.*)

ART. 22.

Les formations sanitaires des pays neutres qui, dans les conditions prévues

ART. 22.

The medical units belonging to neutral countries which may be au-

par l'article 11, auraient été autorisées à fournir leurs services, doivent arborer, avec le drapeau de la Convention, le drapeau national du belligérant dont elles relèvent.

Les dispositions du deuxième alinéa de l'article précédent leur sont applicables.

ART. 23.

L'emblème de la croix rouge sur fond blanc et les mots *Croix-Rouge* ou *Croix de Genève* ne pourront être employés, soit en temps de paix, soit en temps de guerre, que pour protéger ou désigner les formations et établissements sanitaires, le personnel et le matériel protégés par la Convention.

CHAPITRE VII.—*De l'Application et de l'Exécution de la Convention.*

ART. 24.

Les dispositions de la présente Convention ne sont obligatoires que pour les Puissances contractantes, en cas de guerre entre deux ou plusieurs d'entre elles. Ces dispositions cesseront d'être obligatoires du moment où l'une des Puissances belligérantes ne serait pas signataire de la Convention.

ART. 25.

Les commandants en chef des armées belligérantes auront à pourvoir aux

thorized to afford their services under the conditions laid down in Article 11 shall fly, along with the flag of the Convention, the national flag of the belligerent to whose army they are attached.
(*New.*)
The provisions of the second paragraph of the preceding Article are applicable to them.
(*New.*)

ART. 23[1].

The emblem of the red cross on a white ground and the words "Red Cross" or "Geneva Cross" shall not be used, either in time of peace or in time of war, except to protect or to indicate the medical units and establishments and the personnel and material protected by the Convention.
(*New.*)

CHAPTER VII.—*Application and Carrying out of the Convention.*

ART. 24.

The provisions of the present Convention are only binding upon the Contracting Powers in the case of war between two or more of them. These provisions shall cease to be binding from the moment when one of the belligerent Powers is not a party to the Convention.
(*New.*)
(*Cp. 3 H. C.* 1899, *Art.* 11.)

ART. 25.

The Commanders-in-chief of belligerent armies shall arrange the details

---

[1] Great Britain made reservations in regard to Arts. 23, 27 and 28. See *post*, p. 36.

détails d'exécution des articles précédents, ainsi qu'aux cas non prévus, d'après les instructions de leurs Gouvernements respectifs et conformément aux principes généraux de la présente Convention.

for carrying out the preceding Articles, as well as for cases not provided for, in accordance with the instructions of their respective Governments and in conformity with the general principles of the present Convention.

(*Cp. G. C.* 1864, *Art.* 8.
10 *H. C.* 1907, *Art.* 19.)

ART. 26.

Les Gouvernements signataires prendront les mesures nécessaires pour instruire leurs troupes, et spécialement le personnel protégé, des dispositions de la présente Convention et pour les porter à la connaissance des populations.

ART. 26.

The Signatory Governments will take the necessary measures to instruct their troops, especially the personnel protected, in the provisions of the present Convention, and to bring them to the notice of the civil population.

(*Cp.* 10 *H. C.* 1907, *Art.* 20.)

CHAPITRE VIII.—*De la Répression des Abus et des Infractions.*

CHAPTER VIII.—*Prevention of Abuses and Infractions.*

ART. 27.

Les Gouvernements signataires, dont la législation ne serait pas dès à présent suffisante, s'engagent à prendre ou à proposer à leurs législatures les mesures nécessaires pour empêcher en tout temps l'emploi, par des particuliers ou par des sociétés autres que celles y ayant droit en vertu de la présente Convention, de l'emblème ou de la dénomination de *Croix-Rouge* ou *Croix de Genève*, notamment, dans un but commercial, par le moyen de marques de fabrique ou de commerce.

ART. 27[1].

The Signatory Governments, in countries the legislation of which is not at present adequate for the purpose, undertake to adopt or to propose to their legislative bodies such measures as may be necessary to prevent at all times the employment of the emblem or the name of Red Cross or Geneva Cross by private individuals or by Societies other than those which are entitled to do so under the present Convention, and in particular for commercial purposes as a trade-mark or trading mark.

(*New.*)

L'interdiction de l'emploi de l'emblème ou de la dénomination dont il s'agit produira son effet à partir de l'époque déterminée par chaque législation et, au plus tard, cinq ans après

The prohibition of the employment of the emblem or the names in question shall come into operation from the date fixed by each legislature, and at the latest five years after the present

[1] See note, *supra*, p. 29.

la mise en vigueur de la présente Con - vention. Dès cette mise en vigueur, il ne sera plus licite de prendre une marque de fabrique ou de commerce contraire à l'interdiction.

Convention comes into force. From that date it shall no longer be lawful to adopt a trade-mark or trading mark contrary to this prohibition.

(*New.*)

ART. 28.

Les Gouvernements signataires s'engagent également à prendre ou à proposer à leurs législatures, en cas d'insuffisance de leurs lois pénales militaires, les mesures nécessaires pour réprimer, en temps de guerre, les actes individuels de pillage et de mauvais traitements envers des blessés et malades des armées, ainsi que pour punir, comme usurpation d'insignes militaires, l'usage abusif du drapeau et du brassard de la Croix-Rouge par des militaires ou des particuliers non protégés par la présente Convention.

Ils se communiqueront, par l'intermédiaire du Conseil fédéral suisse, les dispositions relatives à cette répression, au plus tard dans les cinq ans de la ratification de la présente Convention.

ART. 28[1].

The Signatory Governments also undertake to adopt, or to propose to their legislative bodies, should their military law be insufficient for the purpose, the measures necessary for the repression in time of war of individual acts of pillage and maltreatment of the wounded and sick of armies, as well as for the punishment, as an unlawful employment of military insignia, of the improper use of the Red Cross flag and armlet (*brassard*) by officers and soldiers or private individuals not protected by the present Convention.

They shall communicate to one another, through the Swiss Federal Council, the provisions relative to these measures of repression at the latest within five years from the ratification of the present Convention.

(*New.*)

(*Cp.* 10 *H. C.* 1907, *Art.* 21.)

Dispositions Générales.

ART. 29.

La présente Convention sera ratifiée aussi tôt que possible.

Les ratifications seront déposées à Berne.

Il sera dressé du dépôt de chaque ratification un procès-verbal dont une copie, certifiée conforme, sera remise

General Provisions.

ART. 29.

The present Convention shall be ratified as soon as possible. The ratifications shall be deposited at Berne.

When each ratification is deposited a *procès-verbal* shall be drawn up, and a copy thereof certified as correct

---

[1] See note, *supra*, p. 29.

par la voie diplomatique à toutes les Puissances contractantes.

shall be forwarded through the diplomatic channel to all the Contracting Powers.

(*Cp. G. C.* 1864, *Art.* 10.)

ART. 30.

La présente Convention entrera en vigueur pour chaque Puissance six mois après la date du dépôt de sa ratification.

ART. 30.

The present Convention shall come into force for each Power six months after the date of the deposit of its ratification.

(*Cp.* 10 *H. C.* 1907, *Art.* 26.)

ART. 31.

La présente Convention, dûment ratifiée, remplacera la Convention du 22 août 1864 dans les rapports entre les États contractants.

La Convention de 1864 reste en vigueur dans les rapports entre les Parties qui l'ont signée et qui ne ratifieraient pas également la présente Convention.

ART. 31.

The present Convention, duly ratified, shall replace the Convention of the 22nd August, 1864, in relations between the Contracting States. The Convention of 1864 remains in force between such of the parties who signed it who may not likewise ratify the present Convention.

(*Cp.* 10 *H. C.* 1907, *Art.* 25.)

ART. 32.

La présente Convention pourra, jusqu'au 31 décembre prochain, être signée par les Puissances représentées à la Conférence qui s'est ouverte à Genève le 11 juin 1906, ainsi que par les Puissances non représentées à cette Conférence qui ont signé la Convention de 1864.

Celles de ces Puissances qui, au 31 décembre 1906, n'auront pas signé la présente Convention, resteront libres d'y adhérer par la suite. Elles auront à faire connaître leur adhésion au moyen d'une notification écrite adressée au Conseil fédéral suisse et communiquée par celui-ci à toutes les Puissances contractantes.

Les autres Puissances pourront demander à adhérer dans la même forme, mais leur demande ne produira effet

ART. 32.

The present Convention may be signed until the 31st December next by the Powers represented at the Conference which was opened at Geneva on the 11th June, 1906, as also by the Powers, not represented at that Conference, which signed the Convention of 1864.

Such of the aforesaid Powers as shall not have signed the present Convention by the 31st December, 1906, shall remain free to accede to it subsequently. They shall notify their accession by means of a written communication addressed to the Swiss Federal Council, and communicated by the latter to all the Contracting Powers.

Other Powers may apply to accede in the same manner, but their request shall only take effect if within a period

que si, dans le délai d'un an à partir de la notification au Conseil fédéral, celui-ci n'a reçu d'opposition de la part d'aucune des Puissances contractantes.

ART. 33.

Chacune des Parties contractantes aura la faculté de dénoncer la présente Convention. Cette dénonciation ne produira ses effets qu'un an après la notification faite par écrit au Conseil fédéral suisse ; celui-ci communiquera immédiatement la notification à toutes les autres Parties contractantes.

Cette dénonciation ne vaudra qu'à l'égard de la Puissance qui l'aura notifiée.

En foi de quoi, les Plénipotentiaires ont signé la présente Convention et l'ont revêtue de leurs cachets.

Fait à Genève, le six juillet mil neuf cent six, en un seul exemplaire, qui restera déposé dans les archives de la Confédération suisse, et dont des copies, certifiées conformes, seront remises par la voie diplomatique aux Puissances contractantes.

PROTOCOLE FINAL DE LA CONFÉRENCE DE REVISION DE LA CONVENTION DE GENÈVE.

La Conférence convoquée par le Conseil fédéral suisse, en vue de la revision de la Convention internationale, du 22 août 1864, pour l'amélioration du sort des militaires blessés

of one year from the notification of it to the Federal Council no objection to it reaches the Council from any of the Contracting Powers.

(*New.*)
(*Cp.* 3 *H. C.* 1899, *Art.* 13.)

ART. 33.

Each of the Contracting Powers shall be at liberty to denounce the present Convention. The denunciation shall not take effect until one year after the written notification of it has reached the Swiss Federal Council. The Council shall immediately communicate the notification to all the other Contracting Parties.

(*New.*)
(*Cp. Add. Art.* 1868, *Art.* 13. 3 *H. C.* 1899, *Art.* 14. 10 *H. C.* 1907, *Art.* 27.)

The denunciation shall only affect the Power which has notified it.

In faith whereof the Plenipotentiaries have signed the present Convention and have affixed thereto their seals.

Done at Geneva the 6th July, 1906, in a single copy, which shall be deposited in the archives of the Swiss Confederation, and of which copies certified as correct shall be forwarded to the Contracting Powers through the diplomatic channel.

FINAL PROTOCOL OF THE CONFERENCE FOR THE REVISION OF THE GENEVA CONVENTION.

The Conference convoked by the Swiss Federal Council with a view to the revision of the International Convention of the 22nd August, 1864, for the amelioration of the condition of

dans les armées en campagne, s'est réunie à Genève le 11 Juin 1906. Les Puissances dont l'énumération suit ont pris part à la Conférence, pour laquelle Elles avaient désigné les Délégués nommés ci-après :

[*Dénomination des Délégués.*]

Dans une série de réunions tenues du 11 juin au 5 juillet 1906, la Conférence a discuté et arrêté, pour être soumis à la signature des Plénipotentiaires, le texte d'une Convention qui portera la date du 6 juillet 1906.

En outre, et en conformité de l'article 16 de la Convention pour le règlement pacifique des conflits internationaux, du 29 juillet 1899, qui a reconnu l'arbitrage comme le moyen le plus efficace et en même temps le plus équitable de régler les litiges qui n'ont pas été résolus par les voies diplomatiques, la Conférence a émis le vœu suivant :

La Conférence exprime le vœu que, pour arriver à une interprétation et à une application aussi exactes que possible de la Convention de Genève, les Puissances contractantes soumettent à la Cour Permanente de La Haye, si les cas et les circonstances s'y prêtent, les différends qui, en temps de paix, s'élèveraient entre elles relativement à l'interprétation de ladite Convention.

Ce vœu a été voté par les États suivants :

Allemagne, République Argentine, Autriche-Hongrie, Belgique, Bulgarie, Chili, Chine, Congo, Danemark, Espagne (*ad ref.*), États-Unis d'Amérique, États-Unis du Brésil, États-Unis

soldiers wounded in armies in the field has assembled at Geneva on the 11th June, 1906. The Powers enumerated below have taken part in the Conference, for which purpose they had designated the under-mentioned Delegates :

[*Names of Delegates.*]

In a series of meetings held from the 11th June to the 5th July, 1906, the Conference has discussed and drawn up, with a view to its being signed by the Plenipotentiaries, the text of a Convention which shall bear the date 6th July, 1906.

In addition, and in accordance with Article 16 of the Convention for the Pacific Settlement of International Disputes of the 29th July, 1899, which recognizes arbitration as the most efficacious and the most equitable means for the settlement of disputes which have not been determined diplomatically, the Conference has framed the following Resolution :—

The Conference expresses the desire that, in order to arrive at an interpretation and application as exact as possible of the Geneva Convention, the Contracting Powers should submit to the Permanent Court at The Hague, if the cases and the circumstances permit, any differences which may, in time of peace, arise between them relative to the interpretation of the said Convention.

This Resolution has been voted by the following States :—

Germany, Argentine Republic, Austria-Hungary, Belgium, Bulgaria, Chile, China, Congo, Denmark, Spain (*ad ref.*), United States of America, United States of Brazil, United States

Mexicains, France, Grèce, Guatémala, Honduras, Italie, Luxembourg, Monténégro, Nicaragua, Norvège, Pays-Bas, Pérou, Perse, Portugal, Roumanie, Russie, Serbie, Siam, Suède, Suisse et Uruguay.

Ce vœu a été rejeté par les États suivants : Corée, Grande-Bretagne et Japon.

En foi de quoi, les Délégués ont signé le présente Protocole.

Fait à Genève, le six juillet mil neuf cent six, en un seul exemplaire, qui sera déposé aux archives de la Confédération suisse et dont des copies, certifiées conformes, seront délivrées à toutes les Puissances représentées à la Conférence.

of Mexico, France, Greece, Guatemala, Honduras, Italy, Luxemburg, Montenegro, Nicaragua, Norway, Netherlands, Peru, Persia, Portugal, Roumania, Russia, Servia, Siam, Sweden, Switzerland, and Uruguay.

This Resolution has been declined by the following States : Corea, Great Britain, and Japan.

In witness whereof the Delegates have signed the present Protocol.

Done at Geneva, the 6th July, 1906, in a single copy, which shall be deposited in the archives of the Swiss Confederation, and of which copies, certified as correct, shall be delivered to all the Powers represented at the Conference.

The following states have up to the present ratified this Convention: Austria-Hungary, Belgium, Brazil, the Congo, Denmark, Germany, Great Britain (under reserve of Articles 23, 27, 28), Italy, Japan and Corea, Luxemburg, Mexico, Russia, Siam, Spain, Switzerland, the United States of America. The following have acceded (under the provisions of Art. 32, par. 3): Colombia, Cuba, Nicaragua, Turkey and Venezuela.

The Convention of 1864 remains in force at present between the following Powers who signed it, and who have not ratified or adhered to the Convention of 1906: the Argentine Republic, Bolivia, Bulgaria, Chili, China, Dominica, Ecuador, France, Greece, Guatemala, Hayti, Holland, Honduras, Montenegro, Norway, Panama, Paraguay, Peru, Persia, Portugal, Roumania, Salvador, Servia, Sweden and Uruguay.

With regard to the position of Corea the following note is appended to the signature of the Japanese Plenipotentiary on behalf of Corea in the British Blue Book on this subject :

"His Majesty's Government have received from the Swiss Minister a notification that by a Declaration dated the 15th October, 1906, the Japanese Chargé d'Affaires at Berne stated that, in virtue of the Agreement between Japan and Corea of the 17th November, 1905, the Imperial Japanese Government has the right of entirely controlling the foreign relations and affairs of Corea. Consequently the inclusion of Corea in the preamble of the Convention and the signature of the latter by the

Japanese Plenipotentiary on behalf of Corea as a separate Contracting Party, being erroneous and incompatible with the aforesaid arrangement, are considered by the Japanese Government as null and void[1]."

It is important to notice that Great Britain ratified the Convention under reserves of Arts. 23, 27, 28. These Articles, it will be seen, provide that the emblem of the Red Cross shall not be used in peace or war, except to protect or indicate medical units and establishments and the personnel and material protected by the Convention, and that the signatory Powers whose legislation is insufficient to prevent the abuse of the name or sign of the Red Cross or Geneva Cross, particularly for commercial purposes as trade marks or commercial labels, shall adopt or propose to their legislative bodies such measures as may be necessary to secure the name and emblem from abuse in peace or war. Several Powers had, previous to the Conference, legislated with this object[2], but the British delegates in signing, and the British Government in their ratification were unable to accept these Articles, though approving of their principles, by reason of the uncertainties of Parliamentary proceedings in this country.

The Hague Conference of 1899 left the initiative in the matter of a Conference for the revision of the Geneva Convention of 1864 to the Swiss Government. This Government, as early as 1901, took steps with a view of calling together a Conference, but owing partly to the dilatoriness of some of the states, and partly to the outbreak of the Russo-Japanese war, it was not until the 11th June, 1906, that the Conference met. The number of Powers represented was larger than that at the Hague in 1899, some of the Powers appearing at an International Conference for the first time. The Conference terminated its labours on the 6th July.

The new Convention contains 33 Articles as against 10 in the Convention of 1864, and is divided into eight chapters dealing with the whole subject. The terminology of the new Convention now harmonises with current usage; the words "neutral" and "neutrality" are no longer used to signify inviolability or immunity from capture, but are restricted to cases of internment, and the personnel of Voluntary Aid Societies of a neutral country whose service is accepted by a belligerent. The terms "ambulances" and "hospitals" are replaced by "mobile sanitary units" or

---

[1] Treaty Series, 1907, No. 15 [Cd. 3502], p. 39.

[2] See two Articles by Prof. Gustave de Rosskowski, *Rev. de dr. int.* (2nd series), Vol. VI. pp. 76, 188. The Powers in question are: The Argentine Republic, Austria, Belgium, Bulgaria, Denmark, Germany, Hungary, Italy, Norway, Portugal, Roumania, Russia, Servia, Spain and the United States. See *Papers relating to the Geneva Convention*, 1906 [1906, Cd. 3933], pp. 64–73.

"sanitary formations" and "fixed establishments of the medical service." The position of Voluntary Aid or Red Cross Societies is made clear. In the case of Societies belonging to one of the belligerents, only when the personnel is recognised by their Government and subject to military laws and regulations do they become entitled to the privileges of the Convention. The position of neutral Societies when rendering assistance to a belligerent is also clearly defined and full protection afforded to their material (Arts. 16, 21 and 22). Such Societies are not entitled to fly the flag of the state to which they belong, but must fly that of the belligerent to which they are attached together with the flag adopted by the Convention, except when they have fallen into the hands of the enemy. The details of the organisation of such Societies and the regulations for their work are not dealt with by the Convention.

The Convention of 1864 left untouched the question of the position of sick and wounded who fell into the hands of the enemy; the Convention of 1906 is explicit on this point, and declares them to be prisoners of war (Art. 2). They thus fall under the *régime* provided by Chapter ii. of the Regulations of the Hague Conventions on the laws of war on land. Provision is made for the identification of the dead, and the return of property found on them, and for the notification of the names of dead, sick and wounded by one belligerent to the other. This had been partially provided for by 2 H. C. 1899 (Regulations), Art. 14.

The Convention makes it clear that not only officers and soldiers, but other persons officially attached to armies, are also to be respected and taken care of, when sick or wounded, by the belligerent in whose power they may be, without distinction of nationality. The subject of convoys of evacuation, which in 1864 was but slightly dealt with, is made the subject of detailed regulations (Art. 17).

Article 5 of the Convention of 1864, and Article 4 of the unratified Convention of 1868, had in practice been found to be unsatisfactory, and in lieu thereof Article 5 now leaves to the discretion of the military authorities appeals to the charitable zeal of the inhabitants to collect and take care of the sick and wounded, as well as the special immunities which may be granted to those who comply with the request.

The Convention also makes it clear that the "Red Cross" has no religious significance (Art. 10), and contains provisions stringently limiting its use (Arts. 18-23).

Article 26 is similar to 2 H. C. 1899, Art. 1, and binds the signatory Powers to take measures to instruct their troops in the provisions of

the present Convention, but it goes farther than this, for the Powers also agree to "bring them to the notice of the civil population."

The Convention of 1864 left the Protocol open unconditionally for the accession of Powers (Art. 9). Article 32 of the new Convention limits the freedom of accession and under it any of the Powers mentioned in paragraphs 1 and 2 of that Article may object to the application of a new Power for leave to accede in cases where its military organisation does not afford sufficient guarantees of its ability to carry out the obligations imposed by the Convention[1].

Great Britain declined to be a party to the *Vœu* that "*if the cases and the circumstances permit*" any differences "which may in time of peace" arise between the contracting Powers relative to the interpretation of the Convention should be submitted to the Permanent Court at the Hague[2].

---

[1] See J. Delpech, *La nouvelle convention de Genève*, pp. 85-7.

[2] Prof. Holland, K.C., who was one of the British Plenipotentiaries at the Conference, states the reasons for the refusal of Great Britain on p. 239 of the Article in the *Fortnightly Review* previously cited.

THE HAGUE PEACE CONFERENCES 1899 AND 1907

THE PEACE CONFERENCE OF 1899[1].

As the Second Peace Conference continued the work of the first and in certain respects was able to make additions to the results attained in 1899, it will be of assistance in the study of the Conventions adopted by the Powers at these two Conferences first to set forth the results of the Conference of 1899.

The first step towards the summoning of the Hague Conference of 1899 was taken when Count Mouravieff, the Russian Foreign Minister, on the 24th Aug. 1898, addressed a circular letter to the representatives of the Powers accredited to St Petersburg in which he referred to the desire which the Emperor had for "the maintenance of the general peace and a possible reduction of the excessive armaments which were burdening all nations." Actuated by the wish to put an end to the increase of such armaments, and to seek for means to avoid the calamities which were threatening the whole world, the Tsar proposed to all the Governments whose representatives were accredited to the Court of St Petersburg to assemble in conference to consider this serious problem. This invitation

---

[1] *The Peace Conference of 1899.* There is a considerable literature on this subject. A few only of the sources of information are here mentioned as most of the modern Text-books deal with this subject. *British Parl. Papers*, Miscellaneous, No. 1 (1899); De Martens, *Nouveau Recueil Général de Traités* (2nd series), Vol. XXVI. pp. 1–920,—the Final Act is printed at p. 258; F. W. Holls; *The Peace Conference at the Hague*; Sir T. Barclay, *Problems of international practice and diplomacy with special reference to the Hague Conferences, etc.*; T. J. Lawrence, *War and neutrality in the Far East*; Idem, *International Problems and Hague Conferences*; G. de Lapradelle, *La Conférence de la Paix*; A. Mérignhac, *La Conférence Internationale de la Paix*; J. B. Scott, *Texts of the Peace Conferences at the Hague*; E. A. Whittuck, *International Documents*. See also F. Despagnet, *La Guerre Sud Africaine*; Sidney Low in *The Nineteenth Century* for September, 1899, p. 888; Prof. T. E. Holland, *Some lessons of the Peace Conference*, Fortnightly Review, Vol. LXVI. (N.S.), p. 944; S. Jules Enthoven in *The Law Magazine and Review*, Vol. XXIV. p. 457; *La Revue Générale de Droit International Public*, Vol. VI. pp. 846, 859, 879, 888; J. B. Moore, *Digest of International Law*, Vol. VII. p. 78.

to disarmament was received with coldness in several important quarters. Count Mouravieff therefore, on the 11th Jan.1899, addressed another circular to the Russian ministers accredited to the states represented at St Petersburg in which he suggested the following topics for the consideration of the Conference, thereby considerably widening its scope. (1) The prohibition for a fixed term of any increase of the armed forces beyond those then maintained. (2) The prohibition of, or limitation in the employment of new firearms or explosives. (3) The restriction of the explosives already existing, and the prohibition of the discharge of projectiles or explosives of any kind from balloons or by any similar means. (4) The prohibition in naval warfare of submarine torpedo-boats or similar engines of destruction, and the ultimate abolition of vessels with rams. (5) The application to naval warfare of the principles of the Geneva Convention of 1864 on the basis of the additional Articles of 1868. (6) The neutralisation of ships and boats employed in saving those shipwrecked during or after an engagement. (7) The revision of the unratified Brussels Declaration of 1874 concerning the laws and customs of war on land. (8) The acceptance in principle of the employment of good offices, of mediation and arbitration with the object of preventing armed conflicts between nations, and the establishment of a uniform practice in their employment.

An important limitation was placed on the discussion of these matters by the statement that all questions concerning the political relations of states and the order of things established by treaties and all questions which did not directly fall within the programme adopted by the Cabinets were to be absolutely excluded from the deliberations of the Conference.

The circular concluded by stating that the Tsar thought it advisable that the Conference should not meet in the capital of one of the great Powers "where so many political interests are centred which might, perhaps, impede the progress of a work in which all the countries of the universe are equally interested[1]."

The Dutch Government having assented to the proposed Conference being held at the Hague, invitations were addressed by it to the states designated by Russia. The Conference met on the 20th May, 1899, under the presidency of M. de Staal, the first Russian Plenipotentiary, and was attended by representatives of the 26 Powers enumerated in the Final Act. Difficulties had been raised as to the status of several Powers to whom invitations had been addressed. Italy declined to attend if the Papal representative was admitted. Great Britain as suzerain objected to the presence of a representative of the Transvaal. The representative of

[1] *Parl. Papers*, Misc. No. 1 (1899), p. 3.

Bulgaria was only admitted in subordination to Turkey. Though the number of Powers represented was large, none of the American Republics, except the United States and Mexico were present. The delegates and their staffs numbered upwards of 100. The representatives were divided into three Committees : the first two being divided into two Sub-Committees. To the First Committee were assigned the matters dealt with in Articles 1-4 of Count Mouravieff's circular of the 11th Jan. 1899 ; to the Second those comprised in Arts. 5, 6 and 7; and to the Third those comprised in Art. 8. The Sub-Committees and Committees held numerous meetings and reported to plenary meetings of the Conference of which there were 10 in all, the last being held on the 31st July. The Conference was thus in session for a little over two months.

The results of the labours of these two months were embodied in a Final Act which is not in itself a Convention, but rather a resumé of the work done by the Conference[1] and as such was signed by all the Powers present, who thus affirmed the authenticity of the record, without binding themselves to sign each of the Conventions or adhere to each of the Declarations or Wishes contained in the Act.

The Final Act of the Hague Conference of 1899.

The following are set forth in the Final Act as having been agreed upon for submission for signature by the Plenipotentiaries[2]: .

(*a*) *Three Conventions*: (1) For the pacific settlement of international disputes, (2) regarding the laws and customs of war on land, (3) for the adaptation to maritime warfare of the principles of the Geneva Convention of the 22nd August, 1864.

(*b*) *Three Declarations*: (1) To prohibit the discharge of projectiles and explosives from balloons or by other similar new methods. (2) To prohibit the use of projectiles, the only object of which is the diffusion of asphyxiating or deleterious gases. (3) To prohibit the use of bullets which expand or flatten easily in the human body, such as bullets with a hard envelope, of which the envelope does not entirely cover the core, or is pierced with incisions.

The Conventions and Declarations to form so many separate Acts.

(*c*) *One Resolution* affirming " that the restriction of military budgets which are at present a heavy burden on the world is extremely desirable for the increase of the material and moral welfare of mankind."

---

[1] The "Acte Final" was described by Sir Julian Pauncefote as " an exposition of the work of the Conference presented to the various Governments for their information and approval " (Sir J. Pauncefote to the Marquess of Salisbury, 31 July, 1899, *Parliamentary Papers*, Misc. No. 1 (1899), p. 278).

[2] For text of Final Act, see *post*, p. 60.

(d) *Six Wishes* (*Vœux*): (1) That a special Conference might be summoned by the Swiss Government for the revision of the Geneva Convention. (2) That the questions of the rights and duties of neutrals might be inserted in the programme of a Conference in the near future. (3) That questions regarding rifles and naval guns, as considered by the Conference, might be studied by the governments with the object of coming to an agreement respecting the employment of new types and calibres. (4) That the governments, taking into consideration the proposals made at the Conference, might examine the possibility of an agreement as to the limitation of armed forces by land and sea, and of war budgets. (5) That the proposal for the exemption of private property from capture in naval warfare might be referred to a subsequent Conference for consideration. (6) That the question of the bombardment of ports, towns and villages by a naval force might be referred to a subsequent Conference for consideration.

As the subjects mentioned in Nos. 2, 5 and 6 were outside the programme of the Conference and as the delegates considered that the Swiss Government had a prior claim to take the initiative in the subjects mentioned in No. 1, the expression of the Wishes on these matters was all that was within the competence of the Conference.

Such is a brief outline of the immediate results of the deliberations of the First Hague Conference. It did not do all that its "August Initiator" had desired, and the question of disarmament or even of the limitation of armaments and budgets which was in the forefront of Count Mouravieff's second circular was found on examination to present "so many difficulties from a practical point of view that it was necessarily abandoned for the present[1]." The passing of a resolution endorsing in general terms the desirability of the restriction of military budgets, and the emission of *Vœux* Nos. 3 and 4 was the method in which this abandonment was notified to the world. But failure in this respect, a failure which had been foreseen from the first, did not mean that 26 Powers had assembled for two months for naught. Idealists had expected too much, and were dissatisfied with the results; but the solid work of the Conference as attested by the three Conventions,

Results of the Hague Conference of 1899.

---

[1] Letter of Sir Julian Pauncefote to the Marquess of Salisbury, *Parl. Papers*, Misc. No. 1 (1899), p. 353. Great Britain was represented at the Conference by the Right Hon. Sir Julian Pauncefote and Sir Henry Howard, with Vice-Admiral Sir John Fisher, Major-Gen. Sir J. C. Ardagh and Lieut.-Col. C. à Court as technical advisers.

The United States delegates were: Mr Andrew D. White, the Hon. Seth Low, Mr Stamford Newell, Captain A. T. Mahan, Captain W. Crozier and Mr F. W. Holls.

two of which were completions of work which previous gatherings[1] had failed to accomplish, cannot but be viewed as marking an important epoch in the development of international law.   It is true that a Conference known as *La Conférence de la Paix* had devoted the greater part of its labours to the elaboration of rules of war.   The Emperor of Russia might have said of it, " I labour for peace, but when I speak unto them thereof, they make them ready for battle."   Many of the members of Peace Societies could not but view the results as discouraging.   But it is not alone by these Conventions, Declarations and *Vœux* that the worth of the Conference is to be appraised.   The results assume a truer perspective when viewed in the light of the years that have passed since the conclusion of the

(i) The laws of war on land.
Conference.   The sanguine prophecy expressed by Sir Julian Pauncefote that the new century was destined to " open with brighter prospects of international peace" was not fulfilled.

Almost before the ink on the Final Act was dry, war broke out between the South African Republics and Great Britain.   Hardly had that terminated, before two of the signatory Powers (one of them the initiator of the Conference) were engaged in a prolonged and sanguinary struggle in the Far East.   The Peace Conference had not maintained the peace of the world.   Its work, however, in humanising the laws of war both on land and sea was now put to the test.   The terms of the two Conventions were well observed, and the bureaux for information relative to prisoners of war, a new creation of the Conference (Art. 13, Regulations for the laws of war), came into existence and operation for the first time[2].   Naturally deficiencies were discovered in the practical application of both Conventions, but in the main they were found to be workable.   War on land was now conducted for the first time under rules previously agreed upon by the parties.

The Convention for the pacific settlement of international disputes is a

(ii) Pacific settlement of international disputes.
greater mark of international progress than the two Conventions just referred to.   This Convention was also put to the test between 1899 and 1907.   Good offices and mediation of friendly powers were not appealed to to prevent the outbreak

of war either in South Africa or the Far East, but twice during the Russo-Japanese war the value of the Convention was manifested.   There is no doubt that the recourse to a Commission of Inquiry, with wider powers than those contemplated by the terms of Title III. of the Con-

---

[1] The Conference of Geneva 1868, and the Brussels Conference 1874.

[2] The Japanese bureau was instituted by Imperial Ordinance No. 44 dated the 21st February, 1904, the Russian by Imperial Ordinance confirmed 18th May, 1904. See S. Takahashi, *International Law applied to the Russo-Japanese War*, p. 114.

vention[1], prevented the outbreak of war between Great Britain and Russia over the Dogger Bank affair of October, 1904. When it is remembered that this was a difference involving "honour and vital interests" which are expressly excluded from the competence of such Commissions by the Convention (Art. 9) the solution of the question in a peaceful manner is the more noteworthy. The long drawn-out struggle between Russia and Japan was ultimately closed by the Treaty of Portsmouth in 1905. It was doubtless the recommendation contained in the third Article of the Convention which furnished President Roosevelt with the means of initiating the negotiations which reached so successful a conclusion[2].

The Permanent Court of Arbitration whose creation was provided for by Title IV. Chapter ii. of the same Convention soon got to work. The Powers nominated their representatives and since its establishment four cases have been heard and settled before a Court composed of Judges who were members of the Permanent Court.

Cases before the Permanent Court at the Hague.

The first case to come before the Court at the Hague was a claim of the United States of America against the Republic of Mexico[3]. By the *Compromis* (agreement of reference) between these states dated the 22nd May, 1902, the subject of the dispute was defined, and terms of proceedings set forth. The question in dispute between the Powers had reference to a charity known as "The Pious Fund of the Californias" which had been instituted in the 17th and 18th centuries for the propagation of the Roman Catholic faith in unsettled portions of Spanish North America called the Californias. After the accomplishment of Mexican independence the administration of the Fund passed to Mexico, and the properties having been sold, the Republic undertook to pay 6 per cent. on the proceeds to the Church. War broke out between the United States and Mexico in 1846, and was terminated by the Treaty of Guadalupe-Hidalgo in 1848, and Upper California was ceded by Mexico to the United States for 15 million dollars and other considerations. During the 20 years succeeding the treaty claims arose by citizens of each republic against the other for damages resulting from injuries of various sorts, and in July, 1868, a Convention was concluded between the two nations under which an international tribunal was constituted for the determination of such claims. Among the claimants were the Roman

(1) The Pious Fund of the Californias.

---

[1] See *post*, pp. 167–9.

[2] Amos S. Hershey, *The international law and diplomacy of the Russo-Japanese War*, pp. 347–8.

[3] J. B. Moore, *International Arbitrations*, Vol. II. pp. 1849–54; De Martens, *Nouveau Recueil Général de Traités* (2nd series), Vol. XXXII. p. 189.

Catholic Archbishop of San Francisco and the Roman Catholic Bishop of Monterey for so much of the interest on the capital of the Pious Fund accrued since the Treaty of Guadalupe-Hidalgo as properly belonged to Upper California. The Arbitrators disagreed, and the question having been referred to the British Minister at Washington as Umpire, he signed an award in favour of the claimants for $904,070.79 in Mexican gold coin, being 21 years' interest at 6 per cent. per ann. on one-half of the capital of the Pious Fund. This award was satisfied. Mexico subsequently made default in payment of the annual interest and the United States Government on behalf of the Bishops claimed payment thereof ($43,050.99) from the year 1868, and contended that the question of liability could not be re-opened as the matter was *res judicata*. In the alternative, the United States contended that if the Permanent Court at the Hague decided against the validity of the Umpire's award, a much larger sum than that originally claimed was due and this was set forth and the method in which it was calculated. Mexico denied liability, and the finality and conclusiveness of the judgment of the Umpire. To this the United States filed a replication. The hearing of the case commenced on the 15th Sept. 1902 before Professor H. Matzen, President of the Danish Landthing, as Umpire and President of the Court, chosen by the Arbitrators, the Right Hon. Sir Edward Fry, a former Lord Justice of Appeal in England, Dr F. de Martens, Privy Councillor of Russia, both nominated by the United States, and Dr T. M. C. Asser, Member of the Council of State of the Netherlands, and Dr A. F. de Savornin Lohman, former Minister of the Interior of the Netherlands, both nominated by Mexico. French was the language of the Tribunal, but the Tribunal decided that both parties might use English. Both states were represented by agents and counsel. The Court sat 11 times and the award was given on the 14th Oct. on the two following points:

1. Whether the claim of the United States on behalf of the Archbishop of San Francisco and the Bishop of Monterey was governed by the principle of *res judicata* in virtue of the decision of the 11 Nov. 1878 given by Sir Edward Thornton in his capacity of Umpire.

2. If *not*, whether the said claim was just; with power to give such judgment as seemed to the Court just and equitable.

The Court unanimously decided in favour of the claim of the United States on the ground that it was governed by the principle of *res judicata* as set forth in the *Compromis*, and awarded the sum of 1,420,682$\frac{67}{100}$ Mexican dollars to the claimants, being the annual interest due from the 2nd Feb. 1869 to the 2nd Feb. 1902.

All friends of international arbitration will re-echo the words of Mr Ralston, the agent for the United States, who in addressing the Court after the delivery of the judgment said: "There has just been determined at the Hague a controversy over money,—a thing which we are told has been the 'slave to thousands,' and the love of which is described as 'the root of all evil.' If a judgment now meant nothing more than the transfer or non-transfer of money from one party to the other, however interesting this might be to those concerned, the world at large would look on with indifference. We believe, however, that a first step has been taken that will count largely for the good of future generations: that following this primal recognition of the existence of a Court competent to settle disputes between nations, will come general references to it, not alone of differences similar to the present, but of other controversies involving larger questions of individual rights and national privileges. We may hope that precisely as questions formerly believed to involve individual honour had in many countries entirely ceased, and in others are ceasing to be settled by formal exercise of force, the same revolution may gradually be effected in the affairs of nations. The Permanent Court of Arbitration, assisting this end, must tend to bring about that 'peace on earth, good will toward men' for which Christians hope[1]."

The members of the Court addressed to the Dutch Minister for Foreign Affairs a note in which they made certain reflections on the procedure before the Tribunal, and recommendations with a view to providing against possible difficulties in the working of the Court. These recommendations will be dealt with in discussing the Convention itself[2].

The next case to come before the Tribunal was a dispute between
(2) Claims against Venezuela.
Great Britain, Germany and Italy on the one side and Venezuela on the other[3]. This case both as regards the questions raised, as well as the procedure to be followed, involved "larger questions of individual rights and national privileges" than the Pious Funds Case. In consequence of the inability of Great Britain, Germany and Italy to obtain satisfaction from Venezuela for claims made on behalf of their subjects, the ports of Venezuela were blockaded in 1902[4]. Ultimately on the intervention of the United States an agreement was arrived at whereby

---

[1] I am indebted to Dr L. H. Ruyssenaers, the Secretary-General of the Permanent Court of Arbitration, for copies of the *Recueil des Actes et Protocoles* of the four cases here dealt with.

[2] See Sir T. Barclay, *Problems, etc.* pp. 276–7.

[3] *Brit. Parl. Papers*, Venezuela, No. 1 (1904) [Cd. 1949]. A. Mallarmé, *L'arbitrage vénézuélien devant la Cour de la Haye*, *Rev. gén. de Droit inter.* Vol. XIII. p. 423; J. B. Moore, *Digest of International Law*, § 967.

[4] See *post*, p. 185, for the circumstances of this blockade

Venezuela recognised in principle the justice of the claims preferred by the three Governments on behalf of their subjects, and agreed for the purpose of their satisfaction to set aside 30 per cent. of the customs revenues of La Guaira and Puerto Cabello, and to submit claims for injury to persons and property to arbitration. Other Powers also claimed against Venezuela, and Protocols containing conditions for the settlement of claims against that country by a Mixed Commission were signed by her Government and those of the following Powers, in addition to the three already mentioned: the United States, France, Spain, Belgium, the Netherlands, Sweden and Norway and Mexico. Great Britain, Germany and Italy having claimed preferential treatment in payment of their claims it was agreed by an additional Protocol of 7th May, 1903, to submit the question of preferential or separate treatment to the Hague Tribunal, and, should it decide against the three Powers, to ask it to determine how the revenue derived from the 30 per cent. customs should be distributed. In consequence of the number of Powers involved the choice of Arbitrators was left to the Tsar (Russia being a disinterested Power), subject to the condition that nationals of interested Powers were to be excluded from membership of the Tribunal. Any nation, moreover, having claims against Venezuela, was allowed to join as a party in the arbitration. As all Venezuela's other creditors had an interest in her success, the case resolved itself into an arbitration between Great Britain, Germany and Italy on the one side, and Venezuela, Belgium, Spain, France, the Netherlands, Sweden and Norway and Mexico on the other. The Arbitrators were M. N. V. Mouravieff, Russian Imperial Secretary of State (President), Professor H. Lammasch, Member of the Upper House of the Austrian Parliament, and Dr F. de Martens, Russian Privy Councillor. The official language used was English in accordance with the terms of the Protocols. The hearing of the case occupied the Court for 13 days during the months of October and November, 1903, and a unanimous decision was given on the 22nd February, 1904, in favour of the three Powers who had claimed preferential treatment by reason of the blockade which they had carried out. This decision in no way affected the Protocols of the 13th Feb. 1903 between Great Britain, Italy and Venezuela for submission of the sums due to a Mixed Commission. The Judges in this case also addressed a note to the Dutch Foreign Minister, containing recommendations in regard to the procedure of the Court[1].

The third case to come before the Court was between Great Britain,

---

[1] See Sir T. Barclay, *Problems, etc.* p. 278.

France and Germany on the one side, and Japan on the other[1].   The Pro-

(3) The case of the Japanese leases.

tocols'for submission were signed on the 28th Aug. 1902.   The question for settlement in this case was the true intent and meaning of the provisions of certain treaties made between the three European Powers and Japan with reference to the exemption of land held under leases in perpetuity granted by Japan from im-posts, taxes, charges, contributions or conditions other than those expressly stipulated in the leases in question.   The Court consisted of three members, Professor Louis Renault (of Paris), nominated by the three European Powers, Dr Itchiro Motono, nominated by the Japanese Government, under the presidency of the Umpire, Mr G. Gram, a former Prime Minister of State of Norway, chosen by the two Arbitrators.   In this case the Court announced that French would be the language of the Tribunal, but that the parties could use either English or French.   At a subsequent sitting, a request was made on behalf of the three European Powers for permission to employ the German language, whereupon the Japanese agent (speaking in English) claimed for the Japanese language the same right as would be accorded to other languages, a claim which the Court admitted.   It does not appear that the Japanese agent availed himself of this right.   The Court held four sittings in November, 1904, and May, 1905.   Judgment was delivered on the 22nd May, 1905.   The Tribunal by two to one decided in favour of the con-tention of the European governments that the provisions of the treaties between them and Japan not only exempted the lands possessed under perpetual leases granted by the Japanese Government or in its name, but they also exempted buildings of every kind erected, or to be erected on these lands from all imposts, taxes, charges, contributions or conditions whatsoever, other than those expressly stipulated in the leases in question. The Japanese member of the Court dissented from this judgment and the reasons for it.

In this case the pleadings were all in writing, and it does not appear that Counsel addressed the Court on the actual points at issue between the parties.

The fourth case to come before the Hague Tribunal was between

(4) The Muscat Dhows Case.

Great Britain and France[2].   The *Compromis* was signed on the 13th Oct. 1904.   It stated that the Government of His Britannic Majesty and that of the French Republic had

---

[1] *Brit. Parl. Papers*, Japan, No. 1 (1905), Vol. CIII. (1905), p. 301.   Anon. *L'arbitrage des baux perpetuels au Japon, Rev. gén. de Droit inter.*, Vol. XII. p. 492.

[2] *Brit. Parl. Papers*, Treaty Series, No. 3, 1905, Vol. CIII. (1905), p. 235 ; Muscat, No. 1 (1905), Vol. CXXXVI. (1906), p. 391.   For a further discussion of the case see an Article by

thought it right, by the Declaration of the 10th March, 1862, " to engage reciprocally to respect the independence " of His Highness the Sultan of Muscat, that difficulties had arisen (1) in relation to the issue by the French Republic, to certain subjects of the Sultan, of papers authorising them to fly the French flag, and (2) as to the nature of the privileges and immunities claimed by subjects of His Highness who are owners or masters of dhows, and in possession of such papers, or are members of the crews of such dhows, and their families, especially as to the manner in which such privileges and immunities affect the jurisdiction of the Sultan over his subjects, and that these questions should be referred to the arbitration of the Hague Tribunal. The *Compromis* provided that each Power should nominate one Arbitrator and these two should choose an Umpire, failing this the choice of the Umpire should be entrusted to the King of Italy. The Arbitrators and Umpire were not to be subjects or citizens of either Great Britain or France and should be chosen from among the members of the Hague Tribunal. It was further agreed that each party should prepare and deliver to the Tribunal a written or printed case supported by arguments and a file containing documents or other evidence on which he relied, and after the delivery of such cases, written or printed counter-cases, similarly supported, and that the Tribunal might require any further oral or written evidence, but in such case the other party had the right to reply. The British Government nominated the Hon. Melville W. Fuller, Chief Justice of the United States, the French Government nominated Dr A. F. de Savornin Lohman, a former Minister of the Interior of the Netherlands, and the King of Italy nominated Professor H. Lammasch, Member of the Upper House of the Austrian Parliament.

The Tribunal held its first meeting on the 25th July, 1905, and sat on four days, the last being the 8th August, when a unanimous decision of the Tribunal was given. The Court held that France by acceding to the General Act of the Brussels Conference of 1890 relative to the African slave trade, was not entitled to authorise vessels belonging to subjects of the Sultan of Muscat to fly the French flag except where their owners or fitters-out had been considered and treated by France as her protégés before 1863, or in the case of owners of dhows, who before 1892 had been authorised by France to fly the French flag, so long as France renews this authorisation to the grantee. On the second point the Court held

Prof. J. Westlake, K.C., in *The Law Quarterly Review*, Vol. xxiii. p. 83; see also M. Bressonnet, *L'arbitrage franco-anglais dans l'affaire des boutres de Mascate*, *Rev. gén. de Droit inter.* Vol. xiii. p. 145.

that dhows of Muscat duly authorised to fly the French flag were entitled in the territorial waters of Muscat to the inviolability provided by the French-Muscat Treaty of 17th Nov. 1844; that the authorisation to fly the French flag could not be transmitted or transferred to any other person or to any other dhow, even if belonging to the same owner; that subjects of the Sultan of Muscat who are owners or masters of dhows authorised to fly the French flag or who are members of the crews of such vessels or who belong to their families, do not enjoy in consequence of that fact any right of exterritoriality exempting them from the sovereignty or jurisdiction of the Sultan.

From the foregoing summary of the points at issue, and the decisions given in the cases which have so far come before the Hague Tribunal, its scope of operations and method of work may in some degree be appreciated. It is not necessary here to deal further with the questions involved.

It will thus be seen that within five years from the conclusion of the First Peace Conference at the Hague all three of the Conventions which emanated therefrom were put to the test. To deficiencies which became apparent in their working reference will be made in discussing the amendments adopted by the Second Conference.

The three Declarations were not adopted with unanimity; Great Britain (iii) The signed none of them, but on the 30th Aug. 1907 she became Declarations a party to Nos. 2 and 3. The first lapsed after 5 years. The of 1899. United States did not sign the second and third, and Portugal only signed on 29th Aug. 1907. Nevertheless Great Britain observed them all during the war in South Africa. They were all observed by Russia and Japan, both of whom had signed the Declarations.

The first Wish was realised in 1906 when a new Geneva Convention was adopted; the others (except No. 3, on which nothing (iv) The appears to have been done) were discussed at the Second Vœux. Peace Conference. The second, regarding the rights and duties of neutrals, and the sixth on the bombardment of unfortified towns by naval forces both resulted in Conventions in 1907.

The foregoing account of the results of the First Conference and their subsequent practical application is sufficient to justify the statement made at the time by Sir Julian Pauncefote that they "greatly surpassed the expectations of its most enthusiastic supporters." The growth of international law has not infrequently been compared to that of municipal law, and in particular to that of the English Common law. As a scientific body of principles it is still in an early stage of development, custom is ripening slowly into law and in some departments of international re-

lations, the work of codification has begun. The "enthusiastic supporters," of whom the British Ambassador spoke, were those who, knowing how exceeding slow is the grinding of the wheels of progress, were prepared for the difficulties which only statesmen, historians and lawyers could fully appreciate; their expectations were chastened by knowledge and experience of the innumerable forces at work in the domain of high politics. It is, therefore, from such a standpoint that a view of the work of the Second Conference must be taken.

THE SECOND PEACE CONFERENCE OF 1907[1].

The Hague Conference of 1899 did nothing definite to ensure a subsequent meeting except to express a wish that certain matters might be inserted in the programme of a Conference in the near future, but it "broke up with the conviction that its work would be completed subsequently by the regular progress of enlightenment among the nations, and as the result of the experience gradually acquired[2]." The Second Conference was, as the Final Act records, first proposed by the President of the United States (Mr Theodore Roosevelt). Several years having elapsed since the termination of the First Conference, and no steps having been taken to convoke another, the Hon. John Hay, American Secretary of State, on the 21st October, 1904, addressed a Circular to the representatives of the United States accredited to the Governments who were

---

[1] *Parl. Papers*, Miscellaneous, Nos. 1, 4, 5 and 6 (1908) ; *La Deuxième Conférence Internationale de la Paix, Actes et Documents* (3 vols.); Sir T. Barclay, *Problems of international practice and diplomacy with special reference to the Hague Conferences and Conventions and other General International Agreements* ; Idem, *The Second Hague Conference, Fortnightly Review*, June and Oct. 1907; Baron d'Estournelles de Constant, *The results of the Second Hague Conference, Am. Independent*, 21 Nov. 1907; A. H. Charteris, *The Second Peace Conference, Juridical Review*, Vol. xix. pp. 223, 347 ; A. Ernst, *L'œuvre de la deuxième Conférence de la Paix* ; A. H. Fried, *Die zweite Haager Konferenz* ; D. J. Hill, *The net result at the Hague, Am. Review of Reviews*, Dec. 1907 ; T. E. Holland, *The Hague Conference 1907, Law Quarterly Review*, Vol. xxiv. p. 76; T. J. Lawrence, *International Problems and Hague Conferences* ; A. de Lapradelle, *La guerre maritime après la nouvelle Conférence de la Paix, Revue des deux Mondes* (1 Aug. 1908), Ernest Lémonon, *La seconde Conférence de la Paix*; J. B. Moore, *Digest of Int. Law*, Vol. vii. p. 96; A. Pillet, *La cause de la Paix*; L. Renault, *Les deux Conférences de la Paix*; J. B. Scott, *The work of the Second Hague Peace Conference, Am. Journal of Int. Law*, Jan. 1908 ; Idem, *Texts of the Peace Conferences at the Hague* ; W. T. Stead, *Notes from the Hague, Review of Reviews* (London), Nov. 1907 ; Idem, *Impressions from the Hague, Contemporary Review*, Dec. 1907; A. Tardieu, *La deuxième Conférence de la Paix, Revue des deux Mondes*, 1st June, 1907; J. Westlake, *International Law, War*, Chapter xi.; Idem, *The Hague Conference, Quarterly Review*, Jan. 1908, p. 225; Anon. *The Second Hague Conference, Edin. Review*, Jan. 1908, p. 224; *Le Courrier de la Conférence*, edited by W. T. Stead ; E. A. Whittuck, *International documents*.

[2] Letter of Count Benckendorff to Sir Edward Grey, 3rd April, 1906.

signatories of the Acts of the Conference of 1899. A preliminary circular had been despatched shortly before by the Assistant Secretary of State.

After referring to the beneficial work done by the Hague Conference of 1899, and the questions which it left over for subsequent discussion, the Circular referred to the work done by the Inter-parliamentary Union in preparing the "minds of governments for an accord in the direction of the assured peace among men." The Annual Meeting of the Union, which was held in 1904 at St Louis, had passed a resolution requesting the several governments of the world to send delegates to an international Conference to be held for the purpose of considering (1) the questions for the consideration of which the Conference at the Hague expressed a wish that a future Conference should be called; (2) the negotiation of arbitration treaties between the nations represented at the Conference to be convened; (3) the advisability of establishing an international congress to be convened periodically for the discussion of international questions: it concluded by inviting the President of the United States to invite nations to send representatives to such a congress. In acceding to the request the President stated that he was not unmindful that a great war was in progress, but he recalled the fact that invitations to the First Hague Conference were sent out while the United States and Spain were at war, though during an armistice for the settlement of terms of peace. The American ministers were directed to bring the foregoing considerations to the attention of the Governments to which they were accredited, without specifically mentioning a programme for such Conference, except those matters which the Hague Conference of 1899 left for further discussion. He referred to the fact that on the 28th April, 1904, the Congress of the United States had resolved that it was desirable, in the interests of uniformity of action by the maritime states of the world in time of war, that the President endeavour to bring about an understanding among the principal maritime Powers with a view of incorporating into the permanent law of civilised nations the principle of the exemption of all private property at sea, not contraband of war, from capture or destruction by belligerents. After mentioning the questions of contraband and inviolability of postal correspondence, and the treatment of refugee belligerent ships in neutral ports, the Circular stated that the overture for a second Conference was not designed to supersede other calls for the consideration of special topics, such as the amendment of the Hague Convention with respect to hospital ships, and concluded by expressing the President's desire and hope that " the undying memories which cling round the Hague as the cradle of the beneficent work which had its

beginning in 1899 may be strengthened by the holding of the Second Peace Conference in that historic city [1]."

Russia, the originator of the First Conference, was, as the American Circular points out, at war with Japan, and the Russian Government stipulated that the Conference should not be held till war was terminated. This was ultimately brought about by the statesmanlike action of President Roosevelt. Meantime the Tsar made known his desire to be allowed to summon the Second Conference. The President at once yielded the precedence to the Emperor Nicholas II, and on the 3rd April, 1906, the following note was addressed with the assent of the Tsar by representatives of the Russian Government abroad to the Governments to which they were accredited [2].

LONDON.
April 3, 1906.

M. LE SECRÉTAIRE D'ETAT,

In convoking a second Peace Conference, the Imperial Government have had in view the necessity of giving a fresh development to the humanitarian principles which formed the basis of the work of the great international meeting of 1899.

They are at the same time of opinion that it is desirable to increase as far as possible the number of states taking part in the labours of the proposed Conference, and the enthusiasm which this appeal has met with proves how deep and widespread is the wish to-day to give effect to ideas having as their object the welfare of humanity.

The first Conference broke up with the conviction that its work would be completed subsequently by the regular progress of enlightenment among the nations and as the result of experience gradually acquired. Its most important creation, the International Court of Arbitration, is an institution which has already been tested, and which has collected for the common weal, as it were in the areopagus Court, jurists enjoying universal respect. It has also been proved how useful the International Commissions of Inquiry have been for settling differences which have arisen between one state and another.

There are, however, improvements to be made in the Convention relative to the pacific settlement of international disputes. As a result of recent arbitrations the jurists on the Tribunal have raised certain

---

[1] Mr Hay's letter is set forth *in extenso* in J. B. Moore, *Digest of Inter. Law*, Vol. VII. p. 96. J. B. Scott, *Texts of the Peace Conferences, etc.* p. 98. See also Sir T. Barclay, *Problems*, *etc.* p. 8.

[2] *Parl. Papers*, Misc. No. 1 (1908), p. 2.

questions of detail about which it is necessary to come to a decision, by giving to the said Convention the necessary developments. It seems, in particular, desirable that fixed principles should be laid down in regard to what languages are to be used in the Court, in view of the difficulties which might arise in the future, as recourse to arbitration jurisdiction became more frequent. There are, similarly, certain improvements to make in the working of the International Commissions of Inquiry.

As regards the codification of the laws and customs of war on land, the provisions adopted by the First Conference must likewise be completed, and so clearly defined as to preclude all possibility of misunderstanding.

In regard to naval warfare, as to which the laws and customs differ in certain particulars in different countries, it is necessary to establish fixed rules to meet both the requirements of the rights of belligerents and the interests of neutrals.

A Convention respecting these matters would have to be elaborated, and would form one of the most important duties of the next Conference.

Consequently, as it is at present desirable to examine only such questions as are of pressing importance, in the light of the experience of recent years, leaving untouched those questions which might affect the limitation of military or naval forces, the Imperial Government puts forward as the programme of the proposed meeting the following principal points :—

1. Improvements to be made in the provisions of the Convention relative to the Pacific Settlement of International Disputes, as far as the Court of Arbitration and the International Commissions of Inquiry are concerned.

2. Additions to be made in the provisions of the Convention of 1899 relative to the Laws and Customs of War on Land, among others, concerning the opening of hostilities, the rights of neutrals on land, etc. Declarations of 1899. One of them having lapsed, question of its renewal.

3. Elaboration of a Convention relative to the Laws and Usages of Naval Warfare concerning—

>Special operations in naval warfare, such as the bombardment of ports, towns, and villages by a naval force, laying torpedoes, etc.;
>Conversion of merchant-vessels into war-ships;
>Private property of belligerents at sea;
>The days of grace accorded to merchant-vessels for leaving neutral or enemy ports after the commencement of hostilities;

The rights and duties of neutrals at sea, among others, questions of contraband, the regulations to be applied to the belligerent vessels in neutral ports; destruction by *force majeure* of neutral merchant-ships detained as prizes.

In the said proposed Convention would be inserted provisions relative to war on land which would be likewise applicable to naval warfare.

4. Additions to be made in the Convention of 1899 for applying to naval warfare the principles of the Geneva Convention of 1864.

As at the Conference of 1899, it is fully understood that the deliberations of the proposed meeting shall not affect either the political relations between one country and another or the existing order of things as established by treaties, or, in general, questions not directly referred to in the programme adopted by the Cabinets.

The Imperial Government wishes it to be clearly understood that this programme and its eventual acceptance by the different states obviously does not prejudice any opinions which may be expressed at the Conference as to the solution to be given to questions submitted for discussion. Similarly it would be the duty of the proposed meeting to define the order in which questions are to be treated and the form which such decisions as are adopted should take, according as it should be considered preferable to include some of them in fresh Conventions or to add them to Conventions already in existence.

In formulating the above-mentioned programme, the Imperial Government has, as far as possible, taken into consideration the opinions expressed at the First Peace Conference, in particular in regard to the rights and duties of neutrals, private property of belligerents at sea, bombardment of ports, towns, etc. They trust that His Britannic Majesty's Government will recognise in the various suggestions an expression of the desire to arrive at that high ideal of international justice which is the constant aim of the whole civilised universe.

Under instructions from my Government, I have the honour to inform you of the above, and I have to add that the date of the assembling of the proposed Conference at the Hague should be the second half of July next (N.S.), the Netherland Government being also of opinion for their part that this date would be the most convenient.

Awaiting a reply from the Government of His Britannic Majesty at an early date, I have, etc.

(*Signed*) BENCKENDORFF.

The First Conference contained no representatives from the Central and South American Republics. In addressing an invitation to these and other states which did not take part in the First Conference a difficulty presented itself. The First Convention of the First Conference on the pacific settlement of international disputes was only open to signature by the Powers present at that Conference. By Article 60 it was provided as follows:—" The conditions upon which those Powers which were not represented in the International Peace Conference may accede to the present Convention shall form the subject of a further agreement between the contracting Powers." No such agreement had been concluded. As it was probable that the projected Conference would take the Conventions of 1899 into consideration, it was necessary to enable the newly-invited states to become parties to the Conventions if they wished. Count Benckendorff therefore suggested in another note of the 3rd April, 1906, that at the opening of the Second Conference the agreement contemplated by Article 60 should be entered into, and as a similar restriction did not exist in the case of the other two Conventions, the Russian Government approached the newly-invited states to signify their adherence to these two Conventions to the Netherland Government[1]. No objection was made to this course and the newly-invited states acceded to the Convention No. 1 of 1899 at the opening of the Conference in 1907, and those states which had hitherto not become parties to the other Conventions also signified their adherence. The date suggested by the Russian Circular was found to be inconvenient for two reasons. A Conference of the South American States had already been fixed for July, 1906, and the Swiss Government had summoned a meeting of the Powers for June, 1906, for the revision of the Geneva Convention of 1864. A further postponement was therefore necessary. Invitations were finally issued by the Dutch Government in May, 1907, to 47 states, and on the 15th June, 1907, the Conference was opened in the Hall of the Knights at the Hague by the Dutch Minister for Foreign Affairs. M. Nélidow, the Russian Ambassador in Paris, was elected President of the Conference. Forty-four states were represented; those who were not represented, though invited, were Abyssinia, Costa Rica and Honduras. The delegates of Corea sought to be included, but owing to the opposition of Japan were excluded[2].

The Programme for the discussion of the Conference had been sketched in the Circular of Count Benckendorff of the 3rd April, 1906, and in replying to it several states intimated their intention to bring forward additional

[1] Letter of Count Benckendorff to Sir Edward Grey, 3rd April, 1906.
[2] See note to Geneva Convention of 1906, p. 35.

subjects. The United States, Great Britain and Spain reserved the right of submitting the question of the reduction or limitation of armaments, and the growing expenditure on them. It is a noteworthy fact that though this question was the prime cause of the meeting of the First Conference and appeared in the forefront of Count Mouravieff's Circular it finds no place in that of Count Benckendorff. This in itself was not a hopeful omen for those who attached great weight to the pacific influence of such gatherings. The United States also intimated their intention of submitting an agreement for restricting the employment of force for the recovery of ordinary public debts resulting from contracts. Japan expressed the opinion that certain questions not specifically mentioned might be usefully included among the subjects to be examined. Bolivia, Denmark, Greece and the Netherlands also reserved the right of submitting to the Conference other subjects similar to those explicitly mentioned in the Circular. It was also clear that several governments did not expect fruitful results from some of the proposals, as the British, Japanese, German and Austro-Hungarian Governments reserved the right of abstaining from discussing questions which they did not consider would lead to useful results. In announcing, before the opening of the Conference, these new subjects for discussion the Russian Government made a similar reservation. Great Britain was represented by four delegates[1]: the Right Hon. Sir Edward Fry, G.C.B., the Right Hon. Sir Ernest Satow, G.C.M.G., the Right Hon. Lord Reay, G.C.S.I., G.C.I.E. and Sir Henry Howard, K.C.M.G., with a staff of seven legal, military and naval technical delegates (Lieut.-Gen. Sir Edmond R. Elles, G.C.I.E., K.C.B., Captain C. L. Ottley, M.V.O., R.N., A.D.C. (now Rear-Admiral Sir Charles Ottley), Mr Eyre Crowe, Mr Cecil Hurst, Lieut.-Col. the Hon. H. Yarde-Buller, D.S.O., Commander J. R. Segrave, R.N. and Major George K. Cockerill). The United States delegates were: the Hon. J. H. Choate, the Hon. Horace Porter, the Hon. U. M. Rose, the Hon. D. J. Hill, Rear-Admiral Sperry, General G. B. Davis, Mr W. I. Buchanan, with two technical delegates (Mr James Brown Scott and Mr C. H. Butler). One hundred and seventy-four names of Plenipotentiaries and delegates are enumerated in the Final Act; being nearly double the number attending the First Peace Conference.

The Second Plenary Meeting was held on the 19th June, when in consequence of the large number of the Plenipotentiaries and delegates it was agreed to adopt a set of 12 rules with a view to facilitate the business. Following the precedent of 1899, Committees were appointed, the Pleni-

---

[1] For the Instructions given to the British delegates see Appendix.

potentiaries of each Power being entitled to place themselves on as many as they chose and to designate their technical delegates. Great Britain and Germany objected to a portion of the eighth rule in the draft which allowed one Power to be represented by the Delegation of another Power, and this was suppressed. It was agreed that each Power should have only one vote. French was recognised as the official language for the deliberations and Acts of the Conference, speeches delivered in any other language to be translated into French through the medium of the Secretariat-General. Four Committees were appointed, and the subjects specified in Count Benckendorff's Circular were allotted among them.

To the First Committee: (1) Arbitration, (2) Commissions of international inquiry, (3) Questions relating to naval prizes; M. Bourgeois (France) was President of this Committee.

To the Second Committee: (1) Revision of the rules of war on land, (2) The three Declarations of 1899, (3) Rights and duties of neutrals in regard to land warfare, (4) The opening of hostilities; M. Beernaert (Belgium) was President of this Committee.

To the Third Committee: (1) The bombardment of ports, towns and villages by a naval force, (2) The placing of torpedoes and submarine mines, (3) Regulations for belligerent ships of war in neutral ports, (4) The revision of the Convention of 1899 applying to naval warfare the principles of the Geneva Convention of 1864 which was revised in 1906; Count Tornielli (Italy) was President of this Committee.

To the Fourth Committee: (1) The conversion of merchant-ships into ships of war, (2) Private property at sea, (3) Days of grace, (4) Contraband of war, (5) Blockade, (6) Destruction of neutral prizes, (7) Application of the rules of war on land to maritime warfare; M. de Martens (Russia) was President of this Committee.

Honorary Presidents and Vice-Presidents were appointed to each Committee. At the Second Plenary Meeting of the Conference the British and German delegates intimated that they proposed to submit projects for the establishment of an International Prize Court. The American delegate announced that he intended to bring before the Conference the question of the forcible collection of public debts, and the British delegate made a general reservation in favour of introducing other subjects during the sitting of the Conference. Besides the Four Committees mentioned there was also a Drafting Committee (*Comité de Rédaction*) and a Committee to examine and report on the numerous addresses, books, etc. presented to the Conference (*Commission des Adresses*). The First, Second and Third Committees were each divided into two Sub-Committees, and

Examining Committees were also appointed.   The size of the Committees as well as the different matters assigned to each made such an arrangement necessary.   The average number of each Committee was 93.   The United States had the largest number of representatives on each, varying from 8 on the Fourth Committee to 5 on the Third.   It will, however, be re-membered that each Power possessed but one vote.

The Conference held eleven plenary meetings; its work as well as that of the Committees whose reports were presented at these meetings will be dealt with in connection with the Conventions and " Wishes " set forth in the Final Act of the Conference adopted on the 18th Oct. 1907, and an endeavour will be made to deal with the results in the concluding chapter.

Actes Finals des Conférences Internationales de da Paix.

Acte Final de la Conférence Internationale de la Paix, 1899.

La Conférence Internationale de la Paix, convoquée dans un haut sentiment d'humanité par Sa Majesté l'Empereur de Toutes les Russies, s'est réunie sur l'invitation du Gouvernement de Sa Majesté la Reine des Pays-Bas, à la Maison Royale du Bois à La Haye, le 18 Mai, 1899.

Les Puissances, dont l'énumération suit, ont pris part à la Conférence, pour laquelle elles avaient désigné les Délégués nommés ci-après :—

[*Dénomination des Délégués des Puissances, dont l'énumération suit.*]

L'Allemagne, l'Autriche-Hongrie, la Belgique, la Chine, le Danemark, l'Espagne, les États-Unis d'Amérique, les États-Unis Mexicains, la France, la Grande-Bretagne et Irlande, la Grèce, l'Italie, le Japon, le Luxembourg, le Monténégro, les Pays-Bas, la Perse, le Portugal, la Roumanie, la Russie, le Serbie, le Siam, la Suède et la Norvège, la Suisse, la Turquie, la Bulgarie.

Acte Final de la Deuxième Conférence Internationale de la Paix, 1907.

La Deuxième Conférence Internationale de la Paix, proposée d'abord par M. le Président des États-Unis d'Amérique, ayant été, sur l'invitation de Sa Majesté l'Empereur de Toutes les Russies, convoquée par Sa Majesté la Reine des Pays-Bas, s'est réunie le 15 Juin, 1907, à La Haye, dans la Salle des Chevaliers, avec la mission de donner un développement nouveau aux principes humanitaires qui ont servi de base à l'œuvre de la Première Conférence de 1899.

Les Puissances, dont l'énumération suit, ont pris part à la Conférence, pour laquelle Elles avaient désigné les Délégués nommés ci-après :—

[*Dénomination des Délégués des Puissances, dont l'énumération suit.*]

L'Allemagne, les Etats-Unis d'Amérique, la République Argentine, l'Autriche-Hongrie, la Belgique, la Bolivie, le Brésil, la Bulgarie, le Chili, la Chine, la Colombie, la République de Cuba, le Danemark, la République Dominicaine, la République de l'Équateur, l'Espagne, la France, la Grande-Bretague, la Grèce, le Guatémala, la République d'Haïti, l'Italie, le Japon, le Luxembourg, le Mexique, le Monténégro, la Nicaragua, la Norvège, le Panama, le Paraguay, les Pays-Bas, le Pérou, la Perse, le Portugal, la Roumanie, la Russie, le Salvador, la Serbie, le Siam, la Suède, la Suisse, la Turquie, l'Uruguay, les États-Unis du Vénézuéla.

FINAL ACTS OF THE INTERNATIONAL PEACE CONFERENCES.

Final Act of the International Peace Conference, 1899.

The International Peace Conference, convoked in the best interests of humanity by His Majesty the Emperor of All the Russias, assembled on the invitation of the Government of Her Majesty the Queen of the Netherlands in the Royal House in the Wood at the Hague, on the 18th May, 1899.

The Powers enumerated in the following list took part in the Conference, to which they appointed the Delegates named below.

[*Names of Delegates of the following Powers.*]

Germany, Austria-Hungary, Belgium, China, Denmark, Spain, the United States of America[1], the United States of Mexico, France, Great Britain[1] and Ireland, Greece, Italy, Japan, Luxemburg, Montenegro, the Netherlands, Persia, Portugal, Roumania, Russia, Servia, Siam, Sweden and Norway, Switzerland, Turkey, Bulgaria.

Final Act of the Second International Peace Conference, 1907.

The Second International Peace Conference, proposed in the first instance by the President of the United States of America, having been convoked, on the invitation of His Majesty the Emperor of All the Russias, by Her Majesty the Queen of the Netherlands, assembled on the 15th June, 1907, at the Hague, in the Hall of the Knights, for the purpose of giving a fresh development to the humanitarian principles which served as a basis for the work of the First Conference of 1899.

The Powers enumerated in the following list took part in the Conference, to which they appointed the Delegates named below :—

[*Names of Delegates of the following Powers.*]

Germany, The United States of America[2], The Argentine Republic, Austria-Hungary, Belgium, Bolivia, Brazil, Bulgaria, Chile, China, Colombia, The Republic of Cuba, Denmark, The Dominican Republic, The Republic of the Ecuador, Spain, France, Great Britain[2], Greece, Guatemala, The Republic of Haïti, Italy, Japan, Luxemburg, Mexico, Montenegro, Nicaragua, Norway, Panama, Paraguay, The Netherlands, Peru, Persia, Portugal, Roumania, Russia, Salvador, Servia, Siam, Sweden, Switzerland, Turkey, Uruguay, The United States of Venezuela.

[1] For names of British and United States delegates in 1899 see *supra*, p. 42.
[2] For names of British and United States delegates in 1907 see *supra*, p. 57.

1899

Dans une série de réunions, tenues du 18 Mai au 29 Juillet, 1899, où les Délégués précités ont été constamment animés du désir de réaliser, dans la plus large mesure possible, les vues généreuses de l'Auguste Initiateur de la Conférence et les intentions de leurs Gouvernements, la Conférence a arrêté, pour être soumis à la signature des Plénipotentiaires, le texte des Conventions et Déclarations énumérées ci-après et annexées au présent Acte :—

I. Convention pour le règlement pacifique des conflits internationaux.

II. Convention concernant les lois et coutumes de la guerre sur terre.

III. Convention pour l'adaptation à la guerre maritime des principes de la Convention de Genève du 22 Août, 1864.

1907

Dans une série de réunions, tenues du 15 Juin au 18 Octobre, 1907, où les Délégués précités ont été constamment animés du désir de réaliser, dans la plus large mesure possible, les vues généreuses de l'Auguste Initiateur de la Conférence et les intentions de leurs Gouvernements, la Conférence a arrêté, pour être soumis à la signature des Plénipotentiaires, le texte des Conventions et de la Déclaration énumérées ci-après et annexées au présent Acte :—

1. Convention pour le règlement pacifique des conflits internationaux.

2. Convention concernant la limitation de l'emploi de la force pour le recouvrement de dettes contractuelles.

3. Convention relative à l'ouverture des hostilités.

4. Convention concernant les lois et coutumes de la guerre sur terre.

5. Convention concernant les droits et les devoirs des puissances et des personnes neutres en cas de guerre sur terre.

6. Convention relative au régime des navires de commerce ennemis au début des hostilités.

7. Convention relative à la transformation des navires de commerce en bâtiments de guerre.

8. Convention relative à la pose de mines sous-marines automatiques de contact.

9. Convention concernant le bombardement par des forces navales en temps de guerre.

10. Convention pour l'adaptation à la guerre maritime des principes de la Convention de Genève.

1899

At a series of meetings, between the 18th May and the 29th July, 1899, in which the above Delegates were throughout animated by the desire to realize, in the fullest possible measure, the generous views of the august initiator of the Conference and the intentions of their Governments, the Conference drew up for submission for signature by the Plenipotentiaries the text of the Conventions and Declarations enumerated below and annexed to the present Act :—

I. Convention for the pacific settlement of international disputes.

II. Convention respecting the laws and customs of war on land.

III. Convention for the adaptation to maritime war of the principles of the Geneva Convention of the 22nd August, 1864.

1907

At a series of meetings, held from the 15th June to the 18th October, 1907, in which the above Delegates were throughout animated by the desire to realize, in the fullest possible measure, the generous views of the august initiator of the Conference and the intentions of their Governments, the Conference drew up for submission for signature by the Plenipotentiaries, the text of the Conventions and of the Declaration enumerated below and annexed to the present Act :—

1. Convention for the pacific settlement of international disputes.

2. Convention respecting the limitation of the employment of force for the recovery of contract debts.

3. Convention relative to the opening of hostilities.

4. Convention respecting the laws and customs of war on land.

5. Convention respecting the rights and duties of neutral powers and persons in case of war on land.

6. Convention relative to the status of enemy merchant-ships at the outbreak of hostilities.

7. Convention relative to the conversion of merchant-ships into warships.

8. Convention relative to the laying of automatic submarine contact mines.

9. Convention respecting bombardment by naval forces in time of war.

10. Convention for the adaptation to maritime war of the principles of the Geneva Convention.

1899

1907

11. Convention relative à certaines restrictions à l'exercice du droit de capture dans la guerre maritime.

12. Convention relative à l'établissement d'une Cour internationale des prises.

13. Convention concernant les droits et les devoirs des Puissances neutres en cas de guerre maritime.

IV. Trois Déclarations concernant :

14. Déclaration relative à l'interdiction de lancer des projectiles et des explosifs du haut de ballons.

1. L'interdiction de lancer des projectiles et des explosifs du haut de ballons ou par d'autres modes analogues nouveaux.

2. L'interdiction de l'emploi des projectiles qui ont pour but unique de répandre des gaz asphyxiants ou délétères.

3. L'interdiction de l'emploi de balles qui s'épanouissent ou s'aplatissent facilement dans le corps humain, telles que les balles à enveloppe dure dont l'enveloppe ne couvrirait pas entièrement le noyau ou serait pourvue d'incisions.

Ces Conventions et Déclarations formeront autant d'Actes séparés. Ces Actes porteront la date de ce jour et pourront être signés jusqu'au 31 Décembre, 1899, par les Plénipotentiaires des Puissances représentées à la Conférence Internationale de la Paix à La Haye.

Ces Conventions et cette Déclaration formeront autant d'Actes séparés. Ces Actes porteront la date de ce jour et pourront être signés jusqu'au 30 Juin, 1908, à la Haye, par les Plénipotentiaires des Puissances représentées à la Deuxième Conférence de la Paix.

La Conférence, se conformant à l'esprit d'entente et de concessions réciproques qui est l'esprit même de ses délibérations, a arrêté la déclaration suivante qui, tout en réservant à chacune des Puissances représentées le bénéfice de ses votes, leur permet à toutes d'affirmer les principes qu'elles considèrent comme unanimement reconnus :—

1899	1907

1907

11. Convention relative to certain restrictions with regard to the exercise of the right of capture in naval war.

12. Convention relative to the creation of an International Prize Court.

13. Convention concerning the rights and duties of neutral Powers in naval war.

IV. Three Declarations :—

1. Prohibiting the discharge of projectiles and explosives from balloons or by other similar new methods.

2. Prohibiting the use of projectiles, the only object of which is the diffusion of asphyxiating or deleterious gases.

3. Prohibiting the use of bullets which expand or flatten easily in the human body, such as bullets with a hard envelope, of which the envelope does not entirely cover the core, or is pierced with incisions.

These Conventions and Declarations shall form so many separate Acts. These Acts shall be dated this day, and may be signed up to the 31st December, 1899, by the Plenipotentiaries of the Powers represented at the International Peace Conference at the Hague.

14. Declaration prohibiting the discharge of projectiles and explosives from balloons.

These Conventions and this Declaration shall form so many separate Acts. These Acts shall be dated this day, and may be signed up to the 30th June, 1908, at The Hague, by the Plenipotentiaries of the Powers represented at the Second Peace Conference.

The Conference, actuated by the spirit of mutual agreement and concession characterizing its deliberations, has agreed upon the following Declaration, which, while reserving to each of the Powers represented full liberty of action as regards voting, enables them to affirm the principles which they regard as unanimously admitted :—

<table>
<tr><td>

1899

</td><td>

1907

</td></tr>
</table>

1899	1907

1899

1907

Elle est unanime—

1. A reconnaître le principe de l'arbitrage obligatoire.

2. A déclarer que certains différends, et notamment ceux relatifs à l'interprétation et à l'application des stipulations conventionnelles internationales, sont susceptibles d'être soumis à l'arbitrage obligatoire sans aucune restriction.

Elle est unanime enfin à proclamer que, s'il n'a pas été donné de conclure dès maintenant une Convention en ce sens, les divergences d'opinion qui se sont manifestées n'ont pas dépassé les limites d'une controverse juridique, et qu'en travaillant ici ensemble pendant quatre mois toutes les Puissances du monde, non seulement ont appris à se comprendre et à se rapprocher davantage, mais ont su dégager, au cours de cette longue collaboration, un sentiment très élevé du bien commun de l'humanité.

Obéissant aux mêmes inspirations, la Conférence a adopté à l'unanimité la Résolution suivante :—

"La Conférence estime que la limitation des charges militaires qui pèsent actuellement sur le monde est grandement désirable pour l'accroissement du bien-être matériel et moral de l'humanité."

En outre, la Conférence a adopté à l'unanimité la Résolution suivante :—

La Deuxième Conférence de la Paix confirme la Résolution adoptée par la Conférence de 1899 à l'égard de la limitation des charges militaires ; et, vu que les charges militaires se sont considérablement accrues dans presque tous les pays depuis la dite année, la Conférence déclare qu'il est hautement désirable de voir les Gouvernements reprendre l'étude sérieuse de cette question.

Elle a, en outre, émis les vœux suivants :—

1. La Conférence, prenant en considération les démarches préliminaires

Elle a de plus émis les Vœux suivants :—

1. La Conférence recommande aux Puissances Signataires l'adoption du

<table>
<tr><td>1899</td><td>1907</td></tr>
</table>

1899

1907

It is unanimous—

1. In admitting the principle of compulsory arbitration.

2. In declaring that certain disputes, in particular those relating to the interpretation and application of the provisions of international agreements, may be submitted to compulsory arbitration without any restriction.

Finally, it is unanimous in proclaiming that, although it has not yet been found feasible to conclude a Convention in this sense, nevertheless the divergences of opinion which have come to light have not exceeded the bounds of judicial controversy, and that, by working together here during the past four months, the collected Powers not only have learnt to understand one another and to draw closer together, but have succeeded in the course of this long collaboration in evolving a very lofty conception of the common welfare of humanity.

Guided by the same sentiments, the Conference has unanimously adopted the following Resolution :—

"The Conference is of opinion that the restriction of military charges, which are at present a heavy burden on the world, is extremely desirable for the increase of the material and moral welfare of mankind."

The Conference has further unanimously adopted the following Resolution :—

The Second Peace Conference confirms the Resolution adopted by the Conference of 1899 in regard to the limitation of military expenditure ; and inasmuch as military expenditure has considerably increased in almost every country since that time, the Conference declares that it is eminently desirable that the Governments should resume the serious examination of this question.

. It has, besides, formulated the following wishes :—

1. The Conference, taking into consideration the preliminary steps

It has besides expressed the following wishes :—

1. The Conference calls the attention of the Signatory Powers to the

5—2

1899

faites par le Gouvernement Fédéral Suisse pour la revision de la Convention de Genève, émet le vœu qu'il soit procédé à bref délai à la réunion d'une Conférence spéciale ayant pour objet la révision de cette Convention.

Ce vœu a été voté à l'unanimité.

2.   La Conférence émet le vœu que la question des droits et des devoirs des neutres soit inscrite au programme d'une prochaine Conférence.

3.   La Conférence émet le vœu que les questions relatives aux fusils et aux canons de marine, telles qu'elles ont été examinées par elle, soient mises à l'étude par les Gouvernements, en vue d'arriver à une entente concernant la mise en usage de nouveaux types et calibres.

4.   La Conférence émet le vœu que les Gouvernements, tenant compte des propositions faites dans la Conférence, mettent à l'étude la possibilité d'une entente concernant la limitation des forces armées de terre et de mer et des budgets de guerre.

5.   La Conférence émet le vœu que la proposition tendant à déclarer l'inviolabilité de la propriété privée dans la guerre sur mer soit renvoyée à l'examen d'une Conférence ultérieure.

1907

projet ci-annexé de Convention pour l'établissement d'une Cour de Justice arbitrale, et sa mise en vigueur dès qu'un accord sera intervenu sur le choix des juges et la constitution de la Cour[1].

2.   La Conférence émet le vœu qu'en cas de guerre, les autorités compétentes, civiles et militaires, se fassent un devoir tout spécial d'assurer et de protéger le maintien des rapports pacifiques et notamment des relations commerciales et industrielles entre les populations des Etats belligérants et les pays neutres.

3.   La Conférence émet le vœu que les Puissances règlent, par des Conventions particulières, la situation, au point de vue des charges militaires, des étrangers établis sur leurs territoires.

4.   La Conférence émet le vœu que l'élaboration d'un règlement relatif aux lois et coutumes de la guerre maritime figure au programme de la prochaine Conférence et que, dans tous les cas, les Puissances appliquent, autant que possible, à la guerre sur mer, les principes de la Convention relative aux lois et coutumes de la guerre sur terre.

Enfin, la Conférence recommande aux Puissances la réunion d'une troisième Conférence de la Paix, qui pourrait avoir lieu dans une période

---

[1] See note 1, page 69.

1899

taken by the Swiss Federal Government for the revision of the Geneva Convention, expresses the wish that steps may be shortly taken for the assembly of a Special Conference having for its object the revision of that Convention.

This wish was voted unanimously.

2. The Conference expresses the wish that the question of the rights and duties of neutrals may be inserted in the programme of a Conference in the near future.

3. The Conference expresses the wish that the questions with regard to rifles and naval guns, as considered by it, may be studied by the Governments with the object of coming to an agreement respecting the employment of new types and calibres.

4. The Conference expresses the wish that the Governments, taking into consideration the proposals made at the Conference, may examine the possibility of an agreement as to the limitation of armed forces by land and sea, and of war budgets.

5. The Conference expresses the wish that the proposal, which contemplates the declaration of the inviolability of private property in naval warfare, may be referred to a subsequent Conference for consideration.

1907

advisability of adopting the annexed draft Convention for the creation of a Judicial Arbitration Court, and of bringing it into force as soon as an agreement has been reached respecting the selection of the Judges and the constitution of the Court[1].

2. The Conference expresses the wish that, in case of war, the responsible authorities, civil as well as military, should make it their special duty to ensure and safeguard the maintenance of pacific relations, more especially of the commercial and industrial relations between the inhabitants of the belligerent States and neutral countries.

3. The Conference expresses the wish that the Powers should regulate, by special Treaties, the position, as regards military charges, of foreigners residing within their territories.

4. The Conference expresses the wish that the preparation of regulations relative to the laws and customs of naval war should figure in the programme of the next Conference, and that in any case, the Powers may apply, as far as possible, to war by sea the principles of the Convention relative to the laws and customs of war on land.

Finally, the Conference recommends to the Powers the assembly of a third Peace Conference, which might be held within a period corresponding to

---

[1] For the draft Convention referred to, see *post*, p. 498.

1899	1907

6. La Conférence émet le vœu que la proposition de régler la question du bombardement des ports, villes, et villages par une force navale soit renvoyée à l'examen d'une Conférence ultérieure.

Les cinq derniers vœux ont été votés à l'unanimité, sauf quelques abstentions.

analogue à celle qui s'est écoulée depuis la précédente Conférence à une date à fixer d'un commun accord entre les Puissances, et elle appelle leur attention sur la nécessité de préparer les travaux de cette troisième Conférence assez longtemps à l'avance pour que ses délibérations se poursuivent avec l'autorité et la rapidité indispensables.

Pour atteindre à ce but, la Conférence estime qu'il serait très désirable que, environ deux ans avant l'époque probable de la réunion, un Comité préparatoire fût chargé par les Gouvernements de recueillir les diverses propositions à soumettre à la Conférence, de rechercher les matières susceptibles d'un prochain règlement international et de préparer un programme que les Gouvernements arrêteraient assez tôt pour qu'il pût être sérieusement étudié dans chaque pays. Ce Comité serait, en outre, chargé de proposer un mode d'organisation et de procédure pour la Conférence elle-même.

En foi de quoi, les Plénipotentiaires ont signé le présent Acte, et y ont apposé leurs cachets.

Fait à La Haye, le 29 Juillet, 1899, en un seul exemplaire, qui sera déposé au Ministère des Affaires Étrangères, et dont des copies, certifiées conformes, seront délivrées à toutes les Puissances représentées à la Conférence.

En foi de quoi les Plénipotentiaires ont signé le présent Acte et y ont apposé leurs cachets.

Fait à La Haye, le 18 Octobre, 1907, en un seul exemplaire, qui sera déposé dans les archives du Gouvernement des Pays-Bas et dont les copies, certifiées conformes, seront délivrées à toutes les Puissances représentées à la Conférence.

1899

6. The Conference expresses the wish that the proposal to settle the question of the bombardment of ports, towns, and villages by a naval force may be referred to a subsequent Conference for consideration.

The last five wishes were voted unanimously, saving some abstentions.

1907

that which has elapsed since the preceding Conference, at a date to be fixed by common agreement between the Powers, and it calls their attention to the necessity of preparing the programme of this third Conference a sufficient time in advance to ensure its deliberations being conducted with the necessary authority and expedition.

In order to attain this object the Conference considers that it would be very desirable that, some two years before the probable date of the meeting, a preparatory Committee should be charged by the Governments with the task of collecting the various proposals to be submitted to the Conference, of ascertaining what subjects are ripe for embodiment in an International Regulation, and of preparing a programme which the Governments should decide upon in sufficient time to enable it to be carefully examined by the countries interested. This Committee should further be intrusted with the task of proposing a system of organization and procedure for the Conference itself.

In faith whereof the Plenipotentiaries have signed the present Act, and have affixed their seals thereto.

Done at the Hague, 29th July, 1899, in a single copy, which shall be deposited in the Ministry for Foreign Affairs, and of which duly certified copies shall be delivered to all the Powers represented at the Conference.

In faith whereof the Plenipotentiaries have signed the present Act and have affixed their seals thereto.

Done at The Hague, the 18th October, 1907, in a single copy, which shall remain deposited in the archives of the Netherland Government, and of which duly certified copies shall be sent to all the Powers represented at the Conference.

THE FINAL ACTS OF THE INTERNATIONAL PEACE CONFERENCES
1899 AND 1907.

The Final Acts of the Conferences are authoritative statements of the
The Final   results arrived at, but the signature thereof by the delegates
Acts.   in no way committed the Powers to a signature of the Con-
ventions. Both in 1899 and 1907 the work of preparing the Final Acts
was entrusted to a Drafting Committee (*Comité de Rédaction*), of which
Professor Louis Renault was " Reporter " on both occasions.

The Final Act of the Second Peace Conference was entrusted to a Sub-
Committee of 8, and finally revised by the Drafting Committee of 29. At
the Ninth Plenary Meeting of the Conference, M. Renault gave an account
of the work of these bodies and explained the form in which the Final Act
was laid before the Conference for signature[1]. The form of the two Acts
is similar, but in that of the Second Conference reference is made to the
fact that the Conference was first proposed by President Roosevelt[2]. Then
follow the names of the Powers and the delegates, and a list of the Conventions and Declarations to be submitted to the Plenipotentiaries for
signature[3].

The name " Convention " was chosen for all the agreements of the
Conference, other designations, such as " Règlement" being not deemed
suitable for international Acts. The term " Règlement" is however
retained in Convention No. 4, on the Laws and Customs of War on
Land, which replaces No. 2 of 1899 on the same subject, but there was
a doubt whether the "Règlement" annexed to this Convention was as
binding on the contracting Powers as the Convention itself (Art. 1)[4].
The Final Acts were left open for signature for some months. In the
case of the Final Act of 1907 the period allowed for signature was about
3 months longer than was the case in 1899; this was in consequence of
the larger number of Powers represented at the Conference. In the case
of Convention No. 12 of 1907, for the establishment of an International
Prize Court, the protocol was left open until the 30th June, 1909. Apart

[1] *Parl. Papers*, Misc. No. 4 (1908), pp. 66–9 ; *La Deuxième Conférence Internationale de
la Paix*, T. I. (*Actes et Documents*), pp. 342–6.   [2] See *ante*, p. 51.

[3] The "Acte Final" is printed after the 13 Conventions and the Declaration in Vol. I.
of the Official Report of the Second Hague Conference, *La Deuxième Conférence Internationale
de la Paix*, T. I.; in the British Blue Book it is printed first, the Conventions and Declaration
following it.

[4] T. E. Holland, *The Laws of War on Land*, p. 5 ; L. Oppenheim, *Int. Law*, Vol. II. p. 77
(note) ; see *post*, p. 260.

from the Final Acts come the various Conventions, and the Declaration, which form so many separate Acts[1].

The question of accession of non-signatory Powers raised considerable discussion both in 1899 and 1907. In the case of the First Conference the system of the "open door" was adhered to except in the case of the Convention for the pacific settlement of international disputes[2]. In this case the special permission of the signatory Powers was required for the accession of non-signatory Powers. The door was closed, but might be opened, though not to everyone who cared to knock. The Powers represented at the First Conference were not willing to contract generally to submit to arbitration disputes which they might have with others than those then present. The accession of the Latin-American States was accepted on the opening of the Second Conference[3].

Accession of non-signatory Powers.

All the Powers present in 1907 were, by the Final Act, enabled to sign until the 30th June, 1908, but as regards those not represented, the question as to their accession was raised, though in a different manner from that in which it presented itself in 1899, by reason of the large increase in the number of the Powers represented, and the very small number which remained outside the deliberations of the Conference. There was no question of modifying the rule laid down by the Conference of 1899 with regard to the Convention for the pacific settlement of international disputes. Article 53 of Convention No. 12, for the establishment of an International Prize Court, reserves to certain Powers, determined beforehand in Article 15 and the annexed table, the right of acceding to the Convention. This provision was necessary so as not to destroy the harmony of the whole project which establishes an agreement between the composition of the Court and the number of the contracting Powers.

But in regard to the other Conventions three alternatives were proposed: (1) To adopt the principle of 1899 and leave the Conventions open. (2) To limit subsequent accession only to the Powers summoned to the Second Conference, which was equivalent to closing the Conventions. (3) To adopt the principle of the Geneva Convention of 1906 under which the Convention is closed, but non-contracting Powers are allowed to accede, and their accession is final unless a formal protest is lodged by one of the contracting Powers within a certain period[4]. The basis of the two latter views was that the signatory states formed a society into which a stranger could not enter without first knocking at the door. The system of the "open door" offered certain inconveniences to the Dutch Government, who

---

[1] *La Deux. Confér.* T. i. p. 343.
[2] *Parl. Papers*, Misc. No. 1 (1899), p. 260 ; Sir T. Barclay, *Problems*, etc. p. 43.
[3] See *ante*, p. 56.   [4] See *ante*, p. 32.

it was thought might find themselves embarrassed if application for accession were made by a Power whose status was doubtful. The Drafting Committee, however, adopted this principle on the grounds that any restrictive system would constitute a retrogressive movement, that the Conventions to which the principle was to apply (and it will be noticed it does not apply to Conventions 1 and 12) do not present the character of mutual concessions as is the case with Conventions made with some states only, for they are general in character, and are declarations of principles, and it is desirable that they should be established by as large a number of states as possible so as to constitute a code of universal law: lastly it was necessary to anticipate the possible case of one state obstinately refusing to allow a new state to become a party to the Conventions. The Conference adopted the recommendation of the Committee for the Conventions other than those mentioned, and each of the Conventions is concluded with a common formula of four Articles, commencing with "Non-signatory Powers may accede to the present Convention," except in the case of Convention No. 10, in which a slight restriction is made by Article 24 which states "Non-signatory Powers *which have accepted the Geneva Convention of the 6th July*, 1906, may accede to the present Convention[1]."

As regards the extent of the application of the Conventions, the general principle adopted is that they are only binding on the contracting Powers, and in case of the Conventions relating to war which contain provisions relative to neutrals, the Conventions only apply when all the belligerents are parties to the Convention except in the case of Convention No. 3 (see Art. 3).

The twenty-six Powers who took part in the First Conference in 1899 are enumerated in the preamble to the Final Act: forty-four Powers are enumerated in the Final Act in 1907. All the Powers who had not participated in the First Conference, and who were present at the Second, signed their accession to the Conventions of the First at the commencement of the Second. The following Powers, who were not parties to the Final Act of 1899, are parties to the Final Act of 1907: the Argentine Republic, Bolivia, Brazil, Chili, Colombia, Cuba, San Domingo, Ecuador, Guatemala, Haïti, Nicaragua, Panama, Paraguay, Peru, Salvador, Uruguay, Venezuela. Norway and Sweden, having dissolved their union in 1905, appear as two separate states. It will also be noticed that Bulgaria, which in 1899 signed after Turkey, is in 1907 placed in alphabetical order with the other Powers. The only state represented at the Second Conference which has not, up to the present, signed the Final Act is Paraguay, though it has signed all the Conventions. Switzerland signed the

Signatory Powers of the Final Acts.

---

[1] *La Deux. Confér.* T. I. pp. 843–4; *Parl. Papers*, Misc. No. 4 (1908), pp. 67–8.

Final Act under reservation of "Wish" No. 1 (for the creation of a Judicial Arbitration Court) which the Swiss Federal Council does not accept.

A slight change was made in the mode of execution of the Conventions of 1907. The long formality of sealing was suppressed for all the Conventions, and only retained for the Final Act. Before dealing with the Conventions and Declaration agreed to at the two Conferences, the Resolutions and Wishes must be referred to.

The Wishes (Vœux).

In the note which Count Mouravieff on the 12th August, 1898, handed to the members of the diplomatic corps at St Petersburg, a note which constituted the first cause of the Hague Conferences, "the maintenance of universal peace and a possible reduction of the excessive armaments which weigh upon all nations," was represented as the ideal towards which the efforts of all Governments should be directed. The second circular of the 12th Jan., 1899, took note of the fact that the political horizon had in the interval undergone a change, but the Imperial Government put forward a programme for discussion in which the limitation of the progressive increase of military and naval armaments appeared as the first item. At the First Conference the Russian proposal was to maintain the *status quo* of the armed forces and military estimates for five years. Count Mouravieff's circular had stated that financial burdens, constantly on the increase, were affecting public prosperity at its source; that the intellectual and physical forces of the peoples, labour and capital were to a large extent diverted from their natural application and were unproductively consumed; and that the armed peace of modern Europe had become a crushing burden which the peoples had more and more difficulty in bearing. This was not the opinion of the German delegate[2], nor of the French, but, said the latter (M. Bourgeois), if both in Germany and France the great resources which are now devoted to military organisation were, at least in part, put to the service of peaceful and productive activity, the grand total of the prosperity of each country would not cease to increase at an even more rapid rate.

The limitation of armaments and military budgets[1].

---

[1] Sir T. Barclay, *Problems*, etc. pp. 123–130; A. Ernst, *L'œuvre de la Deuxième Conférence de la Paix*, p. 55; E. Lémonon, *La seconde Conférence de la Paix*, pp. 719–735; "The limitation of Armaments," *The Times*, 20 July, 1906; R. P. Hobson, *Disarmament*, Am. Journ. of Inter. Law, Vol. II. p. 743; B. F. Trueblood, *The case for limitation of Armaments*, Idem, p. 758. The subject is treated fully in the various works dealing with the Hague Conferences mentioned in the note on p. 51.

[2] *Parl. Papers*, Misc. No. 1 (1899), p. 113.

The limitation of armaments and the reduction of military burdens as means of reducing the chances of war were remedies which appealed to the popular imagination; but the discussions showed that the difficulties in carrying them into effect, which had never been absent from the minds of statesmen, were unsurmountable. The military forces of a nation do not always correspond with the amounts of their military budgets or the numbers of men enrolled in time of peace. The position of no two states is identical: geographical, physical, and political conditions, the density, rapidity of growth, and state of education of the population, the position of a state in regard to colonies, coaling stations and means of communication, its dependence for food supplies on ocean-borne trade, its financial credit and natural resources, are all factors to be taken into account. It was not found possible to frame any formula which could apply to all states, and as M. Nélidow stated in 1907, keen differences of opinion soon broke out, and the debates assumed such a character, that, instead of the desired understanding, there was a danger of a disagreement which might have proved fatal to the rest of the labours of the Conference. Formal homage was paid to the Tsar's ideal by the passing of the Resolution which declared that the restriction of military budgets was extremely (*grandement*) desirable, and by the emission of the *Vœu* that Governments would examine the possibility of an agreement as to the limitation of armed forces and war budgets.

The subject of the reduction of military budgets and disarmament was absent from the circular of Count Benckendorff. Much had happened since 1899. The position of Russia after the termination of the Russo-Japanese war did not permit her to consider that the limitation of armaments was an urgent question. In the interval of the two Conferences the question had however not been allowed to remain dormant. The subject was discussed in the House of Commons on 10th May, 1906, and in the House of Lords on the 25th May, and in the French and Italian Chambers of Deputies in June of the same year[1]. Subsequently Sir H. Campbell-Bannerman, when Prime Minister, expressed himself strongly against the policy of huge armaments and in favour of the reconsideration of the subject by the Powers[2]. Notwithstanding the fact that the British Government had reason to anticipate that the discussion of the question would lead to no fruitful results, the British delegates were instructed to bring it forward at the Conference of 1907[3]. At the Fourth Plenary

[1] Sir T. Barclay, *Problems, etc.* p. 125.
[2] See Article in *The Nation* of 2 March, 1907.
[3] For Instructions on this subject see Appendix.

Meeting of the Conference on the 18th August, Sir Edward Fry proposed that the Conference should confirm the Resolution adopted in 1899 in regard to the limitation of the military charges, and, in view of their great increase, should put it on record that it is eminently (*hautement*) desirable that Governments should resume their study of the question[1]. The British Plenipotentiary in his speech drew attention to the fact that between 1898 and 1906 the military expenditure of Europe, the United States and Japan had increased from £251,000,000 to £320,000,000, and stated that with a view of assisting in a reduction of this non-productive expenditure the British Government would be willing to communicate annually their programme to other Powers who would pursue the same course. The late Lord Goschen in a speech in 1906 in the House of Lords made a somewhat similar proposal, but on this occasion Sir Edward Fry on behalf of the British Government made the offer formally to the whole world. So far no Power seems to have accepted it. Sir Edward Fry's motion received the support of the French delegate, M. Bourgeois, and the President communicated to the Conference a note from the delegates of Argentine and Chili containing the terms of a treaty which had been entered into on the 28th May, 1902, for the mutual reduction of the armaments of their countries for five years[2]. The discussion was felt however to be purely academic. "Contact with reality," said M. Nélidow, "soon showed that the noble ideal of the Tsar concealed practical difficulties when it became a question of putting it into application." The Resolution, which committed no one, was carried unanimously with applause.

The problem of disarmament or the limitation of armaments is one of the greatest difficulty. Armaments are not a cause of war in themselves; often they afford the best guarantee of peace. The sense of insecurity felt by nations, and the increase of their means of defence are due to moral causes; they spring from a lack of international confidence and the instinct of self-preservation. Disarmament, or even the reduction of armaments will not be effected so long as there is the fear that while some Powers adopt this course others will not. The lack of confidence in the protestations of pacific intentions which some of the greatest military Powers make from time to time prevents the reduction of the vast burdens which all the great Powers are increasingly putting on their citizens. Until the causes of international distrust are removed, progress towards the solution of the disarmament problem will be stayed. "La deuxième Conférence," writes M. de Lapradelle, "n'accorde à la limitation des armamens, proclamée

---

[1] *Parl. Papers*, Misc. No. 1 (1908), p. 27 ; *La Deux. Confér.* T. i. p. 90.
[2] A translation of this treaty is given by Sir T. Barclay, *Problems*, etc. pp. 128–9.

grandement désirable en 1899, *hautement* désirable en 1907, qu'une attention indifférente et lointaine, négligemment fixée dans un vœu sceptique, dont la molle formule cherche moins à flatter les amateurs de mirages qu'à leur adoucir la peine de l'illusion déçue[1]."

Of the other *Vœux* which were expressed by the Conference of 1899, No. 1 produced a practical result in the Geneva Convention of 1906, and Nos. 2 and 6 form the basis of Conventions Nos. 5, 9 and 13 of the Conference of 1907. No. 3 appears up to the present to have been fruitless. No. 4 has already been dealt with. There remains only No. 5 in which the Conference expressed the wish that the proposal which contemplates the declaration of the inviolability of private property in naval warfare may be referred to a subsequent Conference for consideration.

The immunity of enemy private property at sea[2].

At the First Hague Conference the United States delegates presented the following proposition: "The private property of all citizens or subjects of the signatory Powers, with the exception of contraband of war, shall be exempt from capture or seizure on the high seas or elsewhere by the armed vessels or the military forces of any of the said signatory Powers. But nothing herein contained shall extend exemption from seizure to vessels and their cargoes which may attempt to enter a port blockaded by the naval forces of any of the said Powers[3]." The Conference did not consider the discussion of this proposition to be within its competence, but adopted the *Vœu* set forth in the Final Act.

At the Second Conference the subject was assigned to the Fourth Committee, and M. Fromageot presented their Report at the Seventh Plenary Meeting[4]. The proposition was again brought forward by the United States Delegation and was framed in similar terms to those in

[1] *La guerre maritime, etc.* in *La Revue des deux Mondes,* 1 Aug. 1908, p. 676.

[2] The literature on this subject is great, and the question is discussed by all writers on Public International Law. L. Oppenheim, *Int. Law,* Vol. II. pp. 179 and 186, gives a list of authors who discuss the question of confiscation of enemy property at sea, and in addition reference may be made to the following: F. W. Holls, *The Peace Conference,* pp. 306–321; J. Westlake, *War,* pp. 129–132, 311–314; Sir T. Barclay, *Problems, etc.* pp. 68–70; C. H. Stockton, *Am. Journ. of Int. Law,* Oct. 1907, p. 930; E. Lémonon, *La seconde Conférence, etc.* p. 623; N. Bentinck, *War and private property,* pp. 85–96; Lord Loreburn's (then Sir R. Reid) letter to *The Times,* 14 Oct. 1905, since edited with notes by F. W. Hirst; A. de Lapradelle, *La guerre maritime, La Revue des deux Mondes,* 1 Aug. 1908, p. 676; *Livre Jaune,* p. 101; Captain Mahan, *National Review,* June, 1907; Julian S. Corbett, *Nineteenth Century and after,* June, 1907.

[3] *Parl. Papers,* Misc. No. 1 (1899), pp. 108–111, 165–8. The United States Government in 1856 refused to accede to the Declaration of Paris in consequence of the non-acceptance of this principle. See *supra,* p. 3.

[4] See *Parl. Papers,* Misc. No. 1 (1908), p. 187; *La Deux. Confér.* T. I. p. 245 for M. Fromageot's Report on which the following summary is based. See also *Livre Jaune,* p. 101.

which it had been presented in 1899 by Mr A. D. White[1], and Mr Choate's
speech in moving it in the Committee followed similar
lines of reasoning. He traced the historical continuity of
the doctrine onwards from 1783 when Benjamin Franklin
proposed to Great Britain a treaty that in case of war between the two
Powers all traders with their unarmed vessels employed in commerce
should be allowed to pass freely unmolested. He cited treaties which
had been entered into embodying the principle of abolition of capture of
private property and the numerous expressions of opinion in its favour
from statesmen, merchants and jurists. He urged the analogy of land
warfare, the lack of military interest in the destruction of commerce,
reasons of humanity, the losses occasioned to neutrals, the need for
limiting war to the armed forces of the belligerents, and the risk
of calling out a spirit of revenge and reprisals, and he concluded by
intimating that President Roosevelt desired a vote of the Conference on
the American proposal. The Russian delegates were of opinion that the
question was not yet ready for solution, for the American proposition
presupposed preparatory agreements and experience which were lacking
up to the present time. The dread of great pecuniary losses both to
belligerents and neutrals by the outbreak of war was, it was pointed out,
one of the strongest guarantees of the peace of the world. The delegates
of Brazil, Sweden and Norway supported the American proposal. The
latter speaking for a Power largely interested in shipping, and for a country
which he hoped would always be neutral, preferred that the self-interest of
neutrals who would certainly gain by the maintenance of the *status quo*
should give place to principles of humanity. The delegates of Holland,
Greece and Austria also spoke on the same side, which received the
qualified support of the German Plenipotentiary, Baron Marschall von
Bieberstein, who, however, contended that the subject could not be
considered by itself, as it was too closely allied to the questions of
blockade and contraband to be able to be settled until these questions
were first solved. The Portuguese delegate expressed a similar view.
Strong opposition to the American proposal came from the Argentine
and Colombian delegates, the latter (M. Triana) observing that the
maintenance of the rule was essential for countries with great natural
wealth which might excite the cupidity of stronger Powers. Sir Ernest
Satow, speaking for Great Britain, opposed the American proposal[2].
He pointed out that the adoption of it would produce an abolition of

The United
States pro-
posal in 1907.

[1] Mr White's speech is printed *in extenso* in Parl. Papers, Misc. No. 1 (1899), p. 166.
[2] For British Instructions on this head see Appendix.

commercial blockade, that attempts to limit blockades would produce friction, but while unable to accept the American proposal Great Britain desired to have the interests of neutrals respected, hence the British proposal for the abolition of contraband.

The unanimous acceptance of the American proposal was obviously not possible, but before a vote was taken on it various proposals for modifying the existing rigour of the law of capture were taken into consideration.

Brazil proposed that pending the acceptance of the American proposition, the Powers should put in force the principles of Articles 23, 28, 46, 47 and 53 of the Convention of 1899 on the laws and customs of war on land. These as further explained by M. Ruy Barbosa would enable a belligerent to capture enemy merchantmen and cargo, even when neutral, if the necessities of war so demanded, receipts being given as if for requisitions: while the crew of a captured enemy were to be put ashore in a neutral port[1].

Other proposals in 1907 for mitigating the rules of capture of private property at sea.

The Belgian proposition consisting of 12 Articles was to substitute sequestration for capture of enemy ships and their cargoes, the crews being liberated on condition of not serving against the captor during the war; and to forbid the destruction of prizes except under special circumstances. At the termination of the war, property so sequestered was to be returned, or if sold or destroyed its value to be handed to the former owners[2].

The Dutch delegate proposed that exemption should be accorded to every ship to which the enemy had delivered a passport certifying that it would not be used as a ship of war, and subject to certain modifications he supported the Belgian proposal.

Lastly, the French delegate, while willing to accept the United States proposition if a unanimous agreement could be reached, suggested certain modifications in the existing rule in the meantime. He argued that as war is a relation of state to state, interference with the commerce of the enemy is perfectly justifiable. It is a powerful means of coercion, but its legitimate exercise should be directed against the resources of the state and not against private individuals, and therefore it should not be used as a means of gain to individuals. With a view of carrying out these ideas, he expressed the desire (*vœu*) that the distribution of prize-money among the crews of the capturing ships should be suppressed, and that means should be taken to ensure that the loss occasioned by the capture of private property should fall on the state.

---

[1] E. Lémonon, *op. cit.* p. 634.   [2] See E. Lémonon, *op. cit.* p. 635.

The American proposition of *absolute immunity from capture of enemy property at sea* was put to the vote, when 21 states voted *for*, 11 *against*, and one abstained; 11 states were absent. The states voting *for* were: Germany (with the reservations before mentioned[1]), the United States, Austria-Hungary, Belgium, Brazil, Bulgaria, China, Cuba, Denmark, Ecuador, Greece, Hayti, Italy, Norway, Holland, Persia, Roumania, Siam, Sweden, Switzerland and Turkey. *Against*: Colombia, Spain, France, Great Britain, Japan, Mexico, Montenegro, Panama, Portugal, Russia and Salvador. *Abstained*, Chili.

Result of the discussion at the Hague in 1907.

On the Brazilian proposition *for the assimilation of the laws of war on sea to those on land*, 13 states voted *for*, 12 *against*. It was therefore withdrawn.

On the Belgian proposition *for the substitution of sequestration for confiscation* 14 states voted *for* the 1st Article, 9 *against*, 7 being absent. It was therefore withdrawn.

The President (M. de Martens) sought to bring about a compromise by proposing the "Wish" that at the commencement of hostilities Powers should declare if, and under what conditions, they would renounce the right of capture, but various objections were raised and it was withdrawn. A vote was then taken on the French proposal *for the suppression of prize-money* as modified by the Austro-Hungarian delegate, who had proposed *the participation by the State in the losses by capture*. The first part expressing the desire that Powers which maintained the right of capture should be invited to consider means of abolishing prize-money was adopted by 16 to 4, 14 states abstaining: on the second part in favour of State indemnity, only 7 states voted *for* (these included Great Britain), while 13 voted *against*, and 14 abstained. Here, so far as the Committee were concerned, the matter terminated, but the Brazilian proposition is largely reflected in the fourth "Wish" adopted in the Final Act which records that the Powers should apply, as far as possible, to war by sea the principles of the Convention relative to the laws and customs of war on land.

An examination of this question in all its bearings is impossible in this connection. The instructions of the British delegates clearly set forth the view which the Government of this country took on the matter before the Conference, and the results of the Conference showed that the questions of the immunity of enemy private property at sea as well as those of contraband and blockade must all be considered together in relation to the proposed creation of an International Prize Court, and the law which it is to administer.

[1] See *ante*, p. 79.

The " Wishes" enumerated in the Final Act of the Second Conference are the summary of its failures to reach any definite conclusion.

The Final Act of 1907, after an enumeration of the 13 Conventions
Obligatory   and the Declaration agreed upon states that the delegates
arbitration.   unanimously admitted the principle of obligatory arbitration, and declares that certain disputes, in particular those relating to the interpretation and application of the provisions of international agreements, may be submitted to obligatory arbitration without any restriction, it ends with the rhetorical statement that though it had not been found feasible to conclude a Convention in this sense the Powers had learnt to understand one another and to draw closer together and had "succeeded in the course of this long collaboration in evolving a lofty conception of the common welfare of humanity." This was adopted at the Ninth Plenary Meeting of the Conference by 41 votes; the United States, Japan and Roumania did not vote.

The problem of obligatory arbitration was considered by the First Committee, and its Sub-Committee, and various propositions were examined by a Special Committee (Committee "A") which held 16 meetings. The Report of Baron Guillaume which was presented to the Ninth Plenary Meeting is a document of great length and contains a *résumé* of the propositions and arguments which the Committees had had under consideration[1].

Article 16 of the Convention of 1899 for the pacific settlement of international disputes recognised arbitration as the most effective, and at the same time the most equitable means of settling disputes which diplomacy has failed to settle in questions of a legal nature, and especially in the interpretation or application of international conventions. It was hoped by many states that the Conference of 1907 would go further and produce a Convention whereby the Powers represented would agree to accept compulsory arbitration in disputes regarding certain definite matters. Various proposals with this object were presented by the Dominican Republic, Brazil, Portugal, Servia, Sweden, Great Britain and the United States, but the discussion chiefly turned on the Portuguese proposal, based upon a draft prepared by the Inter-parliamentary Union which was subsequently amended by, and to a large degree embodied in, a proposal formulated by Great Britain and the United States and supported by France. Under

---

[1] *Parl. Papers*, Misc. No. 4 (1908), pp. 851–428; *La Deux. Confér.* T. ɪ. pp. 455–552; *Livre Jaune*, pp. 42–54; E. Lémonon, *La seconde Conférence*, pp. 121–187; A. B. Fried, *Die zweite Haager Konferenz*, pp. 89–119; W. J. Hull, *Obligatory arbitration and the Hague Conferences*, Am. *Journ. of Int. Law*, Vol. ɪɪ. p. 781.

the Portuguese proposal the contracting Powers agreed to submit to arbitration, without any reservations, disputes on some 18 subjects: the British proposal eliminated several and altered the definitions of others. The draft in this form was called the "Projet du Comité d'Examen" or "Projet anglo-portugais-américain."

The chief opposition came from Germany. Baron Marschall von Bieberstein, while declaring himself favourable to the principle of obligatory arbitration under certain conditions and reservations, made it clear that he was not prepared to go beyond this general acceptance of principle. His main line of argument was as follows. If awards are given of a contradictory character regarding the interpretation of international treaties to which many states are parties, the existence of these treaties will be imperilled. Awards in contradiction with judicial verdicts of national tribunals in respect of the interpretation and application of international treaties will create an impossible situation. Awards to the effect that a state ought to alter its laws in accordance with an international treaty may produce serious conflicts with legislative bodies. And as regards the lists submitted, some matters were too unimportant to include, others were too serious without the reservation of "honour and vital interests[1]."

It was evident that Germany would not fall in line with the great majority of the Powers on these questions, though Baron Marschall's arguments were equally cogent in regard to the proposal to establish an international prize court which he was supporting. Strenuous endeavours were made to frame lists of subjects which would receive the acceptance of the Powers. The British proposal contained a table with a list of 22 subjects against which states should write their acceptance or rejection. Germany, however, was not prepared to accept or formulate any list. The Austro-Hungarian delegate (M. Mérey de Kapos-Mère) proposed that the Conference should content itself with a declaration which accepted the general principle of obligatory arbitration, but should state that, as difficulties were experienced in arriving at an agreement, the Conference would invite the Governments represented to make a further study of the questions and submit them to an international Committee[2]. This failed to receive the unanimous support of the Sub-Committee. Italy submitted another amendment by way of an addition to Article 16 of the Convention for the pacific settlement of disputes, whereby the Powers undertook to study the question and report by the 31st Dec. 1908 to the Dutch Government the matters which they

---

[1] *Parl. Papers*, Misc. No. 4 (1908), p. 868; *La Deux. Confér.* T. i. p. 476.
[2] *Parl. Papers*, Misc. No. 4 (1908), p. 870; *La Deux. Confér.* T. i. p. 479.

were prepared to make the subject of a Convention on obligatory arbitration, but this also was rejected by Germany. Thus the attempts of the two members of the Triple Alliance to facilitate the adhesion of the third to some form of obligatory arbitration were unsuccessful. After weeks of fruitless endeavour to reach unanimity the Anglo-Portuguese-American proposals were submitted to the Committee and voted upon. The debate lasted two days, when this draft was carried by 32 votes against 9: 3 states abstained from voting. The majority agreed to accept obligatory arbitration in disputes concerning the interpretation and application of treaties with regard to the following matters: (1) mutual relief of indigent sick persons; (2) international protection of labour; (3) means of preventing collisions at sea; (4) weights and measures; (5) measurement of vessels; (6) wages and effects of deceased seamen; (7) protection of literary and artistic works; also for claims for pecuniary damages when the principle of indemnity was recognised by the parties. The states which voted against the project were: Germany, Austria-Hungary, Belgium, Bulgaria, Greece, Montenegro, Roumania, Switzerland and Turkey. Italy, Japan and Luxemburg abstained from voting—the Japanese delegate, though not voting, announced that his Government was not prepared to accept obligatory arbitration, as the Court might adopt legal principles in opposition to those which his Government had adopted. The subjects on which the majority agreed to accept compulsory arbitration were not matters of great importance, but even these would have been welcomed as affording evidence of a practical acceptance of the principle. The opposition of Germany and Austria-Hungary, and the abstention of Italy, were fatal to their acceptance.

Notwithstanding the largeness of the majority, the Committee, acting on the principle that unanimity was requisite for a Convention, limited its recommendation to the acceptance of the *Vœu* suggested by Count Tornielli, which the Conference adopted. Mr Choate, however, was unable to accept this, as he considered that it constituted a real and serious retreat, and its adoption would imperil the cause of arbitration; he therefore abstained from voting at the Ninth Plenary Meeting. Japan and Roumania also abstained. The *principle* of obligatory arbitration was therefore accepted *nem. con.*

In one important point, however, the Conference was able to register a success, namely, Convention No. 2, respecting the limitation of force for the recovery of contract debts, which in effect makes arbitration compulsory in such cases[1].

---

[1] See *post*, pp. 180–197.

The first *Vœu* of the Second Conference relates to an annexed draft
Judicial
Arbitration
Court.
for the creation of a Judicial Arbitration Court, and will be discussed in connection with the text of the draft Convention [1].

The second and third *Vœux* emanated from the Second Committee to
Neutrals in
belligerent
territory [2].
which was referred the subject of the rights and duties of neutrals on land. The second *Vœu* expresses the desire that in case of war the responsible authorities, civil and military, should make it their special duty to ensure and safeguard the maintenance of pacific relations, more especially the commercial and industrial relations, between the inhabitants of the belligerent states and neutral countries. By the third the Conference expresses the opinion that the Powers should regulate, by special treaties, the position, as regards military charges of foreigners residing within their territories.

The Second Committee, for which Colonel Borel (Swiss delegate) acted as "Reporter," presented a report to the Fifth Plenary Meeting of the Conference, in which they recommended the addition of two chapters to the Regulations for war on land containing 11 Articles which were based on a draft introduced by the German delegate. Chapter 1, containing draft Articles 61–63, dealt with the definition of a neutral; Chapter 2, containing draft Articles 64–68, dealt with services rendered by neutrals, and the treatment of neutral property. The discussion at the Fifth Plenary Meeting on the 7th Sept. showed so much divergence of opinion with regard to the draft Articles 64 and 65, and so many reservations were made, that the draft was remitted to the Committee for further consideration. The Articles in question proposed to confer special benefits on neutral aliens resident in belligerent territory, both as regards the treatment of their persons and property. It was proposed to enact that belligerents should not requisition neutrals for services having direct bearing on the war except for sanitary services or sanitary police absolutely demanded by the circumstances (64). That such exemption from service should not apply to persons who had voluntarily enlisted in a belligerent army, nor to persons belonging to the army of a belligerent state in virtue of the legislation of that state (65). As regards neutral property it was proposed that no contribution of war should be levied on neutrals (66); that the destruction, injury or seizure of neutral property should be prohibited except in case

[1] See *post*, p. 498.
[2] *Parl. Papers*, Misc. No. 4 (1908), pp. 38–86, 184–145; *La Deux. Confér.* T. I. pp. 125–9, 150–161, 163, 176–8; J. Westlake, *War*, p. 285; *Livre Jaune*, pp. 79–82; A. S. de Bustamente, *Am. Journ. of Int. Law*, Vol. II. p. 115.

of absolute necessity, and then compensation should be paid (67); that belligerents should undertake to grant compensation for use of neutral immoveable property (68); and also for expropriation or use of neutral moveable property (69). The difficulty in regard to the draft Articles 64 and 65 turned partly on the difference of treatment as regards military service by various states of domiciled aliens and their children born within their territory, in which there is a striking lack of uniformity. Several of the Spanish-American states have been engaged in controversies with European Powers who have considered that the principle of nationality by parentage ought to exempt the children of their nationals, born within the territory of such states, from military service [1]. Several states have, by treaties, expressly guarded against the compulsory enrolment of their subjects for other than police purposes [2]. Some states, such as Switzerland, have replaced military service by a tax, and France and Spain have, by treaty of 1862, agreed that Spaniards born in France, and Frenchmen born in Spain are liable for military service in France and Spain respectively, unless they can prove that they have performed the service in their own countries [3]. As regards the special benefits it was proposed to confer on neutral property, Great Britain, France, Russia and Holland contended that aliens by taking up their residence in a state must submit to the treatment accorded to its nationals by the invader, and that contributions were levied *ratione loci* not *ratione personae*. The opposing principles were those of nationality and enemy domicile. Special difficulties in applying the suggested Articles were also pointed out by the British and Japanese delegates. Notwithstanding the hearty support accorded to the draft Articles by the United States and Swiss delegates, they failed of acceptance; Articles 61–63 of the German draft alone were adopted and form Articles 16–19 of Convention No. 5 [4]. The Committee recommended the adoption of the two *Vœux* which were unanimously accepted. We have dealt so far with the second; the fulfilment of the first does not appear to be very probable. The purpose of military operations is to bring the enemy to terms as speedily as possible, and a belligerent can best do this by cutting off the supplies of his adversary from neutral sources. His business is to hamper his opponent by all possible legitimate means, he will not be likely to assist and protect the maintenance of commercial and industrial relations

[1] J. Westlake, *Peace*, p. 218.

[2] See W. E. Hall, *Int. Law*, pp. 207–8 for a discussion of the position of aliens in regard to military service.

[3] Despagnet, *Droit int.* § 342.

[4] For further discussion of this subject see *post*, p. 293.

between the inhabitants of his enemy's state and neutrals, when by so doing he will naturally tend to increase the duration of the struggle[1]. War is more than a relation of state to state.

The fourth *Vœu* covers a wider field than the second and third.

The laws and customs of naval warfare[2]. Questions relating to naval warfare entered into the work of all the four Committees of the Second Conference. The first Committee elaborated a draft Convention for an International Prize Court, the second dealt with declarations of war, a matter common to warfare by land and sea; the third and fourth formed a combined Committee on maritime questions under the presidencies of Count Tornielli and M. de Martens.

Of all departments of international law, that which relates to naval warfare, and the duties of neutrals therein, is in the most unsatisfactory condition. Jurists cannot be entirely acquitted of the charge of having assisted in producing this result. Sometimes the rules adopted by the state of which a publicist is a citizen, have been enunciated by him as if they were universally accepted as international law, and no small number of "incidents" and "strained relations" between states have been produced by the ignorance of the people of one state of the rules of naval warfare observed by another. In the case of land warfare there have been no changes in the weapons in use or the mode of conduct of hostilities during the past century comparable to the change from wooden sailing vessels to great floating metal fortresses propelled by steam power. The rules of maritime warfare, elaborated when wooden walls were the defence of a sea-girt state, are seen to be antiquated, and in some cases useless, when applied to modern conditions. Not only are the problems, by which belligerents themselves are faced, of increasing complexity, but in a still higher degree difficulties are experienced by neutrals in fulfilling their rôle of abstaining from all interference in a pending conflict. The dislocation of neutral trade, springing from an extension of the idea of contraband, the doctrine of "continuous voyage," the divergent views of great naval Powers on the subject of blockade, and the danger to innocent neutral merchantmen from floating mines, produces increasing friction between belligerents and neutrals. The two great wars which had taken place since 1899 had brought these questions into dangerous prominence, and afford sufficient explanation why problems relating to naval warfare occupied so much of the attention of the Second Hague

---

[1] J. Westlake, *War*, p. 285.

[2] *Parl. Papers*, Misc. No. 4 (1908), p. 201; *La Deux. Confér.* T. I. p. 264; *Livre Jaune*, p. 101.

Conference. Unlike the laws of war on land, which, previously to the First Conference, had been considered in detail at the Brussels Conference and by the Institute of International Law, both of which bodies had prepared draft regulations, admirably adapted to form a basis for the work of the Conference, the laws of naval warfare as a whole (and apart from the treatment of the sick and wounded) had never received the careful study of an international gathering of the Powers. In many important points it has long been recognised that there are two divergent views, the Anglo-American and the Continental, and the failure of the Conference to produce a code of laws for naval warfare analogous to that which the First Conference elaborated for land warfare is not a matter for surprise. The "questionnaire," prepared by M. de Martens for the basis of the discussions of the Fourth Committee, was framed in the following terms: "Within what limits are the provisions of the Convention of 1899 relating to the laws of war on land applicable to the operations of war on sea?" Considerable labour and much time were devoted to an examination of the general question of a code of naval warfare, as well as to a consideration of specific subjects which were entrusted to the Committee.

The "questionnaire" of M. de Martens was examined by a Comité d'Examen and a report prepared by M. de Karnebeck, but time did not admit of its being taken into consideration by the whole Committee. The difficulties in the way of arriving at a solution of the numerous questions connected with maritime warfare were explained by M. de Martens at the meeting of the Committee on the 18th Sept. He pointed out that historically there was a sharp line of demarcation between land and sea warfare. That, whereas in the case of the former, soldiers from Epaminondas to Gustavus Adolphus had themselves endeavoured to frame the rules, and the First Conference had before it the work of the Brussels Conference, in the matter of naval warfare the case was quite different. The instructions of a few great naval commanders, the decisions of Prize Courts and especially those of Lord Stowell, and naval manuals prepared by various Governments, were the sources for the law of naval warfare, and all were more or less tainted with national aspirations and the requirements of political expediency. M. Fromageot also pointed out in his report[1] that the attempt to adapt the Rules of Land Warfare of 1899 to naval warfare would necessitate a change not only in drafting and form, but that they would even require fundamental modifications. The principles, however, underlying these regulations were recommended to the Conference as being applicable to maritime warfare, and the fourth *Vœu*

---

[1] *Parl. Papers*, Misc. No. 4 (1908), p. 201; *La Deux. Confér.* T. I. p. 265.

was proposed, and unanimously adopted by the Conference, that the preparation of regulations relative to the laws and customs of naval warfare should be considered at the next Conference, and that meantime the Powers should apply the principles of the Convention of 1899 to war by sea. The Committee prepared a draft in parallel columns showing suggested changes in the application of these rules[1]. The problem relating to blockade and contraband, and the question as to the legality of sinking neutral prizes were however found to be insoluble[2].

On this latter subject the "questionnaire" of M. de Martens was as follows: "Is the destruction of merchant ships under a neutral flag engaged in war time in carrying troops or contraband forbidden by the laws of different countries or by international practice?" "Is the destruction of all neutral prizes illegitimate according to existing national laws and according to the practice in naval wars?"

Destruction of neutral prizes[3].

In examining these questions the Committee refrained from endeavouring to formulate a statement as to what was the existing law, devoting its labours to discussions *de lege ferenda* rather than *de lege lata*, but it considered that there was a close connection between this subject and the question of the free access of prizes to neutral ports which was under consideration by the Third Committee.

In the course of the study of the matter by the Fourth Committee four proposals presented by the delegates of Great Britain, Russia, the United States and Japan came under consideration. These four were subsequently reduced to two, the United States and Japan supporting the British proposals.

The Russian proposal which was the first to be examined by the Examining Committee forbade the destruction of neutral prizes except in cases where the non-destruction would endanger the safety of the captor or the success of his operations. The arguments advanced by Colonel Ovtchinnokow in support of this proposal were that by the fact of

---

[1] *Parl. Papers,* Misc. No. 4 (1908), pp. 202–216; *La Deux. Confér.* T. I. p. 264.

[2] See *ante,* p. 4.

[3] *Parl. Papers,* Misc. No. 1 (1908), p. 17; *Idem,* Misc. No. 4 (1908), p. 199; *La Deux. Confér.* T. I. p. 262; Sir T. Barclay, *Problems,* etc. pp. 99–102; J. Westlake, *War,* p. 318; L. Oppenheim, Vol. II. § 481; T. J. Lawrence, *Int. Law,* § 215; Idem, *War and Neutrality,* etc. p. 255; W. E. Hall, *Int. Law,* p. 735; T. E. Holland, *Prize Law,* § 303; Idem, *Neutral duties in a Maritime War,* pp. 12–18; H. Taylor, *Int. Law,* § 691; A. Hershey, *International Law and Diplomacy of the Russo-Japanese War,* pp. 156–9; F. E. Smith and N. W. Sibley, *International Law as interpreted during the Russo-Japanese War,* Chap. XII.; L. A. Atherley-Jones, *Commerce in War,* pp. 531–8; T. Baty, *La destruction des prises neutres,* Rev. de Dr. int.* (2nd series), Vol. VIII. p. 484; E. Lémonon, *La seconde Conférence,* etc. pp. 684–694.

capture the property in the prize passed to the captor, and that the subsequent decision of a Prize Court confirmed and did not create the right of ownership. The right of destruction should and would naturally be exercised with great reserve, for a captor would not lightly destroy his own property, and when it was exercised, persons and, as far as possible, cargo and papers on board should be preserved for use of Prize Courts, and to assist in fixing indemnities, if any, to neutrals. If the Prize Court subsequently decided against the validity of the capture, that would entail a liability to make compensation. For military or other reasons it might be impossible to take a captured ship into a port for condemnation, and absolutely to forbid its destruction would place states not possessing ports (*hors de leurs côtes métropolitaines*), into which prizes could be conducted, in a position of unjustifiable inferiority, and this would be increased if additional restrictions were adopted, as was proposed, on access of belligerents and their prizes to neutral ports.

The British proposal was framed to carry out the instructions given by Sir Edward Grey "that Great Britain has always maintained that the right to destroy is confined to enemy vessels only[1]," and was that the destruction of neutral prizes is forbidden, and the captor must release a neutral ship which it cannot bring in for adjudication before a Prize Court. Sir Ernest Satow in supporting this proposal contended that destruction of neutral prizes was forbidden by existing practice, and pointed out that the Regulations of the Institute of International Law on maritime prizes, which in 1882 were drafted so as to make no distinction between captured enemy and neutral vessels, were in 1887 altered so that the right to destroy was limited to enemy vessels[2]. The rule of the British Admiralty, based on decisions of Lord Stowell, was clear, and Commanders are directed, when unable to send their prizes in for adjudication, "to release the vessel and cargo without ransom[3]." In answer to the Russian argument based on the difference of the geographical situation of states, the British delegate urged that if this prevented the exercise of the right of capture of neutral ships carrying contraband or guilty of breach of blockade, they ought nevertheless to be set free. He concluded by stating that if

[1] See Appendix.

[2] See Sir T. Barclay, *Problems, etc.* p. 101; *Annuaire*, Vol. IX. (1888), p. 204. *The Règlement international des prises maritimes* allows the destruction of a captured enemy ship in five cases, (1) where she is unseaworthy and the sea is rough, (2) where she sails so badly that she cannot keep up with the captor, (3) on the approach of a stronger enemy fleet endangering her recapture, (4) where the captor cannot spare a prize crew without endangering her own safety, (5) when the port to which it is possible to take the captured ship is too distant.

[3] See The *Actaeon*, 2 Dodson, 48 ; *Felicity*, 2 Dodson, 381 ; *Leucade*, Spinks, 217 ; T. E. Holland, *Manual of Naval Prize Law*, § 303.

the destruction of neutral prizes were allowed, there would be but little difference between neutral and enemy ships, and neutral governments would be almost powerless to protect their merchantmen.

The German delegate "shared entirely" the Russian point of view, while the United States and Japanese delegates supported the British; the Italian delegate pointed out the intimate connection between the subject and the right of using neutral ports, and a combined meeting of the two Examining Committees was held with the following result: free access to neutral ports for belligerent prizes was carried by a small majority (9 for, 3 against, 6 abstentions), prohibition of destruction, made by most conditional to free access, was carried by a slightly larger majority (11 for, 4 against, 2 abstentions), the Russian proposal for right to destroy had a small majority (6 for, 4 against, 7 abstentions)[1].

The subject of the destruction of neutral prizes was brought into striking prominence during the Russo-Japanese war by the sinking by the Russians of various neutral merchantmen, the *Knight Commander*, the *Hip-sang*, the *St Kilda*, the *Ikhoma*, the *Oldhamia*, the *Thea* and others. The British Government entered a strong protest against this procedure, which it characterised as "a serious breach of international law"; and a distinguished English publicist terms it an "outrage" and a "gross breach of international law[2]."

It will be noticed that the "questionnaire" of M. de Martens referred to the "laws of different countries" and "international practice." Sir Ernest Satow asked for the view of the Committee on the existing state of international law, but M. de Martens objected to put this question to the vote[3]. The "laws of different countries" as evidenced by their naval instructions undoubtedly show a lack of uniformity, but such instructions have no international force, as will be seen from Lord Salisbury's correspondence with Germany in 1901 in the cases of the *Herzog* and *Bundesrath*[4]. According to the Naval Codes and Prize Regulations of Russia, the United States and Japan, the sinking of neutral prizes is allowed under certain circumstances[5]; the British proposal was however supported by the delegates of the two latter states. The British Manual of Naval Prize Law prohibits this procedure. From Naval Codes and the opinions of certain writers on international law (chiefly continental), the language of the British Government cannot be wholly

---

[1] See *post*, p. 478. [2] T. J. Lawrence, *War and Neutrality*, p. 257.

[3] See *The Times*, 8th Aug. 1908.

[4] *Parl. Papers*, Cd. (1900); J. Dundas White, The seizure of the *Bundesrath*, 17 *L. Q. R.* 14.

[5] L. Oppenheim, Vol. II. pp. 470–1.

supported, but it is certainly supported by modern international practice. In no modern naval war has any Government put forward such a doctrine as that enunciated by the Russian, and no belligerent since the Declaration of Paris has acted as the Russians. The doctrine of the Russian Government would, as Lord Lansdowne stated, justify the destruction of any neutral ship taken by a belligerent vessel which started on her voyage with a crew sufficient only for her requirements, and therefore unable to furnish prize crews for her captures; it is in effect a negation of the Declaration of Paris.

There is a clear distinction between the right of seizure of enemy and neutral ships. The former is the legitimate exercise of a right of appropriation of all enemy property found on the high seas, the latter is exercised only for the purpose of punishing certain special acts which do not necessarily involve condemnation of the ship[1]. If the destruction of enemy ships is now generally recognised as lawful only in special cases, the list of exceptions should either vanish altogether, or be reduced to the minutest dimensions in the case of neutral prizes. The "Institut de Droit International" in 1887 pronounced in favour of the first alternative which is undoubtedly supported by modern practice. An agreement on this subject would materially aid in maintaining the peace of the world by removing a not improbable cause of war on the part of a neutral Power whose commerce was being ruined by the adoption by a belligerent of the practice advocated by the Russian Government[2].

The Conference was, however, able to make some progress towards a Code of naval warfare by the adoption of the Conventions relating **Beginnings of a Code of naval warfare.** to the status of enemy merchant ships at the outbreak of hostilities (No. 6), the Convention relative to the conversion of merchant ships into war ships (No. 7), the Convention relative to the laying of automatic submarine contact mines (No. 8), the Convention respecting bombardment by naval forces in time of war (No. 9), the Convention placing certain restrictions on the exercise of the right of capture in naval warfare (No. 11), the Convention for the creation of an international prize court (No. 12), and the Convention concerning the rights and duties of neutral Powers in naval war (No. 13). These Conventions are of unequal value, and some bear evident traces of a desire that some agreement on the subject to which they relate might be registered after so many weeks of labour; they will, doubtless, on many points need revision by the next Conference.

---

[1] L. Oppenheim, Vol. II. p. 469.
[2] See *post*, pp. 557, 597.

The First Conference had closed without making any provision for the
summoning of another. The Second Conference was dragging
on, hampered by its want of preparation and of adherence to
parliamentary precedents, and many of those who looked for
solid results were "in genuine anxiety about the consequence of a real
collapse," and possessed by a "genuine desire that the Hague institution
should not perish of what were not, perhaps, essential defects[2]." A
Meeting of the First Delegates was held on the 14th September to
consider the situation, and it was resolved to bring before the next Plenary
Meeting a *Vœu* with reference to a future Conference. The United States
Delegation was instructed to "favour the adoption of a resolution by the
Conference providing for the holding of further Conferences within fixed
periods and arranging the machinery by which such Conferences may be
called and the terms of the programme may be arranged, without awaiting
any new and specific initiative on the part of the powers or any one of
them." This had been recommended by the Inter-parliamentary Congress in 1904. The Conferences would then become real international
assemblies presided over by a President chosen without any regard to the
requirements of diplomatic etiquette, and discussing a programme which
had not been prepared for it, but which it had previously settled for itself.
The actual form in which the *Vœu* found acceptance is as it appears in
the Final Act, and M. Nélidow, the President of the Conference, proposed
it at the Sixth Plenary Meeting on the 21st Sept., but the initiative must
be assigned to the United States Delegation. "The somewhat slow and at
times uncertain progress of our labours," said the President, "as well as
the impossibility which the Conference finds of solving some of the
problems submitted to it, or which have been brought forward in the
course of our labours, have suggested to some of our colleagues the idea
of taking into consideration the advantage of another meeting of the
Conference, and of the necessity of preparing for it in advance a detailed
programme and the method of its working and organisation[3]." In these
words the President concisely specified some of the causes of the want of
success which had attended the wearisome and laborious discussions on
many of the topics which had been under consideration. The Roumanian
delegate, M. Beldiman, in supporting the *Vœu* paid a tribute of homage to
the August Initiator of the First and Second Conferences, adding that the

---

[1] J. B. Scott, *Recommendations for a third Peace Conference at the Hague*, *Am. Journ. of Int. Law*, Vol. II. p. 815.

[2] See Article in *Edin. Review*, Jan. 1908, p. 224.

[3] *Parl. Papers*, Misc. No. 4 (1908), p. 42; *La Deux. Confér.* T. I. p. 169.

Vœu in his opinion did not prejudge the taking of the same august initiative in the future, while the Austro-Hungarian delegate in rendering grateful homage to the Tsar added that they considered the initiative of Russia was definitely accepted in this matter. A general desire was expressed that the Queen of Holland would extend her hospitality to the next Conference. It will be seen that the speeches of the Roumanian and Austro-Hungarian delegates go beyond the actual words of the *Vœu*. To whomsoever the initiative of the next Conference may belong, if in 1915 the Third Conference should meet in accordance with this *Vœu*, two years before that date a preparatory Committee is to collect the various proposals to be submitted, to ascertain the subjects which are ripe for embodiment in an international regulation and to prepare a programme which the Governments shall decide upon in sufficient time to enable it to be carefully examined by the countries interested. The Committee is also to be entrusted with the work of proposing a system of organisation and procedure for the Conference itself. The Second Hague Conference has thus taken an important step, and, taught by its own tedious and cumbersome procedure, it has endeavoured to spare its successor from suffering from the like causes. If Hague Conferences, meeting in the future at specified intervals, are to develope into a world legislature, a veritable "Parliament of man," they can only be certain of producing beneficial and lasting results if the states taking part have thoroughly made up their minds both in regard to the matters to be discussed, and the views which their representatives are to support. The delegates of future Conferences will also be spared the chagrin and annoyance from which on several important occasions Plenipotentiaries suffered in 1907, when, owing to lack of instructions, they were unable to speak with any authority for the states they represented; while the latter will not hurriedly, and without due warning, have to formulate a policy on any topic which may be introduced without previous notice and consideration.

THE CONVENTIONS OF THE HAGUE CONFERENCES OF 1899 AND 1907[1].

I. CONVENTION FOR THE PACIFIC SETTLEMENT OF INTERNATIONAL DISPUTES.

[1] Changes made in the three Conventions of 1899 by the Conference of 1907 are indicated by italics.

1. Règlement Pacifique des Conflits Internationaux.

Convention pour le Règlement Pacifique des Conflits Internationaux.

Sa Majesté le Roi des Belges; Sa Majesté le Roi de Danemark; Sa Majesté le Roi d'Espagne, et en son nom Sa Majesté la Reine-Régente du Royaume; le Président des États-Unis d'Amérique; le Président des États-Unis Mexicains; le Président de la République Française; Sa Majesté le Roi des Hellènes; Son Altesse le Prince de Monténégro; Sa Majesté la Reine des Pays-Bas; Sa Majesté Impériale le Schah de Perse; Sa Majesté le Roi de Portugal et des Algarves; Sa Majesté le Roi de Roumanie; Sa Majesté l'Empereur de Toutes les Russies; Sa Majesté le Roi de Siam; Sa Majesté le Roi de Suède et de Norvège; et Son Altesse Royale le Prince de Bulgarie[1] :

Convention pour le Règlement Pacifique des Conflits Internationaux.

Sa Majesté l'Empereur d'Allemagne, Roi de Prusse; le Président des États-Unis d'Amérique; le Président de la République Argentine; Sa Majesté l'Empereur d'Autriche, Roi de Bohême, &c., et Roi Apostolique de Hongrie; Sa Majesté le Roi des Belges; le Président de la République de Bolivie; le Président de la République des États-Unis du Brésil; Son Altesse Royale le Prince de Bulgarie; le Président de la République de Chili; Sa Majesté l'Empereur de Chine; le Président de la République de Colombie; le Gouverneur provisoire de la République de Cuba; Sa Majesté le Roi de Danemark; le Président de la République Dominicaine; le Président de la République de l'Équateur; Sa Majesté le Roi d'Espagne; le Président de la République Française; Sa Majesté le Roi du Royaume-Uni de Grande-Bretagne et d'Irlande et des Territoires Britanniques au delà des mers, Empereur des Indes; Sa Majesté le Roi des Hellènes; le Président de la République de Guatémala; le Président de la République d'Haïti; Sa Majesté le Roi d'Italie; Sa Majesté l'Empereur du Japon; Son Altesse Royale le Grand-Duc de Luxembourg, Duc de Nassau; le Président des États-Unis Mexicains; Son Altesse Royale le

---

[1] See note 1, p. 97.

1. Pacific Settlement of International Disputes

Convention for the Pacific Settlement of International Disputes.

His Majesty the King of the Belgians; His Majesty the King of Denmark; His Majesty the King of Spain, and in his name Her Majesty the Queen-Regent of the Kingdom; the President of the United States of America; the President of the United States of Mexico; the President of the French Republic; His Majesty the King of the Hellenes; His Highness the Prince of Montenegro; Her Majesty the Queen of the Netherlands; His Imperial Majesty the Shah of Persia; His Majesty the King of Portugal and the Algarves; His Majesty the King of Roumania; His Majesty the Emperor of All the Russias; His Majesty the King of Siam; His Majesty the King of Sweden and Norway; and His Royal Highness the Prince of Bulgaria[1],

Convention for the Pacific Settlement of International Disputes.

His Majesty the German Emperor, King of Prussia; the President of the United States of America; the President of the Argentine Republic; His Majesty the Emperor of Austria, King of Bohemia, &c., and Apostolic King of Hungary; His Majesty the King of the Belgians; the President of the Republic of Bolivia; the President of the Republic of the United States of Brazil; His Royal Highness the Prince of Bulgaria; the President of the Republic of Chile; His Majesty the Emperor of China; the President of the Republic of Colombia; the Provisional Governor of the Republic of Cuba; His Majesty the King of Denmark; the President of the Dominican Republic; the President of the Republic of Ecuador; His Majesty the King of Spain; the President of the French Republic; His Majesty the King of the United Kingdom of Great Britain and Ireland and of the British Dominions beyond the Seas, Emperor of India; His Majesty the King of the Hellenes; the President of the Republic of Guatemala; the President of the Republic of Haïti; His Majesty the King of Italy; His Majesty the Emperor of Japan; His Royal Highness the Grand Duke of Luxemburg, Duke of Nassau; the President of the United States of Mexico; His Royal

---

[1] The list of Powers is as given in *Parl. Papers*, Misc. No. 1 (1899), p. 301. All the Powers enumerated in the Convention of 1907 subsequently signed or acceded.

1899	1907
	Prince de Monténégro ; le Président de la République de Nicaragua ; Sa Majesté le Roi de Norvège ; le Président de la République de Panama ; le Président de la République du Paraguay ; Sa Majesté la Reine des Pays-Bas ; le Président de la République du Pérou ; Sa Majesté Impériale le Schah de Perse ; Sa Majesté le Roi de Portugal et des Algarves, &c. ; Sa Majesté le Roi de Roumanie ; Sa Majesté l'Empereur de Toutes les Russies ; le Président de la République du Salvador ; Sa Majesté le Roi de Serbie ; Sa Majesté le Roi de Siam ; Sa Majesté le Roi de Suède ; le Conseil Fédéral Suisse ; Sa Majesté l'Empereur des Ottomans ; le Président de la République orientale de l'Uruguay ; le Président des États-Unis de Venezuela :
Animés de la ferme volonté de concourir au maintien de la paix générale ;	Animés de la ferme volonté de concourir au maintien de la paix générale ;
Résolus à favoriser de tous leurs efforts le règlement amiable des conflits internationaux ;	Résolus à favoriser de tous leurs efforts le règlement amiable des conflits internationaux ;
Reconnaissant la solidarité qui unit les membres de la société des nations civilisées ;	Reconnaissant la solidarité qui unit les membres de la société des nations civilisées ;
Voulant étendre l'empire du droit et fortifier le sentiment de la justice internationale ;	Voulant étendre l'empire du droit et fortifier le sentiment de la justice internationale ;
Convaincus que l'institution permanente d'une juridiction arbitrale accessible à tous, au sein des Puissances indépendantes, peut contribuer efficacement à ce résultat ;	Convaincus que l'institution permanente d'une juridiction arbitrale accessible à tous, au sein des Puissances indépendantes, peut contribuer efficacement à ce résultat ;
Considérant les avantages d'une organisation générale et régulière de la procédure arbitrale ;	Considérant les avantages d'une organisation générale et régulière de la procédure arbitrale ;

1899	1907

<table>
<tr><td></td><td>Highness the Prince of Montenegro; the President of the Republic of Nicaragua; His Majesty the King of Norway; the President of the Republic of Panamá; the President of the Republic of Paraguay; Her Majesty the Queen of the Netherlands; the President of the Republic of Peru; His Imperial Majesty the Shah of Persia; His Majesty the King of Portugal and of the Algarves, &c.; His Majesty the King of Roumania; His Majesty the Emperor of All the Russias; the President of the Republic of Salvador; His Majesty the King of Servia; His Majesty the King of Siam; His Majesty the King of Sweden; the Swiss Federal Council; His Majesty the Emperor of the Ottomans; the President of the Oriental Republic of Uruguay; the President of the United States of Venezuela:</td></tr>
</table>

1899	1907
animated by the sincere desire to work for the maintenance of the general peace ;	Animated by the sincere desire to work for the maintenance of general peace ;
Resolved to promote by their best efforts the friendly settlement of international disputes ;	Resolved to promote by their best efforts the friendly settlement of international disputes ;
Recognizing the solidarity uniting the members of the society of civilized nations ;	Recognizing the solidarity uniting the members of the society of civilized nations ;
Desirous of extending the empire of law, and of strengthening the appreciation of international justice ;	Desirous of extending the empire of law and of strengthening the appreciation of international justice ;
Convinced that the permanent institution of a Tribunal of Arbitration, accessible to all, in the midst of independent Powers, will contribute effectively to this result ;	Convinced that the permanent institution of a Tribunal of Arbitration accessible to all, in the midst of independent Powers, will contribute effectively to this result ;
Having regard to the advantages of the general and regular organization of the procedure of arbitration ;	Having regard to the advantages of the general and regular organization of the procedure of arbitration ;

7—2

1899	1907
Estimant avec l'Auguste Initiateur de la Conférence Internationale de la Paix qu'il importe de consacrer dans un accord international les principes d'équité et de droit sur lesquels reposent la sécurité des États et le bien-être des peuples ;	Estimant avec l'Auguste Initiateur de la Conférence Internationale de la Paix qu'il importe de consacrer dans un accord international les principes d'équité et de droit sur lesquels reposent la sécurité des États et le bien-être des peuples ;
Désirant conclure une Convention à cet effet, ont nommé pour Leurs Plénipotentiaires, savoir :	*Désireux, dans ce but, de mieux assurer le fonctionnement pratique des Commissions d'enquête et des tribunaux d'arbitrage et de faciliter le recours à la justice arbitrale lorsqu'il s'agit de litiges de nature à comporter une procédure sommaire ;*
	Ont jugé nécessaire de reviser sur certains points et de compléter l'œuvre de la Première Conférence de la Paix pour le règlement pacifique des conflits internationaux ;
	Les Hautes Parties contractantes ont résolu de conclure une nouvelle Convention à cet effet et ont nommé pour Leurs Plénipotentiaires, savoir :
[*Dénomination des Plénipotentiaires.*]	[*Dénomination des Plénipotentiaires.*]
Lesquels, après s'être communiqué leurs pleins pouvoirs, trouvés en bonne et due forme, sont convenus des dispositions suivantes.	Lesquels, après avoir *déposé* leurs pleins pouvoirs, trouvés en bonne et due forme, sont convenus *de ce qui suit* :—

Titre I.
Du Maintien de la Paix Générale.

Art. 1.

En vue de prévenir autant que possible le recours à la force dans les rapports entre les États, les Puissances signataires conviennent d'employer tous leurs efforts pour assurer le règlement pacifique des différends internationaux.

Titre I.
Du Maintien de la Paix Générale.

Art. 1.

(*Aucune modification.*)[1]

---

[1] See note 1, p. 101.

1899	1907
Sharing the opinion of the august Initiator of the International Peace Conference that it is expedient to record in an international agreement the principles of equity and right on which are based the security of States and the welfare of peoples ;	Sharing the opinion of .the august Initiator of the International Peace Conference that it is expedient to record in an international agreement the principles of equity and right on which are based the security of States and the welfare of peoples; and
Being desirous of concluding a Convention to this effect, have appointed as their Plenipotentiaries,	Being desirous, *with this object, of insuring the better working in practice of Commissions of Inquiry and Tribunals of Arbitration, and of facilitating recourse to arbitration in cases which allow of a summary procedure ;*
	Have deemed it necessary to revise in certain particulars and to complete the work of the First Peace Conference for the pacific settlement of international disputes ;
	The High Contracting Parties have resolved to conclude a new Convention for this purpose, and have appointed as their Plenipotentiaries, that is to say :
[*Names of Plenipotentiaries.*]	[*Names of Plenipotentiaries.*]
Who, after communication of their full powers, found in good and due form, have agreed on the following provisions :—	Who, *after having deposited* their full powers, found in good and due form, have agreed upon the following :—

Title I.

On the Maintenance of the General Peace.

Art. 1.

With a view of obviating, as far as possible, recourse to force in the relations between States, the Signatory Powers agree to use their best efforts to insure the pacific settlement of international differences.

Part I.

On the Maintenance of General Peace.

Art. 1.

(*No change.*)[1]

---

[1] For the words "Signatory Powers" in the Convention of 1899 read "*Contracting Powers*" throughout the Convention of 1907.

1899	1907
Titre II.	Titre II.
Des Bons Offices et de la Médiation.	Des Bons Offices et de la Médiation.

ART. 2.

En cas de dissentiment grave ou de conflit, avant d'en appeler aux armes, les Puissances signataires conviennent d'avoir recours, en tant que les circonstances le permettront, aux bons offices ou à la médiation d'une ou de plusieurs Puissances amies.

ART. 2.

(*Aucune modification.*)[1]

ART. 3.

Indépendamment de ce recours, les Puissances signataires jugent utile qu'une ou plusieurs Puissances, étrangères au conflit, offrent de leur propre initiative, en tant que les circonstances s'y prêtent, leurs bons offices ou leur médiation aux États en conflit.

Le droit d'offrir les bons offices ou la médiation appartient aux Puissances étrangères au conflit, même pendant le cours des hostilités.

L'exercice de ce droit ne peut jamais être considéré par l'une ou l'autre des Parties en litige comme un acte peu amical.

ART. 3.

Indépendamment de ce recours, les Puissances signataires jugent utile *et désirable* qu'une ou plusieurs Puissances, étrangères au conflit, offrent de leur propre initiative, en tant que les circonstances s'y prêtent, leurs bons offices ou leur médiation aux États en conflit.

Le droit d'offrir les bons offices ou la médiation appartient aux Puissances étrangères au conflit, même pendant le cours des hostilités.

L'exercice de ce droit ne peut jamais être considéré par l'une ou l'autre des Parties en litige comme un acte peu amical.

ART. 4.

Le rôle du médiateur consiste à concilier les prétentions opposées et à apaiser les ressentiments qui peuvent s'être produits entre les États en conflit.

ART. 4.

(*Aucune modification.*)

ART. 5.

Les fonctions du médiateur cessent du moment où il est constaté, soit par l'une des Parties en litige, soit par le

ART. 5.

(*Aucune modification.*)

---

[1] V. note, *supra*, p. 101.

1899	1907
Title II.	**Part II.**
On Good Offices and Mediation.	**On Good Offices and Mediation.**
ART. 2.	ART. 2.
In case of serious disagreement or dispute, before an appeal to arms, the Signatory Powers agree to have recourse, as far as circumstances allow, to the good offices or mediation of one or more friendly Powers.	(*No change.*)[1]
ART. 3.	ART. 3.
Independently of this recourse, the Signatory Powers deem it expedient that one or more Powers, strangers to the dispute, should, on their own initiative and as far as circumstances may allow, offer their good offices or mediation to the States at variance.	Independently of this recourse, the Contracting Powers deem it expedient *and desirable* that one or more Powers, strangers to the dispute, should, on their own initiative and as far as circumstances may allow, offer their good offices or mediation to the States at variance.
Powers, strangers to the dispute, have the right to offer good offices or mediation, even during the course of hostilities.	Powers, strangers to the dispute, have the right to offer good offices or mediation, even during the course of hostilities.
The exercise of this right can never be regarded by either of the parties at variance as an unfriendly act.	The exercise of this right can never be regarded by either of the parties at variance as an unfriendly act.
ART. 4.	ART. 4.
The part of the mediator consists in reconciling the opposing claims and appeasing the feelings of resentment which may have arisen between the States at variance.	(*No change.*)
ART. 5.	ART. 5.
The duties of the mediator are at an end when once it is declared, either by one of the contending parties, or	(*No change.*)

---

[1] V. note, *supra*, p. 101.

1899	1907
médiateur lui-même, que les moyens de conciliation proposés par lui ne sont pas acceptés.	

ART. 6.	ART. 6.
Les bons offices et la médiation, soit sur le recours des Parties en conflit, soit sur l'initiative des Puissances étrangères au conflit, ont exclusivement le caractère de conseil et n'ont jamais force obligatoire.	(*Aucune modification.*)

ART. 7.	ART. 7.
L'acceptation de la médiation ne peut avoir pour effet, sauf convention contraire, d'interrompre, de retarder ou d'entraver la mobilisation et autres mesures préparatoires à la guerre. Si elle intervient après l'ouverture des hostilités, elle n'interrompt pas, sauf convention contraire, les opérations militaires en cours.	(*Aucune modification.*)

ART. 8.	ART. 8.
Les Puissances signataires sont d'accord pour recommander l'application, dans les circonstances qui le permettent, d'une médiation spéciale sous la forme suivante :— En cas de différend grave compromettant la paix, les États en conflit choisissent respectivement une Puissance à laquelle ils confient la mission d'entrer en rapport direct avec la Puissance choisie d'autre part, à l'effet de prévenir la rupture des relations pacifiques. Pendant la durée de ce mandat dont le terme, sauf stipulation contraire, ne peut excéder trente jours, les États en litige cessent tout rapport	(*Aucune modification.*)[1]

[1] V. note, *supra*, p. 101.

1899

by .the mediator himself, that the means of reconciliation proposed by him are not accepted.

ART. 6.

Good offices and mediation, undertaken either at the request of the contending parties or on the initiative of Powers strangers to the dispute, have exclusively the character of advice, and never have binding force.

ART. 7.

The acceptance of mediation cannot, in default of agreement to the contrary, have the effect of interrupting, delaying or hindering mobilization or other measures of preparation for war.

If mediation takes place after the commencement of hostilities, the military operations in progress are not interrupted, in default of agreement to the contrary.

ART. 8.

The Signatory Powers are agreed in recommending the application, when circumstances allow, of special mediation in the following form :—

In case of a serious difference endangering peace, the contending States choose respectively a Power, to which they intrust the mission of entering into direct communication with the Power chosen on the other side, with the object of preventing the rupture of pacific relations.

For the period of this mandate, the term of which, in default of agreement to the contrary, cannot exceed thirty days, the States at variance cease from

1907

ART. 6.

(*No change.*)

ART. 7.

(*No change.*)

ART. 8.

(*No change.*)[1]

---

[1] V. note, *supra*, p. 101.

1899	1907

direct au sujet du conflit, lequel est considéré comme déféré exclusivement aux Puissances médiatrices. Celles-ci doivent appliquer tous leurs efforts à régler le différend.

En cas de rupture effective des relations pacifiques, ces Puissances demeurent chargées de la mission commune de profiter de toute occasion pour rétablir la paix.

Titre III.	**Titre III.**
Des Commissions Internationales d'Enquête.	**Des Commissions Internationales d'Enquête.**
ART. 9.	ART. 9.

Dans les litiges d'ordre international n'engageant ni l'honneur ni des intérêts essentiels et provenant d'une divergence d'appréciation sur des points de fait, les Puissances signataires jugent utile que les parties qui n'auraient pu se mettre d'accord par les voies diplomatiques instituent, en tant que les circonstances le permettront, une Commission internationale d'enquête chargée de faciliter la solution de ces litiges en éclaircissant, par un examen impartial et consciencieux, les questions de fait.

Dans les litiges d'ordre international n'engageant ni l'honneur ni des intérêts essentiels et provenant d'une divergence d'appréciation sur des points de fait, les Puissances *contractantes* jugent utile *et désirable* que les parties qui n'auraient pu se mettre d'accord par les voies diplomatiques instituent, en tant que les circonstances le permettront, une Commission internationale d'enquête chargée de faciliter la solution de ces litiges en éclaircissant, par un examen impartial et consciencieux, les questions de fait.

ART. 10.	ART. 10.

Les Commissions internationales d'enquête sont constituées par convention spéciale entre les parties en litige.

La convention d'enquête précise les faits à examiner et l'étendue des pouvoirs des commissaires.

Elle règle la procédure.

L'enquête a lieu contradictoirement.

Les Commissions internationales d'enquête sont constituées par convention spéciale entre les parties en litige.

La convention d'enquête précise les faits à examiner ; *elle détermine le mode et le délai de formation de la Commission* et l'étendue des pouvoirs des commissaires.

1899	1907

all direct communication on the subject of the dispute, which is regarded as referred exclusively to the mediating Powers. These Powers shall use their best efforts to settle the dispute.

In case of a definite rupture of pacific relations, these Powers remain jointly charged with the task of taking advantage of any opportunity to restore peace.

Title III.

On International Commissions of Inquiry.

ART. 9.

In disputes of an international nature involving neither honour nor vital interests, and arising from a difference of opinion on points of fact, the Signatory Powers deem it expedient that the parties, who have not been able to come to an agreement by means of diplomacy, should, as far as circumstances allow, institute an International Commission of Inquiry, to facilitate a solution of these disputes by elucidating the facts by means of an impartial and conscientious investigation.

ART. 10.

International Commissions of Inquiry are constituted by special agreement between the contending parties.

The Inquiry Convention defines the facts to be examined and the extent of the powers of the Commissioners.

It settles the procedure.

At the inquiry both sides must be heard.

Part III.

On International Commissions of Inquiry.

ART. 9.

In disputes of an international nature involving neither honour nor vital interests, and arising from a difference of opinion on points of fact, the *Contracting* Powers deem it expedient *and desirable* that the parties who have not been able to come to an agreement by means of diplomacy, should, as far as circumstances allow, institute an International Commission of Inquiry, to facilitate a solution of these disputes by elucidating the facts by means of an impartial and conscientious investigation.

ART. 10.

International Commissions of Inquiry are constituted by special agreement between the contending parties.

The Inquiry Convention defines the facts to be examined: *it determines the manner and period within which the Commission is to be formed* and the extent of the powers of the Commissioners.

1899	1907
La forme et les délais à observer, en tant qu'ils ne sont pas fixés par la convention d'enquête, sont déterminés par la Commission elle-même.	*Elle détermine également, s'il y a lieu, le siège de la Commission et la faculté de se déplacer, la langue dont la Commission fera usage et celles dont l'emploi sera autorisé devant elle, ainsi que la date à laquelle chaque Partie devra déposer son exposé des faits, et généralement toutes les conditions dont les Parties sont convenues.*
	Si les Parties jugent nécessaire de nommer des assesseurs, la convention d'enquête détermine le mode de leur désignation et l'étendue de leurs pouvoirs.

ART. 11.

Si la convention d'enquête n'a pas désigné le siège de la Commission, celle-ci siégera à La Haye.

Le siège une fois fixé ne peut être changé par la Commission qu'avec l'assentiment des Parties.

Si la convention d'enquête n'a pas déterminé les langues à employer, il en est décidé par la Commission.

1899	1907
ART. 11. Les Commissions internationales d'enquête sont formées, sauf stipulation contraire, de la manière déterminée par l'article 32 de la présente Convention.	**ART. 12.** Sauf stipulation contraire, les Commissions d'enquête sont formées de la manière déterminée par *les articles 45 et 57* de la présente Convention.

ART. 13.

En cas de décès, de démission ou d'empêchement, pour quelque cause que ce soit, de l'un des commissaires, ou éventuellement de l'un des assesseurs, il est pourvu à son remplacement selon le mode fixé pour sa nomination.

1899	1907
The form and the periods to be observed, if not stated in the Inquiry Convention, are decided by the Commission itself.	*It also determines, if there is occasion for it, where the Commission is to meet, and whether it may remove to another place, the language the Commission shall use and the languages the use of which shall be authorized before it, as well as the date on which each party must deposit its statement of facts, and, generally speaking, all the conditions upon which the parties have agreed.*

If the parties consider it necessary to appoint Assessors, the Inquiry Convention shall determine the mode of their selection and the extent of their powers.

ART. 11.

If the Inquiry Convention has not determined where the Commission is to sit, it shall sit at The Hague.

The place of sitting, once fixed, cannot be altered by the Commission except with the assent of the parties.

Unless the Inquiry Convention has specified the languages to be employed, the question shall be decided by the Commission.

### ART. 11. International Commissions of Inquiry are formed, unless otherwise stipulated, in the manner determined by Article 32 of the present Convention.	### ART. 12. In default of agreement to the contrary, Commissions of Inquiry shall be formed in the manner determined by *Articles 45 and 57* of the present Convention.

ART. 13

Should one of the Commissioners or one of the Assessors, if there be any, either die, resign, or be unable for any reason whatever to act, the same procedure is followed in filling his place which was followed in appointing him.

1899	1907

Art. 14.

Les Parties ont le droit de nommer auprès de la Commission d'enquête des agents spéciaux avec la mission de Les représenter et de servir d'intermédiaires entre Elles et la Commission.

Elles sont, en outre, autorisées à charger des conseils ou avocats nommés par Elles, d'exposer et de soutenir leurs intérêts devant la Commission.

Art. 15.

Le Bureau International de la Cour permanente d'arbitrage sert de greffe aux Commissions qui siègent à La Haye, et mettra ses locaux et son organisation à la disposition des Puissances contractantes pour le fonctionnement de la Commission d'enquête.

Art. 16.

Si la Commission siège ailleurs qu'à La Haye, elle nomme un Secrétaire général dont le Bureau lui sert de greffe.

Le greffe est chargé, sous l'autorité du Président, de l'organisation matérielle des séances de la Commission, de la rédaction des procès-verbaux et, pendant le temps de l'enquête, de la garde des archives, qui seront ensuite versées au Bureau International de La Haye.

Art. 17.

En vue de faciliter l'institution et le fonctionnement des Commissions d'enquête, les Puissances contractantes recommandent les règles suivantes qui seront applicables à la procédure d'enquête en tant que les Parties n'adopteront pas d'autres règles.

ART. 14.

The parties are entitled to appoint special agents to attend the Commission of Inquiry, whose duty it is to represent them and to act as intermediaries between them and the Commission.

They are further authorized to engage counsel or advocates, appointed by themselves, to state their case and uphold their interests before the Commission.

ART. 15.

The International Bureau of the Permanent Court of Arbitration acts as registry for the Commissions which sit at The Hague, and shall place its offices and staff at the disposal of the Contracting Powers for the use of the Commission of Inquiry.

ART. 16.

If the Commission sits elsewhere than at The Hague, it appoints a Secretary-General, whose office serves as registry.

It is the function of the registry, under the control of the President, to make the necessary arrangements for the sittings of the Commission, the preparation of the Minutes and, while the inquiry lasts, for the custody of the archives, which shall subsequently be transferred to the International Bureau at The Hague.

ART. 17.

In order to facilitate the constitution and working of Commissions of Inquiry, the Contracting Powers recommend the following rules, which shall be applicable to the inquiry procedure in so far as the parties do not adopt other rules.

1899	1907

1907

ART. 18.

La Commission réglera les détails de la procédure non prévus dans la convention spéciale d'enquête ou dans la présente Convention, et procédera à toutes les formalités que comporte l'administration des preuves.

ART. 19.

L'enquête a lieu contradictoirement.
(*Voyez Art.* 10 (1899).)

Aux dates prévues, chaque Partie communique à la Commission et à l'autre Partie les exposés des faits, s'il y a lieu, et, dans tous les cas, les actes, pièces et documents qu'elle juge utiles à la découverte de la vérité, ainsi que la liste des témoins et des experts qu'Elle désire faire entendre.

ART. 20.

La Commission a la faculté, avec l'assentiment des parties, de se transporter momentanément sur les lieux où Elle juge utile de recourir à ce moyen d'information, ou d'y déléguer un ou plusieurs de ses membres. L'autorisation de l'État sur le territoire duquel il doit être procédé à cette information devra être obtenue.

ART. 21.

Toutes constatations matérielles, et toutes visites des lieux doivent être faites en présence des agents et conseils des Parties ou eux dûment appelés.

ART. 22.

La Commission a le droit de solliciter de l'une ou l'autre Partie telles explications ou informations qu'elle juge utiles.

ART. 18.

The Commission shall settle the details of the procedure not covered by the special Inquiry Convention or the present Convention, and shall arrange all the formalities required for dealing with the evidence.

ART. 19.

On the inquiry both sides must be heard.

(*Cp. Art.* 10 (1899).)

At the dates fixed, each party communicates to the Commission and to the other party the statements of facts, if any, and, in all cases, the instruments, papers, and documents which it considers useful for ascertaining the truth, as well as the list of witnesses and experts whose evidence it wishes to be heard.

ART. 20.

The Commission is entitled, with the assent of the parties, to move temporarily to any place where it considers it may be useful to have recourse to taking evidence by this means, or to send thither one or more of its members. Permission must be obtained from the State on whose territory evidence has to be taken in this way.

ART. 21.

Every investigation, and every examination of a locality, must be made in the presence of the agents and counsel of the parties or after they have been duly summoned.

ART. 22.

The Commission is entitled to ask from either party such explanations and information as it thinks fit.

1899	1907
ART. 12.	ART. 23.

Les Puissances en litige s'engagent à fournir à la Commission internationale d'enquête, dans la plus large mesure qu'Elles jugeront possible, tous les moyens et toutes les facilités nécessaires pour la connaissance complète et l'appréciation exacte des faits en question.

Les *Parties* s'engagent à fournir à la Commission d'enquête, dans la plus large mesure qu'Elles jugeront possible, tous les moyens et toutes les facilités nécessaires pour la connaissance complète et l'appréciation exacte des faits en question.

Elles s'engagent à user des moyens dont Elles disposent d'après leur législation intérieure, pour assurer la comparution des témoins ou des experts se trouvant sur leur territoire et cités devant la Commission.

Si ceux-ci ne peuvent comparaître devant la Commission, Elles feront procéder à leur audition devant leurs autorités compétentes.

ART. 24.

Pour toutes les notifications que la Commission aurait à faire sur le territoire d'une tierce Puissance contractante, la Commission s'adressera directement au Gouvernement de cette Puissance. Il en sera de même s'il s'agit de faire procéder sur place à l'établissement de tous moyens de preuve.

Les requêtes adressées à cet effet seront exécutées suivant les moyens dont la Puissance requise dispose d'après sa législation intérieure. Elles ne peuvent être refusées que si cette Puissance les juge de nature à porter atteinte à Sa souveraineté ou à Sa sécurité.

La Commission aura aussi toujours la faculté de recourir à l'intermédiaire de la Puissance sur le territoire de laquelle elle a son siège.

1899	1907
Art. 12.	Art. 23.

The Powers at variance undertake to afford to the International Commission of Inquiry, within the widest limits they may think practicable, all means and facilities necessary to enable it to become completely acquainted with, and to accurately understand the facts at issue.

The *Parties* undertake to afford to the Commission of Inquiry, within the widest limits they may think practicable, all the means and facilities necessary to enable it to become completely acquainted with, and accurately to understand the facts at issue.

They undertake to make use of the means at their disposal under their municipal law, to secure the appearance of the witnesses or experts who are in their territory and have been summoned before the Commission.

If the witnesses or experts are unable to appear before the Commission, the parties shall arrange for their evidence to be taken before the qualified officials of their own country.

Art. 24.

For the service of all notices by the Commission in the territory of a third Contracting Power, the Commission shall apply direct to the Government of such Power. The same rule shall apply in the case of steps being taken in order to procure evidence on the spot.

Requests for this purpose are to be executed so far as the means which the Power applied to possesses under municipal law allow. They cannot be rejected unless the Power in question considers they are calculated to impair its sovereign rights or its safety.

The Commission will also be entitled in all cases to have recourse to the intervention of the Power on whose territory it sits.

ART. 25.

Les témoins et les experts sont appelés à la requête des Parties ou d'office par la Commission, et, dans tous les cas, par l'intermédiaire du Gouvernement de l'État sur le territoire duquel ils se trouvent.

Les témoins sont entendus, successivement et séparément, en présence des agents et des conseils et dans un ordre à fixer par la Commission.

ART. 26.

L'interrogatoire des témoins est conduit par le Président.

Les membres de la Commission peuvent néanmoins poser à chaque témoin les questions qu'ils croient convenables pour éclaircir ou compléter sa déposition, ou pour se renseigner sur tout ce qui concerne le témoin dans les limites nécessaires à la manifestation de la vérité.

Les agents et les conseils des Parties ne peuvent interrompre le témoin dans sa déposition, ni lui faire aucune interpellation directe, mais peuvent demander au Président de poser au témoin telles questions complémentaires qu'ils jugent utiles.

ART. 27.

Le témoin doit déposer sans qu'il lui soit permis de lire aucun projet écrit. Toutefois, il peut être autorisé par le Président à s'aider de notes ou documents si la nature des faits rapportés en nécessite l'emploi.

ART. 25.

The witnesses and experts are summoned on the request of the parties or by the Commission of its own motion, and, in every case, through the Government of the State in whose territory they are.

The witnesses are heard in succession and separately, in the presence of the agents and counsel, and in the order fixed by the Commission.

ART. 26.

The examination of witnesses is conducted by the President.

The members of the Commission may however put to each witness questions which they consider likely to throw light on and complete his evidence, or elicit information on any point concerning the witness within the limits of what is necessary in order to get at the truth.

The agents and counsel of the parties may not interrupt the witness when he is making his statement, nor put any direct question to him, but they may ask the President to put such additional questions to the witness as they think expedient.

ART. 27.

The witness must give his evidence without being allowed to read any written proof. He may, however, be permitted by the President to consult notes or documents if the nature of the facts referred to necessitates their employment.

1899	1907

ART. 28.

Procès-verbal de la déposition du témoin est dressé séance tenante et lecture en est donnée au témoin. Le témoin peut y faire tels changements et additions que bon lui semble et qui seront consignés à la suite de sa déposition.

Lecture faite au témoin de l'ensemble de sa déposition, le témoin est requis de signer.

ART. 29.

Les agents sont autorisés au cours ou à la fin de l'enquête, à présenter par écrit à la Commission et à l'autre Partie tels dires, réquisitions, ou résumés de fait qu'ils jugent utiles à la découverte de la vérité.

ART. 30.

Les délibérations de la Commission ont lieu à huis clos et restent secrètes.

Toute décision est prise à la majorité des membres de la Commission.

Le refus d'un membre de prendre part au vote doit être constaté dans le procès-verbal.

ART. 31.

Les séances de la Commission ne sont publiques et les procès-verbaux et documents de l'enquête ne sont rendus publics qu'en vertu d'une décision de la Commission, prise avec l'assentiment des Parties.

ART. 32.

Les Parties ayant présenté tous les éclaircissements et preuves, tous les témoins ayant été entendus, le Président prononce la clôture de l'enquête et la Commission s'ajourne pour délibérer et rédiger son rapport.

1907

ART. 28.

A Minute of the evidence of the witness is drawn up forthwith and read to the witness. The latter may make such alterations and additions as he thinks necessary, which shall be recorded at the end of his statement.

When the whole of his statement has been read to the witness, he is required to sign it.

ART. 29.

The agents are authorized, in the course of or at the close of the inquiry, to present in writing to the Commission and to the other party such statements, requisitions, or summaries of the facts as they consider useful for ascertaining the truth.

ART. 30.

The Commission considers its decisions in private and the proceedings remain secret.

All questions are decided by a majority of the members of the Commission.

If a member declines to vote, the fact must be recorded in the Minutes.

ART. 31.

The sittings of the Commission are not public, nor are the Minutes and documents connected with the inquiry published, except in virtue of a decision of the Commission taken with the consent of the parties.

ART. 32.

After the parties have presented all the explanations and evidence, and the witnesses have all been heard, the President declares the inquiry terminated, and the Commission adjourns to deliberate and to draw up its Report.

1899	1907

ART. 13.

La Commission internationale d'enquête présente aux Puissances en litige son rapport signé par tous les membres de la Commission.

ART. 33.

Le rapport est signé par tous les membres de la Commission.

Si un des membres refuse de signer, mention en est faite; le rapport reste néanmoins valable.

ART. 34.

Le rapport de la Commission est lu en séance publique, les agents et les conseils des parties présents ou dûment appelés.

Un exemplaire du rapport est remis à chaque partie.

ART. 14.

Le rapport de la Commission internationale d'enquête, limité à la constatation des faits, n'a nullement le caractère d'une sentence arbitrale. Il laisse aux Puissances en litige une entière liberté pour la suite à donner à cette constatation.

ART. 35.

Le rapport de la Commission, limité à la constatation des faits, n'a nullement le caractère d'une sentence arbitrale. Il laisse aux *Parties* une entière liberté pour la suite à donner à cette constatation.

ART. 36.

Chaque Partie supporte ses propres frais et une part égale des frais de la Commission.

Titre IV.

De l'Arbitrage International.

Chapitre I.

De la Justice Arbitrale.

ART. 15.

L'arbitrage international a pour objet le règlement de litiges entre les États par des juges de leur choix et sur la base du respect du droit.

Titre IV.

De l'Arbitrage International.

Chapitre I.

De la Justice Arbitrale.

ART. 37.

L'arbitrage international a pour objet le règlement de litiges entre les États par les juges de leur choix et sur la base du respect du droit.

Le recours à l'arbitrage implique l'engagement de se soumettre de bonne foi à la sentence.

(*Voyez Art.* 18 (1899).)

1899	1907

ART. 13.

The International Commission of Inquiry communicates its Report to the Powers at variance, signed by all the members of the Commission.

ART. 33.

The Report is signed by all the members of the Commission.

If one of the members refuses to sign, the fact is mentioned ; but the validity of the Report is not affected.

ART. 34.

The Report of the Commission is read in open Court, the agents and counsel of the parties being present or duly summoned to attend.

A copy of the Report is furnished to each party.

ART. 14.

The Report of the International Commission of Inquiry being limited to a finding of fact, has in no way the character of an Arbitral Award. It leaves to the Powers at variance entire freedom as to the effect to be given to the finding.

ART. 35.

The Report of the Commission, being limited to a finding of fact, has in no way the character of an Arbitral Award. It leaves to the *Parties* entire freedom as to the effect to be given to the finding.

ART. 36.

Each party pays its own expenses and an equal share of the expenses of the Commission.

Title IV.

On International Arbitration.

Chapter I.

On the System of Arbitration.

ART. 15.

International arbitration has for its object the settlement of differences between States by judges of their own choice, and on the basis of respect for law.

Part IV.

On International Arbitration.

Chapter I.

On the System of Arbitration.

ART. 37.

International arbitration has for its object the settlement of disputes between States by judges of their own choice and on the basis of respect for law.

Recourse to arbitration implies an engagement to submit loyally to the Award.

(*Cp. Art.* 18 (1899).)

1899	1907
ART. 16.	ART. 38.

1899 — ART. 16.

Dans les questions d'ordre juridique, et en premier lieu dans les questions d'interprétation ou d'application des Conventions Internationales, l'arbitrage est reconnu par les Puissances Signataires comme le moyen le plus efficace et en même temps le plus équitable de régler les litiges qui n'ont pas été résolus par les voies diplomatiques.

1907 — ART. 38.

Dans les questions d'ordre juridique, et en premier lieu dans les questions d'interprétation ou d'application des Conventions internationales, l'arbitrage est reconnu par les Puissances *contractantes* comme le moyen le plus efficace et en même temps le plus équitable de régler les litiges qui n'ont pas été résolus par les voies diplomatiques.

En conséquence, il serait désirable que, dans les litiges sur les questions susmentionnées, les Puissances contractantes eussent, le cas échéant, recours à l'arbitrage, en tant que les circonstances le permettraient.

1899 — ART. 17.

La convention d'arbitrage est conclue pour des contestations déjà nées ou pour des contestations éventuelles.

Elle peut concerner tout litige ou seulement les litiges d'une catégorie déterminée.

1899 — ART. 18.

La convention d'arbitrage implique l'engagement de se soumettre de bonne foi à la sentence arbitrale.

(*Voyez Art.* 37 (1907).)

1907 — ART. 39.

(*Aucune modification.*)

1899 — ART. 19.

Indépendamment des Traités généraux ou particuliers qui stipulent actuellement l'obligation du recours à l'arbitrage pour les Puissances signataires, ces Puissances se réservent de conclure, soit avant la ratification du présent Acte, soit postérieurement, des accords nouveaux, généraux, ou particuliers, en vue d'étendre l'arbitrage obligatoire à tous les cas qu'Elles jugeront possible de lui soumettre.

1907 — ART. 40.

Indépendamment des Traités généraux ou particuliers qui stipulent actuellement l'obligation du recours à l'arbitrage pour les Puissances *contractantes*, ces Puissances se réservent de conclure des accords nouveaux, généraux ou particuliers, en vue d'étendre l'arbitrage obligatoire à tous les cas qu'Elles jugeront possible de lui soumettre.

1899	1907
ART. 16.	ART. 38.

In questions of a legal nature, and especially in the interpretation or application of International Conventions, arbitration is recognized by the Signatory Powers as the most effective, and at the same time the most equitable, means of settling disputes which diplomacy has failed to settle.

In questions of a legal nature, and especially in the interpretation or application of International Conventions, arbitration is recognized by the *Contracting* Powers as the most effective, and, at the same time, the most equitable means of settling disputes which diplomacy has failed to settle.

Consequently, it would be desirable that, in disputes regarding the above-mentioned questions, 'the Contracting Powers should, if the case arise, have recourse to arbitration, in so far as circumstances permit.

ART. 17.	ART. 39.

The Arbitration Convention is concluded for questions already existing or for questions which may arise eventually.

(No change.)

It may embrace any dispute or only disputes of a certain category.

ART. 18.

The Arbitration Convention implies the engagement to submit loyally to the Award.

(*See Art.* 37 (1907).)

ART. 19.	ART. 40.

Independently of general or private Treaties expressly stipulating recourse to arbitration as obligatory on the Signatory Powers, these Powers reserve to themselves the right of concluding, either before the ratification of the present Act or later, new agreements, general or private, with a view to extending obligatory arbitration to all cases which they may consider possible to submit to it.

Independently of general or private Treaties expressly stipulating recourse to arbitration as obligatory on the Contracting Powers, the said Powers reserve to themselves the right of concluding new agreements, general or particular, with a view to extending compulsory arbitration to all cases which they may consider possible to submit to it.

1899	1907
Chapitre II.	Chapitre II.
De la Cour permanente d'arbitrage.	De la Cour permanente d'arbitrage.
ART. 20.	ART. 41.
Dans le but de faciliter le recours immédiat à l'arbitrage pour les différends internationaux qui n'ont pu être réglés par la voie diplomatique, les Puissances signataires s'engagent à organiser une Cour permanente d'arbitrage, accessible en tout temps et fonctionnant, sauf stipulation contraire des Parties, conformément aux règles de procédure insérées dans la présente Convention.	Dans le but de faciliter le recours immédiat à l'arbitrage pour les différends internationaux qui n'ont pu être réglés par la voie diplomatique, les Puissances *contractantes s'engagent à maintenir, telle qu'elle a été établie par la Première Conférence de la Paix, la Cour permanente d'arbitrage*, accessible en tout temps et fonctionnant, sauf stipulation contraire des Parties, conformément aux règles de procédure insérées dans la présente Convention.
ART. 21.	ART. 42.
La Cour permanente sera compétente pour tous les cas d'arbitrage, à moins qu'il n'y ait entente entre les Parties pour l'établissement d'une juridiction spéciale.	La Cour permanente *est* compétente pour tous les cas d'arbitrage, à moins qu'il n'y ait entente entre les Parties pour l'établissement d'une juridiction spéciale.
ART. 22.	ART. 43.
	La Cour permanente a son siège à La Haye.
	(*Voyez Art.* 25 (1899).)
Un Bureau international établi à La Haye sert de greffe à la Cour.	Un Bureau international sert de greffe à la Cour ; il est l'intermédiaire des communications relatives aux réunions de celle-ci ; il a la garde des archives et la gestion de toutes les affaires administratives.
Ce Bureau est l'intermédiaire des communications relatives aux réunions de celle-ci.	
Il a la garde des archives et la gestion de toutes les affaires administratives.	
Les Puissances signataires s'engagent à communiquer au Bureau international de La Haye une copie certifiée	Les Puissances *contractantes* s'engagent à communiquer au Bureau, *aussitôt que possible*, une copie certifiée

1899	1907

Chapter II.

On the Permanent Court of Arbitration.

Art. 20.

With the object of facilitating an immediate recourse to arbitration for international differences, which it has not been possible to settle by diplomacy, the Signatory Powers undertake to organize a permanent Court of Arbitration, accessible at all times and acting, in default of agreement to the contrary between the parties, in accordance with the rules of procedure inserted in the present Convention.

Art. 21.

The Permanent Court shall be competent for all arbitration cases, unless the parties agree to institute a special Tribunal.

Art. 22.

An International Bureau, established at the Hague, serves as registry for the Court.

This Bureau is the channel for communications relative to the meetings of the Court.

It has the custody of the archives and conducts all the administrative business.

The Signatory Powers undertake to communicate to the International Bureau at the Hague a duly certified

Chapter II.

On the Permanent Court of Arbitration.

Art. 41.

With the object of facilitating an immediate recourse to arbitration for international differences, which it has not been possible to settle by diplomacy, the *Contracting* Powers undertake *to maintain the Permanent Court of Arbitration, as established by the First Peace Conference,* accessible at all times, and acting, in default of agreement to the contrary between the parties, in accordance with the rules of procedure inserted in the present Convention.

Art. 42.

The Permanent Court *is* competent for all arbitration cases, unless the parties agree to institute a special Tribunal.

Art. 43.

The seat of the Permanent Court is at the Hague.

(*Cp. Art.* 25 (1899).)

An International Bureau serves as registry for the Court. It is the channel for communications relative to the meetings of the Court; it has the custody of the archives and conducts all the administrative business.

The *Contracting* Powers undertake to communicate to the Bureau, *as soon as possible,* a duly certified copy

1899	1907
conforme de toute stipulation d'arbitrage intervenue entre Elles et de toute sentence arbitrale les concernant et rendue par des juridictions spéciales.	conforme de toute stipulation d'arbitrage intervenue entre Elles et de toute sentence arbitrale Les concernant et rendue par des juridictions spéciales.
Elles s'engagent à communiquer de même au Bureau les lois, règlements, et documents constatant éventuellement l'exécution des sentences rendues par la Cour.	Elles s'engagent à communiquer de même au Bureau les lois, règlements, et documents constatant éventuellement l'exécution des sentences rendues par la Cour.

<table>
<tr><td align="center">Art. 23.</td><td align="center">Art. 44.</td></tr>
</table>

Chaque Puissance Signataire désignera, dans les trois mois qui suivront la ratification par elle du présent Acte, quatre personnes au plus, d'une compétence reconnue dans les questions de droit international, jouissant de la plus haute considération morale et disposées à accepter les fonctions d'arbitres.	Chaque Puissance *contractante* désigne quatre personnes au plus, d'une compétence reconnue dans les questions de droit international, jouissant de la plus haute considération morale et disposées à accepter les fonctions d'arbitre.
Les personnes ainsi désignées seront inscrites, au titre de Membre de la Cour, sur une liste qui sera notifiée à toutes les Puissances signataires par les soins du Bureau.	Les personnes ainsi désignées *sont* inscrites, au titre de Membres de la Cour, sur une liste qui sera notifiée à toutes les Puissances *contractantes* par les soins du Bureau.
Toute modification à la liste des arbitres est portée, par les soins du Bureau, à la connaissance des Puissances signataires.	Toute modification à la liste des arbitres est portée, par les soins du Bureau, à la connaissance des Puissances *contractantes*.
Deux ou plusieurs Puissances peuvent s'entendre pour la désignation en commun d'un ou de plusieurs Membres.	Deux ou plusieurs Puissances peuvent s'entendre pour la désignation en commun d'un ou de plusieurs Membres.
La même personne peut être désignée par des Puissances différentes.	La même personne peut être désignée par des Puissances différentes.
Les Membres de la Cour sont nommés pour un terme de six ans. Leur mandat peut être renouvelé.	Les Membres de la Cour sont nommés pour un terme de six ans. Leur mandat peut être renouvelé.
En cas de décès ou de retraite d'un Membre de la Cour, il est pourvu à son remplacement selon le mode fixé pour sa nomination.	En cas de décès ou de retraite d'un membre de la Cour, il est pourvu à son remplacement selon le mode fixé pour sa nomination, *et pour une nouvelle période de six ans.*

1899	1907
copy of any agreement concerning arbitration arrived at between them, and of any award concerning them delivered by a special Tribunal.	of any agreement concerning arbitration arrived at between them and of any award concerning them delivered by a special Tribunal.
They likewise undertake to communicate to the Bureau the laws, regulations, and documents if any, showing the execution of the awards given by the Court.	They likewise undertake to communicate to the Bureau the laws, regulations, and documents if any, showing the execution of the Awards given by the Court.

ART. 23.	ART. 44.
Within the three months following its ratification of the present Act, each Signatory Power shall select four persons at the most, of known competency in questions of international law, of the highest moral reputation, and disposed to accept the duties of Arbitrators.	Each *Contracting* Power selects four persons at the most, of known competency in questions of international law, of the highest moral reputation, and disposed to accept the duties of Arbitrator.
The persons thus selected shall be inscribed, as Members of the Court, in a list which shall be notified by the Bureau to all the Signatory Powers.	The persons thus selected *are* inscribed, as Members of the Court, in a list which shall be notified to all the *Contracting* Powers by the Bureau.
Any alteration in the list of Arbitrators is brought by the Bureau to the knowledge of the Signatory Powers.	Any alteration in the list of Arbitrators is brought by the Bureau to the knowledge of the *Contracting* Powers.
Two or more Powers may agree on the selection in common of one or more Members.	Two or more Powers may agree on the selection in common of one or more Members.
The same person may be selected by different Powers.	The same person may be selected by different Powers.
The Members of the Court are appointed for a term of six years. Their appointments can be renewed.	The Members of the Court are appointed for a term of six years. Their appointments can be renewed.
Should a Member of the Court die or resign, the same procedure is followed in filling the vacancy as was followed in appointing him.	Should a Member of the Court die or resign, the same procedure is followed in filling the vacancy as was followed in appointing him. *In this case the appointment is made for a fresh period of six years.*

1899

ART. 24.

Lorsque les Puissances signataires veulent s'adresser à la Cour permanente pour le règlement d'un différend survenu entre Elles, le choix des arbitres appelés à former le Tribunal compétent pour statuer sur ce différend, doit être fait dans la liste générale des Membres de la Cour.

A défaut de constitution du Tribunal arbitral par l'accord immédiat des Parties, il est procédé de la manière suivante :—

Chaque Partie nomme deux arbitres et ceux-ci choisissent ensemble un surarbitre.

En cas de partage des voix, le choix du surarbitre est confié à une Puissance tierce, désignée de commun accord par les Parties.

Si l'accord ne s'établit pas à ce sujet, chaque Partie désigne une Puissance différente, et le choix du surarbitre est fait de concert par les Puissances ainsi désignées.

Le Tribunal étant ainsi composé, les Parties notifient au Bureau leur dé-

1907

ART. 45.

Lorsque les Puissances *contractantes* veulent s'adresser à la Cour permanente pour le règlement d'un différend survenu entre Elles, le choix des arbitres appelés à former le Tribunal compétent pour statuer sur ce différend, doit être fait dans la liste générale des Membres de la Cour.

A défaut de constitution du Tribunal Arbitral par l'accord des Parties, il est procédé de la manière suivante :

Chaque Partie nomme deux arbitres, *dont un seulement peut être son national ou choisi parmi ceux qui ont été désignés par Elle comme Membres de la Cour Permanente.* Ces arbitres choisissent ensemble un surarbitre.

En cas de partage des voix, le choix du surarbitre est confié à une Puissance tierce, désignée de commun accord par les Parties.

Si l'accord ne s'établit pas à ce sujet, chaque Partie désigne une Puissance différente, et le choix du surarbitre est fait de concert par les Puissances ainsi désignées.

Si, dans un délai de deux mois, ces deux Puissances n'ont pu tomber d'accord, chacune d'Elles présente deux candidats pris sur la liste des Membres de la Cour Permanente, en dehors des Membres désignés par les Parties et n'étant les nationaux d'aucune d'Elles. Le sort détermine lequel des candidats ainsi présentés sera le surarbitre.

ART. 46.

Dès que le Tribunal est composé, les Parties notifient au Bureau leur

1899	1907
ART. 24.	ART. 45.

When the Signatory Powers wish to have recourse to the Permanent Court for the settlement of a difference which has arisen between them, the Arbitrators called upon to form the Tribunal to decide this difference must be chosen from the general list of Members of the Court.

When the *Contracting* Powers wish to have recourse to the Permanent Court for the settlement of a difference which has arisen between them, the Arbitrators called upon to form the Tribunal to decide this difference must be chosen from the general list of Members of the Court.

Failing the composition of the Arbitration Tribunal by direct agreement between the parties, the following course shall be pursued :—

Failing the composition of the Arbitration Tribunal by agreement between the parties, the following course shall be pursued :—

Each party appoints two Arbitrators, and these together choose an Umpire.

Each party appoints two Arbitrators, *of whom one only can be its national or chosen from among the persons selected by it as Members of the Permanent Court.* These Arbitrators together choose an Umpire.

If the votes are equally divided, the choice of the Umpire is intrusted to a third Power, selected by agreement between the parties.

If the votes are equally divided, the choice of the Umpire is intrusted to a third Power, selected by agreement between the parties.

If an agreement is not arrived at on this subject, each party selects a different Power, and the choice of the Umpire is made in concert by the Powers thus selected.

If an agreement is not arrived at on this subject each party selects a different Power, and the choice of the Umpire is made in concert by the Powers thus selected.

If, within two months' time, these two Powers cannot come to an agreement, each of them presents two candidates taken from the list of Members of the Permanent Court, exclusive of the Members selected by the parties and not being nationals of either of them. Which of the candidates thus presented shall be Umpire is determined by lot.

ART. 46.

As soon as the Tribunal has been constituted, the parties notify to the

As soon as the Tribunal has been constituted, the parties notify to the

1899	1907
cision de s'adresser à la Cour et les noms des arbitres.	décision de s'adresser à la Cour, *le texte de leur Compromis*, et les noms des arbitres.
	Le Bureau communique sans délai à chaque arbitre le Compromis et les noms des autres Membres du Tribunal.
Le Tribunal arbitral se réunit à la date fixée par les Parties.	Le Tribunal se réunit à la date fixée par les Parties. *Le Bureau pourvoit à son installation.*
Les Membres de la Cour, dans l'exercice de leurs fonctions et en dehors de leur pays, jouissent des privilèges et immunités diplomatiques.	Les Membres *du Tribunal*, dans l'exercice de leurs fonctions et en dehors de leur pays, jouissent des privilèges et immunités diplomatiques.
(*Voyez Art.* 46 (1907).)	

ART. 25.

Le Tribunal arbitral siège d'ordinaire à La Haye.

(*Voyez Art.* 43 (1907).)

Le siège ne peut, sauf le cas de force majeure, être changé par le Tribunal que de l'assentiment des Parties.

ART. 26.	ART. 47.
Le Bureau international de La Haye est autorisé à mettre ses locaux et son organisation à la disposition des Puissances signataires pour le fonctionnement de toute juridiction spéciale d'arbitrage.	Le Bureau est autorisé à mettre ses locaux et son organisation à la disposition des Puissances *contractantes* pour le fonctionnement de toute juridiction spéciale d'arbitrage.
La juridiction de la Cour permanente peut être étendue, dans les conditions prescrites par les Règlements, aux litiges existant entre des Puissances non-signataires ou entre des Puissances signataires et des Puissances non-signataires, si les Parties sont convenues de recourir à cette juridiction.	La juridiction de la Cour permanente peut être étendue, dans les conditions prescrites par les Règlements, aux litiges existant entre des Puissances non-*contractantes*, ou entre des Puissances *contractantes* et des Puissances non-*contractantes*, si les Parties sont convenues de recourir à cette juridiction.

1899	1907
Bureau their determination to have recourse to the Court and the names of the Arbitrators.	Bureau their determination to have recourse to the Court, *the text of their Compromis*[1], and the names of the Arbitrators. *The Bureau communicates without delay to each Arbitrator the* Compromis, *and the names of the other members of the Tribunal.*
The Tribunal of Arbitration assembles at the date fixed by the parties.	The Tribunal assembles at the date fixed by the parties. *The Bureau makes the necessary arrangements for its meeting.*
The Members of the Tribunal, in the performance of their duties and when outside their own country, enjoy diplomatic privileges and immunities.	The Members of the Tribunal, in the performance of their duties and when outside their own country, enjoy diplomatic privileges and immunities.

ART. 25.

The Tribunal of Arbitration has its ordinary seat at the Hague.

(*See Art.* 43 (1907).)

Except in cases of necessity, the place of session can only be altered by the Tribunal with the assent of the parties.

ART. 26.	ART. 47.
The International Bureau at the Hague is authorized to place its offices and its staff at the disposal of the Signatory Powers for the use of any special Board of Arbitration.	The Bureau is authorized to place its offices and staff at the disposal of the *Contracting* Powers for the use of any special Board of Arbitration.
The jurisdiction of the Permanent Court may, within the conditions laid down in the Regulations, be extended to disputes between non-Signatory Powers, or between Signatory Powers and non-Signatory Powers, if the parties are agreed to have recourse to the Court.	The jurisdiction of the Permanent Court may, within the conditions laid down in the Regulations, be extended to disputes between non-*Contracting* Powers or between *Contracting* Powers and non-*Contracting* Powers, if the parties are agreed to have recourse to the Court.

[1] See Article 52, *infra*, for definition of the word "Compromis."

1899	1907
Art. 27.	Art. 48.

Les Puissances signataires considèrent comme un devoir, dans le cas où un conflit aigu menacerait d'éclater entre deux ou plusieurs d'entre Elles, de rappeler à celles-ci que la Cour permanente leur est ouverte.

En conséquence, Elles déclarent que le fait de rappeler aux Parties en conflit les dispositions de la présente Convention, et le conseil donné, dans l'intérêt supérieur de la paix, de s'adresser à la Cour permanente ne peuvent être considérés que comme actes de bons offices.

Les Puissances *contractantes* considèrent comme un devoir, dans le cas où un conflit aigu menacerait d'éclater entre deux ou plusieurs d'entre Elles, de rappeler à celles-ci que la Cour permanente leur est ouverte.

En conséquence, Elles déclarent que le fait de rappeler aux Parties en conflit les dispositions de la présente Convention, et le conseil donné, dans l'intérêt supérieur de la paix, de s'adresser à la Cour permanente, ne peuvent être considérés que comme actes de bons offices.

En cas de conflit entre deux Puissances, l'une d'Elles pourra toujours adresser au Bureau international une note contenant sa déclaration qu'Elle serait disposée à soumettre le différend à un arbitrage.

Le Bureau devra porter aussitôt la déclaration à la connaissance de l'autre Puissance.

Art. 28.	Art. 49.

Un Conseil administratif permanent composé des Représentants diplomatiques des Puissances signataires accrédités à La Haye et du Ministre des Affaires Étrangères des Pays-Bas qui remplira les fonctions de Président, sera constitué dans cette ville le plus tôt possible après la ratification du présente Acte par neuf Puissances au moins.

Ce Conseil sera chargé d'établir et d'organiser le Bureau international, lequel demeurera sous sa direction et sous son contrôle.

Il notifiera aux Puissances la constitution de la Cour et pourvoira à l'installation de celle-ci.

Le Conseil administratif permanent, composé des Représentants diplomatiques des Puissances *contractantes* accrédités à La Haye et du Ministre des Affaires Étrangères des Pays-Bas, qui *remplit* les fonctions de Président, a la direction et le contrôle du Bureau international.

1899	1907
ART. 27.	ART. 48.

The Signatory Powers consider it their duty, if a serious dispute threatens to break out between two or more of them, to remind these latter that the Permanent Court is open to them.

Consequently, they declare that the fact of reminding the parties at variance of the provisions of the present Convention, and the advice given to them, in the highest interests of peace, to have recourse to the Permanent Court, can only be regarded as in the nature of good offices.

The *Contracting* Powers consider it their duty, if a serious dispute threatens to break out between two or more of them, to remind these latter that the Permanent Court is open to them.

Consequently, they declare that the fact of reminding the parties at variance of the provisions of the present Convention, and the advice given to them, in the highest interests of peace, to have recourse to the Permanent Court, can only be regarded as in the nature of good offices[1].

In case of dispute between two Powers, one of them may always address to the International Bureau a note containing a declaration that it would be ready to submit the dispute to arbitration.

The Bureau must at once inform the other Power of the declaration.

ART. 28.	ART. 49.

A Permanent Administrative Council composed of the Diplomatic Representatives of the Signatory Powers accredited to the Hague and of the Netherland Minister for Foreign Affairs, who will act as President, shall be instituted in this town as soon as possible after the ratification of the present Act by at least nine Powers.

This Council will be charged with the establishment and organization of the International Bureau, which will be under its direction and control.

It will notify to the Powers the constitution of the Court and will provide for its installation.

The Permanent Administrative Council, composed of the Diplomatic Representatives of the *Contracting* Powers accredited to The Hague and of the Netherland Minister for Foreign Affairs, who *acts* as President, *is* charged with the direction and control of the International Bureau.

[1] See Article 2, *supra*.

1899	1907
Il arrêtera son règlement d'ordre ainsi que tous autres règlements nécessaires.	*Le Conseil arrête* son règlement d'ordre ainsi que tous autres règlements nécessaires.

Il décidera toutes les questions administratives qui pourraient surgir touchant le fonctionnement de la Cour.

Il aura tout pouvoir quant à la nomination, la suspension, ou la révocation des fonctionnaires et employés du Bureau.

Il fixera les traitements et salaires et contrôlera la dépense générale.

La présence de cinq membres dans les réunions dûment convoquées suffit pour permettre au Conseil de délibérer valablement. Les décisions sont prises à la majorité des voix.

Le Conseil communique sans délai aux Puissances signataires les règlements adoptés par lui. Il leur adresse chaque année un rapport sur les travaux de la Cour, sur le fonctionnement des services administratifs et sur les dépenses.

Il *décide* toutes les questions administratives qui pourraient surgir touchant le fonctionnement de la Cour.

Il *a* tout pouvoir quant à la nomination, la suspension, ou la révocation des fonctionnaires et employés du Bureau.

Il *fixe* les traitements et salaires, et *contrôle* la dépense générale.

La présence de *neuf* membres dans les réunions dûment convoquées suffit pour permettre au Conseil de délibérer valablement. Les décisions sont prises à la majorité des voix.

Le Conseil communique sans délai aux Puissances *contractantes* les règlements adoptés par lui. Il leur *présente* chaque année un rapport sur les travaux de la Cour, sur le fonctionnement des services administratifs, et sur les dépenses. *Le rapport contient également un résumé du contenu essentiel des documents communiqués au Bureau par les Puissances en vertu de l'article 43, alinéas 3 et 4.*

ART. 29.	ART. 50.
Les frais du Bureau seront supportés par les Puissances signataires dans la proportion établie pour le Bureau international de l'Union postale universelle.	Les frais du Bureau seront supportés par les Puissances *contractantes* dans la proportion établie pour le Bureau international de l'Union postale universelle.

Les frais à la charge des Puissances adhérentes seront comptés à partir du jour où leur adhésion produit ses effets.

1899	1907
It will settle its rules of procedure and all other necessary regulations.	*The Council settles* its rules of procedure and all other necessary regulations.
It will decide all questions of administration which may arise with regard to the business of the Court.	It *decides* all questions of administration which may arise with regard to the business of the Court.
It will have entire control over the appointment, suspension or dismissal of the officials and employés of the Bureau.	It *has* entire control over the appointment, suspension, or dismissal of the officials and employés of the Bureau.
It will fix the payments and salaries, and control the general expenditure.	It *fixes* the payments and salaries, and controls the general expenditure.
At meetings duly summoned the presence of five members is sufficient to render valid the discussions of the Council. The decisions are taken by a majority of votes.	At meetings duly summoned, the presence of *nine* members is sufficient to render valid the discussions of the Council. The decisions are taken by a majority of votes.
The Council communicates to the Signatory Powers without delay the Regulations adopted by it. It furnishes them with an annual Report on the labours of the Court, the working of the staff, and the expenditure.	The Council communicates to the *Contracting* Powers without delay the regulations adopted by it. It furnishes them with an annual Report on the labours of the Court, the working of the staff, and the expenditure. *The Report likewise contains a summary of the more important contents of the documents communicated to the Bureau by the Powers in virtue of Article 43, paragraphs 3 and 4.*

ART. 29.	ART. 50.
The expenses of the Bureau shall be borne by the Signatory Powers in the proportion fixed for the International Bureau of the Universal Postal Union.	The expenses of the Bureau shall be borne by the *Contracting* Powers in the proportion fixed for the International Bureau of the Universal Postal Union. *The expenses to be charged to the acceding Powers shall be reckoned from the date on which their accession takes effect.*

1899	1907
Chapitre III.	Chapitre III.
De la Procédure Arbitrale.	De la Procédure Arbitrale.

ART. 30.	ART. 51.
En vue de favoriser le développement de l'arbitrage, les Puissances signataires ont arrêté les règles suivantes qui seront applicables à la procédure arbitrale, en tant que les Parties ne sont pas convenues d'autres règles.	(*Aucune modification.*)[1]

ART. 31.	ART. 52.
Les Puissances qui recourent à l'arbitrage signent un acte spécial (compromis) dans lequel sont nettement déterminés l'objet du litige ainsi que l'étendue des pouvoirs des arbitres. Cet acte implique l'engagement des Parties de se soumettre de bonne foi à la sentence arbitrale. (*Voyez Art. 37, al. 2 (1907).*)	Les Puissances qui recourent à l'arbitrage signent un compromis dans lequel sont déterminés l'objet du litige, *le délai de nomination des Arbitres, la forme, l'ordre et les délais dans lesquels la communication visée par l'Article 63 devra être faite, et le montant de la somme que chaque Partie aura à déposer à titre d'avance pour les frais.* *Le compromis détermine également, s'il y a lieu, le mode de nomination des arbitres, tous pouvoirs spéciaux éventuels du Tribunal, son siège, la langue dont il fera usage et celles dont l'emploi sera autorisé devant lui, et généralement toutes les conditions dont les Parties sont convenues.*

	ART. 53.
	La Cour permanente est compétente pour l'établissement du compromis, si les Parties sont d'accord pour s'en remettre à elle. *Elle est également compétente, même*

V. note, *supra*, p. 101.

1899	1907
Chapter III.	Chapter III.
On Arbitration Procedure.	On Arbitration Procedure.

ART. 30. ·	ART. 51.

<table>
<tr>
<td>

With a view of encouraging the development of arbitration, the Signatory Powers have agreed on the following Rules, which shall apply to arbitration procedure, except in so far as other Rules shall have been agreed on by the parties.

</td>
<td>

(No change.)[1]

</td>
</tr>
</table>

ART. 31.	ART. 52.

<table>
<tr>
<td>

The Powers which have recourse to arbitration sign a special Act (*Compromis*), in which the subject of the dispute is clearly defined, as well as the extent of the Arbitrators' powers. This Act implies the undertaking of the parties to submit loyally to the award.

(*See Art.* 37, *par.* 2 (1907).)

</td>
<td>

The Powers which have recourse to arbitration sign a *Compromis,* in which the subject of the dispute is clearly defined, *the time allowed for appointing Arbitrators, the form, order, and time in which the communication referred to in Article 63 must be made, and the amount of the sum which each party must deposit in advance to defray the expenses.*

The Compromis *likewise defines, if there is occasion for it, the manner of appointing Arbitrators, the special powers, if any, conferred on the Tribunal, the place of meeting, the language it shall use, and the languages the employment of which shall be authorized before it, and, generally speaking, all the conditions on which the parties are agreed.*

</td>
</tr>
</table>

	ART. 53.

The Permanent Court is competent to settle the Compromis, *if the parties are agreed to have recourse to it for the purpose.*

It is similarly competent, even if the

---

[1] V. note, *supra,* p. 101.

<table>
<tr><td>1899</td><td>1907</td></tr>
</table>

1899   1907

si la demande est faite seulement par l'une des Parties, après qu'un accord par la voie diplomatique a été vainement essayé, quand il s'agit :—

1. *D'un différend rentrant dans un Traité d'arbitrage général conclu ou renouvelé après la mise en vigueur de cette Convention et qui prévoit pour chaque différend un compromis et n'exclut pour l'établissement de ce dernier ni explicitement ni implicitement la compétence de la Cour. Toutefois, le recours à la Cour n'a pas lieu si l'autre Partie déclare qu'à son avis le différend n'appartient pas à la catégorie des différends à soumettre à un arbitrage obligatoire, à moins que le Traité d'arbitrage ne confère au Tribunal arbitral le pouvoir de décider cette question préalable ;*

2. *D'un différend provenant de dettes contractuelles réclamées à une Puissance par une autre Puissance comme dues à ses nationaux, et pour la solution duquel l'offre d'arbitrage a été acceptée. Cette disposition n'est pas applicable si l'acceptation a été subordonnée à la condition que le compromis soit établi selon un autre mode.*

(*Voyez 2 H. C.* 1907.)

Art. 54.

Dans les cas prévus par l'Article précédent, le compromis sera établi par une Commission composée de cinq membres désignés de la manière prévue à l'Article 45, alinéas 3 à 6.

Le cinquième membre est de droit Président de la Commission.

request is only made by one of the parties, when all attempts to reach an understanding through the diplomatic channel have failed, in the case of :—

1. *A dispute covered by a general Treaty of Arbitration concluded or renewed after the present Convention has come into force, and providing for a* Compromis *in all disputes and not either explicitly or implicitly excluding the settlement of the* Compromis *from the competence of the Court. Recourse cannot, however, be had to the Court if the other party declares that in its opinion the dispute does not belong to the category of disputes which can be submitted to obligatory arbitration, unless the Treaty of Arbitration confers upon the Arbitration Tribunal the power of deciding this preliminary question ;*

2. *A dispute arising from contract debts claimed from one Power by another Power as due to its nationals, and for the settlement of which the offer of arbitration has been accepted. This provision is not applicable if acceptance is subject to the condition that the* Compromis *should be settled in some other way.*

(*Cp. 2 H. C.* 1907.)

ART. 54.

In the cases contemplated in the preceding Article, the Compromis *shall be settled by a Commission consisting of five members selected in the manner laid down in Article* 45, *paragraphs* 3 *to* 6.

The fifth member is ex officio *President of the Commission.*

1899	1907
ART. 32.	**ART. 55.**

Les fonctions arbitrales peuvent être conférées à un arbitre unique ou à plusieurs arbitres désignés par les Parties à leur gré, ou choisis par Elles parmi les Membres de la Cour permanente d'arbitrage établie par le présent Acte.

A défaut de constitution du Tribunal par l'accord immédiat des Parties, il est procédé de la manière suivante :

Chaque Partie nomme deux arbitres et ceux-ci choisissent ensemble un surarbitre.

En cas de partage des voix, le choix du surarbitre est confié à une Puissance tierce, désignée de commun accord par les Parties.

Si l'accord ne s'établit pas à ce sujet, chaque Partie désigne une Puissance différente et le choix du surarbitre est fait de concert par les Puissances ainsi désignées.

Les fonctions arbitrales peuvent être conférées à un arbitre unique ou à plusieurs arbitres désignés par les Parties à leur gré, ou choisis par Elles parmi les Membres de la Cour permanente d'arbitrage établie par la présente *Convention*.

A défaut de constitution du Tribunal par l'accord des Parties, il est procédé de la manière *indiquée à l'Article 45, alinéas 3 à 6.*

ART. 33.

Lorsqu'un Souverain ou un Chef d'État est choisi pour arbitre, la procédure arbitrale est réglée par lui.

ART. 56.

(*Aucune modification.*)

ART. 34.

Le surarbitre est de droit Président du Tribunal.

Lorsque le Tribunal ne comprend pas de surarbitre, il nomme lui-même son Président.

ART. 57.

(*Aucune modification.*)

ART. 58.

En cas d'établissement du compromis par une Commission, telle qu'elle est visée à l'Article 54, et sauf stipulation contraire, la Commission elle-même formera le Tribunal d'arbitrage.

1899	1907
ART. 32.	**ART. 55.**
The duties of Arbitrator may be conferred on a single Arbitrator or on several Arbitrators selected by the parties as they please, or chosen by them from the Members of the Permanent Court of Arbitration established by the present Act.	The duties of Arbitrator may be conferred on a single Arbitrator or on several Arbitrators selected by the parties as they please, or chosen by them from the Members of the Permanent Court of Arbitration established by the present *Convention*.
Failing the constitution of the Tribunal by direct agreement between the parties, the following course shall be pursued :	Failing the composition of the Tribunal by agreement between the parties, the course *referred to in Article 45, paragraphs 3 to 6, is followed*.
Each party appoints two Arbitrators, and these latter together choose an Umpire.	
In case of equal voting, the choice of the Umpire is intrusted to a third Power, selected by the parties by common accord.	
If no agreement is arrived at on this subject, each party selects a different Power, and the choice of the Umpire is made in concert by the Powers thus selected.	
ART. 33.	**ART. 56.**
When a Sovereign or the Chief of a State is chosen as Arbitrator, the arbitration procedure is settled by him.	(*No change.*)
ART. 34.	**ART. 57.**
The Umpire is *ex officio* President of the Tribunal.	(*No change.*)
When the Tribunal does not include an Umpire, it appoints its own President.	
	ART. 58.
	When the Compromis is settled by a Commission, as contemplated in Article 54, and in default of agreement to the contrary, the Commission itself shall form the Arbitration Tribunal.

1899	1907

Art. 35.

En cas de décès, de démission ou d'empêchement, pour quelque cause que ce soit, de l'un des arbitres, il est pourvu à son remplacement selon le mode fixé pour sa nomination.

Art. 59.

(*Aucune modification.*)

Art. 36.

Le siège du Tribunal est désigné par les Parties. A défaut de cette désignation le Tribunal siège à La Haye.

Le siège ainsi fixé ne peut, sauf le cas de force majeure, être changé par le Tribunal que de l'assentiment des Parties.

Art. 60.

A défaut de désignation par les Parties, le Tribunal siège à La Haye.

Le Tribunal ne peut siéger sur le territoire d'une tierce Puissance qu'avec l'assentiment de celle-ci.

Le siège *une fois* fixé ne peut être changé par le Tribunal qu'avec l'assentiment des Parties.

Art. 61.

Si le Compromis n'a pas déterminé les langues à employer, il en est décidé par le Tribunal.

(*Voyez Art. 38 (1899).*)

Art. 37.

Les Parties ont le droit de nommer auprès du Tribunal des délégués ou agents spéciaux, avec la mission de servir d'intermédiaires entre Elles et le Tribunal.

Elles sont en outre autorisées à charger de la défense de leurs droits et intérêts devant le Tribunal, des conseils ou avocats nommés par Elles à cet effet.

Art. 62.

Les Parties ont le droit de nommer auprès du Tribunal des agents spéciaux, avec la mission de servir d'intermédiaires entre Elles et le Tribunal.

Elles sont, en outre, autorisées à charger de la défense de leurs droits et intérêts devant le Tribunal des conseils ou avocats nommés par Elles à cet effet.

Les Membres de la Cour permanente ne peuvent exercer les fonctions d'agents, conseils ou avocats, qu'en faveur de la Puissance qui les a nommés Membres de la Cour.

1899	1907
ART. 35.	ART. 59.
In case of the death, retirement or disability from any cause of one of the Arbitrators, the same procedure is followed in filling the vacancy as was followed in appointing him.	(*No change.*)
ART. 36.	ART. 60.
The Tribunal's place of session is selected by the parties. Failing this selection the Tribunal sits at the Hague.	The Tribunal sits at The Hague, unless some other place is selected by the parties.
	The Tribunal may only sit in the territory of a third Power with the latter's consent.
The place of session thus fixed cannot, except in case of necessity, be altered by the Tribunal, except with the assent of the Parties.	The place of session *once* fixed cannot be altered by the Tribunal, except with the assent of the Parties.
	ART. 61.
	Unless the Compromis *has specified the languages to be employed*, the question shall be decided by the Tribunal. (*Cp. Art.* 38 (1899).)
ART. 37.	ART. 62.
The parties are entitled to appoint delegates or special agents to attend the Tribunal, for the purpose of acting as intermediaries between themselves and the Tribunal.	The parties are entitled to appoint special agents to attend the Tribunal, for the purpose of acting as intermediaries between themselves and the Tribunal.
They are further authorized to retain, for the defence of their rights and interests before the Tribunal, counsel or advocates appointed by them for this purpose.	They are further authorized to retain for the defence of their rights and interests before the Tribunal counsel or advocates appointed by them for the purpose.
	The Members of the Permanent Court may not act as agents, counsel or advocates except on behalf of the Power which has appointed them Members of the Court.

1899	1907

Art. 38.

Le Tribunal décide du choix des langues dont il fera usage et dont l'emploi sera autorisé devant lui.
(*Voyez Art.* 61 (1907).)

Art. 39.

La procédure arbitrale comprend en règle générale deux phases distinctes : l'instruction et les débats.

L'instruction consiste dans la communication faite par les agents respectifs, aux Membres du Tribunal et à la Partie adverse, de tous actes imprimés ou écrits et de tous documents contenant les moyens invoqués dans la cause. Cette communication aura lieu dans la forme et dans les délais déterminés par le Tribunal en vertu de l'Article 49.

Les débats consistent dans le développement oral des moyens des Parties devant le Tribunal.

Art. 40.

Toute pièce produite par l'une des Parties doit être communiquée à l'autre Partie.

Art. 63.

La procédure arbitrale comprend en règle générale deux phases distinctes : l'instruction *écrite* et les débats.

L'instruction *écrite* consiste dans la communication faite par les agents respectifs, aux Membres du Tribunal et à la Partie adverse, *des mémoires, des contre-mémoires, et, au besoin, des répliques; les Parties y joignent toutes pièces et* documents invoqués dans la cause. Cette communication aura lieu, *directement ou par l'intermédiaire du Bureau International, dans l'ordre et* dans les délais déterminés par le *Compromis.*

Les délais fixés par le Compromis pourront être prolongés de commun accord par les Parties, ou par le Tribunal quand il le juge nécessaire pour arriver à une décision juste.

Les débats consistent dans le développement oral des moyens des Parties devant le Tribunal.

Art. 64.

Toute pièce produite par l'une des Parties doit être communiquée, *en copie certifiée conforme,* à l'autre Partie.

Art. 65.

A moins de circonstances spéciales, le Tribunal ne se réunit qu'après la clôture de l'instruction.

1899	1907

Art. 38.

The Tribunal decides on the choice of languages to be used by itself, and to be authorized for use before it.
(*See Art.* 61 (1907).)

Art. 39.

As a general rule arbitration procedure comprises two distinct phases; pleadings and oral discussions.

The pleadings consist in the communication by the respective agents to the members of the Tribunal and the opposing party of all printed or written Acts and of all documents containing the pleas relied on in the case. This communication shall be made in the form and within the time fixed by the Tribunal in accordance with Article 49.

Art. 63.

As a general rule, arbitration procedure comprises two distinct phases : *written* pleadings and oral discussions.

The *written* pleadings consist in the communication by the respective agents to the members of the Tribunal and the opposing party, *of cases, counter-cases, and, if necessary, of replies ; the parties annex thereto all papers and* documents relied on in the cause. This communication shall be made *either directly or through the intermediary of the International Bureau*, in the *order* and within the time fixed by the *Compromis.*

The time fixed by the Compromis *may be extended by mutual agreement between the parties, or by the Tribunal when the latter considers it necessary for the purpose of reaching a just decision.*

The discussions consist of the oral development of the pleas of the parties before the Tribunal.

The discussions consist of the oral developments of the pleas of the parties before the Tribunal.

Art. 40.

Every document produced by one party must be communicated to the other party.

Art. 64.

A *duly certified copy* of every document produced by one party must be communicated to the other party.

Art. 65.

Unless special circumstances arise, the Tribunal does not meet until the pleadings are closed.

1899	1907
ART. 41.	ART. 66.

Les débats sont dirigés par le Président.

Ils ne sont publics qu'en vertu d'une décision du Tribunal, prise avec l'assentiment des Parties.

Ils sont consignés dans des procès-verbaux rédigés par des secrétaires que nomme le Président. Ces procès-verbaux ont seuls caractère authentique.

Les débats sont dirigés par le Président.

Ils ne sont publics qu'en vertu d'une décision du Tribunal, prise avec l'assentiment des Parties.

Ils sont consignés dans des procès-verbaux rédigés par des secrétaires que nomme le Président. Ces procès-verbaux *sont signés par le Président et par un des secrétaires ; ils* ont seuls caractère authentique.

ART. 42.	ART. 67.

L'instruction étant close, le Tribunal a le droit d'écarter du débat tous actes ou documents nouveaux qu'une des Parties voudrait lui soumettre sans le consentement de l'autre.

(*Aucune modification.*)

ART. 43.	ART. 68.

Le Tribunal demeure libre de prendre en considération les actes ou documents nouveaux sur lesquels les agents ou conseils des parties appelleraient son attention.

En ce cas, le Tribunal a le droit de requérir la production de ces actes ou documents, sauf l'obligation d'en donner connaissance à la Partie adverse.

(*Aucune modification.*)

ART. 44.	ART. 69.

Le Tribunal peut, en outre, requérir des agents des Parties la production de tous actes et demander toutes explications nécessaires. En cas de refus, le Tribunal en prend acte.

(*Aucune modification.*)

<table>
<tr><td>1899</td><td>1907</td></tr>
</table>

1899	1907
ART. 41.	ART. 66.

The discussions are under the direction of the President.

They are not public unless it be so decided by the Tribunal, with the assent of the parties.

They are recorded in minutes drawn up by the Secretaries appointed by the President. These minutes are the only authentic record.

The discussions are under the direction of the President.

They are not public unless it be so decided by the Tribunal, with the assent of the parties.

They are recorded in minutes drawn up by the Secretaries appointed by the President. These minutes *are signed by the President and by one of the Secretaries and* are the only authentic record.

| ART. 42. | ART. 67. |

After the close of the pleadings, the Tribunal is entitled to exclude from the discussion all fresh papers or documents which one party may wish to submit to it without the consent of the other.

(No change.)

| ART. 43. | ART. 68. |

The Tribunal is free to take into consideration fresh papers or documents to which its attention may be drawn by the agents or counsel of the parties.

In that case, the Tribunal has the right to require the production of such papers or documents, but is obliged to make them known to the opposite party.

(No change.)

| ART. 44. | ART. 69. |

The Tribunal may also call upon the agents of the parties to furnish all necessary papers and explanations. In case of refusal the Tribunal takes note of it.

(No change.)

1899	1907
ART. 45.	ART. 70.
Les agents et les conseils des Parties sont autorisés à présenter oralement au Tribunal tous les moyens qu'ils jugent utiles à la défense de leur cause.	(*Aucune modification.*)
ART. 46.	ART. 71.
Ils ont le droit de soulever des exceptions et des incidents. Les décisions du Tribunal sur ces points sont définitives et ne peuvent donner lieu à aucune discussion ultérieure.	(*Aucune modification.*)
ART. 47.	ART. 72.
Les membres du Tribunal ont le droit de poser des questions aux agents et aux conseils des Parties et de leur demander des éclaircissements sur les points douteux.	(*Aucune modification.*)
Ni les questions posées, ni les observations faites par les Membres du Tribunal pendant le cours des débats ne peuvent être regardées comme l'expression des opinions du Tribunal en général ou de ses Membres en particulier.	
ART. 48.	ART. 73.
Le Tribunal est autorisé à déterminer sa compétence en interprétant le Compromis ainsi que les autres Traités qui peuvent être invoqués dans la matière, et en appliquant les principes du droit international.	Le Tribunal est autorisé à déterminer sa compétence en interprétant le Compromis ainsi que les autres *Actes et documents* qui peuvent être invoqués dans la matière, et en appliquant les principes du droit.
ART. 49.	ART. 74.
Le Tribunal a le droit de rendre des ordonnances de procédure pour la direction du procès, de déterminer les formes et délais dans lesquels chaque Partie devra prendre ses conclusions et de procéder à toutes les formalités que comporte l'administration des preuves.	Le Tribunal a le droit de rendre des ordonnances de procédure pour la direction du procès, de déterminer les formes, *l'ordre* et les délais dans lesquels chaque Partie devra prendre ses conclusions *finales*, et de procéder à toutes les formalités que comporte l'administration des preuves.

1899	1907
ART. 45.	ART. 70.

The agents and counsel of the parties are authorised to present orally to the Tribunal all the arguments they may think expedient in support of their case.

(*No change.*)

ART. 46.

ART. 71.

They are entitled to raise objections and points.

The decisions of the Tribunal thereon are final, and cannot form the subject of any subsequent discussion.

(*No change.*)

ART. 47.

ART. 72.

The members of the Tribunal are entitled to put questions to the agents and counsel of the parties, and to ask them for explanations on doubtful points.

Neither the questions put nor the remarks made by members of the Tribunal in the course of the discussions are to be regarded as an expression of opinion by the Tribunal in general, or by its members in particular.

(*No change.*)

ART. 48.

ART. 73.

The Tribunal is authorised to determine its competence by interpreting the *Compromis* as well as the other Treaties which may be adduced in the matter and by applying the principles of international law.

The Tribunal is authorised to determine its competence by interpreting the *Compromis* as well as the other *papers and documents* which may be adduced in the matter and by applying the principles of law.

ART. 49.

ART. 74.

The Tribunal is entitled to make rules of procedure for the conduct of the case, to decide the forms and time in which each party must conclude its arguments, and to arrange all the formalities required for taking evidence.

The Tribunal is entitled to make rules of procedure for the conduct of the case, to decide the forms, *order*, and time in which each party must conclude its arguments, and to arrange all the formalities for taking evidence.

1899	1907

1907

ART. 75.

Les Parties s'engagent à fournir au Tribunal, dans la plus large mesure qu'elles jugeront possible, tous les moyens nécessaires pour la décision du litige.

ART. 76.

Pour toutes les notifications que le Tribunal aurait à faire sur le territoire d'une tierce Puissance Contractante, le Tribunal s'adressera directement au Gouvernement de cette Puissance. Il en sera de même s'il s'agit de faire procéder sur place à l'établissement de tous moyens de preuve.

Les requêtes adressées à cet effet seront exécutées suivant les moyens dont la Puissance requise dispose d'après sa législation intérieure. Elles ne peuvent être refusées que si cette Puissance les juge de nature à porter atteinte à Sa souveraineté ou à Sa sécurité.

Le Tribunal aura aussi toujours la faculté de recourir à l'intermédiaire de la Puissance sur le territoire de laquelle il a son siège.

ART. 50.

Les agents et les conseils des Parties ayant présenté tous les éclaircissements et preuves à l'appui de leur cause, le Président prononce la clôture des débats.

ART. 51.

Les délibérations du Tribunal ont lieu à huis clos.

Toute décision est prise à la majorité des membres du Tribunal.

Le refus d'un membre de prendre part au vote doit être constaté dans le procès-verbal.

ART. 77.

(*Aucune modification.*)

ART. 78.

Les délibérations du Tribunal ont lieu à huis clos *et restent secrètes.*

Toute décision est prise à la majorité *de ses* membres.

Art. 75.

The parties undertake to supply the Tribunal, within the widest limits they may think practicable, with all the information required for deciding the dispute.

Art. 76.

For the service of all notices by the Tribunal in the territory of a third Contracting Power, the Tribunal shall apply direct to the Government of such Power. The same rule shall apply in the case of steps being taken in order to procure evidence on the spot.

Requests for this purpose are to be executed so far as the means which the Power applied to possesses under its municipal law allow. They cannot be rejected unless the Power in question considers they are calculated to impair its sovereign rights or its safety.

The Tribunal will also be entitled in all cases to act through the Power on whose territory it sits.

Art. 50.

When the agents and counsel of the parties have submitted all the explanations and evidence in support of their case, the President shall declare the discussion closed.

Art. 77.

(*No change.*)

Art. 51.

The deliberations of the Tribunal take place in private

All questions are decided by a majority of members of the Tribunal.

The refusal of a member to vote must be recorded in the *procès-verbal.*

Art. 78.

The deliberations of the Tribunal take place in private *and the proceedings remain secret.*

All questions are decided by a majority of the members of the Tribunal.

1899	1907

ART. 52.

La sentence arbitrale, votée à la majorité des voix, est motivée. Elle est rédigée par écrit et signée par chacun des membres du Tribunal.

Ceux des membres qui sont restés en minorité peuvent constater, en signant, leur dissentiment.

ART. 79.

La sentence arbitrale est motivée. *Elle mentionne les noms des arbitres;* elle est signée par *le Président et par le greffier ou le secrétaire faisant fonctions de greffier.*

ART. 53.

La sentence arbitrale est lue en séance publique du Tribunal, les agents et les conseils des Parties présents ou dûment appelés.

ART. 80.

La sentence est lue en séance publique, les agents et les conseils des Parties présents ou dûment appelés.

ART. 54.

La sentence arbitrale, dûment prononcée et notifiée aux agents des Parties en litige, décide définitivement et sans appel la contestation.

ART. 81.

La sentence, dûment prononcée et notifiée aux agents des Parties, décide définitivement et sans appel la contestation.

ART. 82.

Tout différend qui pourrait surgir entre les Parties, concernant l'interprétation et l'exécution de la sentence, sera, sauf stipulation contraire, soumis au jugement du Tribunal qui l'a rendue.

ART. 55.

Les Parties peuvent se réserver dans le compromis de demander la revision de la sentence arbitrale.

Dans ce cas, et sauf stipulation contraire, la demande doit être adressée au Tribunal qui a rendu la sentence. Elle ne peut être motivée que par la découverte d'un fait nouveau qui eût été de nature à exercer une influence décisive sur la sentence et qui, lors de

ART. 83.

(Aucune modification.)

1899	1907

ART. 52.

The Award, given by a majority of votes, must state the reasons on which it is based. It is drawn up in writing and signed by each member of the Tribunal.

Those members who are in the minority may record their dissent when signing.

ART. 79.

The Award must state the reasons on which it is based. *It recites the names of the Arbitrators and is signed by the President and by the Registrar or the Secretary acting as Registrar.*

ART. 53.

The Award is read out at a public sitting of the Tribunal, the agents and counsel of the parties being present, or duly summoned to attend.

ART. 80.

The Award is read out at a public sitting, the agents and counsel of the parties being present or duly summoned to attend.

ART. 54.

The Award, duly pronounced and notified to the agents of the parties at variance, settles the dispute definitely and without appeal.

ART. 81.

The Award, duly pronounced and notified to the agents of the parties, settles the dispute definitely and without appeal.

ART. 82.

Any dispute arising between the parties as to the interpretation and execution of the Award shall, in default of agreement to the contrary, be submitted to the decision of the Tribunal which pronounced it.

ART. 55.

The parties may in the *Compromis* reserve the right to demand the revision of the Award.

In this case, and unless there be an agreement to the contrary, the demand must be addressed to the Tribunal which pronounced the Award. It can only be made on the ground of the discovery of some new fact which is calculated to exercise a decisive influence upon the Award, and which,

ART. 83.

(*No change.*)

1899	1907

la clôture des débats, était inconnu du Tribunal lui-même et de la Partie qui a demandé la revision.

La procédure de revision ne peut être ouverte que par une décision du Tribunal constatant expressément l'existence du fait nouveau, lui reconnaissant les caractères prévus par le paragraphe précédent et déclarant à ce titre la demande recevable.

Le compromis détermine le délai dans lequel la demande de revision doit être formée.

Art. 56.

La sentence arbitrale n'est obligatoire que pour les Parties qui ont conclu le compromis.

Lorsqu'il s'agit de l'interprétation d'une Convention à laquelle ont participé d'autres Puissances que les Parties en litige, celles-ci notifient aux premières le Compromis qu'elles ont conclu. Chacune de ces Puissances a le droit d'intervenir au procès. Si une ou plusieurs d'entre elles ont profité de cette faculté, l'interprétation contenue dans la sentence est également obligatoire à leur égard.

Art. 84.

La sentence arbitrale n'est obligatoire que pour les Parties *en litige.*

Lorsqu'il s'agit de l'interprétation d'une Convention à laquelle ont participé d'autres Puissances que les Parties en litige, celles-ci *avertissent en temps utile toutes les Puissances Signataires.* Chacune de ces Puissances a le droit d'intervenir au procès. Si une ou plusieurs d'entre elles ont profité de cette faculté, l'interprétation contenue dans la sentence est également obligatoire à leur égard.

Art. 57.

Chaque Partie supporte ses propres frais et une part égale des frais du Tribunal.

Art. 85.

(Aucune modification.)

Chapitre IV.

De la Procédure Sommaire d'Arbitrage.

Art. 86.

En vue de faciliter le fonctionnement de la justice arbitrale, lorsqu'il s'agit de litiges de nature à comporter une

1899	1907

at the time the discussion was closed, was unknown to the Tribunal and to the party demanding revision.

Proceedings for revision can only be instituted by a decision of the Tribunal expressly recording the existence of the new fact, recognizing in it the character described in the preceding paragraph, and declaring the demand admissible on this ground.

The *Compromis* fixes the period within which the demand for revision must be made.

ART. 56.

The Award is only binding on the parties who concluded the *Compromis*.

When there is a question of interpreting a Convention to which Powers other than those at variance are parties, the latter notify to the former the *Compromis* they have concluded. Each of these Powers has the right to intervene in the case. If one or more of them avail themselves of this right, the interpretation contained in the Award is equally binding on them.

ART. 57.

Each party pays its own expenses and an equal share of those of the Tribunal.

ART. 84.

The Award is only binding on the parties *to the proceedings*.

When there is a question of interpreting a Convention to which Powers other than those at variance are parties, the latter *shall inform all the Signatory Powers in good time.* Each of these Powers has the right to intervene in the case. If one or more of them avail themselves of this right, the interpretation contained in the Award is equally binding on them.

ART. 85.

(*No change.*)

Chapter IV.

On Arbitration by Summary Procedure.

ART. 86.

With a view of facilitating the working of the system of arbitration in disputes admitting of a summary

1899	1907
	procédure sommaire, les Puissances contractantes arrêtent les règles ci-après, qui seront suivies en l'absence de stipulations différentes, et sous réserve, le cas échéant, de l'application des dispositions du Chapitre III, qui ne seraient pas contraires.

ART. 87.

Chacune des Parties en litige nomme un arbitre. Les deux arbitres ainsi désignés choisissent un surarbitre. S'ils ne tombent pas d'accord à ce sujet, chacun présente deux candidats pris sur la liste générale des Membres de la Cour permanente en dehors des Membres indiqués par chacune des Parties Elles-mêmes et n'étant les nationaux d'aucune d'Elles; le sort détermine lequel des candidats ainsi présentés sera le surarbitre.

Le surarbitre préside le Tribunal, qui rend ses décisions à la majorité des voix.

ART. 88.

A défaut d'accord préalable, le Tribunal fixe, dès qu'il est constitué, le délai dans lequel les deux Parties devront lui soumettre leurs mémoires respectifs.

ART. 89.

Chaque Partie est représentée devant le Tribunal par un agent qui sert d'intermédiaire entre le Tribunal et le Gouvernement qui l'a désigné.

ART. 90.

La procédure a lieu exclusivement par écrit. Toutefois, chaque Partie a le droit de demander la comparution de témoins et d'experts. Le Tribunal

1899	1907

procedure, the Contracting Powers adopt the following rules, which shall be observed in the absence of other arrangements and with the reservation that the provisions of Chapter III apply so far as they are not inconsistent with these rules.

ART. 87.

Each of the parties at variance appoints an Arbitrator. The two Arbitrators thus selected choose an Umpire. If they do not agree on this point, each of them proposes two candidates taken from the general list of the Members of the Permanent Court exclusive of the Members appointed by either of the parties and not being nationals of either of them; which of the candidates thus proposed shall be the Umpire is determined by lot.

The Umpire presides over the Tribunal, which gives its decisions by a majority of votes.

ART. 88.

In default of previous agreement, the Tribunal, as soon as it is constituted, settles the time within which the two parties shall submit their respective cases to it.

ART. 89.

Each party is represented before the Tribunal by an agent, who serves as intermediary between the Tribunal and the Government which has appointed him.

ART. 90.

The proceedings are conducted exclusively in writing. Each party, however, is entitled to ask that witnesses and experts should be called. The

<table>
<tr><td>1899</td><td>1907</td></tr>
</table>

1899

1907

a, de son côté, la faculté de demander des explications orales aux agents des deux Parties, ainsi qu'aux experts et aux témoins dont il juge la comparution utile.

Titre V.

Dispositions Générales.

Dispositions Finales.

ART. 91.

La présente Convention dûment ratifiée remplacera, dans les rapports entre les Puissances contractantes, la Convention pour le règlement pacifique des conflits internationaux du 29 juillet, 1899.

ART. 58.

La présente Convention sera ratifiée dans le plus bref délai possible.

Les ratifications seront déposées à La Haye.

Il sera dressé du dépôt de chaque ratification un procès-verbal, dont une copie, certifiée conforme, sera remise par la voie diplomatique à toutes les Puissances qui ont été représentées à la Conférence internationale de la Paix de La Haye.

ART. 92.

La présente Convention sera ratifiée *aussitôt que* possible.

Les ratifications seront déposées à La Haye.

Le premier dépôt de ratifications sera constaté par un procès-verbal signé par les représentants des Puissances qui y prennent part et par le Ministre des Affaires Étrangères des Pays-Bas.

Les dépôts ultérieurs de ratifications se feront au moyen d'une notification écrite adressée au Gouvernement des Pays-Bas et accompagnée de l'instrument de ratification.

Copie certifiée conforme du procès-verbal relatif au premier dépôt de ratifications, des notifications mentionnées à l'alinéa précédent, ainsi que des instruments de ratification, sera immédiatement remise, par les soins du Gouvernement des Pays-Bas et par la voie diplomatique, aux Puissances

<table>
<tr><td>1899</td><td>1907</td></tr>
</table>

	Tribunal, on its part, has the right to ask for oral explanations from the agents of the two parties, as well as from the experts and witnesses whose appearance in Court it may consider useful.

	Part V.
General Provisions.	**Final Provisions.**
	ART. 91.
	The present Convention, duly ratified, shall replace, as between the Contracting Powers, the Convention for the Pacific Settlement of International Disputes of the 29th July, 1899.

ART. 58.	**ART. 92.**
The present Convention shall be ratified as speedily as possible.	The present Convention shall be ratified *as soon* as possible.
The ratifications shall be deposited at The Hague.	The ratifications shall be deposited at The Hague.
A *procès-verbal* shall be drawn up recording the receipt of each ratification, and a copy duly certified shall be sent, through the diplomatic channel, to all the Powers who were represented at the International Peace Conference at The Hague.	*The first deposit of ratifications shall be recorded in a* procès-verbal *signed by the Representatives of the Powers which take part therein and by the Nether-land Minister for Foreign Affairs.*
	The subsequent deposits of ratifications shall be made by means of a written notification addressed to the Netherland Government and accompanied by the instrument of ratification.
	A duly certified copy of the procès-verbal *relating to the first deposit of ratifications, of the notifications mentioned in the preceding paragraph, and of the instruments of ratification, shall be immediately sent by the Netherland Government, through the diplomatic*

1899	1907
	conviées à la Deuxième Conférence de la Paix, ainsi qu'aux autres Puissances qui auront adhéré à la Convention. Dans les cas visés par l'alinéa précédent, le dit Gouvernement Leur fera connaître en même temps la date à laquelle il a reçu la notification.

<table>
<tr><td align="center">ART. 59.</td><td align="center">ART. 93.</td></tr>
<tr><td>Les Puissances non-signataires qui ont été représentées à la Conférence internationale de la Paix pourront adhérer à la présente Convention. Elles auront à cet effet à faire connaître Leur adhésion aux Puissances Contractantes, au moyen d'une notification écrite, adressée au Gouvernement des Pays-Bas et communiquée par celui-ci à toutes les autres Puissances contractantes.</td><td>Les Puissances non-signataires qui ont été *conviées* à la *Deuxième* Conférence de la Paix pourront adhérer à la présente Convention.

La Puissance qui désire adhérer notifie par écrit son intention au Gouvernement des Pays-Bas en lui transmettant l'acte d'adhésion, qui sera déposé dans les archives du dit Gouvernement.

Ce Gouvernement transmettra immédiatement à toutes les autres Puissances conviées à la Deuxième Conférence de la Paix copie certifiée conforme de la notification ainsi que de l'acte d'adhésion, en indiquant la date à laquelle il a reçu la notification.</td></tr>
<tr><td align="center">ART. 60.</td><td align="center">ART. 94.</td></tr>
<tr><td>Les conditions auxquelles les Puissances qui n'ont pas été représentées à la Conférence internationale de la Paix, pourront adhérer à la présente Convention, formeront l'objet d'une entente ultérieure entre les Puissances contractantes.</td><td>Les conditions auxquelles les Puissances qui n'ont pas été *conviées* à la *Deuxième* Conférence de la Paix, pourront adhérer à la présente Convention, formeront l'objet d'une entente ultérieure entre les Puissances contractantes.</td></tr>
<tr><td></td><td align="center">ART. 95.</td></tr>
<tr><td></td><td>*La présente Convention produira effet, pour les Puissances qui auront participé au premier dépôt de ratifications, soixante jours après la date du*</td></tr>
</table>

<table>
<tr><td>1899</td><td>1907</td></tr>
</table>

1899	1907

channel, to the Powers invited to the Second Peace Conference, as well as to the other Powers which have acceded to the Convention. In the cases contemplated in the preceding paragraph the said Government shall at the same time inform the Powers of the date on which it received the notification.

ART. 59.

The non-Signatory Powers which were represented at the International Peace Conference can accede to the present Convention. For this purpose they must make known their accession to the Contracting Powers by a written notification addressed to the Netherland Government, and communicated by it to all the other Contracting Powers.

ART. 93.

Non-Signatory Powers which have been *invited to* the *Second* Peace Conference may accede to the present Convention.

A Power which desires to accede notifies its intention in writing to the Netherland Government, forwarding to it the act of accession, which shall be deposited in the archives of the said Government.

The said Government shall immediately forward to all the other Powers invited to the Second Peace Conference a duly certified copy of the notification as well as of the act of accession, mentioning the date on which it received the notification.

ART. 60.

The conditions on which the Powers not represented at the International Peace Conference may accede to the present Convention shall form the subject of a subsequent agreement between the Contracting Powers.

ART. 94.

The conditions on which the Powers not *invited to* the *Second* Peace Conference may accede to the present Convention shall form the subject of a subsequent agreement between the Contracting Powers.

ART. 95.

The present Convention shall take effect, in the case of the Powers which were parties to the first deposit of ratifications, sixty days after the date

1899	1907
	procès-verbal de ce dépôt, et pour les Puissances qui ratifieront ultérieurement ou qui adhéreront, soixante jours après que la notification de leur ratification ou de leur adhésion aura été reçue par le Gouvernement des Pays-Bas.

ART. 61.	ART. 96.
S'il arrivait qu'une des Hautes Parties contractantes dénonçât la présente Convention, cette dénonciation ne produirait ses effets qu'un an après la notification faite par écrit au Gouvernement des Pays-Bas et communiquée immédiatement par celui-ci à toutes les autres Puissances contractantes.	S'il arrivait qu'une des *Puissances* contractantes *voulût dénoncer* la présente Convention, *la* dénonciation *sera notifiée* par écrit au Gouvernement des Pays-Bas, *qui communiquera* immédiatement *copie certifiée conforme de* la notification à toutes les autres Puissances *en leur faisant savoir la date à laquelle il l'a reçue.*
Cette dénonciation ne produira ses effets qu'à l'égard de la Puissance qui l'aura notifiée.	*La* dénonciation ne produira ses effets qu'à l'égard de la Puissance qui l'aura notifiée, *et un an après que la notification en sera parvenue au Gouvernement des Pays-Bas.*

ART. 97.

Un registre tenu par le Ministère des Affaires Étrangères des Pays-Bas indiquera la date du dépôt de ratifications effectué en vertu de l'Article 92, alinéas 3 et 4, ainsi que la date à laquelle auront été reçues les notifications d'adhésion (Article 93, alinéa 2) ou de dénonciation (Article 96, alinéa 1).

Chaque Puissance contractante est admise à prendre connaissance de ce registre, et à en demander des extraits certifiés conformes.

En foi de quoi, les Plénipotentiaires ont signé la présente Convention et l'ont revêtue de leurs sceaux.	En foi de quoi, les Plénipotentiaires ont *revêtu* la présente Convention *de leurs signatures.*

1899	1907
	of the procès-verbal *recording such deposit, and, in the case of the Powers which ratify subsequently or which shall accede, sixty days after the notification of their ratification or of their accession has been received by the Netherland Government.*

<table>
<tr><td align="center">ART. 61.</td><td align="center">ART. 96.</td></tr>
</table>

In the event of one of the High Contracting Parties denouncing the present Convention, this denunciation would not take effect until a year after its notification made in writing to the Netherland Government, and by it communicated at once to all the other Contracting Powers.

This denunciation shall only affect the notifying Power.

In the event of one of the Contracting *Powers wishing to denounce* the present Convention, *the* denunciation *shall be notified* in writing to the Netherland Government, *which shall* immediately *communicate a duly certified copy of the* notification to all the other Powers, *informing them of the date on which it was received.*

The denunciation shall only affect the notifying Power, *and only on the expiry of one year after the notification has reached the Netherland Government.*

ART. 97.

A register kept by the Netherland Minister for Foreign Affairs shall record the date of the deposit of ratifications effected in virtue of Article 92, paragraphs 3 and 4, as well as the date on which the notifications of accession (Article 93, paragraph 2) or of denunciation (Article 96, paragraph 1) have been received.

Each Contracting Power is entitled to have access to this register and to be supplied with duly certified extracts from it.

In faith whereof the Plenipotentiaries have signed the present Convention and affixed their seals to it.

In faith whereof the Plenipotentiaries *have appended their signatures to the present Convention.*

1899	1907
Fait à La Haye, le 29 juillet, 1899, en un seul exemplaire, qui restera déposé dans les archives du Gouvernement des Pays-Bas et dont des copies, certifiées conformes, seront remises par la voie diplomatique aux Puissances contractantes.	Fait à La Haye, *le 18 octobre, 1907*, en un seul exemplaire, qui restera déposé dans les archives du Gouvernement des Pays-Bas, et dont des copies certifiées conformes seront remises par la voie diplomatique aux Puissances contractantes.

I. CONVENTION FOR THE PACIFIC SETTLEMENT OF INTERNATIONAL DISPUTES[1].

The most important result of the First Conference in the opinion of Sir Julian Pauncefote, the First British delegate, was the production of a Convention for the pacific settlement of international disputes. " It was elaborated by a Committee composed of distinguished jurists and diplomatists and it constitutes a complete code on the subject of good offices, mediation and arbitration. Its most striking and novel feature is the establishment of a Permanent Court of international arbitration, which has so long been the dream of the advocates of peace, destined, apparently, until now never to be realized[2]." This Convention was the work of the Third Committee in 1899, which commenced its labours with an examination of a draft communicated to the Conference by the Russian Delegation. This contained no provision for the establishment of a permanent international tribunal of arbitration.

The work of the First Conference.

[1] *Parl. Papers*, Misc. No. 4 (1908), pp. 302–351; *La Deux. Confér.* T. I. pp. 399–454; *Livre Jaune*, pp. 64–68; *Weissbuch*, pp. 2–3; J. B. Scott, *Leading Cases in International Law*, p. xlvi. (bibliography); Sir T. Barclay, *Problems, etc.* pp. 9–45, 191; Idem, *The Hague Court and vital interests*, L. Q. R. Vol. XXI. p. 109; Le Chevalier Descamps, *Rapport sur le Règlement des Conflits internationaux*, Rev. de Droit int. (2nd series), Vol. II. pp. 117, 270, 352, 498; F. Despagnet, *Droit int. public*, Bk. VII. tit. 1; A. Ernst, *L'œuvre de la deuxième Conférence*, p. 8; Bonfils-Fauchille, *Droit international* (5th ed.), Pt. IV. Bk. i. ch. 2; A. S. Hershey, *Convention for the peaceful adjustment of international differences*, Am. Journ. of Int. Law, Vol. II. p. 29; F. W. Holls, *The Peace Conference*, Chap. v.; T. J. Lawrence, *International Problems, etc.* Chap. IV.; C. Meurer, *Uebersicht über die Arbeiten der Haager Friedenskonferenz*; Idem, *Die zweite Haager Friedenskonferenz*, Teil I.; O. Nippold, *Die Fortbildung des Verfahrens in völkerrechtlichen Streitigkeiten*; E. Lémonon, *La seconde Conférence de la Paix*, p. 69; L. Oppenheim, *Int. Law*, Vol. II. Pt. i. chap. 1; E. Nys, *L'arbitrage*, Rev. de Droit int. (2nd series), Vol. VIII. p. 5 (and works cited therein); Idem, *Le Droit inter.* Vol. III. § 12; J. Westlake, *Peace*, appendix; F. E. Smith and N. W. Sibley, *International Law as interpreted by the Russo-Japanese War*, Chap. XIV.; A. Pillet, *La cause de la paix et les deux Conférences de la Haye*; E. A. Whittuck, *International Documents*, pp. xv., xxiv.

[2] *Parl. Papers*, Misc. No. 1 (1899), p. 354.

1899	1907
Done at The Hague, the 29th July, 1899, in a single original, which shall remain in the archives of the Netherland Government, and of which duly certified copies shall be sent through the diplomatic channel to the Contracting Powers.	Done at The Hague, *the 18th October, 1907*, in a single original, which shall remain *deposited* in the archives of the Netherland Government, and of which duly certified copies shall be sent through the diplomatic channel, to the Contracting Powers.

Proposals with this object were submitted to the Conference by the British delegates who worked in collaboration with those of the United States who had received instructions to present a project of an international tribunal not dissimilar to the British in some respects, "though hampered with provisions relating to procedure," but these proposals were not pressed, and the American delegates supported the British draft. In the course of the examination of the various projects, the British proposals were ultimately taken as a basis. The work of the Committee and its results were summarised in the able report of M. le Chevalier Descamps whose labours in the cause of International Arbitration were acknowledged by the Committee, extracts from his Essay on Arbitration being printed and circulated among the members[1].

The Convention is divided into four Titles: (i) on the maintenance of the general peace (1 article); (ii) on good offices and mediation (7 articles); (iii) International Commission of Inquiry (6 articles); (iv) International Arbitration (42 articles).

This Convention is a noteworthy advance on previous attempts to extend the principle of arbitration as a means of settlement of international disputes, and by far the most important part of it is Chapter ii. of the Fourth Title which creates a Permanent Court of Arbitration, the credit for which is chiefly due to the combined labours of the British and United States delegates. The Russian draft contemplated little more than the framing of Rules of Procedure for international tribunals, which, whatever the merit of those rules, would not materially have advanced the cause of arbitration. The expression "Permanent Court" does not accurately describe the institution created by this Convention under which each of the signatory Powers agreed within three months after its ratification to select four persons at the most of known competency in questions of

---

[1] *Parl. Papers*, Misc. No. 1 (1899), pp. 222–248.

international law, of the highest moral reputation, and disposed to accept the duties of arbitrators (Art. 23). When any of the signatory Powers desire to have recourse to the Permanent Court the arbitrators are to be chosen from the list of members of the Court. The Court is only permanent in the sense that there now came into existence a body of duly qualified arbitrators, ready and willing if called upon to undertake the work of assisting in the peaceful settlement of disputes, and provided with general rules of procedure for the fulfilment of their office. Four times since 1899 has a body constituted under the term of this Convention come into being and delivered judgment[1], and certain defects had become apparent in the working of the Court. A Commission of Inquiry, constituted with somewhat wider powers than those provided by Title iii. of the Convention, settled a most important dispute between Great Britain and Russia, and from its proceedings improvements in the Convention were seen to be advisable.

The Circular of Count Benckendorff of the 3rd April, 1906, placed as the first item in the proposed Programme for the consideration of the Second Hague Conference: "(1) Improvements to be made in the provisions of the Convention relative to the pacific settlement of international disputes, so far as the Court of Arbitration and the International Commissions of Inquiry are concerned." These subjects were entrusted to the First Committee under the presidency of M. Léon Bourgeois, and its two Sub-Committees designated as Committee A and C respectively, for which Baron Guillaume acted as Reporter. The Report of the First Committee, containing an account of their discussions and the changes proposed in the Convention of 1899, was presented to the Ninth Plenary Meeting of the Conference on the 16th Oct. 1907[2]. The result was the adoption of a revised Convention of 97 Articles, which when ratified replaces as between the contracting Powers the Convention of 1899. A comparison of the two Conventions shows how far the original Convention remains unchanged, and the additions which the Conference was able to make.

The preamble points out that the object of the revision is to ensure the better working in practice of commissions of inquiry and tribunals of arbitration, and of facilitating recourse to arbitration in cases which allow of a summary procedure. It is on these matters that the chief changes will be found. Chapter iv. of Part IV. on arbitration by summary procedure is wholly new.

The object of the Second Conference.

---

[1] See *ante*, pp. 44–50.

[2] *Parl. Papers*, Misc. No. 4 (1907), pp. 60, 302 ; *La Deux. Confér.* T. I. pp. 399–454.

Except for the substitution of the word "contracting" for "signatory"
Good offices and mediation. Powers, and the addition of the words "and desirable" in Article 3 which now reads that "the contracting Powers deem it expedient *and desirable*" that strangers to a dispute shall as far as circumstances allow offer their good offices or mediation to states at variance, there is no alteration in the first 8 Articles of the 1899 Convention. The addition of the words "and desirable" was made on the proposition of the First Delegate of the United States, Mr Choate. The word "contracting" is throughout the Convention substituted for "signatory."

An endeavour was made by the Haytian delegate to modify Art. 8 in such a way that the two Powers chosen by the states at variance should themselves nominate a third to act as mediator, but it was felt that not only would this increase the difficulty of the situation, but was not in harmony with the scheme of mediation of the Article.

There is according to many writers on international law a theoretical difference between mediation and good offices, but this is not observed in the text of the Convention. The difference is, however, more theoretical than practical, and both consist in a friendly interposition of a third Power to adjust differences and lead to a pacific solution of a dispute between two Powers at variance[1].

The subject of International Commissions of Inquiry was dealt with in
International Commissions of Inquiry. 6 Articles in the Convention of 1899, but in that of 1907 it occupies 28 Articles. The institution had proved its value, and the Conference availed itself of the experience which had been gained by the North Sea Commission which sat in 1905[2]. The occasion of this Commission was an incident which occurred in the progress of the Russian Baltic Fleet to the Far East during the Russo-Japanese War. On the night of October 21–22, 1904, some ships of the Russian Fleet fired on the Hull fishing fleet which was engaged in fishing off the Dogger Bank in the North Sea. Two men were killed, several injured, one boat was sunk and others damaged. The attack had every appearance of a deliberate outrage, and Lord Lansdowne immediately addressed a note to the Russian Minister demanding an apology, compensation and the punishment of the offenders. The tension between Great Britain and Russia was great, and for a short time war appeared

[1] See F. Despagnet, *Cours de Droit international*, §§ 473–6.
[2] *Parl. Papers*, Russia, No. 2 (1905), No. 3 (1905), Vol. cIII. (1905), pp. 369–445; De Martens, *Nouveau recueil général de traités* (2nd series), Vol. xxxiii. p. 641; A. Mandelstam, *Le Commission international d'enquête sur l'incident de la mer du Nord, Rev. gén. de Droit inter.* Vol. xII. pp. 161, 351; Sir T. Barclay, *Problems, etc.* pp. 35–42.

to be inevitable. The Russian Government maintained that Japanese torpedo-boats were concealed among the fishing fleet, and that consequently the firing took place as an operation of war. The presence of Japanese boats was denied by Great Britain. Russia professed her readiness to make compensation if the facts were not as she alleged. The dispute turned therefore on a question of fact, and by a Declaration of Nov. 25, 1904, the two Powers "agreed to entrust to an International Commission of Inquiry, assembled in accordance with Articles ix.-xiv. of the Hague Convention of July 29, 1899, for the pacific settlement of international disputes, the care of elucidating by an impartial and conscientious examination the question of fact relating to the incident which took place during the night of Oct. 21-22, 1904, in the North Sea—in the course of which the firing of cannon of the Russian Fleet occasioned the loss of a boat and the death of two persons belonging to a flotilla of British fishermen, and also damages to the boats of the said flotilla, and wounds to the crew of some of these boats." The Commission was composed of five members: two officers in the British and Russian Navies respectively (Admiral Sir L. A. Beaumont and Admiral Kaznakov); two naval officers chosen by the United States and France (Admirals Davis and Fournier); and a fifth member chosen by the Emperor of Austria (Admiral Baron Spaun). Great Britain and Russia each appointed a jurist as assessor (but without a vote), and agents. By the 52nd Article the terms of the Inquiry were explained to be the following: "The Commission shall make an inquiry into and draw up a report upon all the circumstances relating to the North Sea incident, and particularly upon the question of where the responsibility lies, and upon the degree of the blame affecting the nationals of the two High Contracting Powers, or of other countries, in case their responsibility should be ascertained by the inquiry." The latter part of this clause referred to the alleged liability of Japan. The terms of the reference are thus wider than those contemplated by Art. 14 of the Convention of 1899 which limits the Report of the Commission "to a statement of facts." The Commission was entrusted with the fullest powers even to the extent of apportioning the blame for the occurrence, and this in a matter which both Powers might well have contended to be a difference involving "honour" and "vital interests," which is expressly excluded from the operation of the Convention by the terms of Art. 9.

Details of the procedure were left to the Commission which met in Paris on December 22, 1904, and delivered its award on February 26, 1905.

The Commission was occupied for four days in settling the procedure to be observed, the Convention of 1899 having enacted no such rules.

Both Powers undertook to afford to the Commission all possible means and facilities to enable it to obtain a thorough knowledge and appreciation of the facts, and to bear an equal share of the expenses of the Commission which reported to the two Governments the results of their inquiry.

The Commission reported (the Russian Admiral alone dissenting) that no Japanese torpedo-boats had been present, that the firing was therefore unjustifiable, that the Commander of the Fleet (Admiral Rojdestvensky) was responsible; but these facts were "not of a nature to cast any discredit on the humanity of Admiral Rojdestvensky or the personnel of his squadron." Russia subsequently paid the sum of £65,000 by way of indemnity.

The rules of procedure adopted by the North Sea Commission were communicated to the Committee of the Conference, of which Sir Edward Fry, who had acted as British legal assessor at the Commission, was a member.

Article 9 (99), though the subject of considerable discussion, remains unchanged save for two verbal alterations similar to those made in Article 3. The discussion chiefly turned on two proposals of M. de Martens, (1) to substitute the words "agree" for "deem it expedient," and (2) to add to the functions of Commissions of Inquiry the duty of fixing responsibility, as was done in the North Sea Inquiry, though M. de Martens did not insist on the use of the word "responsibility." The effect of the acceptance would, it was thought by many of the delegates, have been to make the establishment of such Commissions compulsory "as far as circumstances allow," and M. de Martens could not carry his point. The fact that Great Britain and Russia had been able to agree under the terms of the Article of the Convention of 1899, determined the Committee to leave it intact.

Considerable additions are made to Art. 10, which in the main are similar to the rules adopted in the North Sea Commission, to which are also due a number of the subsequent Articles in this Part. The place of meeting is to be the Hague unless the Inquiry Convention decides otherwise; the Commission settles the question of the language to be used unless the Inquiry Convention determines it (Art. 11). Art. 17 recommends a set of rules for use by Commissions of Inquiry, which are embodied in the subsequent Articles and are based on a draft presented by the British and French delegate. The mode of procedure adopted is that usual in continental courts of justice. The witnesses are examined by the President. Article 35 reproduces Art. 14 (99). The Russian delegate proposed to modify this Article as follows: "The Powers at variance, having obtained knowledge of the facts and responsibilities declared by the International Commission of Inquiry, are free either to conclude a friendly

arrangement, or to have recourse to the Permanent Court of Arbitration at the Hague." The object of this proposal was to exclude the possibility of the Powers who had constituted an International Commission of Inquiry which had reported on the facts having recourse to war. It was based on the consideration that, if two Powers had been able to agree to constitute a Commission of Inquiry, they should be able to go farther in the manifestation of their attachment to peace[1]. The Committee was unable to accept this proposal which appeared to imply obligatory arbitration as a necessary consequence of recourse to Commissions of Inquiry, and which they feared would have tended to diminish the number of cases of appeal to this method of peaceful settlement of disputes.

The Articles on the subject of International Commissions of Inquiry mark an advance on those of the Convention of 1899, though the non-acceptance of the amendments mentioned shows that the subject was approached in an extremely conservative spirit. The new rules adopted had for the more part stood the test of actual practice, and were therefore accepted as ready for embodiment in an international Act, but any changes of principle in the nature of an approach to compulsion could find no acceptance. If Great Britain and Russia had, at a time when relations between them were strained almost to breaking point, been enabled to terminate the period of tension in a friendly manner, it was thought that other states might on future occasions do the same.

Part IV. is concerned with International Arbitration and is divided into four chapters, dealing with the system of arbitration, the Permanent Court of Arbitration, arbitration procedure, and arbitration by summary procedure.

International Arbitration.

Article 37 blends Arts. 15 and 18 (99). Article 38 reproduces Art. 16 (99), which recognises that arbitration is the most effective and equitable means of settling disputes in questions of a legal nature and especially in the interpretation or application of international conventions. This Article is, in the words of Sir Edward Fry, "the corner-stone of the Convention." A clause is now added stating that "consequently, it would be desirable that, in disputes regarding the above-mentioned questions, the contracting Powers should in that case have recourse to arbitration, in so far as circumstances permit." It is hardly possible to frame a clause in a more cautious or non-committal form of words. Its author was M. de Mérey, one of the Austro-Hungarian

Chapter I.
The system of arbitration.

---

[1] Report of Baron Guillaume, *Parl. Papers*, Misc. No. 4 (1908), p. 315; *La Deux. Confér.* T. I. p. 415.

delegates. As has already been explained it was round this Article that the various propositions for obligatory arbitration grouped themselves[1]. They all took the form of suggestions making recourse to arbitration (which the Article recognised as an equitable solution of disputes) under certain conditions obligatory. They all failed of acceptance and no change was made save the addition of the clause just mentioned[2]. There are no further changes in Chapter i.

Articles 41 and 42 are re-enactments of Arts. 20 and 21 (99). A slight addition is made in Article 43, where the words "as soon as possible" were added on the proposition of the German delegate in accordance with the recommendation of the arbitrators in the "Pious Funds" case, and with a view of adding precision to the terms of the Article.

Chapter ii.
The Permanent Court.

Article 44 clears up a doubt which existed under Art. 23 (99) as to the length of time for which a member of the Court held office when he had been nominated to fill the place of another who had died or retired[3].

Article 45 contains some slight changes which however were not arrived at without considerable discussion. As a result of these amendments, each party chooses two arbitrators, but only one of them may be a national or chosen from among the persons nominated by it as members of the Permanent Court. This was in the nature of a compromise, as M. Lammasch (Austro-Hungarian delegate) proposed that no national judge should be appointed where the tribunal was composed of only three members.

In connection with the alterations in this Article it may be noticed that under the Protocol of the 7th May, 1903, with reference to the Venezuelan Arbitration, the Tsar was invited to name from among the members of the Permanent Court three arbitrators, none of whom should be subjects of any of the signatory Powers or creditors. It was not without some

[1] See *ante*, p. 82.

[2] Baron Guillaume's Report, *Parl. Papers*, Misc. No. 4 (1908), p. 318; *La Deux. Confér.* T. i. p. 416.

[3] The following are the Members of the Permanent Court nominated by Great Britain:—The Right Hon. Sir Edward Fry, formerly Judge of the Court of Appeal, Member of the Privy Council; the Right Hon. Viscount Selby, formerly Speaker of the House of Commons, Member of the Privy Council; the Right Hon. Sir E. Satow, formerly Envoy Extraordinary and Minister Plenipotentiary at Pekin, Member of the Privy Council; the Hon. Sir Charles Fitzpatrick, Chief Justice of the Supreme Court of the Dominion of Canada. All appointed on the 30th Nov. 1906.

The following are the Members nominated by the United States :—The Hon. Melville W. Fuller, Chief Justice of the United States of America; the Hon. John W. Griggs, Ex-Attorney-General; the Hon. George Gray, Judge of the Circuit Court, formerly a Senator, appointed on the 27th Nov. 1906; and the Hon. Oscar S. Straus, Minister of Commerce and Labour, formerly Envoy Extraordinary and Minister Plenipotentiary at Constantinople, appointed on the 29th Jan. 1908.

difficulty that the Tsar was able to comply with the request. He first nominated, in addition to M. Mouravieff, M. Lardy, Swiss Minister at Paris, and Professor Henning Matzen, Judge of the High Court of Denmark, but the two latter declined, as their countrymen were not disinterested in the litigation. MM. Lammasch and de Martens were then nominated and accepted[1].

In all the four cases, except that of the Japanese leases, the arbitrators were not nationals of the parties to the Arbitration. In the "Pious Funds" and "Venezuela" cases nationals were excluded by the terms of the *Compromis*, and although there was no such exclusion in the "Muscat Dhows" case, nationals of the parties were not included.

Art. 24 (99) provided no solution for the case where in choosing an umpire the different Powers selected by each party failed to agree; consequently a new paragraph is added to Article 45 under which each Power, if they cannot agree within two months, presents *two* candidates, and the drawing of lots decides which of them shall be umpire.

Article 46 contains the last three paragraphs of Art. 24 (99); the words "without delay" were added for the same reasons as in the case of Article 43.

Article 47 contains no material change.

Article 48 marks an important alteration in Art. 27 (99), an alteration not arrived at without considerable discussion. Two amendments to Art. 27 (99) were moved, one by the Delegation of Peru, the other by the Delegation of Chili[2]. It was thought by the Conference of 1899 that the Article would provide a valuable means of assisting in the maintenance of peace, for by it the signatory Powers consider it their duty, if a serious dispute threatens to break out between two or more of them, to remind these latter that the Permanent Court is open to them. The Article had however practically been a dead letter. The Peruvian delegate therefore proposed that in case of dispute between two Powers, one of them can always, by a note addressed to the International Bureau at the Hague, declare that it is disposed to submit the dispute to arbitration; the note to contain a short statement of the question in dispute from the point of view of the Power sending it, and the Bureau to communicate it to the other Power, and place itself at the disposition of both Powers in order to facilitate an exchange of views between them and a possible conclusion of a *Compromis*. The Chilian proposition was in the nature of an amendment to the Peruvian, limiting the cases to

---

[1] *Rev. gén. de Dr. int.* Vol. XIII. pp. 423, 449.

[2] *Parl. Papers*, Misc. No. 4 (1908), p. 320; *La Deux. Confér.* T. I. p. 421.

which it was applicable to disputes subsequent to the present Convention, and allowing the application of the Power to be made by telegraph. It further limited the function of the Bureau to one of administration, whereas the Peruvian proposal seemed to give to it the character of a compulsory mediator, which was going beyond the principle of the Convention of 1899. These proposals received the support of Baron D'Estournelles de Constant on behalf of France, but he suggested that it would be sufficient, and in harmony with the general principles of the Convention, if one Power merely addressed to the Bureau a note announcing its willingness to arbitrate, and the Bureau's function should consist in communicating this to the other Power. The function of the Bureau would thus in no sense be political, it would be " an international letter box." He agreed that this provision should not have a retroactive effect. In the discussion, the French view was supported by the United States, British, Russian and Brazilian delegates, the former pointing out that on several occasions the faculty offered by Art. 27 (99) had been successfully exercised by President Roosevelt in the case of South American States. On the other hand, the delegates of Austria-Hungary and Japan spoke against the proposal. The former contending that Art. 27 (99) had not been appealed to, though occasions for it had certainly not been wanting, it was therefore inopportune to extend it. A vote was taken, when 34 states voted for the Article as it now stands. Germany, Austria-Hungary, Belgium, Japan, Roumania, Sweden and Turkey voted against it; Greece, Luxemburg and Montenegro were absent. It remains to be seen whether the additional paragraph will render the Article more efficacious than Art. 27 of the former Convention.

Mr J. B. Scott on behalf of the United States renewed the Declaration made in 1899 on the subject of Art. 27, which now becomes Article 48.

" The Delegation of the United States of America in signing the Convention for the pacific settlement of international disputes, such as is proposed by the International Conference of the Peace, makes the following declaration:

" Nothing contained in this Convention shall be so construed as to require the United States of America to depart from its traditional policy of not intruding upon, interfering with, or entangling itself in the political questions or policy or internal administration of any foreign state: nor shall anything contained in the said Convention be construed to imply a relinquishment by the United States of its traditional attitude towards purely American questions[1]."

---

[1] In his annual message to Congress in 1901, Mr Roosevelt treated the acceptance of this Declaration by the Conference of 1899 as an acquiescence of the Powers in the Monroe

Article 50 is a modification of Art. 29 (99). The new paragraph was rendered necessary in consequence of the accession to the Convention of 1899 on the 14th June, 1907, of a large number of Powers who had taken no part in the Conference of 1899. The expenses of the Bureau charged to the acceding Powers are to commence from the date of their accession and not from that of the ratification.

In this Part there are a few changes, some of drafting, others of more

Chapter iii.
Arbitration
procedure.

importance. Article 53 is new and gives fuller powers to the Permanent Court in the settlement of the *Compromis* when both parties agree; it also gives it a similar power on the request of one of the parties when attempts to reach an understanding through the diplomatic channel have failed in two classes of disputes. If, however, one of the Powers declares that in its opinion the dispute does not belong to one of the specified classes, this function of the Permanent Court is excluded, a proviso which may have an important limitation on the effectiveness of this Article. (See also Article 73.)

Article 57 re-enacts 34 (99). The judges in the "Pious Funds" case pointed out that in their opinion certain inconveniences existed in reference to Article 32 (99) and the following Articles, under which the arbitrators named by the Powers at variance were obliged to choose an umpire who became by right President of the Tribunal, and they recommended that the arbitrators should be left free to choose the President of the Tribunal from among themselves, and that the nomination of the President should be made at the first sitting of all the members. A proposal in this sense was made by the Russian delegate when Art. 34 (99) was under consideration, but failed to meet with the acceptance of the Committee.

Article 60 makes provision for the case of the Tribunal sitting elsewhere than at the Hague, or on the territory of one of the parties, and adds a clause to 36 (99) providing that the consent of the third Power shall be necessary in such cases.

Article 38 (99) provided that the Tribunal should decide on the choice of language to be used by itself, and to be authorised for use before it. In the arbitration in the "Pious Funds" case and "Venezuela" case, the difficulties in this respect were very apparent, and considerable delay was occasioned by the necessity for translations being made owing to the ignorance of certain of the officials, and in the latter case in consequence of the large number of states with different languages involved

Doctrine (J. B. Moore, *Digest of Int. Law*, Vol. vi. p. 594). It is, however, difficult to see why the Declaration of the United States delegate should be considered to have a bilateral effect, and the principle that " silence gives consent " be invoked in so important a matter.

in the dispute. The arbitrators in the "Pious Funds" case therefore recommended, and the arbitrators in the "Venezuela" case supported the recommendation, that the *Compromis* should make the question of the languages to be employed clear, and that the choice of agents and counsel before the Tribunal should be made in conformity with the desire of the Powers at variance on the question of the languages to be employed before the Tribunal. The question was discussed by the Committee, and a compromise between the view adopted by Art. 38 (99) which left the decision to the judges, and the view advanced by the German and Russian delegates excluding this matter from the decision of the Tribunal, was reached. Article 61 leaves the decision to the Tribunal where the *Compromis* has not determined the languages to be employed.

Article 37 (99) left to the parties an absolute freedom in the choice of agents, counsel and advocates. The arbitrators in the "Venezuela" case, in their note of the 22nd Feb. 1904, drew the attention of the Governments to the inconveniences which may arise from allowing members of the Permanent Court to act as agents or advocates. Counsel acting for Venezuela had, during the proceedings, also addressed a note to the members of the Administrative Council and the judges on the same subject. The arbitrators pointed out that the personal relations existing between all the members of the Permanent Court might have an influence on the progress of the proceedings. "The scientific authority of a member of the Permanent Court would create for him a predominating position in the case when he was charged to represent his own Government before it. Moreover a member of the Permanent Court appearing in one case as agent might in another case be acting as arbitrator, and there might be a danger that the impartiality of the agent and the decision to be pronounced might be compromised, as he who was yesterday appearing as counsel and obtained a favourable verdict might to-day be sitting as judge, and the judge of yesterday appearing before him as counsel." The British Government strongly supported this point of view, and Sir Henry Howard put the question directly to the Secretary-General of the Permanent Court. The British Government lodged a formal protest against the appointment by the French Government of M. Louis Renault, a member of the Permanent Court, as its agent. The French Government equally strongly affirmed their right to appoint M. Renault, and denied that anyone "especially among the other litigants had a right to contest it."

The arbitrators having no power to settle the point drew the attention of the signatories of the Convention to the question which had been raised

and the Conference took it into consideration. Three alternatives were possible, either to leave the Article of 1899 untouched, which was supported by France and Belgium ; or in all cases to forbid members of the Permanent Court to appear as agents or counsel, which was the proposition of Great Britain, the United States and Russia; or to limit the occasions when members of the Permanent Court could appear before it as agents, counsel or advocates to cases where they are employed by the Powers which appointed them members of the Court, which was proposed by Germany. The German compromise was accepted by the addition of a paragraph to Article 62 on the understanding that it did not prevent members of the Permanent Court from giving legal advice to the parties at variance.

Article 63 makes certain changes in Art. 39 (99) on the lines suggested by the arbitrators in the " Pious Funds " case, the third paragraph embodying an amendment moved by Sir Edward Fry, one of the arbitrators in that case.

Article 73. The object of this Article which re-enacts with a slight change Art. 48 (99) is clearly brought out in the Report by M. le Chevalier Descamps in 1899. It is to enable the Tribunal to decide the limits of its own competence. If the Tribunal were not empowered to decide the extent of its own jurisdiction under the *Compromis*, it would be rendered impotent whenever one of the parties, even against the weight of evidence, chose to contest the jurisdiction of the Court[1].

Articles 75 and 76 are new and are based on the Franco-British Draft on Commissions of Inquiry (see Articles 23 and 24).

Articles 51 and 52 (99) were considered together by the Committee, and M. Loeff on behalf of the Netherlands moved the suppression of the second paragraph of Art. 52 (99) which enables the dissentient members of the Court to state their dissent, while the first paragraph requires that all the members shall sign the award. He pointed out that the provisions of this Article were in opposition to the fundamental principle of arbitration procedure which requires the sentence to be final *omni sensu*, so that all discussion on it outside the Tribunal shall cease ; the expression of dissent tended to revive discussion on the matter which had been adjudicated upon, and to endanger the acceptance of the decision. The Committee adopted this point of view and further amended the Article so that the signature of a dissenting member of the Tribunal is no longer required. The award under Article 79 is now to be signed only by the President and the

---

[1] *Parl. Papers*, Misc. No. 1 (1899), p. 246. The official English translation appears to miss this point. The text and translation given in *Parl. Papers*, Misc. No. 1 (1908), are inaccurate.

Registrar, or the Secretary acting as Registrar. The form thus adopted is that in which decisions of the Judicial Committee of the British Privy Council are recorded.

The suppression of Art. 55 (99), which deals with the question of the revision of the award, was moved by M. de Martens who had in 1899 opposed its enactment. The arbitrators in the "Pious Funds" case had expressed the "wish" "that in the *Compromis* the least possible use should be made of the power given by Article 55." M. de Martens urged that the prime object of arbitration is the termination of a dispute. The revision of the award is contrary to this idea as it allows the Powers at variance to continue the dispute; he also pointed out that in no one of the four cases heard before the Hague Tribunal had the demand for revision been made. In opposition to this view of M. de Martens it was pointed out that arbitration is not solely for the purpose of terminating a difference, but that it is before all things a means of settling by agreement a dispute which has been left to the judgment of arbitrators freely chosen. Every stage of arbitration depends upon the voluntary action of the parties. Why then should recourse to revision be forbidden them? Further, the Tribunal might have been misled; new facts unknown at the moment when the award was given might come to light, and it would be regrettable if revision under such circumstances were excluded; and even if Art. 55 (99) were suppressed, the parties might provide for revision in the *Compromis*. M. de Martens' views failed of acceptance, and Article 83 re-enacts Art. 55 (99).

One of the objections to the Permanent Court was the cost of the proceedings which made it difficult for poorer states to avail themselves of it, and also that as the choice of arbitrators was limited to members of the Permanent Court it might render recourse to it impossible in technical disputes. The French Delegation therefore presented a draft intended to be supplementary to the Convention, and in no way destined to replace it, but to adapt its principles to the settlement of disputes of a technical nature, and others not contemplated by the Conference of 1899. The choice of arbitrators in summary cases is therefore not limited to those on the list of the Permanent Court. The Committee adopted the French draft, and embodied it in the present Convention, making certain necessary changes, accepting in Article 87 the principle in regard to the appointment of umpire which they had rejected in the case of the Permanent Court[1].

Chapter iv. Summary arbitration.

The changes made in the Convention are on the whole only in the

[1] See *ante*, p. 174.

nature of developments of the principles adopted in 1899. The influence of the recommendations made by the arbitrators in the "Pious Funds" and "Venezuelan" cases is especially noteworthy. Perhaps the most important change is that in Article 48 to which attention has already been directed. A state conscious of the justice of its claims can now appeal to the Hague Tribunal, and leave it to its opponent either to accept arbitration or face public opinion.

A *protocol de compromis* for the reference to arbitration of the dispute between France and Germany on the Casablanca affair was signed on the 24th Nov. 1908. In matters not specifically regulated by the *Compromis* the parties agreed to be bound by the terms of the foregoing Convention notwithstanding the fact that it had not at the time been ratified by either state. This will apparently be the first case to be heard before the Permanent Court under the new Convention.

Great Britain and the United States signed a Convention on the 27th January, 1909, for submitting to arbitration disputes which have arisen between them as to the interpretation of a Treaty of 1818 on the subject of fishery rights on the coasts of Newfoundland, Labrador, etc.[1] The Tribunal of Arbitration is to be chosen from the general list of members of the Permanent Court at the Hague in accordance with the provisions of Article 45 of the Convention of 1907. The provisions of this Convention, except Articles 53 and 54, are to govern the proceedings. The Tribunal is to be empowered to recommend for the consideration of the parties rules and a method of procedure under which questions which may arise in the future regarding the exercise of liberties under the Convention of 1818 may be determined in accordance with the principles laid down in the award. If the parties shall not adopt the rules and method of procedure recommended, or if they shall not, subsequent to the award, agree upon such rules and procedure, any differences which may arise between them relating to the interpretation of the Treaty of 1818, or the effect and application of the award of the Tribunal, shall be referred informally to the Permanent Court at the Hague for decision by the summary procedure provided by Chapter iv. of the Hague Convention for the Pacific Settlement of International Disputes[2].

None of the states which signed the Convention of 1899 have abstained from signing the new Convention except Nicaragua: the remaining 43 states enumerated in the Preamble have all signed, but eight have made the reservations which follow.

The signatory Powers.

---

[1] *Parl. Papers*, 1909. [Cd. 4528.]
[2] See *ante*, p. 155.

The United States signed under reservation of the declaration made by Mr Scott as set out previously[1], a declaration which was renewed by Mr Hill at the Plenary Meeting on the 16th Oct. 1907.

Reservations.

Brazil signed under reserve of paragraphs 2, 3 and 4 of Article 53 which relate to the powers conferred on the Permanent Court to settle the *Compromis* on the request of one of the parties in the case where the parties have not been able to agree.

Greece and *Switzerland* made similar reserves in the case of paragraph 2 of the same Article.

Chili signed subject to a reservation on Art. 39.

Japan signed under reserve of paragraphs 3 and 4 of Article 48 and paragraph 2 of Article 53 and Article 54.

Roumania signed under reservation on Arts. 37, 38 and 40.

Turkey signed under reservation of the following declarations: "The Ottoman Delegation declares, in the name of his government, that while it is not unmindful of the beneficent influence which good offices, mediation, commissions of inquiry and arbitration are able to exercise on the maintenance of the pacific relations between states; in giving its adhesion to the whole of the Draft, it does so on the understanding that such methods remain, as before, purely optional; it could in no case recognise them as having an obligatory character rendering them susceptible of leading directly or indirectly to an intervention.

"The Imperial Government proposes to remain the sole judge of the occasions when it shall be necessary to have recourse to the different proceedings or to accept them without its determination on the point being liable to be viewed by the signatory states as an unfriendly act.

"It is unnecessary to add that such methods should never be applied in cases of internal order."

---

[1] See *ante*, p. 173.

II. The Recovery of Contract Debts.

II. Convention concernant la Limitation de l'Emploi de la Force pour le Recouvrement de Dettes Contractuelles.

Sa Majesté l'Empereur d'Allemagne, Roi de Prusse &c.[1]

Désireux d'éviter entre les nations des conflits armés d'une origine pécuniaire, provenant de dettes contractuelles, réclamées au Gouvernement d'un pays par le Gouvernement d'un autre pays comme dues à ses nationaux,

Ont résolu de conclure une Convention à cet effet, et ont nommé pour Leurs Plénipotentiaires, savoir :

[*Dénomination des Plénipotentiaires.*]

Lesquels, après avoir déposé leurs pleins pouvoirs, trouvés en bonne et due forme, sont convenus des dispositions suivantes :—

Art. 1.

Les Puissances contractantes sont convenues de ne pas avoir recours à la force armée pour le recouvrement de dettes contractuelles réclamées au Gouvernement d'un pays par le Gouvernement d'un autre pays comme dues à ses nationaux.

Toutefois, cette stipulation ne pourra être appliquée quand l'État débiteur refuse ou laisse sans réponse une offre d'arbitrage, ou, en cas d'acceptation, rend impossible l'établissement du compromis, ou, après l'arbitrage, manque de se conformer à la sentence rendue.

II. Convention respecting the Limitation of the Employment of Force for the Recovery of Contract Debts.

His Majesty the German Emperor, King of Prussia &c.[1]

Being desirous of avoiding between nations armed conflicts originating in a pecuniary dispute respecting contract debts claimed from the Government of one country by the Government of another country as due to its nationals,

Have resolved to conclude a Convention to this effect, and have appointed as their Plenipotentiaries, that is to say :

[*Names of Plenipotentiaries.*]

Who, after having deposited their full powers, found to be in good and due form, have agreed upon the following provisions:—

Art. 1.

The Contracting Powers agree not to have recourse to armed force for the recovery of contract debts claimed from the Government of one country by the Government of another country as being due to its nationals.

This undertaking is, however, not applicable when the debtor State refuses or neglects to reply to an offer of arbitration, or, after accepting the offer, renders the settlement of the *Compromis* impossible, or, after the arbitration, fails to submit to the award.

[1] List of States as in the Final Act, 1907.

Art. 2.

Il est de plus convenu que l'arbitrage, mentionné dans l'alinéa 2 de l'article précédent, sera soumis à la procédure prévue par le titre IV, chapitre 3, de la Convention de La Haye pour le règlement pacifique des conflits internationaux. Le jugement arbitral détermine, sauf les arrangements particuliers des Parties, le bien-fondé de la réclamation, le montant de la dette, le temps, et le mode de paiement.

Art. 3.

La présente Convention sera ratifiée aussitôt que possible.

Les ratifications seront déposées à La Haye.

Le premier dépôt de ratifications sera constaté par un procès-verbal signé par les représentants des Puissances qui y prennent part et par le Ministre des Affaires Étrangères des Pays-Bas.

Les dépôts ultérieurs de ratifications se feront au moyen d'une notification écrite, adressée au Gouvernement des Pays-Bas et accompagnée de l'instrument de ratification.

Copie certifiée conforme du procès-verbal relatif au premier dépôt de ratifications, des notifications mentionnées à l'alinéa précédent, ainsi que des instruments de ratification, sera immédiatement remise, par les soins du Gouvernement des Pays-Bas et par la voie diplomatique, aux Puissances conviées à la Deuxième Conférence de la Paix, ainsi qu'aux

Art. 2.

It is further agreed that the arbitration mentioned in the second paragraph of the preceding Article shall be subject to the procedure laid down in Part IV, Chapter 3, of the Hague Convention for the Pacific Settlement of International Disputes. The award shall determine, except where otherwise agreed between the parties, the validity of the claim, the amount of the debt, and the time and mode of payment.

Art. 3.

The present Convention shall be ratified as soon as possible.

The ratifications shall be deposited at The Hague.

The first deposit of ratifications shall be recorded in a *procès-verbal* signed by the Representatives of the Powers which take part therein and by the Netherland Minister for Foreign Affairs.

The subsequent deposits of ratifications shall be made by means of a written notification addressed to the Netherland Government and accompanied by the instrument of ratification.

A duly certified copy of the *procès-verbal* relating to the first deposit of ratifications, of the notifications mentioned in the preceding paragraph, as well as of the instruments of ratification, shall be immediately sent by the Netherland Government through the diplomatic channel to the Powers invited to the Second Peace Conference, as well as to the other Powers which

autres Puissances qui auront adhéré à la Convention. Dans les cas visés par l'alinéa précédent, le dit Gouvernement leur fera connaître en même temps la date à laquelle il a reçu la notification.

have acceded to the Convention. In the cases contemplated in the preceding paragraph, the said Government shall inform them at the same time of the date on which it received the notification.

ART. 4.

Les Puissances non-signataires sont admises à adhérer à la présente Convention.

La Puissance qui désire adhérer notifie par écrit son intention au Gouvernement des Pays-Bas en lui transmettant l'acte d'adhésion qui sera déposé dans les archives du dit Gouvernement.

Ce Gouvernement transmettra immédiatement à toutes les autres Puissances conviées à la Deuxième Conférence de la Paix copie certifiée conforme de la notification ainsi que de l'acte d'adhésion, en indiquant la date à laquelle il a reçu la notification.

ART. 4.

Non-Signatory Powers may accede to the present Convention.

A Power which desires to accede notifies its intention in writing to the Netherland Government, forwarding to it the act of accession, which shall be deposited in the archives of the said Government.

The said Government shall immediately forward to all the other Powers invited to the Second Peace Conference a duly certified copy of the notification as well as of the act of accession, mentioning the date on which it received the notification.

ART. 5.

La présente Convention produira effet pour les Puissances qui auront participé au premier dépôt de ratifications, soixante jours après la date du procès-verbal de ce dépôt, pour les Puissances qui ratifieront ultérieurement ou qui adhéreront, soixante jours après que la notification de leur ratification ou de leur adhésion aura été reçue par le Gouvernement des Pays-Bas.

ART. 5.

The present Convention shall take effect, in the case of the Powers which were parties to the first deposit of ratifications, sixty days after the date of the *procès-verbal* recording such deposit, in the case of the Powers which shall ratify subsequently or which shall accede, sixty days after the notification of their ratification or of their accession has been received by the Netherland Government.

ART. 6.

S'il arrivait qu'une des Puissances contractantes voulût dénoncer la présente Convention, la dénonciation sera notifiée par écrit au Gouvernement des

ART. 6.

In the event of one of the Contracting Powers wishing to denounce the present Convention, the denunciation shall be notified in writing to the

Pays-Bas, qui communiquera immédiatement copie certifiée conforme de la notification à toutes les autres Puissances en leur faisant savoir la date à laquelle il l'a reçue.

La dénonciation ne produira ses effets qu'à l'égard de la Puissance qui l'aura notifiée, et un an après que la notification en sera parvenue au Gouvernement des Pays-Bas.

Netherland Government, which shall immediately communicate a duly certified copy of the notification to all the other Powers, informing them of the date on which it was received.

The denunciation shall only affect the notifying Power, and only on the expiry of one year after the notification has reached the Netherland Government.

ART. 7.

Un registre tenu par le Ministère des Affaires Étrangères des Pays-Bas indiquera la date du dépôt de ratifications effectué en vertu de l'Article 3, alinéas 3 et 4, ainsi que la date à laquelle auront été reçues les notifications d'adhésion (Article 4, alinéa 2) ou de dénonciation (Article 6, alinéa 1).

Chaque Puissance contractante est admise à prendre connaissance de ce registre, et à en demander des extraits certifiés conformes.

En foi de quoi, les Plénipotentiaires ont revêtu la présente Convention de leurs signatures.

Fait à La Haye, le 18 Octobre, 1907, en un seul exemplaire, qui restera déposé dans les archives du Gouvernement des Pays-Bas, et dont des copies certifiées conformes seront remises par la voie diplomatique aux Puissances contractantes.

ART. 7.

A register kept by the Netherland Ministry for Foreign Affairs shall record the date of the deposit of ratifications effected in virtue of Article 3, paragraphs 3 and 4, as well as the date on which the notifications of accession (Article 4, paragraph 2) or of denunciation (Article 6, paragraph 1) were received.

Each Contracting Power is entitled to have access to this register and to be supplied with duly certified extracts from it.

In faith whereof the Plenipotentiaries have appended their signatures to the present Convention.

Done at The Hague, the 18th October, 1907, in a single original, which shall remain deposited in the archives of the Netherland Government, and of which duly certified copies shall be sent through the diplomatic channel to the Contracting Powers.

CONVENTION No. 2. THE LIMITATION OF THE EMPLOYMENT
OF FORCE FOR THE RECOVERY OF CONTRACT DEBTS[1].

In the course of the correspondence which followed on the Circular of
Count Benckendorff of the 3rd April, 1906, the United States
expressed their intention of raising the question of restricting
the employment of force for the recovery of ordinary public
debts resulting from contracts. The genesis of this proposal
is to be found in the combined blockade by Great Britain,
Germany and Italy of the coasts of Venezuela in 1902, the Note of
Dr Luis Drago of the 29th Dec. of the same year, the message to
Congress of President Roosevelt of the 5th Dec. 1905, and the resolution
passed at the Third Pan-American Congress at Rio de Janeiro in 1906.
The cause of the blockade was the inability of the three Powers to obtain
satisfaction for claims which they made on behalf of their subjects.
Previous to the blockade Germany invited Venezuela to submit the
claims of her subjects to arbitration; Great Britain in calling the
attention of Venezuela to the claims of British subjects, including therein
"an arrangement for the foreign debt," asked for the admission in
principle and payment of some of them, and the acceptance by Venezuela
of the "decisions of a mixed Commission with respect to the amount and
guarantee for payment," and Italy requested Venezuela to "be good
enough to declare itself disposed to give to the claims of her subjects the
attention which may put an end to further discussion, accepting the
opinion of a mixed Commission[2]." To all of these requests Venezuela

Connection of this Convention with the "Drago doctrine."

---

[1] *Parl. Papers*, Misc. No. 4 (1908), p. 423; *The Second International Peace Conference* (*Report to U.S. Congress*, Document 444, 1908), pp. 10, 34, 88; *Livre Jaune*, p. 55; *Weissbuch*, p. 5; *La Deux. Confér.* T. I. p. 336; E. Lémonon, *La seconde Conférence de la Paix*, p. 97; C. Calvo, *La doctrine de Monroe*, Rev. de Droit inter. Vol. V. (2nd series), p. 597; Luis M. Drago, *State loans and their relation to international policy*, *Am. Journ. of Int. Law*, Vol. I. p. 692; see also *Rev. gén. de Dr. int.* Vol. XIV. p. 251; Amos S. Hershey, *The Calvo and Drago Doctrine*, *Am. Journ. of Int. Law*, Vol. I. p. 26; G. W. Scott, *Hague Convention restricting the use of force to recover on contract claims*, id. Vol. II. p. 78; Idem, *International law and the Drago doctrine*, *North American Review*, 15 Oct. 1906; J. Westlake, *The Hague Conference*, *Quarterly Review*, Jan. 1908, p. 236; Sir T. Barclay, *Problems*, etc. pp. 115–122; H. A. Moulin, *La doctrine de Drago*, Rev. gén. de Droit inter. Vol. XIV. p. 417; Idem, *La doctrine de Drago, questions de droit des gens et de politique internationale (with bibliography)*; A. B. Fried, *Die zweite Haager Konferenz*, p. 119; Dachne van Varick, *Le Droit Financier devant la Conférence de la Haye*.

[2] G. W. Scott, *Am. Journ. of Int. Law*, Vol. II. p. 82.

returned answer that her own laws were conclusive on these matters, and the offer of arbitration was ignored. The claims for which the governments were pressing were based on various grounds; injuries sustained during revolutionary proceedings, deferred interest on public debt outstanding on bonds issued by the Venezuelan government for construction of railways and other public works, and special contracts. The three Powers being unable to obtain redress blockaded the ports of La Guaira, Carevero, Guanta, Campano and the mouths of the Orinoco in December, 1902, seized the Venezuelan fleet, and in the course of the operations bombarded La Guaira, Puerto Cabello and Maracaibo[1]. On the 29th Dec. 1902, Dr Luis M. Drago, the Foreign Minister of the Argentine Republic, addressed a Note to Señor Mérou, the Argentine Minister in Washington, with reference to these proceedings. In his note he confined himself to considerations with reference to the forcible collection of public debts suggested by the events then in progress. He argued that creditors in advancing a loan take into account the security offered, the resources of the country, etc., and make their terms accordingly. While admitting that the payment of its public debt is absolutely binding on a state, he maintained that the debtor state has a right to choose the manner and time of payment, in which it has as much interest as the creditor himself, or more, since its credit and national honour are involved. It may be highly inconvenient and detrimental to the best interests of a state to be compelled to pay at a given time, but this is not a defence for bad faith, disorder and deliberate and voluntary insolvency. The Argentine people, he continued, "has felt alarmed on learning that the failure to meet the service of the public debt of Venezuela has been assigned as one of the causes which have led to the seizure of her fleet and the bombardment of one of her ports, and a war blockade rigorously established along her coasts[2]." They were alarmed lest the action of the Powers should establish a precedent dangerous to the security and peace of the nations of South America, for "the collection of loans by military means implies territorial occupation to make it effective, and territorial occupation signifies the suppression over the sphere of such occupation of the government of the country wherein it extended," a situation obviously at variance with the Monroe Doctrine. He then quoted from the famous

---

[1] T. E. Holland, *War sub modo*, *Law Quarterly Review*, Vol. XIX. p. 133; *Parl. Papers*, Venezuela, No. 1 (1904); A. E. Hogan, *Pacific blockade*, pp. 149–157; A. Gaché, *Le conflit Vénézuelin et l'Arbitrage de la Haye*; Bonfils-Fauchille, *Manuel de Droit international public*, § 990.

[2] Dr Drago omits to mention the offers of arbitration which the Powers had made previous to the blockade, and which had been ignored by Venezuela.

message of President Monroe of the 22 Dec. 1823 the declarations on non-colonisation and non-intervention on the American continent and pointed out the tendency of European nations to single out the South American countries as an ample field for future territorial expansion, and the danger lest European nations should make use of "financial intervention" as a pretext for conquest. " The only thing that the Argentine Republic maintains, and which she would see with great satisfaction consecrated...by a nation, such as the United States...is the principle that there cannot be European territorial expansion in America or oppression of the peoples of this continent, because their unfortunate financial condition might oblige one or more of them to put off the fulfilment of its obligations: that is to say... *that a public debt cannot give rise to the right of intervention, and much less to the occupation of the soil of any American nation by any European Power.*" It is this last sentence which contains the principle which has become known as the "Drago Doctrine," a principle which its author considers to be supplementary to or explanatory of the Monroe Doctrine.

Drago and Calvo doctrines distinguished.
Though sometimes confused with a doctrine associated with the name of the late distinguished South American jurist, Dr Calvo[1], it is, as is pointed out by Mr Amos S. Hershey, much narrower in scope. " Calvo absolutely denies that a government is responsible by way of indemnity for any losses or injuries sustained by foreigners in time of internal troubles, civil war, or for injuries resulting from such violence (provided the government is not at fault) on the grounds that the admission of such a principle of responsibility would ' establish an unjustifiable inequality between nationals and foreigners,' and would undermine the independence of weaker states[2]."

The note of Dr Drago was not immediately successful in procuring a pronouncement of the United States such as was desired, but in his message of 5th Dec. 1905 President Roosevelt dealt with the Drago doctrine. After stating that the United States would not enforce contractual obligations on behalf of its citizens by an appeal to arms, and expressing the wish that other states would take the same view, he pointed out that there were two alternatives: "On the one hand, this country would certainly decline to go to war to prevent a foreign government from collecting a just debt; on the other hand, it is very inadvisable to permit any foreign Power to take possession, even temporarily, of the Customs Houses of an American Republic in order to enforce the payment of its obligations, for such temporary occupation

---

[1] *Droit international*, T. 1. liv. iii. §§ 185–206.
[2] *Am. Journ. of Int. Law*, Vol. 1. p. 81.

might turn into a permanent occupation. The only escape from these alternatives may at any time be that we must ourselves undertake to bring about some arrangement by which so much as possible of a just debt shall be paid. It is far better that this country should put through such an arrangement, rather than allow any foreign country to undertake it."

Dr Drago's doctrine was not new, it had been enunciated by "the illustrious Hamilton," and American Secretaries of State from Alexander Hamilton to Colonel Hay have made declarations of varying import in regard to it.

The question of the use of force for the collection of public debts came before the Third Pan-American Conference which met at Rio de Janeiro in July—August, 1906, when a resolution was passed recommending "to the governments represented therein that they consider the point of inviting the Second Peace Conference at the Hague to consider the question of the compulsory collection of public debts: and in general, means tending to diminish between nations conflicts having an exclusively pecuniary origin."

On the eve of the Hague Conference Dr Drago published both in Europe and America an elaborate exposition of the doctrine that had become associated with his name[1]. In it he drew a distinction between ordinary contracts and public loans, and contended that as regards the former, a state acts as a legal person acquiring rights and accepting definite obligations in respect of certain specified individuals, and in case of denial of justice by the national courts the common and accepted principles of international law obtain, a state "avoiding by means of payment the action which, though unjust, a foreign state might take to compel it." In the case of debts arising from domestic or foreign loans through the emission of bonds at a fixed interest, which constitute public debts, the suspension of payment brings with it a profound disturbance of the finances and economic resources of the debtor country, thus giving occasion for intervention and the subordination of the local government to the creditor nation, as has been instanced in the cases of Turkey and Egypt. "This is what the Argentine Republic sought to avoid. Its doctrine is in consequence before all and above all a statement of *policy*[2]."

The subject was one peculiarly well suited for discussion by an international assembly. Divergent views had been expressed by leading

---

[1] *Am. Journ. of Int. Law*, Vol. I. p. 692; *Rev. gén. de Droit inter.* Vol. XIV. p. 251.
[2] *Am. Journ. of Int. Law*, Vol. I. at p. 725.

publicists, and international practice was equally divergent[1]. If there had been a generally accepted practice and doctrine as to the cases when intervention was recognised as legal, the question might have been dealt with by applying these principles, but here, again, international practice and doctrine are in an unsettled condition. There had undoubtedly been cases in which a strong creditor state had bullied a weak one into payment, while the cases which had come before arbitration courts had not infrequently shown that the amount ultimately awarded fell very far short of that claimed[2].

Had Venezuela consented to go to arbitration, instead of flouting the great Powers who were courteously endeavouring to obtain redress for their subjects, she would, as subsequent events showed, have had nothing to fear. Cases which came before the Venezuelan Mixed Commission in 1903 showed that of four claims advanced two only were successful, and in one of these a claim for $8,100,000 resulted in an award of only $668,000, less than one-twelfth of the claim[3].

What was wanted was some mode of procedure which while it prevented poor but honest debtor states from being oppressed by powerful grasping creditors, at the same time ensured that no state should be able to shelter itself behind the aegis of a stronger, and allege possible territorial occupation or political complication as a means of evading the just demands of its creditors.

The subject was introduced at the Hague Conference by General Porter, one of the Plenipotentiaries of the United States, on the 2nd July, but, in accordance with the instructions of the United States Government[4], his proposal made no distinction

The United States proposition.

---

[1] The use of force for the collection of pecuniary claims has in the past generally been subordinated by creditor states to questions of expediency. Some states, more long-suffering than others, rarely, if ever, resorted to extreme measures, but, as was recognised in President Roosevelt's message of 5 December, 1905, such action is undoubtedly within the competence of a state in its sovereign capacity. The divergence of views among publicists was chiefly due to the different views taken of the lawful occasions for intervention. On the 17th April, 1903, M. Calvo, Argentine Minister in Paris, addressed a letter to 12 international jurists, enclosing a copy of Dr Drago's despatch; this letter and the replies which he received are set out in *Rev. de Droit inter.* (2nd series), Vol. v. pp. 597–628.

[2] Compare for example the case of Don Pacifico, whose claim was for the sum of £21,295. 1s. 4d. and who was awarded the sum of £150 by commissioners to whom the matter was referred.

[3] Other instances are given by D. J. Hill, *The Second Peace Conference at the Hague*, *Am. Journ. of Int. Law*, Vol. I. p. 689 ; see also Darby, *Modern Pacific Settlements*.

[4] See *The Second International Peace Conference* (*Report to U.S. Congress*), p. 10. The United States Delegation was instructed to urge the following "if no better solution seems

between public loans and other contractual debts, a distinction which is the essence of the Drago doctrine and for which there is no authority in respect of the means which governments have taken in case of non-fulfilment of obligations. "No such distinction has indeed been drawn by any government," says Professor Westlake[1]. The wording of the United States proposal was as follows:

"With the object of avoiding between nations armed conflicts of a purely pecuniary origin, arising from contract debts claimed from the government of one country by the government of another as due to its subjects or citizens, and in order to guarantee that all contractual debts of this nature which have not been found capable of settlement in a friendly manner by diplomatic means shall be submitted to arbitration, it is agreed that no recourse to a coercive measure implicating the employment of military or naval forces for the recovering of such contractual debts shall be had until an offer of arbitration has been made by the creditor and refused or left unanswered by the debtor state, or until arbitration has taken place and the debtor state has failed to comply with the decision given.

"It is further agreed that this arbitration shall be in conformity with the procedure in Chapter iii. of the Convention for the pacific settlement of international disputes adopted at the Hague, and that it shall determine the justice and the amount of the debt, the time and mode of its settlement, and the guarantee, if necessary, to be given during any delay in the payment[2]."

This proposition, called throughout the discussion the "Porter proposition," was made to the Committee entrusted with the subject of obligatory arbitration. It was accorded a special examination, as while it was evident that the possibility of reaching any definite conclusion on this subject generally was felt to be doubtful, there was good reason to believe that the American proposal would have a favourable reception. Such proved to be the case.

In introducing his proposal, General Porter pointed out the danger to the peace of the world occasioned by the employment of pacific blockade

practicable":—"The use of force for the collection of a contract debt alleged to be due by the Government of any country to the citizen of any other country is not permissible until after: 1. The justice and amount of the debt shall have been determined by arbitration if demanded by the alleged debtor. 2. The time and manner of payment, and the security, if any, to be given pending payment, shall have been fixed by arbitration, if demanded by the alleged debtor."

[1] *The Quarterly Review*, Jan. 1908, p. 238. See also A. Moulin, *La doctrine de Drago, Rev. gén. de Droit inter.* Vol. xiv. at p. 424.

[2] *Parl. Papers*, Misc. No. 4 (1908), p. 428; *La Deux. Confér.* T. i. p. 553.

or the use of force for the purpose of collecting unadjusted contractual debts. The object of the American proposal was to stop the resources of states from being exploited by speculators and adventurers. The forcible collection of debts was detrimental to all states, for if pacific blockade was ineffectual states had recourse to a war blockade as was the case in Venezuela, the trade of the world was for the time being dislocated, and the government of the creditor state often found itself put to great expense for the collection of a comparatively small sum. He instanced a case where the United States had once used 19 warships and spent £760,000 to recover £18,000[1]. If recourse to force were recognised as lawful only when the resources of arbitration had failed, advantages would accrue to all the states of the world.

Dr Drago (Argentine) in the discussion spoke at considerable length, reproducing largely his published views, and making the reservations set out below. M. Ruy Barbosa (Brazil) strongly supported the proposal, though he desired to add words providing that no acquisition of territory should be recognised except after failure to accept arbitration by the state claiming an alteration of boundaries—a matter clearly alien to the subject.

The discussion which followed on General Porter's speech made it evident that a change in the wording would be required. The Italian delegate pointed out that too great emphasis was laid on the forcible remedy, while recourse to arbitration was not made obligatory on the creditor state. The Swedish delegate said that an indirect sanction to the employment of force was given in all cases which were not expressly provided for. The Venezuelan delegate refused to be content with anything less than the absolute prohibition of the use of force in all cases. The Committee finally adopted the proposition in much the same form as that in which it now appears in the Convention, slight changes having been made by the Drafting Committee.

In its final form the Convention came before the 9th Plenary Meeting of the Conference on the 16th Oct. when all the 44 states represented voted for it, except Belgium, Roumania, Sweden, Switzerland and Venezuela: these five states abstained from taking part in the vote.

Up to the present time the Convention has been signed by all the The signatory states enumerated in the Final Act except Belgium, Brazil, States. China, Luxemburg, Nicaragua, Roumania, Siam, Sweden, Switzerland and Venezuela.

The following states have signed with reservations: The Argentine Republic, Bolivia, Colombia, Dominica, Ecuador, Greece, Guatemala, Peru, Salvador and Uruguay.

[1] Report of Gen. Porter's speech in *The Times* of 17 July, 1908.

The reservations are as follow :

The *Argentine Republic* adopts the reservations made by Dr Drago in

The reserva- Committee, viz. (1) "In regard to debts arising from ordinary
tions. contracts between the national of a state and a foreign
government, recourse shall not be had to arbitration except in the specific
case of denial of justice by the tribunals of the country which made
the contract ; the legal remedies must first be exhausted. (2) Public
loans, with issue of bonds, constituting the national debt, cannot in any
circumstances give rise to military aggression or to the effective occupation
of the territory of any American state."

Guatemala and *Salvador* make similar reservations.

Bolivia signs under reservation, as the Convention implies the legali-
sation by the Conference of a certain class of wars or at least interventions,
based on disputes which relate neither to the honour or vital interest of
the creditor states.

Colombia "does not accept in any case the employment of force for the
recovery of debts of any kind. She only accepts arbitration after the final
decision of the courts of the debtor countries."

Dominica makes a reservation in the case of the sentence " or after
accepting the offer, renders the settlement of the *Compromis* impossible "
(*rend impossible le compromis*) as the interpretation may lead to excessive
consequences which would be the more regrettable as they are provided
for and avoided in Art. 53 of the new Convention for the pacific settlement of international disputes[1].

Ecuador signs under reservation of a declaration against any use of
force for the settlement of debts.

Greece signs under the reservation that the provisions contained in
paragraph 2 of Art. 1 and Art. 2 shall in no way affect existing stipulations, nor the laws in force in Greece.

Peru signs under the reserve that the principles laid down in this
Convention cannot apply to claims or differences arising from contracts
entered into by a state with the subjects of a foreign state when it is
expressly stipulated in such contracts that the claims or differences must
be submitted to the judges and tribunals of the country.

Uruguay signs under reserve of the second paragraph of Article 1,
because the Delegation considers that refusal to submit to arbitration can
always be made rightfully if the fundamental law of the debtor state,

---

[1] There appear to be good grounds for this reservation as under the Article referred to "the
Permanent Court is competent to settle the *Compromis*,...even if the request is only made
by one of the parties, when all attempts to reach an understanding through the diplomatic
channel have failed in the case of...(2) a dispute arising from contract debts," etc.

previous to the contract which occasioned the misunderstandings or disputes, or the said contract itself has fixed that such misunderstandings or disputes shall be settled by the tribunals of the said country.

The abstention from signature of 10 states, and the reservations in the case of 10 others, considerably weaken the force of this Convention, especially as the states abstaining or making reservations are mainly those against whom it has been found necessary to exercise force in the past.

The signatory Powers have in effect accepted the principle of obligatory arbitration in one important class of cases, no reservations being made in the Convention regarding "honour and vital interests"—a point emphasised by the Roumanian delegate. The Permanent Court at the Hague will therefore in cases of this kind which come before it have a wide field for its labours which will involve an examination of the whole circumstances of the claim and the validity of the excuses of the debtor. It will thus be enabled to administer justice transcending the mere letter of the law[1]. It is to be regretted that so many states in whose interests the proposal of the United States was chiefly made have thought fit either to abstain altogether, or to sign with such far-reaching reservations as to deprive themselves of the benefit which would accrue to an honest debtor state from an examination of all its circumstances by an independent tribunal.

The Convention provides that recourse shall not be had to armed force The Argentine for the recovery of contract debts claimed from the government reservation. of one country by the government of another country as being due to its nationals except

(1) when the debtor state refuses

or (2) neglects to reply to an offer of arbitration,

or (3) after accepting an offer of arbitration prevents any *Compromis* from being agreed upon,

or (4) after arbitration fails to comply with the award.

The first paragraph of the reservation made by the Argentine delegate[2], and adopted by the delegates of Guatemala, Colombia, Salvador, and Uruguay requires consideration. It was urged strongly in Committee by Venezuela and most of the Latin American states that the Convention would gain in precision, while possible misunderstanding and abuse of its provisions would be prevented, if it was made quite clear that in all cases of contract debts, where the laws of the debtor state allow proceedings to be taken against it in its own courts, such proceedings must first be taken, and an evident denial of justice proved to exist before the state is

---

[1] J. Westlake, *Quarterly Rev.* January, 1908, p. 239.

[2] See p. 191, *supra*.

compelled to appear before an international tribunal, or run the risk of the creditor state having recourse to the employment of armed force to support its national's demands.

During the discussion in the Sub-Committee, General Porter in reply to M. de Martens said that the intention of the authors of the proposal was to limit the application of force to the cases where the subjects of one state who were creditors of another addressed themselves to their government with the object of recovering the amount which was due to them; and that it was understood that it was entirely in the discretion of the government interested to intervene in this dispute between its nationals and a foreign state[1].

It is for every government to appreciate the justice of the claims which any of its nationals may have against another state, before determining whether those claims shall be pressed by diplomatic methods. The fact that such claims have or have not been judicially considered by the tribunals of the debtor state is doubtless of great importance in assisting a government in arriving at a conclusion. But the mere fact of their having been dealt with judicially will not preclude a government from pressing for a settlement. All state judiciaries are not above suspicion; but where no doubts exist as to the impartiality of the tribunal or the competence of the judges the creditor ought to exhaust all the legal resources of the debtor state before appealing to his own state for aid, and this is the course invariably followed.

The temptation to a powerful state with territorial ambitions and an increasing population to seize upon the occasion of a dispute between one of its nationals and the government of a state with a small population but large natural wealth, as a means of obtaining an outlet for its surplus population, was emphasised in the now historic despatch of Dr Drago. The Monroe Doctrine will, in the case of American states, probably prevent actual territorial acquisition, while states outside the Western Hemisphere can rely on the sense of justice, or the self-interest of the other Powers to protect their territory from seizure on such a plea.

In the course of the discussions in Committee[2] the delegates of the Argentine Republic and Servia raised the question of the meaning of the term "dettes contractuelles" which they considered as too vague. The use of these words, they contended, would give rise to misunderstanding, for they would include debts arising from conventions entered into between one

The meaning of "dettes contractuelles."

---

[1] *Parl. Papers*, Misc. No. 4 (1908), p. 428; *La Deux. Confér.* T. i. p. 559.

[2] *Parl. Papers*, Misc. No. 4 (1908), pp. 427–9; *La Deux. Confér.* T. i. pp. 558–9.

state and the subjects of another as well as those arising from contracts between states and states. General Porter replied that the distinction between the two kinds of debts had little importance here, as in the case of public debts, as well as the emission of obligations of *rentes*, the creditors would be sufficiently protected by the general principles of international law; on the other hand in the case of contractual debts, the protection of the rights of creditors would be assured by the American proposition[1]. Nor could he consent to delete all mention of armed force as demanded by his last interlocutors. He desired it however to be understood that this extreme measure was reserved solely for the case of refusal to execute an arbitral award. This reply was not of a nature to satisfy Dr Drago, who thought it dangerous to retain the contested expression. The delegate of Guatemala considered that the American proposition did not refer in any way to state loans, or public debts properly so called. The words of the Convention make no distinction between debts of all kinds arising from contracts.

Obligations are recognised as springing from two main sources, contract and delict. States which borrow money, buy ships and armaments, grant leases or concessions, and generally enter into transactions of the nature which in private law fall under the head of contracts, by so doing purport to create legal relations between themselves and those with whom they deal. When, as is generally the case, a state allows legal proceedings to be taken against it in its own courts, whether technically as an act of grace, as in English law by Petition of Right[2], or under statutory provisions which may provide special formalities, in all such cases as the foregoing contractual obligations may be said to exist.

Under the head of delictual obligations would come claims for injury to person or property of aliens arising from the neglect of a state to protect those who are sojourning within its borders. The Convention excludes such cases, for as the *exposé des motifs* presented by General Porter in support of his proposition stated: "This proposal is concerned solely with claims based on contracts entered into between a state and the individuals of another country and has no reference to claims for injuries done to resident aliens[3]."

---

[1] "He might have answered that the language of the Convention was not susceptible of the former construction," that is, it does not apply to disputes arising from contracts to which *two states* were the direct parties (G. W. Scott, *Am. Journ. of Inter. Law*, Vol. II. p. 90). See also E. Lémonon, *La seconde Conférence*, p. 119.

[2] See *The Bankers' Case, State Trials*, Vol. XIV. p. 1; *Thomas v. The Queen*, L.R. 10 Q.B. 31; 23 and 24 Vic. c. 34.

[3] See H. A. Moulin, *La doctrine de Drago*, p. 309.

The attempt on the part of Dr Drago to distinguish between contractual debts and public debts, such as bonds to bearer in the hands of foreign subjects, appears, as has been already stated, to be ill-founded. The initiative taken by the United States in introducing the subject was the direct result of the intervention in Venezuela when a "public debt" was forcibly collected, and the object of the Porter Proposition was to put an end to the disputes which this intervention had occasioned. The terms of the Convention lend no support to those who would contend that the term "dettes contractuelles" is used only in the sense of contractual obligations other than public debts, and the reservations made by the various Latin American states make it clear that it was understood by them as applying to contractual debts in the widest sense[1]. The indefiniteness of the answer which General Porter gave to the Argentine and Servian delegates, and the variations made in the terminology of the drafts during the course of the examination of the question suggest that the American delegate was not always quite clear in his own mind as to the extent to which the Committee was prepared to go. In the first draft he speaks of debts of a "purely pecuniary origin arising from contractual debts[2]." Subsequently the phrase used is "ordinary *public* debts having their origin in contracts." In the Examining Committee he spoke of "wars having a purely pecuniary origin being avoided" and subsequently at the same sitting he stated that the United States desired that in cases "of debts or claims *of any nature whatever*" recourse should always be had to arbitration[3]. But looking at the Convention as finally adopted and having regard to the fact that Dr Drago formulated reservations clearly indicating that the Convention did not adopt his distinction, and that this has been endorsed by several Latin American states while several others have withheld their signatures altogether, there appears no doubt that the term "dettes contractuelles" is used in the widest sense, including both public debts and ordinary contracts.

The Conference, as has been noticed above, refused to accept the Argentine amendment which required that recourse must first be had to the courts of the debtor state and only permitted a demand for arbitration in case of an evident denial of justice. The rejection of

---

[1] See the 2nd reservation of the Argentine Republic cited above.

[2] *Parl. Papers*, Misc. No. 4, 1908, p. 485 (also p. 423).

[3] *Parl. Papers*, Misc. No. 4, 1908, p. 427. See H. A. Moulin, *La doctrine de Drago*, pp. 316-8. M. Moulin considers that there is considerable doubt whether the expression "dettes contractuelles" is used in the wider sense of including public debts, but he inclines to that opinion and regrets that the Conference did not define the term (p. 320).

this amendment was due to the existence of states whose judiciaries are imperfectly organised and in which it was common knowledge that even in cases where a creditor could in theory sue in the courts of the debtor state, he had no prospects of success, whatever the intrinsic merit of his claim. The decision of a court against a creditor or the suspension of payment by an executive or legislative act deprives a creditor of his right of suit, his debt ceases to be contractual from the municipal standpoint; but such an act of sovereignty may be appreciated by an international tribunal, the debt still remains contractual from the point of view of international law—whenever a wrong has been done to the subject of one state by the organs of another, the state has the right to obtain redress for its national[1]; the method of redress for a wrong ensuing from a breach of a contractual obligation is under this Convention by arbitration. " The intent of the Convention," says Professor G. W. Scott, "is to refer to international tribunals the very delicate and difficult task of determining the liability of one state to another where the public governmental acts of the one have annulled or modified the contracts which it had with the subjects of another[2]." It is however not a case of compulsory arbitration on both sides, the creditor *must* propose, the debtor may reject. But the Convention does not contemplate an immediate and peremptory summons to the debtor to appear on a writ specially endorsed by the creditor as for a claim of a purely pecuniary nature arising from a contract debt. If the debtor state is willing to go to arbitration the *Compromis* is then settled by the two states, and the opinion of the court is taken on a "case stated" by the parties in conflict who may also agree upon the law to be applied. The debtor state may decline to arbitrate. It may be that such a state adopting the view of Dr Drago that "it is particularly difficult to determine the financial position and solvency of a debtor state without the most minute enquiry into its administration, a matter closely bound up with the political and social organisation of the nation," will refuse to allow such an examination to be made with a view of its international liability being determined. The alternative is that the creditor state may have recourse to armed force to recover the contract debt. This as in the past may or may not be treated by the debtor as a *casus belli*, but the creditor having recourse to war, *after* and not *before* attempting a peaceful solution of the dispute, will henceforth occupy a far stronger moral as well as legal position than formerly.

[1] See L. Oppenheim, *Int. Law*, Vol. i. § 162. In the case of a manifest denial of justice the Institut de droit international at its meeting at Neuchatel in Sept. 1900 recommended resort to arbitration before possible action be taken (*Annuaire*, Vol. xviii. p. 256).

[2] *Am. Journ. of Int. Law*, Vol. ii. pp. 92–3.

It is to be noticed that the United States in signing this Convention did not think it necessary, as in the case of the first Convention, to make any reservation embodying the Monroe Doctrine[1]. Dr Drago both in his despatch and his speech at the Hague Conference laid great stress on the intimate connection between the declaration of policy which he was enunciating and that which President Monroe laid down in his famous message.

[1] See *ante*, p. 173.

III. Convention relative to the Commencement of Hostilities.

III. Convention relative à l'Ouverture des Hostilités.	III. Convention relative to the Opening of Hostilities.

Sa Majesté l'Empereur d'Allemagne, Roi de Prusse, &c. &c.

His Majesty the German Emperor, King of Prussia, &c. &c.[1]

Considérant que, pour la sécurité des relations pacifiques, il importe que les hostilités ne commencent pas sans un avertissement préalable ;

Considering that it is important, in order to ensure the maintenance of pacific relations, that hostilities should not commence without previous warning ;

Qu'il importe, de même, que l'état de guerre soit notifié sans retard aux Puissances neutres ;

That it is equally important that the existence of a state of war should be notified without delay to neutral Powers ; and

Désirant conclure une Convention à cet effet, ont nommé pour Leurs Plénipotentiaires, savoir :

Being desirous of concluding a Convention to this effect, have appointed the following as their Plenipotentiaries :

[*Dénomination des Plénipotentiaires.*]

[*Names of Plenipotentiaries.*]

Lesquels, après avoir déposé leurs pleins pouvoirs, trouvés en bonne et due forme, sont convenus des dispositions suivantes :—

Who, after having deposited their full powers, found to be in good and due form, have agreed upon the following provisions :—

Art. 1.

Les Puissances contractantes reconnaissent que les hostilités entre elles ne doivent pas commencer sans un avertissement préalable et non équivoque, qui aura, soit la forme d'une déclaration de guerre motivée, soit celle d'un ultimatum avec déclaration de guerre conditionnelle.

Art. 1.

The Contracting Powers recognize that hostilities between them must not commence without a previous and unequivocal warning, which shall take the form either of a declaration of war, giving reasons, or of an ultimatum with a conditional declaration of war.

[1] List of States as in the Final Act, 1907.

Art. 2.

L'état de guerre devra être notifié sans retard aux Puissances neutres et ne produira effet à leur égard qu'après réception d'une notification qui pourra être faite même par voie télégraphique. Toutefois les Puissances neutres ne pourraient invoquer l'absence de notification, s'il était établi d'une manière non douteuse qu'en fait elles connaissaient l'état de guerre.

Art. 2.

The state of war should be notified to the neutral Powers without delay, and shall not take effect in regard to them until after the receipt of a notification, which may even be made by telegraph. Nevertheless, neutral Powers cannot plead the absence of notification if it be established beyond doubt that they were in fact aware of the state of war.

Art. 3.

L'Article 1 de la présente Convention produira effet en cas de guerre entre deux ou plusieurs des Puissances contractantes.

L'Article 2 est obligatoire dans les rapports entre un belligérant contractant et les Puissances neutres également contractantes.

Art. 3.

Article 1 of the present Convention shall take effect in case of war between two or more of the Contracting Powers.

Article 2 is binding as between a belligerent Power which is a party to the Convention and neutral Powers which are also parties to the Convention.

Art. 4.

La présente Convention sera ratifiée aussitôt que possible.

Les ratifications seront déposées à La Haye.

Le premier dépôt de ratifications sera constaté par un procès-verbal signé par les représentants des Puissances qui y prennent part et par le Ministre des Affaires Étrangères des Pays-Bas.

Les dépôts ultérieurs de ratifications se feront au moyen d'une notification écrite adressée au Gouvernement des Pays-Bas et accompagnée de l'instrument de ratification.

Copie certifiée conforme du procès-verbal relatif au premier dépôt de ratifications, des notifications mentionnées à l'alinéa précédent ainsi que

Art. 4.

The present Convention shall be ratified as soon as possible.

The ratifications shall be deposited at The Hague.

The first deposit of ratifications shall be recorded in a *procès-verbal* signed by the Representatives of the Powers which take part therein and by the Netherland Minister for Foreign Affairs.

The subsequent deposits of ratifications shall be made by means of a written notification, addressed to the Netherland Government and accompanied by the instrument of ratification.

A duly certified copy of the *procès-verbal* relating to the first deposit of ratifications, of the notifications mentioned in the preceding paragraph, as well as

des instruments de ratification, sera immédiatement remise par les soins du Gouvernement des Pays-Bas et par la voie diplomatique aux Puissances conviées à la Deuxième Conférence de la Paix, ainsi qu'aux autres Puissances qui auront adhéré à la Convention. Dans les cas visés par l'alinéa précédent, le dit Gouvernement leur fera connaître en même temps la date à laquelle il a reçu la notification.

of the instruments of ratification, shall be immediately sent by the Netherland Government through the diplomatic channel to the Powers invited to the Second Peace Conference, as well as to the other Powers which have acceded to the Convention. In the cases contemplated in the preceding paragraph, the said Government shall inform them at the same time of the date on which it received the notification.

Art. 5.

Les Puissances non-signataires sont admises à adhérer à la présente Convention.

La Puissance qui désire adhérer notifie par écrit son intention au Gouvernement des Pays-Bas en lui transmettant l'acte d'adhésion, qui sera déposé dans les archives du dit Gouvernement.

Ce Gouvernement transmettra immédiatement à toutes les autres Puissances copie certifiée conforme de la notification ainsi que de l'acte d'adhésion, en indiquant la date à laquelle il a reçu la notification.

Art. 5.

Non-Signatory Powers may accede to the present Convention.

A Power which desires to accede notifies its intention in writing to the Netherland Government, forwarding to it the act of accession, which shall be deposited in the archives of the said Government.

The said Government shall immediately forward to all the other Powers a duly certified copy of the notification as well as of the act of accession, mentioning the date on which it received the notification.

Art. 6.

La présente Convention produira effet, pour les Puissances qui auront participé au premier dépôt de ratifications, soixante jours après la date du procès-verbal de ce dépôt, et, pour les Puissances qui ratifieront ultérieurement ou qui adhéreront, soixante jours après que la notification de leur ratification ou de leur adhésion aura été reçue par le Gouvernement des Pays-Bas.

Art. 6.

The present Convention shall take effect, in the case of the Powers which were parties to the first deposit of ratifications, sixty days after the date of the *procès-verbal* recording such deposit, and, in the case of the Powers which shall ratify subsequently or which shall accede, sixty days after the notification of their ratification or of their accession has been received by the Netherland Government.

ART. 7.

S'il arrivait qu'une des Hautes Parties contractantes voulût dénoncer la présente Convention, la dénonciation sera notifiée par écrit au Gouvernement des Pays-Bas, qui communiquera immédiatement copie certifiée conforme de la notification à toutes les autres Puissances en leur faisant savoir la date à laquelle il l'a reçue.

La dénonciation ne produira ses effets qu'à l'égard de la Puissance qui l'aura notifiée et un an après que la notification en sera parvenue au Gouvernement des Pays-Bas.

ART. 8.

Un registre tenu par le Ministère des Affaires Étrangères des Pays-Bas indiquera la date du dépôt de ratifications effectué en vertu de l'Article 4, alinéas 3 et 4, ainsi que la date à laquelle auront été reçues les notifications d'adhésion (Article 5, alinéa 2) ou de dénonciation (Article 7, alinéa 1).

Chaque Puissance contractante est admise à prendre connaissance de ce registre et à en demander des extraits certifiés conformes.

En foi de quoi les Plénipotentiaires ont revêtu la présente Convention de leurs signatures.

Fait à La Haye, le 18 Octobre, 1907, en un seul exemplaire qui restera déposé dans les archives du Gouvernement des Pays-Bas et dont des copies, certifiées conformes, seront remises par la voie diplomatique aux Puissances qui ont été conviées à la Deuxième Conférence de la Paix.

ART. 7.

In the event of one of the High Contracting Parties wishing to denounce the present Convention, the denunciation shall be notified in writing to the Netherland Government, which shall immediately communicate a duly certified copy of the notification to all the other Powers, informing them of the date on which it was received.

The denunciation shall only affect the notifying Power, and only on the expiry of one year after the notification has reached the Netherland Government.

ART. 8.

A register kept by the Netherland Ministry for Foreign Affairs shall record the date of the deposit of ratifications effected in virtue of Article 4, paragraphs 3 and 4, as well as the date on which the notifications of accession (Article 5, paragraph 2) or of denunciation (Article 7, paragraph 1) have been received.

Each Contracting Power is entitled to have access to this register and to be supplied with duly certified extracts from it.

In faith whereof the Plenipotentiaries have appended their signatures to the present Convention.

Done at The Hague, the 18th October, 1907, in a single original, which shall remain deposited in the archives of the Netherland Government, and of which duly certified copies shall be sent, through the diplomatic channel, to the Powers invited to the Second Peace Conference.

CONVENTION NO. 3.   THE COMMENCEMENT OF HOSTILITIES[1].

The report of the Second Committee on the opening of hostilities was
Declaration   presented by M. Renault at the 5th Plenary Meeting of the
of war.   Conference.   It emanated from an Examining Committee of
eighteen members.

There are few subjects connected with the laws of war on which a greater
amount of divergence has appeared in the writings of publicists than the
necessity for a declaration of war preceding the outbreak of hostilities; it
has also led to frequent recriminations among belligerents.   Russia accused
Japan of gross treachery because her torpedo-boats attacked their war-
ships at Port Arthur before a formal declaration of war had been made,
a charge which was embodied in a Circular of Count Lamsdorff on the
22nd Feb. 1904 to the Russian diplomatic representatives at foreign
courts.   It is unnecessary to enter into a detailed examination of the
practice of states and the theories of writers on this matter.   General
Maurice in his work on this subject which was published in 1883 examines
the commencements of the wars that had taken place from 1700 to 1872,
and during this period he found that less than 10 cases had occurred in
which an actual declaration of war, prior to hostilities, had been made.
In his article on this subject in the *Nineteenth Century and after* (April,
1904) he points out that the practice of not issuing a preliminary
declaration was common to all the great Powers: "Numerically, within

---

[1] *Parl. Papers*, Misc. No. 4 (1908), pp. 33, 120–3; *La Deux. Confér.* T. I. p. 181; *Livre
Jaune*, p. 78; *Weissbuch*, p. 5; *L'Annuaire de l'Institut de Droit International* (1907); Sir T.
Barclay, *Problems, etc.* p. 53; Bonfils-Fauchille, *Droit international* (5th ed.), §§ 1027–1031;
G. B. Davis, *International Law* (3rd ed.), pp. 279, 281, 571; C. Dupuis, *La déclaration de
guerre est-elle requise par le droit positif?* *Rev. gén. de Dr. int.* Vol. XIII. p. 725; Idem, *Le droit
de la guerre maritime, etc.* § 2; H. Ebren, *Obligation juridique de la déclaration de guerre,*
Rev. gén. de Dr. int. Vol. XI. p. 725; A. S. Hershey, *The international law and diplomacy of
the Russo-Japanese War,* Chap. I.; T. E. Holland, *The laws of war on land,* p. 18; T. J.
Lawrence, *War and Neutrality in the Far East,* Chap. II.; Idem, *International problems, etc.*
p. 85; E. Lémonon, *La seconde Conférence de la Paix,* pp. 395–406; F. de Martens, *Les
hostilités sans déclaration de guerre,* *Rev. gén. de Dr. int.* Vol. XI. p. 148; Sir J. F. Maurice,
Hostilities without declaration of war; Idem, *Nineteenth Century and after,* for April, 1904;
A. Mérignhac, *Les lois et coutumes de la guerre sur terre,* p. 29; E. Nys, *La guerre et la
déclaration de la guerre,* *Rev. de Dr. int.* (2nd series), Vol. VII. p. 517; Idem, *Le Droit inter.*
T. III. ch. II.; D. Owen, *Declaration of War*; A. Pillet, *La guerre sans déclaration,* *Rev. pol.
et parlem.* April, 1904; F. E. Smith and N. W. Sibley, *International Law interpreted during
the Russo-Japanese War,* Chap. III.; Ellery C. Stowell, *Am. Journ. of Int. Law,* Vol. II. p. 50;
J. B. Scott, *Leading Cases in Int. Law* (bibliography, p. xlvii.); S. Takahashi, *International
Law applied to the Russo-Japanese War,* p. 1; J. Westlake, *War,* pp. 18, 267.   The subject is
discussed by most of the text writers on Public International Law.

the time I more particularly examined, Britain struck thirty of these blows, France thirty-six, Russia seven (not reckoning her habitual practice towards Turkey and other bordering Asiatic States, including China), Prussia seven, Austria twelve, the United States five at least."

In modern times there has been a tendency to revert to the older order of procedure under which a formal defiance was made before the outbreak of hostilities. The Franco-German War, 1870, and the Russo-Turkish War, 1877, both commenced with a formal declaration, while in the case of the Spanish-American War, 1898, and the Boer War, 1899, ultimatums, which are forms of conditional declaration, were presented.

Amongst this diversity of theory and practice one rule emerged with clearness, namely that "an attack which nothing had foreshadowed would be infamous[1]." A gross violation of international law would be committed by the commencement of hostilities in time of peace without a previous controversy and negotiations with a view to a peaceful settlement[2].

The Committee wisely refrained from a definite pronouncement as to whether there was a positive rule of international law on the subject; "we have," they reported, "only to ask ourselves whether it is advisable to establish one and in what terms." To the first part of this question an affirmative answer was returned. The Committee took as its basis for discussion a proposition of the French delegate, with amendments proposed by the Dutch and Belgian Delegations. The French proposal was based on the resolutions passed by the Institut de Droit International at its meeting at Ghent in September, 1906, when, after a careful examination of the whole question, the following rules were adopted[3].

(1) It is in accordance with the requirements of International Law, and with the spirit of loyalty which nations owe to each other in their mutual relations, as well as in the common interest of all states, that hostilities should not commence without previous and unequivocal notice.

(2) This notice may take the form of a declaration of war pure and simple, or that of an ultimatum, duly notified to the adversary by the state about to commence war.

(3) Hostilities should not begin till after the expiry of a delay sufficient to ensure that the rule of previous and unequivocal notice may not be considered as evaded.

Article 1 of the French draft embodied rules 1 and 2 adopted by the Institut and was framed in the words which now form Article 1 of this Convention. The object of the proposal was to prevent an attack by one Power on another by surprise. The reasons to be given in the declaration are required because "Governments ought not to have recourse to such an extreme measure without giving reasons. Everyone, whether citizens of

---

[1] J. Westlake, *War*, p. 23.   [2] L. Oppenheim, *Int. Law*, Vol. II. p. 105.
[3] *Annuaire*, Vol. XXI. p. 292.

the countries about to become belligerents or of neutral states, ought to know why there is to be a war in order to judge of the conduct of the two adversaries. We, of course, do not cherish the illusion that the real reasons for a war will always be given; but the difficulty of definitely stating reasons, the necessity of advancing those which have no foundation or are out of proportion to the gravity of war, will naturally have the effect of attracting the attention of neutral states and of enlightening public opinion[1]." There was no opposition to the principle of the French proposal, but difficulties of a constitutional order were raised by the Delegations of the United States and Cuba; on further consideration, however, these were seen to be avoided by the form in which the proposition was introduced[2].

The amendment of General den Beer Poortugael, the Dutch plenipotentiary, was proposed with the object of modifying Article 1 by providing that hostilities should not commence until the lapse of 24 hours from the time when an unequivocal declaration of war accompanied by reasons, or an ultimatum with a conditional declaration of war had been received by the government of the adversary. This was supported by Colonel Michelson on behalf of Russia on the ground that if a definite period was recognised it would enable a state to make certain economies, and to this extent might be a step towards the reduction of the military burdens of states which would then not feel the necessity of always keeping their establishments on a war footing and ready for instant mobilisation: and furthermore it would provide an opportunity for neutral Powers to employ their efforts at bringing about a reconciliation. The Dutch amendment was rejected by 16 to 13, with 5 abstentions. The discussions appear only to have dealt with the question from the point of view of land warfare. The position of armies is invariably well-known, but the delay of 24 hours, by enabling a change in the position of naval forces, the whereabouts of which are frequently matters of conjecture, might have most important consequences in the initial stages of belligerent operations[3].

The second Article of the French draft provided that "the state of war must be notified without delay to neutral Powers." The Belgian delegate proposed to add that the notification might be made even by telegraph, and should only take effect as regards neutral Powers forty-eight hours after its receipt. It was felt that this might have been interpreted as permitting neutrals to act during this period in a way contrary to the principles of neutrality, and the amendment was rejected. The proposal that notification might be made by telegraph was accepted, and the Committee added the last sentence of Article 1 to meet the possible case of a neutral

[1] Report of M. Renault, *Parl. Papers*, Misc. No. 4 (1908), p. 121; *La Deux. Confér.* T. 1. pp. 132–3.
[2] See *Parl. Papers*, Misc. No. 4 (1908), p. 122; *La Deux. Confér.* T. 1. p. 182; Ellery C. Stowell, op. cit. p. 55; G. B. Davis, op. cit. p. 572 note.   [3] See *The Times*, 8 July, 1907.

failing to receive notification. The mere absence, therefore, of official notification will not exonerate a neutral Power from the performance of its duties if it can be shown that it was actually aware of the existence of war. It has for many years been the practice of belligerents to issue notifications to neutrals at the commencement of war; the contracting Powers now formally accept the obligation to do so. The importance of notification is apparent both as regards the general principles of neutrality, and the freedom from capture of belligerent ships ignorant of the outbreak of war[1].

The Convention is a useful contribution to the rules of International Law. By Article 1 the contracting Parties recognise that they are now under an obligation[2] to each other to issue an absolute or conditional declaration before the commencement of hostilities, whatever differences of opinion on this point may previously have existed. But although the contracting Powers have agreed on a rule that hostilities are not to commence without previous warning, they have not precluded the possibility of a surprise attack, for the Conference rejected the Dutch proposal for the very limited delay of twenty-four hours between the presentation of the declaration and the outbreak of hostilities. "No forms give security against disloyal conduct[3]."

The Chinese delegate put two very pertinent questions during the discussions. He asked for a definition of war, as distinct from "military expeditions," and he also desired to know what was to happen if a state against which war was declared did not wish to fight: no answer appears to have been made to these enquiries. The difficulty of distinguishing between non-belligerent and belligerent action in cases of reprisals and pacific blockade ("war *sub modo*") was not considered by the Committee[4]. The practice of states, however, enables definite conclusions to be drawn with regard to the second point, and a state not wishing to resist would find itself subjected to all the consequences of a state of belligerency.

Signatory Powers. This Convention has been signed by all the states enumerated in the Final Act except China and Nicaragua.

[1] See 6 H. C. 1907, Art. 8; Declaration of London, Art. 42.

[2] The French Delegation in their report to the Minister for Foreign Affairs enumerate among " Obligations de faire," *Obligation de ne pas commencer les hostilités sans un avertissement préalable et non équivoque* (*Livre Jaune*, p. 111).

[3] " The use of a declaration," says Mr Hall, " does not exclude surprise, but it at least provides that notice shall be served an infinitesimal space of time before a blow is struck " (*Int. Law*, p. 384).

[4] On the question whether a declaration is necessary before the commencement of reprisals see a letter from Dr J. Westlake, K.C., in *The Times* of 21 Dec. 1908, on the occasion of reprisals by Holland against Venezuela. See also Dr Westlake's *War*, pp. 267, 24 for exceptional cases in which he considers the commencement of war still possible without a preceding declaration.

IV. Les Lois et Coutumes de la Guerre sur Terre.

II. Convention concernant les Lois et Coutumes de la Guerre sur Terre.

1899

Sa Majesté le Roi des Belges ; Sa Majesté le Roi de Danemark ; Sa Majesté le Roi d'Espagne, et, en son nom, Sa Majesté la Reine-Régente du Royaume ; le Président des États-Unis Mexicains ; le Président de la République Française ; Sa Majesté le Roi des Hellènes ; Son Altesse le Prince de Monténégro ; Sa Majesté la Reine des Pays-Bas ; Sa Majesté Impériale le Schah de Perse ; Sa Majesté le Roi de Portugal et des Algarves ; Sa Majesté le Roi de Roumanie ; Sa Majesté l'Empereur de Toutes les Russies ; Sa Majesté le Roi de Siam ; Sa Majesté le Roi de Suède et de Norvège, et Son Altesse Royale le Prince de Bulgarie[1] ;

Considérant que, tout en recherchant les moyens de sauvegarder la paix et de prévenir les conflits armés entre les nations, il importe de se préoccuper également du cas où l'appel aux armes serait amené par des évènements que leur sollicitude n'aurait pu détourner ;

Animés du désir de servir encore, dans cette hypothèse extrême, les intérêts de l'humanité et les exigences toujours progressives de la civilisation ;

IV. Convention concernant les Lois et Coutumes de la Guerre sur Terre.

1907

Sa Majesté l'Empereur d'Allemagne, Roi de Prusse ; &c.[2]

Considérant que, tout en recherchant les moyens de sauvegarder la paix et de prévenir les conflits armés entre les nations, il importe de se préoccuper également du cas où l'appel aux armes serait amené par des évènements que leur sollicitude n'aurait pu détourner ;

Animés du désir de servir encore, dans cette hypothèse extrême, les intérêts de l'humanité et les exigences toujours progressives de la civilisation ;

[1] See note 1, p. 207.

[2] See note 2, p. 207.

IV. The Laws and Customs of War on Land.

II. Convention with respect to the Laws and Customs of War on Land.

1899

His Majesty the King of the Belgians; His Majesty the King of Denmark; His Majesty the King of Spain, and in his name Her Majesty the Queen-Regent of the Kingdom; the President of United States of Mexico; the President of the French Republic; His Majesty the King of the Hellenes; His Highness the Prince of Montenegro; Her Majesty the Queen of the Netherlands; His Imperial Majesty the Shah of Persia; His Majesty the King of Portugal and the Algarves; His Majesty the King of Roumania, His Majesty the Emperor of All the Russias; His Majesty the King of Siam; His Majesty the King of Sweden and Norway, and His Royal Highness the Prince of Bulgaria[1];

Considering that, while seeking means to preserve peace and prevent armed conflicts between nations, it is likewise necessary to have regard to cases where an appeal to arms may be caused by events which their solicitude could not avert;

Animated also by the desire to serve, even in this extreme case, the interests of humanity and the ever progressive needs of civilization;

IV. Convention concerning the Laws and Customs of War on Land.

1907

His Majesty the German Emperor, King of Prussia; &c.[2]

Considering that, while seeking means to preserve peace and prevent armed conflicts between nations, it is likewise necessary to have regard to cases where an appeal to arms may be caused by events which their solicitude could not avert;

Animated also by the desire to serve, even in this extreme case, the interests of humanity and the ever-progressive needs of civilization; and

[1] The list of Powers is as given in *Parl. Papers*, Misc. No. 1 (1899), p. 312. All the Powers enumerated in the Final Act of 1907 subsequently signed or adhered.

[2] List of Powers as in Final Act of 1907.

1899

Estimant qu'il importe, à cette fin, de reviser les lois et coutumes générales de la guerre, soit dans le but de les définir avec plus de précision, soit afin d'y tracer certaines limites destinées à en restreindre autant que possible les rigueurs ;

S'inspirant de ces vues recommandées aujourd'hui, comme il y a vingt-cinq ans, lors de la Conférence de Bruxelles de 1874, par une sage et généreuse prévoyance ;

Ont, dans cet esprit, adopté un grand nombre de dispositions qui ont pour objet de définir et de régler les usages de la guerre sur terre.

Selon les vues des Hautes Parties contractantes, ces dispositions, dont la rédaction a été inspirée par le désir de diminuer les maux de la guerre, autant que les nécessités militaires le permettent, sont destinées à servir de règle générale de conduite aux belligérants, dans leurs rapports entre eux et avec les populations.

Il n'a pas été possible toutefois de concerter dès maintenant des stipulations s'étendant à toutes les circonstances qui se présentent dans la pratique.

D'autre part, il ne pouvait entrer dans les intentions des Hautes Parties contractantes que les cas non prévus fussent, faute de stipulation écrite, laissées à l'appréciation arbitraire de ceux qui dirigent les armées.

En attendant qu'un Code plus complet des lois de la guerre puisse être édicté, les Hautes Parties contractantes jugent opportun de constater que, dans les cas non compris dans les

1907

Estimant qu'il importe, à cette fin, de reviser les lois et coutumes générales de la guerre, soit dans le but de les définir avec plus de précision, soit afin d'y tracer certaines limites destinées à en restreindre autant que possible les rigueurs ;

Ont jugé nécessaire de compléter et de préciser sur certains points l'œuvre de la Première Conférence de la Paix qui, s'inspirant, à la suite de la Conférence de Bruxelles de 1874, de ces idées recommandées par une sage et généreuse prévoyance a adopté des dispositions ayant pour objet de définir et de régler les usages de la guerre sur terre.

Selon les vues des Hautes Parties contractantes, ces dispositions, dont la rédaction a été inspirée par le désir de diminuer les maux de la guerre, autant que les nécessités militaires le permettent, sont destinées à servir de règle générale de conduite aux belligérants, dans leurs rapports entre eux et avec les populations.

Il n'a pas été possible toutefois de concerter dès maintenant des stipulations s'étendant à toutes les circonstances qui se présentent dans la pratique ;

. D'autre part, il ne pouvait entrer dans les intentions des Hautes Parties contractantes que les cas non prévus fussent, faute de stipulation écrite, laissées à l'appréciation arbitraire de ceux qui dirigent les armées.

En attendant qu'un Code plus complet des lois de la guerre puisse être édicté, les Hautes Parties contractantes jugent opportun de constater que, dans les cas non compris dans les

1899

Thinking it important, with this object, to revise the laws and general customs of war, either with the view of defining them more precisely, or of laying down certain limits for the purpose of modifying their severity as far as possible;

Inspired by these views which are enjoined at the present day, as they were twenty-five years ago at the time of the Brussels Conference in 1874, by a wise and generous foresight;

Have, in this spirit, adopted a great number of provisions, the object of which is to define and govern the usages of war on land.

According to the view of the High Contracting Parties, these provisions, the wording of which has been inspired by the desire to diminish the evils of war, so far as military necessities permit, are intended to serve as general rules of conduct for belligerents in their relations with each other and with populations.

It has not, however, been possible to agree forthwith on provisions embracing all the circumstances which occur in practice.

On the other hand, it could not be intended by the High Contracting Parties that the cases not provided for should, for want of a written provision, be left to the arbitrary judgment of military Commanders.

Until a more complete code of the laws of war can be issued, the High Contracting Parties think it expedient to declare that in cases not included in

1907

Thinking it important, with this object, to revise the laws and general customs of war, either with the view of defining them more precisely, or of laying down certain limits for the purpose of modifying their severity as far as possible;

Have deemed it necessary to complete and render more precise in certain particulars the work of the First Peace Conference, which, following on the Brussels Conference of 1874, and inspired by the ideas dictated by a wise and generous forethought, adopted provisions, the object of which is to define and govern the usages of war on land.

According to the views of the High Contracting Parties, these provisions, the wording of which has been inspired by the desire to diminish the evils of war, so far as military necessities permit, are intended to serve as general rules of conduct for belligerents in their relations with each other and with populations.

It has not, however, been possible to agree forthwith on provisions embracing all the circumstances which occur in practice;

On the other hand, it could not be intended by the High Contracting Parties that the cases not provided for should, for want of a written provision, be left to the arbitrary judgment of military Commanders.

Until a more complete code of the laws of war can be issued, the High Contracting Parties think it expedient to declare that in cases not included in

14

1899	**1907**

dispositions réglementaires adoptées par elles, les populations et les belligérants restent sous la sauvegarde et sous l'empire des principes du droit des gens, tels qu'ils résultent des usages établis entre nations civilisées, des lois de l'humanité et des exigences de la conscience publique ;

Elles déclarent que c'est dans ce sens que doivent s'entendre notamment les Articles 1 et 2 du Règlement adopté ;

Les Hautes Parties contractantes désirant conclure une Convention à cet effet ont nommé pour leurs Plénipotentiaires, savoir :

[*Dénomination des Plénipotentiaires.*]

Lesquels, après s'être communiqué leurs pleins pouvoirs, trouvés en bonne et due forme, sont convenus de ce qui suit :—

ART. 1.

Les Hautes Parties contractantes donneront à leurs forces armées de terre des instructions qui seront conformes au "Règlement concernant les lois et coutumes de la guerre sur terre," annexé à la présente Convention.

ART. 2.

Les dispositions contenues dans le Règlement visé à l'article 1er ne sont obligatoires que pour les Puissances contractantes, en cas de guerre entre deux ou plusieurs d'entre elles.

Ces dispositions cesseront d'être obligatoires du moment où, dans une guerre entre des Puissances contractantes, une Puissance non-contractante se joindrait à l'un des belligérants.

---

dispositions réglementaires adoptées par elles, les populations et les belligérants restent sous la sauvegarde et sous l'empire des principes du droit des gens, tels qu'ils résultent des usages établis entre nations civilisées, des lois de l'humanité et des exigences de la conscience publique.

Elles déclarent que c'est dans ce sens que doivent s'entendre notamment les Articles 1 et 2 du Règlement adopté.

Les Hautes Parties contractantes, désirant conclure une *nouvelle* Convention à cet effet, ont nommé pour leurs Plénipotentiaires, savoir :

[*Dénomination des Plénipotentiaires.*]

Lesquels, après *avoir déposé* leurs pleins pouvoirs, trouvés en bonne et due forme, sont convenus de ce qui suit :—

ART. 1.

(*Aucune modification.*)[1]

ART. 2.

Les dispositions contenues dans le Règlement visé à l'article 1er *ainsi que dans la présente Convention* ne sont *applicables* qu'entre les Puissances contractantes, *et seulement si les belligérants sont tous parties à la Convention.*

---

[1] Lisez *Puissances* contractantes pour *Hautes Parties* contractantes.

1899	1907

the Regulations adopted by them, populations and belligerents remain under the protection and the rule of the principles of the law of nations, as they result from the usages established between civilized nations, from the laws of humanity, and the requirements of the public conscience ;

They declare that it is in this sense especially that Articles 1 and 2 of the Regulations adopted must be understood ;

The High Contracting Parties, desiring to conclude a Convention to this effect, have appointed as their Plenipotentiaries, that is to say :

[*Names of Plenipotentiaries.*]

Who, after communication of their full powers, found in good and due form, have agreed on the following :—

the Regulations adopted by them, populations and belligerents remain under the protection and the rule of the principles of the law of nations, as they result from the usages established between civilized nations, from the laws of humanity, and the requirements of the public conscience.

They declare that it is in this sense especially that Articles 1 and 2 of the Regulations adopted must be understood.

The High Contracting Parties, desiring to conclude a *fresh* Convention to this effect, have appointed as their Plenipotentiaries, that is to say :

[*Names of Plenipotentiaries.*]

Who, after *having deposited* their full powers, found in good and due form, have agreed upon the following:—

ART. 1.

The High Contracting Parties will issue to their armed land forces, instructions which shall be in conformity with the "Regulations respecting the Laws and Customs of War on Land" annexed to the present Convention.

ART. 1.

(*No change.*)[1]

ART. 2.

The provisions contained in the Regulations mentioned in Article 1 are only binding on the Contracting Powers, in case of war between two or more of them.

These provisions shall cease to be binding from the time when, in a war between Contracting Powers, a non-Contracting Power joins one of the belligerents.

ART. 2.

The provisions contained in the Regulations referred to in Article 1, *as well as in the present Convention,* are only binding between Contracting Powers, *and only if all the belligerents are parties to the Convention.*

[1] For "High Contracting Parties" read "Contracting Powers."

<table>
<tr><td>1899</td><td>1907</td></tr>
</table>

1899

1907

Art. 3.

La Partie belligérante qui violerait les dispositions du dit Règlement sera tenue à indemnité, s'il y a lieu. Elle sera responsable de tous actes commis par les personnes faisant partie de sa force armée.

Art. 4.

La présente Convention dûment ratifiée remplacera, dans les rapports entre les Puissances contractantes, la Convention du 29 juillet, 1899, concernant les lois et coutumes de la guerre sur terre.

La Convention de 1899 reste en vigueur dans les rapports entre les Puissances qui l'ont signée et qui ne ratifieraient pas également la présente Convention.

Art. 3.

La présente Convention sera ratifiée dans le plus bref délai possible.

Les ratifications seront déposées à La Haye.

Il sera dressé du dépôt de chaque ratification un procès-verbal, dont une copie, certifiée conforme, sera remise par la voie diplomatique à toutes les Puissances contractantes.

Art. 5.

La présente Convention sera ratifiée *aussitôt que possible.*

Les ratifications seront déposées à La Haye.

Le premier dépôt de ratifications sera constaté par un procès-verbal signé par les représentants des Puissances qui y prennent part et par le Ministre des Affaires Étrangères des Pays-Bas.

Les dépôts ultérieurs de ratifications se feront au moyen d'une notification écrite adressée au Gouvernement des Pays-Bas et accompagnée de l'instrument de ratification.

Copie certifiée conforme du procès-verbal relatif au premier dépôt de

1899	1907

1907

ART. 3.

A belligerent party which violates the provisions of the said Regulations shall, if the case demands, be liable to make compensation. It shall be responsible for all acts committed by persons forming part of its armed forces.

ART. 4.

The present Convention, when duly ratified, shall replace, as between the Contracting Powers, the Convention of the 29th July, 1899, respecting the Laws and Customs of War on Land.

The Convention of 1899 remains in force as between the Powers which signed it, but which do not ratify also the present Convention.

1899

ART. 3.

The present Convention shall be ratified as speedily as possible.

The ratifications shall be deposited at the Hague.

A *procès-verbal* shall be drawn up recording the receipt of each ratification, and a copy, duly certified, shall be sent through the diplomatic channel, to all the Contracting Powers.

1907

ART. 5.

The present Convention shall be ratified as soon as possible.

The ratifications shall be deposited at The Hague.

The first deposit of ratifications shall be recorded in a Procès-verbal *signed by the Representatives of the Powers which take part therein and by the Netherland Minister for Foreign Affairs.*

The subsequent deposits of ratifications shall be made by means of a written notification, addressed to the Netherland Government and accompanied by the instrument of ratification.

A duly certified copy of the Procès-verbal *relating to the first deposit of*

1899

1907

ratifications, des notifications mention-
nées à l'alinéa précédent, ainsi que des
instruments de ratification, sera im-
médiatement remise par les soins du
Gouvernement des Pays-Bas et par la
voie diplomatique aux Puissances
conviées à la Deuxième Conférence de
la Paix, ainsi qu'aux autres Puissances
qui auront adhéré à la Convention.
Dans les cas visés par l'alinéa précédent,
le dit Gouvernement leur fera connaître
en même temps la date à laquelle il a
reçu la notification.

Art. 4.

Les Puissances non-signataires sont
admises à adhérer à la présente
Convention.

Elles auront, à cet effet, à faire
connaître leur adhésion aux Puissances
contractantes au moyen d'une notification écrite, adressée au Gouvernement
des Pays-Bas, et communiquée par
celui-ci à toutes les autres Puissances
contractantes.

Art. 6.

Les Puissances non-signataires sont
admises à adhérer à la présente Convention.

La Puissance qui désire adhérer
notifie par écrit son intention au
Gouvernement des Pays-Bas en lui
transmettant l'acte d'adhésion, qui sera
déposé dans les archives du dit
Gouvernement.

Ce Gouvernement transmettra im-
médiatement à toutes les autres Puis-
sances copie certifiée conforme de la
notification ainsi que de l'acte d'adhé-
sion, en indiquant la date à laquelle il
a reçu la notification.

Art. 7.

La présente Convention produira
effet, pour les Puissances qui auront
participé au premier dépôt de ratifica-
tions, soixante jours après la date du

1899	1907
	ratifications, of the notifications mentioned in the preceding paragraph, as well as of the instruments of ratification, shall be immediately sent by the Netherland Government through the diplomatic channel to the Powers invited to the Second Peace Conference, as well as to the other Powers which have acceded to the Convention. In the cases contemplated in the preceding paragraph, the said Government shall inform them at the same time of the date on which it received the notification.

<table>
<tr>
<td>

Art. 4.

Non-Signatory Powers are allowed to accede to the present Convention.

For this purpose they must make their accession known to the Contracting Powers by means of a written notification addressed to the Netherland Government, and by it communicated to all the other Contracting Powers.

</td>
<td>

Art. 6.

Non-Signatory Powers may accede to the present Convention.

A Power which desires to accede notifies its intention in writing to the Netherland Government, forwarding to it the act of accession, which shall be deposited in the archives of the said Government.

The said Government shall immediately forward to all the other Powers a duly certified copy of the notification as well as of the act of accession, mentioning the date on which it received the notification.

Art. 7.

The present Convention shall take effect, in the case of the Powers which were parties to the first deposit of ratifications, sixty days after the date

</td>
</tr>
</table>

procès-verbal de ce dépôt et, pour les Puissances qui ratifieront ultérieurement ou qui adhéreront, soixante jours après que la notification de leur ratification ou de leur adhésion aura été reçue par le Gouvernement des Pays-Bas.

Art. 5.

S'il arrivait qu'une des Hautes Parties contractantes dénonçât la présente Convention, cette dénonciation ne produirait ses effets qu'un an après la notification faite par écrit au Gouvernement des Pays-Bas et communiquée immédiatement par celui-ci à toutes les autres Puissances contractantes.

Cette dénonciation ne produira ses effets qu'à l'égard de la Puissance qui l'aura notifiée.

Art. 8.

S'il arrivait qu'une des Puissances contractantes *voulût dénoncer* la présente Convention, *la* dénonciation *sera notifiée* par écrit au Gouvernement des Pays-Bas, *qui communiquera immédiatement copie certifiée conforme de la notification* à toutes les autres Puissances *en leur faisant savoir la date à laquelle il l'a reçue.*

La dénonciation ne produira ses effets qu'à l'égard de la Puissance qui l'aura notifiée *et un an après que la notification en sera parvenue au Gouvernement des Pays-Bas.*

Art. 9.

Un registre tenu par le Ministère des Affaires Étrangères des Pays-Bas indiquera la date du dépôt de ratifications effectué en vertu de l'Article 5, alinéas 3 et 4, ainsi que la date à laquelle auront été reçues les notifications d'adhésion (Article 6, alinéa 2) ou de dénonciation (Article 8, alinéa 1).

Chaque Puissance contractante est admise à prendre connaissance de ce registre et à en demander des extraits certifiés conformes.

En foi de quoi, les Plénipotentiaires ont signé la présente Convention et l'ont revêtue de leurs cachets.

En foi de quoi les Plénipotentiaires ont revêtu la présente Convention de leurs *signatures.*

1899	1907
	of the Procès-verbal *recording such deposit, and, in the case of the Powers which shall ratify subsequently or which shall accede, sixty days after the notification of their ratification or of their accession has been received by the Netherland Government.*

<table>
<tr><td>ART. 5.</td><td>ART. 8.</td></tr>
</table>

ART. 5.

In the event of one of the High Contracting Parties denouncing the present Convention, such denunciation would not take effect until a year after the written notification made to the Netherland Government, and by it at once communicated to all the other Contracting Powers.

This denunciation shall only affect the notifying Power.

ART. 8.

In the event of one of the Contracting *Powers wishing to denounce* the present Convention, *the* denunciation *shall be notified in writing to the Netherland Government, which shall immediately communicate a duly certified copy of the notification to all the other Powers, informing them of the date on which it was received.*

The denunciation shall only operate in respect of the notifying Power, *and only on the expiry of one year after the notification has reached the Netherland Government.*

ART. 9.

A register kept by the Netherland Ministry for Foreign Affairs shall record the date of the deposit of ratifications effected in virtue of Article 5, paragraphs 3 and 4, as well as the date on which the notifications of accession (Article 6, paragraph 2) or of denunciation (Article 8, paragraph 1) have been received.

Each Contracting Power is entitled to have access to this register and to be supplied with duly certified extracts from it.

In faith of which the Plenipotentiaries have signed the present Convention and affixed their seals thereto.

In faith whereof the Plenipotentiaries have appended *their signatures* to the present Convention.

1899	1907
Fait à La Haye, le 29 juillet, 1899, en un seul exemplaire, qui restera déposé dans les archives du Gouvernement des Pays-Bas et dont des copies, certifiées conformes, seront remises par la voie diplomatique aux Puissances contractantes.	Fait à La Haye, *le 18 octobre, 1907,* en un seul exemplaire, qui restera déposé dans les archives du Gouvernement des Pays-Bas et dont des copies, certifiées conformes, seront remises par la voie diplomatique aux Puissances *qui ont été conviées à la Deuxième Conférence de la Paix.*

<table>
<tr><td>

Annexe à la Convention.

Règlement concernant les Lois et Coutumes de la Guerre sur Terre.

Section I.

Des Belligérants.

Chapitre I.

De la Qualité de Belligérant.

ART. 1.

Les lois, les droits et les devoirs de la guerre ne s'appliquent pas seulement à l'armée, mais encore aux milices et aux corps de volontaires réunissant les conditions suivantes :—

1. D'avoir à leur tête une personne responsable pour ses subordonnés ;

2. D'avoir un signe distinctif fixe et reconnaissable à distance ;

3. De porter les armes ouvertement ; et

4. De se conformer dans leurs opérations aux lois et coutumes de la guerre.

Dans les pays où les milices ou des corps de volontaires constituent l'armée ou en font partie, ils sont compris sous la dénomination "d'armée."

</td><td>

Annexe à la Convention.

Règlement concernant les Lois et Coutumes de la Guerre sur Terre.

Section I.

Des Belligérants.

Chapitre I.

De la Qualité de Belligérant.

ART. 1.

(Aucune modification.)

</td></tr>
</table>

1899

Done at the Hague, the 29th July, 1899, in a single original, which shall remain deposited in the archives of the Netherland Government, and of which duly certified copies shall be sent, through the diplomatic channel, to the Contracting Powers.

1907

Done at The Hague, *the 18th October, 1907*, in a single original, which shall remain deposited in the archives of the Netherland Government, and of which duly certified copies shall be sent, through the diplomatic channel, to the Powers *invited to the Second Peace Conference.*

Annex to the Convention.

Regulations respecting the Laws and Customs of War on Land.

Section I.

Belligerents.

Chapter I.

The Qualifications of Belligerents.

ART. 1.

The laws, rights, and duties of war apply not only to the army, but also to militia and corps of volunteers, fulfilling the following conditions :—

1. That of being commanded by a person responsible for his subordinates;

2. That of having a distinctive emblem fixed and recognizable at a distance;

3. That of carrying arms openly; and

4. That of conducting their operations in accordance with the laws and customs of war.

In countries where militia or corps of volunteers constitute the army, or form part of it, they are included under the denomination "army."

Annex to the Convention.

Regulations respecting the Laws and Customs of War on Land.

Section I.

Belligerents.

Chapter I.

The Qualifications of Belligerents.

ART. 1.

(*No change.*)

(*Cp. Brussels Draft Declaration, Art. 9.*)

1899	1907
Art. 2.	Art. 2.

La population d'un territoire non occupé qui, à l'approche de l'ennemi, prend spontanément les armes pour combattre les troupes d'invasion sans avoir eu le temps de s'organiser conformément à l'Article 1er, sera considérée comme belligérante si elle respecte les lois et coutumes de la guerre.

La population d'un territoire non occupé qui, à l'approche de l'ennemi, prend spontanément les armes pour combattre les troupes d'invasion sans avoir eu le temps de s'organiser conformément à l'Article 1er, sera considérée comme belligérante *si elle porte les armes ouvertement* et si elle respecte les lois et coutumes de la guerre.

Art. 3.	Art. 3.

Les forces armées des Parties belligérantes peuvent se composer de combattants et de non-combattants. En cas de capture par l'ennemi, les uns et les autres ont droit au traitement des prisonniers de guerre.

(Aucune modification.)

Chapitre II.
Des Prisonniers de Guerre.

Chapitre II.
Des Prisonniers de Guerre.

Art. 4.	Art. 4.

Les prisonniers de guerre sont au pouvoir du Gouvernement ennemi, mais non des individus ou des corps qui les ont capturés.

Ils doivent être traités avec humanité.

Tout ce qui leur appartient personnellement, excepté les armes, les chevaux, et les papiers militaires, reste leur propriété.

(Aucune modification.)

Art. 5.	Art. 5.

Les prisonniers de guerre peuvent être assujettis à l'internement dans une ville, forteresse, camp, ou localité quelconque, avec obligation de ne pas s'en éloigner au delà de certaines limites déterminées ; mais ils ne peuvent être enfermés que par mesure de sûreté indispensable.

Les prisonniers de guerre peuvent être assujettis à l'internement dans une ville, forteresse, camp, ou localité quelconque, avec obligation de ne pas s'en éloigner au delà de certaines limites déterminées ; mais ils ne peuvent être enfermés que par mesure de sûreté indispensable, *et seulement*

1899	1907
ART. 2.	ART. 2.
The population of a territory which has not been occupied who, on the approach of the enemy, spontaneously take up arms to resist the invading troops without having had time to organize themselves in accordance with Article 1, shall be regarded as belligerents if they respect the laws and customs of war.	The population of a territory which has not been occupied who, on the approach of the enemy, spontaneously take up arms to resist the invading troops without having had time to organize themselves in accordance with Article 1, shall be regarded as belligerents *if they carry arms openly* and if they respect the laws and customs of war.
	(*Cp. B. D. Art.* 10.)
ART. 3.	ART. 3.
The armed forces of the belligerent parties may consist of combatants and non-combatants. In case of capture by the enemy both have a right to be treated as prisoners of war.	(*No change.*)
	(*Cp. B. D. Art.* 11.)

Chapter II.

Prisoners of War.

ART. 4.	ART. 4.
Prisoners of war are in the power of the hostile Government, but not in that of the individuals or corps who captured them.	(*No change.*)
They must be humanely treated.	
All their personal belongings, except arms, horses, and military papers, remain their property.	(*Cp. B. D. Art.* 23.)
ART. 5.	ART. 5.
Prisoners of war may be interned in a town, fortress, camp, or any other locality, and are bound not to go beyond certain fixed limits; but they can only be confined as an indispensable measure of safety.	Prisoners of war may be interned in a town, fortress, camp, or any other locality, and are bound not to go beyond certain fixed limits; but they can only be confined as an indispensable measure of safety, *and only while*

1899

ART. 6.

L'État peut employer, comme travailleurs, les prisonniers de guerre, selon leur grade et leurs aptitudes. Ces travaux ne seront pas excessifs et n'auront aucun rapport avec les opérations de la guerre.

Les prisonniers peuvent être autorisés à travailler pour le compte d'administrations publiques ou de particuliers, ou pour leur propre compte.

Les travaux faits pour l'État sont payés d'après les tarifs en vigueur pour les militaires de l'armée nationale exécutant les mêmes travaux.

Lorsque les travaux ont lieu pour le compte d'autres administrations publiques ou pour des particuliers, les conditions en sont réglées d'accord avec l'autorité militaire.

Le salaire des prisonniers contribuera à adoucir leur position, et le surplus leur sera compté au moment de leur libération, sauf défalcation des frais d'entretien.

ART. 7.

Le Gouvernement au pouvoir duquel se trouvent les prisonniers de guerre est chargé de leur entretien.

A défaut d'une entente spéciale entre les belligérants, les prisonniers de guerre seront traités, pour la nourriture, le couchage et l'habillement, sur le même pied que les troupes du Gouvernement qui les aura capturés.

1907

pendant la durée des circonstances qui nécessitent cette mesure.

ART. 6.

L'État peut employer, comme travailleurs, les prisonniers de guerre, selon leur grade et leurs aptitudes, *à l'exception des officiers.* Ces travaux ne seront pas excessifs et n'auront aucun rapport avec les opérations de la guerre.

Les prisonniers peuvent être autorisés à travailler pour le compte d'administrations publiques ou de particuliers, ou pour leur propre compte.

Les travaux faits pour l'État sont payés d'après les tarifs en vigueur pour les militaires de l'armée nationale exécutant les mêmes travaux, *ou, s'il n'en existe pas, d'après un tarif en rapport avec les travaux exécutés.*

Lorsque les travaux ont lieu pour le compte d'autres administrations publiques ou pour des particuliers, les conditions en sont réglées d'accord avec l'autorité militaire.

Le salaire des prisonniers contribuera à adoucir leur position, et le surplus leur sera compté au moment de leur libération, sauf défalcation des frais d'entretien.

ART. 7.

(Aucune modification.)

1899	1907
	the circumstances which necessitate the measure continue to exist. (*Cp. B. D. Art.* 24.)

ART. 6.	ART. 6.

The State may utilize the labour of prisoners of war according to their rank and capacities.   Their tasks shall not be excessive, and shall have nothing to do with the operations of war.

The State may utilize the labour of prisoners of war, *other than officers*, according to their rank and capacities. Their tasks shall not be excessive and shall have nothing to do with the operations of the war.

Prisoners may be authorized to work for the public service, for private persons, or on their own account.

Prisoners may be authorized to work for the public service, for private persons, or on their own account.

Work done for the State shall be paid for according to the tariffs in force for soldiers of the national army employed on similar tasks.

Work done for the State shall be paid for according to the tariffs in force for soldiers of the national army employed on similar tasks, *or, if there are no such tariffs in force, at rates proportional to the work executed.*

When the work is for other branches of the public service or for private persons, the conditions shall be settled in agreement with the military authorities.

When the work is for other branches of the public service or for private persons, the conditions shall be settled in agreement with the military authorities.

The earnings of the prisoners shall go towards improving their position, and the balance shall be paid them at the time of their release, after deducting the cost of their maintenance.

The earnings of the prisoners shall go towards improving their position, and the balance shall be paid them at the time of their release, after deducting the cost of their maintenance.

(*Cp. B. D. Arts.* 25, 26.)

ART. 7.	ART. 7.

The Government into whose hands prisoners of war have fallen is bound to maintain them.

(*No change.*)

Failing a special agreement between the belligerents, prisoners of war shall be treated as regards food, quarters, and clothing, on the same footing as the troops of the Government which has captured them.

(*Cp. B. D. Art.* 27.)

1899	1907

Art. 8.

Les prisonniers de guerre seront soumis aux lois, règlements et ordres en vigueur dans l'armée de l'État au pouvoir duquel ils se trouvent.

Tout acte d'insubordination autorise, à leur égard, les mesures de rigueur nécessaires.

Les prisonniers évadés, qui seraient repris avant d'avoir pu rejoindre leur armée ou avant de quitter le territoire occupé par l'armée qui les aura capturés, sont passibles de peines disciplinaires.

Les prisonniers qui, après avoir réussi à s'évader, sont de nouveau faits prisonniers, ne sont passibles d'aucune peine pour la fuite antérieure.

Art. 8.

(*Aucune modification.*)

Art. 9.

Chaque prisonnier de guerre est tenu de déclarer, s'il est interrogé à ce sujet, ses véritables noms et grade et, dans le cas où il enfreindrait cette règle, il s'exposerait à une restriction des avantages accordés aux prisonniers de guerre de sa catégorie.

Art. 9.

(*Aucune modification.*)

Art. 10.

Les prisonniers de guerre peuvent être mis en liberté sur parole, si les lois de leur pays les y autorisent, et, en pareil cas, ils sont obligés, sous la garantie de leur honneur personnel, de remplir scrupuleusement, tant vis-à-vis de leur propre Gouvernement que vis-à-vis de celui qui les a faits prisonniers, les engagements qu'ils auraient contractés.

Dans le même cas, leur propre Gouvernement est tenu de n'exiger ni accepter d'eux aucun service contraire à la parole donnée.

Art. 10.

(*Aucune modification.*)

1899	1907

Art. 8.

Prisoners of war shall be subject to the laws, regulations, and orders in force in the army of the State into whose hands they have fallen.

Any act of insubordination warrants the adoption, as regards them, of such measures of severity as may be necessary.

Escaped prisoners, recaptured before they have succeeded in rejoining their army, or before quitting the territory occupied by the army that captured them, are liable to disciplinary punishment.

Prisoners who, after succeeding in escaping, are again taken prisoners, are not liable to any punishment for the previous flight.

Art. 8.

(*No change.*)

(*Cp. B. D. Art.* 28.)

Art. 9.

Every prisoner of war, if questioned, is bound to declare his true name and rank, and if he disregards this rule, he is liable to a curtailment of the advantages accorded to the prisoners of war of his class.

Art. 9.

(*No change.*)

(*Cp. B. D. Art.* 29.)

Art. 10.

Prisoners of war may be set at liberty on parole if the laws of their country authorize it, and, in such a case, they are bound, on their personal honour, scrupulously to fulfil, both as regards their own Government and the Government by which they were made prisoners, the engagements they have contracted.

In such cases, their own Government is bound not to require of nor to accept from them any service incompatible with the parole given.

Art. 10.

(*No change.*)

(*Cp. B. D. Art.* 31.)

1899	1907
Art. 11.	Art. 11.

Un prisonnier de guerre ne peut être contraint d'accepter sa liberté sur parole ; de même le Gouvernement ennemi n'est pas obligé d'accéder à la demande du prisonnier réclamant sa mise en liberté sur parole.

(Aucune modification.)

Art. 12.	Art. 12.

Tout prisonnier de guerre, libéré sur parole et repris portant les armes contre le Gouvernement envers lequel il s'était engagé d'honneur, ou contre les alliés de celui-ci, perd le droit au traitement des prisonniers de guerre et peut être traduit devant les tribunaux.

(Aucune modification.)

Art. 13.	Art. 13.

Les individus qui suivent une armée sans en faire directement partie, tels que les correspondants et les reporters de journaux, les vivandiers, les fournisseurs, qui tombent au pouvoir de l'ennemi et que celui-ci juge utile de détenir, ont droit au traitement des prisonniers de guerre, à condition qu'ils soient munis d'une légitimation de l'autorité militaire de l'armée qu'ils accompagnaient.

(Aucune modification.)

Art. 14.	Art. 14.

Il est constitué, dès le début des hostilités, dans chacun des États belligérants et, le cas échéant, dans les pays neutres qui auront recueilli des belligérants sur leur territoire, un bureau de renseignements sur les prisonniers de guerre. Ce bureau, chargé de répondre à toutes les demandes qui les concernent, reçoit des divers services compétents toutes les

Il est constitué, dès le début des hostilités, dans chacun des États belligérants, et, le cas échéant, dans les pays neutres qui auront recueilli des belligérants sur leur territoire, un bureau de renseignements sur les prisonniers de guerre. Ce bureau, chargé de répondre à toutes les demandes qui les concernent, reçoit des divers services compétents toutes les indications

1899	1907
ART. 11.	ART. 11.

A prisoner of war cannot be forced to accept his liberty on parole; similarly the hostile Government is not obliged to assent to the prisoner's request to be set at liberty on parole.

(No change.)

(Cp. B. D. Art. 32.)

ART. 12.   ART. 12.

Any prisoner of war, who is liberated on parole and recaptured bearing arms against the Government to which he had pledged his honour, or against the allies of that Government, forfeits his right to be treated as a prisoner of war, and can be brought before the Courts.

(No change.)

(Cp. B. D. Art. 33.)

ART. 13.   ART. 13.

Individuals who follow an army without directly belonging to it, such as newspaper correspondents and reporters, sutlers, contractors, who fall into the enemy's hands, and whom the latter thinks fit to detain, have a right to be treated as prisoners of war, provided they can produce a certificate from the military authorities of the army they were accompanying.

(No change.)

(Cp. B. D. Art. 34.)

ART. 14.   ART. 14.

A Bureau for information relative to prisoners of war is instituted, on the commencement of hostilities, in each of the belligerent States and, should it so happen, in the neutral countries in whose territory belligerents have been received. The duty of this Bureau is to answer all inquiries about prisoners of war, it is furnished by the various services concerned with all the

A bureau for information relative to prisoners of war is instituted on the commencement of hostilities in each of the belligerent States, and, should it so happen, in the neutral countries in whose territory belligerents have been received. The duty of this bureau is to answer all inquiries about prisoners of war, it is furnished by the various services concerned with all the information

1899	1907
indications nécessaires pour lui permettre d'établir une fiche individuelle pour chaque prisonnier de guerre. Il est tenu au courant des internements et des mutations, ainsi que des entrées dans les hôpitaux et des décès.	*relatives* aux internements et aux mutations, *aux mises en liberté sur parole, aux échanges, aux évasions,* aux entrées dans les hôpitaux, aux décès, ainsi que les autres renseignements nécessaires pour établir *et tenir à jour* une fiche individuelle pour chaque prisonnier de guerre. *Le bureau devra porter sur cette fiche le numéro matricule, les nom et prénom, l'âge, le lieu d'origine, le grade, le corps de troupe, les blessures, la date et le lieu de la capture, de l'internement, des blessures et de la mort, ainsi que toutes les observations particulières. La fiche individuelle sera remise au Gouvernement de l'autre belligérant après la conclusion de la paix.*
Le Bureau de Renseignements est également chargé de recueillir et de centraliser tous les objets d'un usage personnel, valeurs, lettres, &c., qui seront trouvés sur les champs de bataille ou délaissés par des prisonniers décédés dans les hôpitaux et ambulances, et de les transmettre aux intéressés.	Le bureau de renseignements est également chargé de recueillir et de centraliser tous les objets d'un usage personnel, valeurs, lettres, &c., qui seront trouvés sur les champs de bataille ou délaissés par des prisonniers *libérés sur parole, échangés, évadés, ou* décédés dans les hôpitaux et ambulances, et de les transmettre aux intéressés.

Art. 15.

Les Sociétés de Secours pour les prisonniers de guerre, régulièrement constituées selon la loi de leur pays et ayant pour objet d'être les intermédiaires de l'action charitable, recevront, de la part des belligérants, pour elles et pour leurs agents dûment accrédités, toute facilité, dans les limites tracées par les nécessités militaires et les règles administratives, pour accomplir efficacement leur tâche d'humanité. Les Délégués de ces	Art. 15. (*Aucune modification.*)

1899	1907
information to enable it to keep an individual return for each prisoner of war. It is kept informed of internments and changes, as well as of admissions into hospital and deaths.	respecting internments and transfers, *releases on parole, exchanges, escapes,* admissions into hospital, deaths, as well as all other information necessary to enable it to make out *and keep up to date* an individual return for each prisoner of war. *The bureau must state in this return the regimental number, surname and name, age, place of origin, rank, unit, wounds, date and place of capture, of internment, the wounds, and the death, as well as any observations of a special character. The individual return shall be sent to the Government of the other belligerent after the conclusion of peace.*
It is also the duty of the Information Bureau to gather and keep together all objects of personal use, valuables, letters, &c., found on the battlefields or left by prisoners who have died in hospitals or ambulances, and to forward them to those interested.	It is also the duty of the Information Bureau to gather and keep together all objects of personal use, valuables, letters, &c., found on the battlefields or left by prisoners who have *been released on parole, or exchanged, or who have escaped*, or died in hospitals or ambulances, and to forward them to those interested.

ART. 15.	ART. 15.
Relief Societies for prisoners of war, regularly constituted in accordance with the law of their country with the object of serving as the intermediaries for charity, shall receive from the belligerents, for themselves and their duly accredited agents, every facility, within the bounds of military necessities and administrative regulations, for the effective accomplishment of their humane task. Delegates of these Societies may be	(*No change.*)

1899	1907

sociétés pourront être admis à distribuer des secours dans les dépôts d'internement, ainsi qu'aux lieux d'étape des prisonniers repatriés, moyennant une permission personnelle délivrée par l'autorité militaire, et en prenant l'engagement par écrit de se soumettre à toutes les mesures d'ordre et de police que celle-ci prescrirait.

ART. 16.

Les bureaux de renseignements jouissent de la franchise de port. Les lettres, mandats et articles d'argent, ainsi que les colis postaux destinés aux prisonniers de guerre ou expédiés par eux, seront affranchis de toutes taxes postales, aussi bien dans les pays d'origine et de destination que dans les pays intermédiaires.

Les dons et secours en nature destinés aux prisonniers de guerre seront admis en franchise de tous droits d'entrée et autres, ainsi que des taxes de transport sur les chemins de fer exploités par l'État.

ART. 16.

(*Aucune modification.*)

ART. 17.

Les officiers prisonniers pourront recevoir le complément, s'il y a lieu, de la solde qui leur est attribuée dans cette situation par les Règlements de leur pays, à charge de remboursement par leur Gouvernement.

ART. 17.

Les officiers prisonniers recevront *la solde à laquelle ont droit les officiers de même grade du pays où ils sont retenus,* à charge de remboursement par leur Gouvernement.

ART. 18.

Toute latitude est laissée aux prisonniers de guerre pour l'exercice de leur religion, y compris l'assistance aux offices de leur culte, à la seule condition de se conformer aux mesures d'ordre et de police prescrites par l'autorité militaire.

ART. 18.

(*Aucune modification.*)

1899

admitted to distribute relief at the places of internment, as also at the halting places of repatriated prisoners, if furnished with a personal permit by the military authorities, and on giving an engagement in writing to comply with all regulations for order and police which the latter may prescribe.

ART. 16.

The Information Bureaux shall have the privilege of free postage. Letters, money orders, and valuables, as well as postal parcels destined for the prisoners of war or dispatched by them, shall be free of all postal rates, alike in the countries of origin and destination, as well as in those they pass through.

Gifts and relief in kind for prisoners of war shall be admitted free of all duties of entry and others, as well as of payments for carriage by the Government railways.

ART. 17.

Officers taken prisoners shall receive, in proper cases, the full pay allowed them in this position by their country's regulations, the amount to be repaid by their Government.

ART 18.

Prisoners of war shall enjoy every latitude for the exercise of their religion, including attendance at their own church services, provided only they comply with the regulations for order and police issued by the military authority.

1907

ART. 16.

(*No change.*)

ART. 17.

Officers taken prisoners shall receive *the same pay as officers of corresponding rank in the country where they are detained;* the amount shall be repaid by their Government.

ART. 18.

(*No change.*)

1899	1907

Art. 19.

Les testaments des prisonniers de guerre sont reçus ou dressés dans les mêmes conditions que pour les militaires de l'armée nationale.

On suivra également les mêmes règles en ce qui concerne les pièces relatives à la constatation des décès, ainsi que pour l'inhumation des prisonniers de guerre, en tenant compte de leur grade et de leur rang.

Art. 19.

(*Aucune modification.*)

Art. 20.

Après la conclusion de la paix, le repatriement des prisonniers de guerre s'effectuera dans le plus bref délai possible.

Art. 20.

(*Aucune modification.*)

Chapitre III.

Des Malades et des Blessés.

Art. 21.

Les obligations des belligérants concernant le service des malades et des blessés sont régies par la Convention de Genève du 22 Août, 1864, sauf les modifications dont celle-ci pourra être l'objet.

Chapitre III.

Des Malades et des Blessés.

Art. 21.

Les obligations des belligérants concernant le service des malades et des blessés sont régies par la Convention de Genève.

Section II.

Des Hostilités.

Chapitre I.

Des moyens de nuire à l'Ennemi, des Sièges et des Bombardements.

Art. 22.

Les belligérants n'ont pas un droit illimité quant au choix des moyens de nuire à l'ennemi.

Section II.

Des Hostilités.

Chapitre I.

Des Moyens de Nuire à l'Ennemi, des Sièges et des Bombardements.

Art. 22.

(*Aucune modification.*)

1899	1907

ART. 19.

The wills of prisoners of war are received or drawn up on the same conditions as for soldiers of the national army.

The same rules shall be observed regarding certificates of death, as well as for the burial of prisoners of war, due regard being paid to their grade and rank.

ART. 19.

(*No change.*)

ART. 20.

After the conclusion of peace, the repatriation of prisoners of war shall take place as speedily as possible.

ART. 20.

(*No change.*)

Chapter III.

The Sick and Wounded.

ART. 21.

The obligations of belligerents with regard to the sick and wounded are governed by the Geneva Convention of the 22nd August, 1864, subject to any modifications which may be introduced into it.

Chapter III.

The Sick and Wounded.

ART. 21.

The obligations of belligerents with regard to the sick and wounded are governed by the Geneva Convention.

(*Cp. B. D. Art.* 35.)

Section II.

Hostilities.

Chapter I.

The means of injuring the Enemy, Sieges and Bombardments.

ART. 22.

The right of belligerents to adopt means of injuring the enemy is not unlimited.

Section II.

Hostilities.

Chapter I.

The means of injuring the Enemy, Sieges and Bombardments.

ART. 22.

(*No change.*)

(*Cp. B. D. Art.* 12.)

1899	1907
ART. 23.	ART. 23.

Outre les prohibitions établies par des Conventions spéciales, il est notamment interdit :—

(*a*) D'employer du poison ou des armes empoisonnées ;

(*b*) De tuer ou de blesser par trahison des individus appartenant à la nation ou à l'armée ennemie ;

(*c*) De tuer ou de blesser un ennemi qui, ayant mis bas les armes ou n'ayant plus les moyens de se défendre, s'est rendu à discrétion ;

(*d*) De déclarer qu'il ne sera pas fait de quartier ;

(*e*) D'employer des armes, des projectiles ou des matières propres à causer des maux superflus ;

(*f*) D'user indûment du pavillon parlementaire, du pavillon national ou des insignes militaires et de l'uniforme de l'ennemi, ainsi que des signes distinctifs de la Convention de Genève ;

(*g*) De détruire ou de saisir des propriétés ennemies, sauf les cas où ces destructions ou ces saisies seraient impérieusement commandées par les nécessités de la guerre.

Outre les prohibitions établies par des Conventions spéciales, il est notamment interdit—

(*a*) D'employer du poison ou des armes empoisonnées ;

(*b*) De tuer ou de blesser par trahison des individus appartenant à la nation ou à l'armée ennemie ;

(*c*) De tuer ou de blesser un ennemi qui, ayant mis bas les armes ou n'ayant plus les moyens de se défendre, s'est rendu à discrétion ;

(*d*) De déclarer qu'il ne sera pas fait de quartier ;

(*e*) D'employer des armes, des projectiles ou des matières propres à causer des maux superflus ;

(*f*) D'user indûment du pavillon parlementaire, du pavillon national ou des insignes militaires et de l'uniforme de l'ennemi, ainsi que des signes distinctifs de la Convention de Genève ;

(*g*) De détruire ou de saisir des propriétés ennemies, sauf les cas où ces destructions ou ces saisies seraient impérieusement commandées par les nécessités de la guerre ;

(*h*) *De déclarer éteints, suspendus ou non recevables en justice, les droits et actions des nationaux de la Partie adverse.*

Il est également interdit à un belligérant de forcer les nationaux de la Partie adverse à prendre part aux opérations de guerre dirigées contre leur pays, même dans le cas où ils auraient été à son service avant le commencement de la guerre.

1899	1907
ART. 23.	ART. 23.

Besides the prohibitions provided by special Conventions, it is especially forbidden :—

(*a*) To employ poison or poisoned arms ;

(*b*) To kill or wound treacherously individuals belonging to the hostile nation or army ;

(*c*) To kill or wound an enemy who, having laid down arms, or having no longer means of defence, has surrendered at discretion ;

(*d*) To declare that no quarter will be given ;

(*e*) To employ arms, projectiles, or material of a nature to cause superfluous injury ;

(*f*) To make improper use of a flag of truce, the national flag, or military ensigns and the enemy's uniform, as well as the distinctive badges of the Geneva Convention ;

(*g*) To destroy or seize the enemy's property, unless such destruction or seizure be imperatively demanded by the necessities of war.

Besides the prohibitions provided by special Conventions, it is especially forbidden—

(*a*) To employ poison or poisoned arms ;

(*b*) To kill or wound treacherously individuals belonging to the hostile nation or army ;

(*c*) To kill or wound an enemy who, having laid down his arms, or having no longer means of defence, has surrendered at discretion ;

(*d*) To declare that no quarter will be given ;

(*e*) To employ arms, projectiles, or material of a nature to cause superfluous injury ;

(*f*) To make improper use of a flag of truce, the national flag, or military ensigns and the enemy's uniform, as well as the distinctive badges of the Geneva Convention ;

(*g*) To destroy or seize the enemy's property, unless such destruction or seizure be imperatively demanded by the necessities of war ;

(*h*) *To declare extinguished, suspended, or unenforceable in a court of law the rights and rights of action of the nationals of the adverse party.*

A belligerent is likewise forbidden to compel the nationals of the adverse party to take part in the operations of war directed against their country, even when they have been in his service before the commencement of the war.

(*Cp. B. D. Art.* 13.)

1899	1907

ART. 24.

Les ruses de guerre et l'emploi des moyens nécessaires pour se procurer des renseignements sur l'ennemi et sur le terrain sont considérés comme licites.

ART. 24.

(*Aucune modification.*)

ART. 25.

Il est interdit d'attaquer ou de bombarder des villes, villages, habitations ou bâtiments qui ne sont pas défendus.

ART. 25.

Il est interdit d'attaquer ou de bombarder, *par quelque moyen que ce soit*, des villes, villages, habitations ou bâtiments qui ne sont pas défendus.

ART. 26.

Le Commandant des troupes assaillantes, avant d'entreprendre le bombardement, et sauf le cas d'attaque de vive force, devra faire tout ce qui dépend de lui pour en avertir les autorités.

ART. 26.

(*Aucune modification.*)

ART. 27.

Dans les sièges et bombardements, toutes les mesures nécessaires doivent être prises pour épargner, autant que possible, les édifices consacrés aux cultes, aux arts, aux sciences et à la bienfaisance, les hôpitaux et les lieux de rassemblement de malades et de blessés, à condition qu'ils ne soient pas employés en même temps à un but militaire.

Le devoir des assiégés est de désigner ces édifices ou lieux de rassemblement par des signes visibles spéciaux qui seront notifiés d'avance à l'assiégeant.

ART. 27.

Dans les sièges et bombardements, toutes les mesures nécessaires doivent être prises pour épargner, autant que possible, les édifices consacrés aux cultes, aux arts, aux sciences et à la bienfaisance, *les monuments historiques*, les hôpitaux et les lieux de rassemblement de malades et de blessés, à condition qu'ils ne soient pas employés en même temps à un but militaire.

Le devoir des assiégés est de désigner ces édifices ou lieux de rassemblement par des signes visibles spéciaux qui seront notifiés d'avance à l'assiégeant.

ART. 28.

Il est interdit de livrer au pillage même une ville ou localité prise d'assaut.

ART. 28.

(*Aucune modification.*)

1899	1907

Art. 24.

Ruses of war and the employment of methods necessary to obtain information about the enemy and the country, are considered lawful.

Art. 24.

(*No change.*)

(*Cp. B. D. Art.* 14.)

Art. 25.

The attack or bombardment of towns, villages, habitations or buildings which are not defended, is forbidden.

Art. 25

The attack or bombardment, *by any means whatever*, of towns, villages, habitations, or buildings which are not defended is forbidden.

(*Cp. B. D. Art.* 15 ; *see also* 9 *H. C.* 1907, *Art.* 1.)

Art. 26.

The Commander of an attacking force, before commencing a bombardment, except in the case of an assault, should do all he can to warn the authorities of it.

Art. 26.

(*No change.*)

(*Cp. B. D. Art.* 16.)

Art. 27.

In sieges and bombardments all necessary steps should be taken to spare, as far as possible, buildings devoted to religion, art, science and charity, hospitals and places where the sick and wounded are collected, provided they are not used at the same time for military purposes.

The besieged should indicate these buildings or places by some special visible signs, which shall previously be notified to the assailants.

Art. 27.

In sieges and bombardments all necessary steps should be taken to spare, as far as possible, buildings devoted to religion, art, science and charity, *historic monuments*, hospitals and places where the sick and wounded are collected, provided they are not used at the same time for military purposes.

The besieged should indicate these buildings or places by some special visible signs, which shall previously be notified to the assailants.

(*Cp. B. D. Art.* 17 ; *see also* 9 *H. C.* 1907, *Arts.* 3 *and* 5.)

Art. 28.

The giving up to pillage of a town or place, even when taken by assault, is forbidden.

Art. 28.

(*No change.*)
(*Cp. B. D. Art.* 18 ; *see also* 9 *H. C.* 1907, *Art.* 7.)

1899	1907
Chapitre II.	Chapitre II.
Des Espions.	Des Espions.

ART. 29.

Ne peut être considéré comme espion que l'individu qui, agissant clandestinement ou sous de faux prétextes, recueille ou cherche à recueillir des informations dans la zone d'opérations d'un belligérant, avec l'intention de les communiquer à la partie adverse.

Ainsi les militaires non déguisés qui ont pénétré dans la zone d'opérations de l'armée ennemie, à l'effet de recueillir des informations, ne sont pas considérés comme espions. De même, ne sont pas considérés comme espions : les militaires et les non-militaires, accomplissant ouvertement leur mission, chargés de transmettre des dépêches destinées, soit à leur propre armée, soit à l'armée ennemie. A cette catégorie appartiennent également les individus envoyés en ballon pour transmettre les dépêches, et, en général, pour entretenir les communications entre les diverses parties d'une armée ou d'un territoire.

ART. 29.

(*Aucune modification.*)

ART. 30.

L'espion pris sur le fait ne pourra être puni sans jugement préalable.

ART. 30.

(*Aucune modification.*)

ART. 31.

L'espion qui, ayant rejoint l'armée à laquelle il appartient, est capturé plus tard par l'ennemi, est traité comme prisonnier de guerre et n'encourt aucune reponsabilité pour ses actes d'espionnage antérieurs.

ART. 31.

(*Aucune modification.*)

1899	1907
Chapter II.	Chapter II.
Spies.	Spies.

ART. 29.

An individual can only be considered a spy if, acting clandestinely, or on false pretences, he obtains, or seeks to obtain information in the zone of operations of a belligerent, with the intention of communicating it to the hostile party.

Thus, soldiers not in disguise who have penetrated into the zone of operations of a hostile army to obtain information are not considered spies. Similarly, the following are not considered spies : soldiers or civilians, carrying out their mission openly, charged with the delivery of despatches destined either for their own army or for that of the enemy. To this class belong likewise individuals sent in balloons to deliver despatches, and generally to maintain communication between the various parts of an army or a territory.

ART. 29.

(*No change.*)

(*Cp. B. D. Arts.* 19, 22.)

ART. 30.

A spy taken in the act cannot be punished without previous trial.

ART. 30.

(*No change.*)
(*Cp. B. D. Art.* 20.)

ART. 31.

A spy who, after rejoining the army to which he belongs, is subsequently captured by the enemy, is treated as a prisoner of war, and incurs no responsibility for his previous acts of espionage.

ART. 31.

(*No change.*)

(*Cp. B. D. Art.* 21.)

1899	1907
Chapitre III.	Chapitre III.
Des Parlementaires.	Des Parlementaires.

Art. 32.

Est considéré comme parlementaire l'individu autorisé par l'un des belligérants à entrer en pourparlers avec l'autre et se présentant avec le drapeau blanc. Il a droit à l'inviolabilité ainsi que le trompette, clairon ou tambour, le porte-drapeau et l'interprète qui l'accompagneraient.

Art. 32.

(*Aucune modification.*)

Art. 33.

Le chef auquel un parlementaire est expédié n'est pas obligé de le recevoir en toutes circonstances.

Il peut prendre toutes les mesures nécessaires afin d'empêcher le parlementaire de profiter de sa mission pour se renseigner.

Il a le droit, en cas d'abus, de retenir temporairement le parlementaire.

Art. 33.

(*Aucune modification.*)

Art. 34.

Le parlementaire perd ses droits d'inviolabilité, s'il est prouvé, d'une manière positive et irrécusable, qu'il a profité de sa position privilégiée pour provoquer ou commettre un acte de trahison.

Art. 34.

(*Aucune modification.*)

Chapitre IV.	Chapitre IV.
Des Capitulations.	Des Capitulations.

Art. 35.

Les capitulations arrêtées entre les Parties contractantes doivent tenir compte des règles de l'honneur militaire.

Une fois fixées, elles doivent être scrupuleusement observées par les deux Parties.

Art. 35.

(*Aucune modification.*)

1899	1907
Chapter III.	Chapter III.
Flags of Truce.	Flags of Truce.
Art. 32.	Art. 32.
A person is considered as the bearer of a flag of truce who is authorized by one of the belligerents to enter into communication with the other, and who comes with a white flag. He has a right to inviolability, as well as the trumpeter, bugler, or drummer, the flag-bearer and the interpreter who may accompany him.	*(No change.)* *(Cp. B. D. Art. 43.)*
Art. 33.	. Art. 33.
The Commander to whom a bearer of a flag of truce is sent is not obliged to receive him in all circumstances. He can take all steps necessary to prevent the bearer taking advantage of his mission to obtain information. In case of abuse, he has the right to detain the bearer temporarily.	*(No change.)* *(Cp. B. D. Art. 44.)*
Art. 34.	Art. 34.
The bearer of a flag of truce loses his rights of inviolability if it is proved in a clear and incontestable manner that he has taken advantage of his privileged position to instigate or commit an act of treachery.	*(No change.)* *(Cp. B. D. Art. 45.)*
Chapter IV.	Chapter IV.
Capitulations.	Capitulations.
Art. 35.	Art. 35.
Capitulations agreed on between the Contracting Parties must be in accordance with the rules of military honour. When once settled, they must be scrupulously observed by both the parties.	*(No change.)* *(Cp. B. D. Art. 46.)*

1899	1907
Chapitre V.	Chapitre V.
De l'Armistice.	De l'Armistice.

ART. 36.

L'armistice suspend les opérations de guerre par un accord mutuel des parties belligérantes. Si la durée n'en est pas déterminée, les parties belligérantes peuvent reprendre en tout temps les opérations, pourvu toutefois que l'ennemi soit averti en temps convenu, conformément aux conditions de l'armistice.

ART. 36.

(Aucune modification.)

ART. 37.

L'armistice peut être général ou local. Le premier suspend partout les opérations de guerre des États belligérants ; le second, seulement entre certaines fractions des armées belligérantes et dans un rayon déterminé.

ART. 37.

(Aucune modification.)

ART. 38.

L'armistice doit être notifié officiellement et en temps utile aux autorités compétentes et aux troupes. Les hostilités sont suspendues immédiatement après la notification ou au terme fixé.

ART. 38.

(Aucune modification.)

ART. 39.

Il dépend des Parties contractantes de fixer, dans les clauses de l'armistice, les rapports qui pourraient avoir lieu, sur le théâtre de la guerre, avec les populations et entre elles.

ART. 39.

(Aucune modification.)

ART. 40.

Toute violation grave de l'armistice, par l'une des Parties, donne à l'autre le droit de le dénoncer et même, en cas d'urgence, de reprendre immédiatement les hostilités.

ART. 40.

(Aucune modification.)

1899	1907

Chapter V.

Armistices.

Chapter V.

Armistices.

ART. 36.

An armistice suspends military operations by mutual agreement between the belligerent parties. If its duration is not fixed, the belligerent parties can resume operations at any time, provided always the enemy is warned within the time agreed upon, in accordance with the terms of the armistice.

ART. 36.

(No change.)

(Cp. B. D. Art. 47.)

ART. 37.

An armistice may be general or local. The first suspends all military operations of the belligerent States; the second, only those between certain fractions of the belligerent armies and in a fixed radius.

ART. 37.

(No change.)

(Cp. B. D. Art. 48.)

ART. 38.

An armistice must be notified officially, and in good time, to the competent authorities and the troops. Hostilities are suspended immediately after the notification, or at a fixed date.

ART. 38.

(No change.)

(Cp. B. D. Art. 49.)

ART. 39.

It is for the Contracting Parties to settle, in the clauses of the armistice, what relations may be had, within the theatre of war, with the population and with each other.

ART. 39.

(No change.)

(Cp. B. D. Art 50.)

ART. 40.

Any serious violation of the armistice by one of the parties gives the other party the right to denounce it, and even, in case of urgency, to recommence hostilities at once.

ART. 40.

(No change.)

(Cp. B. D. Art. 51.)

1899	1907

ART. 41.

La violation des clauses de l'armistice, par des particuliers agissant de leur propre initiative, donne droit seulement à réclamer la punition des coupables et, s'il y a lieu, une indemnité pour les pertes éprouvées.

ART. 41.

(*Aucune modification.*)

Section III.

De l'Autorité Militaire sur le Territoire de l'État Ennemi.

Section III.

De l'Autorité Militaire sur le Territoire de l'État Ennemi.

ART. 42.

Un territoire est considéré comme occupé lorsqu'il se trouve placé de fait sous l'autorité de l'armée ennemie.

L'occupation ne s'étend qu'aux territoires où cette autorité est établie et en mesure de s'exercer.

ART. 42.

(*Aucune modification.*)

ART. 43.

L'autorité du pouvoir légal ayant passé de fait entre les mains de l'occupant, celui-ci prendra toutes les mesures qui dépendent de lui en vue de rétablir et d'assurer, autant qu'il est possible, l'ordre et la vie publics en respectant, sauf empêchement absolu, les lois en vigueur dans le pays.

ART. 43.

(*Aucune modification.*)

ART. 44.

Il est interdit de forcer la population d'un territoire occupé à prendre part aux opérations militaires contre son propre pays.

ART. 44.

Il est interdit à un belligérant de forcer la population d'un territoire occupé à *donner des renseignements sur l'armée de l'autre belligérant ou sur ses moyens de défense.*

ART. 45.

Il est interdit de contraindre la population d'un territoire occupé à prêter serment à la Puissance ennemie.

ART. 45.

(*Aucune modification.*)

1899	1907
Art. 41.	Art. 41.

1899 — Art. 41.

A violation of the terms of the armistice by individuals acting on their own initiative, only confers the right of demanding the punishment of the offenders, and, if necessary, indemnity for the losses sustained.

1907 — Art. 41.

(*No change.*)

(*Cp. B. D. Art.* 52.)

Section III.

Military Authority over the Territory of the Hostile State.

Section III.

Military Authority over the Territory of the Hostile State.

1899 — Art. 42.

Territory is considered to be occupied when it is actually placed under the authority of the hostile army.

The occupation applies only to the territories where such authority is established, and can be exercised.

1907 — Art. 42.

(*No change.*)

(*Cp. B. D. Art.* 1.)

1899 — Art. 43.

The authority of the legitimate power having actually passed into the hands of the occupant, the latter shall take all steps in his power to re-establish and insure, as far as possible, public order and safety, while respecting, unless absolutely prevented, the laws in force in the country.

1907 — Art. 43.

(*No change.*)

(*Cp. B. D. Arts.* 2, 3.)

1899 — Art. 44.

Any compulsion on the population of occupied territory to take part in military operations against its own country is forbidden.

1907 — Art. 44.

Any compulsion on the population of occupied territory to *furnish information about the army of the other belligerent, or about his means of defence is forbidden.*

(*Cp. B. D. Art.* 36.)

1899 — Art. 45.

Any compulsion on the population of occupied territory to take the oath to the hostile Power is forbidden.

1907 — Art. 45.

(*No change.*)

(*Cp. B. D. Art.* 37.)

1899	1907
ART. 46.	**ART. 46.**

L'honneur et les droits de la famille, la vie des individus et la propriété privée, ainsi que les convictions religieuses et l'exercice des cultes, doivent être respectés.

La propriété privée ne peut pas être confisquée.

(Aucune modification.)

ART. 47.   **ART. 47.**

Le pillage est formellement interdit.

(Aucune modification.)

ART. 48.   **ART. 48.**

Si l'occupant prélève, dans le territoire occupé, les impôts, droits et péages établis au profit de l'État, il le fera, autant que possible, d'après les règles de l'assiette et de la répartition en vigueur, et il en résultera pour lui l'obligation de pourvoir aux frais de l'administration du territoire occupé dans la mesure où le Gouvernement légal y était tenu.

(Aucune modification.)

ART. 49.   **ART. 49.**

Si, en dehors des impôts visés à l'article précédent, l'occupant prélève d'autres contributions en argent dans le territoire occupé, ce ne pourra être que pour les besoins de l'armée ou de l'administration de ce territoire.

(Aucune modification.)

ART. 50.   **ART. 50.**

Aucune peine collective, pécuniaire ou autre, ne pourra être édictée contre les populations à raison de faits individuels dont elles ne pourraient être considérées comme solidairement responsables.

(Aucune modification.)

1899	1907
ART. 46.	ART. 46.

Family honour and rights, the lives of individuals and private property, as well as religious convictions and liberty of worship, must be respected.

Private property cannot be confiscated.

(No change.)

(Cp. B. D. Art. 38.)

ART. 47. — ART. 47.

Pillage is formally prohibited.

(No change.)
(Cp. B. D. Art. 39.)

ART. 48. — ART. 48.

If, in the territory occupied, the occupant collects the taxes, dues, and tolls imposed for the benefit of the State, he shall do it, as far as possible, in accordance with the rules in existence and the assessment in force, and will in consequence be bound to defray the expenses of the administration of the occupied territory on the same scale as that to which the legitimate Government was bound.

(No change.)

(Cp. B. D. Art. 5.)

ART. 49. — ART. 49.

If, besides the taxes referred to in the preceding Article, the occupant levies other money contributions in the occupied territory, this can only be for military necessities or the administration of such territory.

(No change.)

(Cp. B. D. Art. 40.)

ART. 50. — ART. 50.

No general penalty, pecuniary or otherwise, can be inflicted on the population on account of the acts of individuals for which it cannot be regarded as collectively responsible.

(No change.)

(Cp. B. D. Arts. 40, 41.)

1899	1907
ART. 51.	ART. 51.

Aucune contribution ne sera perçue qu'en vertu d'un ordre écrit et sous la responsabilité d'un général-en-chef.

Il ne sera procédé, autant que possible, à cette perception que d'après les règles de l'assiette et de la répartition des impôts en vigueur.

Pour toute contribution, un reçu sera délivré aux contribuables.

(*Aucune modification.*)

ART. 52.	ART. 52.

Des réquisitions en nature et des services ne pourront être réclamés des communes ou des habitants, que pour les besoins de l'armée d'occupation. Ils seront en rapport avec les ressources du pays et de telle nature qu'ils n'impliquent pas pour les populations l'obligation de prendre part aux opérations de la guerre contre leur patrie.

Ces réquisitions et ces services ne seront réclamés qu'avec l'autorisation du commandant dans la localité occupée.

Les prestations en nature seront, autant que possible, payées au comptant; sinon, elles seront constatées par des reçus.

Des réquisitions en nature et des services ne pourront être réclamés des communes ou des habitants, que pour les besoins de l'armée d'occupation. Ils seront en rapport avec les ressources du pays et de telle nature qu'ils n'impliquent pas pour les populations l'obligation de prendre part aux opérations de la guerre contre leur patrie.

Ces réquisitions et ces services ne seront réclamés qu'avec l'autorisation du commandant dans la localité occupée.

Les prestations en nature seront, autant que possible, payées au comptant; sinon, elles seront constatées par des reçus, *et le paiement des sommes dues sera effectué le plus tôt possible.*

ART. 53.	ART. 53.

L'armée qui occupe un territoire ne pourra saisir que le numéraire, les fonds et les valeurs exigibles appartenant en propre à l'État, les dépôts d'armes, moyens de transport, magasins et approvisionnements et, en

L'armée qui occupe un territoire ne pourra saisir que le numéraire, les fonds et les valeurs exigibles appartenant en propre à l'État, les dépôts d'armes, moyens de transport, magasins et approvisionnements et, en

1899	1907

ART. 51.

No contribution shall be collected except under a written order and on the responsibility of a Commander-in-chief.

This levy shall only take place, as far as possible, in accordance with the rules in existence and the assessment in force for taxes.

For every contribution a receipt shall be given to the payer.

ART. 51.

(*No change.*)

(*Cp. B. D. Art.* 41.)

ART. 52.

Neither requisitions in kind nor services can be demanded from communes or inhabitants except for the necessities of the army of occupation. They must be in proportion to the resources of the country, and of such a nature as not to imply for the population any obligation to take part in military operations against their country.

These requisitions and services shall only be demanded on the authority of the Commander in the locality occupied.

Supplies in kind shall, as far as possible, be paid for in ready money; if not, their receipt shall be acknowledged.

ART. 52.

Neither requisitions in kind nor services can be demanded from communes or inhabitants except for the necessities of the army of occupation. They must be in proportion to the resources of the country, and of such a nature as not to imply for the population any obligation to take part in military operations against their country.

These requisitions and services shall only be demanded on the authority of the Commander in the locality occupied.

Supplies in kind shall as far as possible be paid for in ready money; if not, their receipt shall be acknowledged *and the payment of the amount due shall be made as soon as possible.*

(*Cp. B. D. Art.* 42.)

ART. 53.

An army of occupation can only take possession of the cash, funds and realizable securities which are strictly the property of the State, depôts of arms, means of transport, stores and

ART. 53.

An army of occupation can only take possession of cash, funds and realizable securities which are strictly the property of the State, depôts of arms, means of transport, stores and

1899

général, toute propriété mobilière de l'État de nature à servir aux opérations de la guerre.

Le matériel des chemins de fer, les télégraphes de terre, les téléphones, les bateaux à vapeur et autres navires, en dehors des cas régis par la loi maritime, de même que les dépôts d'armes et en général toute espèce de munitions de guerre, même appartenant à des sociétés ou à des personnes privées, sont également des moyens de nature à servir aux opérations de la guerre, mais devront être restitués, et les indemnités seront réglées à la paix.

1907

général, toute propriété mobilière de l'État de nature à servir aux opérations de la guerre.

Tous les moyens affectés sur terre, sur mer et dans les airs à la transmission des nouvelles, au transport des personnes ou des choses, en dehors des cas régis par le droit maritime, les dépôts d'armes et, en général, toute espèce de munitions de guerre, peuvent être saisis, même s'ils appartiennent à des personnes privées, mais devront être restitués et les indemnités seront réglées à la paix.

Art. 54.

Le matériel des chemins de fer provenant d'États neutres, qu'il appartienne à ces États ou à des sociétés ou personnes privées, leur sera renvoyé aussitôt que possible.

Art. 54.

Les câbles sous-marins reliant un territoire occupé à un territoire neutre ne seront saisis ou détruits que dans le cas d'une nécessité absolue. Ils devront également être restitués et les indemnités seront réglées à la paix.

Art. 55.

L'État occupant ne se considérera que comme administrateur et usufruitier des édifices publics, immeubles, forêts et exploitations agricoles appartenant à l'État ennemi et se trouvant dans le pays occupé.   Il devra sauvegarder le fonds de ces propriétés et les administrer conformément aux règles de l'usufruit.

Art. 55.

(*Aucune modification.*)

Art. 56.

Les biens des communes, ceux des établissements consacrés aux cultes, à la charité et à l'instruction, aux arts et aux sciences, même appartenant à l'État, seront traités comme la propriété privée.

Art. 56.

(*Aucune modification.*)

1899	1907

supplies, and, generally, all movable property of the State which may be used for operations of war.

Railway plant, land telegraphs, telephones, steamers, and other ships, apart from cases governed by maritime law, as well as depôts of arms and, generally, all kinds of war material, even though belonging to companies or to private persons, are likewise means of a nature to be used in the operations of war, but they must be restored and indemnities for them regulated at the peace.

supplies, and, generally, all movable property of the State which may be used for operations of war.

All appliances, whether on land, at sea, or in the air, adapted for the transmission of news or for the transport of persons or goods apart from cases governed by maritime law, depôts of arms, and, generally, all kinds of war material may be seized, even though belonging to private persons, but they must be restored and indemnities for them regulated at the peace.

(Cp. B. D. Art. 6.)

ART. 54.

Railway material coming from neutral States, whether the property of those States, or of companies, or of private persons, shall be sent back to them as soon as possible.

(Cp. B. D. Art. 6.)

ART. 54.

Submarine cables connecting a territory occupied with a neutral territory shall not be seized or destroyed except in the case of absolute necessity. They also must be restored and indemnities for them regulated at the peace.

ART. 55.

The occupying State shall regard itself only as administrator and usufructuary of the public buildings, immovable property, forests and agricultural undertakings belonging to the hostile State, and situated in the occupied country. It must protect the capital of these properties, and administer it according to the rules of usufruct.

ART. 55.

(No change.)

(Cp. B. D. Art. 7.)

ART. 56.

The property of the communes, that of institutions dedicated to religious worship, charity, education, art and science, even when belonging to the State, shall be treated as private property.

ART. 56.

(No change.)

Toute saisie, destruction ou dégra-
dation intentionnelle de semblables
établissements, de monuments historiques, d'œuvres d'art et de science, est
interdit et doit être poursuivie.

Section IV.

Des Belligérants Internés et des Blessés Soignés chez les Neutres.

ART. 57.

L'État neutre qui reçoit sur son
territoire des troupes appartenant aux
armées belligérantes, les internera,
autant que possible, loin du théâtre de
la guerre.

Il pourra les garder dans des camps,
et même les enfermer dans des forteresses ou dans des lieux appropriés à
cet effet.

Il décidera si les officiers peuvent
être laissés libres en prenant l'engagement sur parole de ne pas quitter
le territoire neutre sans autorisation.

ART. 58.

A défaut de convention spéciale,
l'État neutre fournira aux internés les
vivres, les habillements et les secours
commandés par l'humanité.

Bonification sera faite, à la paix, des
frais occasionnés par l'internement.

1899	1907
All seizure of, and destruction, or intentional damage done to such institutions, historical monuments, works of art or science, is forbidden, and should be made the subject of legal proceedings.	
	(*Cp. B. D. Art.* 8.)

Section IV.

The Internment of Belligerents and the Care of the Wounded in Neutral Countries.

ART. 57.

(*Transferred to* 5 *H. C.* 1907, *Art.* 11.)[1]

A neutral State which receives in its territory troops belonging to the belligerent armies shall intern them, as far as possible, at a distance from the theatre of war.

It can keep them in camps, and even confine them in fortresses or places assigned for this purpose.

It shall decide whether officers may be left at liberty on giving their parole not to leave the neutral territory without permission.

(*Cp. B. D. Art.* 53.)

ART. 58.

(*Transferred to* 5 *H. C.* 1907, *Art.* 12.)[1]

In the absence of a special Convention, the neutral State shall supply the interned with the food, clothing, and relief which the dictates of humanity prescribe.

At the conclusion of peace, the expenses caused by the internment shall be made good.

(*Cp. B. D. Art.* 54.)

[1] See post, p. 284.

Art. 59.

L'État neutre pourra autoriser le passage sur son territoire des blessés ou malades appartenant aux armées belligérantes, sous la réserve que les trains qui les amèneront ne transporteront ni personnel ni matériel de guerre. En pareil cas, l'État neutre est tenu de prendre les mesures de sûreté et de contrôle nécessaires à cet effet.

Les blessés ou malades amenés dans ces conditions sur le territoire neutre par un des belligérants, et qui appartiendraient à la partie adverse, devront être gardés par l'État neutre, de manière qu'ils ne puissent de nouveau prendre part aux opérations de la guerre. Celui-ci aura les mêmes devoirs quant aux blessés ou malades de l'autre armée qui lui seraient confiés.

Art. 60.

La Convention de Genève s'applique aux malades et aux blessés internés sur territoire neutre.

1899	1907
ART. 59.	(*Transferred to* 5 *H. C.* 1907, *Art.* 14.)[1]

A neutral State may authorize the passage over its territory of wounded or sick belonging to the belligerent armies, on condition that the trains bringing them shall carry neither personnel nor material of war. In such a case, the neutral State is bound to adopt such measures of safety and control as may be necessary for the purpose.

Wounded and sick brought under these conditions into neutral territory by one of the belligerents, and belonging to the adverse party, must be guarded by the neutral State, so as to insure their not taking part again in the operations of war. The same duty shall devolve on the neutral State with regard to wounded or sick of the other army who may be committed to its care.

(*Cp. B. D. Art.* 55.)

ART. 60.	(*Transferred to* 5 *H. C.* 1907, *Art.* 15.)[1]

The Geneva Convention applies to the sick and wounded interned in neutral territory.

(*Cp. B. D. Art.* 56.)

[1] See post, p. 260.

CONVENTION NO. 4.   CONCERNING THE LAWS AND CUSTOMS OF
WAR ON LAND[1].

The rules for the conduct of hostilities on land are still in many
cases to be sought for in historical treatises, the writings
Codification of laws relating to land warfare. of publicists, and from "unwritten custom and tradition;
but within the last forty years, attempts of two kinds have
been made to deal with the topic in a more authoritative
manner[2]." National manuals have been compiled for the use of officers
and armies in the field, and international Conventions have produced
something like a Code of law which is almost universally accepted.

The starting-point for the codification of the rules of war on land
is the "Instructions for the government of armies of the United States in
the field" drawn up by Dr Francis Lieber and revised by a Board of officers
of the United States Army at the instance of President Lincoln and
issued from the office of the Adjutant-General to the army as General
Order, No. 100, of 1863[3]. It was "a deed of great moment in the history
of international law and of civilisation," and although Dr Lieber's
expectation that it would be adopted as a "basis for similar works by
the English, French and Germans[4]" was not fully realised, its influence

---

[1] *Parl.?Papers*, Misc. No. 4 (1908), pp. 24–26, 100–112 ; *La Deux. Confér.* T. I. pp. 85–7,
96–110; *Livre Jaune*, pp. 75–7 ; *Weissbuch*, No. 527 (1907), pp. 6–7 ; J. B. Atlay, *Legitimate
modes of warfare, Journal of the Soc. of Comp. Legislation*, New Series, No. XIII. p. 10 ; Sir
T. Barclay, *Problems, etc.* p. 51 ; G. B. Davis, *The amelioration of the rules of war on land, Am.
Journ. of Int. Law*, Vol. II. p. 63 ; Idem, *Elements of International Law*, pp. 573–584 ; T. E.
Holland, *The laws and customs of war on land* (1904); Idem, *The laws of war on land* (1908) ;
Idem, *Studies in international law*, Nos. 2, 3 and 4 ; F. W. Holls, *The Peace Conference, etc.*
Chapters III. and IV.; E. Lémonon, *La seconde Conférence de la Paix*, pp. 341–381;
A. Mérignhac, *Les lois et coutumes de la guerre sur terre* ; Idem, *Les théories du grand état-major
allemand sur les lois de la guerre continentale, Rev. gén. de Dr. inter.* Vol. XIV. p. 197;
L. Oppenheim, *Inter. Law*, Vol. II. §§ 67, 97, 103–172 (with bibliography) ; A. Pillet, *Les lois
actuelles de la guerre*; J. Westlake, *War*, pp. 60–119, 268–270 ; *Les lois de la guerre
continentale (publication de la section historique du grand état-major allemand*, 1902) *traduites
et annotées par* Paul Carpentier (1904).

[2] T. E. Holland, *The laws of war on land*, p. 1.   Professor Holland's work contains a
lucid and concise exposition of the Articles in the Convention and Regulations dealt with
in this Section.   I have therefore confined my observations to the changes made in 1907.

[3] See G. B. Davis, *Doctor Francis Lieber's Instructions, Am. Journ. of Int. Law*, Vol. I.
p. 13.   The full text of the instructions will be found in Vol. II. of *The Institutes of the Law
of Nations*, by J. Lorimer, pp. 303–336; G. B. Davis, *Elements of International Law*,
Appendix A ; J. B. Scott, *Texts of the Peace Conferences*, p. 350.

[4] "Doctor Lieber's rules were also adopted by the German government with a view to
regulating the conduct of its armies in the field during the war of 1870," G. B. Davis, *Am.
Journ. of Int. Law*, p. 22.

is to be seen in the attempts which ultimately were successful in 1899 in producing a Code acceptable to nearly all the members of the family of nations.

The horror at the treatment to which prisoners of war had in some cases

The Brussels draft Declaration[1].

been subjected during the American Civil War, had led to the formation in France, in 1872, of a society for the amelioration of the condition of prisoners of war. In 1874 this society invited the Powers of Europe to send two delegates to a Conference to be held at Paris to endeavour to carry out their objects. Meantime the Tsar, Alexander II, proposed a Conference to consider the wider and more general question of the conduct of war. The first meeting of the Conference was held on the 27th July, 1874, at Brussels, and was attended by delegates of Austria, Belgium, France, Germany, Great Britain, Greece, Italy, the Netherlands, Russia, Spain, Switzerland and Sweden. The Portuguese and Turkish delegates attended the later meetings of the Conference, but did not arrive in time to take part in the earlier meetings.

The Russian Plenipotentiary, Baron Jomini, was elected President. With the circular addressed to the Powers by the Tsar was enclosed a draft project for the consideration of the Conference, and this was taken as a basis. Dr Bluntschli, one of the German delegates, filled the post of Chairman of the Committee on Codification, and in preparing the final draft, considerable use was made of Dr Lieber's "Instructions[2]." The Conference terminated its labours on the 27th August, 1874, and the delegates signed the *Projet de Déclaration* merely as a record of the proceedings and without pledging their Governments[3]. The Declaration was never ratified. Many causes have been assigned for this failure ; among

---

The French Government issued in 1877 a *Manuel de Droit International à l'usage des officiers de l'armée de Terre* ; Russia issued a similar set of instructions in 1877 ; the Netherlands in 1871 issued a Manual prepared by General den Beer Poortugael. At a Congress held at Madrid in 1892, representatives of Spain, Portugal and the Latin American states prepared regulations for their armies ; Spain in 1893 adopted a Manual based on this draft. The *British Manual of Military Law*, issued in 1888, contained a Chapter on "The customs of war" prepared by Lord Thring. (F. Despagnet, *Cours de Droit International Public*, p. 545 ; Sir H. Maine, *Int. Law*, Lectures VII. and VIII.; A. Merignhac, *Les lois et coutumes de la guerre sur terre*, p. 24 ; T. E. Holland, *The laws of war on land*, p. 72)

[1] See post, p. 270, for translation of the Brussels draft Declaration.

[2] G. B. Davis, *Am. Journ. of Int. Law*, Vol. I. p. 22.

[3] For text, see *Parl. Papers*, 1875, LXXII. [c. 1120] ; and for other information as to the Conference, *Parl. Papers*, 1874, LXXVI. [c. 1010], 1875 [c. 1129, 1136]; T. E. Holland, *Studies in International Law*, pp. 59-95 ; J. Lorimer, *Institutes of the Law of Nations*, Vol. II. pp. 337-402 ; J. Westlake, *Chapters on International Law*, Chap. XI. ; Sir H. Maine, *Int. Law*, Chaps. VII.-XI. ; Holtzendorff, § 80, and (for history of attempts at codification), §§ 70-8 ; Bluntschli, pp. 303, 529 et seq.

others, the British Government declined to accept the Declaration on the ground that the Articles contained many innovations, while Germany saw in some of its rules, a condemnation of her recent practices in the conduct of the Franco-German war. The Conference was held too soon after this war "which probably never had a rival in the violence of the passions which it excited[1]." The sections on the occupation of belligerent territory, and the definition of combatants (especially Articles 9 and 10), were fought most keenly, the contest being chiefly between the great military Powers and the smaller ones. Though never forming part of international law, the Declaration has nevertheless had considerable influence, which is reflected in many of the Manuals prepared for the use of armies in the field. But what is even more important, it formed the basis of the "Regulations concerning the laws and customs of war on land" adopted as the annex to the Second Convention of the Hague Conference 1899[2].

The Circular of Count Mouravieff of 11th January, 1899, enumerated

The Hague Conference 1899.

among the subjects for consideration by the Conference "the Declaration concerning the laws and customs of war elaborated in 1874 by the Conference of Brussels, which has remained unratified to the present day." The Brussels Declaration was considered by the Second Sub-Commission of the Second Commission under the presidency of M. de Martens and after a prolonged examination and considerable protests, especially on the part of some of the smaller states, particularly as regards Articles 9, 10 and 11 of the Declaration, the Convention concerning the laws and customs of war on land was agreed to. M. de Martens' appeal to the Committee at the meeting on the 6th June, 1899, was a masterly summary of the reasons for the acceptance by the Powers of a set of rules for land warfare. He said that if their attempt was again to be unsuccessful the result would be fatal and disastrous in the highest degree to the whole of their work, for belligerent governments and their Generals would say, "Twice, in 1874 and 1899, two great International Conferences composed of the most competent and eminent men in the civilised world in this matter have met. They have not been able to determine the laws and customs of war. They have separated, leaving in absolute vagueness all these questions. These eminent men, in discussing these questions of occupation and the rights and duties over invaded territories, have found no solution but to leave everything

---

[1] Sir H. Maine, *Int. Law*, p. 128.

[2] The Institut de Droit International at its meeting at Oxford in 1880 prepared a Manual of the laws of war, a Spanish edition of which was adopted by the Argentine Republic in 1881 for its army (T. E. Holland, *The laws of war on land*, p. 78).

vague and within the domain of the law of nations. How shall we, the Commanders-in-Chief of armies, we who are in the midst of action, find time to settle these disputes when they have been unable to do so in time of peace, when a profound calm reigned in the whole world, and when Governments had met to lay the solid foundation for a common life of peace and concord." At the meeting on the 10th June, Sir John Ardagh on behalf of Great Britain said that in order to avoid a fruitless result of the Conference, it was better to accept the Declaration as a general basis for the instruction of the troops in the laws and customs of war without any express engagement to accept all the Articles which were accepted by the majority. M. de Martens said, "In order to clearly express what is, in the view of the Russian Government, the object of this Conference in this matter, I cannot find a better illustration than that of a 'Mutual Insurance Society against the abuse of force in time of war.' Well, gentlemen, one is free to participate or not in a Society, but for its existence Statutes are necessary. In such Insurance Societies as those against fire, hail, or other calamities the Statutes which anticipate such disasters do not legalise them, but state existing dangers. So it is that in founding by common agreement the 'Society against the abuse of force in time of war' with the object of safeguarding the interests of populations against the greatest disasters, we do not legalise the disasters: we only state them. It is not against the necessities of war, it is solely against the abuse of force that we wish to provide a guarantee[1]."

These explanations appear to provide a sufficient reason for the unique character of the Conventions both of 1899 and 1907. Unlike the others, this Convention does not embody the rules of war to be observed by the belligerents, but a detached *Règlement* contains rules "suitable for communication, disencumbered of alien matter, to troops and others, who have no concern with the mechanism of diplomacy[2]."

The object of the Convention is set forth in the preamble, namely "to revise the laws and general customs of war, either with the view of defining them more precisely, or of laying down certain limits for the purpose of modifying their severity as far as possible." The wording of these provisions was "inspired by the desire to diminish the evils of war so far as military necessities permit" and the Regulations "are intended to serve as general rules of conduct for belligerents in their relations with each other and with populations." The *Règlement* is admittedly incomplete,

The Conventions.

---

[1] *Parl. Papers*, Misc. No. 1 (1899), pp. 56–8.
[2] T. E. Holland, *The laws of war on land*, p. 5.

and the "high contracting Parties think it right to declare that in cases
not included in the regulations adopted by them, populations and belligerents remain under the protection and the rule of the principles of
the law of nations, as they result from the usages established between
civilised nations, from the laws of humanity, and the requirements of
the public conscience." It is in this sense, especially, that Articles 1 and 2
of the *Règlement*, over which so much controversy took place, are to be
understood. By the Convention (Art. 1) the Parties agree to issue to their
armed land forces instructions which shall be in conformity with the
"Regulations respecting the laws and customs of war on land" annexed
to the Convention[1]. The Regulations are therefore to form the basis of
the instructions to be issued to the troops, but it was open to doubt
whether they had the same literal binding force as if they had been
embodied in a Convention, though the Convention binds the signatory
Powers to an essential observance of all these rules[2].

The Convention of 1899 contained five Articles, that of 1907 contains
nine. The change in Article 3 (1907) is important, a sanction
is now provided for the Regulations. "A belligerent party
which violates the provisions of the said Regulations shall, if
the case demands, be liable to pay compensation. It shall be responsible
for all acts committed by persons forming part of its armed forces." This
would appear to determine the obligatory character of the Regulations.
This proposition was introduced by the German delegate, but as originally
presented it made a distinction between the populations of belligerent states
and neutral persons which appeared to be to the advantage of the latter[3],
but the Conference recognised that in both cases there was a breach of
law and that consequently reparation should as a rule be the same. It
will be noticed that it is the government, and not the individual wrong-
doer from whom reparation is to be demanded. The German draft
fixed the time and mode of the settlement; in the case of violations of the
laws of war as against a belligerent the settlement of the question was to

Changes in the Conven- tion in 1907.

---

[1] T. E. Holland, *op. cit.*, Appendix I. gives a list of countries which have published Regulations for their armies: they include Great Britain (*Handbook of the laws and customs of
war on land* prepared by Professor Holland in 1904), France and Italy. For Russian
and Japanese Rules of Warfare see A. S. Hershey, *International law and diplomacy of the
Russo-Japanese War*, Chapter X.

[2] See on this subject, F. Despagnet, *Droit International*, § 510; T. E. Holland, *op. cit.*
p. 6; L. Oppenheim, *Int. Law*, Vol. II. p. 77 (note 2); E. A. Whittuck, *International
documents*, p. xviii.; J. Westlake, *War*, p. 57.

[3] For original German proposal see *Parl. Papers*, Misc. No. 4 (1908), p. 105; *La Deux.
Confér.* T. I. p. 103. The German military delegate explained that the distinction drawn had
reference only to the settlement of the mode of payment of indemnities.

be postponed until the conclusion of the war, but in the case of injuries to a neutral, the necessary measures were to be taken to assure the promptest reparation compatible with military necessities[1].

The other changes in the Convention are in reference to the arrangements for accession and denunciation, and are in accordance with the scheme adopted in most of the other Conventions.

The Second Committee of the Conference of 1907 was entrusted with

Change in the Regulations in 1907. the subjects comprised in the second paragraph of the Russian programme; the amelioration of the existing laws and usages of war as embodied in the Convention of the First Conference, together with additions relating thereto, such as questions relating to the commencement of war, rights of neutrals on land etc., and the Declarations of 1899. The work was allotted to two Sub-Committees: the first presided over by M. Beernaert (Belgium) took into consideration the Convention concerning the laws and usages of war of 1899 and the Declarations of 1899; the Reporter was Baron von Gieslingen (Austria-Hungary). The Report was presented to the Fourth Plenary Meeting of the Conference on the 17th August, 1907, when the amendments now to be referred to were adopted with certain reservations which will be mentioned subsequently. As Baron von Gieslingen states in his Report, the revision of the Convention and Regulations was not undertaken with a view of re-casting them but only in order to make amendments in points of detail, and the alterations make no very material changes in the work of the Conference of 1899. It was only at the last moment that amendments were forthcoming; when the Sub-Committee commenced its labours there were none before it. Questions affecting the position of neutral persons were transferred to the Second Sub-Committee, and Articles 57 to 60 (99) now form Articles 11, 12, 14 and 15 of the new Convention (No. 5) with regard to neutrals in land warfare.

ARTICLE 2. The amendment in this Article relating to levies *en masse* requires that in addition to respecting the laws and usages of war such persons as have not had time to organise themselves in accordance with Article 1 "must carry arms openly." This amendment was inserted on the proposition of the German delegate. This was carried in Committee by 30 to 3, with 2 abstentions.

ARTICLE 5 relates to the internment of prisoners. There is a difference between internment and confinement[2]; the latter is the more rigorous, and

---

[1] *Livre Jaune*, p. 77; E. Lémonon, *La seconde Conférence de la Paix*, p. 381.

[2] See G. B. Davis, *Am. Journ. of Int. Law*, Vol. II. p. 68; T. E. Holland, *Laws of war on land*, p. 21.

the Cuban amendment which was adopted unanimously[1] now provides that this closer form of detention of prisoners can only be continued so long as the circumstances which necessitate the measure continue to exist.

ARTICLE 6.   There are two slight changes in this Article.   The first proposed by the Spanish delegate exempts officers who are prisoners of war from being compelled to work.   The second proposed by the Japanese delegate provided for cases where the laws of states make no provision for payment to prisoners of war, and says that where no schedule of rates of payment exists, the remuneration shall be proportionate to the work done.

ARTICLE 14.   Articles 14–20 (99) were additions to the Brussels Declaration and made provision for a Bureau for information relative to prisoners of war, and gave relief societies for prisoners facilities to carry out their objects.   Certain defects in the working of these Bureaux which both Russia and Japan had established during the war were considered, and especially in the case of Article 14[2].   The Japanese and Cuban delegates proposed the amendments which were adopted, and which require additional details to be kept regarding prisoners of war, including those who have been released on parole, or exchanged or who have escaped.

ARTICLE 17.   The alteration in this Article was also the result of a Japanese proposal slightly modified in Committee[3].   Article 17 (99) provided that officers who were prisoners might receive, in proper cases, the full pay allowed them while in this position by the regulations of their own country, the amount to be repaid by their Government.   There appear to have been doubts as to the actual meaning of this Article and some Governments, e.g. the United States, make no provision for such a case[4].   The original Japanese draft left the matter in a very equivocal condition and the Sub-Committee, having referred to the corresponding Article in the Geneva Convention of 1906 as regards the pay of the *personnel* of the Medical Service in the enemy's hands (Chapter iii. Art. 13)[5],

---

[1] In *La Deux. Confér.* T. I. p. 97; *Parl. Papers*, Misc. No. 4 (1908), p. 101. E. Lémonon, *op. cit.* p. 349, states that the United States Delegation voted against the alteration.

[2] For text of Imperial Japanese Ordinance relating to the Bureau of information see A. S. Hershey, *International law and diplomacy, etc.* p. 289; see also S. Takahashi, *International law applied to the Russo-Japanese War*, pp. 94–146.

[3] The original Japanese proposal was as follows : " Le Gouvernement accordera, s'il y a lieu, aux officiers prisonniers entre ses mains une solde convenable, à charge de remboursement par leur Gouvernement."   *Parl. Papers*, Misc. No. 4 (1908), p. 101; *La Deux. Confér.* T. I. p. 98.

[4] G. B. Davis, *Am. Journ. of Int. Law*, Vol. II. p. 69.

[5] See *supra*, p. 25.

proposed the Article in the form in which it now stands, so that officers taken prisoner receive the pay allowed to officers of the same rank of the country whose prisoners they are, the amount to be repaid by their Government.

ARTICLE 23 (paragraph *h*).   This addition to Article 23 of the Regulations of 1899 which contains a list of seven acts a belligerent is forbidden to perform was made on the proposition of the German delegate.   The meaning to be attributed to this clause is open to doubt.   At the meeting of the *Comité de rédaction* of the First Sub-Committee of the Second Committee on the 3rd July the President asked for further information with reference to the proposal.   Herr Göppert, the German delegate, explained that the proposal was intended not to confine the inviolability of enemy property to corporeal property and that it had in view the whole domain of obligations by prohibiting all legislative measures which, in time of war, would place the subject of an enemy state in a position of being unable to prosecute the execution of a contract before the courts of the adverse party.   On the 13th July, in the First Sub-Committee, General Yermolow (Russian) proposed to introduce an amendment to the German proposition allowing in certain cases during the war the seizure of debts or documents (*de saisir des créances ou des titres*) belonging to the enemy which might assist in the continuance of the hostilities.   This proposal was not accepted, and the text as it now stands was adopted.   In the Report of Baron von Gieslingen to the Fourth Plenary Meeting of the Conference he states that " this addition [i.e. paragraph *h*] was considered to define in felicitous terms one of the consequences of the principles admitted in 1899[1]."   The introduction to the German *Weissbuch* states that by this paragraph " the principle of the inviolability in the department of justice is recognised.   According to the legislation of some states the consequences of war are that the claims of states or their subjects against the nationals of the enemy are extinguished or suspended or inadmissible in a Court of Law.   Such provisions are henceforth by Article 23 (*h*) declared to be invalid[2]."

General Davis in discussing the meaning of this paragraph states that the purport of the whole Convention was to impose reasonable and wholesome restrictions upon the authority of commanding generals and their subordinates in the theatre of belligerent activity.   "It is more than probable that this humane and commendable purpose would fail of accomplishment if a military commander conceived it to be within his authority to suspend

---

[1] *Parl. Papers*, Misc. No. 4 (1907), p. 104; *La Deux. Confér.* T. I. p. 101.

[2] *Weissbuch*, p. 7.

or nullify their operation, or to regard their application in certain cases as a matter falling within his administrative discretion. Especially is this true where a military officer refuses to receive well grounded complaints, or declines to receive demands for redress, in respect to the acts or conduct of the troops under his command, from persons subject to the jurisdiction of the enemy who find themselves, for the time being, in the territory which he holds in military occupation. To provide against such a contingency it was deemed wise to add an appropriate declaratory clause to the prohibition of Article 23[1]."

Professor Holland in commenting on this new prohibition remarks that " if this clause is intended only for the guidance of an invading commander it needs careful re-drafting: if, as would rather appear, it is of general application, besides being quite out of place where it stands, it is so revolutionary of the doctrine which denies to an enemy any *persona standi in judicio* that although it is included in the ratification of the Convention by the United States on March 10, 1908, and the signature of the same on June 29, 1908, by Great Britain, it can hardly, till its policy has been seriously discussed, be treated as rule of international law[2]." In his introductory chapter to "The Laws of War on Land" Professor Holland cites this paragraph as an instance of the inconvenience of inter-mixing rules relating to the duties of belligerent Governments at home with those intended to serve for the guidance of armies in the field; he adds that the clause seems to require the signatory Powers to legislate for the abolition of an enemy's disability to sustain a *persona standi in judicio*[3].

In favour of the view propounded by General Davis it may be pointed out that the instruction is one addressed to commanders of armies in the field, and therefore such a prohibition has only reference to their pro-ceedings in an enemy country. Article 32 of Dr Lieber's "Instructions for the government of the armies of the United States" provides that "a victorious army, by the martial power inherent in the same, may suspend, change or abolish, as far as the martial power extends, the relations which arise from the services due, according to the existing laws of the invaded country, from one citizen, subject or native of the same to another." The object of this provision was to enable .the Federal Generals to set aside slavery in the Confederate territory occupied, and the Article of the

---

[1] *Am. Journ. of Int. Law*, Vol. II. p. 70; also *Elements of International Law* (1908), p. 578. The Report in *The Times* of the 1st Aug. 1907 is as follows, " The Committee adopted unanimously without a vote a German proposal imposing upon belligerents the duty to respect contractual obligations in an enemy's country."

[2] *The laws of war on land*, p. 44.   [3] *Op. cit.* p. 5.

"Instructions" attributed to them a power which was not theirs by the general rules of law. The paragraph under consideration would have the effect of negativing the view contained in the Article of the "Instructions," but it appears to do more than this. Dr Lieber's Article refers to "relations...from one citizen, subject or native of the same to another"; Article 23 (*h*) of the present Convention refers to the "rights...of the adverse party."

If the view taken by the German *Weissbuch* be correct, and so far as I have been able to ascertain from the official records of the proceedings at the Conference it was the only view expressed during the discussions, Article 23 (*h*) constitutes a reversal of a rule of the English and American Common Law that contracts entered into by British subjects and subjects of the belligerent states, before the outbreak of war, become extinguished or suspended according to their nature[1]; in England it has been stated by writers of great authority that statutes of limitation run during a war as against enemies, though the contrary has been decided in the United States[2]. According to the strict wording of this paragraph some states may read it either with the restrictive meaning attached to it by General Davis, others with the more extended meaning given by the German *Weissbuch*[3] if the latter view is taken by Great Britain legislation will probably be required to give it effect.

ARTICLE 23 (2nd paragraph) and ARTICLE 44. The alterations in these two Articles both have relation to the limits of compulsion which an invader may apply to the inhabitants of the invaded territory. They are dealt with together in the Report of Baron von Gieslingen.

The second paragraph of Article 23 is based on a proposal introduced by the German delegate. Originally it was intended to form a new Article between 22 and 23, and to take the place of Article 44; it is throughout the discussion referred to as 22 *a*. As introduced by Germany the proposal was as follows: "A belligerent is also forbidden to compel the

---

[1] W. E. Hall, *Int. Law*, p. 393; T. J. Lawrence, *Int. Law*, § 165; H. Taylor, *Int. Law*, § 465; J. Westlake, *War*, p. 44; Wheaton, *Int. Law*, § 305; J. B. Scott, *Leading Cases in Int. Law*, pp. 498–554. L. Oppenheim, *Int. Law*, Vol. II. § 101, considers the rules of the English and American Courts are merely rules of municipal law and not of international law, and that such a rule of international law as that prohibiting peaceful intercourse between subjects of the belligerent states does not exist, and never has existed, but he appears to be almost alone in this opinion among British writers. See F. Despagnet, *Droit inter.* p. 631, who states the rule of non-intercourse as one generally admitted.

[2] See authorities cited by J. Westlake, *War*, p. 49.

[3] M. Fauchille appears to understand the paragraph in the latter sense (Bonfils-Fauchille, *Droit international* (5th ed.), § 1065).

subjects (*ressortissants*)[1] of the enemy to take part in the operations of war directed against their own country (*contre leur propre pays*) even in cases where they are in the service of the other belligerent before the commencement of the war." The Austro-Hungarian delegate moved to insert the words "as combatants" after the words "take part." The Austrian amendment was opposed by the French, Belgian and Swiss delegates as legalising the employment of guides taken from the population of the invaded country. The Austro-Hungarian and Russian delegates supported this amendment on the ground that frequently in mountainous countries, maps were practically valueless, and local guides were essential to an invading army. The Austrian amendment was rejected by 11 to 2, and the German proposal accepted with a slight verbal alteration. The Committee decided to suppress Article 44 (99) and in its place to insert a Dutch proposal moved by General den Beer Poortugael as 44 a. This proposal was as follows : " It is forbidden to compel the inhabitants (*population*) of an occupied territory to give information (*éclaircissements*) about their own army or the means of defence of their country."

Forced guides.

The German proposal for Article 22 a was a development of the principle accepted in 1899, as regards the forced participation of the inhabitants of an occupied territory in military operations against their own country, by extending to all persons therein (*ressortissants*) the prohibition in which the Regulation did not expressly give them the benefit. It even extended it to foreign subjects who might have been in the service of the other belligerent before the commencement of the war. It was on account of the general application of the Article that the German delegate proposed its insertion in the 2nd section of the Regulations, relating to the means of injuring the enemy. The German proposal had an extensive character ; the Austrian had a quite different meaning, as it permitted the compulsion of the inhabitants to render assistance of every kind short of fighting, and especially the employment of forced guides, and the giving of military information. The Austro-Hungarian delegate desired to draw a clear distinction between "operations of war" in which the inhabitants of the enemy state could not be compelled to take part, and " military services" which it was sought in exceptional cases to be able to impose on them[2].

At the meeting of the Sub-Committee on the 24th July Baron von

---

[1] The word *ressortissant* appears to have a wider meaning than subject, and to include all over whom a state claims to exercise jurisdiction either by virtue of allegiance or domicile.

[2] *Parl. Papers*, Misc. No. 4 (1908), p. 102; *La Deux. Confér.* T. I. p. 99.

Gieslingen presented his report on the foregoing, and the President (M. Beernaert) summarised the position which had been reached. Baron von Gieslingen defended with considerable vehemence the Austrian amendment before mentioned. General Yermolow (Russia) again supported the Austrian view. "The services of the inhabitants," he said, "are often indispensable to the army in the form of road mending, for camps, hospital trains, etc. Such services are already authorised by Article 52 which provides that they may be required from the inhabitants for the needs of the army. Consequently if the German proposal is accepted without the addition of the Austro-Hungarian amendment, there will be a contradiction to Article 52 and the whole question will be brought into ambiguity, obscurity and confusion. Either maintain the existing rules or accept Article 22 a with the Austro-Hungarian amendment."

General den Beer Poortugael (Holland) supported the recommendation of the Committee, and urged that it was immoral to authorise the practice of exacting the service of guides. General Amourel (France) spoke in the same sense, supporting the German and Dutch proposals, because their objects were to definitely forbid (*de consacrer l'interdiction*) the use of forced guides. Colonel Borel (Switzerland) also supported the German-Dutch proposal.

M. Beernaert (Belgium) with a view to combine the two proposals moved the following: "To replace Article 44 (or whatever be the number assigned to it) and Article 44 a proposed by the Dutch delegate by the following: 'It is forbidden to force the inhabitants (*habitants*) of an occupied territory to take part personally either directly or indirectly, collectively or individually in military operations against their country and to demand from them information in view of such operations[1].'" The advantages claimed for this were that the word *habitants* was less equivocal than *populations*, and that the words "directly or indirectly, collectively or individually" left no doubt as to the meaning of "military operations." The Russian delegate proposed to leave Article 44 (99) intact, and to place the German proposition 22 a without the Austrian amendment in a chapter by itself headed "*Des ressortissants d'un belligérant dans le territoire de la Partie adverse*". Baron von Gieslingen still maintained his point, but professed his willingness to accept the Russian amendment if his own failed to be carried. The Belgian compromise was finally carried by the small majority of 3 (18 *for*, 15 *against*), but this was not sufficient and once more the subject was sent to the *Comité de rédaction* which finally decided to retain the separate propositions 22 a and 44 a with the two following changes of "contre leur pays" instead of "contre leur *propre* pays" in Article 22 a,

[1] E. Lémonon, *op. cit.* p. 361.

and the substitution of the words *les habitants* for *la population* in Article 44 a. M. Beernaert pointed out that the Russian amendment avoided the question of the employment of guides and forced information without providing a solution either way. General den Beer Poortugael then made an eloquent appeal in support of the proposed alteration. He pleaded that the greatest respect should be shown to the inhabitants of occupied districts, a principle on which Wellington had acted, and which inspired the proclamation of the King of Prussia issued at Saarbrücken in 1870. War was between states and not between individuals, the peaceful inhabitants must not be compelled to take part in it. The German proposition 22 a was carried as was also the Dutch 44 a, the latter by 23 to 9 with 1 abstention.

The Report came before the Conference at its Fourth Plenary Meeting on the 17th August, 1908, when Article 22 a was accepted unanimously, but when Article 44 a was reached Baron Marschall (Germany) explained that he was unable to accept it on the ground that it was impossible to specify particular instances of acts already prohibited by Article 22 a [i.e. Article 23, par. 2 of the present Regulations]. In endeavouring to do this there was a risk either of unduly limiting the freedom of military action, or of producing an interpretation which according to the maxim " qui dicit de uno, negat de altro " would allow all acts being considered lawful which were not expressly forbidden[1].

In signing the Convention, Germany, Austria-Hungary, Japan, Montenegro and Russia made reservations on the subject of this Article. In the introduction to the German *Weissbuch* the non-acceptance of Article 44 by Germany is explained as being due to the fact that it selects in an undesirable manner single instances from the cases to which the principles contained in Article 23, par. 2, are applicable[2].

Reservations on Article 44.

All the Powers, except China, Spain and Nicaragua, have signed this Convention and the signatory Powers in accepting these two amendments have registered a distinct advance in ameliorating the conditions of the inhabitants of invaded districts. As a result of these two Articles such persons cannot be compelled to take part in "operations of war." This expression is unsatisfactorily vague, but from the discussions there can be no doubt that it was understood to include the employment of the enemy's subjects as guides; and Article 44 forbids a belligerent to force the inhabitants of "occupied" territory to furnish information about the army of the

---

[1] *Parl. Papers*, Misc. No. 4 (1908), p. 94; *La Deux. Confér.* T. 1. p. 86.
[2] See *Weissbuch*, p. 7.

other belligerent, or about its means of defence, thus specifying in detail certain of the prohibitions expressed in more general terms in Article 23.

Article 44 (99) was ambiguous, and the employment of guides was by many authorities deemed not to be prohibited. The German General Staff treated their employment as permissible; Professor Holland also considered that their employment was not rendered unlawful by it: the Japanese resorted to this practice in their war against China[1]. Professor Holland considers that the question is still doubtful, but Article 44 of the new Convention is much more definite than the old Article, and the amendment moved by the Austrian delegate, and supported by the Russian, was with the express object of legalising the employment of forced guides which these delegates clearly thought was forbidden[2]. The new paragraph to Article 23 makes use of the phrase "operations of war" which may be taken to cover a wider range than "military operations." The same expression is used in Article 52, to which reference was made by the Russian delegate, and it is therein provided that the services permitted to be demanded from localities or inhabitants can only be required for the needs of the army of occupation, and must be of such a nature as not to imply any obligation on the population to take part in "operations of war" against their country.

Under Article 2 of the Convention, the Regulations only apply as between the Contracting Powers, and then only if all the belligerents are parties to the Convention. Germany, Austria, Japan, Montenegro and Russia have expressly refused to accept Article 44, but if the view above expressed is correct they are all now by virtue of their acceptance of the other Articles bound for the future to refrain from forcing inhabitants of an invaded enemy territory to act as guides to their armies.

In another direction, Article 23, par. 2, also makes an important alteration by providing that the subjects of a state in the service of the other belligerent before the outbreak of war cannot be compelled to take part in operations of war directed against their own country[3].

ARTICLE 25. The addition to this Article of the words "by any

---

[1] See J. Westlake, *War*, p. 91; T. E. Holland, *The laws and customs of war on land* (1904), p. 34; L. Oppenheim, *Int. Law*, Vol. II. p. 175.

[2] "*Par l'article 44 notamment une des pratiques les plus odieuses de la guerre, l'emploi des guides forcés et la contrainte exercée sur les populations envahies pour en obtenir des renseignements militaires, a été solennellement interdite.*" (Report of French Delegation, *Livre Jaune*, p. 107.)

[3] I desire to acknowledge my indebtedness to the work of M. Lémonon already cited; the account of the discussions on this subject are extremely valuable (see pp. 358–364). See also *Parl. Papers*, Misc. No. 4 (1908), pp. 24, 102; *La Deux. Confér*. T. I. pp. 86, 99–101; *Livre Jaune*, p. 76; *Weissbuch*, p. 7.

means whatever" was understood to cover the case of bombardment of undefended towns by projectiles from balloons. The first Declaration of 1899 against the discharge of projectiles and explosives from balloons, a Declaration which was not limited to undefended places, was renewed in 1907, but it has not been accepted by many of the great military Powers[1]. The words "by any means whatever" were introduced on the proposition of the French delegate, in order to make clear the illegality of employing such a method of attack against an undefended town. These words take the place of a much more lengthy proposal introduced by the Russian and Italian delegates. The prohibition is therefore of unlimited duration, whereas the Declaration lasts only until the termination of the next Conference, unless it is renewed by it.

ARTICLE 27.   With a view of bringing the recommendation of the Second Committee into harmony with those of the Third Committee relating to naval bombardments[2] the Greek delegate suggested the inclusion of "historical monuments" in the list of buildings which are to be spared, as far as possible, in bombardments. This was unanimously accepted.

ARTICLE 52.   M. Tcharkyow (Russia) proposed to complete this Article by a provision that commanders should be authorised to settle as soon as possible *during* the continuance of hostilities the receipts given for requisition. The wording of the addition was settled by the *Comité de rédaction*, leaving the time and mode of payment indefinite (*le plus tôt possible*).

ARTICLE 53, par. 2.   This paragraph which deals with the property which an army of occupation may appropriate is based on a proposal made by the Austro-Hungarian delegate.   His proposition was to add to the paragraph referring to the means of transport the words "sur terre, sur mer et dans les airs."   The *Comité de rédaction* proposed a new paragraph enumerating various modes of transport, but the Committee thought it advisable not to make a specific enumeration owing to the dangers of incompleteness.   A general formula which did not lend itself to any ambiguity was thought preferable, and this was adopted.   The military delegate of Japan raised the question of the appropriateness of including means of transport by sea in regulations for land warfare, but the Committee considered it advisable to retain the words "sur mer" as the right of maritime capture was applicable in land warfare in the case of ships seized in a port by a body of troops, especially as regards those destined for river navigation.

ARTICLE 54.   This Article was originally proposed by the Danish delegate as a third paragraph to Article 53.   It now takes the place of

---

Article 54 (99) which related to neutral railway plant, and which is transferred to the 5th Convention, where it stands, with certain alterations, as Article 19[1].

The subject of submarine cables was introduced at the Conference of 1899, when the Danish delegate proposed to add after the words "télégraphes de terre" the words "y compris les fils d'atterrissage établis dans les limites du territoire maritime de l'État." This was objected to by the British delegate as involving the discussion of matters relating to maritime warfare, which were outside the scope of Articles dealing exclusively with land warfare. The Article then under discussion (which subsequently became Article 53 (99)) was drafted so as to include "câbles d'atterrissage." In a Memorandum from the War Office to the Foreign Office of 19th July, 1899, on this subject, it was stated that "Lord Lansdowne does not consider that their exclusion [i.e. the exclusion of the words 'câbles d'atterrissage'] affects military interests in any way, as the dominant military Power on land would, under any circumstances, have adequate control over the landing places of cables in an occupied territory, whether the words were inserted or not; and he is further of opinion that if submarine cables are dealt with internationally as a whole, the particular case of the 'câbles d'atterrissage' should be considered whenever that subject may come under discussion." The words were subsequently excluded from the Article[2].

The question was again raised in 1907 by the Danish delegate, and the proposal was accepted with the omission of the words "ou ennemi" after "occupé." Submarine cables which connect an occupied territory with a neutral are not to be seized or destroyed except in case of absolute necessity. They must be restored and the compensation to be paid for them is to be arranged for on the conclusion of peace. This is the only international agreement affecting submarine cables in time of war. The Institut de Droit International devoted considerable attention to the subject, and at the meeting at Brussels in 1902 adopted five resolutions for the treatment of cables by belligerents[3]. There appears to be a general

Submarine Cables.

---

[1] See *post*, p. 286.
[2] *Parl. Papers*, Misc. No. 1 (1899), pp. 88, 178.
[3] *Annuaire*, Vol. XIX. p. 331. 1. A submarine cable connecting neutral territories is inviolable. 2. A cable connecting the territories of the two belligerents or two parts of the territory of one of the belligerents may be cut anywhere except in territorial waters or the neutralised waters of a neutral. 3. A cable connecting the territories of a neutral may in no case be cut in neutral waters, and only in the high seas if there is an effective blockade, subject to the duty of its being re-established within the shortest possible time. A cable can always be cut within enemy territory or territorial waters. 4. A neutral state must only allow the transmission of despatches which clearly do not lend assistance to one of the

agreement that cables connecting neutral territory are inviolable, that cables connecting enemy territory may be cut anywhere except in neutral waters, and that under this Article, in case of necessity, cables connecting an occupied enemy territory may be cut within such territory. The foregoing rules were adopted by the United States Naval Code of 1900, which was withdrawn in 1904. The International Convention for the protection of submarine cables of 1884 expressly states that its provisions in no way limit the liberty of actions of belligerents (Art. 15)[1].

The changes made in the Regulations will be seen to be on the whole slight. The most important, namely, the additions to Article 23 and the alteration in Article 44, are open to different constructions, and the non-acceptance of the latter by several important military Powers prevents it from ranking as a rule of universal international law. The alterations in the other Articles are on points of detail, or are legitimate deductions from admitted principles. The changes are all in the direction of ameliorating the conditions of land warfare, and strengthening the terms of the " Policy of Insurance against the abuse of force in time of war."

Signatory Powers. All the states present at the Conference have signed the Convention except China, Spain and Nicaragua, and the only reservations of importance made are those already referred to in connection with Article 23, par. 2. Turkey made a reservation as regards Article 3.

belligerents. 5. In applying the above rules, no difference is to be made between cables owned by the state and private individuals, nor between cables which are enemy and neutral property.

[1] De Martens, *Nouveau Recueil Général* (2nd series), Vol. xi. p. 281 ; 48 and 49 Vic., c. 49. For a further discussion of this topic see J. Westlake, *War*, p. 280 ; A. S. Hershey, *International law and diplomacy, etc.* p. 122; O. Phillipson, *Two studies in international law*, pp. 55–116; also the report of the discussions at the Institut de Droit International, *Annuaire*, Vol. xix.

Appendix to Note on the Laws and Customs of War on Land.

Translation of the Draft of an International Declaration concerning the Laws and Customs of War adopted by the Conference of Brussels, 27th August, 1874[1].

Of Military Authority over the Hostile State.

Art. 1. A territory is considered as occupied when it is actually placed under the authority of the hostile army.

The occupation applies only to the territory where such authority is established, and in a position to assert itself. (*See Art. 42 of Hague Regulations, No. 3, 1899.*)

Art. 2. The authority of the legitimate power being suspended and having actually passed into the hands of the occupant, the latter shall take all steps in his power to re-establish and insure, as far as possible, public order and safety. (*See Art. 43 of H. R., which combines Arts. 2 and 3.*)

Art. 3. With this object he will maintain the laws which were in force in the country in time of peace, and will only modify, suspend or replace them by others if necessity obliges him to do so.

Art. 4. The functionaries and officials of every class who at the instance of the occupier consent to continue to perform their duties shall be under his protection. They shall not be dismissed or liable to summary punishment (*punis disciplinairement*) unless they fail in fulfilling the obligations they have undertaken, and shall be handed over to justice only if they violate those obligations by unfaithfulness. (*Omitted from H. R.*)

Art. 5. The army of occupation shall only levy such taxes, dues, duties and tolls as are already established for the benefit of the State, or their equivalent, if it be impossible to collect them, and this shall be done so far as possible in the form of and according to existing practice. It shall devote them to defraying the expenses of the administration of the country to the same extent as was obligatory on the legitimate government. (*See Art. 48 of H. R.*)

Art. 6. The army occupying a territory shall take possession only of the specie, the funds and realisable securities (*valeurs exigibles*) which are the property of the State in its own right, the depôts of arms, means of transport, magazines and supplies, and, in general, all the personal property of the State which is of a nature to aid in carrying on the war.

Railway plant, land telegraphs, steam and other vessels, not included in

· [1] See *ante*, p. 257.

cases regulated by maritime law, as well as depôts of arms, and generally every kind of munitions of war, although belonging to companies or to private individuals, are to be considered equally as means of a nature to aid in carrying on war, which cannot be left by the army of occupation at the disposal of the enemy. Railway plant, land telegraphs, as well as the steam and other vessels above mentioned, shall be restored and indemnities be regulated on the conclusion of peace. (*See Art. 53 of H. R.*)

Art. 7. The occupying State shall only consider itself in the light of an administrator and usufructuary of the public buildings, real property, forests, and agricultural undertakings belonging to the hostile State, and situated in the occupied territory. It should protect the capital of these properties (*fonds de ces propriétés*), and administer them according to the laws of usufruct. (*See Art. 55 of H. R.*)

Art. 8. The property of communes, institutions devoted to religion, charity and education, to arts and sciences, even when State property, shall be treated as private property.

All seizure of, and destruction of, or intentional damage to such institutions, to historical monuments, works of art or science, should be made the subject of proceedings by the competent authorities. (*See Art. 56 of H. R.*)

Of those who are to be recognized as Belligerents ; of Combatants and Non-combatants.

Art. 9. The laws, rights and duties of war apply not only to armies, but likewise to militia and corps of volunteers, fulfilling the following conditions :—

1. That they have at their head a person responsible for his subordinates;
2. That they wear some fixed distinctive badge recognizable at a distance ;
3. That they carry arms openly ; and
4. That in their operations they conform to the laws and customs of war.

In those countries where the militia form the whole or part of the army, they shall be included under the denomination of "army." (*See Art. 1 of H. R.*)

Art. 10. The population of a non-occupied territory, who on the approach of the enemy spontaneously take up arms to resist the invading troops, without having had time to organize themselves in conformity with Article 9, shall be considered as belligerents, if they respect the laws and customs of war. (*See Art. 2 of H. R.*)

Art. 11. The armed forces of the belligerents may be composed of combatants and non-combatants. In the event of being captured by the enemy, both shall enjoy the rights of prisoners of war. (*See Art. 3 of H. R.*)

Of means of Injuring the Enemy.

ART. 12. The laws of war do not allow to belligerents an unlimited power as to the choice of means of injuring the enemy. (*See Art. 22 of H. R.*)

ART. 13. According to this principle are strictly forbidden—

(*a*) The use of poison or poisoned weapons.

(*b*) Murder by treachery of individuals belonging to the hostile nation or army.

(*c*) Murder of an enemy, who, having laid down his arms or having no longer the means of defending himself, has surrendered at discretion.

(*d*) The declaration that no quarter will be given.

(*e*) The use of arms, projectiles or material which may cause unnecessary suffering, as well as the use of the projectiles prohibited by the Declaration of St Petersburg in 1868.

(*f*) Abuse of the flag of truce, the national flag, or the military insignia or uniform of the enemy, as well as the distinctive badges of the Geneva Convention.

(*g*) All destruction or seizure of the property of the enemy which is not imperatively required by the necessity of war. (*See Art. 23 of H. R.*)

ART. 14. Ruses of war and the employment of means necessary to procure intelligence respecting the enemy and the country (subject to the provisions of Article 36) are considered as lawful. (*See Art. 24 of H. R.*)

Of Sieges and Bombardments.

ART. 15. Fortified places are alone liable to be besieged. Towns, agglomerations of houses or open villages which are undefended, cannot be attacked or bombarded. (*See Art. 25 of H. R.*)

ART. 16. But if a town or fortress, agglomeration of houses, or village, be defended, the commander of the attacking forces should, before commencing a bombardment, and except in the case of surprise (*l'attaque de vive force*), do all in his power to warn the authorities. (*See Art. 26 of H. R.*)

ART. 17. In the like case, all necessary steps should be taken to spare, as far as possible, buildings devoted to religion, arts, sciences and charity, hospitals, and places where sick and wounded are collected, on condition that they are not used at the same time for military purposes.

It is the duty of the besieged to indicate these buildings by special visible signs, to be notified beforehand by the besieged. (*See Art. 27 of H. R.*)

ART. 18. A town taken by storm shall not be given up to the victorious troops to plunder. (*See Art. 28 of H. R.*)

Of Spies.

ART. 19. An individual shall be considered as a spy if, acting secretly or under false pretences, he collects, or tries to collect, information in districts occupied by the enemy, with the intention of communicating it to the hostile party. (*See Art.* 29 *of H. R.*)

ART. 20. A spy, if taken in the act, shall be tried and treated according to the laws in force in the army which captures him. (*See Art.* 30 *of H. R.*)

ART. 21. A spy who rejoins the army to which he belongs and who is subsequently captured by the enemy is to be treated as a prisoner of war, and incurs no responsibility for his previous acts. (*See Art.* 31 *of H. R.*)

ART. 22. Soldiers (*les militaires*) not in disguise who have penetrated within the zone of operations of the enemy's army, with the intention of collecting information, are not considered as spies.

In like manner, soldiers (and also non-military persons carrying out their mission openly) charged with the transmission of despatches, either to their own army or to that of the enemy, shall not be considered as spies if captured by the enemy.

To this class belong also, if captured, individuals sent in balloons to carry despatches, and generally to keep up communications between the different parts of an army or of a territory. (*See Art.* 29 *of H. R.*)

Of Prisoners of War.

ART. 23. Prisoners of war are lawful and disarmed enemies. They are in the power of the enemy's Government, but not of the individuals or of the corps who made them prisoners.

They should be treated with humanity.

Every act of insubordination authorizes the necessary measures of severity to be taken with regard to them.

All their personal effects except their arms are considered to be their own property. (*See Art.* 4 *of H. R.*)

ART. 24. Prisoners of war are liable to internment in a town, fortress, camp, or any locality whatever, under an obligation not to go beyond certain fixed limits; but they may not be placed in confinement (*enfermés*) unless absolutely necessary as a measure of security. (*See Art.* 5 *of H. R.*)

ART. 25. Prisoners of war may be employed on certain public works which have no immediate connection with the operations on the theatre of war, provided the employment be not excessive, nor humiliating to their military rank if they belong to the army, or to their official or social position if they do not belong to it.

They may also, subject to such regulations as may be drawn up by the military authorities, undertake private work.

The pay they receive will go towards ameliorating their position, or will be paid to them at the time of their release. In this case the cost of their maintenance may be deducted from their pay. (*See Art. 6 of H. R.*)

ART. 26. Prisoners of war cannot be compelled in any way to take any part whatever in carrying on the operations of war. (*See Art. 6 of H. R.*)

ART. 27. The Government, in whose power are the prisoners of war, undertakes to provide for their maintenance.

The conditions of such maintenance may be settled by a mutual understanding between the belligerents.

In default of such an understanding, and as a general principle, prisoners of war shall be treated, as regards food and clothing, on the same footing as the troops of the Government who made them prisoners. (*See Art. 7 of H. R.*)

ART. 28. Prisoners of war are subject to the laws and regulations in force in the army in whose power they are.

Arms may be used, after summoning, against a prisoner attempting to escape. If retaken, he is subject to summary punishment (*peines disciplinaires*), or to a stricter surveillance.

If, after having succeeded in making his escape, he is again made prisoner, he is not liable to any punishment for his previous escape. (*See Art. 8 of H. R.*)

ART. 29. Every prisoner is bound to declare, if questioned on the point, his true names and rank, and in the case of his infringing this rule he will incur a restriction of the advantages granted to the prisoners of the class to which he belongs. (*See Art. 9 of H. R.*)

ART. 30. The exchange of prisoners of war is regulated by mutual agreement between the belligerents. (*Omitted from H. R.*)

ART. 31. Prisoners of war may be released on parole if the laws of their country allow of it, and in such a case they are bound on their personal honour to fulfil scrupulously, as regards their own Government as well as that which made them prisoners, the engagements they have undertaken.

In the same case their own Government should neither demand nor accept from them any service contrary to their parole. (*See Art. 10 of H. R.*)

ART. 32. A prisoner of war cannot be forced to accept release on parole, nor is the enemy's Government obliged to comply with the request of a prisoner claiming to be released on parole. (*See Art. 11 of H. R.*)

ART. 33. Every prisoner of war liberated on parole, and retaken carrying arms against the Government to which he had pledged his honour, may be deprived of the rights accorded to prisoners of war, and may be brought before the courts. (*See Art. 12 of H. R.*)

ART. **34.** Persons who are with armies, but who do not directly form part of them, such as correspondents, newspaper reporters, sutlers, contractors, &c., may also be made prisoners of war.

These persons should, however, be furnished with a permit issued by a competent authority, as well as with a certificate of identity. (*See Art.* 13 *of H. R.*)

Of the Sick and Wounded.

ART. **35.** The duties of belligerents with regard to the treatment of sick and wounded are regulated by the Convention of Geneva of the 22nd August, 1864, subject to the modifications which may be introduced into that Convention. (*See Art.* 21 *of H. R.*)

Of the Military Power with respect to Private Individuals.

ART. **36.** The population of an occupied territory cannot be compelled to take part in military operations against its own country. (*See Art.* 44 *of H. R.*)

ART. **37.** The population of occupied territories cannot be compelled to swear allegiance to the enemy Power. (*See Art.* 45 *of H. R.*)

ART. **38.** The honour and rights of the family, the life and property of individuals, as well as their religious convictions and the exercise of their religion, should be respected.

Private property cannot be confiscated. (*See Art.* 46 *of H. R.*)

ART. **39.** Pillage is formally forbidden. (*See Art.* 47 *of H. R.*)

Of Contributions and Requisitions.

ART. **40.** As private property should be respected, the enemy will demand from parishes (*communes*), or the inhabitants, only such payments and services as are connected with the necessities of war generally acknowledged, in proportion to the resources of the country, and which do not imply, with regard to the inhabitants, the obligation of taking part in the operations of war against their own country. (*Arts.* 49–52 *of H. R. are new, and deal with the subjects of Arts.* 40–42.)

ART. **41.** The enemy, in levying contributions, whether as equivalents for taxes (see Art. 5) or for payments which should be made in kind, or as fines, will proceed, as far as possible, according to the rules of the distribution and assessment of the taxes in force in the occupied territory.

The civil authorities of the legal government shall afford their assistance, if they have remained in office.

Contributions can be imposed only on the order and on the responsibility of

the general-in-chief, or of the superior civil authority established by the enemy in the occupied territory.

For every contribution a receipt shall be given to the person furnishing it.

ART. 42. Requisitions shall be made only by the authority of the commander of the locality occupied.

For every requisition an indemnity shall be granted or a receipt given.

Of Flags of Truce.

ART. 43. An individual is considered as bearing a flag of truce who is authorized by one of the belligerents to confer with the other, on presenting himself with a white flag, accompanied by a trumpeter (bugler or drummer), or also by a flag-bearer. He shall have the right to inviolability as well as the trumpeter (bugler or drummer), and the flag-bearer, who accompany him. (*See Art. 32 of H. R.*)

ART. 44. The commander to whom a bearer of a flag of truce is despatched is not obliged to receive him under all circumstances and conditions.

It is lawful for him to take all measures necessary for preventing the bearer of the flag of truce taking advantage of his stay within the radius of the enemy's position, to the prejudice of the latter; and if the bearer of the flag of truce is found guilty of such a breach of confidence, he has the right to detain him temporarily. (*See Art. 33 of H. R.*)

He may equally declare beforehand that he will not receive bearers of flags of truce during a certain period. Envoys presenting themselves after such a notification from the side to which it has been given forfeit their right to inviolability. (*Omitted from H. R.*[1])

ART. 45. The bearer of a flag of truce forfeits his right of inviolability if it be proved in a positive and irrefutable manner that he has taken advantage of his privileged position to provoke or commit an act of treachery. (*See Art. 34 of H. R.*)

Of Capitulations.

ART. 46. The conditions of capitulations shall be discussed by the contracting parties.

These conditions should not be contrary to military honour.

When once settled by a convention they shall be scrupulously observed by both sides. (*See Art. 35 of H. R.*)

Of Armistices.

ART. 47. An armistice suspends warlike operations by a mutual agreement between the belligerents. Should the duration thereof not be fixed, the belligerents may resume operations at any moment; provided, however, that

---

[1] This paragraph was omitted from the Regulations adopted at the Hague Conference of 1899 as being contrary to the principles of international law. (See *Parl. Papers*, Misc. No. 1 (1899), p. 147.

proper warning be given to the enemy in accordance with the conditions of the armistice. (*See Art. 36 of H. R.*)

ART. 48. An armistice may be general or local. The former suspends all warlike operations between the belligerents; the latter only those between certain portions of the belligerent armies, and within a fixed radius. (*See Art. 37 of H. R.*)

ART. 49. An armistice should be notified officially and without delay to the competent authorities and to the troops. Hostilities are suspended immediately after the notification. (*See Art. 38 of H. R.*)

ART. 50. It rests with the contracting parties to define in the clauses of the armistice the relations which shall exist between the populations. (*See Art. 39 of H. R.*)

ART. 51. The violation of the armistice by either of the parties gives to the other the right of terminating it (*le dénoncer*). (*See Art. 40 of H. R.*)

ART. 52. The violation of the clauses of an armistice by private individuals, on their own initiative, only affords the right of demanding the punishment of the guilty persons, and, if there is occasion for it, an indemnity for losses sustained. (*See Art. 41 of H. R.*)

Of Belligerents interned, and of Wounded interned, in Neutral Territory.

ART. 53. The neutral State which receives on its territory troops belonging to the belligerent armies shall intern them, so far as possible, away from the theatre of war.

It may keep them in camps, or even confine them in fortresses or in places appropriated to this purpose.

It will decide whether the officers may be left at liberty on giving their parole not to quit the neutral territory without authority. (*See Art. 57 of H. R.*)

ART. 54. In default of a special convention, the neutral State shall furnish the interned with provisions, clothing, and relief which the dictates of humanity prescribe.

The expenses incurred by the internment shall be made good at the conclusion of peace. (*See Art. 58 of H. R.*)

ART. 55. The neutral State may authorize the transport across its territory of the wounded and sick belonging to the belligerent armies, provided that the trains which convey them do not carry either the *personnel* or *matériel* of war.

In this case the neutral State is bound to take the measures necessary for the safety and control of the operation. (*See Art. 59 of H. R.*)

ART. 56. The Convention of Geneva applies to the sick and wounded interned on neutral territory. (*See Art. 60 of H. R.*)

V. Convention concernant les Droits et les Devoirs des Puissances et des Personnes Neutres en cas de Guerre sur Terre.

Sa Majesté l'Empereur d'Allemagne, Roi de Prusse, &c.[1]

En vue de mieux préciser les droits et les devoirs des Puissances neutres en cas de guerre sur terre et de régler la situation des belligérants réfugiés en territoire neutre ;

Désirant également définir la qualité de neutre en attendant qu'il soit possible de régler dans son ensemble la situation des particuliers neutres dans leurs rapports avec les belligérants ;

Ont résolu de conclure une Convention à cet effet et ont, en conséquence, nommé pour Leurs Plénipotentiaires, savoir :

[*Dénomination des Plénipotentiaires.*]

Lesquels, après avoir déposé leurs pleins pouvoirs, trouvés en bonne et due forme, sont convenus des dispositions suivantes :—

V. Convention respecting the Rights and Duties of Neutral Powers and Persons in War on Land.

His Majesty the German Emperor, King of Prussia, &c.[1]

With the view of laying down more clearly the rights and duties of neutral Powers in case of war on land and of regulating the position of belligerents who have taken refuge in neutral territory ;

Being likewise desirous of defining the meaning of the term "neutral," pending the possibility of settling, in its entirety, the position of neutral persons in their relations with belligerents ;

Have resolved to conclude a Convention to this effect, and have, in consequence, appointed as their Plenipotentiaries, that is to say :

[*Names of Plenipotentiaries.*]

Who, after having deposited their full powers, found in good and due form, have agreed upon the following provisions :—

Chapitre I.

Des Droits et des Devoirs des Puissances Neutres.

Art. 1.

Le territoire des Puissances neutres est inviolable.

Chapter I.

The Rights and Duties of Neutral Powers.

Art. 1.

The territory of neutral Powers is inviolable.

[1] List of States as in Final Act, 1907.

ART. 2.

Il est interdit aux belligérants de faire passer à travers le territoire d'une Puissance neutre des troupes ou des convois, soit de munitions, soit d'approvisionnements.

ART. 3.

Il est également interdit aux belligérants :

(a) D'installer sur le territoire d'une Puissance neutre une station radiotélégraphique ou tout appareil destiné à servir comme moyen de communication avec des forces belligérantes sur terre ou sur mer ;

(b) D'utiliser toute installation de ce genre établie par eux avant la guerre sur le territoire de la Puissance neutre dans un but exclusivement militaire, et qui n'a pas été ouverte au service de la correspondance publique.

ART. 4.

Des corps de combattants ne peuvent être formés, ni des bureaux d'enrôlement ouverts, sur le territoire d'une Puissance neutre au profit des belligérants.

ART. 5.

Une Puissance neutre ne doit tolérer sur son territoire aucun des actes visés par les articles 2 à 4.

Elle n'est tenue de punir des actes contraires à la neutralité que si ces actes ont été commis sur son propre territoire.

ART. 6.

La responsabilité d'une Puissance neutre n'est pas engagée par le fait que des individus passent isolément la frontière pour se mettre au service de l'un des belligérants.

ART. 2.

Belligerents are forbidden to move across the territory of a neutral Power troops or convoys, either of munitions of war or of supplies.

ART. 3.

Belligerents are also forbidden :

(a) To erect on the territory of a neutral Power a wireless telegraphy station or any apparatus intended to serve as a means of communication with belligerent forces on land or sea ;

(b) To make use of any installation of this kind established by them before the war on the territory of a neutral Power, for purely military purposes and not previously opened for the service of public messages.

ART. 4.

Corps of combatants cannot be formed, nor recruiting offices opened, on the territory of a neutral Power, in the interest of the belligerents.

ART. 5.

A neutral Power ought not to allow on its territory any of the acts referred to in Articles 2 to 4.

It is not bound to punish acts in violation of neutrality unless such acts have been committed on its own territory.

ART. 6.

A neutral Power does not incur responsibility by the fact that persons cross the frontier singly in order to place themselves at the service of one of the belligerents.

ART. 7.

Une Puissance neutre n'est pas tenue d'empêcher l'exportation ou le transit, pour le compte de l'un ou de l'autre des belligérants, d'armes, de munitions, et, en général, de tout ce qui peut être utile à une armée ou à une flotte.

ART. 7.

A neutral Power is not bound to prevent the export or transit, on behalf of one or other of the belligerents, of arms, munitions of war, or, in general, of anything which can be of use to an army or fleet.

ART. 8.

Une Puissance neutre n'est pas tenue d'interdire ou de restreindre l'usage, pour les belligérants, des câbles télégraphiques ou téléphoniques, ainsi que des appareils de télégraphie sans fil, qui sont, soit sa propriété, soit celle de compagnies ou de particuliers.

ART. 8.

A neutral Power is not bound to forbid or restrict the employment on behalf of belligerents of telegraph or telephone cables or of wireless telegraphy apparatus whether belonging to it, or to companies or to private individuals.

ART. 9.

Toutes mesures restrictives ou prohibitives prises par une Puissance neutre à l'égard des matières visées par les articles 7 et 8 devront être uniformément appliquées par elle aux belligérants.

La Puissance neutre veillera au respect de la même obligation par les compagnies ou particuliers propriétaires de câbles télégraphiques ou téléphoniques ou d'appareils de télégraphie sans fil.

ART. 9.

Every restrictive or prohibitive measure taken by a neutral Power in regard to the matters referred to in Articles 7 and 8 must be applied impartially by it to the belligerents.

The neutral Power shall see to the same obligation being observed by companies or private owners of telegraph or telephone cables or wireless telegraphy apparatus.

ART. 10.

Ne peut être considéré comme un acte hostile le fait, par une Puissance neutre, de repousser, même par la force, les atteintes à sa neutralité.

ART. 10.

The fact of a neutral Power repelling, even by force, attacks on its neutrality cannot be considered as a hostile act.

Chapitre II.

Des Belligérants internés et des Blessés soignés chez les Neutres.

ART. 11.

La Puissance neutre qui reçoit sur son territoire des troupes appartenant aux armées belligérantes, les internera, autant que possible, loin du théâtre de la guerre.

Elle pourra les garder dans des camps, et même les enfermer dans les forteresses ou dans des lieux appropriés à cet effet.

Elle décidera si les officiers peuvent être laissés libres en prenant l'engagement sur parole de ne pas quitter le territoire neutre sans autorisation.

ART. 12.

A défaut de convention spéciale, la Puissance neutre fournira aux internés les vivres, les habillements, et les secours commandés par l'humanité.

Bonification sera faite, à la paix, des frais occasionnés par l'internement.

ART. 13.

La Puissance neutre qui reçoit des prisonniers de guerre évadés les laissera en liberté. Si elle tolère leur séjour sur son territoire, elle peut leur assigner une résidence.

La même disposition est applicable aux prisonniers de guerre amenés par des troupes se réfugiant sur le territoire de la Puissance neutre.

Chapter II.

Internment of Belligerents and Care of the Wounded in Neutral Territory.

ART. 11.

A neutral Power which receives in its territory troops belonging to the belligerent armies shall intern them, as far as possible, at a distance from the theatre of war.

It can keep them in camps, and even confine them in fortresses or places assigned for this purpose.

It shall decide whether officers may be left at liberty on giving their parole not to leave the neutral territory without permission.

(*Cp.* 3 *H. C.* 1899, *Art.* 57.)

ART. 12.

In the absence of a special Convention, the neutral Power shall supply the interned with the food, clothing, and relief which the dictates of humanity prescribe.

At the conclusion of peace, the expenses caused by the internment shall be made good.

(*Cp.* 3 *H. C.* 1899, *Art.* 58.)

ART. 13.

A neutral Power which receives prisoners of war who have escaped shall leave them at liberty. If it allows them to remain in its territory, it may assign them a place of residence.

The same rule applies to prisoners of war brought by troops taking refuge in the territory of a neutral Power.

ART. 14.

Une Puissance neutre pourra autoriser le passage sur son territoire des blessés ou malades appartenant aux armées belligérantes, sous la réserve que les trains qui les amèneront ne transporteront ni personnel, ni matériel de guerre. En pareil cas, la Puissance neutre est tenue de prendre les mesures de sûreté et de contrôle nécessaires à cet effet.

Les blessés ou malades amenés dans ces conditions sur le territoire neutre par un des belligérants, et qui appartiendraient à la partie adverse, devront être gardés par la Puissance neutre de manière qu'ils ne puissent de nouveau prendre part aux opérations de la guerre. Cette Puissance aura les mêmes devoirs quant aux blessés ou malades de l'autre armée qui lui seraient confiés.

ART. 14.

A neutral Power may authorize the passage over its territory of wounded or sick belonging to the belligerent armies, on condition that the trains bringing them shall carry neither personnel nor material of war. In such a case, the neutral Power is bound to adopt such measures of safety and control as may be necessary for the purpose.

Wounded and sick brought under these conditions into neutral territory by one of the belligerents, and belonging to the adverse party, must be guarded by the neutral Power, so as to insure their not taking part again in the operations of war. The same duty shall devolve on the neutral Power with regard to wounded or sick of the other army who may be committed to its care.

(*Cp.* 3 *H. C.* 1899, *Art.* 59.)

ART. 15.

La Convention de Genève s'applique aux malades et aux blessés internés sur territoire neutre.

ART. 15.

The Geneva Convention applies to the sick and wounded interned in neutral territory.

(*Cp.* 3 *H. C.* 1899, *Art.* 60.)

Chapitre III.

Des Personnes Neutres.

ART. 16.

Sont considérés comme neutres les nationaux d'un État qui ne prend pas part à la guerre.

Chapter III.

Neutral Persons.

ART. 16[1].

The nationals of a State which is not taking part in the war are considered to be neutrals.

ART. 17.

Un neutre ne peut pas se prévaloir de sa neutralité :

ART. 17[1].

A neutral cannot claim the benefit of his neutrality :

[1] On signing this Convention Great Britain made reservations in regard to Articles 16, 17 and 18. See *Parl. Papers*, Misc. No. 5 (1908).

(a) S'il commet des actes hostiles contre un belligérant ;

(b) S'il commet des actes en faveur d'un belligérant, notamment s'il prend volontairement du service dans les rangs de la force armée de l'une des parties.

En pareil cas, le neutre ne sera pas traité plus rigoureusement par le belligérant contre lequel il s'est départi de la neutralité que ne pourrait l'être, à raison du même fait, un national de l'autre État belligérant.

ART. 18.

Ne seront pas considérés comme actes commis en faveur d'un des belligérants, dans le sens de l'article 17, lettre (b) :

(a) Les fournitures faites ou les emprunts consentis à l'un des belligérants, pourvu que le fournisseur ou le prêteur n'habite ni le territoire de l'autre partie, ni le territoire occupé par elle, et que les fournitures ne proviennent pas de ces territoires ;

(b) Les services rendus en matière de police ou d'administration civile.

Chapitre IV.

Du Matériel des Chemins de Fer.

ART. 19.

Le matériel des chemins de fer provenant du territoire de Puissances neutres, qu'il appartienne à ces Puissances ou à des sociétés ou personnes privées, et reconnaissable comme tel, ne pourra être réquisitionné et utilisé

(a) If he commits hostile acts against a belligerent ;

(b) If he commits acts in favour of a belligerent, particularly if he voluntarily enlists in the ranks of the armed force of one of the parties.

In such a case, the neutral shall not be more severely treated by the belligerent as against whom he has abandoned his neutrality than a national of the other belligerent State could be for the same act.

ART. 18[1].

The following acts shall not be considered as committed in favour of one of the belligerents within the meaning of Article 17, letter (b) :

(a) The furnishing of supplies or the making of loans to one of the belligerents, provided that the person so furnishing or lending neither lives in the territory of the other party nor in territory in the occupation of that party, and that the supplies do not come from these territories ;

(b) The rendering of services in matters of police or of civil administration.

Chapter IV.

Railway Material.

ART. 19.

Railway material coming from the territory of neutral Powers, whether belonging to those Powers or to companies or private persons, and recognizable as such, shall not be requisitioned or utilized by a belligerent

---

[1] On signing this Convention Great Britain made reservations in regard to Articles 16, 17 and 18. See *Parl. Papers*, Misc. No. 5 (1908).

par un belligérant que dans le cas et la mesure où l'exige une impérieuse nécessité. Il sera renvoyé aussitôt que possible dans le pays d'origine.

La Puissance neutre pourra de même, en cas de nécessité, retenir et utiliser, jusqu'à due concurrence, le matériel provenant du territoire de la Puissance belligérante.

Une indemnité sera payée de part et d'autre en proportion du matériel utilisé et de la durée de l'utilisation.

except in the case of and to the extent required by absolute necessity. It shall be sent back as soon as possible to the country of origin.

A neutral Power may likewise, in case of necessity, retain and make use of, to a corresponding extent, railway material coming from the territory of the belligerent Power.

Compensation shall be paid on either side in proportion to the material used, and to the period of usage.

(*Cp.* 3 *H. C.* 1899, *Art.* 54.)

Chapitre V.

Dispositions Finales.

ART. 20.

Les dispositions de la présente Convention ne sont applicables qu'entre les Puissances contractantes et seulement si les belligérants sont tous parties à la Convention.

ART. 21.

La présente Convention sera ratifiée aussitôt que possible.

Les ratifications seront déposées à La Haye.

Le premier dépôt de ratifications sera constaté par un procès-verbal signé par les représentants des Puissances qui y prennent part et par le Ministre des Affaires Étrangères des Pays-Bas.

Les dépôts ultérieurs de ratifications se feront au moyen d'une notification écrite, adressée au Gouvernement des Pays-Bas et accompagnée de l'instrument de ratification.

Copie certifiée conforme du procès-verbal relatif au premier dépôt de

Chapter V.

Final Provisions.

ART. 20.

The provisions of the present Convention are only applicable between the Contracting Powers, and only if all the belligerents are parties to the Convention.

ART. 21.

The present Convention shall be ratified as soon as possible.

The ratifications shall be deposited at The Hague.

The first deposit of ratifications shall be recorded in a *procès-verbal* signed by the Representatives of the Powers which take part therein and by the Netherland Minister for Foreign Affairs.

The subsequent deposits of ratifications shall be made by means of a written notification, addressed to the Netherland Government and accompanied by the instrument of ratification.

A duly certified copy of the *procès-verbal* relating to the first deposit of

ratifications, des notifications mentionnées à l'alinéa précédent, ainsi que des instruments de ratification sera immédiatement remise par les soins du Gouvernement des Pays-Bas et par la voie diplomatique aux Puissances conviées à la Deuxième Conférence de la Paix, ainsi qu'aux autres Puissances qui auront adhéré à la Convention. Dans les cas visés ·par l'alinéa précédent, le dit Gouvernement leur fera connaître en même temps la date à laquelle il a reçu la notification.

ART. 22.

Les Puissances non-signataires sont admises à adhérer à la présente Convention.

La Puissance qui désire adhérer notifie par écrit son intention au Gouvernement des Pays-Bas en lui transmettant l'acte d'adhésion, qui sera déposé dans les archives du dit Gouvernement.

Ce Gouvernement transmettra immédiatement à toutes les autres Puissances copie certifiée conforme de la notification ainsi que de l'acte d'adhésion, en indiquant la date à laquelle il a reçu la notification.

ART. 23.

La présente Convention produira effet, pour les Puissances qui auront participé au premier dépôt de ratifications, soixante jours après la date du procès-verbal de ce dépôt et, pour les Puissances qui ratifieront ultérieurement ou qui adhéreront, soixante jours après que la notification de leur ratification ou de leur adhésion aura été reçue par le Gouvernement des Pays-Bas.

ratifications, of the notifications mentioned in the preceding paragraph, as well as of the instruments of ratification shall be immediately sent by the Netherland Government through the diplomatic channel, to the Powers invited to the Second Peace Conference, as well as to the other Powers which have acceded to the Convention. In the cases contemplated in the preceding paragraph, the said Government shall inform them at the same time of the date on which it received the notification.

ART. 22.

Non-Signatory Powers may accede to the present Convention.

A Power which desires to accede notifies its intention in writing to the Netherland Government, forwarding to it the act of accession, which shall be deposited in the archives of the said Government.

The said Government shall immediately forward to all the other Powers a duly certified copy of the notification as well as of the act of accession, mentioning the date on which it received the notification.

ART. 23.

The present Convention shall take effect, in the case of the Powers which were parties to the first deposit of ratifications, sixty days after the date of the *procès-verbal* recording such deposit, and, in the case of the Powers which shall ratify subsequently or which shall accede, sixty days after the notification of their ratification or of their accession has been received by the Netherland Government.

Art. 24.

S'il arrivait qu'une des Puissances contractantes voulût dénoncer la présente Convention, la dénonciation sera notifiée par écrit au Gouvernement des Pays-Bas, qui communiquera immédiatement copie certifiée conforme de la notification à toutes les autres Puissances, en leur faisant savoir la date à laquelle il l'a reçue.

La dénonciation ne produira ses effets qu'à l'égard de la Puissance qui l'aura notifiée et un an après que la notification en sera parvenue au Gouvernement des Pays-Bas.

Art. 25.

Un registre tenu par le Ministère des Affaires Étrangères des Pays-Bas indiquera la date du dépôt des ratifications effectué en vertu de l'article 21, alinéas 3 et 4, ainsi que la date à laquelle auront été reçues les notifications d'adhésion (article 22, alinéa 2) ou de dénonciation (article 24, alinéa 1).

Chaque Puissance contractante est admise à prendre connaissance de ce registre et à en demander des extraits certifiés conformes.

En foi de quoi les Plénipotentiaires ont revêtu la présente Convention de leurs signatures.

Fait à la Haye, le 18 octobre, 1907, en un seul exemplaire, qui restera déposé dans les archives du Gouvernement des Pays-Bas et dont des copies, certifiées conformes, seront remises par la voie diplomatique aux Puissances qui ont été conviées à la Deuxième Conférence de la Paix.

Art. 24.

In the event of one of the Contracting Powers wishing to denounce the present Convention, the denunciation shall be notified in writing to the Netherland Government, which shall immediately communicate a duly certified copy of the notification to all the other Powers, informing them of the date on which it was received.

The denunciation shall only affect the notifying Power, and only on the expiry of one year after the notification has reached the Netherland Government.

Art. 25.

A register kept by the Netherland Ministry of Foreign Affairs shall record the date of the deposit of ratifications effected in virtue of Article 21, paragraphs 3 and 4, as well as the date on which the notifications of accession (Article 22, paragraph 2) or of denunciation (Article 24, paragraph 1) have been received.

Each Contracting Power is entitled to have access to this register and to be supplied with duly certified extracts from it.

In faith whereof the Plenipotentiaries have appended their signatures to the present Convention.

Done at The Hague, the 18th October, 1907, in a single original, which shall remain deposited in the archives of the Netherland Government, and of which duly certified copies shall be sent, through the diplomatic channel, to the Powers invited to the Second Peace Conference.

CONVENTION No. 5. RESPECTING THE RIGHTS AND DUTIES OF
NEUTRAL POWERS AND PERSONS IN WAR ON LAND[1].

The regulations on the laws and customs of war on land annexed to the
Convention of 1899 contained four Articles dealing with neutrals. The
subject was not further dealt with, but the Conference expressed a " Wish "
that the question of the rights and duties of neutrals might be inserted in
the programme of a future Conference and it appears under the second
heading of suggested topics in Count Benckendorff's circular. The subject
was entrusted to the Second Sub-Committee of the Second Committee
which was concerned with the laws of war on land. The object which the
Committee kept in view was to effect a reasonable compromise between the
interests of belligerents and the rights of neutrals, and it was also felt that
it would be well not to endeavour to settle disputed points in the laws of
neutrality, but to make a beginning in codification by converting into a
written law such of the existing usages as regarded neutral Powers and
persons as were of general acceptance.

The subject fell naturally into two divisions, (1) the position of neutral
Powers, their rights and duties in regard to the belligerent Powers, and
(2) the position of neutral persons and their relations with the belligerents.

Chapter i., consisting of 10 Articles, is based on a draft presented
by the French Delegation and explained by General Amourel
on the 19th July, 1907. He stated that it contained only provisions generally admitted by publicists and established by
usage. There were, undoubtedly, many cases not provided for,
but if the draft was accepted it would form a starting-point for their discussions, and for future developments. One very important matter had to be
settled before the examination of the subject could be undertaken. Should
the provisions be addressed to neutral states marking out the conduct they
should pursue, or should they be of a more general character addressed to
all parties? It was thought preferable not only to provide that neutrals
must prevent certain acts from being done on their territory, but to
declare that belligerents are under a corresponding duty not to do such
acts. The 10 Articles of Chapter i. commence with the fundamental

*The rights
and duties of
Neutral
Powers.*

---

[1] *Parl. Papers*, Misc. No. 4 (1908), pp. 82-9, 134-145, and No. 5 (1908); *La Deux. Confér.*
T. I. pp. 125-9, 136-161; *Livre Jaune*, pp. 79-82; *Weissbuch*, pp. 7-9; A. S. de Bustamente,
Am. Journ. of Int. Law, Vol. II. pp. 95-120; A. Ernst, *L'œuvre de la deuxième Conférence*,
pp. 42-9; E. Lémonon, *La seconde Conférence*, pp. 409-470; Sir T. Barclay, *Problems*, etc.
p. 83; J. Westlake, *War*, p. 284; T. E. Holland, *The laws of war on land*, pp. 62-8.

principle inserted on the suggestion of the Belgian delegate of the inviolability of the neutral territory (Article 1). The second Article which is a direct consequence of the first was proposed by the British delegate and forbids belligerents to send troops and war material through neutral territory. The experiences of the Russo-Japanese War suggested the prohibition in Article 3. The Russians, having erected a wireless telegraphy apparatus on one of the hills of Port Arthur, had established a receiving station at Chefoo on the Chinese side of the Gulf of Pechili, and the besieged garrison at Port Arthur was thus enabled to communicate with their home Government and the outside world generally[1]. This Article forbids the establishment by a belligerent on neutral territory of a radio-telegraphic station, or the use by a belligerent of any such installation made by him "for purely military purposes" before the war on territory of a neutral and not previously opened for the service of public messages. The limitation in paragraph (b) "and not previously opened" is taken from the Radio-telegraphic Convention of 1906 and was for the purpose of enabling the British and Japanese delegates to abandon the reservations they had made on Articles 3 and 9. Article 4 forbids the formation of bodies of combatants for one of the belligerents on neutral territory and the establishment of offices there for the purpose of enlistment. A neutral Power by Article 6 does not incur any responsibility if persons cross the frontier singly from the neutral state and enlist with one of the belligerents. Article 5 lays a duty on neutral Powers corresponding to those imposed on belligerents by Articles 2–4 to prevent such acts as are enumerated in those Articles from being done on its territory. The Japanese delegate desired to extend the neutral obligation to territory over which a neutral had jurisdiction. This question of the rights of jurisdiction exercised by a state over territory not its own raised difficult points for solution which the Committee thought it unwise to attempt to solve. What, for instance, is the position of Cyprus or Wei-hai-wei? The complex problems relating to acts done on leased or "occupied" or "administered" territory had to be passed over in order to arrive at an agreement on generally accepted principles.

Articles 6–8 relate to acts for which a neutral state is not responsible. Articles 7 and 8 expressly provide that a neutral is not under any obligation to prevent the export of contraband of war by its subjects, nor to prevent belligerents using telegraphs or telephone cables or wireless telegraphy apparatus belonging to the neutral state or private individuals. It will be

---

[1] See T. J. Lawrence, *War and Neutrality, etc.* p. 218 ; A. S. Hershey, *International law and diplomacy, etc.* pp. 122, 124, 259, 266.

noticed that the installations prohibited by Article 3 are those which belong to belligerents. A neutral cannot in practice distinguish among the various persons who make use of telegraphic and other similar means of communication within its territory. Strict impartiality in regard to the matters referred to in Articles 7 and 8 is enjoined, and the duty is laid on the neutral Power to see that the use of privately owned telegraphic and other similar means of communication is regulated in the same impartial manner (Article 9). Neutrals are however under no obligation to allow belligerents to use such means of communication, but impartiality of prohibition is necessary. Lord Reay desired that it should be stated in the Report that the liberty of a neutral state to transmit despatches by land telegraphs or submarine cables or wireless-telegraphic apparatus does not imply the right of making use of them or of allowing them to be used in order to lend any assistance to one of the belligerents[1]. Article 10 recognises that the fact of a neutral Power repelling by force attempts to violate its neutrality cannot be regarded as a hostile act. The Belgian delegate deemed this superfluous, but his objection was over-ruled and the foregoing 10 Articles received unanimous acceptance. The Danish delegate desired to add an Article providing that the mere fact of a neutral state mobilising its forces with a view to prevent infractions of its neutrality should not be considered a hostile act, but the Committee deemed it unnecessary, as each sovereign state has the indisputable right to take such steps within its own territory for its defence as it may deem fit.

Articles 11–15 are based upon Section IV. of the Regulations annexed to the Hague Convention on the laws and usages of war on land of 1899. Articles 11, 12, 14 and 15 are re-enactments of Articles 57, 58, 59 and 60 of these Regulations. Article 13 is new. An attempt was made by Japan to make a change in Article 11 (57 of the Regulations of 1899) by providing that officers and other members of the armed forces of a belligerent interned in a neutral state should not be given their liberty or authorised to return to their country except with the consent and under conditions laid down by the other belligerent, and that the parole given to a neutral state by such individuals should be deemed equivalent to a pledge given to the enemy. This was rejected, the Committee preferring to leave the Articles in their original form, and for special cases to be settled according to circumstances.

Chapter ii. Belligerents interned, and wounded tended in neutral territory.

Article 13 deals with cases not covered by the Articles in the

---

[1] *Parl. Papers*, Misc. No. 4 (1908), p. 128; *La Deux. Confér.* T. I. p. 142.

Convention of 1899. Prisoners of war escape and take refuge on neutral territory; belligerent troops that have taken refuge on neutral territory have with them prisoners of war; what is the duty of the neutral state? In the first case, it has long been a rule of international law that a prisoner of war escaping and taking refuge in a neutral state is free, but it was not settled whether the neutral state could restrain him from rejoining his army if he subsequently wished to do so[1]. The first paragraph of Article 13 leaves the neutral state liberty of action. It may receive escaped prisoners, and allow them to remain in its territory, and may assign them a place of residence. If the prisoner will not conform to neutral regulations is he at liberty to leave? The second paragraph was objected to by the Russian military delegate as being contrary to Article 59 of the Regulations for land warfare of 1899 and Article 15 of the Convention adapting to maritime warfare the principles of the Geneva Convention of 1906, which require that sick and wounded belonging to belligerent armies and navies committed to the care of neutrals must be guarded by the latter and not allowed to take part again in the war. The case dealt with by this paragraph is quite different. A body of belligerent troops with prisoners of war enter a neutral territory with the object of avoiding surrender to the enemy[2]; if such troops surrender to the enemy their prisoners are freed; the same rule now applies where they enter neutral territory and are interned. Their prisoners are dealt with in the same way as escaped prisoners of war.

Articles 16, 17 and 18 are all that remain of a German draft of 12
Chapter iii. Neutral persons. Articles originally intended to form Chapter v. of the Regulations for the laws of war on land. The failure of the German delegate to obtain acceptance for his proposals has already been referred to in discussing the Second and Third *Vœux*[3]. The draft Articles proposed to establish a *régime* highly favourable both to the persons and property of neutrals in belligerent states. Great Britain, having large colonies with populations drawn from many states, would have been considerably handicapped if she had never been able to avail herself of the services of immigrants freely offered, who, not having resided long enough to acquire British nationality, still remained technically subjects of a neutral Power. The British delegate strongly objected to the German proposals

---

[1] See L. Oppenheim, *Int. Law*, Vol. ii. § 337.

[2] The most striking example of internment occurred in 1871 during the Franco-Prussian war when over 80,000 French troops under General Clinchant entered Swiss territory and were interned for the remainder of the war; France at the conclusion of the war paid to Switzerland some 11 million francs for their maintenance.

[3] See *supra*, p. 85.

and he was supported by the delegates of France, Russia and Japan, who also declined to accept the favoured position created for subjects of neutral Powers in belligerent states. The three Articles which found acceptance and which constituted the 1st Chapter of the German draft have not been accepted by Great Britain.

Article 19 replaces Article 54 of the Regulations of 1899 and is a compromise between contradictory views. Luxemburg and Belgium denied the right of belligerents to requisition and make use of neutral railway material within their territory. Germany and Austria desired to have the right to use it admitted, on the understanding that an indemnity was paid for its use after the close of the war. France and Luxemburg as an alternative claimed both an indemnity and the right, in case of need, to retain and make use of a corresponding quantity of railway material coming from the territory of a belligerent state. The Conference took the middle course, allowing belligerents to requisition and use neutral railway material only when absolutely necessary, on condition that it be returned as soon as possible, the neutral being given a corresponding right over belligerent material within its territory, compensation to be paid by one party to the other in proportion to the material used and the period of use. The terms used in this Article leave the neutral very much at the mercy of the belligerent as regards the requisition and use of railway material. Who is to be the judge of the necessity, and what is the meaning of "as soon as possible"? M. Eyschen (Luxemburg) proposed that within a certain time after the outbreak of war all neutral railway material should be returned to the country of its origin. General von Gündell (Germany) objected that this would entirely disorganise the transport and mobilisation of troops in the belligerent country on the outbreak of war; the latter view prevailed.

This Convention affords within modest limits a starting-point for future Conferences, and a basis on which may be built further rules safeguarding neutral interests. It contains on the whole well accepted principles which were ready for codification.

All the Powers except China and Nicaragua have signed this Convention, but Great Britain has made reservations in regard to Articles 16, 17 and 18, and the Argentine Republic in regard to Article 18.

VI. Enemy Merchant-Ships at the Outbreak of Hostilities.

VI. Convention relative au Régime des Navires de Commerce Ennemis au Début des Hostilités.

Sa Majesté l'Empereur d'Allemagne, Roi de Prusse, &c.[1]

Désireux de garantir la sécurité du commerce international contre les surprises de la guerre et voulant, conformément à la pratique moderne, protéger autant que possible les opérations engagées de bonne foi et en cours d'exécution avant le début des hostilités ;

Ont résolu de conclure une Convention à cet effet et ont nommé pour Leurs Plénipotentiaires, savoir :

[*Dénomination des Plénipotentiaires.*]

Lesquels, après avoir déposé leurs pleins pouvoirs trouvés en bonne et due forme, sont convenus des dispositions suivantes :—

Art. 1.

Lorsqu'un navire de commerce relevant d'une des Puissances belligérantes se trouve, au début des hostilités, dans un port ennemi, il est désirable qu'il lui soit permis de sortir librement, immédiatement ou après un délai de faveur suffisant, et de gagner directement, après avoir été muni d'un laissez-passer, son port de destination ou tel autre port qui lui sera désigné.

VI. Convention relative to the Status of Enemy Merchant-ships at the Outbreak of Hostilities.

His Majesty the German Emperor, King of Prussia, &c.[1]

Anxious to ensure the security of international commerce against the surprises of war and wishing, in accordance with modern practice, to protect as far as possible operations undertaken in good faith and in process of being carried out before the outbreak of hostilities ;

Have resolved to conclude a Convention to this effect, and have appointed as their Plenipotentiaries, that is to say :

[*Names of Plenipotentiaries.*]

Who, after having deposited their full powers, found in good and due form, have agreed upon the following provisions :—

Art. 1.

When a merchant-ship of one of the belligerent Powers is at the commencement of hostilities in an enemy port, it is desirable that it should be allowed to depart freely, either immediately, or after a sufficient term of grace, and to proceed direct, after being furnished with a passport, to its port of destination or such other port as shall be named for it.

[1] List of States as in the Final Act, 1907.

Il en est de même du navire ayant quitté son dernier port de départ avant le commencement de la guerre et entrant dans un port ennemi sans connaître les hostilités.

The same applies in the case of a ship which left its last port of departure before the commencement of the war and enters an enemy port in ignorance of the hostilities.

ART. 2.

Le navire de commerce qui, par suite de circonstances de force majeure, n'aurait pu quitter le port ennemi pendant le délai visé à l'article précédent, ou auquel la sortie n'aurait pas été accordée, ne peut être confisqué.

Le belligérant peut seulement le saisir moyennant l'obligation de le restituer après la guerre sans indemnité, ou le réquisitionner moyennant indemnité.

ART. 2.

A merchant-ship which, owing to circumstances of *force majeure*, may have been unable to leave the enemy port during the period contemplated in the preceding Article, or which may not have been allowed to leave, may not be confiscated.

The belligerent may only detain it, under an obligation of restoring it after the war, without indemnity, or he may requisition it on condition of paying an indemnity.

ART. 3.

Les navires de commerce ennemis qui ont quitté leur dernier port de départ avant le commencement de la guerre et qui sont rencontrés en mer ignorants des hostilités, ne peuvent être confisqués. Ils sont seulement sujets à être saisis, moyennant l'obligation de les restituer après la guerre sans indemnité, ou à être réquisitionnés, ou même à être détruits, à charge d'indemnité et sous l'obligation de pourvoir à la sécurité des personnes ainsi qu'à la conservation des papiers de bord.

Après avoir touché à un port de leur pays ou à un port neutre, ces navires sont soumis aux lois et coutumes de la guerre maritime.

ART. 3.

Enemy merchant-ships which left their last port of departure before the commencement of the war, and which are met at sea while ignorant of the hostilities, cannot be confiscated. They are only liable to be detained under an obligation to restore them after the war without indemnity, or to be requisitioned, or even destroyed, with indemnity and under the obligation of providing for the safety of the persons as well as the preservation of the papers on board.

After having touched at a port of their own country or at a neutral port, such ships are subject to the laws and customs of naval war.

ART. 4.

Les marchandises ennemies se trouvant à bord des navires visés aux

ART. 4.

Enemy cargo on board the vessels referred to in Articles 1 and 2 is like-

articles 1 et 2 sont également sujettes à être saisies et restituées après la guerre sans indemnité, ou à être réquisitionnées moyennant indemnité, conjointement avec le navire ou séparément.

Il en est de même des marchandises se trouvant à bord des navires visés à l'article 3.

ART. 5.

La présente Convention ne vise pas les navires de commerce dont la construction indique qu'ils sont destinés à être transformés en bâtiments de guerre.

ART. 6.

Les dispositions de la présente Convention ne sont applicables qu'entre les Puissances contractantes et seulement si les belligérants sont tous parties à la Convention.

ART. 7.

La présente Convention sera ratifiée aussitôt que possible.

Les ratifications seront déposées à La Haye.

Le premier dépôt de ratifications sera constaté par un procès-verbal signé par les représentants des Puissances qui y prennent part et par le Ministre des Affaires Étrangères des Pays-Bas.

Les dépôts ultérieurs de ratifications se feront au moyen d'une notification écrite, adressée au Gouvernement des Pays-Bas et accompagnée de l'instrument de ratification.

Copie certifiée conforme du procès-verbal relatif au premier dépôt de ratifications, des notifications mention-

wise liable to be detained and restored after the war without indemnity, or to be requisitioned on payment of indemnity, with the ship or separately.

The same applies in the case of cargo on board the vessels referred to in Article 3.

ART. 5.

The present Convention does not affect merchant-ships whose construction indicates that they are intended to be converted into ships of war.

ART. 6.

The provisions of the present Convention are only applicable between the Contracting Powers, and only if all the belligerents are parties to the Convention.

ART. 7.

The present Convention shall be ratified as soon as possible.

The ratifications shall be deposited at The Hague.

The first deposit of ratifications shall be recorded in a *procès-verbal* signed by the Representatives of the Powers which take part therein and by the Netherland Minister for Foreign Affairs.

The subsequent deposits of ratifications shall be made by means of a written notification, addressed to the Netherland Government and accompanied by the instrument of ratification.

A duly certified copy of the *procès-verbal* relating to the first deposit of ratifications, of the notifications men-

nées à l'alinéa précédent, ainsi que des instruments de ratifications, sera immédiatement remise par les soins du Gouvernement des Pays-Bas et par la voie diplomatique aux Puissances conviées à la Deuxième Conférence de la Paix, ainsi qu'aux autres Puissances qui auront adhéré à la Convention. Dans les cas visés par l'alinéa précédent, le dit Gouvernement leur fera connaître en même temps la date à laquelle il a reçu la notification.

tioned in the preceding paragraph, as well as of the instruments of ratification, shall be immediately sent by the Netherland Government, through the diplomatic channel, to the Powers invited to the Second Peace Conference, as well as to the other Powers which have acceded to the Convention. In the cases contemplated in the preceding paragraph, the said Government shall inform them at the same time of the date on which it received the notification.

Art. 8.

Les Puissances non-signataires sont admises à adhérer à la présente Convention.

La Puissance qui désire adhérer notifie par écrit son intention au Gouvernement des Pays-Bas en lui transmettant l'acte d'adhésion, qui sera déposé dans les archives du dit Gouvernement.

Ce Gouvernement transmettra immédiatement à toutes les autres Puissances copie certifiée conforme de la notification ainsi que de l'acte d'adhésion, en indiquant la date à laquelle il a reçu la notification.

Art. 8.

Non-Signatory Powers may accede to the present Convention.

A Power which desires to accede notifies its intention in writing to the Netherland Government, forwarding to it the act of accession, which shall be deposited in the archives of the said Government.

The said Government shall immediately forward to all the other Powers a duly certified copy of the notification as well as of the act of accession, mentioning the date on which it received the notification.

Art. 9.

La présente Convention produira effet, pour les Puissances qui auront participé au premier dépôt de ratifications, soixante jours après la date du procès-verbal de ce dépôt et, pour les Puissances qui ratifieront ultérieurement ou qui adhéreront, soixante jours après que la notification de leur ratification ou de leur adhésion aura été reçue par le Gouvernement des Pays-Bas.

Art. 9.

The present Convention shall take effect, in the case of the Powers which were parties to the first deposit of ratifications, sixty days after the date of the *procès-verbal* recording such deposit, and, in the case of the Powers which shall ratify subsequently or which shall accede, sixty days after the notification of their ratification or of their accession has been received by the Netherland Government.

ART. 10.

S'il arrivait qu'une des Puissances Contractantes voulût dénoncer la présente Convention, la dénonciation sera notifiée par écrit au Gouvernement des Pays-Bas, qui communiquera immédiatement copie certifiée conforme de la notification à toutes les autres Puissances en leur faisant savoir la date à laquelle il l'a reçue.

La dénonciation ne produira ses effets qu'à l'égard de la Puissance qui l'aura notifiée et un an après que la notification en sera parvenue au Gouvernement des Pays-Bas.

ART. 11.

Un registre tenu par le Ministère des Affaires Étrangères des Pays-Bas indiquera la date du dépôt de ratifications effectué en vertu de l'article 7, alinéas 3 et 4, ainsi que la date à laquelle auront été reçues les notifications d'adhésion (article 8, alinéa 2) ou de dénonciation (article 10, alinéa 1).

Chaque Puissance contractante est admise à prendre connaissance de ce registre et à en demander des extraits certifiés conformes.

En foi de quoi les Plénipotentiaires ont revêtu la présente Convention de leurs signatures.

Fait à La Haye, le 18 octobre, 1907, en un seul exemplaire qui restera déposé dans les archives du Gouvernement des Pays-Bas et dont des copies, certifiées conformes, seront remises par la voie diplomatique aux Puissances qui ont été conviées à la Deuxième Conférence de la Paix.

ART. 10.

In the event of one of the Contracting Powers wishing to denounce the present Convention, the denunciation shall be notified in writing to the Netherland Government, which shall immediately communicate a duly certified copy of the notification to all the other Powers, informing them of the date on which it was received.

The denunciation shall only affect the notifying Power, and only on the expiry of one year after the notification has reached the Netherland Government.

ART. 11.

A register kept by the Netherland Ministry for Foreign Affairs shall record the date of the deposit of ratifications effected in virtue of Article 7, paragraphs 3 and 4, as well as the date on which the notifications of accession (Article 8, paragraph 2) or of denunciation (Article 10, paragraph 1) have been received.

Each Contracting Power is entitled to have access to this register and to be supplied with duly certified extracts from it.

In faith whereof the Plenipotentiaries have appended their signatures to the present Convention.

Done at The Hague, the 18th October, 1907, in a single original, which shall remain deposited in the archives of the Netherland Government, and of which duly certified copies shall be sent, through the diplomatic channel, to the Powers invited to the Second Peace Conference.

CONVENTION No. 6. RELATIVE TO THE STATUS OF ENEMY
MERCHANT-SHIPS AT THE OUTBREAK OF HOSTILITIES[1].

The third subject on the list of matters assigned to the Fourth
Committee was that of "days of grace" (*délai de faveur*) to be granted
to vessels to leave neutral or enemy ports after the commencement of
hostilities.

It is a well recognised rule of international law that private property
belonging to the enemy on the sea is liable to capture.
This rule applies to both ships and cargoes. At the beginning
of the last century ships whether public or private in territorial
waters of the enemy on the outbreak of war were also liable
to capture, and it was no uncommon thing for a state to lay an embargo
on ships belonging to the subjects of another state with which it was at
variance in anticipation of the outbreak of war. This embargo was at
first a civil embargo and equivocal in character, but if the dispute ended in
war, its effect was retroactive and impressed a "hostile character on the
original seizure[2]." This practice has however not been followed during the
past half-century. A custom has arisen according to which states, on the
commencement of war, issue proclamations allowing enemy ships in harbour
to depart within a specified time, either after loading, or unloading, and to
be free from capture under certain specified conditions. Such proclamations often made provision for the freedom from capture of enemy ships
which had sailed from foreign ports before the proclamation. Turkey in
1853 on the outbreak of war with Russia allowed Russian merchant-ships
to leave her ports. France and Great Britain in 1854 allowed Russian
ships of commerce six weeks, and granted concessions to those bound for
their ports for a similar period. Russia made analogous concessions to
French and British ships. Six weeks were also allowed by Prussia to

Development of practice of "days of grace."

---

[1] *Parl. Papers*, Misc. No. 4 (1908), pp. 190–3, and No. 5 (1908); *La Deux. Confér.*, etc.
T.' I. pp. 250–5; T. III. pp. 825–830, 852–3, 884–6; *Livre Jaune*, p. 96; *Weissbuch*, p. 9;
Sir T. Barclay, *Problems*, etc. p. 67; N. Bentwich, *War and private property*, p. 82; A. Ernst,
L'œuvre de la deux. Confér. p. 30; Halleck, *Int. law* (4th ed.), Vol. I. p. 587; A. S. Hershey,
International law and diplomacy of the Russo-Japanese War, pp. 269, 281–2, 295–7; T. J.
Lawrence, *International Problems*, etc. p. 110; Idem, *War and Neutrality*, etc. Chap. III.;
E. Lémonon, *La seconde Conférence*, etc. pp. 647–661; J. B. Moore, *Digest of Int. Law*,
Sec. 1196; E. Nys, *Le droit inter.* Vol. III. p. 140; J. B. Scott, *Status of enemy merchant
ships*, *Am. Journ. of Int. Law*, Vol. II. p. 259; S. Takahashi, *International Law applied to the
Russo-Japanese War*, pp. 60–9; H. Taylor, *Int. Law*, Sec. 464; J. Westlake, *War*, pp. 39, 307;
H. Wheaton, *International Law* (Atlay's edition), Sec. 304.

[2] The *Boedes Lust*, 5 C. Robinson's Reports, 245. See also the *Johanna Emilie* (1854),
Spinks, p. 14; J. B. Scott, *Leading Cases*, Section 25 and note on p. 498.

Austrian ships in 1866. In 1870 France allowed 30 days to German merchant vessels in French ports, or which entered the ports in ignorance of the war. The most liberal concessions were those of the United States to Spanish ships at the outbreak of the war in 1898. President McKinley's Proclamation issued on the 26th April allowed Spanish merchant-ships in American ports until the 21st May for loading their cargoes and departing, and such vessels were not to be captured on their voyage if it appeared from their papers that the cargoes were taken on board within the time allowed. There was an express exclusion of vessels having on board military or naval enemy officers, contraband of war, or despatches to or from the Spanish Government[1]. Spain was not so liberal in her concessions, and allowed only five days for American merchant-ships to leave her ports. The United States Proclamation received a liberal construction in the case of the *Buena Ventura*, a ship which had sailed before the outbreak of war and was captured the day before the issue of the Proclamation. Days of grace were also allowed by both Japan and Russia at the outbreak of the war of 1904 but the time allowed was very short. Japan allowed a week's grace to Russian vessels in Japanese ports at the date of the Proclamation to enable them to discharge or load cargo and depart, and exempted such ships from capture, if they were provided with a certificate and proved that they were on their way back to the nearest Russian port or a leased port or their original destination[2]. The Russian concessions were still less favourable to enemy merchantmen found in Russian ports at the outbreak of war. They were allowed to remain "for a period of 48 hours from the time of publication of the declaration by the local authorities." Carriage of contraband of war was prohibited by both states.

The foregoing instances represent the mitigations of the severity of the rule of capture of enemy ships at the commencement of war which had been introduced by various states since the Crimean War. The periods allowed varied from the liberal concessions made by the United States, to the period of 48 hours allowed by Russia. The granting of days of grace in the latter case was merely a formal acknowledgment of the existence of the practice.

The motive for the concession was that of "conciliating the interests of commerce with the necessities of war" and "of protecting in as large a measure as possible operations entered into in good faith and in process of being carried out before the war[3]." The

Proceedings in Committee.

---

[1] J. B. Scott, *Am. Journ. of Int. Law*, Vol. II. p. 264; *La Deux. Confér.* T. III. p. 826.

[2] S. Takahashi, *op. cit.* p. 64.

[3] Pistoye et Duverdy, *Traité des prises maritimes*, T. II. p. 467 (quoted by M. Fromageot).

question to be considered by the Committee was formulated by M. de Martens: "Is it a rule of war (*Est-il de bonne guerre*) on the opening of hostilities to detain and confiscate enemy merchant-ships in the ports of one of the belligerent states? Should the vessels be recognised as having a right to leave freely, within a given fixed time, the ports in which they were at the commencement of war, with or without their cargoes?" Russia proposed four Articles declaring the granting of a period of delay to merchantmen in an enemy port at the outbreak of war to be obligatory, and that they should be allowed to complete their commercial operations and be free from capture till they reached the nearest port of their own country or a neutral port (Art. 1). Ships which in consequence of *force majeure* were unable to avail themselves of this advantage should not be confiscated (Art. 2). Merchant-ships on the high seas having left their port of origin or another port before the commencement of war are not to be confiscated, but if military circumstances demand it, they may be detained by the enemy for such a time as might be required by the necessities of war (Art. 3). Ships mentioned in the foregoing Article arriving in an enemy port to enjoy the periods of grace and immunities previously mentioned (Art. 4)[1]. Captain Qttley (Great Britain) contended that the allowance of time which Great Britain had accorded was only an act of grace, and must not be regarded as a right, and that it would be impossible to formulate any rule which would give satisfaction to every one under all circumstances. He put the case of a war between two Powers, one with a large mercantile navy, the other with but small commercial interests; the former would wish for as long a period as possible, the latter would be anxious to commence operations as soon as possible against the merchant-ships of its enemy[2]. (This was the case in the Russo-Japanese War.) The Japanese delegate re-echoed the words of Captain Ottley.

Russian proposals.

M. Renault (France) proposed to maintain the existing optional system, but desired to exclude from capture ships whose exit had been prohibited, allowing them to be requisitioned and indemnities to be paid. The Dutch delegate wished to fix the delay at not less than five days and to exempt from the concession vessels obviously designed or capable of being converted into ships of war, vessels which M. Lammasch had termed "hermaphrodites."

French proposal.

Dutch proposal.

The Swedish delegate proposed as a compromise to combine the Russian and French propositions, limiting them to an expression of the *desirability* of granting a period of grace.

Swedish proposal.

Four different propositions were therefore before the Committee, Russian, French, Dutch and Swedish, but the preliminary dis-

[1] *La Deux. Confér.* T. III. p. 1150.   [2] *Idem,* T. III. p. 828.

cussions turned entirely on the question whether the concessions to be made to enemy shipping should be made obligatory or left optional. The Swedish proposition formed the starting-point for the Examining Committee, the obligatory character of the concessions to be made having failed to receive a unanimous acceptance chiefly owing to the opposition of Great

British proposal.

Britain, France and Japan[1]. In the course of the examination of the Swedish draft the British Delegation presented a draft in five Articles. The draft Convention was adopted by the Committee, and subsequently by the Conference at its Seventh Plenary Meeting on the 27th September, 1907.·

Article 1.

The first Article states that *it is desirable* that merchant-ships belonging to one of the belligerents at the commencement of hostilities in an enemy port should be allowed to depart freely at once, or after a sufficient number of days of grace, and after being furnished with a pass to proceed direct to a port indicated. The words *de faveur* were added to *délai* at the request of the British delegate to show that the granting of the period of delay was not obligatory. By six to five, the Committee rejected the Swedish proposal to grant the days of grace for the purpose of allowing a ship to complete the unloading or loading of her cargo, other than contraband.

The practice of granting of days of grace remains therefore as it was before the Conference. The Powers have recognised its *desirability*, but no merchant-ship can demand it, nor will there be a legal ground of complaint if all enemy merchant-ships within a belligerent's ports at the outbreak of war are ordered to leave immediately or after a "sufficient" period. Whether the expression "it is desirable" will be considered as equivalent to a command[2] remains to be seen. States will probably act in the future as they have acted in the past. Captain Ottley stated that the British Government had every intention of adhering to the practice which it had observed during the past 50 years in granting days of grace, subject always to the reservation that the time allowed should not compromise its national interests[3]. It was doubtless with a similar mental reservation that the other Powers accepted this Article. States will in the future as in the past consult their own interests in this matter, but their interests may not infrequently involve a consideration for the interests of neutrals.

---

[1] The obligatory view was voted for by eight states, Germany, The United States, Austria-Hungary, Belgium, Norway, Holland, Russia and Servia. Four states voted against it, Great Britain, France, Japan and the Argentine Republic. Sweden did not vote. *La Deux. Confér.* T. iii. p. 936.

[2] J. B. Scott, *Am. Journ. of Int. Law*, Vol. ii. p. 266.

[3] *La Deux. Confér.* T. iii. p. 828.

Each state will determine for itself whether the desire to injure its enemy by detaining his merchant-ships, which might be of the greatest value as auxiliary ships for the fleet, will "prevail over the fear of offending neutrals by causing a great dislocation of trade in which some of them are sure to be interested[1]."

The second paragraph of Article 1 recognises that it is desirable to allow days of grace to a ship which left its last port of departure before the commencement of the war and entered an enemy port in ignorance of the existence of hostilities. This has been the practice of states since the Crimean War. If such a ship has been visited by an enemy cruiser and an entry made in its log-book, that will be conclusive against its claim to any exemption from capture.

Article 2 deals with the case of enemy ships of commerce unable to leave within the allotted time, or not permitted to leave.

Article 2.

Such vessels would formerly have been liable to confiscation. Under this Article they cannot be confiscated, but are to be kept and handed back to the owners at the conclusion of the war, or if they are requisitioned, compensation is to be made.

Article 3 exempts from capture enemy merchantmen met on the high seas which left their last port of departure before the outbreak of war and are in ignorance of its existence. They may

Article 3.

be requisitioned or even destroyed subject to indemnities being paid. If they are aware of the outbreak of war, they can still be confiscated. This Article encountered considerable opposition from Germany and Russia, and at the Seventh Plenary Meeting of the Conference Baron Marschall von Bieberstein said: "The German Delegation is of opinion that these provisions establish an inequality between states in imposing financial burdens on those Powers which, in default of naval stations in different parts of the world, are not in a position to take vessels which they have seized into a port, but find themselves compelled to destroy them[2]." Germany and Russia made a reservation of this Article in signing the Convention.

The German delegate (Dr Kriege) had previously explained the views of his Government in Committee. Only the Powers, he said, which possess naval stations in different parts of the world can regularly exercise this right of seizure. Other Powers will often be unable to take ships they detain into port, and will have to destroy them, and therefore to bear the cost of such vessels; they will therefore have their financial burdens unduly increased as against Powers able to take such vessels into port and retain them till the end of the war[3]. It would appear that Germany and Russia

---

[1] T. J. Lawrence, *War and Neutrality, etc.* (2nd ed.), p. 55.
[2] *La Deux. Confér.* T. i. p. 285.   [3] *Idem*, T. iii. p. 954.

by not accepting this Article retain the right to capture enemy merchant-ships on the high seas which have left their last port before the outbreak of war, subject to any modifications which they may make by proclamation at the commencement of war. Furthermore German and Russian merchant-ships will under similar circumstances also remain liable to be captured subject to a like modification by the other belligerent (see Article 6).

The Article is an amelioration of the strict rules of existing law, though it falls short of recent practice. The exemption from capture provided by it will probably be found however not to be of much value in practice, as it will not often happen under modern conditions that ships will long remain in ignorance of the existence of war in any part of the world. The permission to destroy vessels ignorant of the existence of war was inserted on the suggestion of the Italian delegate to meet the case of states unable to take such vessels into their own ports for detention. Provision must be made for the safety of the persons and papers on board such ships.

Article 4 provides that enemy cargo on the vessels mentioned in
Article 4. Articles 1, 2 and 3 is subject to the same treatment as the vessel. Germany and Russia made reservations on the second paragraph of the Article relating to cargoes on board the enemy merchantmen referred to in Article 3. The provision relating to cargo must be read subject to the Declaration of Paris.

Article 5 imposes an important limitation on the foregoing Articles
Article 5. which it declares are inapplicable to merchant-ships whose construction indicates that they are destined for conversion into war-ships. This Article was inserted at the instance of the British delegate Lord Reay. The words originally proposed were, "*navires marchands ennemis susceptibles d'être transformés en vaisseaux de combat.*" This was altered by the *Comité de rédaction* to "*navires marchands qui ont été désignés d'avance pour être transformés en bâtiments de guerre.*" This phraseology was objected to by the German delegate who contended that all steamships, not only the great ocean-liners but smaller craft, might be of use in war for purpose of mine-laying and other subsidiary operations. He moved the rejection of the whole Article[1]. This was opposed by the British and Japanese delegates. The French and Swedish delegates contended that ships of the class intended were always constructed under special orders of a Government, but the Belgium delegate denied this and desired to modify the phrase by substituting "*susceptibles d'après leur état pour d'être*" etc., but this was rejected and the motion of the German delegate for the

[1] *La Deux. Confér.* T. III. p. 1033.

rejection of the Article was carried by 8 votes to 5 with 2 abstentions. At a subsequent meeting, on the proposition of the Swedish delegate the Article was restored in the form in which it now appears. Russia and Germany have accepted this Article. The discussion, however, brought out the difficulties that may be expected to arise in construing the language in which the Article is framed, "*dont la construction indique qu'ils sont destinés à être transformés en bâtiments de guerre*[1]." The terms of this Article recall those of the Treaty of Washington whereby Great Britain and the United States agreed to use due diligence to prevent the fitting out, arming or equipping within the jurisdiction of either of the Powers of any vessel "which it has reasonable ground to believe is intended *to cruise or to carry on war*" against a Power with which it is at peace[2]. The two Governments could not agree as to the meaning of this language; is there a likelihood of agreement on the meaning of the words "merchant-ships whose construction indicates that they are intended for conversion to war-ships"? "Experts are perfectly able to distinguish vessels built primarily for warlike use," says Mr Hall, writing of the words cited from the Treaty of Washington, "but it is otherwise with many vessels primarily fitted for commerce. Perhaps few fast ships are altogether incapable of being so used as to inflict damage to trade.... Mail steamers of large size are fitted by their strength and build to receive, without much special adaptation, one or two guns of sufficient calibre to render the ships carrying them dangerous cruisers against merchantmen[3]." Subsidised liners were the ships the Committee appear to have had in view; in the case of other vessels M. Fromageot states "the build (*construction*) of ships must serve to indicate the eventual destination." The vessels referred to in the Article are not "primarily built for warlike use" but for commerce; will it be equally easy for experts to distinguish such of these as were built with a view to their eventual conversion into ships of war? Furthermore, what is a ship of war[4]?

The important alteration made in the rules of international law by the Convention is the abrogation of the rule of confiscation of enemy merchant-ships found in a belligerent port at the outbreak of war, unless they are "ships whose construction indicates that they are intended for conversion into warships," but these can be requisitioned and must be paid for. Even if such ships are detained until the end of the war, and not used, immense

---

[1] The German official translation is "*deren Bau ersehen lässt, dass sie zur Umwandlung in Kriegschiffe bestimmt sind.*"

[2] Treaty of Washington, Art. VI., De Martens, *Nouv. Rec. Gén.* Vol. XX. p. 702.

[3] *Int. Law* (5th ed.), p. 616. See also T. J. Lawrence, *Int. Law*, § 262.

[4] See also the discussion on the meaning of the expression *bâtiments de guerre* in the next Convention, *post*, p. 316.

loss will still be occasioned to their owners. The important qualification of Article 5 will probably considerably limit the application of this Convention.

The only Powers which have not signed this Convention are the United
Signatory States, China and Nicaragua. The United States' refusal is
Powers and based on the ground that the Convention is an unsatisfactory
reservations. compromise between those who believe in the existence of
a right and those who refuse to recognise the legal validity of the custom which has grown up in recent years. "The Convention cannot be called progressive, for it questions a custom which seems generally established, and its adoption would seem to sanction less liberal and enlightened practice[1]." The reservations of Germany and Russia, the only two Powers making any, have already been dealt with[2].

[1] J. B. Scott, *Am. Journ. of Int. Law*, Vol. II. p. 270.
[2] See *supra*, p. 304.

VII. Conversion of Merchant-ships into War-ships.

VII. Convention relative à la Transformation des Navires de Commerce en Bâtiments de Guerre.

VII. Convention relative to the Conversion of Merchant-ships into War-ships.

Sa Majesté l'Empereur d'Allemagne, Roi de Prusse, &c.[1]

His Majesty the German Emperor, King of Prussia, &c.[1]

Considérant qu'en vue de l'incorporation en temps de guerre de navires de la marine marchande dans les flottes de combat, il est désirable de définir les conditions dans lesquelles cette opération pourra être effectuée;

Considering that in view of the incorporation in time of war of merchant-ships in the fighting fleet it is desirable to define the conditions subject to which this operation may be effected;

Que, toutefois, les Puissances Contractantes n'ayant pu se mettre d'accord sur la question de savoir si la transformation d'un navire de commerce en bâtiment de guerre peut avoir lieu en pleine mer, il est entendu que la question du lieu de transformation reste hors de cause et n'est nullement visée par les règles ci-dessous;

As, however, the Contracting Powers having been unable to come to an agreement on the question whether the conversion of a merchant-ship into a war-ship may take place upon the high seas, it is understood that the question of the place where such conversion is effected remains outside the scope of this Agreement and is in no way affected by the following rules;

Désirant conclure une Convention à cet effet, ont nommé pour leurs Plénipotentiaires, savoir:

Being desirous of concluding a Convention to this effect, have appointed as their Plenipotentiaries, that is to say:

[*Dénomination des Plénipotentiaires.*]

[*Names of Plenipotentiaries.*]

Lesquels, après avoir déposé leurs pleins pouvoirs, trouvés en bonne et due forme, sont convenus des dispositions suivantes :—

Who, after having deposited their full powers, found to be in good and due form, have agreed upon the following provisions :—

---

[1] List of States as in the Final Act, 1907.

ART. 1.

Aucun navire de commerce transformé en bâtiment de guerre ne peut avoir les droits et les obligations attachés à cette qualité s'il n'est placé sous l'autorité directe, le contrôle immédiat et la responsabilité de la Puissance dont il porte le pavillon.

ART. 2.

Les navires de commerce transformés en bâtiments de guerre doivent porter les signes extérieurs distinctifs des bâtiments de guerre de leur nationalité.

ART. 3.

Le commandant doit être au service de l'État et dûment commissionné par les autorités compétentes. Son nom doit figurer sur la liste des officiers de la flotte militaire.

ART. 4.

L'équipage doit être soumis aux règles de la discipline militaire.

ART. 5.

Tout navire de commerce transformé en bâtiment de guerre est tenu d'observer, dans ses opérations, les lois et coutumes de la guerre.

ART. 6.

Le belligérant qui transforme un navire de commerce en bâtiment de guerre, doit, le plus tôt possible, mentionner cette transformation sur la liste des bâtiments de sa flotte militaire.

ART. 7.

Les dispositions de la présente Convention ne sont applicables qu'entre les Puissances contractantes et seulement si les belligérants sont tous parties à la Convention.

ART. 1.

No merchant-ship converted into a war-ship can have the rights and duties appertaining to that status unless it is placed under the direct authority, immediate control and responsibility of the Power whose flag it flies.

ART. 2.

Merchant-ships converted into war-ships must bear the external marks which distinguish the war-ships of their nationality.

ART. 3.

The commander must be in the service of the State and duly commissioned by the proper authorities. His name must figure on the list of the officers of the military fleet.

ART. 4.

The crew must be subject to the rules of military discipline.

ART. 5.

Every merchant-ship converted into a war-ship is bound to observe, in its operations, the laws and customs of war.

ART. 6.

A belligerent who converts a merchant-ship into a war-ship must, as soon as possible, announce such conversion in the list of the ships of its military fleet.

ART. 7.

The provisions of the present Convention are only applicable between the Contracting Powers, and only if all the belligerents are parties to the Convention.

<table>
<tr><td>

ART. 8.

La présente Convention sera ratifiée aussitôt que possible.

Les ratifications seront déposées à La Haye.

Le premier dépôt de ratifications sera constaté par un procès-verbal signé par les Représentants des Puissances qui y prennent part et par le Ministre des Affaires Étrangères des Pays-Bas.

Les dépôts ultérieurs de ratifications se feront au moyen d'une notification écrite, adressée au Gouvernement des Pays-Bas et accompagnée de l'instrument de ratification.

Copie certifiée conforme du procès-verbal relatif au premier dépôt de ratifications, des notifications mentionnées à l'alinéa précédent, ainsi que des instruments de ratification, sera immédiatement remise, par les soins du Gouvernement des Pays-Bas, et par la voie diplomatique, aux Puissances conviées à la Deuxième Conférence de la Paix, ainsi qu'aux autres Puissances qui auront adhéré à la Convention. Dans les cas visés par l'alinéa précédent, le dit Gouvernement leur fera connaître en même temps la date à laquelle il a reçu la notification.

</td><td>

ART. 8.

The present Convention shall be ratified as soon as possible.

The ratifications shall be deposited at The Hague.

The first deposit of ratifications shall be recorded in a *procès-verbal* signed by the Representatives of the Powers which take part therein and by the Netherland Minister for Foreign Affairs.

The subsequent deposits of ratifications shall be made by means of a written notification, addressed to the Netherland Government and accompanied by the instrument of ratification.

A duly certified copy of the *procès-verbal* relating to the first deposit of ratifications, of the notifications mentioned in the preceding paragraph, and of the instruments of ratification, shall be immediately sent by the Netherland Government, through the diplomatic channel, to the Powers invited to the Second Peace Conference, as well as to the other Powers which have acceded to the Convention. In the cases contemplated in the preceding paragraph, the said Government shall inform them at the same time of the date on which it received the notification.

</td></tr>
</table>

ART. 9.

Les Puissances non-signataires sont admises à adhérer à la présente Convention.

La Puissance qui désire adhérer notifie par écrit son intention au Gouvernement des Pays-Bas en lui transmettant l'acte d'adhésion, qui sera déposé dans les archives du dit Gouvernement.

ART. 9.

Non-Signatory Powers may accede to the present Convention.

A Power which desires to accede notifies its intention in writing to the Netherland Government, forwarding to it the act of accession, which shall be deposited in the archives of the said Government.

Ce Gouvernement transmettra immédiatement à toutes les autres Puissances copie certifiée conforme de la notification ainsi que de l'acte d'adhésion, en indiquant la date à laquelle il a reçu la notification.

The said Government shall immediately forward to all the other Powers a duly certified copy of the notification as well as of the act of accession, mentioning the date on which it received the notification.

Art. 10.

La présente Convention produira effet, pour les Puissances qui auront participé au premier dépôt de ratifications, soixante jours après la date du procès-verbal de ce dépôt, et pour les Puissances qui ratifieront ultérieurement ou qui adhéreront, soixante jours après que la notification de leur ratification ou de leur adhésion aura été reçue par le Gouvernement des Pays-Bas.

Art. 10.

The present Convention shall take effect, in the case of the Powers which were parties to the first deposit of ratifications, sixty days after the date of the *procès-verbal* recording such deposit, and, in the case of the Powers which shall ratify subsequently or which shall accede, sixty days after the notification of their ratification or of their accession has been received by the Netherland Government.

Art. 11.

S'il arrivait qu'une des Puissances contractantes voulût dénoncer la présente Convention, la dénonciation sera notifiée par écrit au Gouvernement des Pays-Bas, qui communiquera immédiatement copie certifiée conforme de la notification à toutes les autres Puissances en leur faisant savoir la date à laquelle il l'a reçue.

La dénonciation ne produira ses effets qu'à l'égard de la Puissance qui l'aura notifiée et un an après que la notification en sera parvenue au Gouvernement des Pays-Bas.

Art. 11.

In the event of one of the Contracting Powers wishing to denounce the present Convention, the denunciation shall be notified in writing to the Netherland Government, which shall immediately communicate a duly certified copy of the notification to all the other Powers, informing them of the date on which it was received.

The denunciation shall only affect the notifying Power, and only on the expiry of one year after the notification has reached the Netherland Government.

Art. 12.

Un registre tenu par le Ministère des Affaires Étrangères des Pays-Bas indiquera la date du dépôt de ratifications effectué en vertu de l'Article 8, alinéas 3 et 4, ainsi que la date à laquelle auront été reçues les notifica-

Art. 12.

A register kept by the Netherland Ministry for Foreign Affairs shall record the date of the deposit of ratifications effected in virtue of Article 8, paragraphs 3 and 4, as well as the date on which the notifications

tions d'adhésion (Article 9, alinéa 2) ou de dénonciation (Article 11, alinéa 1).

Chaque Puissance contractante est admise à prendre connaissance de ce registre et à en demander des extraits certifiés conformes.

En foi de quoi les Plénipotentiaires ont revêtu la présente Convention de leurs signatures.

Fait à La Haye, le 18 Octobre, 1907, en un seul exemplaire qui restera déposé dans les archives du Gouvernement des Pays-Bas, et dont des copies, certifiées conformes, seront remises par la voie diplomatique aux Puissances qui ont été conviées à la Deuxième Conférence de la Paix.

of accession (Article 9, paragraph 2) or of denunciation (Article 11, paragraph 1) have been received.

Each Contracting Power is entitled to have access to this register and to be supplied with duly certified extracts from it.

In faith whereof the Plenipotentiaries have appended their signatures to the present Convention.

Done at The Hague, the 18th October, 1907, in a single original, which shall remain deposited in the archives of the Netherland Government, and of which duly certified copies shall be sent, through the diplomatic channel, to the Powers invited to the Second Peace Conference.

CONVENTION NO. 7.   CONVENTION RELATIVE TO THE CONVERSION OF
MERCHANT-SHIPS INTO WAR-SHIPS[1].

It is suggested that this Convention should be entitled " A Convention

Privateering and Volunteer Navies.

to secure the observance of the Declaration of Paris in regard to privateering[2]." Privateering was abolished as between the signatory Powers to the Declaration of Paris. Nearly all the civilised states of the world have become parties to

[1] *Parl. Papers*, Misc. No. 4 (1908), pp. 47, 183 ; *La Deux. Confér.* T. I. pp. 232, 239 ; *Livre Jaune*, p. 97 ; *Weissbuch*, p. 10 ; L. A. Atherley-Jones, *Commerce in War*, pp. 538–543 ; Sir T. Barclay, *Problems, etc.* p. 204 ; Bonfils-Fauchille, *Droit international* (5th ed.), § 1395 ; F. Despagnet, *Droit international*, §§ 641–3 ; C. Dupuis, *Le droit de la guerre maritime*, Chap. III. § 2 ; W. E. Hall, *Inter. Law*, p. 527 ; Halleck, *International Law* (4th ed.), Vol. II. p. 136 ; A. S. Hershey, *International law and diplomacy of the Russo-Japanese War*, Chap. V. ; T. J. Lawrence, *International Law*, § 224 ; Idem, *International Problems, etc.* p. 125 ; Idem, *War and Neutrality*, Chap. IX. ; A. de Lapradelle, *La guerre maritime, etc. Revue des deux Mondes* (1 Aug. 1908) ; E. Lémonon, *La seconde Conférence*, p. 611 ; J. B. Moore, *Digest of Int. Law*, Vol. VII. p. 542 ; L. Oppenheim, *Int. Law*, Vol. II. § 84 ; F. E. Smith and N. W. Sibley, *International Law, etc.* Chap. II. ; J. Westlake, *War*, p. 304 ; G. G. Wilson, *Conversion of merchant ships, etc.*, Am. Journ. of Int. Law, Vol. II. p. 271.

[2] G. G. Wilson, *op. cit.* p. 272.

this Declaration, but in many continental states opinions have been expressed that accession to the Declaration was far from being advantageous, and the creation of Volunteer Navies in some states has raised delicate questions as to the evasion of the Declaration. Prussia

Prussian proposals in 1870. in 1870 decided to address an appeal to all German sailors and shipowners, inviting them to put their resources and ships at the disposal of their country. Volunteer ships were to be placed under naval discipline during the war. Officers and crew were to enter for the duration of the war into the Navy of the Confederation, to wear its uniform and marks of rank, and swear to the articles of war ; they were to be entitled to pensions like regular members of the Navy. Officers were to receive Commissions of their rank and in case of meritorious service permanent Commissions were promised. The vessels were to fly the war-flag of the North German Confederation. Large premiums were offered for the destruction of enemy ships[1]. France protested, but the British Law Officers when consulted by the Government gave their opinion that there were substantial differences between the Volunteer Navy sanctioned by the Prussian Government and the system which it was the object of the Declaration of Paris to suppress. Prussia had announced her intention not to capture private property at sea, but as France would not agree to this proposal the Prussian offer was withdrawn, and with it the formation of a Volunteer Navy was abandoned. But the incident was far-reaching in its influence. In 1877–8 relations between Great Britain and

Russian Volunteer Navy. Russia were strained ; there was for a time every prospect of war breaking out. The Russian Fleet was small, and the mercantile marine insignificant. A patriotic association was formed with the object of raising money and buying fast ships to act as auxiliaries to the Imperial Navy. The vessels purchased were to be placed under the command of the officers of the Navy, and the crews to be subjected to military discipline. This institution still exists, and is subsidised by the Government. The commander of the ship and at least one other officer hold the Imperial Commission, and their crews receive training so as to enable them to perform the duties allotted to crews of men of war. In time of peace they carry the merchant flag and are usually engaged in ordinary mercantile traffic, though many of the vessels are also employed by the state as transport-ships[2].

---

[1] See W. E. Hall, *op. cit.* p. 527 ; T. J. Lawrence, *Int. Law*, § 224 ; C. Dupuis, *op. cit.* §§ 82–4.· For official details of the Prussian-proposals see Geffcken in 4 Holtzendorff, *Handbuch des Völkerrechts*, p. 560 (quoting from *Staatsarchiv*, Vol. xx. No. 4345).

[2] T. J. Lawrence, *Int. Law*, § 224 ; C. Dupuis, *op. cit.* § 85.

In France some of the mail-boats are commanded by officers of the
French Navy. The companies receive a subsidy from the state,
Auxiliary and they are constructed on plans sanctioned by the French
Cruisers. Admiralty. On the outbreak of war they are to be incor-
porated into the regular Navy[1].

Great Britain in 1887 entered into arrangements with several of the
great Navigation Steamship Companies, such as the Cunard,
British. White Star, Peninsular and Oriental, etc. In return for an
annual subsidy the companies undertake to sell or charter to the Government certain fast vessels at a fixed price and on short notice, and to build
new ships on plans approved by the Admiralty. Half the crews are to be
engaged from the Royal Naval Reserve, and the Admiralty has the right
of placing on board fittings and arrangements to facilitate their speedy
conversion into ships of war[2].

The United States in 1892 entered into similar agreements with
American companies and in the Spanish-American War of 1898 they
made use of these vessels[3].

The arrangements made by these Powers in regard to their incorporation into the regular navy vary, but where they are placed under the
command of the regular Naval Authorities of the state, and carry the
national flag of the State Navy and are commanded by duly commissioned
officers, and the crews wear a distinctive uniform and observe the laws
of war, there is no doubt that they are entitled to treatment as regular
belligerents[4]. It was however desirable, as is stated in the preamble to
this Convention, "in view of the incorporation in time of war of merchant-
ships in the fighting fleet, to define the conditions subject to which this
operation may be effected." The immediate cause of the insertion of the
subject in the Programme of the Conference[5] was an incident which
The Peter- occurred during the Russo-Japanese War. Two vessels, the
burg and *Peterburg* and *Smolensk*, belonging to the Russian Volunteer
Smolensk. Navy stationed in the Black Sea, on the 4th and 6th July,
1904, passed through the Bosphorus and Dardanelles flying the flag of the
Russian mercantile marine. These Straits are under the Treaties of Paris,
London and Berlin closed to vessels of war. The vessels also passed through

<hr>

[1] C. Dupuis, *op. cit.* p. 114; W. E. Hall, *Int. Law*, p. 529.

[2] T. J. Lawrence, *Int. Law*, § 224; *Parl. Papers*, 1887, *Subvention of Merchant Steamers for State purposes.*

[3] Sir T. Barclay, *Problems*, etc. p. 294.

[4] F. Despagnet, *Droit inter.* § 643; C. Dupuis, *op. cit.* § 84; Guihéneue, *La marine auxiliaire.*

[5] See Count Benckendorff's Circular, *ante*, p. 54.

the Suez Canal under the same flag. " The *Peterburg* certainly, and possibly the *Smolensk* also, engaged pilots for the Red Sea as a vessel of commerce[1]." When in the Red Sea they hoisted the flag of the Imperial Navy, and the *Peterburg* captured the *Malucca*, a P. and O. Mail Boat. Ultimately after strong protests by the British Government these vessels were ordered to haul down the flag of the Imperial Navy and to cease to act as cruisers, and Russia agreed that all vessels captured by them should be restored.

The first question mentioned in the Programme of the Fourth Com-

The Problems for the Conference. mittee was that of the conversion of merchant-ships into ships of war[2], and M. de Martens, the President, framed his questionnaire in the following terms :

(1) Is it admitted by practice and the laws of states that belligerent states can convert merchant-ships into ships of war ?

(2) In cases of conversion of merchant-ships into ships of war, what are the legal conditions which belligerent states ought to observe ?

From the sketch already given there was no doubt as to the answer which the Committee would give to the first question. The laws of various states make provision for the incorporation into their navies of merchant-ships under varying conditions. The terms on which such vessels are to be obtained are matters to be settled by municipal law. But international law is concerned with the question as to what conditions are to be observed so that private vessels may become entitled to all the privileges and subject to the restrictions imposed by neutrals on ships of war[2]. The questions which the Committee discussed were five in number. (1) Can merchant-ships be converted into ships of war ? (2) What is a ship of war ? (3) Where can conversion take place ? (4) How long does the conversion last ? (5) What regulations shall be applied to merchant-ships converted into ships of war ?

No difficulty was occasioned in giving an affirmative answer to the first

The terms of the Convention. question; very little also was occasioned in framing the regulations to be applied to such vessels, and any doubt which may have been raised as to the re-introduction of privateering under the guise of volunteer fleets has been effectually dispelled by the acceptance of the six rules embodied in this Convention— " Privateering is and remains abolished." The converted merchant-ship in

---

[1] T. J. Lawrence, *War and Neutrality*, p. 205 ; for the career of these vessels and an examination of the legality of their proceedings, see pp. 205–217 of this work. See also Smith and Sibley, *op. cit.* Chap. II.; A. S. Hershey, *International Law, etc.* Chap. V.; Halleck, *International Law* (4th ed.), Vol. II. p. 187.

[2] *Parl. Papers*, Misc. No. 4 (1908), p. 188; *La Deux. Confér.* T. I. p. 240 ; *Idem*, T. III. p. 745.

order to be entitled to the status of a ship of war must be under the direct control and responsibility of the state converting it (Art. 1), and must notify its character by external marks such as the use of the flag of the State Navy (Art. 2). Its commander must be in the service of the state and duly commissioned, and his name must appear on the official list of officers of the state (Art. 3). The proposal that he must be in personal possession of his commission and of papers showing the regular conversion of the vessel was rejected. The crew must be subject to military discipline (Art. 4). The ship must in its operations conform to the laws and customs of war (Art. 5). This was objected to by the United States Delegation as constituting an invidious distinction as regards certain vessels bought and regularly commissioned in time of peace as forming part of the United States Navy. M. Renault, however, pointed out that the Article was in complete harmony with Article 1 of the Regulations on the laws and customs of war on land. Lastly the conversion of the merchant-ship must be notified publicly as soon as possible (Art. 6). The question of the duration of the conversion does not appear to be touched by this Article. These Articles embody the general principles which had been accepted by states, and except for the points raised on Articles 3 and 5 were accepted without discussion. The Convention does not go very far, but it may be welcomed as a beginning of a set of written rules on the subject. The other questions discussed were found to be insoluble.

Lord Reay desired to go to the root of the whole matter at the beginning. The legality of the conversion of merchant-ships into "ships of war" was not doubted, but the fundamental question, which, acting on the instructions of the British Government[1], he sought to have settled was—what is a ship of war? The difficulty is not peculiar to this question, but is equally important as regards the meaning to be attributed to the exemption from capture provided for in Article 5 of the previous Convention by which "merchant-ships whose construction indicates that they are intended for conversion into war-ships" in an enemy port at the outbreak of war remain liable to capture[2]. A modern navy to be effective must contain more than battle-ships, fast cruisers, torpedo-boats and destroyers and submarines. If a fleet is to remain for any length of time at sea, especially if its state does not possess a large number of coaling stations within the area of its operations, it needs a whole auxiliary fleet of colliers, repairing ships, supply ships, despatch vessels, transports for the carriage of men, ammunition, etc. The

Unsolved problems.

What is a ship of war?

---

[1] See Instructions in Appendix.

[2] See *ante*, p. 306.

following proposition introduced by Lord Reay was framed to meet modern conditions. "There are two classes of ships of war: (A) fighting ships (*vaisseaux de combat*), (B) auxiliary ships (*vaisseaux auxiliaires*)." He proposed to assimilate to the status of the fighting ships of the Navy the auxiliary ships used for any purpose of the fleet. Objection was taken to this on the ground that the principles of "unneutral service" were involved, and that this subject was not included in the Programme of the Conference; Lord Reay subsequently withdrew his proposed definition[1]. The question of the length of the period of the conversion of merchant-ships is important in this connection and this point was also discussed in connection with the place of conversion. Lord Reay, having abandoned the

Where may attempt to include auxiliary ships under the head of ships of
conversion war, developed his proposals in regard to Class A "fighting
take place,
and how long ships" which were defined as: "Every ship flying a recog-
does it last? nised flag, armed at the expense of the state for attacking
the enemy and the officers and crews of which are duly authorised for the purpose by the Government to which they belong. It shall not be lawful for a ship to be invested with this character save before its departure from a national port, nor to be divested of it, save after return to a national port[2]." It was urged in support of this view that for a neutral to allow

(a) Conver- the conversion to take place in one of its ports would be an
sion in na- infraction of its neutrality, and for a belligerent to make the
tional ports.
change within neutral waters would be a breach by a belligerent of his duties to a neutral, and that vessels so converted did not acquire the character of a regular ship of war[3]. Against conversion on the high seas Lord Reay urged that as ships of war were accorded rights of search of neutral vessels, a neutral has the right to know what ships are authorised to exercise this right. If it be permitted to all ships which have left a neutral port as merchantmen to suddenly appear in a new character (and as the Japanese delegate pointed out the converse case would be equally possible) "regrettable incidents" would be occasioned, complications in regard to breach of neutrality laws would occur and an intolerable situation would be created. The Dutch delegate supported the proposition to limit conversion to national ports. The United States and Japanese delegates also concurred with the addition of "ports or territorial waters in the naval or military occupation" of the Power making the conversion.

---

[1] See *La Deux. Confér.* T. III. pp. 847, 917.　　[2] *La Deux. Confér.* T. III. p. 822.
[3] See *The Santissima Trinidad* (7 Wheaton, 283, J. B. Scott, *Leading Cases*, p. 701), *The Gran Para* (7 Wheaton, 471).

The delegates of Germany, Russia and France opposed these proposals and contended that such conversion was permissible on the high seas. They urged that there was no existing rule of international law against it, that as the laws of many states allowed the private property of nationals to be employed for operations of war, such states could exercise this right within territories under their jurisdiction and also on the high seas which are subject to the jurisdiction of no one Power. A prize captured from the enemy on the high seas, and suitable for conversion, could at once be turned into a ship of war by placing her under the command of an officer of the capturing ship and transferring to her a crew, and if this is *ex hypothesi* allowable, it is equally allowable for a ship of war meeting a merchantman of its own state on the high seas to make a conversion in a similar manner. M. Renault (France) agreed that conversion must not take place in neutral ports or territorial waters but otherwise he supported the German and Russian point of view.

(b) Conversion on the high seas.

The Italian delegate (Count Tornielli), as on other occasions, endeavoured to bring about a compromise between the opposing views of Germany and Great Britain; he moved " That ships which leave the territorial waters of their country *after* the opening of hostilities cannot change their character either on the high seas or in the territorial waters of another state[1]." M. Fusinato (Italy) in supporting this proposal pointed out that it would be a serious matter for a merchant-ship which had enjoyed the right of entry of a neutral port to be able to take advantage of its commercial character there and immediately on reaching the high seas to throw it off. Such a proceeding was nothing less than an abuse of neutral hospitality. The Italian proposition thus accepted the Russo-German view only to the extent of allowing the conversion of merchant-ships on the high seas in case they had left the territorial waters of their own state before the outbreak of war. The Mexican delegate supported the Italian proposition. The debates on these points were renewed in the *Comité d'Examen* and finally a division on the Italian proposition was taken with the result that 9 states voted *for* (Great Britain, the United States, Belgium, Brazil, Italy, Japan, Norway, Holland and Sweden) and 7 *against* (Germany, Austria, Argentine, Chili, France, Russia and Servia)[2]. The vote was indecisive and the preamble records that " whereas the contracting Powers have been unable to come to an agreement on the question whether the conversion of a merchant-ship into a war-ship may take place upon the high seas, it is

(c) The Italian compromise.

Problem left unsolved.

---

[1] *La Deux. Confér.* T. III. pp. 824, 1136.　　[2] *Idem*, T. I. p. 243, note 2.

understood that the question of the place where such conversion is effected remains outside the scope of this agreement[1]."

The really important question was therefore left undecided. A similar fate befell the attempt to settle the period of duration of the conversion. The Austro-Hungarian delegate proposed that a ship once converted could not be re-converted until the termination of the war; this was supported by the Mexican delegate. The Austrian proposal was meant to prevent the not impossible case of a converted merchantman which had entered a neutral port as a ship of war, leaving and returning in a few hours having divested herself of her character on the high seas, for as was pointed out by the Japanese delegate if conversion on the high seas is allowed, it would be equally possible for the act of re-conversion or divestment of the public character to take place there also. Lord Reay's proposition allowed the character of the converted ship to be divested only in a national port. As no agreement had been reached as to the place of conversion the Committee decided to leave this question in its present (uncertain) position[2].

In this case, as in so many other questions discussed at the Conference, the conflict of political interests was found to be too acute to allow of a settlement of a problem which, if it is allowed to remain in its present extremely unsatisfactory condition, will be certain on the outbreak of a naval war to bring about strained relations between the states which hold such divergent views. Every principle of the law of neutrality demands that the conversion of merchant-ships in neutral waters should be recognised as illegal; but there was not absolute unanimity even on this. The British proposal started with an endeavour to obtain the acceptance of such a definition of ship of war as would "prove sufficient to prevent the issue by any Power of letters of marque" (British Instructions). The Articles agreed to by the Conference have formulated principles which will have this effect. The Italian proposal was one which, while being wholly consistent with principle, allowed for the exceptional case of "convertible"

---

[1] The late Professor M. Bernard was of opinion "that a vessel may be built, equipped, armed, commissioned and employed as a cruiser, without even having entered a port of the nation under whose flag she sails. Whether it is just or expedient for all nations that this should be prohibited, is an open question: at present it is not prohibited" (*British Neutrality* p. 401). Sir William Harcourt was of opinion that for all reasons it is wise to discourage such a practice as that of granting commissions to vessels on the high seas, by which such vessels become at once raised to the position of lawful belligerent cruisers. (See quotation from Memorandum on the Report of the Neutrality Laws Commission cited by T. Baty, *Some questions in the Law of Neutrality, Journ. of the Soc. of Comparative Legislation* (New Series), No. xiv. p. 216.

[2] *La Deux. Confér.* T. i. p. 243; *Idem*, T. iii. p. 1014.

vessels which were on the high seas at the outbreak of war. This proposal, embodying the British, Japanese and American views, would have allowed the conversion of merchant-ships only in the national ports and territorial waters of the converting Power or in ports and territorial waters occupied by it. Conversion on the high seas would have been prohibited in the case of all ships leaving their national ports after the outbreak of war, but allowed in the case of those which left a port before the outbreak of war. If these proposals, and the Austrian proposition that conversion when once effected should continue for the duration of the war, had been added to the rules adopted by the Conference, a valuable and important addition would have been made to the Law of Nations. Neutral rights, wholly ignored by the Russo-German proposals, would have been safeguarded, and belligerents would have avoided the friction with neutrals which must inevitably take place so long as the present uncertainty exists.

This Convention has been signed by all Powers mentioned in the Final
Signatory Powers. Act except the United States of America (which has not acceded to the Declaration of Paris), China, Dominica, Nicaragua, and Uruguay. Turkey signed under a general reservation which was made by her delegate at the Seventh Plenary Meeting of the Conference on the 27th Sept. 1907 and which is applicable to all the Conventions recommended to the Conference by the Fourth Committee[1].

The subject of the conversion of merchant vessels into war-ships on
The Conference of London[2]. the high seas was examined at the Naval Conference which sat in London during December, 1908, and January and February, 1909. The conflicting views which were so strongly marked at the Hague recurred at that Conference. Similar arguments to those adduced at the Hague were again advanced by the delegates of the different states, but though all were agreed that it would be a great advantage to put an end to an uncertainty, all attempts to bring about an understanding were unsuccessful. States claiming an unrestricted right of conversion on the high seas "refused to make any concessions or to abate one jot from the claim to the absolutely unfettered exercise of the right which its advocates vindicate as a rule forming part of the existing law of nations[3]." The British Delegation declined to admit the right.

At one point of the proceedings it appeared possible to come to an agreement on the subject of *re-conversion*, so as to prevent a "war-ship (generally a recently converted merchant vessel) doffing its character so as

---

[1] *La Deux. Confér.* T. I. p. 235.
[2] *Parl. Papers*, Misc. No. 4 (1909), pp. 10, 35, 101; No. 5, p. 340.
[3] *Idem*, No. 4, p. 101 (Report of British Delegation).

to be able to revictual or refit in a neutral port without being bound by the restrictions imposed on war-ships." The delicate position of a neutral state in such circumstances was admitted. "Agreement might perhaps have been reached on this proposal, but it seemed very difficult to deal with this secondary aspect of a question which there was no hope of settling as a whole.......The question of conversion on the high seas and that of re-conversion therefore remain open[1]."

[1] *Parl. Papers*, Misc. No. 4 (1909), p. 35 (Report of M. Renault).

VIII. AUTOMATIC SUBMARINE CONTACT MINES.

VIII. Convention relative à la Pose de Mines Sous-marines Automatiques de Contact.

Sa Majesté l'Empereur d'Allemagne, Roi de Prusse, &c.[1]

S'inspirant du principe de la liberté des voies maritimes, ouvertes à toutes les nations ;

Considérant que, si dans l'état actuel des choses, on ne peut interdire l'emploi de mines sous-marines automatiques de contact, il importe d'en limiter et réglementer l'usage, afin de restreindre les rigueurs de la guerre et de donner, autant que faire se peut, à la navigation pacifique la sécurité à laquelle elle a droit de prétendre, malgré l'existence d'une guerre ;

En attendant qu'il soit possible de régler la matière d'une façon qui donne aux intérêts engagés toutes les garanties désirables ;

Ont résolu de conclure une Convention à cet effet et ont nommé pour leurs Plénipotentiaires, savoir :

[*Dénomination des Plénipotentiaires.*]

Lesquels, après avoir déposé leurs pleins pouvoirs, trouvés en bonne et due forme, sont convenus des dispositions suivantes :—

VIII. Convention relative to the Laying of Automatic Submarine Contact Mines.

His Majesty the German Emperor, King of Prussia, &c.[1]

Inspired by the principle of the freedom of the seas as the common highway of all nations ;

Seeing that, while the existing position of affairs makes it impossible to forbid the employment of automatic submarine contact mines, it is nevertheless expedient to restrict and regulate their employment in order to mitigate the severity of war and to ensure, as far as possible, to peaceful navigation the security to which it is entitled, despite the existence of war ;

Until such time as it may be found possible to formulate rules on the subject which shall ensure to the interests involved all the guarantees desirable ;

Have resolved to conclude a Convention to this effect, and have appointed as their Plenipotentiaries, that is to say :

[*Names of Plenipotentiaries*]

Who, after having deposited their full powers, found to be in good and due form, have agreed upon the following provisions :—

[1] List of States as in the Final Act, 1907.

ART. 1.

Il est interdit :

1. De placer des mines automatiques de contact non amarrées, à moins qu'elles ne soient construites de manière à devenir inoffensives une heure au maximum après que celui qui les a placées en aura perdu le contrôle ;

2. De placer des mines automatiques de contact amarrées qui ne deviennent pas inoffensives dès qu'elles auront rompu leurs amarres ;

3. D'employer des torpilles, qui ne deviennent pas inoffensives lorsqu'elles auront manqué leur but.

ART. 1.

It is forbidden :

1. To lay unanchored automatic contact mines, unless they be so constructed as to become harmless one hour at most after those who laid them have lost control over them ;

2. To lay anchored automatic contact mines which do not become harmless as soon as they have broken loose from their moorings ;

3. To use torpedoes which do not become harmless when they have missed their mark.

ART. 2.

Il est interdit de placer des mines automatiques de contact devant les côtes et les ports de l'adversaire, dans le seul but d'intercepter la navigation de commerce.

ART. 2.

It is forbidden to lay automatic contact mines off the coasts and ports of the enemy, with the sole object of intercepting commercial navigation.

ART. 3.

Lorsque les mines automatiques de contact amarrées sont employées, toutes les précautions possibles doivent être prises pour la sécurité de la navigation pacifique.

Les belligérants s'engagent à pourvoir, dans la mesure du possible, à ce que ces mines deviennent inoffensives après un laps de temps limité, et, dans le cas où elles cesseraient d'être surveillées, à signaler les régions dangereuses aussitôt que les exigences militaires le permettront, par un avis à la navigation, qui devra être aussi communiqué aux Gouvernements par la voie diplomatique.

ART. 3.

When anchored automatic contact mines are employed, every possible precaution must be taken for the security of peaceful navigation.

The belligerents undertake to provide, as far as possible, for these mines becoming harmless after a limited time has elapsed, and, where the mines cease to be under observation, to notify the danger zones as soon as military exigencies permit, by a notice to mariners, which must also be communicated to the Governments through the diplomatic channel.

Art. 4.

Toute Puissance neutre qui place des mines automatiques de contact devant ses côtes, doit observer les mêmes règles et prendre les mêmes précautions que celles qui sont imposées aux belligérants.

La Puissance neutre doit faire connaître à la navigation, par un avis préalable, les régions où seront mouillées des mines automatiques de contact. Cet avis devra être communiqué d'urgence aux Gouvernements par voie diplomatique.

Art. 4.

Neutral Powers which lay automatic contact mines off their coasts must observe the same rules and take the same precautions as are imposed on belligerents.

The neutral Power must give notice to mariners in advance of the places where automatic contact mines have been laid. This notice must be communicated at once to the Governments through the diplomatic channel.

Art. 5.

A la fin de la guerre, les Puissances contractantes s'engagent à faire tout ce qui dépend d'elles pour enlever, chacune de son côté, les mines qu'elles ont placées.

Quant aux mines automatiques de contact amarrées que l'un des belligérants aurait posées le long des côtes de l'autre, l'emplacement en sera notifié à l'autre partie par la Puissance qui les a posées, et chaque Puissance devra procéder dans le plus bref délai à l'enlèvement des mines qui se trouvent dans ses eaux.

Art. 5.

At the close of the war, the Contracting Powers undertake to do their utmost to remove the mines which they have laid, each Power removing its own mines.

As regards anchored automatic contact mines laid by one of the belligerents off the coast of the other, their position must be notified to the other party by the Power which laid them, and each Power must proceed with the least possible delay to remove the mines in its own waters.

Art. 6.

Les Puissances contractantes qui ne disposent pas encore de mines perfectionnées telles qu'elles sont prévues dans la présente Convention, et qui, par conséquent, ne sauraient actuellement se conformer aux règles établies dans les Articles 1 et 3, s'engagent à transformer, aussitôt que possible, leur matériel de mines, afin qu'il réponde aux prescriptions susmentionnées.

Art. 6.

The Contracting Powers which do not at present own perfected mines of the description contemplated in the present Convention, and which, consequently, could not at present carry out the rules laid down in Articles 1 and 3, undertake to convert the *matériel* of their mines as soon as possible, so as to bring it into conformity with the foregoing requirements.

ART. 7.

Les dispositions de la présente Convention ne sont applicables qu'entre les Puissances contractantes et seulement si les belligérants sont tous parties à la Convention.

ART. 8.

La présente Convention sera ratifiée aussitôt que possible.

Les ratifications seront déposées à La Haye.

Le premier dépôt de ratifications sera constaté par un procès-verbal signé par les représentants des Puissances qui y prennent part et par le Ministre des Affaires Étrangères des Pays-Bas.

Les dépôts ultérieurs de ratifications se feront au moyen d'une notification écrite, adressée au Gouvernement des Pays-Bas et accompagnée de l'instrument de ratification.

Copie certifiée conforme du procès-verbal relatif au premier dépôt de ratifications, des notifications mentionnées à l'alinéa précédent, ainsi que des instruments de ratification, sera immédiatement remise, par les soins du Gouvernement des Pays-Bas et par la voie diplomatique, aux Puissances conviées à la Deuxième Conférence de la Paix, ainsi qu'aux autres Puissances qui auront adhéré à la Convention. Dans les cas visés par l'alinéa précédent, le dit Gouvernement leur fera connaître en même temps la date à laquelle il a reçu la notification.

ART. 9.

Les Puissances non-signataires sont admises à adhérer à la présente Convention.

La Puissance qui désire adhérer

ART. 7.

The provisions of the present Convention are only applicable between the Contracting Powers, and only if all the belligerents are parties to the Convention.

ART. 8.

The present Convention shall be ratified as soon as possible.

The ratifications shall be deposited at The Hague.

The first deposit of ratifications shall be recorded in a *procès-verbal* signed by the Representatives of the Powers which take part therein and by the Netherland Minister for Foreign Affairs.

The subsequent deposits of ratifications shall be made by means of a written notification addressed to the Netherland Government and accompanied by the instrument of ratification.

A duly certified copy of the *procès-verbal* relating to the first deposit of ratifications, of the notifications mentioned in the preceding paragraph, as well as of the instruments of ratification, shall be immediately sent, by the Netherland Government through the diplomatic channel, to the Powers invited to the Second Peace Conference, as well as to the other Powers which have acceded to the Convention. In the cases contemplated in the preceding paragraph, the said Government shall inform them at the same time of the date on which it received the notification.

ART. 9.

Non-Signatory Powers may accede to the Present Convention.

A Power which desires to accede

notifie par écrit son intention au Gouvernement des Pays-Bas en lui transmettant l'acte d'adhésion, qui sera déposé dans les archives du dit Gouvernement.

Ce Gouvernement transmettra immédiatement à toutes les autres Puissances copie certifiée conforme de la notification ainsi que de l'acte d'adhésion, en indiquant la date à laquelle il a reçu la notification.

ART. 10.

La présente Convention produira effet pour les Puissances qui auront participé au premier dépôt de ratifications, soixante jours après la date du procès-verbal de ce dépôt, et pour les Puissances qui ratifieront ultérieurement ou qui adhéreront, soixante jours après que la notification de leur ratification ou de leur adhésion aura été reçue par le Gouvernement des Pays-Bas.

ART. 11.

La présente Convention aura une durée de sept ans à partir du soixantième jour après la date du premier dépôt de ratifications.

Sauf dénonciation, elle continuera d'être en vigueur après l'expiration de ce délai.

La dénonciation sera notifiée par écrit au Gouvernement des Pays-Bas, qui communiquera immédiatement copie certifiée conforme de la notification à toutes les Puissances, en leur faisant savoir la date à laquelle il l'a reçue.

La dénonciation ne produira ses effets qu'à l'égard de la Puissance qui l'aura notifiée et six mois après que la notification en sera parvenue au Gouvernement des Pays-Bas.

notifies its intention in writing to the Netherland Government, forwarding to it the act of accession, which shall be deposited in the archives of the said Government.

The said Government shall immediately forward to all the other Powers a duly certified copy of the notification, as well as of the act of accession, mentioning the date on which it received the notification.

ART. 10.

The present Convention shall take effect, in the case of the Powers which were parties to the first deposit of ratifications, sixty days after the date of the *procès-verbal* recording such deposit, and, in the case of the Powers which shall ratify subsequently or which shall accede, sixty days after the notification of their ratification or of their accession has been received by the Netherland Government.

ART. 11.

The present Convention shall remain in force for seven years, dating from the sixtieth day after the date of the first deposit of ratifications.

Unless denounced, it shall continue in force after the expiry of this period.

The denunciation shall be notified in writing to the Netherland Government, which shall immediately communicate a duly certified copy of the notification to all the Powers, informing them of the date on which it was received.

The denunciation shall only operate in respect of the denouncing Power, and only on the expiry of six months after the notification has reached the Netherland Government.

ART. 12.

Les Puissances contractantes s'engagent à reprendre la question de l'emploi des mines automatiques de contact six mois avant l'expiration du terme prévu par l'alinéa premier de l'Article précédent, au cas où elle n'aurait pas été reprise et résolue à une date antérieure par la Troisième Conférence de la Paix.

Si les Puissances contractantes concluent une nouvelle Convention relative à l'emploi des mines, dès son entrée en vigueur, la présente Convention cessera d'être applicable.

ART. 13.

Un registre tenu par le Ministère des Affaires Étrangères des Pays-Bas indiquera la date du dépôt de ratifications effectué en vertu de l'Article 8, alinéas 3 et 4, ainsi que la date à laquelle auront été reçues les notifications d'adhésion (Article 9, alinéa 2) ou de dénonciation (Article 11, alinéa 3).

Chaque Puissance contractante est admise à prendre connaissance de ce registre et à en demander des extraits certifiés conformes.

En foi de quoi les Plénipotentiaires ont revêtu la présente Convention de leurs signatures.

Fait à La Haye, le 18 Octobre, 1907, en un seul exemplaire, qui restera déposé dans les archives du Gouvernement des Pays-Bas, et dont des copies, certifiées conformes, seront remises par la voie diplomatique aux Puissances qui ont été conviées à la Deuxième Conférence de la Paix.

ART. 12.

The Contracting Powers agree to reopen the question of the employment of automatic contact mines six months before the expiry of the period contemplated in the first paragraph of the preceding Article, in the event of the question not having been already taken up and settled by the Third Peace Conference.

If the Contracting Powers conclude a fresh Convention relative to the employment of mines, the present Convention shall cease to be applicable from the moment when it comes into force.

ART. 13.

A register kept by the Netherland Ministry for Foreign Affairs shall record the date of the deposit of ratifications effected in virtue of Article 8, paragraphs 3 and 4, as well as the date on which the notifications of accession (Article 9, paragraph 2) or of denunciation (Article 11, paragraph 3) have been received.

Each Contracting Power is entitled to have access to this register and to be supplied with duly certified extracts from it.

In faith whereof the Plenipotentiaries have appended their signatures to the present Convention.

Done at The Hague, the 18th October, 1907, in a single original, which shall remain deposited in the archives of the Netherland Government, and of which duly certified copies shall be sent, through the diplomatic channel, to the Powers invited to the Second Peace Conference.

CONVENTION No. 8. RELATIVE TO THE LAYING OF AUTOMATIC
SUBMARINE CONTACT MINES[1].

The Russo-Japanese War drew the attention of the world to the
Submarine deadly results produced by floating mines. Though not
mines. expressly mentioned in Count Benckendorff's Circular, the
laying of torpedoes, etc. (*pose de torpilles, etc.*) was included among the
subjects for consideration[2]. Automobile torpedoes were practically excluded
from the discussions: they are referred to only in the 1st Article of this
Convention; the lengthy debates in the Committees were all concerned
with submarine mines[3]. Mines are of three different kinds: (1) Observation
mines which are anchored along the coast and connected therewith by
wires by which they can be exploded electrically. These are not dealt
with in the Convention. They are innocuous to peaceful shipping.
(2) Anchored automatic contact mines which are attached to heavy
weights, and which can be placed at any required depth below the surface;
these mines are exploded automatically by contact with heavy bodies such
as ships. (3) Unanchored automatic contact mines which also explode
by contact.

Mines were employed in the Russo-Japanese War by both belligerents,
Danger of and hundreds either broke adrift from their moorings
mines to or, not being anchored at all, floated into the high seas and
neutrals. caused serious loss of life to neutrals long after the conclusion

---

[1] *Parl. Papers*, Misc. No. 4 (1908), pp. 51, 227; *La Deux. Confér.* T. I. pp. 277, 287;
T. III. pp. 292, 364–459, 517–537, 660–680; *Livre Jaune*, p. 83; *Weissbuch*, p. 10; Sir
T. Barclay, *Problems, etc.* pp. 57, 158; A. S. Hershey, *International Law and Diplomacy, etc.*
pp. 124–135; T. J. Lawrence, *War and Neutrality, etc.* pp. 94–101; Idem, *International
Problems*, pp. 121, 162, 190, 199; E. Lémonon, *La seconde Conférence*, pp. 472–502;
C. H. Stockton, *Submarine mines and torpedoes in war*, *Am. Journ. of Int. Law*, Vol. II. p. 276;
J. Westlake, *War*, p. 322; Halleck's *International Law* (4th edition), Vol. I. p. 620;
Bonfils-Fauchille, *Droit international* (5th ed.), f. 1273[1]; L. Oppenheim, *International Law*,
Vol. II. p. 189; L. A. Atherley-Jones, *Commerce in War*; M. Sueter, *The evolution of the
submarine boat, mine and torpedo*; Schücking, *Die Verwendung von Minen im Seekrieg*,
Ztschr. für int. Priv. u. Strafrecht, XVI. (1906), p. 121; v. Martitz, *Minen im Seekrieg*, 23rd
Report Int. Law Association (1906), p. 47.

[2] The word "torpille" until recently appears to have meant any sort of receptacle
containing an explosive intended to operate against the hull of a ship by contact either
on or below the water-line. Thus there were *torpilles fixes, torpilles mouillées, torpilles
mobiles* and finally *torpilles automobiles*. It would appear that latterly the word has come to
mean only "automobile torpedo," e.g. in the Convention now under consideration the word
"mine" is used when an automobile torpedo is not implied.

[3] Fuller accounts are given of the proposals and discussions in connection with this
Convention than in the case of the others by reason of the great importance of the subject to
neutrals.

of the war. In the course of the discussion of the British proposals in Committee the Chinese delegate made the following declaration which brings out strongly the dangers to which neutral shipping is exposed by their employment:

"At the same time the Delegation [of China] desires to bring to the knowledge of the delegates certain facts which it ventures to hope will suggest the examination of this important proposition in a widely humanitarian sense.

"The Chinese Government is even to-day obliged to furnish vessels engaged in coastal navigation with special apparatus to raise and destroy floating mines which are found not only on the open sea but even in its territorial waters. In spite of the precautions which have been taken a very considerable number of coasting vessels, fishing boats, junks and sampans have been lost with all hands without the details of these disasters being known to the western world. It is calculated from five to six hundred of our countrymen engaged in their peaceful occupations have there met a cruel death in consequence of these dangerous engines of war[1]."

The subject of mines was entrusted to the Third Committee presided

Mines and the Hague Conference. over by Count Tornielli. This Committee also dealt with naval bombardments, the adaptation to naval warfare of the principles of the Geneva Convention and the right and duty of neutrals in naval warfare. The Committee was divided into two Sub-Committees, the first of which, presided over by M. Hagerup (Norway) with M. Streit (Greece) as Reporter, dealt with submarine mines and naval bombardments.

The British Delegation in accordance with their instructions[2] pre-

Various proposals: (a) British. sented the following draft consisting of six Articles which was the most complete and at the same time the most restrictive of any laid before the Committee:

1. The employment of unanchored automatic submarine contact mines is forbidden.

2. Automatic submarine contact mines which on breaking from their moorings do not become harmless are forbidden.

3. The employment of automatic submarine contact mines to establish or maintain a commercial blockade is forbidden.

4. Belligerents may only lay mines in their territorial waters or those of their enemies. Before fortified military ports (*ports de guerre*), however, this zone may be extended to a distance of 10 miles from shore batteries

---

[1] *La Deux. Confér.* T. III. p. 663.
[2] See paragraph 15 of Instructions in Appendix.

(*canons à terre*), provided that the belligerent laying such mines gives notice to neutrals and also takes such steps as circumstances allow to prevent, as far as possible, merchant-ships which have not had notice, being exposed to destruction.

Only ports which possess at least one large graving-dock and are provided with the equipment necessary for the construction and repair of ships of war, and in which a staff of workmen paid by the state to construct and repair ships of war is maintained in time of peace, shall be considered as coming within the meaning of the term "ports de guerre."

5. Generally, the necessary precautions shall be taken to safeguard neutral ships engaged in lawful commerce; and it is desirable that automatic submarine contact mines shall be so constructed as to cease to be dangerous after a reasonable period.

6. At the conclusion of the war the belligerents will communicate to each other the necessary information as to the places where each has laid mines on the coasts of the other, and each belligerent must take steps as soon as possible to remove mines in his territorial waters[1].

The Italian Delegation handed in a preliminary motion[2]: (1) that un-anchored mines should be provided with apparatus whereby they became harmless within an hour after they were laid; (2) that as regards anchored mines they should be so constructed as to become harmless on breaking adrift from their moorings[3]. The latter part of the Italian proposal was already covered by the British draft, but the first part allowed the use of unanchored floating mines which were forbidden by the British proposal, if they became harmless within an hour.

(b) Italian.

In support of the British draft Captain Ottley stated that no objection could be raised to the use of mines controlled by electric wires from the shore, but that the interests of humanity demanded that the lives and interests of neutrals and non-combatants should be protected as far as was consistent with belligerent rights as regards the use of automatic contact mines. Referring to the loss of life occasioned in the China Seas which were frequented by a comparatively small number of ships, he said that had the number been anything like that frequenting the entrance to the Baltic, the Dardanelles, the Straits of Gibraltar or Dover a series of catastrophes would have occurred which would have attracted the attention of the whole civilised world[4].

---

[1] *La Deux. Confér.* T. III. p. 660.   [2] *Ibid.* p. 661.

[3] In this connection it was suggested that mines, like torpedoes, might be made to sink by infiltration after the lapse of a given time (*Ibid.* p. 519).

[4] *La Deux. Confér.* T. III. pp. 519–520.

The Italian naval delegate (Captain Castiglia) in support of his "motion préalable" pointed out that mines provided a cheap form of defence for states with a weak navy, and that those possessing a large navy and a long coast line also found them a valuable assistance to their coastal defences. The danger to neutrals was however so great that it was natural that a limit should be imposed on the unrestricted use of such terrible instruments of destruction, and he asked for the acceptance of his preliminary amendment to the British proposals as neutrals were safeguarded while a belligerent could still use a weapon which might as a last resort, especially where a weaker vessel was being pursued by a stronger, prove its salvation[1].

(c) Japanese. The Japanese Delegation proposed an amendment in the same sense as the Italian, and this was accepted by the British Delegation[2].

(d) Dutch. The Dutch Delegation proposed amendments to Articles 4, 5 and 6 of the British draft allowing neutrals to place mines in their own waters to prevent access to their territory, but prohibiting the laying of mines in straits connecting two open seas. It was also proposed to add a seventh Article providing that in case of loss of either neutral persons or property, the state laying the mines should make compensation[3].

(e) Brazilian. The Brazilian Delegation also proposed an amendment allowing neutrals to lay mines in their waters for self-defence[4].

(f) German. The German Delegation proposed an amendment to Article 4 of the British draft allowing mines to be laid in the theatre of war which was defined in the following terms: "*l'espace de mer sur lequel se fait ou vient de se faire une opération de guerre ou sur lequel une pareille opération pourra avoir lieu par suite de la présence ou de l'approche des forces armées des deux belligérants*[5]."

(g) Spanish. The Spanish Delegation proposed an amendment to Article 2 of the British draft that until an international technical commission had discovered means of rendering automatic contact mines harmless on breaking from their moorings they should be forbidden; and an amendment to Article 4 allowing belligerents only to employ mines in their own territorial waters or in those of their enemy *when they exercise effective power there*[6].

(h) United States. At the third Meeting of the First Sub-Committee on the 11th July General Porter (United States) presented the following draft:

---

[1] *La Deux. Confér.* T. III. p. 518.   [2] *Ibid.* p. 661.   [3] *Ibid.* p. 661.
[4] *Ibid.* p. 662.   [5] *Ibid.* p. 663.   [6] *Ibid.* p. 663.

1.   Unanchored automatic contact mines are prohibited.

2.   Anchored automatic contact mines, which do not become innocuous on getting adrift, are prohibited.

3.   If anchored automatic contact mines are used within belligerent jurisdiction or within the area of immediate belligerent activities, due precautions shall be taken for the safety of neutrals[1].

At the same meeting a Russian amendment was presented which provided that (1) belligerents shall make use of anchored automatic submarine contact mines constructed in such a way that, as far as it is possible, they shall become harmless when they have broken from their moorings; (2) their automatic floating mines shall be constructed in such a way that, as far as possible, they become harmless after the lapse of a certain time from their being launched; (3) torpedoes shall be constructed in such a way that, as far as possible, they become harmless when they have missed their mark; (4) a sufficient delay shall be accorded to governments to bring into use perfected mines[2].

(i) Russian.

It will be evident from the foregoing list that the proposals of several states, notably Holland, Germany and Russia, considerably widened the area of discussion. The various proposals were sent for consideration to an Examining Committee composed of one representative from each of the Delegations of the following states: Great Britain, China, France, Germany, The United States, Brazil, Italy, Spain, Japan, Holland and Russia. This Committee held ten long meetings and during the course of their deliberation numerous amendments and proposals were tabled[3]. To

Difficulties of the Examining Committee.

---

[1] *La Deux. Confér.* T. III. p. 664.

[2] *Ibid.* p. 664. The subject was considered by the Institut de Droit International at the meeting at Ghent in 1906 and by the International Law Association in the same year. The Institut adopted by 17 votes to 3 the following rules :

1.   The placing of anchored or floating mines on the high seas is prohibited.

2.   Belligerents may place mines in their own territorial waters or in those of the enemy, with the exception of floating or anchored mines liable on displacement to be a danger to navigation outside the waters of the belligerents.

3.   (1) The above also applies to neutral states placing in their waters any means (*engins*) to prevent the violation of their neutrality.

(2) Neutral states may not place such mines in the passage of straits leading into the open sea.

4.   The obligation of notification is incumbent on the belligerent state as well as on the neutral state.

5.   Violation of any of the above rules entails the responsibility of the state which commits such violation. *Annuaire*, Vol. XXI. pp. 88–99, 330–345.

The official Report of the Conference does not contain reports of the meetings of the Examining Committee, but gives the various proposals brought before it. (*La Deux. Confér.* T. III. pp. 668–680. The Report of M. Streit summarises the discussions (pp. 397–428).)

increase the difficulties of their work doubts were raised as to the competence of the Examining Committee. Some members doubted not only whether the Committee but even the Conference was competent to deal with the question of the laying of mines by *neutrals* as this did not definitely appear in the programme of the Conference. The question was referred to a full meeting of the Third Committee on the 23rd August and after a lengthy discussion the competence of the Examining Committee was affirmed[1]. The Report of the First Sub-Committee of the Third Committee on the work of its Examining Committee containing a draft Convention of 10 Articles was presented to a full meeting of the Third Committee on the 17th September[2].

The draft Convention in its first Article forbade (*a*) the use of unanchored mines which do not become harmless within the maximum of one hour after the party laying them has lost control over them, (*b*) the use of anchored mines which do not become harmless after they have broken loose from their moorings, (*c*) the use of torpedoes which do not become harmless when they have missed their mark.

First draft Convention[3].

Articles 2–5 dealt with the area in which floating unanchored mines might be laid. Article 2 prohibited the laying of such mines beyond a distance of three marine miles from low-water mark along the whole extent of the coast and dependent islands and small islands. As regards bays, the three-mile limit was to be measured from a straight line drawn across the bay at the point nearest the entrance where the width does not exceed 10 miles[4].

Article 3 extended the limits for placing unanchored mines to 10 miles off naval ports (*ports de guerre*) and ports where there are military arsenals, ship-building yards or graving-docks. Naval ports are defined as those which have been declared to be such by the state to which they belong.

Article 4 allowed belligerents to lay unanchored mines off the coasts and ports of the enemy within the limits provided by the two preceding Articles, but not beyond the three-mile limit where the ports are not *ports de guerre* as above defined, unless they contained ship-building yards or graving-docks belonging to the state; belligerents were also prohibited

---

[1] *La Deux. Confér.* T. III. pp. 364–374.

[2] *Ibid.* p. 375. The report is given pp. 397–428; see also *The Times*, 2, 3, 18, 19, 20 Sept. 1907.

[3] *La Deux. Confér.* T. III. pp. 427–8.

[4] The definition of territorial waters and bays was taken, with the substitution of *ilots* for *bancs*, from Art. 2 of the North Sea Fishery Convention of 6 May, 1882. See *La Deux. Confér.* T. III. p. 409.

from laying mines off the coasts and ports of the enemy with the sole object of intercepting commercial navigation.

Article 5 provided that within the sphere of their immediate activity belligerents have the same right of laying anchored mines outside the limits prescribed by Articles 2–4; such mines must be constructed in such a way as to become harmless within a maximum of two hours after they have been abandoned by those who laid them.

Article 6 stated that when anchored mines are used every precaution should be taken for the safety of navigation: the belligerents undertake when the mines cease to be under observation to notify to governments as soon as possible the dangerous areas and to provide as far as possible that they shall become harmless within a limited time.

By Article 7 neutrals laying mines off their coasts must follow the same rules and observe the same precautions as belligerents: they may not lay mines outside the limits indicated in Article 2, and must notify in advance the areas of danger to other governments at once.

Article 8 provided that at the conclusion of the war states shall remove mines they have laid: and as regards moored mines laid by one belligerent on the coasts of the other each shall notify their position to the other and shall proceed as soon as possible to remove those in its own waters.

Article 9 placed an important limit on the prohibition of Articles 1, 5 and 6 by providing that states which did not as yet possess mines of the perfected type dealt with in the draft and therefore not conforming to those Articles undertook as soon as possible to transform their mines so that they should answer to these requirements; until a belligerent was provided with such mines he was prohibited from laying them outside the limits fixed by Articles 2–4; the use of unanchored mines which did not conform to the requirements of Article 1 was prohibited a year after the Convention came into force.

According to Article 10 the Convention was to last for five years, and the signatory Powers undertook to reopen the question of the employment of mines six months before its expiration.

From the Report of M. Streit it appears that most of the Articles were adopted only by majorities, sometimes very small, and the debates on the draft at the meetings of the Third Committee in their 5th, 6th and 7th sittings[1] show the general trend of the debates before the smaller body. The discussion of the draft was commenced by Admiral Siegel (Germany)[2] who drew attention to the great

Discussion of first draft Convention.

---

[1] *La Deux. Confér.* T. III. pp. 375 *et seq.*, 429 *et seq.* and 445 *et seq.*   [2] *Ibid.* p. 377.

diversity of opinion manifested in the Examining Committee and the fact that none of the Articles were unanimously adopted. The question in his opinion was not ripe for solution; that attempted was not satisfactory. He then passed to a criticism of the draft, particularly the limits imposed on the area of mine-laying operations, and urged that the restriction to territorial waters did not meet the case of the defence of a blockaded coast by mines which to be effective must be laid near the blockading squadron lying perhaps 20 miles or more off the land. Nor could he accept the rule that *unanchored* mines must be rendered innocuous within a given length of time. That principle was sound as regards *anchored* mines which broke loose from their moorings but the limit of one hour was useless where a weak naval force was flying from a stronger and dropped unanchored mines in defence.

Sir Ernest Satow[1] followed in a lengthy and detailed criticism of the draft which he contended was quite inadequate as a safeguard to legitimate neutral rights. The permission to belligerents to lay mines anywhere in "the sphere of their immediate activity" was a permission to strew the high seas with mines. On the outbreak of war a catastrophe to a neutral ship would at once create a situation which in all probability diplomacy would be impotent to solve; if therefore the draft were adopted the Conference instead of diminishing would increase the causes of war. He strongly urged that the Conference ought only to allow belligerents to lay anchored mines in their own territorial waters or those of their adversary and then only if they became harmless as soon as they broke loose; that belligerents should only be allowed to use floating mines during a battle on condition that they became harmless within a short period; that anchored mines should not be allowed beyond territorial waters or more than 10 miles off military ports, etc., otherwise the navigation of a great part of the Baltic, the North Sea, the Mediterranean, etc. might all be rendered full of dangers beyond these limits, for the provision that anchored mines should be rendered harmless within two hours after they were laid was impracticable. The prohibition to lay mines outside belligerent ports to intercept commerce was equivocal as appearing to countenance blockade by mines which was contrary alike to the spirit and letter of the Declaration of Paris. The British proposal in regard to "ports de guerre" was preferable. Finally he proposed to extend the duration of the Convention for seven years or until the end of the Third Peace Conference.

Baron Marschall von Bieberstein (Germany)[2] supported the views of Admiral Siegel. He said Germany did not mean to demand an unlimited

---

[1] *La Deux. Confér.* T. III. pp. 378–382.   [2] *Ibid.* p. 382.

liberty in the use of mines or desire to "sow mines in profusion in all the seas"; he fully admitted the great responsibility of belligerents in their use of mines. Germany, to show her desire to conform to public opinion, was willing to forbid the use of floating (unanchored) mines for five years, and he concluded by moving an amendment to the first Article of the draft to this effect[1].

The Japanese[2] and Russian[3] delegates supported the prohibition of floating mines contained in Article 1 of the draft Convention. General Porter (United States) criticised in detail the draft Convention in which he found numerous technical difficulties and stated that there were only a few Articles which the American Delegation was prepared to accept[4].

The German amendment prohibiting floating mines for five years was then put to the vote with the result that 15 Delegations including Great Britain and the United States voted for it, 9 against, 14 abstained and 6 were absent[5]. This voting not being conclusive the discussion was continued on the first Article which was carried[6].

The second Article prohibiting the laying of anchored mines outside territorial waters was carried by a small majority (15 to 11, 10 abstentions and 8 absent)[7].

The third and fourth Articles were also carried by small majorities[8].

The rejection of Article 5 which had been moved by Sir E. Satow was supported by the Brazilian delegate (Captain Burlamaqui de Moura) and was carried by 28 votes, 4 abstaining and 12 absent[9].

Article 6 was adopted with a reservation by the Turkish delegate in regard to the Dardanelles and Bosphorus[10].

Article 7 was under discussion when the Committee adjourned till the 19th September. The discussions were then resumed and Articles 7 and 8 and part of 9 were adopted[11]. Article 10 was amended in accordance with Sir Ernest Satow's motion, and the duration of the Convention was fixed at seven years instead of five as originally proposed[12].

A long debate took place on the results of the divisions on Articles 2–4

---

[1] Baron Marschall repeated the greater part of this speech at the 8th Plenary Meeting of the Conference (9 Oct. 1908). See post, page 342.

[2] La Deux. Confér. T. III. p. 382.   [3] Ibid. p. 384.   [4] Ibid. pp. 384–7.

[5] The following voted for: Austria-Hungary, Belgium, Brazil, Bulgaria, Cuba, Dominica, Equador, Germany, Great Britain, Hayti, Panama, Portugal, Roumania, Spain and the United States. Against: Argentine, Chili, Colombia, Greece, Holland, Italy, Japan, Norway and Salvador. Abstained from voting: Bolivia, Denmark, France, Montenegro, Nicaragua, Paraguay, Persia, Russia, Servia, Siam, Sweden, Switzerland, Turkey and Venezuela. Absent: China, Guatemala, Luxemburg, Mexico, Peru and Uruguay. Op. cit. T. III. p. 388.

[6] La Deux. Confér. T. III. pp. 389–390.   [7] Ibid. p. 390.   [8] Ibid. p. 391.

[9] Ibid. pp. 393–4.   [10] Ibid. p. 395.   [11] Ibid. pp. 436–7.   [12] Ibid. p. 439.

as to the effect of the small majorities[1]. The German delegate held that a relative majority should be decisive. The Italian delegate advocated an absolute majority, that is where more than half of the delegates voted on the same side. The Committee ultimately decided to adjourn for the preparation of another draft which it was hoped might prove acceptable to the Conference[2].

The Committee met again on the 26th September and took into consideration a revised draft prepared as the result of the previous discussions and embodying those Articles or amendments which had received an absolute majority in the full meeting of the Committee. The second draft was accepted and became the Convention now under consideration[3].

The second draft Convention.

Article 1. The first Article remains as in the first draft except for slight changes in the wording. The distinction between anchored and unanchored mines and torpedoes is maintained[4], and the Article was unanimously accepted by the Committee, subject to reservations by Russia, Germany, Sweden and Turkey.

The Convention.

Article 2 reproduces paragraph 3 of the fourth Article of the original draft. It is all that remains of the attempts to limit the area in which mines may be laid. The German delegate in Committee objected to this Article which forbids the laying of mines before the shores and ports of the enemy with the sole object of intercepting commercial navigation. He urged that the subjective element in this Article was absent from the others and would give rise to difficulties in its application[5]. The Austro-Hungarian delegate expressed himself in a similar sense. Sir Ernest Satow pointed out that the prohibition to lay mines off commercial ports would have avoided this difficulty[6]. The objection appears to be a valid one, as it will only be necessary to allege some other reason to avoid the application of the rule.

When this Article was under discussion in Committee the delegate of Colombia (M. Triana) moved the following amendment[7]:

The Colombian amendment.

"*To suppress Article 2 and Article 5 (2) and replace them by the following provisions :—*

---

[1] *La Deux. Confér.* T. III. pp. 441–4. [2] *Ibid.* p. 444. [3] *Ibid.* pp. 445–454.

[4] Generally speaking, automobile torpedoes can be adjusted so as to become harmless after they have missed their aim. Anchored floating mines which may drift while still attached to their moorings remain dangerous for an indefinite period ; those in use in the British Navy become harmless as soon as they have broken from their moorings. Unanchored mines have ceased to be used by the British Navy ; they can be rendered harmless in a short time after they are laid by methods fully explained to the Committee by Captain Ottley and Captain Castiglia (of the Italian Navy) (*La Deux. Confér.* T. III. p. 404).

[5] *La Deux. Confér.* T. III. p. 447. [6] *Ibid.* p. 451. [7] *Ibid.* p. 447.

"*The employment of anchored mines is absolutely forbidden except as a means of defence.*

"*Belligerents may not employ such mines except for the protection of their own coasts and only within a distance of the greatest range of cannon.*

"*In the case of arms of the sea or navigable maritime channels leading exclusively to the shores of a single Power, that Power may bar the entrance for its own protection by laying anchored mines.*

"*Belligerents are absolutely forbidden to lay anchored mines in the open sea or in the waters of the enemy.*"

In support of this amendment M. Triana made an eloquent and forcible speech in which he pointed out that the essential object of the Conference was peace. War could not be suppressed but its horrors could be diminished, though not all at once, but every rule adopted tended towards the object in view. Mines were, of all modern methods of war, the most devastating and treacherous. It was pitiable to think of "the mass of courage marching on the foe" overwhelmed and annihilated by a murderous agent laid by an absent enemy. The horror was increased when mines floated at the will of wind and wave, a menace not only to belligerents but to all that sail the seas. "It is the hatred of man extended like a curse over the waves of the ocean." If mines could not be suppressed, their use should be limited to mines anchored for the purpose of defending ports, coasts and mouths of rivers, etc.; the law allows homicide in self-defence. It was for the Great Powers to set an example; they should prove their sincerity in the cause of humanity. If such a concession were not made, the sincerity of the Conference would be open to doubt, and the greatest responsibility would rest on the strongest Powers; it was to them he appealed. If they could not agree to diminish in some way one of the most horrible possibilities of war, if they lacked the courage or the generosity to do so, where was the justification for their power? *La force comme la noblesse oblige*[1].

This impressive appeal was warmly applauded, and was supported by the British and Chinese delegates. The Austro-Hungarian and German delegates objected on the ground of the difficulty of distinguishing between attack and defence and on a division 16 states voted for and 15 against the Colombian amendment, 6 abstained and 7 were absent. As the majority was not absolute the amendment failed. Article 2 was then adopted by 33 votes, 3 Powers abstaining and 7 being absent. Germany reserved her vote[2].

Article 3. This Article was unanimously adopted. Throughout the

---

[1] *La Deux. Confér.* T. III. p. 448.   [2] *Ibid.* p. 450.

discussions all the delegates in their speeches supported the proposition that all possible precautions should be taken to safeguard neutral interests, and the present Article reproduces with verbal amendments Article 6 of the original draft. The Turkish delegate made reservations on the subject of the Bosphorus and Dardanelles[1].

Article 4. This Article was unanimously adopted; it reproduces Article 7 of the original draft as modified at the full meeting of the Committee when the limits of the area within which neutrals can lay mines were suppressed.

Article 5. This Article (Article 8 of the original draft) completes the two previous Articles and was unanimously adopted[2].

Article 6. This Article reproduces Article 9 of the original draft with the omission of the time limit as originally recommended. The engagement taken by the Powers to transform as soon as possible their *matériel* so that they should answer to the technical conditions in these Regulations was unanimously adopted. Sir Ernest Satow however, with a view of fixing a definite time within which such transformation should be effected, proposed to add to this Article the following paragraph: "The prohibition to employ mines which do not answer to the conditions of Article 1 shall come into force in the case of unanchored mines within *one* year, and in the case of anchored mines within *three* years after the ratification of the present Convention." The original draft had proposed to allow *one* year for the transformation of both anchored and unanchored mines. The result of the voting was as follows: 17 for, 9 against, 10 abstentions, 8 absent. The amendment was therefore not proceeded with[3].

Articles 7, 8, 9 and 10 call for no remarks.

Articles 11 and 12. The first paragraph of Article 11 is the result of an amendment moved in Committee by Sir Ernest Satow, which together with Article 12 were unanimously accepted at the seventh meeting of the Third Committee. The Convention is to last for seven years and the Contracting Powers undertake to reopen the question of the employment of mines six months before the termination of this period, in the event of the question not having been already reopened and settled by the Third Peace Conference[4].

Before passing to the last stage in the adoption of the draft which became the present Convention, the fate of the proposal deposited by the Dutch delegate in reference to the laying of mines in straits must

---

[1] *La Deux. Confér.* T. III. p. 452.
[2] *Ibid.* p. 452. [3] *Ibid.* p. 453.
[4] *Ibid.* T. I. p. 291; *Parl. Papers*, Misc. No. 4 (1908), p. 230.

be mentioned[1].   The Dutch naval delegate (Admiral Röell) desired that

The position of straits. Dutch amendment.

the prohibition of mine-laying in straits connecting the high seas should be clearly enunciated in the interests of neutrals. The right of innocent passage was generally admitted, he said, but it was desirable that the principle should be definitely adopted in a conventional stipulation, clearly providing that straits should not be barred in such a way as not to leave communication open to peaceful navigation.   The Japanese, United States, and Turkish delegates all made reservations as regards the Islands of the Japanese Empire, the Philippines, the Bosphorus and the Dardanelles which form integral parts of their respective states.   The German and Spanish delegates stated that they had no instructions on the subject, and the Russian naval delegate (Captain Behr) expressed doubts as to the competence of the Conference to deal with the question.   The Dutch proposal, he said, laid down a general rule for all straits.   Certain straits are dealt with by international agreements based on political considerations and these were outside their competence; it would be unwise to lay down general rules for some straits, leaving out others, as thereby a new source of difficulty would be occasioned.   He concluded by saying that he was instructed to state that the consideration of the question was not competent to the Conference and that he should not take part in the discussion.   The Committee therefore decided to suppress all provision relating to straits.   The Report by M. Streit to the Conference states that it was clearly understood that nothing was changed by the Convention as regards the actual situation of straits.   "But, it has been considered as natural that the technical conditions established by the Regulations should be of general application[2]."

The Report of the Third Committee and the draft Convention came

The Conference and the Convention.

before the 8th Plenary Meeting of the Conference on the 9th October, 1908, when the draft was adopted with certain reservations.

Sir Ernest Satow then made the following declaration:

Sir Ernest Satow's declaration.

"Having voted for the Mines Convention which the Conference has just accepted, the British Delegation desires to declare that it cannot regard this arrangement as furnishing a final solution of the question, but only as marking a stage in international legislation on the subject.   It does not consider that adequate account has been taken in the Convention of the right of neutrals to protection, nor of

---

[1] *La Deux. Confér.* T. III. pp. 661–2, *supra*, p. 331.   See also Chapter V. of the Report of M. Streit, *La Deux. Confér.* T. III. pp. 405–7.

[2] *Parl. Papers*, Misc. No. 4 (1908), p. 230 ; *La Deux. Confér.* T. I. p. 293.

humanitarian sentiments which cannot be neglected; it has done all that is possible to bring the Conference to share its views, but its efforts in this direction have remained without result.

"The high seas, Gentlemen, are a great international highway. If in the present state of international law and custom belligerents are permitted to fight their battles there, it is none the less incumbent on them to do nothing which might, long after their departure from a particular place, render this highway dangerous to neutrals who have an equal right to use it. We declare without hesitation that the right of the neutral to security of navigation of the high seas ought to take precedence of the transitory right of the belligerent to employ these seas as the scene of the operations of war.

"This Convention, however, as it has been adopted, imposes on the belligerent no restriction as to the placing of anchored mines, which consequently may be laid wherever the belligerent chooses, in his own waters for self-defence, in the waters of the enemy as a means of attack, or lastly on the high seas, so that neutral navigation will inevitably run great risks in time of naval war and may be exposed to many a disaster. We have already on several occasions insisted on the danger of a situation of this kind. We have endeavoured to show what would be the effect produced by the loss of a great liner belonging to a neutral Power. We have not failed to produce every argument in favour of limiting the field of action of these mines, while we called special attention to the advantages which the civilised world would gain from this restriction, as it would diminish to a certain extent the causes of armed conflicts. It appeared to us that by accepting the proposal made by us at the beginning of the discussion dangers would have been obviated which in every maritime war of the future will threaten to disturb friendly relations between neutrals and belligerents. But since the Conference has not shared our views, it remains for us to declare in the most formal manner that these dangers exist and that the certainty that they will make themselves felt in the future is due to the incomplete character of the present Convention. As, in our opinion, this constitutes only a partial and insufficient solution of the problem, it cannot, as has already been pointed out, be regarded as a complete exposition of international law on the subject. Therefore the legitimacy of a given act cannot be presumed for the mere reason that the Convention has not forbidden it. That is a principle which we desired to affirm, and which could never be ignored by any state, whatever its power[1]."

---

[1] *Parl. Papers*, Misc. No. 4 (1908), p. 54; *La Deux. Confér.* T. I. p. 281.

Baron Marschall von Bieberstein replied as follows:

Baron Marschall von Bieberstein's reply.
 "In view of the declaration just made by His Excellency the delegate of Great Britain, I wish to repeat what I have already said in the Committee[1].

"A belligerent who lays mines assumes a very heavy responsibility towards neutrals and peaceful shipping. On that point we are all agreed. No one will resort to such means unless for military reasons of an absolutely urgent character. But military acts are not governed solely by principles of international law. There are other factors: conscience, good sense and the sentiment of duty imposed by principles of humanity will be the surest guides for the conduct of sailors, and will constitute the most effective guarantee against abuses. The officers of the German Navy, I emphatically affirm (*je le dis à voix haute*), will always fulfil, in the strictest fashion, the duties which emanate from the unwritten law of humanity and civilisation.

"I have no need to tell you that I recognise entirely the importance of the codification of rules to be followed in war. But it would be well not to issue rules the strict observation of which might be rendered impossible by the force of things. It is of the first importance that the international maritime law which we desire to create should only contain clauses the execution of which is possible from a military point of view, even in exceptional circumstances. Otherwise the respect for law will be lessened and its authority undermined. Also it would seem to us to be preferable to preserve at present a certain reserve, in the expectation that, seven years hence, it will be easier to find a solution which will be acceptable to the whole world.

"As to the sentiments of humanity and civilisation, I cannot admit that there is any government or country which is superior in these sentiments to that which I have the honour to represent[2]."

Signatory Powers.
 This Convention has been signed by all the Powers represented at the Conference except China, Spain, Montenegro, Nicaragua, Portugal, Russia and Sweden.

The following Powers made reservations:

Reservations.
 France and Germany, Article 2.
 The Dominican Republic and Siam, Article 1, paragraph 1.

Great Britain. "In placing their signatures to this Convention the British Plenipotentiaries declare that the mere fact that the said Convention does not prohibit a particular act or proceeding must not be

---

[1] See *ante*, p. 336.
[2] *Parl. Papers*, Misc. No. 4 (1908), p. 55; *La Deux. Confér.* T. I. pp. 280-1.

held to debar His Britannic Majesty's Government from contesting its legitimacy[1]."

Turkey under reserves of the declarations made at the 8th Plenary Meeting of the Conference on the 9th October, 1907. These declarations relate to Articles 1 and 6 in regard to which the Ottoman delegate would enter into no undertaking to transform the *matériel* of mines into any system not generally known. Also in regard to Article 3 the Ottoman delegate declared that in the exceptional circumstances of the Dardanelles and Bosphorus the Turkish Government would enter into no engagement tending to limit the means of defence which it might deem necessary to employ for these straits in time of war, or to protect their neutrality.

The declaration of Sir Ernest Satow and the speeches made by the British, Japanese and Chinese delegates during the various

Defects of the Convention. discussions draw attention in a striking manner to the defects of the Convention. Baron Marschall's contention that conscience, good sense and the unwritten law of humanity and civilisation afford a better guarantee for the observance of international law than a Convention is unconvincing. States are not content to rely on such principles for the maintenance of internal order; life and property are safeguarded by definite enactments embodying the old commands "Thou shalt not kill, thou shalt not steal." The interests of neutrals demand that the law of humanity and civilisation in a matter in which they are so deeply concerned should also form part of the written law of nations though the absence of the *litera scripta* cannot be adduced to justify proceedings against this unwritten law. It is impossible to under-estimate the risks to neutrals from the use of mines in ways not prohibited by this Convention. There is nothing in its provisions to forbid a belligerent placing mines, floating or anchored, on the high seas; nothing to prohibit him from placing mines off the coasts of the enemy without regard to neutral shipping, for the proviso that danger zones shall be notified "as soon as military exigencies allow" is of little value. The prohibition of the use of mines off the coasts of the enemy with the sole object of intercepting commercial shipping, is, as has been pointed out, futile, for a belligerent has only to allege a different object to make it illusory and none of the safeguards which the laws of blockade require in the interests of neutrals are mentioned in this Convention. The prohibitions contained in the first Article are in effect nullified by the sixth, for no time is specified within which states are to cause their *matériel* to conform to the requirements of Article 1, and where neutrals suffer from the use of imperfectly constructed

---

[1] *Parl. Papers*, Misc. No. 5 (1909).

mines it is not likely that they will be satisfied with the belligerent's plea that he has been prevented by lack of funds or time from making the needful changes.

Neutrals have a right to demand that the high seas, the great international highway of all nations, shall be protected from belligerent operations to their detriment, and it was with this object that the British proposals were framed. They were not accepted, and Sir Ernest Satow's declaration is a clear notification that the Convention is wholly inadequate as a guarantee of neutral interests, and also that the legitimacy of acts such as those above mentioned cannot be presumed merely because a Convention has not forbidden them.

Owing to the action of some of the Great Powers to whom the Colombian delegate addressed his appeal to prove their sincerity in the cause of humanity, the Convention is a wholly unsatisfactory attempt to deal with a question of vital importance to neutrals and has only been accepted by many states for want of a better. The requirements of humanity and the methods by which states should realise them are better stated by M. de Lapradelle: "Chasser la mine amarrée de la haute mer, exiger que la mine flottante, jetée pendant le combat, perde rapidement son pouvoir nocif, et que la mine fixe d'usage côtier devienne inoffensive dès qu'elle a rompu ses amarres, puis, défendre le blocus par mines, parcequ'en cas d'infraction il substituerait la mort à la capture: tels sont les principes que l'humanité commande[1]." These were the principles of the British proposals.

The question of mines was again considered by the Institut de Droit International at its meeting at Florence in September, 1908, as since its meeting at Ghent in 1906 the present Convention had been agreed on. A draft series of regulations was adopted by the Institut and is to be reconsidered at its meeting at Paris in 1910[2].

---

[1] *La guerre maritime, etc., Revue des deux Mondes,* July, 1908, p. 688.

[2] Article 1. It is forbidden to place anchored and unanchored automatic contact mines in the high seas.

Article 2. Belligerents may for strategical reasons (1) place mines in their own territorial water or in those of their enemy: (2) but it is forbidden

(a) To place unanchored automatic contact mines unless they are so constructed as to become harmless one hour at most after the party laying them has lost control over them.

(b) To place anchored automatic contact mines which do not become harmless as soon as they have broken adrift from their moorings.

Article 3. It is always forbidden both in the high seas and in territorial waters to use torpedoes which do not become harmless when they have missed their mark.

Article 4. It is forbidden to lay automatic contact mines off the coasts and ports of the enemy with the sole object of intercepting commercial navigation.

Article 5. Where anchored automatic contact mines are laid, every precaution must be taken for the security of peaceful navigation.

Article 6. Every neutral Power which lays automatic contact mines off its coasts must observe the same rules and take the same precautions as are imposed on belligerents.

Article 7. The obligation of notification is incumbent on a belligerent as well as on a neutral state.

Article 8. At the termination of the war, contracting Powers undertake to do all in their power, each on his own side, to remove mines which they have laid.

As regards anchored automatic contact mines which one of the belligerents has laid along the coasts of the other, the locality thereof shall be notified to the other Party by the Power which has laid them and each Power must proceed as quickly as possible to remove mines found in his waters.

Article 9. The contracting Powers, which do not yet possess perfected mines such as are provided for in the present Convention and which consequently are unable at present to conform to the rules laid down in Articles 1 to 3 undertake to transform as soon as possible their *matériel* of mines, so as to make it answer to the above mentioned requirements.

Article 10. The violation of any of the preceding rules involves the responsibility of the state making default. (See *Am. Journ. of Int. Law*, Vol. III. p. 187; *Annuaire*, Vol. XXII.)

IX. Convention cóncernant le Bombardement par des Forces Navales en Temps de Guerre.

Sa Majesté l'Empereur d'Allemagne, Roi de Prusse, &c.[1]

Animés du désir de réaliser le vœu exprimé par la Première Conférence de la Paix, concernant le bombardement, par des forces navales, de ports, villes, et villages, non défendus ;

Considérant qu'il importe de soumettre les bombardements par des forces navales à des dispositions générales qui garantissent les droits des habitants et assurent la conservation des principaux édifices, en étendant à cette opération de guerre, dans la mesure du possible, les principes du Règlement de 1899 sur les Lois et Coutumes de la Guerre sur Terre ;

S'inspirant ainsi du désir de servir les intérêts de l'humanité et de diminuer les rigueurs et les désastres de la guerre ;

Ont résolu de conclure une Convention à cet effet et ont, en conséquence, nommé pour leurs Plénipotentiaires, savoir :

[*Dénomination des Plénipotentiaires.*]

Lesquels, après avoir déposé leurs pleins pouvoirs, trouvés en bonne et due forme, sont convenus des dispositions suivantes :—

IX. Convention respecting Bombardment by Naval Forces in Time of War.

His Majesty the German Emperor, King of Prussia, &c.[1]

Animated by the desire to realise the wish expressed by the First Peace Conference respecting the bombardment by naval forces of undefended ports, towns, and villages ;

Deeming it expedient that bombardments by naval forces should be subject to rules of general application which would safeguard the rights of the inhabitants and assure the preservation of the more important buildings, by applying as far as possible to this operation of war the principles of the Regulations of 1899 respecting the Laws and Customs of Land War ;

Actuated, accordingly, by the desire to serve the interests of humanity and to diminish the severity and disasters of war ;

Have resolved to conclude a Convention to this effect, and have, for this purpose, appointed as their Plenipotentiaries, that is to say :

[*Names of Plenipotentiaries.*]

Who, after having deposited their full powers, found to be in good and due form, have agreed upon the following provisions :—

----

[1] List of States as in Final Act, 1907.

Chapitre I.

Du Bombardement des Ports, Villes, Villages, Habitations ou Bâtiments non défendus.

ART. 1.

Il est interdit de bombarder, par des forces navales, des ports, villes, villages, habitations ou bâtiments qui ne sont pas défendus.

Une localité ne peut pas être bombardée à raison du seul fait que, devant son port, se trouvent mouillées des mines sous-marines automatiques de contact.

ART. 2.

Toutefois, ne sont pas compris dans cette interdiction les ouvrages militaires, établissements militaires ou navals, dépôts d'armes ou de matériel de guerre, ateliers et installations propres à être utilisés pour les besoins de la flotte ou de l'armée ennemies, et les navires de guerre se trouvant dans le port. Le commandant d'une force navale pourra, après sommation avec délai raisonnable, les détruire par le canon, si tout autre moyen est impossible et lorsque les autorités locales n'auront pas procédé à cette destruction dans le délai fixé.

Il n'encourt aucune responsabilité dans ce cas pour les dommages involontaires qui pourraient être occasionnés par le bombardement.

Si des nécessités militaires exigeant une action immédiate, ne permettaient pas d'accorder de délai, il reste entendu que l'interdiction de bombarder la ville non défendue subsiste comme

Chapter I.

Bombardment of Undefended Ports, Towns, Villages, Dwellings, or Buildings.

ART. 1.

The bombardment by naval forces of undefended ports, towns, villages, dwellings, or buildings is forbidden.
(*Cp. 4 H. C.* 1907 (*Regulations*), *Art.* 25.)
A place cannot be bombarded solely because automatic submarine contact mines are anchored off the harbour.

ART. 2.

Military works, military or naval establishments, depôts of arms or war material, workshops or plant which could be utilized for the needs of the hostile fleet or army, and ships of war in the harbour, are not, however, included in this prohibition. The commander of a naval force may destroy them with artillery, after a summons followed by a reasonable interval of time, if all other means are impossible, and when the local authorities have not themselves destroyed them within the time fixed.

He incurs no responsibility for any unavoidable damage which may be caused by a bombardment under such circumstances.

If for military reasons, immediate action is necessary, and no delay can be allowed to the enemy, it is nevertheless understood that the prohibition to bombard the undefended town holds

dans le cas énoncé dans l'alinéa 1ᵉʳ, et que le commandant prendra toutes les dispositions voulues pour qu'il en résulte pour cette ville le moins d'inconvénients possible.

good, as in the case given in the first paragraph, and that the commander shall take all due measures in order that the town may suffer as little harm as possible.

ART. 3.

Il peut, après notification expresse, être procédé au bombardement des ports, villes, villages, habitations ou bâtiments non défendus, si les autorités locales, mises en demeure par une sommation formelle, refusent d'obtempérer à des réquisitions de vivres ou d'approvisionnements nécessaires au besoin présent de la force navale qui se trouve devant la localité.

Ces réquisitions seront en rapport avec les ressources de la localité. Elles ne seront réclamées qu'avec l'autorisation du commandant de la dite force navale et elles seront, autant que possible, payées au comptant ; sinon elles seront constatées par des reçus.

ART. 3.

After due notice has been given, the bombardment of undefended ports, towns, villages, dwellings, or buildings may be commenced, if the local authorities, on a formal summons being made to them, decline to comply with requisitions for provisions or supplies necessary for the immediate use of the naval force before the place in question.

These requisitions shall be proportional to the resources of the place. They shall only be demanded in the name of the commander of the said naval force, and they shall, as far as possible, be paid for in ready money ; if not, their receipt shall be acknowledged.

(*Cp. 4 H. C.* 1907 (*Regulations*), *Art.* 52.)

ART. 4.

Est interdit le bombardement, pour le non-paiement des contributions en argent, des ports, villes, villages, habitations ou bâtiments non défendus.

ART. 4.

The bombardment of undefended ports, towns, villages, dwellings, or buildings, for the non-payment of money contributions, is forbidden.

Chapitre II.

Dispositions Générales.

ART. 5.

Dans le bombardement par des forces navales, toutes les mesures nécessaires doivent être prises par le commandant pour épargner, autant que possible, les édifices consacrés aux cultes, aux arts, aux sciences, et à la bienfaisance, les monuments historiques, les hôpitaux

Chapter II.

General Provisions.

ART. 5.

In bombardments by naval forces all necessary steps should be taken by the commander to spare as far as possible, buildings devoted to public worship, art, science or charitable purposes, historic monuments, hospitals and places where the sick or

et les lieux de rassemblement de malades ou de blessés, à condition qu'ils ne soient pas employés en même temps à un but militaire.

Le devoir des habitants est de désigner ces monuments, ces édifices ou lieux de rassemblement, par des signes visibles, qui consisteront en grands panneaux rectangulaires rigides, partagés, suivant une des diagonales, en deux triangles de couleur, noire en haut et blanche en bas.

wounded are collected, provided they are not used at the time for military purposes.

It is the duty of the inhabitants to indicate such monuments, edifices, or places by visible signs, which shall consist of large stiff rectangular panels divided diagonally into two coloured triangular portions, the upper portion black, the lower portion white.

(*Cp.* 4 *H. C.* 1907 (*Regulations*), *Art.* 27.)

ART. 6.

Sauf le cas où les exigences militaires ne le permettraient pas, le commandant de la force navale assaillante doit, avant d'entreprendre le bombardement, faire tout ce qui dépend de lui pour avertir les autorités.

ART. 6.

Unless military exigencies render it impossible, the commander of an attacking naval force must, before commencing the bombardment, do all in his power to warn the authorities.

(*Cp.* 4 *H. C.* 1907 (*Regulations*), *Art.* 26.)

ART. 7.

Il est interdit de livrer au pillage une ville ou localité même prise d'assaut.

ART. 7.

The giving over to pillage of a town or place, even when taken by assault, is forbidden.

(*Cp.* 4 *H. C.* 1907 (*Regulations*), *Art.* 28.)

Chapitre III.

Dispositions Finales.

ART. 8.

Les dispositions de la présente Convention ne sont applicables qu'entre les Puissances contractantes et seulement si les belligérants sont tous parties à la Convention.

Chapter III.

Final Provisions.

ART. 8.

The provisions of the present Convention are only applicable between Contracting Powers, and only if all the belligerents are parties to the Convention.

ART. 9.

La présente Convention sera ratifiée aussitôt que possible.

ART. 9.

The present Convention shall be ratified as soon as possible.

Les ratifications seront déposées à La Haye.

Le premier dépôt de ratifications sera constaté par un procès-verbal signé par les Représentants des Puissances qui y prennent part et par le Ministre des Affaires Étrangères des Pays-Bas.

Les dépôts ultérieurs de ratifications se feront au moyen d'une notification écrite, adressée au Gouvernement des Pays-Bas et accompagnée de l'instrument de ratification.

Copie certifiée conforme du procès-verbal relatif au premier dépôt de ratifications, des notifications mentionnées à l'alinéa précédent, ainsi que des instruments de ratification, sera immédiatement remise, par les soins du Gouvernement des Pays-Bas et par la voie diplomatique, aux Puissances conviées à la Deuxième Conférence de la Paix, ainsi qu'aux autres Puissances qui auront adhéré à la Convention. Dans les cas visés par l'alinéa précédent, le dit Gouvernement leur fera connaître en même temps la date à laquelle il a reçu la notification.

ART. 10.

Les Puissances non-signataires sont admises à adhérer à la présente Convention.

La Puissance qui désire adhérer notifie par écrit son intention au Gouvernement des Pays-Bas en lui transmettant l'acte d'adhésion, qui sera déposé dans les archives du dit Gouvernement.

Ce Gouvernement transmettra immédiatement à toutes les autres

The ratifications shall be deposited at The Hague.

The first deposit of ratifications shall be recorded in a *procès-verbal* signed by the Representatives of the Powers which take part therein and by the Netherland Minister for Foreign Affairs.

The subsequent deposits of ratifications shall be made by means of a written notification addressed to the Netherland Government and accompanied by the instrument of ratification.

A duly certified copy of the *procès-verbal* relating to the first deposit of ratifications, of the notifications mentioned in the preceding paragraph, and of the instruments of ratification, shall be immediately sent by the Netherland Government, through the diplomatic channel, to the Powers invited to the Second Peace Conference, as well as to the other Powers which have acceded to the Convention. In the cases contemplated in the preceding paragraph, the said Government shall inform them at the same time of the date on which it received the notification.

ART. 10.

Non-Signatory Powers may accede to the present Convention.

A Power which desires to accede notifies its intention in writing to the Netherland Government, forwarding to it the act of accession, which shall be deposited in the archives of the said Government.

The said Government shall immediately forward to all the other Powers

Puissances copie certifiée conforme de la notification ainsi que de l'acte d'adhésion, en indiquant la date à laquelle il a reçu la notification.

Art. 11.

La présente Convention produira effet pour les Puissances qui auront participé au premier dépôt de ratifications, soixante jours après la date du procès-verbal de ce dépôt et, pour les Puissances qui ratifieront ultérieurement ou qui adhéreront, soixante jours après que la notification de leur ratification ou de leur adhésion aura été reçue par le Gouvernement des Pays-Bas.

Art. 12.

S'il arrivait qu'une des Puissances contractantes voulût dénoncer la présente Convention, la dénonciation sera notifiée par écrit au Gouvernement des Pays-Bas, qui communiquera immédiatement copie certifiée conforme de la notification à toutes les autres Puissances en leur faisant savoir la date à laquelle il l'a reçue.

La dénonciation ne produira ses effets qu'à l'égard de la Puissance qui l'aura notifiée et un an après que la notification en sera parvenue au Gouvernement des Pays-Bas.

Art. 13.

Un registre tenu par le Ministère des Affaires Étrangères des Pays-Bas indiquera la date du dépôt de ratifications effectué en vertu de l'Article 9, alinéas 3 et 4, ainsi que la date à laquelle auront été reçues les notifications d'adhésion (article 10, alinéa 2) ou de dénonciation (article 12, alinéa 1).

a duly certified copy of the notification, as well as of the act of accession, mentioning the date on which it received the notification.

Art. 11.

The present Convention shall take effect, in the case of the Powers which, were parties to the first deposit of ratifications, sixty days after the date of the *procès-verbal* recording such deposit, and in the case of the Powers which shall ratify subsequently or which shall accede, sixty days after the notification of their ratification or of their accession has been received by the Netherland Government.

Art. 12.

In the event of one of the Contracting Powers wishing to denounce the present Convention, the denunciation shall be notified in writing to the Netherland Government, which shall immediately communicate a duly certified copy of the notification to all the other Powers informing them of the date on which it was received.

The denunciation shall only affect the notifying Power, and only on the expiry of one year after the notification has reached the Netherland Government.

Art. 13.

A register kept by the Netherland Ministry for Foreign Affairs shall record the date of the deposit of ratifications effected in virtue of Article 9, paragraphs 3 and 4, as well as the date on which the notifications of accession (Article 10, paragraph 2) or of denunciation (Article 12, paragraph 1) have been received.

Chaque Puissance contractante est admise à prendre connaissance de ce registre et à en demander des extraits certifiés conformes.

En foi de quoi les Plénipotentiaires ont revêtu la présente Convention de leurs signatures.

Fait à La Haye, le 18 Octobre, 1907, en un seul exemplaire, qui restera déposé dans les archives du Gouvernement des Pays-Bas, et dont des copies, certifiées conformes, seront remises par la voie diplomatique aux Puissances qui ont été conviées à la Deuxième Conférence de la Paix.

Each Contracting Power is entitled to have access to this register and to be supplied with duly certified extracts from it.

In faith whereof the Plenipotentiaries have appended their signatures to the present Convention.

Done at The Hague, the 18th October, 1907, in a single original, which shall remain deposited in the archives of the Netherland Government, and of which duly certified copies shall be sent, through the diplomatic channel, to the Powers invited to the Second Peace Conference.

CONVENTION No. 9.   RESPECTING BOMBARDMENT BY NAVAL FORCES IN
TIME OF WAR[1].

The first Conference expressed the " Wish " that the proposal to settle the question of the bombardment of ports, towns and villages by a naval force might be referred to a subsequent Conference for consideration.   The subject was embodied in the Circular of Count Benckendorff and was dealt with by the Third Committee of the Conference of 1907, presided over by M. Hagerup (Norway), Professor G. Streit (Greece) acting as Reporter.

Coast warfare continued to be conducted with great brutality long after many of the excesses of land warfare had been modified and an attack on undefended commercial coast towns was recommended by the Prince de Joinville in 1844 in case of war with England.   The Duke of Wellington rejected such a method of conducting hostilities as one which had been " disclaimed by the civilised portions of mankind."

[1] *Parl. Papers*, Misc. No. 4 (1908), pp. 27, 113–119 ; *La Deux. Confér.* T. i. pp. 111–119 ; T. iii. pp. 341–364, 518, 538–550, 655–9 ; *Livre Jaune*, p. 86 ; *Weissbuch*, p. 10 ; *Annuaire de l'Institut de Droit International*, Vol. xv. p. 313 ; Sir T. Barclay, *Problems, etc.* p. 51 ; Bonfils-Fauchille, *Droit international* (5th ed.), § 1277 ; T. E. Holland, *Studies in International Law*, p. 96 ; W. E. Hall, *Int. Law*, pp. 433, 537 ; C. Dupuis, *Le droit de la guerre maritime*, §§ 67–72 ; T. J. Lawrence, *International Problems, etc.* p. 119 ; Idem, *Int. Law*, p. 443 ; E. Lémonon, *La seconde Conférence, etc.* pp. 503–525 ; L. Oppenheim, *Int. Law*, Vol. ii. § 213 ; J. W. Scott, *Bombardment by Naval Forces*, Am. Journ. of Int. Law, Vol. ii. p. 285 ; H. Taylor, *Int. Law*, p. 499 ; J. Westlake, *War*, pp. 76, 315.

In 1882 Admiral Aube wrote an article in the *Revue des deux Mondes*[1] expressing the opinion that "armoured fleets in possession of the sea will turn their powers of attack and destruction against the coast towns of the enemy...and will burn them and lay them in ruins, or at the very least will hold them mercilessly to ransom." The question was again reopened in 1888 on the occasion of the manœuvres executed by the British fleet, the enemy part of which feigned to hold to ransom, under the threat of bombardment, great commercial towns, such as Liverpool, and to cause unnecessary devastation to pleasure towns and bathing-places, such as Folkestone, by means of throwing bombs. Professor Holland addressed a series of letters to the *Times* contending that such proceedings were contrary to the modern rules of international law, and that the bombardment of an open town ought only to be allowed for the purpose of obtaining requisitions in kind necessary for the enemy fleet and contributions instead of requisitions, further by way of reprisals, and in case the town defends itself against occupation by enemy troops approaching on land[2]. A similar view was expressed by Mr Hall. "An undefended town may fairly be summoned by a vessel or squadron to pay a contribution: if it refuses a force must be landed; and if it still refuses, like measures may be taken with those which are taken by armies in the field....A levy of money made in any other manner than this is not properly a contribution at all. It is a ransom from destruction. If it is permissible, it is permissible because there is a right to devastate, and because ransom is a mitigation of that right[3]."

The subject was examined by the Institut de Droit International in 1896, and a set of rules was formulated by it. These rules started from the principle that bombardment of all undefended towns is prohibited and added some special rules required by the exigencies of naval warfare[4]. The United States Naval War Code of 1900 adopted in the main the recommendations of the Institut and laid down that "the bombardment by a naval force, of unfortified and undefended towns, villages or buildings is forbidden, except when such bombardment is incidental to the destruction of military or naval establishments, public depôts of munitions of war, or vessels of war in ports, or unless reasonable requisitions for provisions and supplies essential, at the same time, to such naval vessel or vessels are forcibly withheld, in which case due notice of bombardment shall be given. The bombardment of unfortified and undefended towns and places for the non-payment of ransom is forbidden" (Article 4).

[1] Vol. L. p. 831.
[2] *Studies in International Law*, p. 96.
[3] *International Law*, p. 436.
[4] See *Annuaire*, Vol. xv. (1896), pp. 145, 148.

Such was the position of the question when the Conference of 1907 took it into consideration. Propositions were handed in to the Third Committee by the delegates of the United States, Spain, Italy, Holland and Russia. These proposals were embodied by their authors in a draft of seven Articles which was issued for the deliberations of the Committee[1].

Discussions at the Hague.

The draft dealt with two separate matters, the first part relating to the bombardment of undefended ports, towns, villages, dwellings or buildings, the second laying down general rules applicable to bombardments by naval forces. The Convention follows this order.

The first paragraph of the first Article is based on Article 25 of 2 H. C. 1899 (Regulations), and does not contain the words "by any means whatever" added in 1907. The meaning of the term "undefended" engaged the attention of the Committee but owing to the difficulty of distinguishing between the defence of a coast and of a town near the coast no definition was attempted[2]. The second paragraph, however, treats as undefended towns, those before which automatic submarine contact mines are anchored. This paragraph was strongly opposed by Captain Ottley who was supported by the delegates of Germany, France, China, Japan and Spain. Mines, it was pointed out, being a general danger to navigation, and far more destructive than guns, it was illogical to render inviolable a town defended by mines and to refuse inviolability to one defended by guns. Moreover, if undefended towns are free from bombardment, what is the need of laying mines on the sea front? A belligerent who has undertaken not to bombard an undefended coast town is entitled to make use of the coast without expecting to run the danger of destruction on approaching it[3]. This argument is sound and unanswerable. A town which has mines moored before its harbour has taken most effective steps to defend itself against occupation, and "the price of immunity from bombardment is that the place shall be left open to the enemy to enter[4]." Captain Ottley, however, failed to convince the Committee and the paragraph was retained by 21 votes to 5, 11 delegates not voting.

Chapter 1. Article 1.

The first Article having laid down the rule of non-bombardment of undefended coast towns, the second and third Articles proceed to make exceptions. These exceptions were considered necessary owing to the special character of naval warfare. Military works,

Article 2.

---

[1] *La Deux. Confér.* T. III. pp. 655–9.

[2] The question of the bombardment of the Hague from the sea was mentioned during the discussion, by General den Beer Poortugael (*La Deux. Confér.* T. III. p. 546). Professor Holland's opinion on the subject given in 1890 may be referred to in this connection, *Studies, etc.* p. 105.

[3] *La Deux. Confér.* T. III. p. 343.   [4] J. Westlake, *War*, p. 315.

military or naval establishments, depôts of arms or war material, workshops or plant which can be utilised for the needs of the hostile fleet or army, as well as ships of war in the harbour, are not included in the prohibition against bombardment. Considerable difficulty was experienced in framing the first paragraph. The word "installations" was adopted to cover such works as are not solely for warlike purposes. An undefended coast town may be an important railway centre, or have floating-docks of great value for the repair of vessels; these are intended to be included under "installations." The word "provisions" was inserted in one of the drafts but "matériel de guerre," an extremely wide term, was ultimately substituted. This Article might, and probably will, be held to confer a right on a commander to destroy by bombardment railway stations, bridges, entrepôts, coal stacks, whether belonging to public authorities or private persons. The commander of a naval force may destroy the military works, etc. with artillery, if the local authorities after due warning do not destroy them, and where military necessity demands they may be destroyed with artillery without any warning. The commander incurs no liability for unavoidable damage caused by such bombardments; he must, however, take measures in order that the town may suffer as little harm as possible.

Article 3 provides the second exception to the prohibition of Article 1.

Article 3. Bombardment is allowed if, after formal demand, the authorities of an undefended coast town do not furnish provisions and supplies necessary for the immediate use of the naval force, but the requisitions must be in proportion to the resources of the place. The requisitions demanded can only be for the supply of the naval force before the place.

This Article adopts the principles of Article 4 of the Draft Regulations of the Institut de Droit International, but these are in excess of the measures allowed for land warfare. In case of undefended towns if requisitions are not forthcoming, the army proceeds to take them. Mr Hall was of opinion that where a naval force demanded requisitions they should send a landing party and follow a similar course[1]. In land warfare, the General can usually from observations on the spot form an accurate estimate of the capacity of a place to provide the requisitions demanded, but in the case of a naval commander this will in many cases prove an impossibility. Under this Article, if after due notice, the amount of requisitions which the naval commander deems to be within the resources of the locality are not provided, he can at once open fire as a punishment for the refusal. The punishment

[1] See *ante*, p. 353.

appears excessive. A naval commander may have largely over-estimated the capabilities of a town, which may already be in a state of want, but on failure to comply with his demands the inhabitants will find themselves not only faced by hunger but by the further terror of a naval bombardment.

Article 4 corresponds to one which was contained in the original **Article 4.** proposition of the United States, and forbade the bombardment of a town on account of the non-payment of a *ransom*. The Committee preferred to suppress the word, as to forbid it in this connection might have led to the inference that the demand of a ransom was not prohibited in principle.

Articles 5, 6 and 7, which refer to naval bombardments generally and not **Chapter II.** only to cases allowed by the preceding Articles, correspond, **Articles 5,** with modifications to suit naval warfare, to Articles 26–28 of **6 and 7.** the Regulations on the laws and customs of war on land. The distinctive sign to be affixed to buildings devoted to religion, art, science, etc. is expressly described in this case, whereas in land warfare the sign is to be notified beforehand by the besieged to the besiegers. An objection was made by the delegates of the United States and Japan on the grounds of the difficulty of providing a distinctive mark which would be suitable under all circumstances, and of the possibility of its being abused. The sign described in Article 5 was devised by a Committee of three naval officers, Admiral Arago (France), Captain Castiglia (Italy) and Captain Behr (Russia)[1].

The form of the sixth Article is due to Captain Ottley's representation, in which he received the support of the Japanese delegate (M. Tsudzuki). The original draft laid down that previous warning of a bombardment should be given to the authorities, but Captain Ottley pointed out that it was frequently of the greatest importance to attack and destroy as speedily as possible a fortress or arsenal of the enemy or war-ships in port. Notice would in many cases be fatal to the success of an attack. A fleet, for instance, arrives before a fortress or naval port without having been observed by the enemy; to give warning of the bombardment would nullify the effect of the manoeuvre[2]. Under the Article as it now stands, the commander of the attacking force must, *except where military exigencies do not permit it*, do his utmost to warn the authorities before commencing the bombardment. This exception brings the Article into harmony with the corresponding Article in 4 H. C. 1007, Regulations (Art. 26).

---

[1] *La Deux. Confér.* T. I. p. 117; T. III. p. 352.
[2] *Ibid.* T. III. p. 542.

Article 7 by the transposition of the word "even" emphasises the prohibition against pillage contained in 4 H. C. 1907, Regulations (Art. 27).

The Convention has been signed by all the Powers represented at the **Signatory Powers and reservations.** Conference except China, Spain and Nicaragua. Great Britain, France, Germany and Japan made reservations of the second paragraph of Article 1, which provides that a place cannot be bombarded for the sole fact that automatic submarine contact mines are moored before its port. Chili made a reservation of Article 3.

The value of this Convention will depend greatly on the spirit in which it is executed by naval commanders. Like most of the other Conventions of the Conference it is tentative. The bold and categorical prohibition of Article 1 is weakened by the two following Articles. Towns which are undefended can avoid bombardment if after due notice they carry out the destruction of the military works, etc. mentioned in Article 2, paragraph 1, but "military necessities" may not always allow of this notice being given, and then the towns where such military works, etc. exist will find themselves without any warning, and although "undefended," subjected to bombardment; not directly, it is true, for the guns of the attacking fleet will be turned on the military works, etc., but some parts of the town cannot escape destruction.

Undefended coast towns are still in many cases left to be dealt with as the "necessities of war" require, but it cannot be denied that it is a distinct gain to have obtained a definite agreement prohibiting the attack or bombardment by naval forces of undefended ports, towns, villages, habitations and buildings, and to have the prohibition made applicable in cases of non-payment of a money contribution.

X. La Convention de Genève et la Guerre Maritime[1].

1899	1907
III. Convention pour l'adaptation à la Guerre Maritime des principes de la Convention de Genève du 22 Août, 1864.	**X. Convention pour l'adaptation à la Guerre Maritime des principes de la Convention de Genève.**

Sa Majesté le Roi des Belges, &c.[2]

Également animés du désir de diminuer autant qu'il dépend d'eux les maux inséparables de la guerre et voulant dans ce but adapter à la guerre maritime les principes de la Convention de Genève du 22 Août, 1864, ont résolu de conclure une Convention à cet effet :

Ils ont, en conséquence, nommé pour Leurs Plénipotentiaires, savoir :

[*Dénomination des Plénipotentiaires.*]

Lesquels, après s'être communiqué leurs pleins pouvoirs, trouvés en bonne et due forme, sont convenus des dispositions suivantes :—

Sa Majesté l'Empereur d'Allemagne, Roi de Prusse, &c.[3]

Également animés du désir de diminuer, autant qu'il dépend d'eux, les maux inséparables de la guerre ;

Et voulant, dans ce but, adapter à la guerre maritime les principes de la Convention de Genève du *6 Juillet, 1906* ;

Ont résolu de conclure une Convention *à l'effet de reviser la Convention du 29 Juillet, 1899, relative à la même matière* et ont nommé pour Leurs Plénipotentiaires, savoir :

[*Dénomination des Plénipotentiaires.*]

Lesquels, après *avoir déposé* leurs pleins pouvoirs, trouvés en bonne et due forme, sont convenus des dispositions suivantes :—

Art. 1.

Les bâtiments-hôpitaux militaires, c'est-à-dire, les bâtiments construits ou aménagés par les États spécialement et uniquement en vue de porter secours aux blessés, malades et naufragés, et dont les noms auront été communiqués, à l'ouverture ou au cours des

Art. 1.

(*Aucune modification.*)

---

[1] See note 1, page 95 *ante*.   [2] See note 1, p. 359.   [3] See note 2, p. 359.

X. The Geneva Convention and Maritime Warfare[1].

<table>
<tr><td align="center">1899</td><td align="center">1907</td></tr>
</table>

III. Convention for the adaptation to Maritime Warfare of the principles of the Geneva Convention of August 22, 1864.

His Majesty the King of the Belgians, &c.[2]

Animated alike by the desire to diminish, as far as depends on them, the evils inseparable from war, and wishing with this object to adapt to maritime warfare the principles of the Geneva Convention of the 22nd August, 1864, have resolved to conclude a Convention to this effect:

They have, in consequence, appointed as their Plenipotentiaries, that is to say:

[*Names of Plenipotentiaries.*]

Who, after communication of their full powers, found in good and due form, have agreed upon the following provisions :—

Art. 1.

Military hospital-ships, that is to say, ships constructed or adapted by States specially and solely with the view of aiding the wounded, sick, and shipwrecked, the names of which have been communicated to the belligerent Powers at the commencement

---

X. Convention for the Adaptation of the Principles of the Geneva Convention to Maritime War.

His Majesty the German Emperor, King of Prussia, &c.[3]

Animated alike by the desire to diminish, as far as depends on them, the evils inseparable from war ;

And wishing with this object to adapt to maritime warfare the principles of the Geneva Convention of the *6th July, 1906* ;

Have resolved to conclude a Convention *for the purpose of revising the Convention of the 29th July, 1899, relative to this subject,* and have appointed as their Plenipotentiaries, that is to say :

[*Names of Plenipotentiaries.*]

Who, after *having deposited* their full powers, found in good and due form, have agreed upon the following provisions :—

Art. 1.

(*No change.*)

---

[1] See note 1, page 95 *ante.*

[2] For List of Powers see Convention No. 2 (1899), *ante*, p. 207. All the Powers enumerated in the Final Act of 1907 subsequently signed or acceded.

[3] List of Powers as in Final Act of 1907.

1899	1907

hostilités, en tout cas avant toute mise en usage, aux Puissances belligérantes, sont respectés et ne peuvent être capturés pendant la durée des hostilités.

Ces bâtiments ne sont pas non plus assimilés aux navires de guerre au point de vue de leur séjour dans un port neutre.

Art. 2.

Les bâtiments-hospitaliers, équipés en totalité ou en partie aux frais des particuliers ou des sociétés de secours officiellement reconnues, sont également respectés et exempts de capture si la Puissance belligérante dont ils dépendent leur a donné une commission officielle et en a notifié les noms à la Puissance adverse à l'ouverture ou au cours des hostilités, en tout cas avant toute mise en usage.

Ces navires doivent être porteurs d'un document de l'autorité compétente déclarant qu'ils ont été soumis à son contrôle pendant leur armement et à leur départ final.

Art. 2.
(*Aucune modification.*)

Art. 3.

Les bâtiments-hospitaliers, équipés en totalité ou en partie aux frais des particuliers ou des sociétés officiellement reconnues de pays neutres, sont respectés et exempts de capture si la Puissance neutre dont ils dépendent leur a donné une commission officielle et en a notifié les noms aux Puissances belligérantes à l'ouverture ou au cours des hostilités, en tout cas avant toute mise en usage.

Art. 3.

Les bâtiments hospitaliers, équipés en totalité ou en partie aux frais des particuliers ou des sociétés officiellement reconnues de pays neutres, sont respectés et exempts de capture, *à condition qu'ils se soient mis sous la direction de l'un des belligérants, avec l'assentiment préalable de leur propre Gouvernement et avec l'autorisation du belligérant lui-même, et que ce dernier* en ait notifié le nom *à son adversaire dès* l'ouverture ou dans le cours des hostilités, en tout cas, avant tout emploi.

1899	1907

or during the course of hostilities, and in any case before they are employed, shall be respected, and cannot be captured while hostilities last.

These ships, moreover, are not on the same footing as war-ships as regards their stay in a neutral port.

ART. 2.

Hospital-ships, equipped wholly or in part at the expense of private individuals or officially recognized relief societies, shall likewise be respected and exempt from capture, if the belligerent Power to whom they belong has given them an official commission and has notified their names to the hostile Power at the commencement of or during hostilities, and in any case before they are employed.

Such ships must be provided with a document from the proper authorities declaring that the vessels have been under their control while fitting out and on final departure.

ART. 2.

(*No change.*)

ART. 3.

Hospital-ships, equipped wholly or in part at the cost of private individuals or officially recognized societies of neutral countries, shall be respected and exempt from capture, if the neutral Power to whom they belong has given them an official commission and notified their names to the belligerent Powers at the commencement of or during hostilities, and in any case before they are employed.

(*Cp. Draft Additional Articles (Geneva), 1868, Art.* 13.)

ART. 3.

Hospital-ships, equipped wholly or in part at the cost of private individuals or officially recognized societies of neutral countries, shall be respected and exempt from capture, *on condition that they are placed under the control of one of the belligerents, with the previous consent of their own Government and with the authorization of the belligerent himself, and that the latter* has notified their name *to his adversary* at the commencement of or during hostilities, and in any case, before they are employed.

(*Cp. Geneva Convention,* 1906, *Art.* 11.)

1899	1907
Art. 4.	Art. 4.

Les bâtiments qui sont mentionnés dans les Articles 1, 2 et 3, porteront secours et assistance aux blessés, malades et naufragés des belligérants sans distinction de nationalité.

Les Gouvernements s'engagent à n'utiliser ces bâtiments pour aucun but militaire.

Ces bâtiments ne devront gêner en aucune manière les mouvements des combattants.

Pendant et après le combat, ils agiront à leurs risques et périls.

Les belligérants auront sur eux le droit de contrôle et de visite; ils pourront refuser leur concours, leur enjoindre de s'éloigner, leur imposer une direction déterminée et mettre à bord un commissaire, même les détenir, si la gravité des circonstances l'exigeait.

Autant que possible, les belligérants inscriront sur le journal de bord des bâtiments-hospitaliers les ordres qu'ils leur donneront.

(Aucune modification.)

Art. 5.	Art. 5.

Les bâtiments-hôpitaux militaires seront distingués par une peinture extérieure blanche avec une bande horizontale verte d'un mètre et demi de largeur environ.

Les bâtiments qui sont mentionnés dans les Articles 2 et 3, seront distingués par une peinture extérieure blanche avec une bande horizontale rouge d'un mètre et demi de largeur environ.

Les embarcations des bâtiments qui viennent d'être mentionnés, comme les petits bâtiments qui pourront être

Les bâtiments-hôpitaux militaires seront distingués par une peinture extérieure blanche avec une bande horizontale verte d'un mètre et demi de largeur environ.

Les bâtiments qui sont mentionnés dans les Articles 2 et 3, seront distingués par une peinture extérieure blanche avec une bande horizontale rouge d'un mètre et demi de largeur environ.

Les embarcations des bâtiments qui viennent d'être mentionnés, comme les petits bâtiments qui pourront être

1899	1907
ART. 4.	ART. 4.

The ships mentioned in Articles 1, 2 and 3 shall afford relief and assistance to the wounded, sick and shipwrecked of the belligerents without distinction of nationality.

(No change.)

The Governments undertake not to use these ships for any military purpose.

Such vessels must in no wise hamper the movements of the combatants.

During and after an engagement they will act at their own risk and peril.

The belligerents shall have the right to control and search them ; they may decline their assistance, order them off, make them take a certain course, and put a commissioner on board ; they may even detain them, if the gravity of the circumstances require it.

As far as possible the belligerents shall enter in the log book of the hospital-ships the orders which they give them.

(*Cp. Draft Additional Articles (Geneva)*, 1868, *Arts.* 10 *and* 13.)

ART. 5.

Military hospital-ships shall be distinguished by being painted white outside with a horizontal band of green about a metre and a half in breadth.

(*Cp. Draft Additional Articles (Geneva)*, 1868, *Art.* 12.)

ART. 5.

Military hospital-ships shall be distinguished by being painted white outside with a horizontal band of green about a metre and a half in breadth.

The ships mentioned in Articles 2 and 3 shall be distinguished by being painted white outside with a horizontal band of red about a metre and a half in breadth.

The ships mentioned in Articles 2 and 3 shall be distinguished by being painted white outside with a horizontal band of red about a metre and a half in breadth.

The boats of the ships above mentioned, as also small craft which may

The boats of the ships abovementioned, as also small craft which

affectés au service hospitalier, se distingueront par une peinture analogue.

Tous les bâtiments-hospitaliers se feront reconnaître en hissant, avec leur pavillon national, le pavillon blanc à croix rouge prévu par la Convention de Genève.

affectés au service hospitalier, se distingueront par une peinture analogue.

Tous les bâtiments hospitaliers se feront reconnaître en hissant, avec leur pavillon national, le pavillon blanc à croix-rouge prévu par la Convention de Genève, *et, en outre, s'ils ressortissent à un État neutre, en arborant au grand mât le pavillon national du belligérant sous la direction duquel ils se sont placés.*

Les bâtiments hospitaliers qui, dans les termes de l'Article 4, sont détenus par l'ennemi, auront à rentrer le pavillon national du belligérant dont ils relèvent.

Les bâtiments et embarcations ci-dessus mentionnés, qui veulent s'assurer la nuit le respect auquel ils ont droit, ont, avec l'assentiment du belligérant qu'ils accompagnent, à prendre les mesures nécessaires pour que la peinture qui les caractérise soit suffisamment apparente.

Art. 6.

Les signes distinctifs prévus à l'Article 5 ne pourront être employés, soit en temps de paix, soit en temps de guerre, que pour protéger ou désigner les bâtiments qui y sont mentionnés.

Art. 7.

Dans le cas d'un combat à bord d'un vaisseau de guerre, les infirmeries seront respectées et ménagées autant que faire se pourra.

Ces infirmeries et leur matériel demeurent soumis aux lois de la guerre, mais ne pourront être détournés de leur emploi, tant qu'ils seront nécessaires aux blessés et malades.

1899	1907
be used for hospital work, shall be distinguished by similar painting.	may be used for hospital work, shall be distinguished by similar painting.

All hospital-ships shall make themselves known by hoisting, with their national flag, the white flag with a red cross provided by the Geneva Convention.

All hospital-ships shall make themselves known by hoisting, with their national flag, the white flag with a red cross provided by the Geneva Convention, *and further, if they belong to a neutral State, by flying at the mainmast the national flag of the belligerent under whose control they are placed.*

Hospital-ships which under the terms of Article 4 are detained by the enemy must haul down the national flag of the belligerent to whom they belong.

(*Cp. G. C.* 1906, *Arts.* 21 *and* 22.)

The ships and boats above mentioned which wish to ensure by night the freedom from interference to which they are entitled, must, subject to the assent of the belligerent they are accompanying, take the necessary measures to render their special painting sufficiently plain.

ART. 6.

The distinguishing signs referred to in Article 5 can only be used, whether in time of peace or war, for protecting or indicating the ships therein mentioned.

(*Cp. G. C.* 1906, *Art.* 23.)

ART. 7.

In the case of a fight on board a war-ship, the sick-bays shall be respected and spared as far as possible.

The said sick-bays and the matériel belonging to them remain subject to the laws of war; they cannot, however, be used for any purpose other than that for which they were originally intended, so long as they are required for the wounded and sick.

1899	1907

Toutefois le commandant, qui les a en son pouvoir, a la faculté d'en disposer, en cas de nécessité militaire importante, en assurant au préalable le sort des blessés et malades qui s'y trouvent.

Art. 8.

La protection due aux bâtiments hospitaliers et aux infirmeries des vaisseaux cesse si l'on en use pour commettre des actes nuisibles à l'ennemi.

N'est pas considéré comme étant de nature à justifier le retrait de la protection le fait que le personnel de ces bâtiments et infirmeries est armé pour le maintien de l'ordre et pour la défense des blessés ou malades, ainsi que le fait de la présence à bord d'une installation radio-télégraphique.

Art. 6.

Les bâtiments de commerce, yachts ou embarcations neutres, portant ou recueillant des blessés, des malades, ou des naufragés des belligérants, ne peuvent être capturés pour le fait de ce transport, mais ils restent exposés à la capture pour les violations de neutralité qu'ils pourraient avoir commises.

Art. 9.

Les belligérants pourront faire appel au zèle charitable des commandants de bâtiments de commerce, yachts ou embarcations neutres, pour prendre à bord et soigner des blessés ou des malades.

Les bâtiments qui auront répondu à cet appel ainsi que ceux qui spontanément auront recueilli des blessés, des malades, ou des naufragés, jouiront d'une protection spéciale et de certaines immunités. En aucun cas ils ne pourront être capturés pour le fait d'un tel transport; mais, sauf les promesses qui leur auraient été faites, ils restent exposés à la capture pour les violations de neutralité qu'ils pourraient avoir commises.

1899	1907

1899 column (left) continues below; 1907 column (right):

The commander into whose power they have fallen may, however, if the military situation requires it, apply them to other purposes, after first seeing that the wounded and sick on board are properly provided for.

(*Cp. G. C.* 1906, *Arts.* 6 *and* 15.)

ART. 8.

The protection to which hospital-ships and sick-bays of vessels are entitled ceases if they are made use of to commit acts harmful to the enemy.

(*Cp. G. C.* 1906, *Art.* 7.)

The fact of the staff of the said ships and sick-bays being armed for maintaining order and for defending the wounded and sick, and the presence of wireless telegraphy apparatus on board, are not sufficient reasons for withdrawing protection.

(*Cp. G. C.* 1906, *Art.* 8.)

ART. 6.

Neutral merchantmen, yachts, or boats, having, or taking on board, wounded, sick, or shipwrecked of the belligerents, cannot be captured for carrying them, but they are liable to capture for any violation of neutrality they may have committed.

(*Cp. Draft Additional Articles* (*Geneva*), 1868, *Arts.* 6 *and* 10.)

ART. 9.

Belligerents may appeal to the charity of the commanders of neutral merchant-ships, yachts, or boats to take on board and tend the wounded and sick.

Vessels responding to this appeal, and also vessels which have of their own accord rescued wounded, sick, or shipwrecked men, shall enjoy special protection and certain immunities. In no case can they be captured for the sole reason of having such persons on board; but, subject to any undertaking that may have been given to them, they remain liable to capture for any violations of neutrality they may have committed.

(*Cp. G. C.* 1906, *Art.* 5.)

1899	1907
ART. 7.	ART. 10.

<table>
<tr><td>

Le personnel religieux, médical et hospitalier de tout bâtiment capturé est inviolable et ne peut être fait prisonnier de guerre. Il emporte, en quittant le navire, les objets et les instruments de chirurgie qui sont sa propriété particulière.

Ce personnel continuera à remplir ses fonctions tant que cela sera nécessaire, et il pourra ensuite se retirer lorsque le Commandant-en-chef le jugera possible.

Les belligérants doivent assurer à ce personnel tombé entre leurs mains, la jouissance intégrale de son traitement.

</td><td>

Le personnel religieux, médical et hospitalier de tout bâtiment capturé est inviolable et ne peut être fait prisonnier de guerre. Il emporte, en quittant le navire, les objets et les instruments de chirurgie qui sont sa propriété particulière.

Ce personnel continuera à remplir ses fonctions tant que cela sera nécessaire et il pourra ensuite se retirer, lorsque le commandant en chef le jugera possible.

Les belligérants doivent assurer à ce personnel tombé entre leurs mains, *les mêmes allocations et la même solde qu'au personnel des mêmes grades de leur propre marine.*

</td></tr>
</table>

ART. 8.	ART. 11.

<table>
<tr><td>

Les marins et les militaires embarqués blessés ou malades, à quelque nation qu'ils appartiennent, seront protégés et soignés par les capteurs.

</td><td>

Les marins et les militaires embarqués, *et les autres personnes officiellement attachées aux marines ou aux armées,* blessés ou malades, à quelque nation qu'ils appartiennent, seront *respectés* et soignés par les capteurs.

</td></tr>
</table>

	ART. 12.

Tout vaisseau de guerre d'une partie belligérante peut réclamer la remise des blessés, malades ou naufragés, qui sont à bord de bâtiments-hôpitaux militaires, de bâtiments hospitaliers de société de secours ou de particuliers, de navires de commerce, yachts et embarcations, quelle que soit la nationalité de ces bâtiments.

	ART. 13.

Si des blessés, malades ou naufragés sont recueillis à bord d'un vaisseau de guerre neutre, il devra être pourvu,

1899	1907
Art. 7.	Art. 10.

The religious, medical and hospital staff of any captured ship is inviolable, and its members cannot be made prisoners of war. On leaving the ship they take with them the objects and surgical instruments which are their own private property.

The religious, medical, and hospital staff of any captured ship is inviolable, and its members cannot be made prisoners of war. On leaving the ship they take with them the objects and surgical instruments which are their own private property.

This staff shall continue to discharge its duties while necessary, and can afterwards leave when the Commander-in-chief considers it possible.

This staff shall continue to discharge its duties while necessary, and can afterwards leave when the Commander-in-chief considers it possible.

The belligerents must guarantee to the said staff that has fallen into their hands the enjoyment of their salaries intact.

The belligerents must guarantee to the said staff that has fallen into their hands *the same allowances and the same pay as are granted to the persons holding the same rank in their own navy.*

(*Cp. Draft Additional Articles (Geneva), 1868, Arts. 7 and 8.*)

(*Cp. G. C. 1906, Art. 13.*)

Art. 8.	Art. 11.

Sailors and soldiers who are taken on board when sick or wounded, whatever their nationality, shall be protected and tended by the captors.

Sailors and soldiers *and other persons officially attached to fleets or armies* who are taken on board when sick or wounded, whatever their nationality, shall be *respected* and tended by the captors.

(*Cp. Draft Additional Articles (Geneva), 1868, Art. 11.*)

(*Cp. G. C. 1906, Art. 1.*)

Art. 12.

Any war-ship belonging to a belligerent may demand the surrender of the wounded, sick, or shipwrecked who are on board military hospital-ships, hospital-ships belonging to relief societies or to private individuals, merchant-ships, yachts and boats, whatever the nationality of such vessels.

Art. 13.

If wounded, sick, or shipwrecked persons are taken on board a neutral

1899	1907
	dans la mesure du possible, à ce qu'ils ne puissent pas de nouveau prendre part aux opérations de la guerre.

<table>
<tr><td>

ART. 9.

Sont prisonniers de guerre les naufragés, blessés ou malades, d'un belligérant qui tombent au pouvoir de l'autre. Il appartient à celui-ci de décider, suivant les circonstances, s'il convient de les garder, de les diriger sur un port de sa nation, sur un port neutre ou même sur un port de l'adversaire. Dans ce dernier cas, les prisonniers ainsi rendus à leur pays ne pourront servir pendant la durée de la guerre.

</td><td>

ART. 14.

(*Aucune modification.*)

</td></tr>
</table>

<table>
<tr><td>

ART. 10[1].

Les naufragés, blessés ou malades, qui sont débarqués dans un port neutre, du consentement de l'autorité locale, devront, à moins d'un arrangement contraire de l'État neutre avec les États belligérants, être gardés par l'État neutre de manière qu'ils ne puissent pas de nouveau prendre part aux opérations de la guerre.

Les frais d'hospitalisation et d'internement seront supportés par l'État dont relèvent les naufragés, blessés ou malades.

</td><td>

ART. 15.

(*Aucune modification.*)

</td></tr>
</table>

ART. 16.

Après chaque combat, les deux parties belligérantes, en tant que les intérêts militaires le comportent, prendront des mesures pour rechercher les naufragés, les blessés et les malades et pour les faire protéger, ainsi que les morts, contre le pillage et les mauvais traitements.

[1] See note, p. 371.

1899	1907
	war-ship, precaution must be taken, so far as possible, that they do not again take part in the operations of the war.

ART. 9.

The shipwrecked, wounded, or sick of one of the belligerents who fall into the power of the other belligerent are prisoners of war. The captor must decide, according to circumstances, whether to keep them, send them to a port of his own country, to a neutral port, or even to an enemy port. In this last case, prisoners thus repatriated cannot serve again while the war lasts.

ART. 14.

(*No change.*)

ART. 10¹.

The shipwrecked, wounded, or sick, who are landed at a neutral port with the consent of the local authorities, must, in default of arrangement to the contrary between the neutral State and the belligerent States, be guarded by the neutral State so as to prevent them from again taking part in the operations of the war.

The expenses of tending them in hospital and interning them shall be borne by the State to which the shipwrecked, wounded, or sick persons belong.

ART. 15.

(*No change.*)

ART. 16.

After each engagement, the two belligerents shall, so far as military interests permit, take measures to search for the shipwrecked, wounded and sick, and to ensure them, as also the dead, protection against pillage and maltreatment.

¹ Excluded from ratification.

1899	1907

Elles veilleront à ce que l'inhumation, l'immersion ou l'incinération des morts soit précédé d'un examen attentif de leurs cadavres.

ART. 17.

Chaque belligérant enverra, dès qu'il sera possible, aux autorités de leur pays, de leur marine ou de leur armée les marques ou pièces militaires d'identité trouvées sur les morts et l'état nominatif des blessés ou malades recueillis par lui.

Les belligérants se tiendront réciproquement au courant des internements et des mutations, ainsi que des entrées dans les hôpitaux et des décès survenus parmi les blessés et malades en leur pouvoir. Ils recueilleront tous les objets d'un usage personnel, valeurs, lettres, &c., qui seront trouvés dans les vaisseaux capturés, ou délaissés par les blessés ou malades décédés dans les hôpitaux, pour les faire transmettre aux intéressés par les autorités de leur pays.

ART. 11.

Les règles contenues dans les articles ci-dessus ne sont obligatoires que pour les Puissances contractantes, en cas de guerre entre deux ou plusieurs d'entre elles.

Les dites règles cesseront d'être obligatoires du moment où, dans une guerre entre des Puissances contractantes, une Puissance non-contractante se joindrait à l'un des belligérants.

ART. 18.

Les dispositions de la présente Convention ne sont applicables qu'entre les Puissances contractantes et seulement si les belligérants sont tous parties à la Convention.

ART. 19.

Les commandants en chef des flottes des belligérants auront à pourvoir aux détails d'exécution des articles précédents, ainsi qu'aux cas non prévus,

1899	1907

1907 (continued)

They shall see that the burial, whether by land or sea, or cremation of the dead shall be preceded by a careful examination of the corpses.

(*Cp. G. C.* 1906, *Art.* 3.)

ART. 17.

Each belligerent shall send, as early as possible, to the authorities of their country, navy or army, the military identification marks or tokens found on the dead and a list of the names of the sick and wounded picked up by him.

The belligerents shall keep each other informed as to internments and transfers as well as to the admissions into hospital and deaths which have occurred among the sick and wounded in their hands. They shall collect all the objects of personal use, valuables, letters, &c., which are found in the captured ships, or which have been left by the wounded or sick who died in hospital, in order to have them forwarded to the persons concerned by the authorities of their own country.

(*Cp. G. C.* 1906, *Art.* 4.)

ART. 11.

The rules contained in the above Articles are binding only on the Contracting Powers, in case of war between two or more of them.

The said rules shall cease to be binding from the time when, in a war between the Contracting Powers, one of the belligerents is joined by a non-Contracting Power.

ART. 18.

The provisions of the present Convention do not *apply* except between Contracting Powers, *and only if all the belligerents are parties to the Convention.*

ART. 19.

The Commanders-in-chief of the belligerent fleets shall arrange the details for carrying out the preceding Articles as well as for cases not provided for, in

1899	1907

d'après les instructions de leurs Gouvernements respectifs et conformément aux principes généraux de la présente Convention.

Art. 20.

Les Puissances signataires prendront les mesures nécessaires pour instruire leurs marines, et spécialement le personnel protégé, des dispositions de la présente Convention et pour les porter à la connaissance des populations.

Art. 21.

Les Puissances signataires s'engagent également à prendre ou à proposer à leurs législatures, en cas d'insuffisance de leurs lois pénales, les mesures nécessaires pour réprimer en temps de guerre les actes individuels de pillage et de mauvais traitements envers des blessés et malades des marines, ainsi que pour punir, comme usurpation d'insignes militaires, l'usage abusif des signes distinctifs désignés à l'article 5 par des bâtiments non protégés par la présente Convention.

Ils se communiqueront, par l'intermédiaire du Gouvernement des Pays-Bas, les dispositions relatives à cette répression, au plus tard dans les cinq ans de la ratification de la présente Convention.

Art. 22.

En cas d'opérations de guerre entre les forces de terre et de mer des belligérants, les dispositions de la présente Convention ne seront applicables qu'aux forces embarquées.

1899	1907

accordance with the instructions of their respective Governments and in conformity with the general principles of the present Convention.

(*Cp. G. C.* 1906, *Art.* 25.)

ART. 20.

The Signatory Powers shall take the necessary measures to instruct their naval forces, especially the personnel protected, in the provisions of the present Convention, and to bring them to the notice of the public.

(*Cp. G. C.* 1906, *Art.* 26.)

ART. 21.

The Signatory Powers likewise undertake to enact or to propose to their Legislatures, if their criminal laws are inadequate, the measures necessary for checking in time of war individual acts of pillage and ill-treatment in respect to the wounded and sick in the fleet, as well as for punishing, as an unjustifiable adoption of naval or military marks, the unauthorized use of the distinctive marks mentioned in Article 5 by vessels not protected by the present Convention.

They shall communicate to each other, through the Netherland Government, the enactments for preventing such acts at the latest within five years of the ratification of the present Convention.

(*Cp. G. C.* 1906, *Arts.* 27 and 28.)

ART. 22.

In the case of operations of war between the land and sea forces of belligerents, the provisions of the present Convention are only applicable to the forces on board ship.

1899	1907
Art. 12.	Art. 23.

La présente Convention sera ratifiée dans le plus bref délai possible.

Les ratifications seront déposées à La Haye.

Il sera dressé du dépôt de chaque ratification un procès-verbal, dont une copie, certifiée conforme, sera remise par la voie diplomatique à toutes les Puissances contractantes.

La présente Convention sera ratifiée *aussitôt que* possible.

Les ratifications seront déposées à La Haye.

Le premier dépôt de ratifications sera constaté par un procès-verbal signé par les Représentants des Puissances qui y prennent part et par le Ministre des Affaires Étrangères des Pays-Bas.

Les dépôts ultérieurs de ratifications se feront au moyen d'une notification écrite, adressée au Gouvernement des Pays-Bas et accompagnée de l'instrument de ratification.

Copie certifiée conforme du procès-verbal relatif au premier dépôt de ratifications, des notifications mentionnées à l'alinéa précédent, ainsi que des instruments de ratification, sera immédiatement remise par les soins du Gouvernement des Pays-Bas et par la voie diplomatique aux Puissances conviées à la Deuxième Conférence de la Paix, ainsi qu'aux autres Puissances qui auront adhéré à la Convention. Dans les cas visés par l'alinéa précédent, le dit Gouvernement leur fera connaître en même temps la date à laquelle il a reçu la notification.

Art. 13.	Art. 24.

Les Puissances non-signataires, qui auront accepté la Convention de Genève du 22 Août, 1864, sont admises à adhérer à la présente Convention.

Elles auront, à cet effet, à faire connaître leur adhésion aux Puissances contractantes, au moyen d'une notification écrite, adressée au Gouverne-

Les Puissances non-signataires qui auront accepté la Convention de Genève du *6 Juillet, 1906*, sont admises à adhérer à la présente Convention.

La Puissance qui désire adhérer, notifie par écrit son intention au Gouvernement des Pays-Bas en lui transmettant l'acte d'adhésion qui sera

1899	1907
ART. 12.	ART. 23.

The present Convention shall be ratified as soon as possible.

The ratifications shall be deposited at the Hague.

On the receipt of each ratification a *procès-verbal* shall be drawn up, a copy of which, duly certified, shall be sent through the diplomatic channel to all the Contracting Powers.

The present Convention shall be ratified as soon as possible.

The ratifications shall be deposited at The Hague.

The first deposit of ratifications shall be recorded in a procès-verbal signed by the Representatives of the Powers which take part therein and by the Netherland Minister for Foreign Affairs.

The subsequent deposits of ratifications shall be made by means of a written notification, addressed to the Netherland Government and accompanied by the instrument of ratification.

A duly certified copy of the procès-verbal relative to the first deposit of ratifications, of the notifications mentioned in the preceding paragraph, and of the instruments of ratification, shall be immediately sent by the Netherland Government through the diplomatic channel to the Powers invited to the Second Peace Conference, as well as to the other Powers which have acceded to the Convention. In the cases contemplated in the preceding paragraph the said Government shall inform them at the same time of the date on which it received the notification.

ART. 13.	ART. 24.

Non-Signatory Powers which have accepted the Geneva Convention of the 22nd August, 1864, may accede to the present Convention.

For this purpose they must make their accession known to the Contracting Powers by means of a written notification addressed to the Nether-

Non-Signatory Powers which have accepted the Geneva Convention of the *6th July, 1906*, may accede to the present Convention.

A Power which desires to accede notifies its intention in writing to the Netherland Government, forwarding to it the act of accession, which shall be

1899	1907
ment des Pays-Bas et communiquée par celui-ci à toutes les autres Puissances contractantes.	*déposé dans les archives du dit Gouvernement.*

Ce Gouvernement transmettra immédiatement à toutes les autres Puissances copie certifiée conforme de la notification ainsi que de l'acte d'adhésion, en indiquant la date à laquelle il a reçu la notification.

ART. 25.

La présente Convention, dûment ratifiée, remplacera dans les rapports entre les Puissances contractantes, la Convention du 29 Juillet, 1899, pour l'adaptation à la guerre maritime des principes de la Convention de Genève.

La Convention de 1899 reste en vigueur dans les rapports entre les Puissances qui l'ont signée et qui ne ratifieraient pas également la présente Convention.

ART. 26.

La présente Convention produira effet pour les Puissances qui auront participé au premier dépôt de ratifications, soixante jours après la date du procès-verbal de ce dépôt, et, pour les Puissances qui ratifieront ultérieurement ou qui adhéreront, soixante jours après que la notification de leur ratification ou de leur adhésion aura été reçue par le Gouvernement des Pays-Bas.

ART. 14.

S'il arrivait qu'une des Hautes Parties contractantes dénonçât la présente Convention, cette dénonciation ne produirait ses effets qu'un an après la notification faite par écrit au Gouvernement des Pays-Bas et com-

ART. 27.

S'il arrivait qu'une des Puissances contractantes *voulût dénoncer* la présente Convention, *la* dénonciation *sera notifiée* par écrit au Gouvernement des Pays-Bas, *qui communiquera* immédiatement *copie certifiée conforme de*

1899	1907
land Government, and by it communicated to all the other Contracting Powers.‾	*deposited in the archives of the said Government.*

The said Government shall immediately forward to all the other Powers a duly certified copy of the notification, as well as of the act of accession, mentioning the date on which it received the notification.

ART. 25.

The present Convention, duly ratified, shall replace as between Contracting Powers, the Convention of the 29th July, 1899, for the adaptation to naval warfare of the principles of the Geneva Convention.

The Convention of 1899 remains in force as between the Powers which signed it but which may not also ratify the present Convention.

(Cp. G. C. 1906, Art. 31.)

ART. 26.

The present Convention shall take effect, in the case of the Powers which were parties to the first deposit of ratifications, sixty days after the date of the procès-verbal *recording such deposit, and, in the case of the Powers which shall ratify subsequently or which shall accede, sixty days after the notification of their ratification or of their accession has been received by the Netherland Government.*

ART. 14.

In the event of one of the High Contracting Parties denouncing the present Convention, such denunciation shall not take effect until a year after the notification made in writing to the Netherland Government, and forthwith

ART. 27.

In the event of one of the Contracting Powers *wishing to* denounce the present Convention, *the* denunciation *shall be notified* in writing to the Netherland Government, *which shall* immediately *communicate a duly certi-*

1899	1907

muniquée immédiatement par celui-ci à toutes les autres Puissances contractantes.

Cette dénonciation ne produira ses effets qu'à l'égard de la Puissance qui l'aura notifiée.

la notification à toutes les autres Puissances *en leur faisant savoir la date à laquelle il l'a reçue.*

La dénonciation ne produira ses effets qu'à l'égard de la Puissance qui l'aura notifiée *et un an après que la* notification *en sera parvenue au Gouvernement des Pays-Bas.*

Art. 28.

Un registre tenu par le Ministère des Affaires Étrangères des Pays-Bas indiquera la date du dépôt des ratifications effectué en vertu de l'Article 23, alinéas 3 et 4, ainsi que la date à laquelle auront été reçues les notifications d'adhésion (article 24, alinéa 2) ou de dénonciation (article 27, alinéa 1).

Chaque Puissance contractante est admise à prendre connaissance de ce registre et à en demander des extraits certifiés conformes.

En foi de quoi, les Plénipotentiaires respectifs ont signé la présente Convention et l'ont revêtue de leurs sceaux.

En foi de quoi les Plénipotentiaires ont revêtu la présente Convention de *leurs signatures.*

Fait à La Haye, le 29 Juillet, 1899, en un seul exemplaire, qui restera déposé dans les archives du Gouvernement des Pays-Bas, et dont des copies, certifiées conformes, seront remises par la voie diplomatique aux Puissances contractantes.

Fait à La Haye, le *18 Octobre, 1907,* en un seul exemplaire qui restera déposé dans les archives du Gouvernement des Pays-Bays, et dont des copies, certifiées conformes, seront remises par la voie diplomatique aux Puissances *qui ont été conviées à la Deuxième Conférence de la Paix.*

1899	1907
communicated by it to all the other Contracting Powers.	*fied copy of the notification* to all the other Powers, *informing them of the date on which it was received.*
This denunciation shall only affect the notifying Power.	The denunciation shall only affect the notifying Power, *and* only on the expiry of one year after the notification *has reached the Netherland Government.*

ART. 28.

A register kept by the Netherland Ministry for Foreign Affairs shall record the date of the deposit of ratifications effected in virtue of Article 23, paragraphs 3 and 4, as well as the date on which the notifications of accession (Article 24, paragraph 2) or of denunciation (Article 27, paragraph 1) have been received.

Each Contracting Power is entitled to have access to this register and to be supplied with duly certified extracts from it.

1899	1907
In faith whereof the respective Plenipotentiaries have signed the present Convention and affixed their seals thereto.	In faith whereof the Plenipotentiaries *have appended their signatures to the present Convention.*
Done at The Hague the 29th July, 1899, in a single original, which shall remain deposited in the archives of the Netherland Government, and of which duly certified copies shall be sent through the diplomatic channel to the Contracting Powers.	Done at The Hague, *the 18th October, 1907,* in a single original, which shall remain deposited in the archives of the Netherland Government, and of which duly certified copies shall be sent through the diplomatic channel, to the Powers *invited to the Second Peace Conference.*

CONVENTION No. 10.　THE ADAPTATION OF THE PRINCIPLES OF THE
GENEVA CONVENTION TO MARITIME WARFARE[1].

The attempt which was unsuccessfully made in 1868 to apply the
principles of the Geneva Convention of 1864 to naval warfare has already been referred to[2]. The additional Articles
then prepared afforded a basis for states during the period
between 1868 and 1899 when the first Hague Conference prepared a
Convention which was signed by all the Powers represented thereat, and
was subsequently acceded to by all the Powers represented at the Second
Peace Conference. The 10th Article was, however, excluded from ratification by all the signatory Powers[3].

The Convention of 1899.

A new Geneva Convention for land warfare having been agreed upon
in 1906, the Conference of 1907 found it necessary to revise the Convention
of 1899 in order to apply its principles to naval warfare, and also to make
certain additions and amendments which experience had shown to be
necessary.

The German Delegation presented a draft which was taken as the basis
of the deliberations of the Conference. Some amendments
were made by the French Delegation, and several of the
Articles of the German draft were modified after examination
by the naval delegates who formed a large proportion of the Examining
Committee.

The Convention of 1907.

The Report[4] made to the Third Committee presided over by Count
Tornielli (Italy) was prepared by Professor L. Renault, who had also
prepared the Report on this subject in 1899. It was taken into consideration at the third Plenary Meeting of the Conference on the 20th July, 1907.
With certain slight reservations which will be subsequently mentioned it
was adopted. This Convention was the first voted by the Conference.

---

[1] *Parl. Papers*, Misc. No. 1 (1899), p. 67; *Parl. Papers*, Misc. No. 4 (1908), pp. 18, 87;
La Deux. Confér. T. I. pp. 66, 70; T. III. pp. 293, 305, 313, 558, 683, 686, 689; *Livre Jaune*,
p. 89; *Weissbuch*, p. 11; Sir T. Barclay, *Problems, etc.* p. 199; A. S. Hershey, *International
Law and Diplomacy, etc.* p. 75; F. W. Holls, *The Peace Conference at the Hague*, Chap. IV.
and App. C; T. J. Lawrence, *War and Neutrality, etc.* Chap. IV.; Idem, *International
Problems, etc.* p. 114; E. Lémonon, *La seconde Conférence*, p. 526; L. Renault, *The Geneva
Convention and Maritime Warfare*, Am. Journ. of Int. Law, Vol. II. p. 295 [This is a
translation of M. Renault's Report to the Conference]; S. Takahashi, *International Law
applied to the Russo-Japanese War*, Part II. Chap. IV.; J. Westlake, *War*, p. 275.

[2] See *ante*, p. 13.　　　　　　　[3] See *post*, p. 390.

[4] *Parl. Papers*, Misc. No. 4 (1908), p. 87; *La Deux. Confér.* T. I. p. 70; T. III. p. 305.

The Committee adopted the wise plan of preparing a wholly new Convention instead of drafting supplementary Articles to the Convention of 1899, a proceeding which would have caused confusion and disturbed the balance and elegance of the agreement. The new Convention contains 26 Articles as compared with 14 in that of 1899.

The first three Articles deal with the three different classes of hospital ships to which the Convention applies, namely (*a*) military hospital ships constructed or adapted by *states* specially and solely with the view of aiding the wounded, sick and shipwrecked in naval war (Article 1); (*b*) hospital ships, equipped wholly or in part at the expense of private individuals or officially recognised relief societies of *belligerent* states (Article 2); (*c*) hospital ships, equipped wholly or in part at the cost of private individuals or officially recognised relief societies of *neutral* states (Article 3).

The various classes of hospital ships.

No changes are made in the first two Articles.

ARTICLE 3 contains modifications of the corresponding Article of the Convention of 1899, based on Article 11 of the Geneva Convention of 1906. The Conference of 1899 left unsettled the relations which should exist between neutral hospital ships and belligerents. The question was also raised as regards the flag which such ships ought to fly. In 1907 similar difficulties were experienced by some members of the Committee who felt that the text of Article 11 of the Convention of 1906 was not enough to remove them. The difference in the circumstances under which aid is rendered by a neutral ambulance in land warfare and a neutral hospital ship in naval warfare was felt by some of the Committee to call for different treatment, as hospital ships enjoy greater freedom of action than the neutral ambulances can claim in land warfare. The majority of the Committee considered that, for reasons of military necessity, it was inadvisable to allow neutral hospital ships to operate apart from the special authorisation of one of the belligerents, the view that such ships might desire to aid both belligerents indiscriminately being inacceptable on the ground that to allow complete independence of action to such neutral ships would leave the way open to serious abuses. The alteration in Article 3 now requires such ships to be placed under the control of one of the belligerents, after having received the previous consent of the neutral government. Such ships will henceforth form part of the sanitary service of the belligerent and be placed under his direction. The Report of M. Renault points out that this Article and Article 5 are not quite in harmony with Articles 11 and 22 of the Geneva Convention of 1906; under the latter a

Flags of neutral hospital ships.

neutral ambulance flies two flags, that of the Geneva Convention and that of the belligerent to whose army it is attached, but the neutral hospital ship must fly three flags, namely the two mentioned as well as its own national (neutral) flag. The German draft proposed that neutral hospital ships should be placed *au service* of one of the belligerents, but on the proposition of M. Van den Heuvel (Belgium) this expression was altered to *sous la direction* which was deemed to be less stringent.

ARTICLE 4 contains a general statement of the duties which are incumbent on hospital ships, namely, to render aid to all needing it irrespective of nationality. Belligerents are given power of control and detention where necessary. There is no change in this Article.

The duty of hospital ships.

ARTICLE 5 deals with the distinctive colours by which hospital ships are to be distinguished. In paragraph 4 a change was made in accordance with the agreement arrived at in Article 3 as to the flags which a neutral hospital ship is to fly, the principle applied being that of Article 21, par. 2 of the Geneva Convention, 1906. The provision applies to ships detained under Article 4. Under that Article when a hospital ship is detained by a belligerent, if it is a military hospital ship it hauls down its national flag and retains the flag of the Geneva Convention only, but if it is a neutral hospital ship it only hauls down the flag of the belligerent under whose direction it is, retaining its own national flag and the Red Cross flag.

Distinguishing marks of hospital ships.

The sixth paragraph of Article 5 is new and refers to the distinctive marks which may be applied to hospital ships at night. The German proposal was that all hospital ships should carry three lights—green, white, green—placed vertically one above the other and separated by at least three metres[1]. The question had been raised during the Russo-Japanese War. Russia notified to Japan through the intermediary of the French Government that she proposed to use by night three vertical lights for her hospital ships—white, red, white—but the Japanese Government declined to accept these distinguishing marks as conferring special privileges, " being apprehensive of various possible dangers which might arise as the result of such a contrivance being availed of by an unprincipled enemy[2]." Objections were also raised in Committee to the German proposal which made the carrying of distinctive lights obligatory. A light on a hospital ship may betray the presence of the fleet, and hospital ships must conform to the order for "lights out" in the same way as the ships under a belligerent's

---

[1] *La Deux. Confér.* T. III. p. 684.
[2] S. Takahashi, *op. cit.* p. 878.

command. During the Japanese attack off Genzan, Korea, even the slightest sign of light was prohibited. "Though almost intolerable for the sick and wounded, especially in the hot season, to have windows and apertures shut up, yet under such circumstances the directions of the authorities should be observed[1]." A warship might also make illicit use of the lights to effect its escape. The Convention leaves the steps which hospital ships and their boats are to take to ensure freedom from interference to be regulated by the belligerent by the special painting being rendered sufficiently plain. This is possible by means of phosphorescent paint or the employment of electric reflectors in case of attack[2].

ARTICLE 6 is based on Article 23 of the Geneva Convention of 1906, and has not been accepted by Great Britain. At the Third Plenary Meeting of the Conference Sir Edward Fry said that in signing the Geneva Convention of 1906 his Government had made a reservation of Articles 23, 27 and 28 because a legislative enactment was necessary to give effect to them, and without the assent of Parliament no law could be made in Great Britain. As Articles 6 and 21 of the present Convention were based on these Articles, his Government were for the time obliged to make reservations on them[3].

ARTICLE 7 is new and provides for a situation analogous to that dealt with by Articles 6 and 15 of the Geneva Convention of 1906.

Sick-bays on warships. In case of a fight *on board* a warship the sick-bays are to be respected and spared as much as possible. This recalls a condition of warfare more common a century ago than now, when hand-to-hand fighting on board a vessel is an extremely rare occurrence in naval engagements. It is not to be expected that in engagements where the combatants remain at a distance from each other the sick-bays can be respected, and the text of the Article makes it clear that it only refers to conflicts taking place on board the ships themselves.

ARTICLE 8 is new; the principle of paragraph 1 is taken from Article 7 of the Geneva Convention of 1906. Hospital ships and sick-

Abuse of hospital ships. bays lose their inviolability if they are employed for purposes of injuring the enemy (see also Article 4, paragraph 2 of the present Convention). A case of this kind occurred during the Russo-Japanese War. The Japanese seized, and secured the condemnation of, the Russian hospital ship *Orel* on 27 May, 1905, because she had been used a

---

[1] See views of Japanese physicians on lights of hospital ships cited by S. Takahashi, *op. cit.* pp. 379–381.

[2] See report of discussions at the Hague in *The Times*, 14 July, 1907.

[3] *Parl. Papers*, Misc. No. 4 (1908), p. 21; *La Deux. Confér.* T. I. p. 67.

short time previously for the accommodation of able-bodied prisoners taken from a captured merchantman, and had otherwise assisted in the hostile operations of the Russians[1].

The second paragraph of Article 8 is based on Article 8 of the Geneva Convention of 1906, but it was not thought necessary to reproduce its provisions in detail. The fact that the staff of the hospital ship or sick-bay are armed for maintaining order or defending sick or wounded, and the presence of wireless telegraphic apparatus on board are not sufficient reasons for withdrawing the protection accorded to such ships or sick-bays. The German draft proposed to allow hospital ships to carry light pieces of artillery as a protection against the dangers of navigation and particularly of piracy[2], but the Committee considered that there was no necessity for the arming of such ships, especially as merchant-ships which run no greater risks are unarmed. The paragraph regarding the presence of wireless telegraphic apparatus on board was inserted on the proposition of the Dutch delegate. The apparatus may often be of great value in enabling hospital ships to communicate either with ships of their own squadron or with land. Any abuse of it can easily be prevented by agents being placed on board, and, if necessary, the apparatus may be removed temporarily under the general powers of control conferred on belligerent commanders by Article 4.

ARTICLE 9 is new, though it retains the substance of Article 6 of the

Assistance rendered by merchant-ships on request.

Convention of 1899; it is based on Article 5 of the Geneva Convention of 1906. By paragraph 1 belligerents may appeal to the charitable zeal of neutral merchantmen to take on board and care for sick and wounded. The assistance thus rendered is purely voluntary, a belligerent cannot compel it. Paragraph 2 governs the situation of ships which have responded to this appeal, as well as those which have of their own accord taken on board shipwrecked, sick and wounded. Such ships are to enjoy "special protection and certain immunities." These expressions which are borrowed from Article 5 of the Geneva Convention of 1906 are vague but as the Report of M. Renault remarks: " it is scarcely possible to proceed otherwise: everything depends on circumstances. A warship may call upon a ship possibly from a distance, promising, for instance, not to search it. It is obvious that the advantages of the immunities are not so great in naval as in land warfare in which the inhabitants to whom such an appeal is made are exposed to a series of

---

[1] T. J. Lawrence, *International Problems, etc.* p. 115. For a full report of this case see S. Takahashi, *op. cit.* p. 620, where the name of the vessel is given as *Aryol*.

[2] *La Deux. Confér.* T. I. p. 74; T. III. p. 685.

rigorous measures on the part of the invader or occupant. It is before all else a question of good faith. A belligerent should keep the promise which he has made to obtain a service, and the neutral ought not by an appearance of zeal to be able to escape the risk to which his conduct may have rendered him liable. It is, however, certain, on the one hand, that the ships in question may not be captured for the transport of ship-wrecked, wounded or sick of a belligerent, and on the other hand, as is expressly stated by Article 6 of the Convention of 1899, they remain subject to capture for violations of neutrality which they may have committed (e.g. contraband of war, breach of blockade)[1]."

There is no immunity accorded to a merchantman belonging to one of the belligerents conveying sick and wounded[2].

Inviolability of hospital staff. ARTICLE 10 which deals with the inviolability of the hospital staff is a reproduction of Article 7 of the Convention of 1899 with a slight modification introduced from Article 13 of the Geneva Convention of 1906 as regards the payments to be made to members of the hospital staff temporarily detained by the enemy. "Only the official staff is concerned, that of a relief society having no claim to receive a salary" (Report of M. Renault).

Inviolability of sick and wounded. ARTICLE 11 reproduces Article 8 of the Convention of 1899 with the additional words intended to bring under the shelter of inviolability not only wounded and sick sailors and soldiers on board but also other persons officially attached to fleets or armies. Their addition is in harmony with Article 1 of the Geneva Convention of 1906.

Surrender to warship of sick and wounded. ARTICLE 12 is new, and settles a very important point which the Convention of 1899 had left unsolved. At the First Peace Conference, Captain Mahan, the United States naval delegate, endeavoured to obtain the insertion of Articles to meet the case of men who by any accident connected with a naval engagement were picked up by a neutral vessel. The commander and some of the crew of the Confederate cruiser *Alabama*, after her last fight with the *Kearsarge* off Cherbourg, were picked up by the British yacht *Deerhound*, the captain of which claimed for the rescued seamen the inviolability of the neutral flag, and their surrender was refused[3]. Captain Mahan's proposal was that in such cases the neutral vessel must surrender

---

[1] *Parl. Papers*, Misc. No. 4 (1908), p. 90 ; *La Deux. Confér.* T. I. p. 74 ; T. II. p. 309.

[2] *Parl. Papers*, Misc. No. 1 (1899), p. 73.

[3] See M. Bernard, *The Neutrality of Great Britain during the American Civil War*, p. 429 ; A. S. Hershey, *International Law and Diplomacy, etc.* p. 77 (note).

the rescued persons, if demand should be made by the other belligerent, or in case no demand was made, that they should not be allowed to serve again during the war. The attempt of the United States delegate was unsuccessful and the Convention of 1899 is silent on this point[1]. Under the new Article a belligerent cruiser meeting a hospital ship of any description or a merchant-ship, yacht or boat of any nationality may demand the surrender of the wounded, sick or shipwrecked men on board. M. Renault in the Report to the Committee states that "we do not think that the rule is new; if the formula is not found in the Convention of 1899, the sense of the latter is not doubtful." This view was combated by Sir Edward Fry who at the Third Plenary Meeting of the Conference stated that "the British Government cannot agree to the opinion expressed in the Report as to the right of a belligerent ship of war to require the surrender of wounded, sick and shipwrecked combatants on board a merchant-ship sailing under a neutral flag. In default of a special Convention, the British Government considers that the recognition of such a right cannot be based on the existing principles of international law[2]." M. Renault in reply stated that he considered that the conclusions of his Report were the expression of existing positive law. The Report contains the following comment on this Article: "A belligerent cruiser meets a military hospital ship, a hospital ship, or a merchant-ship; whatever be the nationality of these ships, it has, either by virtue of Article 4 of the Convention or by virtue of the common law of nations, the right to visit them. It exercises it and finds on board shipwrecked, wounded or sick; it has the right to have them delivered up to it, because they are its prisoners, as is stated in Article 9 of the Convention of 1899, reproduced in Article 14 of our draft. This is only an application of a general principle by virtue of which the combatants of one belligerent who fall into the power of the other are by that fact its prisoners. Obviously, it will not always be to the interest of the belligerent to make use of this right. It will often be to his advantage to leave the wounded and sick where they are and not to take charge of them. But, in such a case, it will be indispensable not to allow wounded or sick to go free who are still in a condition to render great services to their country: and this applies even more strongly in the case of shipwrecked men who are able-bodied. It has been said that it would be inhuman to force a neutral vessel to deliver up wounded which it had charitably picked up. To meet this objection, it is only necessary to reflect on what would be the position in the absence of a Convention. The positive law of nations would permit not only the seizure

---

[1] F. W. Holls, *The Peace Conference*, pp. 497–506; *Parl. Papers*, Misc. No. 1 (1899), p. 92.
[2] *Parl. Papers*, Misc. No. 4 (1908), p. 21; *La Deux. Confér.* T. I. p. 68.

of individuals who are enemy combatants, found on board a neutral vessel, but the seizure and confiscation of the vessel for having rendered an *un-neutral* service. We may add that if the shipwrecked men were, for example, permitted to escape captivity by the sole fact that they had been taken on board a neutral vessel, the belligerents would disregard the philanthropic action of the neutrals the moment such action might have the result of causing them an irreparable injury. Humanity would not be the gainer[1]."

A strict application of the principles of neutrality would imply, apart from a Convention, that belligerents taken on board neutral ships should not be allowed to take part again in hostilities during the course of the war: but the statement of M. Renault that the mere fact of picking up shipwrecked or wounded men would render a neutral merchant-ship liable to seizure for unneutral service appears incapable of being substantiated as a rule of international law[2]. The question was discussed by the United States and Great Britain in regard to the rescue (already referred to) by the *Deerhound* of the captain and members of the crew of the *Alabama* on the 19th June, 1864. The solution of the difficulty provided by this Article is, however, one which may be justified by practical considerations. Among those on board a hospital or merchant ship may be found the "brain" of one of the belligerent navies, and "military necessity" might be appealed to as a justification for his removal. A belligerent would take the risk of complications with the neutral Power. Moreover, the neutral captain might from unforeseen circumstances be unable to land the sick, wounded or shipwrecked at a neutral port where they would be interned[3].

Although a belligerent may under this Article remove wounded, sick or shipwrecked combatants, he cannot change the course of a neutral merchant-ship or impose any definite course on it; such orders can only be given to the commanders of hospital ships.

In signing this Convention on behalf of Great Britain Sir Edward Fry did not fully maintain the reservation made at the Plenary Meeting. The final reservation is as follows: "In affixing their signatures to this Convention, the British Plenipotentiaries declare that His Majesty's Government understands Article 12 to apply only to the case of combatants rescued during or after a naval engagement in which they have taken part[4]."

British reservation on Article 12.

---

[1] *Parl. Papers*, Misc. No. 4 (1908), p. 91; *La Deux. Confér.* T. I. p. 75; T. III. p. 310.
[2] See J. Westlake, *War*, p. 278; E. Lémonon, *La seconde Conférence*, p. 551.
[3] See T. J. Lawrence, *International Problems, etc.* p. 116.
[4] *Parl. Papers*, Misc. No. 5 (1908); No. 6 (1908), p. 148.

This Article therefore would not apply as regards rescues by British merchant-ships of belligerents at a distance from the scene of an engagement, as for instance of men rescued from a ship which had sunk in a storm or as the result of contact with an unanchored floating mine.

ARTICLE 13 fills a gap left in the Convention of 1899. At the outbreak of the Russo-Japanese War on the 8th February, 1904, the captains of the British, French and Italian cruisers at Chemulpo rescued the sailors of the Russian vessels *Korietz* and *Variag*, and refused to surrender them to the Japanese. Ultimately after negotiations, the rescued sailors in the possession of the British authorities were, with the consent of the Japanese Government, handed over to the Russians at a neutral port[1]. Article 13, which was proposed by the French delegate, now provides that the shipwrecked, sick or wounded picked up by a neutral ship of war are in the same position as that of combatants who take refuge in a neutral territory. They are not to be given up to the adversary, but they should be detained.

Rescue by neutral war-vessel.

ARTICLE 14 reproduces Article 9 of the Convention of 1899. It only deals with the treatment of persons, not of ships.

ARTICLE 15 reproduces Article 10 of the Convention of 1899 which was excluded from ratification. At the Conference of 1899 this Article was carried only by a bare majority, and in signing the treaty Great Britain, Germany, the United States and Italy reserved liberty of action in regard to it. In consequence of these reservations the Netherland Government suggested that with a view to uniformity—a uniformity which would be endangered by the reservations of these four Powers—the Article should be excluded from ratification by all Powers. This suggestion was acted upon[2].

At the Conference of 1907 the restoration of this Article was proposed by the French delegate and accepted. Under this Article where shipwrecked, wounded or sick are landed at a neutral port with the consent of the local authorities, they must, in default of arrangements to the contrary between the neutral and belligerent states, be guarded by the neutral state so as to prevent them from again taking part in the war. The expenses are to be borne by the state to which such persons belong. M. Renault states that if a neutral merchant vessel, having occasionally picked up wounded or sick, or even shipwrecked persons, arrives at a neutral port without having met a cruiser or without having entered into any agree-

---

[1] A. S. Hershey, *International Law and Diplomacy*, p. 76; T. J. Lawrence, *War and Neutrality*, etc. Chap. IV.

[2] F. W. Holls, *The Peace Conference at the Hague*, p. 128.

ment, the persons which it lands do not fall under the provisions of this Article: they are free.

ARTICLE 16 is new, and is based on Article 3 of the Geneva Convention of 1906. The provisions as to the burial or cremation of the dead on land will apply to cases where engagements have taken place near land.

Search for shipwrecked and wounded.

ARTICLE 17 is also new, and is reproduced from Article 4 of the Geneva Convention of 1906.

ARTICLE 18 corresponds to Article 11 of the Convention of 1899.

ARTICLE 19 is new, and corresponds to Article 25 of the Geneva Convention of 1906.

ARTICLE 20 is new, and corresponds to Article 26 of the Geneva Convention of 1906. It is obviously of great importance, and M. Renault emphasises this in his Report. "The best of rules become a dead letter if measures are not taken in advance for the instruction of those who will have to apply them. The staff of hospital ships or floating hospitals will often have to fulfil a very difficult mission. They must be convinced of the necessity of not taking advantage of the immunities accorded them to commit acts of belligerency: for, to do so would result in the ruin of the Convention and all the humanitarian work of the two Peace Conferences[1]."

Application of the Convention.

ARTICLE 21 is new and corresponds to Articles 27 and 28 of the Geneva Convention of 1906, and has not been accepted by Great Britain for the reasons given under Article 6.

ARTICLE 22 is new. In case 'of combined military and naval operations, the present Convention applies to forces afloat and the Geneva Convention of 1906 to the land forces.

ARTICLE 23 corresponds to Article 12 of the Convention of 1899 with the additional formulae adopted in the diplomatic clauses of the Conventions of the Conference of 1907.

The remaining Articles call for no observations.

This Convention has been signed by all the Powers represented at the Conference except Nicaragua. China makes a reservation of Article 21, and Great Britain of Articles 6 and 21 and also the declaration quoted above on Article 12. Persia reserved the right recognised by the Conference to use the Lion and the Red Sun instead of the Red Cross, and Turkey made a similar reservation for the Red Crescent[2].

Signatory Powers.

---

[1] *Parl. Papers*, Misc. No. 4 (1908), p. 92; *La Deux. Confér.* T. I. p. 77.
[2] *Parl. Papers*, Misc. No. 6 (1908), p. 148.

A Conference of maritime Powers was held at the Hague in December, 1904, to discuss the status of hospital ships in time of war in regard to their freedom from port dues, etc.

Exemption of hospital ships from port dues.

Great Britain did not take part in the Conference, owing to the fact that dues are levied by different authorities in the United Kingdom and legislation would be necessary to give effect to any Convention entered into. The British Minister at the Hague, Sir Henry Howard, in his reply to the invitation of the Netherland Government, stated that his Government was disposed to consider the proposal favourably[1].

The following is a translation of

A CONVENTION RELATING TO HOSPITAL SHIPS, SIGNED AT THE HAGUE, THE 21ST DECEMBER, 1904[2].

His Majesty the German Emperor, etc.[3]

Considering that the Convention concluded at the Hague on the 29th July, 1899, for the adaptation to maritime warfare of the principles of the Geneva Convention of the 22nd August, 1864, has sanctioned the principle of the intervention of the Red Cross in naval wars by the provisions for the benefit of hospital ships;

Desiring to conclude a Convention in order to facilitate by additional provisions the mission of such ships;

Have named as their Plenipotentiaries the following: [*Names of Plenipotentiaries.*]

Who, after communication of their full powers, found to be in good and due form, have agreed to the following provisions:

Article 1.

Hospital ships fulfilling the conditions of Articles 1, 2 and 3 of the Convention concluded at the Hague on the 29th July, 1899, for the adaptation to maritime warfare of the principles of the Geneva Convention of the 22nd August, 1864, shall be exempted, in time of war, in the ports of the contracting Parties, from all dues and taxes levied on ships for the benefit of the state.

Article 2.

The provision of the preceding Article does not prevent the application,

---

[1] Sir T. Barclay, *Problems, etc.* pp. 198, 257.

[2] Sir T. Barclay, *op. cit.* pp. 257-9; L. Oppenheim, *International Law*, Vol. II. p. 213; J. B. Scott, *Texts of the Peace Conferences*, pp. 400-2.

[3] For list of signatory Powers see *post*, p. 394.

by means of visitation and other formalities, of the fiscal or other laws in force in such ports.

Article 3.

The rule laid down in the first Article is only binding on the contracting Powers in case of war between two or more of them.

The said rule shall cease to be binding from the time when, in a war between the contracting Powers, a non-contracting Power shall join one of the belligerents.

Article 4.

The present Convention, which, bearing date this day, may be signed until the 1st October, 1905, by the Powers which shall have expressed a wish to do so, shall be ratified within the shortest possible time.

The ratifications shall be deposited at the Hague. A *procès-verbal* of the deposit of the ratifications shall be drawn up and a copy thereof, duly certified, shall be delivered through the diplomatic channel to all the contracting Powers.

Article 5.

Non-signatory Powers are permitted to accede to the present Convention after the 1st October, 1905.

They must, for this purpose, make known their accession to the contracting Powers by means of a written notification addressed to the Netherland Government and communicated by the latter to the other contracting Powers.

Article 6.

In the event of one of the high contracting Powers denouncing the present Convention, this denunciation shall not take effect until one year after the notification has been made in writing to the Netherland Government and communicated at once by the latter to all the other contracting Powers. Such denunciation shall only take effect in regard to the notifying Power.

In faith whereof, the Plenipotentiaries have signed the present Convention and affixed their seals thereto.

Done at the Hague the 21st December, 1904, in a single original which shall remain deposited in the archives of the Netherland Government, and of which duly certified copies shall be sent through the diplomatic channel to the contracting Powers.

Final Act.

At the moment of proceeding to sign the Convention whose object is the exemption of hospital ships in time of war in the ports of the contracting Parties from all dues and taxes imposed on ships for the benefit of the state, the Plenipotentiaries signing the present Act express the wish that, in view of the highly humanitarian mission of such ships, the contracting Governments may take the necessary measures for the exemption, within a short time, of such ships also from the payment of dues and taxes collected in their ports for the benefit of others than the state, especially those collected for the benefit of municipalities, private companies or persons.

In faith whereof the Plenipotentiaries have signed the present *procès-verbal* which, bearing date this day, may be signed up to the 1st October, 1905.

Done at the Hague, the 21st December, 1904, in a single original which shall remain deposited in the archives of the Netherland Government, and of which duly certified copies shall be sent through the diplomatic channel to the Powers signing the foregoing Convention.

Ratifications have been deposited at the Hague by the following Powers: Germany, Austria-Hungary, Belgium, China, Denmark, the United States of America, Mexico, Greece, Japan and Corea, Luxemburg, Montenegro, the Netherlands, Peru, Portugal, Roumania, Russia, Siam, Switzerland, France, Spain, Italy and Persia.

The following Powers have also acceded: Guatemala, Norway and Sweden. Servia is the only Power represented at the Conference which has not ratified the Convention.

XI. Convention relative à certaines Restrictions à l'Exercice du Droit de Capture dans la Guerre Maritime.

Sa Majesté l'Empereur d'Allemagne, Roi de Prusse, &c.

Reconnaissant la nécessité de mieux assurer que par le passé l'application équitable du droit aux relations maritimes internationales en temps de guerre ;

Estimant que, pour y parvenir, il convient, en abandonnant ou en conciliant, le cas échéant, dans un intérêt commun certaines pratiques divergentes anciennes, d'entreprendre de codifier dans des règles communes les garanties dues au commerce pacifique et au travail inoffensif, ainsi que la conduite des hostilités sur mer ; qu'il importe de fixer dans des engagements mutuels écrits les principes demeurés jusqu'ici dans le domaine incertain de la controverse ou laissés à l'arbitraire des Gouvernements ;

Que, dès à présent, un certain nombre de règles peuvent être posées, sans qu'il soit porté atteinte au droit actuellement en vigueur concernant les matières qui n'y sont pas prévues ;

Ont nommé pour Leurs plénipotentiaires, savoir :

[*Dénomination des Plénipotentiaires.*]

Lesquels, après avoir déposé leurs pleins pouvoirs, trouvés en bonne et due forme, sont convenus des dispositions suivantes :—

XI. Convention relative to certain Restrictions on the Exercise of the Right of Capture in Maritime War.

His Majesty the German Emperor, King of Prussia, &c.

Recognizing the necessity of ensuring more effectively than hitherto the equitable application of law to maritime international relations in time of war ;

Considering that, for this purpose, it is expedient, in giving up or, if necessary, in harmonizing for the common interest certain conflicting practices of long standing, to undertake to codify in regulations of general application the guarantees due to peaceful intercourse and legitimate business, as well as the conduct of hostilities by sea ; that it is expedient to lay down in written mutual engagements the principles which have hitherto remained in the uncertain domain of controversy or have been left to the discretion of Governments ;

That from henceforth a certain number of rules may be made, without thereby affecting the law now in force with regard to the matters which these rules do not touch ;

Have appointed as their Plenipotentiaries, that is to say :

[*Names of Plenipotentiaries.*]

Who, after having deposited their full powers, found to be in good and due form, have agreed upon the following provisions :—

<table>
<tr><td>

Chapitre I.

De la Correspondance Postale.

ART. 1.

La correspondance postale des neutres ou des belligérants, quel que soit son caractère officiel ou privé, trouvée en mer sur un navire neutre ou ennemi, est inviolable. S'il y a saisie du navire, elle est expédiée avec le moins de retard possible par le capteur.

Les dispositions de l'alinéa précédent ne s'appliquent pas, en cas de violation de blocus, à la correspondance qui est à destination ou en provenance du port bloqué.

ART. 2.

L'inviolabilité de la correspondance postale ne soustrait pas les paquebots-poste neutres aux lois et coutumes de la guerre sur mer concernant les navires de commerce neutres en général. Toutefois, la visite n'en doit être effectuée qu'en cas de nécessité, avec tous les ménagements et toute la célérité possibles.

</td><td>

Chapter I.

Postal Correspondence.

ART. 1.

The postal correspondence of neutrals or belligerents, whether official or private in character, which may be found on board a neutral or enemy ship at sea, is inviolable. If the ship is detained, the correspondence is forwarded by the captor with the least possible delay.

The provisions of the preceding paragraph do not apply, in case of violation of blockade, to correspondence destined for or proceeding from the blockaded port.

ART. 2.

The inviolability of postal correspondence does not exempt a neutral mail-ship from the laws and customs of naval war respecting neutral merchant-ships in general. The ship, however, may not be searched except when absolutely necessary, and then only with as much consideration and expedition as possible.

</td></tr>
<tr><td>

Chapitre II.

De l'Exemption de Capture pour certains Bateaux.

ART. 3.

Les bateaux exclusivement affectés à la pêche côtière ou à des services de petite navigation locale sont exempts de capture, ainsi que leurs engins, agrès, apparaux et chargement.

Cette exemption cesse de leur être applicable dès qu'ils participent d'une façon quelconque aux hostilités.

</td><td>

Chapter II.

Exemption from Capture of certain Vessels.

ART. 3.

Vessels employed exclusively in coast fisheries, or small boats employed in local trade, are exempt from capture together with their appliances, rigging, tackle, and cargo.

This exemption ceases as soon as they take any part whatever in hostilities.

</td></tr>
</table>

Les Puissances contractantés s'interdisent de profiter du caractère inoffensif
desdits bateaux pour les employer
dans un but militaire en leur con-
servant leur apparence pacifique.

The Contracting Powers bind themselves not to take advantage of the
harmless character of the said vessels
in order to use them for military purposes while preserving their peaceful
appearance.

Art. 4.

Sont également exempts de capture
les navires chargés de missions religieuses, scientifiques, ou philanthro-
piques.

Art. 4.

Vessels charged with religious,
scientific, or philanthropic missions
are likewise exempt from capture.

Chapitre III.

Du Régime des Équipages des Navires de Commerce Enne-mis capturés par un Belligé-rant.

Chapter III.

Regulations regarding the Crews of Enemy Merchant-ships captured by a Belligerent.

Art. 5.

Lorsqu'un navire de commerce
ennemi est capturé par un belligérant,
les hommes de son équipage, nationaux
d'un État neutre, ne sont pas faits
prisonniers de guerre.

Il en est de même du capitaine et
des officiers, également nationaux d'un
État neutre, s'ils promettent formellement par écrit de ne pas servir sur un
navire ennemi pendant la durée de la
guerre.

Art. 5.

When an enemy merchant-ship is
captured by a belligerent, such of its
crew as are nationals of a neutral
State are not made prisoners of war.

The same rule applies in the case
of the captain and officers, likewise
nationals of a neutral State, if they
give a formal promise in writing not
to serve on an enemy ship while the
war lasts.

Art. 6.

Le capitaine, les officiers, et les
membres de l'équipage, nationaux de
l'État ennemi, ne sont pas faits prisonniers de guerre, à condition qu'ils
s'engagent, sous la foi d'une promesse
formelle écrite, à ne prendre, pendant
la durée des hostilités, aucun service
ayant rapport avec les opérations de la
guerre.

Art. 6.

The captain, officers, and members
of the crew, when nationals of the
enemy State, are not made prisoners of
war, provided that they undertake, on
the faith of a formal written promise,
not to engage, while hostilities last, in
any service connected with the operations of the war.

ART. 7.

Les noms des individus laissés libres dans les conditions visées à l'article 5, alinéa 2, et à l'article 6, sont notifiés par le belligérant capteur à l'autre belligérant. Il est interdit à ce dernier d'employer sciemment lesdits individus.

ART. 8.

Les dispositions des trois articles précédents ne s'appliquent pas aux navires qui prennent part aux hostilités.

Chapitre IV.

Dispositions Finales.

ART. 9.

Les dispositions de la présente Convention ne sont applicables qu'entre les Puissances contractantes et seulement si les belligérants sont tous parties à la Convention.

ART. 10.

La présente Convention sera ratifiée aussitôt que possible.

Les ratifications seront déposées à La Haye.

Le premier dépôt de ratifications sera constaté par un procès-verbal signé par les représentants des Puissances qui y prennent part et par le Ministre des Affaires Étrangères des Pays-Bas.

Les dépôts ultérieurs de ratifications se feront au moyen d'une notification écrite, adressée au Gouvernement des Pays-Bas et accompagnée de l'instrument de ratification.

Copie certifiée conforme du procès-verbal relatif au premier dépôt de

ART. 7.

The names of the persons retaining their liberty under the conditions laid down in Article 5, paragraph 2, and in Article 6, are notified by the belligerent captor to the other belligerent. The latter is forbidden knowingly to employ the said persons.

ART. 8.

The provisions of the three preceding Articles do not apply to ships taking part in hostilities.

Chapter IV.

Final Provisions.

ART. 9.

The provisions of the present Convention are only applicable between Contracting Powers, and only if all the belligerents are parties to the Convention.

ART. 10.

The present Convention shall be ratified as soon as possible.

The ratifications shall be deposited at The Hague.

The first deposit of ratifications shall be recorded in a *procès-verbal* signed by the Representatives of the Powers which take part therein and by the Netherland Minister for Foreign Affairs.

The subsequent deposits of ratifications shall be made by means of a written notification, addressed to the Netherland Government and accompanied by the instrument of ratification.

A duly certified copy of the *procès-verbal* relating to the first deposit of

ratifications, des notifications mentionnées à l'alinéa précédent ainsi que des
instruments de ratification, sera immédiatement remise par les soins du
Gouvernement des Pays-Bas et par la
voie diplomatique aux Puissances conviées à la Deuxième Conférence de la
Paix, ainsi qu'aux autres Puissances
qui auront adhéré à la Convention.
Dans les cas visés par l'alinéa précédent,
le dit Gouvernement leur fera connaître
en même temps la date à laquelle il a
reçu la notification.

ratifications, of the notifications mentioned in the preceding paragraph, and
of the instruments of ratification, shall
be immediately sent by the Netherland
Government, through the diplomatic
channel, to the Powers invited to the
Second Peace Conference, as well as to
the other Powers which have acceded
to the Convention. In the cases contemplated in the preceding paragraph,
the said Government shall inform them
at the same time of the date on which
it received the notification.

Art. 11.

Les Puissances non-signataires sont
admises à adhérer à la présente Convention.

La Puissance qui désire adhérer
notifie par écrit son intention au
Gouvernement des Pays-Bas en lui
transmettant l'acte d'adhésion, qui
sera déposé dans les archives du dit
Gouvernement.

Ce Gouvernement transmettra immédiatement à toutes les autres Puissances copie certifiée conforme de la notification ainsi que de l'acte d'adhésion,
en indiquant la date à laquelle il a
reçu la notification.

Art. 11.

Non-Signatory Powers may accede
to the present Convention.

A Power which desires to accede
notifies its intention in writing to the
Netherland Government, forwarding to
it the act of accession, which shall be
deposited in the archives of the said
Government.

The said Government shall immediately forward to all the other Powers
a duly certified copy of the notification,
as well as of the act of accession,
mentioning the date on which it
received the notification.

Art. 12.

La présente Convention produira
effet pour les Puissances qui auront
participé au premier dépôt de ratifications, soixante jours après la date du
procès-verbal de ce dépôt et, pour les
Puissances qui ratifieront ultérieurement ou qui adhéreront, soixante jours
après que la notification de leur ratification ou de leur adhésion aura été
reçue par le Gouvernement des Pays-
Bas.

Art. 12.

The present Convention shall take
effect, in the case of the Powers which
were parties to the first deposit of
ratifications, sixty days after the date
of the Protocol recording such deposit,
and, in the case of the Powers which
shall ratify subsequently or which
shall accede, sixty days after the
notification of their ratification or of
their accession, has been received by
the Netherland Government.

ART. 13.

S'il arrivait qu'une des Puissances contractantes voulût dénoncer la présente Convention, la dénonciation sera notifiée par écrit au Gouvernement des Pays-Bas, qui communiquera immédiatement copie certifiée conforme de la notification à toutes les autres Puissances en leur faisant savoir la date à laquelle il l'a reçue.

La dénonciation ne produira ses effets qu'à l'égard de la Puissance qui l'aura notifiée et un an après que la notification en sera parvenue au Gouvernement des Pays-Bas.

ART. 14.

Un registre tenu par le Ministère des Affaires Étrangères des Pays-Bas indiquera la date du dépôt des ratifications effectué en vertu de l'article 10, alinéas 3 et 4, ainsi que la date à laquelle auront été reçues les notifications d'adhésion (article 11, alinéa 2) ou de dénonciation (article 13, alinéa 1).

Chaque Puissance contractante est admise à prendre connaissance de ce registre et à en demander des extraits certifiés conformes.

En foi de quoi, les Plénipotentiaires ont revêtu la présente Convention de leurs signatures.

Fait à La Haye, le 18 Octobre, 1907, en un seul exemplaire, qui restera déposé dans les archives du Gouvernement des Pays-Bas, et dont des copies, certifiées conformes, seront remises par la voie diplomatique aux Puissances qui ont été conviées à la Deuxième Conférence de la Paix.

ART. 13.

In the event of one of the Contracting Powers wishing to denounce the present Convention, the denunciation shall be notified in writing to the Netherland Government, which shall immediately communicate a duly certified copy of the notification to all the other Powers informing them of the date on which it was received.

The denunciation shall only operate in respect of the denouncing Power, and only on the expiry of one year after the notification has reached the Netherland Government.

ART. 14.

A register kept by the Netherland Ministry for Foreign Affairs shall record the date of the deposit of ratifications effected in virtue of Article 10, paragraphs 3 and 4, as well as the date on which the notifications of accession (Article 11, paragraph 2) or of denunciation (Article 13, paragraph 1) have been received.

Each Contracting Power is entitled to have access to this register and to be supplied with duly certified extracts from it.

In faith whereof the Plenipotentiaries have appended their signatures to the present Convention.

Done at The Hague, the 18th October, 1907, in a single original, which shall remain deposited in the archives of the Netherland Government, and of which duly certified copies shall be sent, through the diplomatic channel, to the Powers invited to the Second Peace Conference.

CONVENTION NO. 11. RELATIVE TO CERTAIN RESTRICTIONS ON THE EXERCISE OF THE RIGHT OF CAPTURE IN MARITIME WAR.

Postal correspondence[1].

The subject of the protection of postal correspondence did not appear in the Programme of the Conference or of the Questionnaire of the Fourth Committee. It was introduced by the German delegate (Herr Kriege) by way of a supplement to his draft proposition on contraband[2].

In the existing state of international law, apart from this Convention, the carriage of mails is not protected by any definite guarantees. Neutral mail packets are subject to visit and search, a right which was exercised during the Russo-Japanese war. During the Spanish-American war President McKinley stated in his proclamation of the 26th April, 1898, that "the voyages of mail steamers were not to be interfered with, except on the clearest grounds of suspicion of a violation of law in respect of contraband or blockade[3]." Great Britain observed a similar practice in regard to German mail boats during the Boer war. Besides the practice of granting immunities by some Powers to mail boats during war, Great Britain and the United States in 1848, and Great Britain and France in 1856 entered into treaties granting immunities to the mail steamers of the contracting Powers in case of war between them. Notwithstanding the growing practice there is no rule of international law granting immunity to enemy mail boats from attack and seizure, or excluding neutral mail boats from visit and search. The increase of postal communication, and the fact that so many interests, commercial and other, are based on the regular service of the mails, render it highly desirable to shelter it from the disturbance which might be caused by a maritime war. "It is hardly possible," said Herr Kriege in support of his proposals, "that the belligerents who control the means of telegraphic and radio-telegraphic

[1] *Parl. Papers*, Misc. No. 4 (1908), p. 217; *La Deux. Confér.* T. I. p. 266; T. III. pp. 921, 1121, 1127, 1173; *Livre Jaune*, p. 98; *Weissbuch*, p. 12; L. A. Atherley-Jones, *Commerce in War*, p. 801; Simeon E. Baldwin, *Eleventh Convention of the Hague Conference*, 1907, *Am. Journ. of Int. Law*, Vol. II. p. 307; Bonfils-Fauchille, *Droit int. public* (5th ed.), § 1854; C. Dupuis, *Le Droit de la guerre maritime*, p. 177; W. E. Hall, *Int. Law*, p. 675; A. S. Hershey, *International Law*, etc. p. 153; H. Taylor, *Public International Law*, § 668; T. J. Lawrence, *International Problems*, p. 118; Idem, *International Law*, p. 627; Idem, *War and Neutrality*, etc. Chap. IX.; E. Lémonon, *La seconde Conférence de la Paix*, p. 698; L. Oppenheim, *Int. Law*, Vol. II. § 191; J. Westlake, *War*, pp. 265, 308; The *Panama* (176 *U.S. Rep.* 535), J. B. Scott, *Leading Cases*, p. 788.

[2] *La Deux. Confér.* T. III. pp. 860, 1178.

[3] E. J. Benton, *International Law and Diplomacy of the Spanish American War*, p. 131.

communication will have recourse to the use of the ordinary mail for official communications as to military operations. The advantage to be drawn by belligerents from the control of the postal service is not in proportion to the prejudicial effect which that control entails on legitimate-commerce[1]." The principles of the German proposal to grant immunity to postal correspondence of neutrals or belligerents, whether of an official or private character and whether on board neutral or enemy ships, met with almost unanimous acceptance in the Committee, and the dissent of the Russian delegate was not renewed when the draft Convention came before the Conference. Russia, however, has not signed the Convention.

It will be noticed that the inviolability is granted to the *correspondence* and not to the vessel itself. It would have been the best guarantee for the uninterrupted service of the mails to have exempted all duly certified mail boats from visit and search, but the Conference was not prepared to go to that length; many of the largest mail boats are built for the special purpose of being converted into ships of war, and if not built for that purpose are capable of being used for many others of considerable value to belligerents. A vessel carrying mails still remains subject to all the laws and customs of maritime war. The only postal correspondence not covered by the immunity is that destined for or proceeding from a blockaded port. " Postal correspondence " is not intended, according to Herr Kriege, to include parcels sent by post (*les colis postaux*)[2].

The second Article provides that a mail ship is not to be searched except when absolutely necessary and then with all the consideration and speed possible, and by the first Article it is laid down that if the ship is seized the correspondence is to be forwarded with the least possible delay. The action of the Commander of the *Smolensk* on the 15th July, 1904, in taking from the German mail boat *Prinz Heinrich* a number of mail bags for examination, and then stopping the P. and O. steamer *Persia* and putting them on board for transmission to their destination, is strongly to be reprobated. The belligerent must make his own arrangements for transmission of mails when the mail boat is seized[3].

The second chapter of this Convention deals with the exemption from capture of boats employed in coast fisheries or in petty local coasting trade (Art. 3), and vessels charged with religious, scientific or philanthropic missions (Art. 4).

Chapter ii.
Fishing
boats[4], etc.

[1] *La Deux. Confér.* T. iii. p. 861.   [2] *Ibid.* p. 1122.

[3] T. J. Lawrence, *War and Neutrality*, pp. 195-7.

[4] *Parl. Papers*, Misc. No. 4 (1908), p. 220; *La Deux. Confér.* T. i. p. 269; T. iii. pp. 896, 909, 916, 967, 980, 987, 1000, 1131, 1148, 1177, 1179; Simeon E. Baldwin, *op. cit.* p. 309; Bonfils-Fauchille, *Droit international*, § 1350; C. Dupuis, *Le droit de la guerre maritime*,

In most states the exemption from capture of fishing boats engaged in coast fisheries has been recognised as a rule of law, but in Great Britain the exemption has never been considered as a right but as "a rule of courtesy only, and not of legal decision[1]." The United States in this matter followed the rule generally adopted in continental countries[2]. Although, Great Britain does not recognise the immunity as one of law, there has not in recent years been any real difference in the practice of maritime countries. All are willing to spare fishing vessels so long as they are harmless. The reasons for the exemption given by Mr Hall, and repeated in similar words by M. Fromageot in his Report to the Conference on the 27th September, 1907, are that "it is indisputable that coasting fishery is the sole means of livelihood of a very large number of families as inoffensive as cultivators of the soil or mechanics, and that the seizure of boats, while inflicting extreme hardship on their owners, is as a measure of general application wholly ineffective against the hostile state[3]." The Committee, however, felt that the favour accorded must not become an obstacle to naval operations, and that it ceases to be justified whenever the fishermen take any part in hostilities.

Articles 3 and 4 of this Convention owe their origin to different sources. The Belgian delegate introduced a proposal for the immunity of fishing boats which was further elaborated by the Portuguese delegate; the Austro-Hungarian delegate proposed the inclusion of boats engaged in the local coasting trade, and the Italian delegate the inclusion of ships charged with religious, scientific or philanthropic missions (Art. 4)[4]. As regards fishing boats the immunity only applies to those engaged in coast fisheries, a limitation which has generally been recognised in the past. It does not apply to

§ 153; W. E. Hall, *Int. Law*, p. 449; T. E. Holland, *Naval Prize Law*, § 36; T. J. Lawrence, *Int. Law*, § 105; E. Lémonon, *La seconde Conférence*, p. 702; L. Oppenheim, *Int. Law*, Vol. II. §§ 186, 187; J. Westlake, *War*, pp. 133, 138, 310; The *Paquette Habana*, The *Lola* (J. B. Scott's *Leading Cases*, p. 19).

[1] See Lord Stowell's judgment in The *Young Jacob and Joanna* (1 Rob. *Rep.* 20).

[2] The most recent United States decision is The *Paquette Habana* (175 *U. S. Reports*, p. 677, and 189 *U. S. Reports*, p. 453, J. B. Scott's *Leading Cases*, p. 19, when the majority of the Court held that "At the present day, by the general consent of the civilised nations of the world, and independently of any express treaty or public act, it is an established rule of international law that coast fishing vessels, with their implements and supplies, cargoes and crews, unarmed and honestly pursuing their peaceful calling of catching and bringing in fresh fish, are exempt from capture as prize of war." A minority of the Court dissented on the ground that a rule of maritime law to which Great Britain did not assent could not be regarded as universal trading. Mr Choate in his speech at the Meeting of the Fourth Committee on 7th August, 1907, drew the attention of the Committee to Mr Justice Gray's judgment from which he read extracts (*La Deux. Confér.* T. III. p. 913).

[3] *Int. Law*, p. 451. [4] *La Deux. Confér.* T. III. p. 1177.

deep sea fishing. "Nor has the exemption been extended to ships or vessels employed on the high seas in taking whales or seals, or cod or other fish which are not brought fresh to market, but are salted or otherwise cured and made a regular article of commerce[1]." The Committee found it impossible to lay down any rules as regards the size of fishing boats, or to fix any limits as to tonnage, number of the crew or the class of boats used; these vary in different places, but are all considerations of importance in deciding whether a given vessel is one to which exemption is to be accorded. It was also found impossible to lay down any rules as to the mode of propulsion of such boats, as these also differ in different countries, some using sails, others oars, others steam or petrol motors and some sails and mechanical means of propulsion.

The term "coast fishery" is also left undefined. The British delegate (Sir Ernest Satow) pointed out that British fishermen have to go far beyond the limits of territorial waters and are often found in the Straits of Dover more than ten miles from land. The "coast" need not be that of the fishermen's own country, it may be that of a third state in which there is a right or a custom of fishing,—the Portuguese delegate instanced the case of the fisheries off the coast of Morocco.

There is a similar indefiniteness in the term "petty local navigation" (*petite navigation locale*) to which the foregoing observations as to size and mode of propulsion of the boats apply. The term originally suggested by Admiral Haus (Austro-Hungary) was *bateaux et barques affectés dans les eaux territoriales de quelques pays au service de l'économie rurale ou à celui du petit trafic local*, which he stated was meant to include ships and boats of small dimension, used in the transport of agricultural produce or of persons along the coasts, or between the coast and adjacent islands or in archipelagoes[2]. This Article does not appear to confer immunity from capture on coasting steamers such as those plying on the west coast of Scotland or the Norwegian fjords, nor the cross-channel boats between Great Britain and Ireland. The Portuguese naval delegate expressly stated that *la petite navigation locale ne comprend pas le cabotage mais les bateaux qui transportent les produits de la pêche et ceux qui vise la proposition du Contre-Amiral Haus*[3].

All the boats mentioned in the first paragraph of Article 3, together with the appliances, rigging, tackle and cargoes, are exempt from capture, but the exemption ceases as soon as they take any part directly or indirectly in hostilities.

---

[1] See judgment of Mr Justice Gray in The *Paquette Habana* and The *Lola* (Scott's *Leading Cases*, p. 20).

[2] *La Deux. Confér.* T. III. p. 1178.   [3] *Ibid.* p. 970.

Mindful of the Dogger Bank incident the Japanese delegate obtained the insertion of the third paragraph of Article 3 whereby the contracting Powers agree not to take advantage of the innocent character of the vessels in question to execute any ruses of war.

Article 4, exempting from capture vessels charged with religious,

Vessels on scientific missions[1], etc. scientific or philanthropic missions, was introduced by the Italian delegate[2]. Numerous instances of the exemption from capture of such vessels during the past 150 years may be cited: the French explorers Bougainville in 1766, and La Pérouse in 1785, Captain Cook in 1776, the Austrian cruiser *Novara* in 1859 were all exempt from seizure. The custom of granting immunities has now been converted into a definite rule of international law, but the conditions, although not mentioned in the Article, must be understood to be the same as those on which the immunities to fishing boats, etc. are granted, namely, abstention from all interference in hostilities.

Chapter iii. marks an important alteration in the law of maritime

Chapter iii. Immunity of crews of captured enemy merchantmen[3]. warfare. It is, apart from this Convention, a well-recognised rule of international law that the officers and crews of captured enemy merchantmen are prisoners of war[4]. The practice was justified on the ground that it deprived the enemy of men who might render service on board ships which might be used as transports or for purposes of supply, or in the fighting navy. The rule was generally applied without regard to the nationality of the persons captured.

The subject was not mentioned in the Programme of Count Benckendorff, but was introduced in the Fourth Committee by the British delegate, who proposed to exempt from capture sailors who are nationals of neutral countries serving on board captured enemy merchantmen[5]. The Belgian delegate proposed to extend this immunity to nationals of the enemy, and this extension was accepted by Sir Ernest Satow on behalf of Great Britain. The combined proposal was then sent to the Drafting Committee,

---

[1] C. Dupuis, *Le droit de la guerre maritime*, § 152; T. J. Lawrence, *Int. Law*, § 205; L. Oppenheim, *Int. Law*, Vol. ɪɪ. § 186; J. Westlake, *War*, p. 138. For a case which occurred during the Russo-Japanese war see S. Takahashi, *International Law applied to the Russo-Japanese War*, p. 353.

[2] *La Deux. Confér.* T. ɪɪɪ. p. 1180.

[3] *Parl. Papers*, Misc. No. 4 (1908), p. 218; *La Deux. Confér.* T. ɪ. p. 267; T. ɪɪɪ. pp. 916, 958, 975, 986, 1174–5; E. Lémonon, *op. cit.* p. 710; J. Westlake, *War*, p. 309.

[4] W. E. Hall, *Int. Law*, p. 407; T. J. Lawrence, *Int. Law*, § 171; J. Westlake, *War*, p. 180.

[5] *La Deux. Confér.* T. ɪɪɪ. p. 1174.

when a proposal to make the distinction which appears in Article 5 between the officers and crew who are nationals of a *neutral* state was accepted by the British delegate.   It had at first been proposed to require from all an undertaking in writing not to serve on an enemy ship during the continuance of the war; the Convention only requires this in the case of officers who are nationals of a neutral state.   The crew are to be liberated without giving any such undertaking.   But in the case of the captain, officers and members of the crew, being nationals of the *enemy* state, they are not to be made prisoners of war if they promise *in writing* not to engage, during the hostilities, in any service having relation to the operations of war (Article 6).   This was stated by the Reporter (M. Fromageot) to include both service on board a ship of war as well as in the arsenals or land army or any other military or naval service.

The names of all persons who retain their liberty under Articles 5 and 6 are to be notified by the captor to the other belligerent who is forbidden knowingly to employ such persons (Article 7).

The provisions of the foregoing Articles only apply to the crews of ships who have not either directly or indirectly taken part in hostilities (Article 8).   The question whether a ship is engaged in a purely commercial undertaking or participating in hostilities is a question of fact on which the Convention makes no attempt to lay down any definite rule.

Signatory Powers.   All the Powers represented at the Conference have signed this Convention except China, Montenegro, Nicaragua and Russia.

The Convention makes a definite and important change in a long established rule of international law, and confirms other usages which had been almost universally observed in regard to a class of persons who take no part in hostilities, who are for the most part poor men, and whose imprisonment while inflicting extreme hardship on their families did not afford a corresponding gain to their captors.   The distinction between combatants and non-combatants which has for many years been recognised in the case of land warfare has now become recognised also in naval warfare. This Convention, which curiously enough deals with matters none of which were mentioned in the Russian Programme, is the most important result of the labours of the Fourth Committee.

**XII. Convention relative à l'Éta-
blissement d'une Cour Internationale des Prises.**

Sa Majesté l'Empereur d'Allemagne,
Roi de Prusse, &c.[1]

Animés du désir de régler d'une
manière équitable les différends qui
s'élèvent, parfois, en cas de guerre
maritime, à propos des décisions des
tribunaux de prises nationaux ;

Estimant que, si ces Tribunaux
doivent continuer à statuer suivant les
formes prescrites par leur législation,
il importe que, dans des cas déterminés,
un recours puisse être formé sous des
conditions qui concilient, dans la
mesure du possible, les intérêts publics
et les intérêts privés engagés dans
toute affaire de prises ;

Considérant, d'autre part, que l'institution d'une cour internationale,
dont la compétence et la procédure
seraient soigneusement réglées, a paru
le meilleur moyen d'atteindre ce but ;

Persuadés, enfin, que de cette façon
les conséquences rigoureuses d'une
guerre maritime pourront être atté-
nuées ; que notamment les bons
rapports entre les belligérants et les
neutres auront plus de chance d'être
maintenus et qu'ainsi la conservation
de la paix sera mieux assurée ;

**XII. Convention relative to the
Establishment of an International Prize Court.**

His Majesty the German Emperor,
King of Prussia, &c.[1]

Animated by the desire to settle in
an equitable manner the differences
which sometimes arise in the course
of a naval war in connection with the
decisions of national Prize Courts ;

Considering that, if these Courts
are to continue to exercise their
functions in the manner determined
by national legislation, it is expedient
that in certain cases an appeal should
be provided under conditions conciliating, as far as possible, the public and
private interests involved in matters
of prize ;

Being of opinion, moreover, that the
institution of an International Court,
whose jurisdiction and procedure would
be carefully defined, would be the best
method of attaining this object ;

Convinced, finally, that in this
manner, the hardships consequent on
naval war might be mitigated ; that, in
particular, good relations will be more
easily maintained between belligerents
and neutrals and peace better assured
in consequence ;

---

[1] List of States as in Final Act, 1907.

Désirant conclure une Convention à cet effet, ont nommé pour Leurs Plénipotentiaires, savoir :

[*Dénomination des Plénipotentiaires.*]

Lesquels, après avoir déposé leurs pleins pouvoirs, trouvés en bonne et due forme, sont convenus des dispositions suivantes :—

Desirous of concluding a Convention to this effect, have appointed as their Plenipotentiaries, that is to say :

[Names of Plenipotentiaries.]

Who, after having deposited their full powers, found to be in good and due form, have agreed upon the following provisions :—

Titre I.
Dispositions Générales.

ART. 1.

La validité de la capture d'un navire de commerce ou de sa cargaison est, s'il s'agit de propriétés neutres ou ennemies, établie devant une juridiction des prises conformément à la présente Convention.

Part I.
General Provisions.

ART. 1.

The validity of the capture of a merchant-ship or its cargo, when neutral or enemy property is involved, is decided before a Prize Court in accordance with the present Convention.

ART. 2.

La juridiction des prises est exercée d'abord par les tribunaux de prises du belligérant capteur.

Les décisions de ces tribunaux sont prononcées en séance publique ou notifiées d'office aux parties neutres ou ennemies.

ART. 2.

Jurisdiction in matters of prize is exercised in the first instance by the Prize Courts of the belligerent captor.

The judgments of these Courts are pronounced in public or are officially notified to the parties concerned who are neutrals or enemies.

ART. 3.

Les décisions des tribunaux de prises nationaux peuvent être l'objet d'un recours devant la Cour internationale des prises :—

(1) Lorsque la décision des tribunaux nationaux concerne les propriétés d'une Puissance ou d'un particulier neutres ;

(2) Lorsque la dite décision concerne des propriétés ennemies et qu'il s'agit—

(*a*) De marchandises chargées sur un navire neutre ;

ART. 3.

The judgments of National Prize Courts may be brought before the International Prize Court—

(1) When the judgment of the National Prize Courts affects the property of a neutral Power or individual;

(2) When the judgment affects enemy property and relates to—

(*a*) Cargo on board a neutral ship;

(*b*) D'un navire ennemi qui aurait été capturé dans les eaux territoriales d'une Puissance neutre, dans le cas où cette Puissance n'aurait pas fait de cette capture l'objet d'une réclamation diplomatique ;

(*c*) D'une réclamation fondée sur l'allégation que le capture aurait été effectuée en violation, soit d'une disposition conventionnelle en vigueur entre les Puissances belligérantes, soit d'une disposition légale édictée par le belligérant capteur.

Le recours contre la décision des tribunaux nationaux peut être fondé sur ce que cette décision ne serait pas justifiée, soit en fait, soit en droit.

(*b*) An enemy ship captured in the territorial waters of a neutral Power, when that Power has not made the capture the subject of a diplomatic claim ;

(*Cp.* 13 *H. C.* 1907, *Art.* 3.)

(*c*) A claim based upon the allegation that the seizure has been effected in violation, either of the provisions of a convention in force between the belligerent Powers, or of an enactment issued by the belligerent captor.

The appeal against the judgment of the National Courts can be based on the ground that the judgment was wrong either in fact or in law.

ART. 4.

Le recours peut être exercé :—

(1) Par une Puissance neutre, si la décision des tribunaux nationaux a porté atteinte à ses propriétés ou à celles de ses ressortissants (article 3 (1)), ou s'il est allégué que la capture d'un navire ennemi a eu lieu dans les eaux territoriales de cette Puissance (article 3 (2) (*b*)) ;

(2) Par un particulier neutre, si la décision des tribunaux nationaux a porté atteinte à ses propriétés (article 3 (1)), sous réserve toutefois du droit de la Puissance dont il relève de lui interdire l'accès de la Cour ou d'y agir elle-même en ses lieu et place ;

(3) Par un particulier relevant de la Puissance ennemie, si la décision des tribunaux nationaux a porté atteinte à ses propriétés dans les conditions visées à l'article 3 (2), à l'exception du cas prévu par l'alinéa (*b*).

ART. 4.

An appeal may be brought—

(1) By a neutral Power, if the judgment of the National Courts injuriously affects its property or the property of its nationals (Article 3 (1)), or if the capture of an enemy vessel is alleged to have taken place in the territorial waters of that Power (Article 3 (2) (*b*)) ;

(2) By a neutral individual, if the judgment of the National Courts injuriously affects his property (Article 3 (1)), subject, however, to the reservation that the Power to which he belongs may forbid him to bring the case before the Court, or may itself undertake the proceedings in his place ;

(3) By an individual subject or citizen of an enemy Power, if the judgment of the National Courts injuriously affects his property in the cases referred to in Article 3 (2), except that mentioned in paragraph (*b*).

Art. 5.

Le recours peut aussi être exercé, dans les mêmes conditions qu'à l'article précédent, par les ayants droit, neutres ou ennemis, du particulier auquel le recours est accordé, et qui sont intervenus devant la juridiction nationale. Ces ayants droit peuvent exercer individuellement le recours dans la mesure de leur intérêt.

Il en est de même des ayants droit, neutres ou ennemis, de la Puissance neutre dont la propriété est en cause.

Art. 5.

An appeal may also be brought on the same conditions as in the preceding Article, by persons belonging either to neutral States or to the enemy, deriving their rights from and entitled to represent an individual qualified to appeal, when they have taken part in the proceedings before the National Court. Persons so entitled may appeal separately to the extent of their interest.

The same rule applies in the case of persons belonging either to neutral States or to the enemy, who derive their rights from and are entitled to represent a neutral Power whose property was the subject of the decision.

Art. 6.

Lorsque, conformément à l'article 3 ci-dessus, la Cour internationale est compétente, le droit de juridiction des tribunaux nationaux ne peut être exercé à plus de deux degrés. Il appartient à la législation du belligérant capteur de décider si le recours est ouvert après la décision rendue en premier ressort ou seulement après la décision rendue en appel ou en cassation.

Faute par les tribunaux nationaux d'avoir rendu une décision définitive dans les deux ans à compter du jour de la capture, la Cour peut être saisie directement.

Art. 6.

When, in accordance with the above Article 3, the International Court has jurisdiction, the National Courts cannot deal with a case in more than two instances. The municipal law of the belligerent captor shall decide whether the case may be brought before the International Court after judgment has been given in first instance or only after an appeal.

If the National Courts fail to give final judgment within two years from the date of capture, the case may be carried direct to the International Court.

Art. 7.

Si la question de droit à résoudre est prévue par une Convention en vigueur entre le belligérant capteur et la Puissance qui est elle-même partie au litige ou dont le ressortissant est

Art. 7.

If the question of law to be decided is covered by a Treaty in force between the belligerent captor and a Power which is itself, or whose national is, a party to the proceedings, the Court

partie au litige, la Cour se conforme aux stipulations de la dite Convention.

A défaut de telles stipulations, la Cour applique les règles du droit international. Si des règles généralement reconnues n'existent pas, la Cour statue d'après les principes généraux de la justice et de l'équité.

Les dispositions ci-dessus sont également applicables en ce qui concerne l'ordre des preuves ainsi que les moyens qui peuvent être employés.

Si, conformément à l'article 3 (2) (c), le recours est fondé sur la violation d'une disposition légale édictée par le belligérant capteur, la Cour applique cette disposition.

La Cour peut ne pas tenir compte des déchéances de procédure édictées par la législation du belligérant capteur, dans les cas où elle estime que les conséquences en sont contraires à la justice et à l'équité.

is governed by the provisions of the said Treaty.

In the absence of such provisions, the Court shall apply the rules of international law. If no generally recognized rule exists, the Court shall give judgment in accordance with the general principles of justice and equity.

The above provisions apply equally to questions relating to the order and mode of proof.

If, in accordance with Article 3 (2) (c), the ground of appeal is the violation of an enactment issued by the belligerent captor, the Court will enforce such enactment.

The Court may disregard failure to comply with the procedure laid down by the laws of the belligerent captor, when it is of opinion that its consequences are unjust and inequitable.

ART. 8.

Si la Cour prononce la validité de la capture du navire ou de la cargaison, il en sera disposé conformément aux lois du belligérant capteur.

Si la nullité de la capture est prononcée, la Cour ordonne la restitution du navire ou de le cargaison et fixe, s'il y a lieu, le montant des dommages-intérêts. Si le navire ou la cargaison ont été vendus ou détruits, la Cour détermine indemnité à accorder de ce chef au propriétaire.

Si la nullité de la capture avait été prononcée par la juridiction nationale, la Cour n'est appelée à statuer que sur les dommages et intérêts.

ART. 8.

If the Court pronounces the capture of the vessel or cargo to be valid, they shall be disposed of in accordance with the laws of the belligerent captor.

If it pronounces the capture to be null, the Court shall order restitution of the vessel or cargo, and shall fix, if there is occasion, the amount of the damages. If the vessel or cargo have been sold or destroyed, the Court shall determine the compensation to be given to the owner on this account.

If the National Prize Court pronounced the capture to be null, the Court can only be asked to decide as to the damages.

<table>
<tr><td>

ART. 9.

Les Puissances contractantes s'engagent à se soumettre de bonne foi aux décisions de la Cour internationale des prises et à les exécuter dans le plus bref délai possible.

</td><td>

ART. 9.

The Contracting Powers undertake to submit in good faith to the decisions of the International Prize Court and to carry them out with the least possible delay.

</td></tr>
</table>

Titre II.

Organisation de la Cour Internationale des Prises.

Part II.

Constitution of the International Prize Court.

<table>
<tr><td>

ART. 10.

La Cour internationale des prises se compose de juges et de juges suppléants, nommés par les Puissances contractantes, et qui tous devront être des jurisconsultes d'une compétence reconnue dans les questions de droit international maritime et jouissant de la plus haute considération morale.

La nomination de ces juges et juges suppléants sera faite dans les six mois qui suivront la ratification de la présente Convention.

</td><td>

ART. 10.

The International Prize Court is composed of Judges and Deputy Judges, who will be appointed by the Contracting Powers, and must all be jurists of known proficiency in questions of international maritime law, and of the highest moral reputation.

The appointment of these Judges and Deputy Judges shall be made within six months after the ratification of the present Convention.

(*Cp.* 1 *H. C.* 1907, *Art.* 44.)

</td></tr>
</table>

<table>
<tr><td>

ART. 11.

Les juges et juges suppléants sont nommés pour une période de six ans, à compter de la date où la notification de leur nomination aura été reçue par le Conseil administratif institué par la Convention pour le règlement pacifique des conflits internationaux du 29 Juillet, 1899. Leur mandat peut être renouvelé.

En cas de décès ou de démission d'un juge ou d'un juge suppléant, il est pourvu à son remplacement selon le mode fixé pour sa nomination.

</td><td>

ART. 11.

The Judges and Deputy Judges are appointed for a period of six years, reckoned from the date on which the notification of their appointment is received by the Administrative Council established by the Convention for the Pacific Settlement of International Disputes of the 29th July, 1899. Their appointments can be renewed.

Should one of the Judges or Deputy Judges die or resign, the same procedure is followed in filling the vacancy as was followed in appointing him.

</td></tr>
</table>

Dans ce cas, la nomination est faite pour une nouvelle période de six ans.	In this case, the appointment is made for a fresh period of six years. (*Cp.* 1 *H. C.* 1907, *Art.* 44.)

ART. 12.

Les juges de la Cour internationale des prises sont égaux entre eux et prennent rang d'après la date où la notification de leur nomination aura été reçue (article 11, alinéa 1), et, s'ils siègent à tour de rôle (article 15, alinéa 2), d'après la date de leur entrée en fonctions. La préséance appartient au plus âgé, au cas où la date est la même.

Les juges suppléants sont, dans l'exercice de leurs fonctions, assimilés aux juges titulaires. Toutefois ils prennent rang après ceux-ci.

ART. 12.

The Judges of the International Prize Court are all equal in rank and have precedence according to the date on which the notification of their appointment was received (Article 11, paragraph 1), and if they sit by rota (Article 15, paragraph 2), according to the date on which they entered upon their duties. When the date is the same, the senior in age takes precedence.

The Deputy Judges when acting are in the same position as the Judges. They rank, however, after them.

ART. 13.

Les juges jouissent des privilèges et immunités diplomatiques dans l'exercice de leurs fonctions et en dehors de leur pays.

Avant de prendre possession de leur siège, les juges doivent, devant le Conseil administratif, prêter serment ou faire une affirmation solennelle d'exercer leurs fonctions avec impartialité et en toute conscience.

ART. 13.

The Judges enjoy diplomatic privileges and immunities in the performance of their duties and when outside their own country.

(*Cp.* 1 *H. C.* 1907, *Art.* 46, *par.* 4.)

Before taking their seat, the Judges must take an oath, or make a solemn affirmation before the Administrative Council, to discharge their duties impartially and conscientiously.

ART. 14.

La Cour fonctionne au nombre de quinze juges ; neuf juges constituent le quorum nécessaire.

Le juge absent ou empêché est remplacé par le suppléant.

ART. 14.

The Court is composed of fifteen Judges : nine Judges constitute a quorum.

A Judge who is absent or prevented from sitting is replaced by the Deputy Judge.

ART. 15.

Les juges nommés par les Puissances contractantes dont les noms suivent : l'Allemagne, les États-Unis d'Amérique, l'Autriche-Hongrie, la France, la Grande-Bretagne, l'Italie, le Japon et la Russie, sont toujours appelés à siéger.

Les juges et les juges suppléants nommés par les autres Puissances contractantes siègent à tour de rôle d'après le tableau annexé à la présente Convention ; leurs fonctions peuvent être exercées successivement par la même personne. Le même juge peut être nommé par plusieurs desdites Puissances.

ART. 15.

The Judges appointed by the following Contracting Powers : Germany, the United States of America, Austria-Hungary, France, Great Britain, Italy, Japan and Russia, are always summoned to sit.

The Judges and Deputy Judges appointed by the other Contracting Powers sit by rota as shown in the Table annexed to the present Convention ; their duties may be performed successively by the same person. The same Judge may be appointed by several of the said Powers.

ART. 16.

Si une Puissance belligérante n'a pas, d'après le tour de rôle, un juge siégeant dans la Cour, elle peut demander que le juge nommé par elle prenne part au jugement de toutes les affaires provenant de la guerre. Dans ce cas, le sort détermine lequel des juges siégeant en vertu du tour de rôle doit s'abstenir. Cette exclusion ne saurait s'appliquer au juge nommé par l'autre belligérant.

ART. 16.

If a belligerent Power has, according to the rota, no Judge sitting in the Court, it may ask that the Judge appointed by it shall take part in the settlement of all cases arising from the war. Lots shall then be drawn as to which of the Judges entitled to sit according to the rota shall withdraw. This arrangement does not affect the Judge appointed by the other belligerent.

ART. 17.

Ne peut siéger le juge qui, à un titre quelconque, aura concouru à la décision des tribunaux nationaux ou aura figuré dans l'instance comme conseil ou avocat d'une partie.

Aucun juge, titulaire ou suppléant, ne peut intervenir comme agent ou comme avocat devant la Cour internationale des prises ni y agir pour une

ART. 17.

No Judge can sit who has been a party, in any way whatever, to the sentence pronounced by the National Courts, or has taken part in the case as counsel or advocate for one of the parties.

No Judge or Deputy Judge can, during his tenure of office, appear as agent or advocate before the International Prize Court, nor act for one

partie, en quelque qualité que ce soit, pendant toute la durée de ses fonctions.

of the parties in any capacity whatever.

(*Cp.* 1 *H.· C.* 1907, *Art.* 62, *par.* 3.)

ART. 18.

Le belligérant capteur a le droit de désigner un officier de marine d'un grade élevé, qui siégera en qualité d'assesseur avec voix consultative. La même faculté appartient à la Puissance neutre qui est elle-même partie au litige, ou à la Puissance dont le ressortissant est partie au litige ; s'il y a, par application de cette dernière disposition, plusieurs Puissances intéressées, elles doivent se concerter, au besoin par le sort, sur l'officier à désigner.

ART. 18.

` The belligerent captor is entitled to appoint a naval officer of high rank to sit as Assessor, but with no voice in the decision. A neutral Power, which is a party to the proceedings or whose national is a party, has the same right of appointment ; if in applying this last provision more than one Power is concerned, they must agree among themselves, if necessary by lot, on the officer to be appointed.

ART. 19.

La Cour élit son Président et son Vice-Président à la majorité absolue des suffrages exprimés. Après deux tours de scrutin, l'élection se fait à la majorité relative, et, en cas de partage des voix, le sort décide.

ART. 19.

The Court elects its President and Vice-President by an absolute majority of the votes cast. After two ballots, the election is made by a bare majority, and, in case the votes are equal, by lot.

ART. 20.

Les juges de la Cour internationale des prises touchent une indemnité de voyage fixée d'après les règlements de leur pays, et reçoivent, en outre, pendant la session ou pendant l'exercice de fonctions conférées par la Cour, une somme de cent florins néerlandais par jour.

Ces allocations, comprises dans les frais généraux de la Cour prévus par l'article 47, sont versées par l'entremise du Bureau international institué par la Convention du 29 Juillet, 1899.

ART. 20.

The Judges of the International Prize Court are entitled to travelling allowances in accordance with the regulations in force in their own country, and in addition thereto receive, while the Court is sitting or while they are carrying out duties conferred upon them by the Court, a sum of 100 Netherland florins per diem.

These payments are included in the general expenses of the Court dealt with in Article 47, and are paid through the International Bureau established by the Convention of the 29th July, 1899.

Les juges ne peuvent recevoir de leur propre Gouvernement ou de celui d'une autre Puissance aucune rémunération comme membres de la Cour.

The Judges may not receive from their own Government or from that of any other Power any remuneration in their capacity of members of the Court.

ART. 21.

La Cour internationale des prises a son siège à La Haye et ne peut, sauf le cas de force majeure, le transporter ailleurs qu'avec l'assentiment des parties belligérantes.

ART. 21.

The seat of the International Prize Court is at The Hague and it cannot, except in the case of *force majeure*, be transferred elsewhere without the consent of the belligerents.

(*Cp.* 1 *H. C.* 1907, *Art.* 60.)

ART. 22.

Le Conseil administratif, dans lequel ne figurent que les représentants des Puissances contractantes, remplit, à l'égard de la Cour internationale des prises, les fonctions qu'il remplit à l'égard de la Cour permanente d'arbitrage.

ART. 22.

The Administrative Council fulfils the same functions with regard to the International Prize Court as with regard to the Permanent Court of Arbitration, but only Representatives of Contracting Powers shall be members of it.

(*Cp.* 1 *H. C.* 1907, *Art.* 49.)

ART. 23.

Le Bureau international sert de greffe à la Cour internationale des prises et doit mettre ses locaux et son organisation à la disposition de la Cour. Il a la garde des archives et la gestion des affaires administratives.

Le Secrétaire-Général du Bureau international remplit les fonctions de greffier.

Les secrétaires adjoints au greffier, les traducteurs et les sténographes nécessaires sont désignés et assermentés par la Cour.

ART. 23.

The International Bureau acts as registry to the International Prize Court and must place its offices and staff at the disposal of the Court. It has the custody of the archives and carries out the administrative work.

The Secretary-General of the International Bureau acts as Registrar.

The necessary secretaries to assist the Registrar, translators and shorthand writers are appointed and sworn in by the Court.

ART. 24.

La Cour décide du choix de la langue dont elle fera usage et des langues dont l'emploi sera autorisé devant elle.

ART. 24.

The Court determines which language it will itself use and what languages may be used before it.

(*Cp.* 1 *H. C.* 1907, *Art.* 61.)

Dans tous les cas, la langue officielle des tribunaux nationaux, qui ont connu de l'affaire, peut être employée devant la Cour.

In all cases, the official language of the National Courts which have had cognizance of the case can be used before the Court.

ART. 25.

Les Puissances intéressées ont le droit de nommer des agents spéciaux ayant mission de servir d'intermédiaires entre elles et la Cour. Elles sont, en outre, autorisées à charger des conseils ou avocats de la défense de leurs droits et intérêts.

ART. 25.

Powers which are concerned in a case may appoint special agents to act as intermediaries between themselves and the Court. They may also engage counsel or advocates to defend their rights and interests.

(*Cp.* 1 *H. C.* 1907, *Art.* 62.)

ART. 26.

Le particulier intéressé sera représenté devant la Cour par un mandataire qui doit être, soit un avocat autorisé à plaider devant une Cour d'appel ou une Cour suprême de l'un des Pays contractants, soit un avoué exerçant sa profession auprès d'une telle Cour, soit enfin un professeur de droit à une école d'enseignement supérieur d'un de ces pays.

ART. 26.

A private person concerned in a case will be represented before the Court by an attorney, who must be either an advocate qualified to plead before a Court of Appeal or a High Court of one of the Contracting States, or a lawyer practising before a similar Court, or lastly, a professor of law at one of the higher teaching centres of those countries.

ART. 27.

Pour toutes les notifications à faire, notamment aux parties, aux témoins, et aux experts, la Cour peut s'adresser directement au Gouvernement de la Puissance sur le territoire de laquelle la notification doit être effectuée. Il en est de même s'il s'agit de faire procéder à l'établissement de tout moyen de preuve.

Les requêtes adressées à cet effet seront exécutées suivant les moyens dont la Puissance requise dispose d'après sa législation intérieure. Elles ne peuvent être refusées que si cette Puissance les juge de nature à porter atteinte à sa souveraineté ou à sa

ART. 27.

For all notices to be served, in particular on the parties, witnesses, or experts, the Court may apply direct to the Government of the State on whose territory the service is to be carried out. The same rule applies in the case of steps being taken to procure evidence.

Requests for this purpose are to be executed so far as the means at the disposal of the Power applied to under its municipal law allow. They cannot be rejected unless the Power in question considers them calculated to impair its sovereign rights or its safety. If the

sécurité. S'il est donné suite à la requête, les frais ne comprennent que les dépenses d'exécution réellement effectuées.

La Cour a également la faculté de recourir à l'intermédiaire de la Puissance sur le territoire de laquelle elle a son siège.

Les notifications à faire aux parties dans le lieu où siège la Cour peuvent être exécutées par le Bureau international.

request is complied with, the fees charged must only comprise the expenses actually incurred.

The Court is equally entitled to act through the Power on whose territory it sits.

(*Cp.* 1 *H. C.* 1907, *Art.* 76.)

Notices to be given to parties in the place where the Court sits may be served through the International Bureau.

Titre III.

Procédure devant la Cour Internationale des Prises.

Art. 28.

Le recours devant la Cour internationale des prises est formé au moyen d'une déclaration écrite, faite devant le tribunal national qui a statué, ou adressée au Bureau international; celui-ci peut être saisi même par télégramme.

Le délai du recours est fixé à 120 jours à dater du jour où la décision a été prononcée ou notifiée (article 2, alinéa 2).

Art. 29.

Si la déclaration de recours est faite devant le tribunal national, celui-ci, sans examiner si le délai a été observé, fait, dans les sept jours qui suivent, expédier le dossier de l'affaire au Bureau international.

Si la déclaration de recours est adressée au Bureau international, celui-ci en prévient directement le tribunal national, par télégramme s'il

Part III.

Procedure in the International Prize Court.

Art. 28.

An appeal to the International Prize Court is entered by means of a written declaration made in the National Court which has already dealt with the case, or addressed to the International Bureau; in the latter case the appeal can be entered by telegram.

The period within which the appeal must be entered is fixed at 120 days, counting from the day the decision is delivered or notified (Article 2, paragraph 2).

Art. 29.

If the notice of appeal is entered in the National Court, such Court, without considering the question whether the appeal was entered in due time, will transmit within seven days the record of the case to the International Bureau.

If the notice of appeal is sent to the International Bureau, the Bureau will immediately inform the National Court, when possible by telegraph. The latter

est possible. Le tribunal transmettra le dossier comme il est dit à l'alinéa précédent.

Lorsque le recours est formé par un particulier neutre, le Bureau international en avise immédiatement par télégramme la Puissance dont relève le particulier, pour permettre à cette Puissance de faire valoir le droit que lui reconnait l'article 4 (2).

ART. 30.

Dans le cas prévu à l'article 6, alinéa 2, le recours ne peut être adressé qu'au Bureau international. Il doit être introduit dans les trente jours qui suivent l'expiration du délai de deux ans.

ART. 31.

Faute d'avoir formé son recours dans le délai fixé à l'article 28 ou à l'article 30, la partie sera, sans débats, déclarée non recevable.

Toutefois, si elle justifie d'un empêchement de force majeure et si elle a formé son recours dans les soixante jours qui ont suivi la cessation de cet empêchement, elle peut être relevée de la déchéance encourue, la partie adverse ayant été dûment entendue.

ART. 32.

Si le recours a été formé en temps utile, la Cour notifie d'office, et sans délai, à la partie adverse une copie certifiée conforme de la déclaration.

ART. 33.

Si, en dehors des parties qui se sont pourvues devant la Cour, il y a d'autres intéressés ayant le droit

will transmit the record as provided in the preceding paragraph.

When the appeal is brought by a neutral individual the International Bureau immediately informs by telegraph the individual's Government, in order to enable it to avail itself of the right it enjoys under Article 4, paragraph 2.

ART. 30.

In the case provided for in Article 6, paragraph 2, the notice of appeal can be addressed to the International Bureau only. It must be entered within thirty days of the expiry of the period of two years.

ART. 31.

If the appellant does not enter his appeal within the period laid down in Articles 28 or 30, it shall be rejected without discussion.

Provided that if he can show that he was prevented from so doing by *force majeure*, and that the appeal was entered within sixty days after the circumstances which prevented him entering it before had ceased to operate, the Court can, after hearing the respondent, grant relief from the effect of the above provision.

ART. 32.

If the appeal has been entered in time, a certified copy of the notice of appeal is forthwith officially transmitted by the Court to the respondent.

ART. 33.

If, in addition to the parties who are before the Court, there are other parties concerned who are entitled to

d'exercer le recours, ou si, dans le cas prévu à l'article 29, alinéa 3, la Puissance qui a été avisée, n'a pas fait connaître sa résolution, la Cour attend, pour se saisir de l'affaire, que les délais prévus à l'article 28 ou à l'article 30 soient expirés.

appeal, or if, in the case referred to in Article 29, paragraph 3, the Government which has received notice of an appeal has not announced its decision, the Court will await, before dealing with the case, the expiry of the periods laid down in Articles 28 or 30.

Art. 34.

La procédure devant la Cour Internationale comprend deux phases distinctes : l'instruction écrite et les débats oraux.

L'instruction écrite consiste dans le dépôt et l'échange d'exposés, de contre-exposés, et, au besoin, de répliques, dont l'ordre et les délais sont fixés par la Cour. Les parties y joignent toutes pièces et documents dont elles comptent se servir.

Toute pièce, produite par une partie, doit être communiquée en copie certifiée conforme à l'autre partie par l'intermédiaire de la Cour.

Art. 34.

The procedure before the International Court comprises two distinct phases : written pleadings and oral discussions.

The written pleadings consist of the deposit and exchange of cases, counter-cases, and, if necessary, of replies, the order of which is fixed by the Court, as also the periods within which they must be delivered. The parties annex thereto all papers and documents of which they intend to make use.

(*Cp.* 1 *H. C.* 1907, *Art.* 63.)

A certified copy of every document produced by one party must be communicated to the other party through the medium of the Court.

(*Cp.* 1 *H. C.* 1907, *Art.* 64.)

Art. 35.

L'instruction écrite étant terminée, il y a lieu à une audience publique, dont le jour est fixé par la Cour.

Dans cette audience, les parties exposent l'état de l'affaire en fait et en droit.

La Cour peut, en tout état de cause, suspendre les plaidoiries, soit à la demande d'une des parties, soit d'office, pour procéder à une information complémentaire.

Art. 35.

After the close of the pleadings, a public sitting is held on a day fixed by the Court.

At this sitting the parties state their view of the case both as to the law and as to the facts.

The Court may, at any stage of the proceedings, suspend the speeches of counsel, either at the request of one of the parties, or on their own initiative, in order that supplementary evidence may be obtained.

ART. 36.

La Cour internationale peut ordonner que l'information complémentaire aura lieu, soit conformément aux dispositions de l'article 27, soit directement devant elle ou devant un ou plusieurs de ses membres en tant que cela peut se faire sans moyen coercitif ou comminatoire.

Si des mesures d'information doivent être prises par des membres de la Cour en dehors du territoire où elle a son siège, l'assentiment du Gouvernement étranger doit être obtenu.

ART. 36.

The International Court may order the supplementary evidence to be taken either in the manner provided by Article 27, or before itself, or one or more of the members of the Court, provided that this can be done without resort to compulsion or intimidation.

If steps are to be taken for the purpose of obtaining evidence by members of the Court outside the territory where it is sitting, the consent of the foreign Government must be obtained.

ART. 37.

Les parties sont appelées à assister à toutes mesures d'instruction. Elles reçoivent une copie certifiée conforme des procès-verbaux.

ART. 37.

The parties are summoned to take part in all stages of the proceedings. They receive certified copies of the Minutes.

ART. 38.

Les débats sont dirigés par le Président ou le Vice-Président, et, en cas d'absence ou d'empêchement de l'un et de l'autre, par le plus ancien des juges présents.

Le juge nommé par une partie belligérante ne peut siéger comme Président.

ART. 38.

The discussions are under the direction of the President or Vice-President, or, in case they are absent or cannot act, of the senior Judge present.

(*Cp.* 1 *H. C.* 1907, *Art.* 66.)

The Judge appointed by a belligerent party may not preside.

ART. 39.

Les débats sont publics, sauf le droit pour une Puissance en litige de demander qu'il y soit procédé à huis clos.

Ils sont consignés dans des procès-verbaux, que signent le Président et le greffier, et qui seuls ont caractère authentique.

ART. 39.

The discussions take place in public, subject to the right of a Government which is a party to the case to demand that they be held in private.

They are recorded in Minutes which are signed by the President and Registrar, and these alone have an authentic character.

(*Cp.* 1 *H. C.* 1907, *Art.* 66.)

ART. 40.

En cas de non-comparution d'une des parties, bien que régulièrement citée, ou faute par elle d'agir dans les délais fixés par la Cour, il est procédé sans elle, et la Cour décide d'après les éléments d'appréciation qu'elle a à sa disposition.

ART. 41.

La Cour notifie d'office aux parties toutes décisions ou ordonnances prises en leur absence.

ART. 42.

La Cour apprécie librement l'ensemble des actes, preuves et déclarations orales.

ART. 43.

Les délibérations de la Cour ont lieu à huis clos et restent secrètes.

Toute décision est prise à la majorité des juges présents. Si la Cour siège en nombre pair et qu'il y ait partage des voix, la voix du dernier des juges dans l'ordre de préséance établi d'après l'article 12, alinéa 1, n'est pas comptée.

ART. 44.

L'arrêt de la Cour doit être motivé. Il mentionne les noms des juges qui y ont participé, ainsi que les noms des assesseurs, s'il y a lieu ; il est signé par le Président et par le greffier.

ART. 45.

L'arrêt est prononcé en séance publique, les parties présentes ou

ART. 40.

If a party does not appear, despite the fact that he has been duly cited, or if a party fails to comply with some step within the period fixed by the Court, the case proceeds without that party, and the Court gives judgment in accordance with the materials at its disposal.

ART. 41.

The Court officially notifies to the parties all judgments or orders made in their absence.

ART. 42.

The Court takes into consideration in arriving at its decision all the documents, evidence, and oral statements.

ART. 43.

The Court considers its decisions in private and the proceedings remain secret.

(*Cp.* 1 *H. C.* 1907, *Art.* 78.)

All questions are decided by a majority of the Judges present. If the number of Judges is even and equally divided, the vote of the junior Judge in the order of precedence laid down in Article 12, paragraph 1, is not counted.

ART. 44.

The judgment of the Court must state the reasons on which it is based. It contains the names of the Judges taking part in it, and also of the Assessors, if any ; it is signed by the President and Registrar.

(*Cp.* 1 *H. C.* 1907, *Art.* 79.)

ART. 45.

The judgment is delivered in open Court, the parties concerned being

dûment appelées ; il est notifié d'office aux parties.

Cette notification une fois faite, la Cour fait parvenir au tribunal national de prises le dossier de l'affaire, en y joignant une expédition des diverses décisions intervenues, ainsi qu'une copie des procès-verbaux de l'instruction.

ART. 46.

Chaque partie supporte les frais occasionnés par sa propre défense.

La partie qui succombe supporte, en outre, les frais causés par la procédure. Elle doit, de plus, verser un centième de la valeur de l'objet litigieux à titre de contribution aux frais généraux de la Cour internationale. Le montant de ces versements est déterminé par l'arrêt de la Cour.

Si le recours est exercé par un particulier, celui-ci fournit au Bureau international un cautionnement dont le montant est fixé par la Cour et qui est destiné à garantir l'exécution éventuelle des deux obligations mentionnées dans l'alinéa précédent. La Cour peut subordonner l'ouverture de la procédure au versement du cautionnement.

ART. 47.

Les frais généraux de la Cour internationale des prises sont supportés par les Puissances contractantes dans la proportion de leur participation au fonctionnement de la Cour, telle qu'elle est prévue par l'article 15 et par le tableau y annexé. La désignation des juges suppléants ne donne pas lieu à contribution.

present or duly summoned to attend ; it is officially communicated to the parties.

(*Cp.* 1 *H. C.* 1907, *Art.* 80.)

When this communication has been made, the Court transmits to the National Prize Court the record of the case, together with copies of the various decisions arrived at and of the Minutes of the proceedings.

ART. 46.

Each party pays its own costs.

(*Cp.* 1 *H. C.* 1907, *Art.* 85.)

The party against whom the Court decides bears, in addition, the costs of the trial, and also pays 1 per cent. of the value of the subject-matter of the case as a contribution to the general expenses of the International Court. The amount of these payments is fixed in the judgment of the Court.

If the appeal is brought by an individual, he will furnish the International Bureau with security to an amount fixed by the Court, for the purpose of guaranteeing the eventual fulfilment of the two obligations mentioned in the preceding paragraph. The Court is entitled to postpone the opening of the proceedings until the security has been furnished.

ART. 47.

The general expenses of the International Prize Court are borne by the Contracting Powers in proportion to their share in the composition of the Court as laid down in Article 15 and in the annexed Table. The appointment of Deputy Judges does not involve any contribution.

Le Conseil administratif s'adresse aux Puissances pour obtenir les fonds nécessaires au fonctionnement de la Cour.

The Administrative Council applies to the Powers for the funds requisite for the working of the Court.

ART. 48.

Quand la Cour n'est pas en session, les fonctions qui lui sont conférées par l'article 32, l'article 34, alinéas 2 et 3, l'article 35, alinéa 1, et l'article 46, alinéa 3, sont exercées par une délégation de trois juges désignés par la Cour. Cette délégation décide à la majorité des voix.

ART. 48.

When the Court is not sitting, the duties conferred upon it by Article 32, Article 34, paragraphs 2 and 3, Article 35, paragraph 1, and Article 46, paragraph 3, are discharged by a delegation of three Judges appointed by the Court. This delegation decides by a majority of votes.

ART. 49.

La Cour fait elle-même son règlement d'ordre intérieur, qui doit être communiqué aux Puissances contractantes.

Dans l'année de la ratification de la présente Convention, elle se réunira pour élaborer ce règlement.

ART. 49.

The Court itself draws up its own rules of procedure, which must be communicated to the Contracting Powers.

(*Cp.* 1 *H. C.* 1907, *Art.* 74.)

It will meet to draw up these rules within a year of the ratification of the present Convention.

ART. 50.

La Cour peut proposer des modifications à apporter aux dispositions de la présente Convention qui concernent la procédure. Ces propositions sont communiquées, par l'intermédiaire du Gouvernement des Pays-Bas, aux Puissances contractantes qui se concerteront sur la suite à y donner.

ART. 50.

The Court may propose modifications in the provisions of the present Convention concerning procedure. These proposals are communicated, through the medium of the Netherland Government, to the Contracting Powers, which will confer together as to the measures to be adopted.

Titre IV.

Dispositions Finales.

ART. 51.

La présente Convention ne s'applique de plein droit que si les Puissances belligérantes sont toutes parties à la Convention.

Part IV.

Final Provisions.

ART. 51.

The present Convention does not apply as of right except when the belligerent Powers are all parties to the Convention.

Il est entendu, en outre, que le recours devant la Cour internationale des prises ne peut être exercé que par une Puissance contractante ou le ressortissant d'une Puissance contractante.

Dans les cas de l'article 5, le recours n'est admis que si le propriétaire et l'ayant droit sont également des Puissances contractantes ou des ressortissants de Puissances contractantes.

It is further understood that an appeal to the International Prize Court can only be brought by a Contracting Power, or the national of a Contracting Power.

In the cases mentioned in Article 5 the appeal is only admitted when both the owner and the person entitled to represent him are equally Contracting Powers or the nationals of Contracting Powers.

ART. 52.

La présente Convention sera ratifiée et les ratifications en seront déposées à La Haye dès que toutes les Puissances désignées à l'article 15 et dans son annexe seront en mesure de le faire.

Le dépôt des ratifications aura lieu, en tout cas, le 30 Juin, 1909, si les Puissances prêtes à ratifier peuvent fournir à la Cour neuf juges et neuf juges suppléants, aptes à siéger effectivement. Dans le cas contraire, le dépôt sera ajourné jusqu'au moment où cette condition sera remplie.

Il sera dressé du dépôt des ratifications un procès-verbal, dont une copie, certifiée conforme, sera remise par la voie diplomatique à chacune des Puissances désignées à l'alinéa premier.

ART. 52.

The present Convention shall be ratified and the ratifications shall be deposited at The Hague as soon as all the Powers mentioned in Article 15 and in the Table annexed are in a position to do so.

The deposit of the ratifications shall take place, in any case, on the 30th June, 1909, if the Powers which are ready to ratify furnish nine Judges and nine Deputy Judges to the Court, duly qualified to constitute a Court. If not, the deposit shall be postponed until this condition is fulfilled.

A Minute of the deposit of the ratifications shall be drawn up, of which a certified copy shall be forwarded, through the diplomatic channel, to each of the Powers referred to in the first paragraph.

ART. 53.

Les Puissances désignées à l'article 15 et dans son annexe sont admises à signer la présente Convention jusqu'au dépôt des ratifications prévu par l'alinéa 2 de l'article précédent.

Après ce dépôt, elles seront toujours

ART. 53.

The Powers referred to in Article 15 and in the Table annexed are entitled to sign the present Convention up to the deposit of the ratifications contemplated in paragraph 2 of the preceding Article.

After this deposit, they can at any

admises à y adhérer, purement et simplement. La Puissance qui désire adhérer notifie par écrit son intention au Gouvernement des Pays-Bas en lui transmettant, en même temps, l'acte d'adhésion, qui sera déposé dans les archives dudit Gouvernement. Celui-ci enverra, par la voie diplomatique, une copie certifiée conforme de la notification et de l'acte d'adhésion à toutes les Puissances désignées à l'alinéa précédent, en leur faisant savoir la date où il a reçu la notification.

time accede to it, purely and simply. A Power wishing to accede, notifies its intention in writing to the Netherland Government, transmitting to it at the same time the act of accession, which shall be deposited in the archives of the said Government. The latter shall send, through the diplomatic channel, a certified copy of the notification and of the act of accession to all the Powers referred to in the preceding paragraph, informing them of the date on which it has received the notification.

Art. 54.

La présente Convention entrera en vigueur six mois à partir du dépôt des ratifications prévu par l'article 52, alinéas 1 et 2.

Les adhésions produiront effet soixante jours après que la notification en aura été reçue par le Gouvernement des Pays-Bas et, au plus tôt, à l'expiration du délai prévu par l'alinéa précédent.

Toutefois, la Cour internationale aura qualité pour juger les affaires de prises décidées par la juridiction nationale à partir du dépôt des ratifications ou de la réception de la notification des adhésions. Pour ces décisions, le délai fixé à l'article 28, alinéa 2, ne sera compté que de la date de la mise en vigueur de la Convention pour les Puissances ayant ratifié ou adhéré.

Art. 54.

The present Convention shall come into force six months from the deposit of the ratifications contemplated in Article 52, paragraphs 1 and 2.

The accessions shall take effect sixty days after the notification of such accession has been received by the Netherland Government, or as soon as possible on the expiry of the period contemplated in the preceding paragraph.

The International Court shall, however, have jurisdiction to deal with prize cases decided by the National Courts at any time after the deposit of the ratifications or of the receipt of the notification of the accessions. In such cases, the period fixed in Article 28, paragraph 2, shall only be reckoned from the date when the Convention comes into force as regards a Power which has ratified or acceded.

Art. 55.

La présente Convention aura une durée de douze ans à partir de sa mise en vigueur, telle qu'elle est déterminée

Art. 55.

The present Convention shall remain in force for twelve years from the date at which it comes into force, as de-

par l'article 54, alinéa 1, même pour les Puissances ayant adhéré postérieurement.

Elle sera renouvelée tacitement de six ans en six ans sauf dénonciation.

La dénonciation devra être, au moins un an avant l'expiration de chacune des périodes prévues par les deux alinéas précédents, notifiée par écrit au Gouvernement des Pays-Bas, qui en donnera connaissance à toutes les autres Parties contractantes.

La dénonciation ne produira ses effets qu'à l'égard de la Puissance qui l'aura notifiée. La Convention subsistera pour les autres Puissances contractantes, pourvu que leur participation à la désignation des Juges soit suffisante pour permettre le fonctionnement de la Cour avec neuf juges et neuf juges suppléants.

termined by Article 54, paragraph 1, even for the Powers acceding to it subsequently.

It shall be renewed tacitly from six years to six years unless denounced.

Denunciation must be notified in writing, one year at least before the expiry of each of the periods mentioned in the two preceding paragraphs, to the Netherland Government, which will inform all the other Contracting Powers.

The denunciation shall only operate in respect of the notifying Power. The Convention shall remain in force in the case of the other Contracting Powers, provided that their share in the appointment of Judges be still sufficient to allow the work of the Court to be discharged by nine Judges and nine Deputy Judges.

Art. 56.

Dans le cas où la présente Convention n'est pas en vigueur pour toutes les Puissances désignées dans l'article 15 et le tableau qui s'y rattache, le Conseil administratif dresse, conformément aux dispositions de cet article et de ce tableau, la liste des juges et des juges suppléants pour lesquels les Puissances contractantes participent au fonctionnement de la Cour. Les juges appelés à siéger à tour de rôle seront, pour le temps qui leur est attribué par le tableau susmentionné, répartis entre les différentes années de la période de six ans, de manière que, dans la mesure du possible, la Cour fonctionne chaque année en nombre égal. Si le nombre des juges suppléants dépasse celui des juges, le nombre de

Art. 56.

In case the present Convention is not in operation as regards all the Powers referred to in Article 15 and the annexed Table, the Administrative Council shall draw up a list on the lines of that Article and Table of the Judges and Deputy Judges through whom the Contracting Powers will share in the composition of the Court. The times allotted by the said Table to Judges who are summoned to sit in rota will be redistributed between the different years of the six-year period in such a way that, as far as possible, the number of the Judges of the Court in each year shall be the same. If the number of Deputy Judges is greater than that of the Judges, the number of the latter can be completed

ces derniers pourra être complété par des juges suppléants désignés par le sort parmi celles des Puissances qui ne nomment pas de juge titulaire.

La liste ainsi dressée par le Conseil administratif sera notifiée aux Puissances contractantes. Elle sera revisée quand le nombre de celles-ci sera modifié par suite d'adhésions ou de dénonciations.

Le changement à opérer par suite d'une adhésion ne se produira qu'à partir du 1ᵉʳ Janvier qui suit la date à laquelle l'adhésion a son effet, à moins que la Puissance adhérente ne soit une Puissance belligérante, cas auquel elle peut demander d'être aussitôt représentée dans la Cour, la disposition de l'article 16 étant du reste applicable, s'il y a lieu.

Quand le nombre total des juges est inférieur à onze, sept juges constituent le quorum nécessaire.

by Deputy Judges chosen by lot among those Powers which do not nominate a Judge.

The list drawn up in this way by the Administrative Council shall be notified to the Contracting Powers. It shall be revised when the number of these Powers is modified as the result of accessions or denunciations.

The change resulting from an accession is not made until the 1st January after the date on which the accession takes effect, unless the acceding Power is a belligerent Power, in which case it can ask to be at once represented in the Court, the provision of Article 16 being, moreover, applicable if necessary.

When the total number of Judges is less than eleven, seven Judges form a quorum.

ART. 57.

Deux ans avant l'expiration de chaque période visée par les alinéas 1 et 2 de l'article 55, chaque Puissance contractante pourra demander une modification des dispositions de l'article 15 et du tableau y annexé, relativement à sa participation au fonctionnement de la Cour. La demande sera adressée au Conseil administratif, qui l'examinera et soumettra à toutes les Puissances des propositions sur la suite à y donner. Les Puissances feront, dans le plus bref délai possible, connaître leur résolution au Conseil administratif. Le résultat sera immédiatement, et au moins un an et trente jours avant

ART. 57.

Two years before the expiry of each period referred to in paragraphs 1 and 2 of Article 55, any Contracting Power may demand a modification of the provisions of Article 15 and of the annexed Table, relative to its participation in the composition of the Court. The demand shall be addressed to the Administrative Council, which shall examine it and submit to all the Powers proposals as to the measures to be adopted. The Powers shall inform the Administrative Council of their decision with the least possible delay. The result shall be at once, and at least one year and thirty days before the expiry of the said period of

l'expiration dudit délai de deux ans, communiqué à la Puissance qui a fait la demande.

Le cas échéant, les modifications adoptées par les Puissances entreront en vigueur dès le commencement de la nouvelle période.

En foi de quoi, les Plénipotentiaires ont revêtu la présente Convention de leurs signatures.

Fait à La Haye, le 18 Octobre, 1907, en un seul exemplaire, qui restera déposé dans les archives du Gouvernement des Pays-Bas et dont des copies, certifiées conformes, seront remises par la voie diplomatique aux Puissances désignées à l'article 15 et dans son annexe.

two years, communicated to the Power which made the demand.

When necessary, the modifications adopted by the Powers shall come into force from the commencement of the new period.

In faith whereof the Plenipotentiaries have appended their signatures to the present Convention.

Done at The Hague, the 18th October, 1907, in a single original, which shall remain deposited in the archives of the Netherland Government, and duly certified copies of which shall be sent, through the diplomatic channel, to the Powers designated in Article 15 and in the Table annexed.

ANNEXE DE L'ARTICLE 15.	ANNEX TO ARTICLE 15.
DISTRIBUTION des Juges et Juges suppléants par Pays pour chaque année de la période de six ans.	DISTRIBUTION of Judges and Deputy Judges by Countries for each Year of the period of Six Years.

Juges	Juges Suppléants	Judges	Deputy Judges
	Première Année		*First Year*
1 Argentine	Paraguay	1 Argentina	Paraguay
2 Colombie	Bolivie	2 Colombia	Bolivia
3 Espagne	Espagne	3 Spain	Spain
4 Grèce	Roumanie	4 Greece	Roumania
5 Norvège	Suède	5 Norway	Sweden
6 Pays-Bas	Belgique	6 Netherlands	Belgium
7 Turquie	Perse	7 Turkey	Persia
	Deuxième Année		*Second Year*
1 Argentine	Panama	1 Argentina	Panama
2 Espagne	Espagne	2 Spain	Spain
3 Grèce	Roumanie	3 Greece	Roumania
4 Norvège	Suède	4 Norway	Sweden
5 Pays-Bas	Belgique	5 Netherlands	Belgium
6 Turquie	Luxembourg	6 Turkey	Luxemburg
7 Uruguay	Costa Rica	7 Uruguay	Costa Rica
	Troisième Année		*Third Year*
1 Brésil	Dominicaine	1 Brazil	Santo Domingo
2 Chine	Turquie	2 China	Turkey
3 Espagne	Portugal	3 Spain	Portugal
4 Pays-Bas	Suisse	4 Netherlands	Switzerland
5 Roumanie	Grèce	5 Roumania	Greece
6 Suède	Danemark	6 Sweden	Denmark
7 Venezuela	Haïti	7 Venezuela	Haïti
	Quatrième Année		*Fourth Year*
1 Brésil	Guatémala	1 Brazil	Guatemala
2 Chine	Turquie	2 China	Turkey
3 Espagne	Portugal	3 Spain	Portugal
4 Pérou	Honduras	4 Peru	Honduras
5 Roumanie	Grèce	5 Roumania	Greece
6 Suède	Danemark	6 Sweden	Denmark
7 Suisse	Pays-Bas	7 Switzerland	Netherlands
	Cinquième Année		*Fifth Year*
1 Belgique	Pays-Bas	1 Belgium	Netherlands
2 Bulgarie	Monténégro	2 Bulgaria	Montenegro
3 Chili	Nicaragua	3 Chile	Nicaragua
4 Danemark	Norvège	4 Denmark	Norway
5 Mexique	Cuba	5 Mexico	Cuba
6 Perse	Chine	6 Persia	China
7 Portugal	Espagne	7 Portugal	Spain
	Sixième Année		*Sixth Year*
1 Belgique	Pays-Bas	1 Belgium	Netherlands
2 Chili	Salvador	2 Chile	Salvador
3 Danemark	Norvège	3 Denmark	Norway
4 Mexique	Equateur	4 Mexico	Ecuador
5 Portugal	Espagne	5 Portugal	Spain
6 Serbie	Bulgarie	6 Servia	Bulgaria
7 Siam	Chine	7 Siam	China

CONVENTION No. 12. RELATIVE TO THE ESTABLISHMENT OF AN
INTERNATIONAL PRIZE COURT[1].

Decisions of belligerent Prize Courts, though they purport to follow
the rules of international law, are not infrequently determined by orders from the supreme authority of the state.
" Prize Courts are subject to the instructions of their own
sovereign[2]," and Prize Courts during the era of the Napoleonic wars were forced to follow the changing views of their Governments as recorded in such enactments as the various orders in Council
and the Milan and Berlin decrees. Neutral states do not consider
themselves bound by decisions of Prize Courts, and not infrequently
judgments adverse to the claims of their nationals give rise to diplomatic
negotiations of an acrimonious character whereby peace itself is endangered.
The objections to the present system of national Prize Courts are that the
captor is both judge and party in his own cause with a natural leaning in
favour of his own side, and that though nominally administering international law they are dominated by the laws of their own country[3].
These considerations do not appear so striking in the case of captures
from an enemy as when neutral property is concerned, and various

*The need
for an
International
Prize Court.*

---

[1] *Parl. Papers*, Misc. No. 4 (1908), pp. 41, 146–182; *La Deuxième Confér.* T. I. pp. 165,
188–229; T. II. pp. 11–33, 783–856, 1071–1106; *Livre Jaune*, pp. 68–74; Sir T. Barclay, *Problems
of international practice, etc.* p. 105; Bonfils-Fauchille, *Droit international public* (5th ed.),
§§ 1440¹, 1691¹; Bulmerincq, *Le droit des prises maritimes, Rev. de droit intern.* Vol. x.
pp. 185, 384, 595; Vol. XI. pp. 152, 321, 561; Vol. XII. p. 187; Vol. XIII. p. 447; Vol. XIV. p. 114;
J. Pawley Bate, *Prize Courts and an International Prize Court of Appeal, International Law
Association*, 23rd Report (1906), p. 151; H. B. Brown, *The proposed International Prize Court,
Am. Journ. of Int. Law*, Vol. II. p. 476; F. D. Curtius, *La Cour international des prises, Rev.
de droit intern.* Vol. XI. (2nd series), p. 5; G. B. Davis, *International Law*, p. 372; F. Despagnet,
Cours de Droit international public (3rd ed.), § 683 (with bibliography); Ch. Dupuis, *Le
droit de la guerre maritime, etc.* § 289; A. Ernst, *L'œuvre de la deuxième Conférence*, p. 36;
A. H. Fried, *Die zweite Haager Konferenz*, pp. 121–130; C. N. Gregory, *The proposed inter-
national prize court and some of its difficulties, Am. Journ. of Int. Law*, Vol. II. p. 458;
T. J. Lawrence, *International Problems, etc.* pp. 141–159, 182–197; E. Lémonon, *La seconde
Conférence de la Paix*, pp. 280–335; L. Oppenheim, *International Law*, Vol. II. § 438; *Tableau
général de l'Institut de droit international*, p. 195; T. R. White, *Constitutionality of the
proposed international prize court, Am. Journ. of Int. Law*, Vol. II. p. 490; J. Westlake,
War, p. 288; J. B. Scott, *The Hague Peace Conferences*, pp. 465–511.

[2] The *Amy Warwick* (2 Sprague, 123).

[3] F. Despagnet, *op. cit.* p. 794; Dr Pawley Bate, however, points out that two out of every
five of the decisions of Lord Stowell collected in Roscoe's *English Prize Cases* (1905) and
numbering between 150 and 160, were given in favour of neutrals (*op. cit.* p. 157).

proposals from the time of Hübner, a Danish publicist, in 1759[1], have been made for a reform of Prize Court procedure. The most important suggestions came from the Institut de Droit International, which in Articles 100-9 of the " Règlement international des prises maritimes," adopted at its meeting at Heidelberg in 1877, proposed that a Court of Appeal should be established at the commencement of a war by either belligerent, consisting of five judges, two to be appointed by the belligerents and the remainder by three neutral Powers named by the belligerents[2]. The question of an International Prize Court was also discussed by the International Law Association at Christiania in 1905, when opinions on the advisability or feasibility of establishing such a Court were divided.

The subject of an International Prize Court was not mentioned in Count Benckendorff's Circular of the 3rd April, 1906, but at the Second Plenary Meeting of the Conference on the 19th June, 1907, Baron Marschall von Bieberstein announced that he had been charged by the German Government to present to the Conference proposals for the establishment of an international court to discuss the lawfulness of the capture of prizes in maritime wars. No objection was raised; on the contrary, Sir Edward Fry welcomed the announcement and stated that he also had been entrusted by the British Government with proposals for the same object and would gladly co-operate with Baron Marschall to extend the principles of arbitration[3]. General Porter, on behalf of the United States, supported the proposals[4]. The subject was assigned to the Second Sub-Committee of the First Committee, under the presidency of M. Léon Bourgeois (France), M. Renault being Reporter, and at the first meeting of the Committee the proposals of Germany and Great Britain were handed in.

The German draft contained 31 Articles[5]. It proposed that a Tribunal

The German draft. should be composed of five members, two admirals and three members of the Permanent Court of Arbitration. Each belligerent within a fortnight after the commencement of war should nominate an admiral, and ask two neutral Powers to nominate one member each, the fifth member to be nominated by the two neutral Powers. The Court was thus to be one constituted *ad hoc*, on the outbreak of hostilities, and was competent to deal with matters affecting belligerents. Appeal

---

[1] *De la saisie des bâtiments neutres.*   [2] *Annuaire*, Vol. IX. 1877), p. 289.
[3] See *Instructions* (No. 10), Appendix.
[4] *Parl. Papers*, Misc. No. 4 (1908), p. 14 ; *La Deux. Confér.* T. I. p. 58.
[5] *La Deux. Confér.* T. II. p. 1071.

lay directly to it from the National Prize Court of first instance by a private individual aggrieved.

The British draft contained 16 Articles. The essential principle was

The British draft. the following : " Each of the signatory Powers whose mercantile marine at the date of signature of the proposed agreement exceeds a total of 800,000 tons, shall, in the course of three months following the ratification of the present Act, nominate a jurisconsult of recognised competence in international maritime law, enjoying the highest moral reputation and disposed to accept the function of Judge of the Court. Each Power shall also nominate a Deputy Judge with similar qualifications" (Art. 4)[1]. The Court was therefore to be permanent and composed solely of lawyers and, unlike that of the German scheme, it was competent only where neutrals were concerned. It was also intended only to be a Court of final appeal from the highest National Prize Court, and again differing from the German proposal, which contemplated action being taken by the aggrieved individual, it was to be endowed with competence for all cases where a Prize Court had given a decision which directly affected the interests of a neutral Power or its subjects, and where that Power asserted that the decision was not just either in point of law or in point of fact (Art. 2).

As the British and German proposals were based on different principles

The Questionnaire. M. Renault proposed that a small Committee should be appointed to prepare a Questionnaire for solution by the Sub-Committee. This was done, and Sir Edward Fry, Herr Kriege and M. Renault, who composed the Committee, after several meetings agreed upon eight questions[2]. The Questionnaire was discussed at the meetings of the Second Sub-Committee on the 4th and 11th July[3]. On the first question, *Is it advisable to institute an international Court of Appeal ?*, Baron Marschall and Sir Edward Fry spoke in support of their respective proposals, and the discussion was favourable to the establishment of a Court[4].

The second question : *Shall the Court to be established deal only with cases between the belligerent state which has captured the prize and the state which claims for its subjects injured by the capture, or can it be seized of the case directly by individuals who assert that they have suffered injury ?* Sir Edward Fry supported the British view that states, the subjects of international law, should be parties to the proceedings before the proposed

[1] *La Deux. Confér.* T. II. p. 1076.   [2] *Ibid.* p. 1078.
[3] *Ibid.* pp. 785–813.   [4] *Ibid.* pp. 785–9.

Court, while Herr Kriege defended the German proposal to allow individuals to appear[1].

The third question: *Is the Court to take cognizance of all prize cases or only of cases in which the interests of neutral Governments or neutral individuals are concerned?* Sir Edward Fry argued in favour of the latter, Herr Kriege of the former of these two positions.

The fourth question: *When does the jurisdiction of the International Prize Court begin? Should it be seized of the case from the time when the Courts of first instance shall have given their verdict on the validity of the capture, or must it wait until the final decision has been given by the captor's state?* Sir Edward Fry supported the latter view, which Herr Kriege admitted from the theoretical point of view, but urged that owing to the long delays which often occurred in obtaining a definitive decision appeals should be allowed from Courts of first instance[2].

The fifth question: *Shall the International Court have a permanent character or shall it only be constituted at the outbreak of each war?* The German delegate, while admitting that a permanent Court would be more likely to ensure continuity of international legal principles, considered that the difficulties in constituting such a Court were insuperable, as it should for this purpose contain representatives from all states, and this would make it too unwieldy. He then proceeded to criticise the British proposal to exclude from membership states with a small mercantile marine. M. Ruy Barbosa (Brazil) supported the British proposal for a permanent institution[3].

The sixth question: *Whether the Court be permanent or temporary what elements shall enter into its composition? Only jurists nominated by nations having a mercantile marine of definite importance, or admirals and lawyers who are members of the Permanent Court of Arbitration nominated by the belligerents and neutral states? Should judges of the nationality of an interested state be excluded?* Herr Kriege put forward the views of the German Delegation in favour of the two admirals and three jurists, urging the necessity of the former for giving technical explanations, and of the latter for safeguarding neutral rights. He was supported by M. de Martens. Mr Choate at this stage spoke at some length with a view of conciliating the opposing views of the British and German proposals, and suggested their consideration by a small Committee ; M. Huber (Switzerland) urged the inclusion of inland Powers in the Court as their commercial interests were important[4].

---

[1] *La Deux. Confér.* T. II. pp. 789–791.   [2] *Ibid.* p. 793.   [3] *Ibid.* p. 796.
[4] *Ibid.* pp. 799–805. Mr Choate's speech in English is given on pp. 810–813.

The seventh question : *What legal principles should the international High Court apply?* Baron Marschall considered this question answered by the British proposals. In the first place any treaties to which the contending Powers are parties must be applied, failing these the general principles of international law. Sir Edward Fry welcomed this view of the German delegate and accepted it as an augury of success of the scheme[1].

The eighth question : *Is it advisable to settle the order and method of taking evidence in the High Court?* M. Hagerup (Norway) urged that the general rule of evidence throwing the burden of proof on the captor should apply, though there was a presumption in favour of the captor. M. Nélidow (Russia) raised the question whether the law of the country of the captor should apply, to which Sir Edward Fry replied that the object was to avoid the multiplicity of national laws in prize cases and to establish a uniform international law. M. Nélidow agreed. Other speakers having supported the general principle of the establishment of an International Prize Court, M. Bourgeois closed the discussion, and in accordance with Mr Choate's suggestion a Committee consisting of the three authors of the Questionnaire, the members of the Bureau of the Sub-Committee, together with three representatives of states nominated by the British and German Delegations respectively, was appointed to prepare a draft for consideration of the Committee. Sir Edward Fry nominated the United States, Italy and Portugal, Baron Marschall von Bieberstein proposed Russia, Norway and Holland. Russia declined the nomination and Sweden was substituted[2].

The Committee was appointed on the 11th July and during the next month negotiations took place between the British and German delegates and those of the United States and France, and when the Examining Committee met on the 12th August a draft Convention consisting of 57 Articles was submitted for its consideration[3]. This draft was with slight modifications adopted and approved by the Committee and presented to the Sixth Plenary Meeting of the Conference on the 21st Sept. 1907, with an interesting Report prepared by M. Renault which, after sketching the various suggestions previously made for the establishment of an International Prize Court, summarises the work of the Committee and adds an explanatory note to each of the Articles of the Convention[4].

The Convention is divided into four parts : 1. General provisions.
The Convention. 2. Organisation of the International Prize Court. 3. Procedure before the International Prize Court. 4. Final provisions.

---

[1] *La Deux. Confér.* T. ii. pp. 505-6.   [2] *Ibid.* pp. 806-9.   [3] *Ibid.* p. 1079.
[4] *Parl. Papers,* Misc. No. 4 (1908), pp. 146-174 ; *La Deux. Confér.* T. i. pp. 180-218.

Each Article will not here be discussed separately, especially as many of those relating to procedure are based on the Convention for the Pacific Settlement of International Disputes, as noted in the text of the Convention.

The order in which the Convention deals with matters of prize is in the main that of the Questionnaire.

The general principle that every case of prize shall be decided by the National Prize Court of the captor, whether neutral or enemy property is concerned, is laid down by Article 1. Any questions affecting a belligerent's treatment of his own subjects for such matters as trading with an enemy are excluded from this Convention. Such matters are governed by national not by international law[1]. National Prize Courts will therefore continue as in the past to be governed as regards their constitution and procedure by the laws of their own countries. Precautions for avoiding the too frequently long delays before appeals can reach the International Court are provided in Article 6. The British and German schemes are combined and questions affecting both neutrals and belligerents may come before the newly established Court.

The competence of the International Prize Court.

Articles 3–5 deal with the cases which may be brought before the International Prize Court (Art. 3) and the parties by whom such appeals may be brought (Arts. 4 and 5).

Appeals from National Prize Courts.

When the judgment of the National Court affects property of a neutral Power or individual there is always a right of appeal; the Court is to be established for the purpose of more easily maintaining good relations between neutrals and belligerents. When it affects belligerents there is only an appeal in the three special cases set forth in Article 3 :—

(*a*) When the judgment relates to *enemy* cargo on board a neutral ship. This under the Declaration of Paris is free from capture unless it is contraband of war, or unless the condemnation of the ship involves condemnation of the cargo as may happen in certain cases of breach of blockade or unneutral service.

(*b*) When the judgment relates to an *enemy* ship captured in the territorial waters of a neutral Power, when that Power has not made the capture the subject of a diplomatic claim. Attention must be drawn to 13 H. C. 1907, Art. 3, in which it is laid down that if the prize is not within the neutral jurisdiction the captor Government, on the demand of the neutral Power, must release the prize with its officers and crew. If the neutral Power does not make the demand, and weak neutrals have

---

[1] *La Deux. Confér.* T. i. p. 185.

sometimes found it difficult to enforce their claims against strong belligerents for such violation of their territory, the neutral Power, not the enemy owner, may appeal to the International Prize Court[1]. The enemy owner would have no rights in the belligerent's Prize Court, for a capture in violation of neutral territory is valid as between the belligerents[2].

(c) When the claim of an enemy is based on the allegation that the seizure has been effected in violation, either of the provisions of a Convention in force between the belligerent Powers, or of an enactment issued by the belligerent captor. In this case also the enemy would have no rights in the belligerent's Court, but under this Article he will be enabled to appeal to the International Prize Court and the fact of this procedure being open will ensure the more careful examination of the case before the National Court[3].

The appeal in all cases may be in the nature of a rehearing, as the International Prize Court has jurisdiction in questions of law and fact and may order supplementary evidence to be taken (Art. 36). Such a question as Did the capture take place in territorial waters? may well involve a combination of law and fact, so also would the question whether a ship had been guilty of a breach of blockade.

One of the points of difference between the German and British proposals was whether states or individuals should have the right of appeal. A compromise is made in Article 4. Individuals may appeal, but a neutral Government may in some cases think it necessary to intervene to protect the interests of a subject, or even to prevent him from appealing. The Court itself is judge of its own competence as to matters coming before it under the Convention. Article 6 allows of only two trials of a case in the National Courts and provides that if no final judgment is given within two years from the date of capture by the National Courts the case may go direct to the International Court.

Who may appeal ?

The question as to what rules of law shall be applied by the International Prize Court is one of the greatest importance. The absence of a code of maritime international law, and the uncertainty of the rules on many important questions threatened

The law to be administered[4].

---

[1] See Article 4 (3) and *post*, p. 462.

[2] The *Florida*, 101 U.S. p. 37. The capture of a vessel in neutral waters "might constitute a ground of claim by the neutral Power whose territory had suffered trespass, for apology or indemnity. But neither an enemy, nor a neutral acting the part of an enemy, can demand restitution on the sole ground of capture in neutral waters" (The *Sir William Peel*, 5 Wallace, p. 535).

[3] *La Deux. Confér.* T. i. p. 186.

[4] See on this topic J. Westlake, *War*, pp. 293–6; T. J. Lawrence, *International Problems*, etc. pp. 141–9; J. B. Scott, *The Hague Peace Conferences*, Vol. i. pp. 488–497.

to render the Convention nugatory. Clearly where a question of law to be decided is covered by a relevant Convention the Court will be governed by the principles of the treaty, and where generally recognised rules of international law exist the Court will apply them, but if none exist what are the "general principles of justice and equity" in accordance with which the Court is to decide? M. Renault says "the situation will to a great extent resemble the condition which has for a long time existed in Courts of countries where the laws, chiefly customary, were still rudimentary. They made the law at the same time as they applied it, their decisions formed precedents which became an important source of law. The essential is to have magistrates who inspire every confidence." The analogy to the growth of such systems as the English Common Law does not appear to be well founded. English judges were controlled by the sovereign power in the state, and the Austinian doctrine that the sovereign commands what he permits receives its best illustration in England.

The possibility of a codification of the rules of international law applicable to naval warfare seemed to M. Renault to be extremely remote: "ce serait une perspective sur laquelle ne pourraient guère compter les plus jeunes d'entre nous." Some few points in dispute were settled by the Conference but as has already been noted agreement was not reached on the more important such as blockade, contraband, sinking of neutral prizes, etc. A strong feeling was manifested in Great Britain and other important naval Powers against the signature of this Convention so long as vagueness and uncertainty existed as to the principles which the Court, in dealing with appeals brought before it, would apply to questions of far-reaching importance affecting naval policy. On the invitation of the British Government delegates from the great Powers of Europe, the United States, Japan, Spain and Holland met in London during the months of December, 1908—February, 1909, and signed a Declaration consisting of 71 Articles dealing with and settling many of the most important points on which divergence had been expressed[1]. M. Renault himself prepared the Report on the Declaration, which if acceded to and ratified by the states of the world will form a solid basis of international law which the International Prize Court will, in the last resort, be called upon to administer.

Articles 8 and 9 called forth no discussion in Committee. If the Court declares the capture of vessel or cargo to be valid, the laws of the belligerent captor decide their ultimate destination. If not, there are various alternatives dealt with, restitution of vessel with or without the cargo and with or without damages. In case of destruction of either,

---

[1] See *post*, pp. 540–566.

compensation to the successful appellant. Lastly, the National Prize Court may have annulled the capture, but not given damages or given what the appellant thinks insufficient: the Appeal Court in either of these cases may be asked to make an award. If the captor has failed before the National Prize Court there is no appeal[1].

Part II., containing Articles 10–27, deals with the constitution of the International Prize Court. The Judges and Deputy Judges are appointed by the contracting Powers, the appointments to be made within six months after the ratification of the Convention (Art. 10). They are appointed for a period of six years, and in case of death or resignation the newly appointed Judge or Deputy is appointed for a full period of six years (Art. 11). They are all equal in rank and have precedence according to the date of notification of their appointment, and if they sit by rota, according to the date on which they enter on their duties. When the date is the same, the senior in age has the precedence, but Deputy Judges when acting as Judges rank after the Judges (Art. 12). The Court is composed of 15 Judges, nine of whom constitute a quorum, any Judge absent or prevented from sitting being replaced by a Deputy Judge (Art. 14). The method of appointment is dealt with in Article 15, which is the governing Article of this part and round which the discussions centred. This Article provides that the Judges appointed by Great Britain, Germany, the United States of America, Austria-Hungary, France, Italy, Japan and Russia—in other words, the eight great Powers of the world—are always summoned to sit. The Judges and Deputy Judges appointed by the other contracting Powers sit by rota as shown in the Table annexed to the Convention.

Constitution of the International Prize Court.

There was no difficulty in reaching an agreement on Articles 10–14. The number of 15 Judges for the Court is the maximum, but nine constitute the necessary quorum. How were these 15 to be obtained? The proposals of Germany and Great Britain were, as has already been noticed, based on totally different principles, the former providing for a Court to be established at the commencement of each war and composed of five members (two admirals and three lawyers), the latter providing for a permanent Court composed of Judges or Deputy Judges nominated by states whose mercantile marine exceeded 800,000 tons. The Court established by the Convention is to be a really permanent tribunal (unlike the body called into being for the purposes of arbitration under the First Convention of 1899), therein following the British principles,

---

[1] *Parl. Papers*, Misc. No. 4 (1908), p. 155; *La Deux. Confér.* T. I. p. 193. (Report of M. Renault.)

but its members instead of being chosen from states possessing a great mercantile marine are provided from the ranks of the great Powers, lesser Powers contributing in proportions settled by the annexed Table. The German scheme provided for the belligerent's representation; the Convention adopts this principle by providing that if a belligerent Power has, according to the rota, no Judge sitting in the Court, it may ask that a Judge appointed by it shall take part in the settlement of all cases arising from the war. Lots are then drawn as to which of the Judges entitled to sit according to the rota shall be withdrawn, but this does not affect the other belligerent. It must be noticed also that this does not affect the members of the Court nominated by the eight great Powers enumerated in Article 15 (Art. 16). The German proposal for the presence of a naval officer is adopted in Article 18, but with the proviso that he sits as Assessor and has no vote.

The adoption of Article 15 was not effected without prolonged and strenuous objections on the part of the smaller states whose case was ably put forward by M. Ruy de Barbosa (Brazil). Mr Eyre Crowe at the first meeting of the Examining Committee on the 12th August explained the principle on which the Committee had proceeded, namely a combination of political power and mercantile shipping, and M. Renault's Report deals with the same point. Numerous ingenious schemes, he says, were put forward, but were not acceptable to those Powers whose support was indispensable for the success of the project, and smaller states are reminded that if they consider their treatment unfavourable the states which are privileged in being always represented are those which are making the most real sacrifice in supporting the institution of an International Court. It is they who are most likely to be belligerents, and it is they who consent that the decisions of their Prize Courts shall be brought before the International Court, and that the actions of their naval officers shall be adjudicated by it. The commercial interests of small states have much to gain and little to lose; they can count on the impartiality of the Court and different legal systems will always be represented. The belligerent will always be entitled to have a Judge of his own country as a member of the Court[1].

M. Ruy de Barbosa (Brazil) fought the principle of Article 15 throughout, and recorded the only vote given against the draft Convention at the Sixth Plenary Meeting of the Conference on the 21st Sept. 1907. In a long and elaborate speech at the second meeting of the Examining Committee on the 17th August he argued that the extent of the mercantile

[1] *La Deux. Confér.* T. I. p. 198.

marine should be taken into consideration in fixing the rota of Judges. He produced a table of the merchant fleets of the world in support of his contention, and he concluded by pointing out that under the scheme of the Convention, out of the three states, Switzerland, Luxemburg and Servia not possessing a single ship, Switzerland was in a better position than Brazil with a mercantile marine of 217,000 tons[1]. The Norwegian delegate (M. Hagerup), as representing a country with a mercantile marine third on the list, supported the proposals of the Committee in order to assist in the accomplishment of a work which it was hoped would have so great consequences for the development of international law[2]. M. Ruy Barbosa subsequently returned to the subject and argued that on the ground both of commercial interests and ships of war his country was entitled to a higher rank than that assigned to it[3]. Again, before the full meeting of the First Committee on the 10th September the Brazilian delegate, on behalf of his own and other American states, criticised the proposed composition of the Court. There were three methods, he said, on which to proceed: the value of the mercantile marine, the value of sea-borne commerce and the value of the fighting navy; he had taken all three into account and Brazil was inequitably treated in every respect. "This palpable iniquity in the foundations of a judicial institution, this ostensible affirmation of the power of force against reason in the work of the most august assembly in the world, convoked for the organisation of peace by means of law, is infinitely sad for the victims. My country will not resign itself to it[4]."

On signing the Convention the following states made reservations on Article 15, thereby refusing to accept the principle of the composition of the Court therein laid down: Chili, Cuba, Ecuador, Guatemala, Hayti, Persia, Salvador, Siam, Turkey and Uruguay.

Parts III. and IV. occasioned but slight discussion; their general principles are those adopted in the Convention for the Pacific Settlement of Disputes, and more especially in the projected Judicial Arbitration Court. By Article 52 it is provided that the Convention shall be ratified and the ratification shall be deposited at the Hague as soon as the Powers mentioned in Article 15 and in the Table annexed are in a position to do so. The deposit of ratifications shall take place, in any case, on the 30th June, 1909, if the Powers which are ready to ratify can furnish nine Judges and nine Deputy Judges to the Court, duly qualified to constitute

---

[1] *La Deux. Confér.* T. II. pp. 832–6. [2] *Ibid.* p. 836.
[3] *Ibid.* pp. 849–852. [4] *Ibid.* pp. 11–13.

a Court. If not the deposit shall be postponed until this condition is fulfilled. By Article 53 the Powers referred to in Article 15 and in the Table annexed are entitled to sign up to the date of the deposit of the ratification contemplated in the second paragraph of Article 52. After this deposit, they can at any time accede to it purely and simply. The Convention shall come into force six months from the deposit of ratification contemplated in Article 52, paragraphs 1 and 2 (Art. 54).

The Convention is to endure for 12 years from the date at which it comes into force as determined by Article 54, paragraph 1, even for Powers acceding to it subsequently, and there shall be a tacit prolongation for periods of six years unless denounced by notification a year before the expiry of the period for which it is to last. If all the Powers referred to in Article 15 are not parties to the Convention provision is made in Article 56 enabling the Administrative Council to draw up a list of Judges and Deputy Judges in accordance with the principles of that Article. A desire having been expressed in the Sub-Committee for a revision in the future of Article 15 it is provided in Article 57 that two years before the periods of expiry of the Convention a demand for revision may be addressed to the Administrative Council.

The Convention has been signed by all the Powers represented at the Conference except Brazil, China, Dominica, Greece, Luxemburg, Montenegro, Nicaragua, Roumania, Russia, Servia and Venezuela. The ten Powers previously mentioned[1] have made a reservation in regard to Article 15. Eleven states, therefore, have not signed the Convention, and ten more have refused to accept the composition of the Court under Article 15.

Signatory Powers.

The future of the International Prize Court is not yet assured. It remains to be seen whether the signatory Powers will also ratify, and in many cases there may be difficulties in passing legislation necessary to give effect to its provisions in states where such legislation is necessary.

If the Declaration of London and the Conventions signed at the Hague are ratified, the Court will have a considerable body of written law to administer. That they may be ratified is a wish which all who desire a peaceful settlement of international difficulties and the due maintenance of the rights of neutrals will cherish. The Convention provides for the creation for the first time of a really permanent Court with obligatory jurisdiction and is a distinct evidence of the progress towards a more definite rule of law in international matters.

---

[1] See *ante*, p. 441.

There are however constitutional difficulties in some states, notably
Constitution- the United States of America, which stand in the way of the
al difficulties ratification of a Convention to submit the judgment of a
regarding the
establishment National Final Court of Appeal to an International Tribunal.
of the Court. The question was raised at the Naval Conference held in
London, Dec. 1908—Feb. 1909, and with a view of solving the problem,
the delegates included in the *Protocole de Clôture* signed on the
26th February, 1909, the following *Vœu*:

"The delegates of the Powers represented at the Naval Conference, which have signed or have expressed the intention of signing
the Hague Convention of the 18th October, 1907, for the establishment of
an International Prize Court, taking into consideration the difficulties of
a constitutional nature which, as regards certain states, stand in the
way of the ratification of that Convention in its present form, agree to
call the attention of their respective Governments to the advantage of concluding an arrangement under which the said states would, at the time of
the deposit of their ratifications, have the power to add thereto a
reservation to the effect that the right of recourse to the International
Prize Court in connection with the decisions of their National Courts,
shall take the form of a direct claim for compensation, provided, however,
that the effect of this reservation shall not be such as to impair the rights
guaranteed by the said Convention either to individuals or to their
Governments, and that the terms of the reservation shall form the subject
of a subsequent understanding between the signatory Powers of the same
Convention[1]."

The explanation of the situation by M. Renault at the meeting of the
Conference on the 25th February, 1909, which was confirmed by Rear-
Admiral Stockton, one of the United States delegates, was the following.
The working of the International Prize Court is not reconcilable with the
constitutions of some states; the decisions of National Prize Courts
cannot be annulled by foreign decision in certain countries, such as the
United States of America. Recourse to the International Prize Court
might have the effect of annulling a decision of the Supreme Court of
the United States of America, a conclusion which is incompatible with
their constitution. The United States Delegation has therefore endeavoured to find a way out of the difficulty. When there is a complaint
with reference to a decision of a Prize Court of their country, application
shall be made to the International Prize Court to obtain compensation on
account of an alleged illegal capture. The Court would decide the case

[1] *Parl. Papers*, Misc. No. 4 (1909), p. 71; *Ibid.* Misc. No. 5 (1909), pp. 222, 379.

de novo, and if it came to the conclusion that the prize was illegal it would award compensation to the party injured. In this way national decisions will be respected. But the essential object of the establishment of the International Prize Court would be attained, by allowing a party interested to be protected against unjust decisions of a national tribunal. According to the *Vœu,* the delegates are to point out to their Governments the advantage there will be in arriving at an agreement of a kind to dispel the difficulties of a constitutional nature which face some of them. It is a question of attaining the same end under another form; instead of annulling a decision, the International Court will award compensation. The result however remains the same: the individual affected will be able to obtain a new trial which will in the end do him justice. The method is different, that is all.

In order to attain the object desired by the United States, it will be necessary to modify the Prize Court Convention in this sense that the signatory states can, on ratifying, reserve to themselves the right of recourse to a procedure different from that which is provided for by this Convention; only the 31 signatory Powers[1] will be able to decide on these modifications if they all agree.

The United States Government will be able, after the Conference, to make a proposal in accordance with the spirit of the *Vœu,* and this proposal must be accepted by the whole of the signatory states[2].

---

[1] There are now 33 signatory Powers; Great Britain and Japan signed the Prize Court Convention after the conclusion of the International Naval Conference.

[2] *Parl. Papers,* Misc. No. 5 (1909), pp. 222–3.

XIII. Convention concernant les Droits et les Devoirs des Puissances Neutres en cas de Guerre Maritime.

Sa Majesté l'Empereur d'Allemagne, Roi de Prusse; &c.[1]

En vue de diminuer les divergences d'opinion qui, en cas de guerre maritime, existent encore au sujet des rapports entre les Puissances neutres et les Puissances belligérantes, et de prévenir les difficultés auxquelles ces divergences pourraient donner lieu;

Considérant que, si l'on ne peut concerter dès maintenant des stipulations s'étendant à toutes les circonstances qui peuvent se présenter dans la pratique, il y a néanmoins une utilité incontestable à établir, dans la mesure du possible, des règles communes pour le cas où malheureusement la guerre viendrait à éclater;

Considérant que, pour les cas non prévus par la présente Convention, il y a lieu de tenir compte des principes généraux du droit des gens;

Considérant qu'il est désirable que les Puissances édictent des prescriptions précises pour régler les conséquences de l'état de neutralité qu'elles auraient adopté;

XIII. Convention respecting the Rights and Duties of Neutral Powers in Maritime War.

His Majesty the German Emperor, King of Prussia; &c.[1]

With the view of harmonizing the divergent views which, in the event of naval war, still exist as to the relations between neutral Powers and belligerent Powers, and of providing for the difficulties to which such divergence of views might give rise;

Seeing that even if it is not possible at present to concert measures applicable to all circumstances which may arise in practice, there is nevertheless an undeniable advantage in framing, as far as may be possible, rules of general application to meet the case where war has unfortunately broken out;

Seeing that in cases not covered by the present Convention, account must be taken of the general principles of the law of nations;

Seeing that it is desirable that the Powers should issue specific enactments regulating the consequences of the status of neutrality whenever adopted by them;

[1] List of States as in Final Act, 1907.

Considérant que c'est, pour les Puissances neutres, un devoir reconnu d'appliquer impartialement aux divers belligérants les règles adoptées par elles ;

Considérant que, dans cet ordre d'idées, ces règles ne devraient pas, en principe, être changées, au cours de la guerre, par une Puissance neutre, sauf dans le cas où l'expérience acquise en démontrerait la nécessité pour la sauvegarde de ses droits ;

Sont convenus d'observer les règles communes suivantes qui ne sauraient, d'ailleurs, porter aucune atteinte aux stipulations des traités généraux existants, et ont nommé pour Leurs Plénipotentiaires, savoir :

[*Dénomination des Plénipotentiaires.*]

Lesquels, après avoir déposé leurs pleins pouvoirs, trouvés en bonne et due forme, sont convenus des dispositions suivantes :—

Seeing that there is a recognized obligation on neutral Powers to apply to the several belligerents impartially the rules adopted by them ; and

Seeing that it is in conformity with these ideas that these rules should not, in principle, be altered, in the course of the war, by a neutral Power, except in a case where experience has shown the necessity for such change for the protection of the rights of that Power ;

Have agreed to observe the following common rules, which cannot, however, modify provisions of existing general Treaties, and have appointed as their Plenipotentiaries, that is to say :

[*Names of Plenipotentiaries.*]

Who, after having deposited their full powers, found to be in good and due form, have agreed upon the following provisions :—

ART. 1.

Les belligérants sont tenus de respecter les droits souverains des Puissances neutres et de s'abstenir, dans le territoire ou les eaux neutres, de tous actes qui constitueraient de la part des Puissances qui les toléreraient un manquement à leur neutralité.

ART. 1.

Belligerents are bound to respect the sovereign rights of neutral Powers and to abstain, in neutral territory or neutral waters, from any act which would, if knowingly permitted by any Power, constitute a violation of neutrality.

(*Cp.* 5 *H. C.* 1907, *Art.* 1.)

ART. 2.

Tous actes d'hostilité, y compris la capture et l'exercice du droit de visite, commis par des vaisseaux de guerre belligérants dans les eaux territoriales d'une Puissance neutre, constituent une violation de la neutralité et sont strictement interdits.

ART. 2.

Any act of hostility, including therein capture and the exercise of the right of search, committed by belligerent war-ships in the territorial waters of a neutral Power, constitutes a violation of neutrality and is strictly forbidden.

ART. 3.

Quand un navire a été capturé dans les eaux territoriales d'une Puissance neutre, cette Puissance doit, si la prise est encore dans sa juridiction, user des moyens dont elle dispose pour que la prise soit relâchée avec ses officiers et son équipage, et pour que l'équipage mis à bord par le capteur soit interné.

Si la prise est hors de la juridiction de la Puissance neutre, le Gouvernement capteur, sur la demande de celle-ci, doit relâcher la prise avec ses officiers et son équipage.

ART. 3.

When a ship has been captured in the territorial waters of a neutral Power, such Power must, if the prize is still within its jurisdiction, employ the means at its disposal to release the prize with its officers and crew, and to intern the prize crew.

If the prize is not within the jurisdiction of the neutral Power, the captor Government, on the demand of that Power, must liberate the prize with its officers and crew.
(*Cp. 12 H. C. 1907, Art. 3.*)

ART. 4.

Aucun tribunal des prises ne peut être constitué par un belligérant sur un territoire neutre ou sur un navire dans des eaux neutres.

ART. 4.

A Prize Court cannot be set up by a belligerent on neutral territory or on a vessel in neutral waters.

ART. 5.

Il est interdit aux belligérants de faire des ports et des eaux neutres la base d'opérations navales contre leurs adversaires, notamment d'y installer des stations radio-télégraphiques ou tout appareil destiné à servir comme moyen de communication avec des forces belligérantes sur terre ou sur mer.

ART. 5.

Belligerents are forbidden to use neutral ports and waters as a base of naval operations against their adversaries, and in particular to erect wireless telegraphy stations or any apparatus intended to serve as a means of communication with the belligerent forces on land or sea.
(*Cp. 5 H. C. 1907, Art. 3 (a).*)

ART. 6.

La remise, à quelque titre que ce soit, faite directement ou indirectement par une Puissance neutre à une Puissance belligérante, de vaisseaux de guerre, de munitions, ou d'un matériel de guerre quelconque, est interdite.

ART. 6.

The supply, in any manner, directly or indirectly, by a neutral Power to a belligerent Power, of war-ships, ammunition, or war material of any kind whatever, is forbidden.

ART. 7.

Une Puissance neutre n'est pas tenue d'empêcher l'exportation ou le transit, pour le compte de l'un ou de l'autre des belligérants, d'armes, de munitions, et, en général, de tout ce qui peut être utile à une armée ou à une flotte.

ART. 7.

A neutral Power is not bound to prevent the export or transit, on behalf of either belligerent, of arms, munitions of war, or, in general, of anything which could be of use to an army or fleet.

(*Cp.* 5 *H. C.* 1907, *Art.* 7.)

ART. 8.

Un Gouvernement neutre est tenu d'user des moyens dont il dispose pour empêcher dans sa juridiction l'équipement ou l'armement de tout navire, qu'il a des motifs raisonnables de croire destiné à croiser ou à concourir à des opérations hostiles contre une Puissance avec laquelle il est en paix. Il est aussi tenu d'user de la même surveillance pour empêcher le départ hors de sa juridiction de tout navire destiné à croiser ou à concourir à des opérations hostiles, et qui aurait été, dans la dite juridiction, adapté en tout ou en partie à des usages de guerre.

ART. 8.

A neutral Government is bound to employ the means at its disposal to prevent the fitting out or arming of any vessel within its jurisdiction which it has reason to believe is intended to cruise, or engage in hostile operations, against a Power with which that Government is at peace. It is also bound to display the same vigilance to prevent the departure from its jurisdiction of any vessel intended to cruise, or engage in hostile operations, which has been adapted in whole or in part within the said jurisdiction to warlike use.

ART. 9.

Une Puissance neutre doit appliquer également aux deux belligérants les conditions, restrictions, ou interdictions, édictées par elle pour ce qui concerne l'admission dans ses ports, rades, ou eaux territoriales, des navires de guerre belligérants ou de leurs prises.

Toutefois, une Puissance neutre peut interdire l'accès de ses ports et de ses rades au navire belligérant qui aurait négligé de se conformer aux ordres et prescriptions édictés par elle ou qui aurait violé la neutralité.

ART. 9.

A neutral Power must apply impartially to the two belligerents the conditions, restrictions, or prohibitions issued by it in regard to the admission into its ports, roadsteads or territorial waters, of belligerent war-ships or of their prizes.

Nevertheless, a neutral Power may forbid a belligerent vessel which has failed to conform to the orders and regulations made by it, or which has violated neutrality, to enter its ports or roadsteads.

ART. 10.

La neutralité d'une Puissance n'est pas compromise par le simple passage dans ses eaux territoriales des navires de guerre et des prises des belligérants.

ART. 11.

Une Puissance neutre peut laisser les navires de guerre des belligérants se servir de ses pilotes brevetés.

ART. 12.

A défaut d'autres dispositions spéciales de la législation de la Puissance neutre, il est interdit aux navires de guerre des belligérants de demeurer dans les ports et rades ou dans les eaux territoriales de la dite Puissance, pendant plus de vingt-quatre heures, sauf dans les cas prévus par la présente Convention.

ART. 13.

Si une Puissance avisée de l'ouverture des hostilités apprend qu'un navire de guerre d'un belligérant se trouve dans un de ses ports et rades ou dans ses eaux territoriales, elle doit notifier au dit navire qu'il devra partir dans les vingt-quatre heures ou dans le délai prescrit par la loi locale.

ART. 14.

Un navire de guerre belligérant ne peut prolonger son séjour dans un port neutre au delà de la durée légale que pour cause d'avaries ou à raison de l'état de la mer. Il devra partir dès que la cause du retard aura cessé.

Les règles sur la limitation du séjour dans les ports, rades et eaux neutres, ne s'appliquent pas aux navires de guerre exclusivement affectés à une

ART. 10.

The neutrality of a Power is not affected by the mere passage through its territorial waters of war-ships or prizes belonging to belligerents.

ART. 11.

A neutral Power may allow belligerent war-ships to employ its licensed pilots.

ART. 12.

In default of special provisions to the contrary in the laws of a neutral Power, war-ships of the belligerent are forbidden to remain in the ports, roadsteads, or territorial waters of the said Power for more than twenty-four hours, except in the cases covered by the present Convention.

ART. 13.

If a Power which has been informed of the outbreak of hostilities learns that a war-ship of a belligerent is in one of its ports or roadsteads, or in its territorial waters, it must notify the said ship to depart within twenty-four hours or within the time prescribed by the local law.

ART. 14.

A belligerent war-ship may not prolong its stay in a neutral port beyond the time permitted except on account of damage or stress of weather. It must depart as soon as the cause of the delay is at an end.

The regulations as to the length of time which such vessels may remain in neutral ports, roadsteads, or waters, do not apply to war-ships devoted ex-

mission religieuse, scientifique ou philanthropique.

clusively to religious, scientific, or philanthropic purposes.

ART. 15.

A défaut d'autres dispositions spéciales de la législation de la Puissance neutre, le nombre maximum des navires de guerre d'un belligérant qui pourront se trouver en même temps dans un de ses ports ou rades, sera de trois.

ART. 15.

In default of special provisions to the contrary in the laws of a neutral Power, the maximum number of war-ships belonging to a belligerent which may be in one of the ports or roadsteads of that Power simultaneously shall be three.

ART. 16.

Lorsque des navires de guerre des deux parties belligérantes se trouvent simultanément dans un port ou une rade neutres, il doit s'écouler au moins vingt-quatre heures entre le départ du navire d'un belligérant et le départ du navire de l'autre.

L'ordre des départs est déterminé par l'ordre des arrivées, à moins que le navire arrivé le premier ne soit dans le cas où la prolongation de la durée légale du séjour est admise.

Un navire de guerre belligérant ne peut quitter un port ou une rade neutres moins de vingt-quatre heures après le départ d'un navire de com-. merce portant le pavillon de son adversaire.

ART. 16.

When war-ships belonging to both belligerents are present simultaneously in a neutral port or roadstead, a period of not less than twenty-four hours must elapse between the departure of the ship belonging to one belligerent and the departure of the ship belonging to the other.

The order of departure is determined by the order of arrival, unless the ship which arrived first is so circumstanced that an extension of its stay is permissible.

A belligerent war-ship may not leave a neutral port or roadstead until twenty-four hours after the departure of a merchant-ship flying the flag of its adversary.

ART. 17.

Dans les ports et rades neutres, les navires de guerre belligérants ne peuvent réparer leurs avaries que dans la mesure indispensable à la sécurité de leur navigation et non pas accroître, d'une manière quelconque, leur force militaire. L'autorité neutre constatera la nature des réparations à effectuer, qui devront être exécutées le plus rapidement possible.

ART. 17.

In neutral ports and roadsteads belligerent war-ships may only carry out such repairs as are absolutely necessary to render them seaworthy, and may not add in any manner whatever to their fighting force. The local authorities of the neutral Power shall decide what repairs are necessary, and these must be carried out with the least possible delay.

ART. 18.

Les navires de guerre belligérants ne peuvent pas se servir des ports, rades et eaux territoriales neutres, pour renouveler ou augmenter leurs approvisionnements militaires ou leur armement ainsi que pour compléter leurs équipages.

ART. 18.

Belligerent war-ships may not make use of neutral ports, roadsteads and territorial waters for replenishing or increasing their supplies of war material or their armament, or for completing their crews.

ART. 19[1].

Les navires de guerre belligérants ne peuvent se ravitailler dans les ports et rades neutres que pour compléter leur approvisionnement normal du temps de paix.

Ces navires ne peuvent, de même, prendre du combustible que pour gagner le port le plus proche de leur propre pays. Ils peuvent, d'ailleurs, prendre le combustible nécessaire pour compléter le plein de leurs soutes proprement dites, quand ils se trouvent dans les pays neutres qui ont adopté ce mode de détermination du combustible à fournir.

Si, d'après la loi de la Puissance neutre, les navires ne reçoivent du charbon que vingt-quatre heures après leur arrivée, la durée légale de leur séjour est prolongée de vingt-quatre heures.

ART. 19[1].

Belligerent war-ships may only revictual in neutral ports or roadsteads to bring up their supplies to the peace standard.

Similarly these vessels may only ship sufficient fuel to enable them to reach the nearest port in their own country. They may, on the other hand, fill up their bunkers built to carry fuel, in neutral countries which have adopted this method of determining the amount of fuel to be supplied.

If, in accordance with the law of the neutral Power, the ships are only supplied with coal twenty-four hours after their arrival, the permissible duration of their stay is extended by twenty-four hours.

ART. 20.

Les navires de guerre belligérants qui ont pris du combustible dans le port d'une Puissance neutre ne peuvent renouveler leur approvisionnement qu'après trois mois dans un port de la même Puissance.

ART. 20.

Belligerent war-ships which have shipped fuel in a port belonging to a neutral Power may not within the succeeding three months replenish their supply in a port of the same Power.

---

[1] On signing this Convention Great Britain made reservations in regard to Articles 19 and 23. (*Parl. Papers*, Misc. No. 5 (1908).)

Art. 21.

Une prise ne peut être amenée dans un port neutre que pour cause d'innavigabilité, de mauvais état de la mer, de manque de combustible ou de provisions.

Elle doit repartir aussitôt que la cause qui en a justifié l'entrée a cessé. Si elle ne le fait pas, la Puissance neutre doit lui notifier l'ordre de partir immédiatement ; au cas où elle ne s'y conformerait pas, la Puissance neutre doit user des moyens dont elle dispose pour la relâcher avec ses officiers et son équipage et interner l'équipage mis à bord par le capteur.

Art. 22.

La Puissance neutre doit, de même, relâcher la prise qui aurait été amenée en dehors des conditions prévues par l'Article 21.

Art. 23[1].

Une Puissance neutre peut permettre l'accès de ses ports et rades aux prises escortées ou non, lorsqu'elles y sont amenées pour être laissées sous séquestre en attendant la décision du tribunal des prises. Elle peut faire conduire la prise dans un autre de ses ports.

Si la prise est escortée par un navire de guerre, les officiers et les hommes mis à bord par le capteur sont autorisés à passer sur le navire d'escorte.

Si la prise voyage seule, le personnel placé à son bord par le capteur est laissé en liberté.

Art. 21.

A prize may only be brought into a neutral port on account of unseaworthiness, stress of weather, or want of fuel or provisions.

It must leave as soon as the circumstances which justified its entry are at an end. If it does not, the neutral Power must order it to leave at once ; should it fail to obey, the neutral Power must employ the means at its disposal to release it with its officers and crew and to intern the prize crew.

Art. 22.

A neutral Power must, similarly, release a prize brought into one of its ports under circumstances other than those referred to in Article 21.

Art. 23[1].

A neutral Power may allow prizes to enter its ports and roadsteads, whether under convoy or not, when they are brought there to be sequestrated pending the decision of a Prize Court. It may have the prize taken to another of its ports.

If the prize is convoyed by a warship, the prize crew may go on board the convoying ship.

If the prize is not under convoy, the prize crew are left at liberty.

---

[1] On signing this Convention Great Britain made reservations in regard to Articles 19 and 23. (*Parl. Papers*, Misc. No. 5 (1908).)

ART. 24.

Si, malgré la notification de l'autorité neutre, un navire de guerre belligérant ne quitte pas un port dans lequel il n'a pas le droit de rester, la Puissance neutre a le droit de prendre les mesures qu'elle pourra juger nécessaires pour rendre le navire incapable de prendre la mer pendant la durée de la guerre et le commandant du navire doit faciliter l'exécution de ces mesures.

Lorsqu'un navire belligérant est retenu par une Puissance neutre, les officiers et l'équipage sont également retenus.

Les officiers et l'équipage ainsi retenus peuvent être laissés dans le navire ou logés, soit sur un autre navire, soit à terre, et ils peuvent être assujettis aux mesures restrictives qu'il paraîtrait nécessaire de leur imposer. Toutefois, on devra toujours laisser sur le navire les hommes nécessaires à son entretien.

Les officiers peuvent être laissés libres en prenant l'engagement sur parole de ne pas quitter le territoire neutre sans autorisation.

ART. 25.

Une Puissance neutre est tenue d'exercer la surveillance, que comportent les moyens dont elle dispose, pour empêcher dans ses ports ou rades et dans ses eaux toute violation des dispositions qui précèdent.

ART. 26.

L'exercice par une Puissance neutre des droits définis par la présente Convention ne peut jamais être considéré comme un acte peu amical par l'un ou

ART. 24.

If, notwithstanding the notification of the neutral Power, a belligerent ship of war does not leave a port where it is not entitled to remain, the neutral Power is entitled to take such measures as it considers necessary to render the ship incapable of putting to sea so long as the war lasts, and the commanding officer of the ship must facilitate the execution of such measures.

When a belligerent ship is detained by a neutral Power, the officers and crew are likewise detained.

The officers and crew so detained may be left in the ship or kept either on another vessel or on land, and may be subjected to such measures of restriction as it may appear necessary to impose upon them. A sufficient number of men must, however, be always left on board for looking after the vessel.

The officers may be left at liberty on giving their word not to quit the neutral territory without permission. (*Cp.* 5 *H. C.* 1907, *Art.* 11, *par.* 3.)

ART. 25.

A neutral Power is bound to exercise such vigilance as the means at its disposal permit to prevent any violation of the provisions of the above Articles occurring in its ports or roadsteads or in its waters.

ART. 26.

The exercise by a neutral Power of the rights laid down in the present Convention can never be considered as an unfriendly act by either belligerent

par l'autre belligérant qui a accepté
les articles qui s'y réfèrent.

who has accepted the Articles relating
thereto.

(*Cp.* 5 *H. C.* 1907, *Art.* 10.)

ART. 27.

Les Puissances contractantes se communiqueront réciproquement, en temps
utile, toutes les lois, ordonnances et
autres dispositions réglant chez elles
le régime des navires de guerre
belligérants dans leurs ports et leurs
eaux, au moyen d'une notification
adressée au Gouvernement des Pays-
Bas et transmise immédiatement par
celui-ci aux autres Puissances contractantes.

ART. 27.

The Contracting Powers shall communicate to each other in due course
all statutes, orders, and other enactments regulating in their respective
countries the situation of belligerent
war-ships in their ports and waters, by
means of a communication addressed
to the Government of the Netherlands,
and forwarded immediately by that
Government to the other Contracting
Powers.

ART. 28.

Les dispositions de la présente Convention ne sont applicables qu'entre
les Puissances contractantes et seulement si les belligérants sont tous
parties à la Convention.

ART. 28.

The provisions of the present Convention are only applicable to the
Contracting Powers, and only if all
the belligerents are parties to the
Convention.

ART. 29.

La présente Convention sera ratifiée
aussitôt que possible.

Les ratifications seront déposées à
La Haye.

Le premier dépôt de ratifications
sera constaté par un procès-verbal
signé par les représentants des Puissances qui y prennent part et par le
Ministre des Affaires Étrangères des
Pays-Bas.

Les dépôts ultérieurs de ratifications
se feront au moyen d'une notification
écrite, adressée au Gouvernement des
Pays-Bas et accompagnée de l'instrument de ratification.

Copie certifiée conforme du procès-
verbal relatif au premier dépôt de
ratifications, des notifications men-

ART. 29.

The present Convention shall be
ratified as soon as possible.

The ratifications shall be deposited
at The Hague.

The first deposit of ratifications shall
be recorded in a *procès-verbal* signed
by the Representatives of the Powers
which take part therein and by the
Netherland Minister for Foreign
Affairs.

The subsequent deposits of ratifications shall be made by means of a
written notification addressed to the
Netherland Government and accompanied by the instrument of ratification.

A duly certified copy of the *procès-
verbal* relating to the first deposit of
ratifications, of the notifications men-

tionnées à l'alinéa précédent, ainsi que des instruments de ratification, sera immédiatement remise par les soins du Gouvernement des Pays-Bas et par la voie diplomatique aux Puissances conviées à la Deuxième Conférence de la Paix, ainsi qu'aux autres Puissances qui auront adhéré à la Convention. Dans les cas visés par l'alinéa précédent, le dit Gouvernement leur fera connaître en même temps la date à laquelle il a reçu la notification.

tioned in the preceding paragraph, and of the instruments of ratification, shall be immediately sent by the Netherland Government, through the diplomatic channel, to the Powers invited to the Second Peace Conference, as well as to the other Powers which have acceded to the Convention. The said Government shall, in the cases contemplated in the preceding paragraph, inform them at the same time of the date on which it received the notification.

ART. 30.

Les Puissances non-signataires sont admises à adhérer à la présente Convention.

La Puissance qui désire adhérer notifie par écrit son intention au Gouvernement des Pays-Bas en lui transmettant l'acte d'adhésion, qui sera déposé dans les archives dudit Gouvernement.

Ce Gouvernement transmettra immédiatement à toutes les autres Puissances copie certifiée conforme de la notification ainsi que de l'acte d'adhésion, en indiquant la date à laquelle il a reçu la notification.

ART. 30.

Non-Signatory Powers may accede to the present Convention.

A Power which desires to accede notifies its intention in writing to the Netherland Government, forwarding to it the act of accession, which shall be deposited in the archives of the said Government.

The said Government shall immediately forward to all the other Powers a duly certified copy of the notification as well as of the act of accession, mentioning the date on which it received the notification.

ART. 31.

La présente Convention produira effet pour les Puissances qui auront participé au premier dépôt des ratifications, soixante jours après la date du procès-verbal de ce dépôt et, pour les Puissances qui ratifieront ultérieurement ou qui adhéreront, soixante jours après que la notification de leur ratification ou de leur adhésion aura été reçue par le Gouvernement des Pays-Bas.

ART. 31.

The present Convention shall take effect, in the case of the Powers which were parties to the first deposit of the ratifications, sixty days after the date of the *procès-verbal* recording such deposit, and, in the case of the Powers which shall ratify subsequently or which shall accede, sixty days after the notification of their ratification or of their accession has been received by the Netherland Government.

ART. 32.

S'il arrivait qu'une des Puissances contractantes voulût dénoncer la présente Convention, la dénonciation sera notifiée par écrit au Gouvernement des Pays-Bas, qui communiquera immédiatement copie certifiée conforme de la notification à toutes les autres Puissances en leur faisant savoir la date à laquelle il l'a reçue.

La dénonciation ne produira ses effets qu'à l'égard de la Puissance qui l'aura notifiée et un an après que la notification en sera parvenue au Gouvernement des Pays-Bas.

ART. 33.

Un registre tenu par le Ministère des Affaires Étrangères des Pays-Bas indiquera la date du dépôt de ratifications effectué en vertu de l'article 29, alinéas 3 et 4, ainsi que la date à laquelle auront été reçues les notifications d'adhésion (article 30, alinéa 2) ou de dénonciation (article 32, alinéa 1).

Chaque Puissance contractante est admise à prendre connaissance de ce registre et à en demander des extraits certifiés conformes.

En foi de quoi les Plénipotentiaires ont revêtu la présente Convention de leurs signatures.

Fait à La Haye, le 18 Octobre, 1907, en un seul exemplaire, qui restera déposé dans les archives du Gouvernement des Pays-Bas, et dont des copies, certifiées conformes, seront remises par la voie diplomatique aux Puissances qui ont été conviées à la Deuxième Conférence de la Paix.

ART. 32.

In the event of one of the Contracting Powers wishing to denounce the present Convention, the denunciation shall be notified in writing to the Netherland Government, which shall immediately communicate a duly certified copy of the notification to all the other Powers, informing them of the date on which it was received.

The denunciation shall only operate in respect of the notifying Power, and only on the expiry of one year after the notification has reached the Netherland Government.

ART. 33.

A register kept by the Netherland Ministry for Foreign Affairs shall record the date of the deposit of ratifications effected in virtue of Article 29, paragraphs 3 and 4, as well as the date on which the notifications of accession (Article 30, paragraph 2) or of denunciation (Article 32, paragraph 1) have been received.

Each Contracting Power is entitled to have access to this register and to be supplied with duly certified extracts from it.

In faith whereof the Plenipotentiaries have appended their signatures to the present Convention.

Done at The Hague, the 18th October, 1907, in a single original, which shall remain deposited in the archives of the Netherland Government, and of which duly certified copies shall be sent, through the diplomatic channel, to the Powers which have been invited to the Second Peace Conference.

CONVENTION NO. 13. THE RIGHTS AND DUTIES OF NEUTRAL
POWERS IN MARITIME WAR[1].

The second *Vœu* adopted by the First Peace Conference was that "the question of the rights and duties of neutrals may be inserted in the programme of a Conference in the near future[2]." The Circular of Count Benckendorff of the 3rd April, 1906, suggested among topics for the consideration of the Conference the "Elaboration of a Convention relative to the laws and usages of naval warfare concerning...the rights and duties of neutrals at sea, among others...the regulations to be applied to belligerent vessels in neutral ports[3]."

The preamble to the Declaration of Paris bore witness to the fact that maritime law in time of war had long been the subject of deplorable disputes, and much of the time of the Second Conference was spent in endeavouring to clear up the uncertainty of the law and duties of states in such matters which give rise to differences of opinion between neutrals and belligerents, differences which may occasion and have occasioned serious difficulties and even conflicts[4].

The development of the law of neutrality during the 19th century **Development** reveals changes in the attitudes of the Powers towards neu- **of law of** tral rights. During the Napoleonic wars belligerent rights **neutrality.** were predominant, but the long peace which was broken by the Crimean War terminating with the Treaty and Declaration of Paris of 1856 marked a movement in the direction of greater recognition of the

[1] *Parl. Papers*, Misc. No. 4 (1908), pp. 51, 223; *La Deux. Confér.* T. i. pp. 282, 295; T. iii. pp. 460–518, 569–652, 695–735; *Livre Jaune*, p. 91; Sir T. Barclay, *Problems of international law and diplomacy, etc.* pp. 83, 89, 160; E. J. Benton, *International law and diplomacy of the Spanish-American War*, Chap. vii.; Bonfils-Fauchille, *Droit international* (5th ed.), Book v. Chap. i.; C. Dupuis, *Le droit de la guerre maritime*, Chap. xii.; *Edinburgh Review*, Jan. 1908, pp. 239–242; W. E. Hall, *International Law*, Part iv. Chap. iii.; A. S. Hershey, *International law and diplomacy of the Russo-Japanese War*, Chap. vii.; T. E. Holland, *Neutral duties in a maritime war, as illustrated by recent events*; C. C. Hyde, *The Hague Convention respecting the rights of neutral Powers in naval war*, Am. Journ. of Int. Law, Vol. ii. p. 507; T. J. Lawrence, *War and neutrality in the far East*, Chap. vi. ; Idem, *International Law*, Part iv. Chaps. ii. and iii.; Idem, *International problems and Hague Conferences*, p. 127; E. Lémonon, *La seconde Conférence de la Paix*, pp. 555–603; J. B. Moore, *Digest of International Law*, Vol. vii. pp. 859–1109; L. Oppenheim, *International Law*, Vol. ii. §§ 313–319, 329–335, 342–8, 357–363; J. B. Scott, *The Hague Peace Conferences of 1899 and 1907*, Vol. i. pp. 620–648; S. Takahashi, *International Law applied to the Russo-Japanese War*, Part iv. Chaps. i., ii. and iii.; J. Westlake, *War*, Chap. viii. and pp. 327–331; Idem, *Quarterly Review*, Jan. 1908, pp. 247–9.

[2] See *ante*, p. 69.   [3] See *ante*, p. 55.
[4] See preamble to Declaration of Paris, *ante*, p. 1.

rights of neutrals. The relinquishment of privateering, and the protection accorded to neutral goods under an enemy flag and enemy goods under a neutral flag were acknowledgments of neutral rights. The Neutrality Regulations of Great Britain in 1862 limiting the amount of coal and the frequency of supplies to belligerent ships marked an important stage in the development of the position of neutrals. Important questions affecting neutrals were raised during the course of the Spanish-American and Boer wars, and more especially during the Russo-Japanese war. Meantime the political situation was undergoing a change; states which formerly viewed maritime questions chiefly from the standpoint of neutrals were themselves becoming naval Powers and beginning to take a different attitude. There was a noticeable reluctance on the part of some of these during the last-mentioned war to refrain from speaking distinctly as to certain acts which *prima facie* seemed to conflict with the duty of neutrals, or to do anything which might hinder their Governments in the event of war doing all that expediency might in unforeseen circumstances dictate[1]. This is also noticeable in the attitude of certain Powers in the discussions which resulted in the preparation of the Convention now under consideration.

The subject of the rights and duties of neutrals at sea, and the regulations to be applied to belligerent vessels in neutral ports was assigned to the Second Sub-Committee of the Third Committee under the presidency of Count Tornielli (Italy), M. Renault being the Reporter.

Proposals at the Conference.

Four proposals were handed in to the Sub-Committee: (1) A Japanese draft defining the position of belligerent ships in neutral waters (seven Articles)[2], (2) a Spanish draft on the same subject (five Articles)[3], (3) a British draft for a Convention concerning the rights and duties of neutral states in maritime warfare (thirty-two Articles)[4], (4) a Russian draft defining the position of belligerent war-ships in neutral ports (seven Articles)[5]. The British draft was the most elaborate, and was a general statement of neutral rights and duties, and the Committee not feeling itself bound by the strict terms of its instructions took into consideration not only the position of belligerent war-ships in neutral ports but the wider question of neutral rights and duties.

A Questionnaire consisting of 17 questions was prepared on the basis of the four drafts[6], and was discussed on the 27th and 30th July and 1st August[7]. Copies of the Three Rules of

The Questionnaire.

---

[1] On this subject see Sir J. Macdonell in *The Nineteenth Century and after*, July, 1904, p. 148.

[2] *La Deux. Confér.* T. III. p. 700.   [3] *Ibid.* p. 701.   [4] *Ibid.* p. 695.
[5] *Ibid.* p. 702.   [6] *Ibid.* p. 703.   [7] *Ibid.* pp. 569–618.

the Treaty of Washington, 1871, and of Chapter vii. of the Italian Code for the Merchant Navy, 1877, were circulated among the Committee.

The Questionnaire related to the following matters, each question being accompanied by the answers provided by the several drafts. (1) Is there a general principle underlying the whole question? (2) What are the rights of neutral states as regards the entry of belligerent ships of war into their ports? (3) To what extent should ships of war be prohibited from using neutral ports or territorial waters, in regard to places of observation, assembling, passage, base of warlike operations, establishment of Prize Courts, military objects of every kind? (4) If a prize is taken in neutral waters what are the rights and duties of the neutral state, (*a*) if the prize is still within its jurisdiction, (*b*) if it has left it? (5) Should the period of stay of belligerent ships of war in neutral waters be limited? (6) If the principle of a limitation is admitted, what exceptions should be made? In respect of stress of weather (*l'état de la mer*)? In respect of repairs? (7) What is the position of a belligerent war-ship which has taken refuge in a neutral port to escape the pursuit of the enemy? (8) What rule should be applied in case ships of both belligerents are in a neutral port simultaneously? How should the order of departure be fixed? (9) Is it necessary to distinguish between single ships and groups of ships? (10) Is any special rule required for ships accompanied by prizes? (11) Can belligerent war-ships effect repairs in a neutral port? (12) What amount of provisions and coal may they take on board? (13) Should a second supply be allowed in the same neutral country unless there is reason to fix some definite period? (14) Should special provision be made for war-ships proceeding to the seat of war or being in proximity to the zone of hostilities? (15) How should belligerent war-ships be dealt with for not conforming to the rules as to the duration and conditions of their stay in neutral ports and waters? (16) What is the duty of neutral states to ensure respect for the rules adopted? (17) Should the same rules be adopted for territorial waters as for neutral ports? (This last question was added at the request of the Norwegian delegate[1].)

The discussions on these questions were lengthy and detailed, and it was recognised that the need for their solution had been emphasized by the occurrences during the Russo-Japanese war, but the methods of the solution proposed differed widely. On the one hand the British proposals, supported generally by the United States and Japan, put great restrictions on the use of neutral ports, whereas other Powers were for leaving the

[1] *La Deux. Confér.* T. III. p. 713.

greatest latitude to neutrals. This difference of standpoint was not derived solely from theoretical conceptions, but from political interests and geographical conditions, which rendered the conciliation of the opposing views particularly difficult[1].

It is the duty of a neutral to take no part in hostilities, to remain absolutely impartial and not to render aid to either belligerent. The admission of belligerent vessels of war into neutral ports and harbours and their passage through territorial waters have long been recognised as standing on a different footing from the admission or passage of troops. In the case of land warfare international practice has decided against it[2], in the case of naval warfare it is permitted. International law however requires that what a neutral allows to one belligerent he must allow to the other. The entrance and length of stay of belligerent ships of war in neutral ports are favours which neutral states may withhold or grant conditionally, and during the Russo-Japanese war Norway, Sweden and Denmark closed certain of their ports to all belligerent war-ships (except in cases of distress)[3]. The rules which neutrals intend to observe during a war in respect to the conditions of admission of belligerent war-ships are usually notified shortly after the commencement of a war by a Declaration of Neutrality, but it has been the practice of some states not to issue any special rules for the stay of belligerent war-ships in their ports. The Declarations of Neutrality lay down different rules, and the same neutral in the course of a war sometimes changes the conditions of admission. The problem in all cases is, as M. Renault states in his Report, to reconcile the neutral right to give asylum to foreign ships with the duty of abstaining from all participation in hostilities[4]. States desire definite rules elaborated before the outbreak of war, the observance of which will be a good defence to recriminations made by either of the belligerents. It was the realisation of this principle, even though it led to an "all round agreement to fetter sovereign power to the extent of making application of some principle obligatory[5]," that was desirable. It will be seen from an examination of the contents of this Convention how far this is carried out.

The Questionnaire reserved several points in the British draft which dealt more particularly with the rights and duties of neutrals, and, in the course of the discussion, the Sub-Committee added others bearing on the same subject. These were sent to an Examining Committee together with the other draft Articles dealing with the regulations for

---

[1] *Livre Jaune*, p. 91.   [2] See 5 H. C. 1907, Articles 2 and 5 (*ante*, p. 282).
[3] T. J. Lawrence, *War and Neutrality*, p. 133; A. S. Hershey, *International Law, etc.* p. 89 n.
[4] *La Deux. Confér.* T. I. p. 297.   [5] *Edinburgh Review*, Jan. 1908, p. 241.

belligerent ships in neutral waters; the British draft was taken as the basis of the draft Convention which was prepared and submitted to the Examining Committee on the 11th, 12th and 28th September[1]. It was further discussed at a full meeting of the Third Committee on the 4th October[2], and after various amendments had been made during the course of the discussion it was adopted at the Eighth Plenary Meeting of the Conference on the 9th October, 1907[3].

The fundamental principle enunciated in Article 1 is the obligation incumbent on belligerent states to respect the sovereign rights of neutral Powers. This right of sovereignty is one springing from the nature of states, but one which is liable to be infringed in time of war. The principle is therefore safeguarded at the commencement of this Convention as also in Article 1 of 5 H. C. 1907. Neutral territory and territorial waters are inviolable, and belligerents must abstain from committing acts therein in violation of neutrality. Article 1 is taken almost verbatim from Article 2 of the British draft and occasioned no discussion[4]. If a violation of neutrality occurs it is a neutral's duty to take steps to obtain redress, especially where the other belligerent is injuriously affected, but this is not definitely stated in the Convention.

Governing principle.

Article 2 follows from the first Article. Every act of hostility, every operation of naval warfare, and in, particular capture of ships and the exercise of the right of visit within neutral waters are forbidden, the more serious act being placed first. It is unnecessary to enter into details of the cases in British and American Prize Courts in which captures in neutral waters have been set aside. The principle has received general recognition for over a century[5].

Article 3 deals with the case where a violation of neutrality has been committed and a vessel has been captured by a belligerent in the territorial waters of a neutral state. Two cases are considered in this Article:—(a) where the prize is still within neutral jurisdiction, (b) where it is not. This Article gave rise to considerable discussion[6]. Article 28 of the British draft was as follows: "Where a prize has been captured in territorial waters in violation of neutrality, the neutral Power shall, if the prize is still within its jurisdiction,

Ship captured in territorial waters.

---

[1] *La Deux. Confér.* T. III. pp. 619–652.

[2] *Ibid.* T. III. pp. 460–485. [3] *Ibid.* T. I. p. 285.

[4] *Ibid.* T. I. pp. 297–8; T. III. p. 622. M. Renault's Report is contained in *Parl. Papers*, Misc. No. 4 (1908), pp. 233–256; *La Deux. Confér.* T. I. pp. 295–326; T. III. pp. 486–514.

[5] See The *Anna* (5 C. Rob. 373), The *Anne* (3 Wheaton, 435), The *Eliza Ann* (1 Dod. 244), The *Florida* (101 U.S. 37).

[6] *La Deux. Confér.* T. III. pp. 622–4.

release it, as well as the officers and crew, and intern the prize crew put
on board by the captor: if the prize has left the neutral jurisdiction, the
neutral Power shall address a protest to the belligerent Government, asking
for the release of the prize with its officers and crew, and the belligerent
shall take means for this purpose[1]." Article 3 of the Convention is
based on this Article with important omissions. The neutral Power
is to employ the means *at its disposal* for the release of the prize if
within its jurisdiction: this expression was substituted for the British as
it was understood that the neutral Power may not always have the
necessary means.

As regards the second case, the British draft proposed, as stated above,
that the neutral should demand the release of the prize, but it was pointed
out in Committee by Admiral Siegel (Germany) that Article 3 of Convention 12 allows such a case to be brought before the International Prize
Court where the neutral has not made a diplomatic remonstrance and
demand. Doubt was expressed as to the mode of procedure to be adopted
where a neutral state was not a party to the Prize Court Convention.
M. Renault stated that in such case the neutral state would proceed by
way of diplomatic request: but if it was a party to the Convention there
were two courses open, either the diplomatic request by the state, or an
appeal to the International Prize Court. The neutral has a choice, " Even
in cases where it does not wish to pursue a diplomatic request strictly
speaking, it will notify the fact to the state of the captor who will
possibly release the prize himself to avoid further difficulties, diplomatic
or judicial[2]." In view of the divergencies of opinion M. Tcharykow
(Russia) moved the suppression of the 2nd paragraph but this was not
carried[3]; the amendment proposed by Count Tornielli to render optional
the claim of the neutral Power, which now appears in the text, was
adopted by nine to four and finally adopted unanimously at the meeting
of the Examining Committee on 28th September, when Sir Ernest Satow,
who had maintained the view of the British draft, reserved his vote[4]. The
difficulty in arriving at a solution was due to the Article in the Prize
Court Convention already mentioned; the duty of the neutral Power, not
a party to the Convention, to demand reparation for the violation of its
neutrality by diplomatic representations was not disputed but is not
expressly stated in the Convention. Cases of this nature have not
infrequently arisen. The capture of the *General Armstrong*, an American
privateer, by a British squadron in the neutral Portuguese harbour of

---

[1] *La Deux. Confér.* T. III. p. 698.   [2] *Ibid.* T. I. p. 299.
[3] *Ibid.* T. III. p. 623.   [4] *Ibid.* p. 644.

Fayal in 1814 led to a long dispute between the United States and Portugal and was finally submitted to the arbitration of Prince Louis Napoleon, then President of the French Republic, who in 1852 decided against the United States on the ground that the American ship did not apply " from the beginning for the intervention of the neutral sovereign[1]." The case of the *Florida*, a Confederate ship, which was captured in 1864 in the territorial waters of Brazil by the Federal cruiser *Wachusett*, is another instance of a neutral state at once demanding reparation, which was given by the United States Government[2]. The most recent case on this subject is the *Ryeshitelni* which occurred during the Russo-Japanese war. This ship, a Russian destroyer, took refuge in Chefoo harbour and was captured there by the Japanese destroyers *Asashiwo* and *Kasumi*. The vacillating policy of China, the neutral Power, in enforcing her neutral rights and compelling disarmament, appears to have caused the Japanese to take the matter into their own hands, and Japan was guilty of a violation of Chinese neutrality (Chefoo being outside the region of the war). The circumstances do not however seem to warrant a severe condemnation of the action of the commanders of the Japanese torpedo-boats. Japan made no reparation to China, though that Power demanded the restoration of the *Ryeshitelni*, and lodged a protest against the violation of her neutrality[3].

Article 4 forbids the establishment by belligerents of Prize Courts
Prize Courts on neutral territory. in neutral territory or waters. This rule has long been recognised as a rule of international law towards the establishment of which the action of the United States in 1793 contributed in a great degree[4]. The words "by a belligerent" were inserted to exclude the case of the International Prize Court which will sit in a neutral territory[5].

The British, Japanese and Russian drafts all contained Articles

---

[1] T. J. Lawrence, *International Law*, p. 540; W. E. Hall, *International Law*, p. 624. This decision is however adversely criticised by several writers of authority ; see Dana's note to § 208 of Wheaton's *International Law*; J. B. Scott, *op. cit.* Vol. I. p. 236.

[2] T. J. Lawrence, *op. cit.* p. 515; W. E. Hall, *op. cit.* p. 620. See also the case of the *Chesapeake* captured by a United States cruiser in the territorial waters of Nova Scotia, W. E. Hall, *op. cit.* p. 620.

[3] T. J. Lawrence, *War and Neutrality*, pp. 291–4; A. S. Hershey, *op. cit.* pp. 258–263; L. Oppenheim, *International Law*, Vol. II. p. 343; S. Takahashi, *op. cit.* pp. 437–444; Professor Westlake (*War*, p. 210) says of the action of the Japanese, "it seems to us impossible to assert that the Japanese exceeded their rights in this, although it was an extreme exercise of them."

[4] T. J. Lawrence, *International Law*, pp. 399, 481.

[5] *La Deux. Confér.* T. I. p. 800.

embodying the principle enunciated in Article 5, the latter part of which is also similar to Article 3 (*a*) of 5 H. C. 1907. The second rule of the Treaty of Washington, 1871, stated this principle from
the standpoint of a neutral's duty: "A neutral government is bound...Secondly, not to permit or suffer either belligerent to make use of its ports or waters as the base of naval operations against the other, or for the purpose of the renewal or augmentation of military supplies or arms or recruitment of men."

Neutral territory as base of belligerent operations.

Article 6 enacts the principle of the second part of the second rule of the Treaty of Washington. Article 3 of the British draft referred only to "sale" by a neutral, the word *supply* (*remise*) has a wider import. Sir Ernest Satow proposed to add a second paragraph prohibiting belligerents from revictualling their *auxiliary* ships in neutral waters. The British delegate contended that while it was allowable for belligerents to purchase food for their crews, the revictualling of belligerent auxiliaries constituted an operation of war. This was opposed by the Russian delegate. This proposal was carried by small majorities but ultimately withdrawn, though its disappearance was understood not to be taken as an acceptance of the whole of the draft by the British or Russian delegates[1]. The supply either directly or indirectly by a neutral Power to a belligerent Power of war-ships, munitions or material of war which had in practice been long forbidden is now definitely prohibited as a rule of law. The sale by auction of Government stores, such as took place in the United States in 1870, during the Franco-German War, is not likely to occur in the future[2]. If a purchase of ships of war from a state has been concluded before the purchasing state becomes a belligerent, it will be the neutral's duty to decline to deliver until the restoration of peace[3].

Supply of instruments of warfare by neutrals.

The supply directly or indirectly by a neutral Power of war-ships and weapons of war is prohibited by Article 6; Article 7, however, recognises that the furnishing of munitions of war etc. by private persons is to be treated differently. Such goods when shipped by a private person are susceptible of capture as contraband; such contraband trade is not internationally unlawful, though in some systems of national law it may involve punishment

Export of arms etc. from neutral states.

---

[1] *Parl. Papers*, Misc. No. 4 (1908), p. 288; *La Deux. Confér.* T. I. p. 301.

[2] See T. E. Holland, *Neutral duties in a maritime war, Proceedings of the British Academy*, Vol. II. p. 2.

[3] For alleged attempt of Russia to purchase war vessels from the Argentine Republic during the Russo-Japanese war, see S. Takahashi, *op. cit.* p. 486.

and, as is frequently pointed out in Neutrality Declarations, is always liable to belligerent capture. A neutral state may forbid its subjects to trade in articles of the class referred to in Article 7, but it is under no international duty to do so. "The supply of materials of war, such as arms and ammunition, to either party to an armed conflict, although neutral governments are not obliged to prevent it, constitutes, on the part of the individuals who engage in it, a participation in hostilities, and as such is confessedly an unneutral act. Should the government of the individual itself supply such articles it would clearly depart from its position of neutrality. The private citizen undertakes the business at his own risk, and against this risk his government cannot assure him protection without making itself a party to his unneutral act[1]."

The first rule of the Treaty of Washington, 1871, is as follows:

Fitting out or arming of ships in neutral jurisdiction. "A neutral Government is bound; first, to use due diligence[2] to prevent the fitting out, arming or equipping within its jurisdiction, of any vessel which it has reasonable grounds to believe is intended to cruise or to carry on war against a power with which it is at peace; and also to use the like diligence to prevent the departure from its jurisdiction of any vessel intended to cruise or carry on war as above, such vessel having been specially adapted, in whole or in part, within such jurisdiction to warlike use." Articles 5, 7 and 8 of the British draft reproduced these rules with certain additions[3]. Article 8 of the Convention also reproduces this rule with two small but important variations. "The expression 'due diligence' which has become celebrated by its obscurity since it was solemnly interpreted has been omitted[4]"; and the Article says in the first place the neutral is "bound to employ the means at its disposal..." and in the second "to employ the same vigilance" to prevent the acts enumerated in the latter part of the Article.

During the discussions on this subject on the 30th July the Brazilian delegate (Captain Burlamaqui de Moura) proposed to insert an Article providing that war-ships in the course of construction in the ship-building yards of a neutral country may be supplied with all their armament to the

---

[1] J. B. Moore, *Digest of International Law*, Vol. VII. p. 748–9. As to the question raised by the purchase by Russia of ships during the Russo-Japanese war from the North German Lloyd and Hamburg-American Companies which are subsidised by the German Government see L. Oppenheim, *op. cit.* Vol. II. p. 344, and S. Takahashi, *op. cit.* pp. 485–9. T. E. Holland, *op. cit.* p. 2.

[2] See on this T. J. Lawrence, *Int. Law*, §§ 259, 263.

[3] *La Deux. Confér.* T. III. p. 695.

[4] Report by M. Renault, *La Deux. Confér.* T. I. p. 302.

officers and crew appointed to receive them, when they have been ordered six months before the declaration of the war[1]. The discussion on this proposal took place on the 1st August, when the Brazilian delegate supported his motion by reference to the French Instructions of the 26th April, 1898, on the occasion of the Spanish-American war (*Rev. Gén. de Droit Inter.* Vol. v. docum. p. 29). It was opposed by the Argentine delegate (M. Drago)[2] and rejected by the Examining Committee on the 26th August[3]. The subject was again introduced by M. Ruy Barbosa at the full meeting of the Third Committee on the 4th October, but no amendment was moved[4]. The British practice is opposed to the Brazilian proposal, and on the outbreak of the Spanish-American war, the British Government prevented the *Amazonas*, renamed by the United States the *Somers*, and the *Almirante Abreu*, two ships building in English ship-building yards which the United States had purchased from Brazil before the commencement of the war, from leaving the country[5].

This Article now converts into a rule of international law the first rule of the Treaty of Washington, but there still remains the difficulty of interpreting the phrase "any vessel intended to cruise or carry on hostile operations" or "which has been adapted in whole or in part, within such jurisdiction, to warlike use[6]." Great Britain has by the Foreign Enlistment Act, 1870, made it a criminal offence to build, equip, dispatch or issue or deliver a commission to any ship with intent or knowledge, or with reasonable cause to believe that the same shall or will be employed in the naval or military service of any foreign state at war with any friendly state (Sec. 8). The United States Neutrality Acts of 1794 and 1818, on which the British Statute of 1819 was modelled, contain similar provisions[7].

The principle of Article 9, which lays on neutrals the duty of impartial

Neutral's impartiality of treatment. treatment to both belligerents, met with no difficulty in acceptance but the form in which it should be stated occasioned some discussion[8]. The British delegate proposed that a neutral Power may, if it thinks necessary, forbid all access to its

---

[1] *La Deux. Confér.* T. I. p. 302; T. III. p. 597.

[2] *Ibid.* T. III. p. 614.   [3] *Ibid.* T. I. p. 302.

[4] *Ibid.* T. III. pp. 468–474.

[5] J. B. Moore, *op. cit.* Vol. VII. p. 861; E. J. Benton. *op. cit.* p. 182.

[6] For the three different constructions put upon these words by the British and United States Governments, and the award of the Arbitrators in the Geneva Arbitration, see T. J. Lawrence, *Inter. Law*, § 263; also W. E. Hall, *op. cit.* pp. 613–4.

[7] Revised Statutes, § 5289. For interpretation of this section by the U.S. Courts during the Spanish-American war see E. J. Benton, *op. cit.* pp. 46–58. See also J. B. Moore, *op. cit.* Vol. VII. § 1320.

[8] *La Deux. Confér.* T. I. p. 303.

ports or certain of them or the passage of its territorial waters to war-ships or prizes of the belligerents. The first draft stated that " A neutral state may allow under definite conditions, and even forbid, if it deems it necessary, access to its ports or certain of its ports by war-ships and prizes of the belligerents, etc." The Japanese delegate contended that this suggested that neutral ports would be freely open to belligerent war-ships, whereas the increasing tendency of writers was to recognise that it was a duty for neutrals to admit them only in cases of distress, etc. The wording of the draft was slightly changed and finally adopted in the present form[1]. The first paragraph, therefore, lays down the general rule that where a neutral admits belligerent war-ships to its ports, roadsteads, or territorial waters, impartial treatment must be given to both; but adds in the second paragraph that one of the belligerents, by failure to conform to the orders and regulations of the neutral or through violation of its neutrality, may forfeit this claim to equal treatment. "The right of a state to forbid in a general way access to its ports by the belligerents is not in question in Article 9, and follows from its right of issuing general regulations and prohibitions[2]."

Article 10 provides that a Power's neutrality is not compromised by the mere passage through its territorial waters of belligerent war-ships or prizes. "Article 32 of the British draft said 'no provisions contained in the preceding Articles shall be interpreted so as to prohibit the innocent passage (*le passage simple*) of neutral waters in time of war by a war-ship or auxiliary ship of a belligerent.' This might have been understood to mean that a neutral had not the right to forbid war-ships from passing through its waters, and it has been previously explained that according to the meaning of the British proposal this innocent passage must be distinguished from access or stay in neutral waters.

Passage of belligerent ships through territorial waters.

" On the 27th July, the first delegate of Sweden, referring to Article 30 of the British draft recognising that a neutral state has the right to forbid in whole or in part access to its ports and territorial waters, had called attention to the special condition of straits which might be situated within the area of territorial waters and suggested the addition of the rule voted by the 'Institut de Droit International' in 1894: 'Straits which form a channel from one open sea to another can never be closed[3].'"

The Danish delegate made a proposition in a similar sense to that of

---

[1] *La Deux. Confér.* T. I. p. 303; T. III. p. 626.

[2] Reply of M. Renault to Sir Ernest Satow, *Ibid.* T. III. p. 626. For the general prohibition of the Scandinavian States in the Russo-Japanese war see *ante*, p. 460.

[3] Report of M. Renault, *Parl. Papers*, Misc. No. 4 (1908), p. 240; *La Deux. Confér.* T. I. p. 304.

the Swedish delegate. He said that to accord to belligerents the right of innocent passage through territorial waters, but to authorise neutrals to prohibit their entry was to take away with one hand what was given with the other. The laying of mines by neutrals being under consideration by another Committee, he would therefore merely draw attention to the connection between the two subjects and the consequent interest which there was in not limiting by the Convention the exercise of the sovereign rights of the neutral over his territorial waters, in such a way as to deprive him of one of the most effective means for maintaining the provisions of the same Convention[1].

The question was discussed by the Examining Committee but no resolutions were passed on these points. From the opinions expressed there it appeared to be the general feeling that a neutral state could forbid even the innocent passage through parts of its territorial waters so far as it was necessary to maintain its neutrality, but that this prohibition could not extend to straits uniting two open seas[2].

Article 10 leaves these questions unsettled, they remain "*sous l'empire du droit des gens général.*" All that it provides is that a state's neutrality is not compromised by the passage through its territorial waters of belligerent ships of war[3].

Admiral Sperry on behalf of the United States declared that he could not accept this Article by reason of the political considerations involved in the question of the passage through territorial waters.

At the meeting of the Sub-Committee on the 30th July Turkhan Pascha made the following declaration: "The Ottoman Delegation thinks it its duty to declare that under the exceptional condition created for the Straits of the Dardanelles and the Bosphorus by the treaties in force, these straits, which are an integral part of Turkish territory, can in no

---

[1] See *ante*, p. 340.

[2] *Parl. Papers*, Misc. No. 4 (1908), p. 240; *La Deux. Confér.* T. I. p. 305.

[3] As will be gathered from the account given by the Report of the discussion on the "right of innocent passage" there is no unanimity among states on this important subject; *le droit des gens général* is not clear, as will be seen from the following statement of Professor Oppenheim: "The right of foreign States for their men-of-war to pass unhindered through the maritime belt is not generally recognised. Although many writers assert the existence of such a right, many others emphatically deny it...it may safely be stated, that...it is now a customary rule of International Law that the right of passage through such parts of the maritime belt as form part of the highway for international traffic cannot be denied to foreign men-of-war" (*International Law*, Vol. I. pp. 243–4). See also on this subject W. E. Hall, *op. cit.* p. 159; T. J. Lawrence, *Intern. Law*, p. 178; J. Westlake, *Peace*, p. 192; Wheaton's *International Law* (Atlay's edition), § 190; F. Despagnet, *Droit international*, § 417; Bonfils-Fauchille, *Droit international*, § 507; H. Taylor, *International Law*, § 282.

case be brought within Article 32 of the British proposals. The Imperial Government could undertake no engagement whatever tending to limit its undoubted rights over these straits."

M. Tsudzuki also declared that the Japanese Government could undertake no engagement concerning the straits which separate the numerous islands or islets which compose the Japanese Empire and which are simply integral parts of the Empire[1].

The 11th Article provides that a neutral Power may allow belligerent war-ships to employ its licensed pilots. It is not bound to provide them, but there are many cases where if a neutral allows belligerents to enter its territorial waters, it requires the employment of its pilots; under this Article no breach of neutrality is committed by granting leave to employ them. "The term ' *brevetés* ' is used not ' *autorisés* ' to indicate that it is a case of official pilots, not of pilots who might be authorised in each particular case " (M. Renault's Report). This permission does not appear to extend to piloting belligerents in the open sea. "Great Britain prohibited her pilots, during the Franco-German War in 1870, from conducting German and French men-of-war outside the maritime belt, the case of vessels in distress excepted[2]."

Employment of neutral pilots.

The question of the length of stay allowed to belligerent ships in neutral ports occasioned the greatest difficulty. The account of the discussion is clearly summarised by M. Renault in his Report to the Conference[3]. Two proposals were before the Committee: (a) the Russian which allowed the neutral state to fix the period of stay allowed to belligerent ships of war[4], and (b) the British, Spanish and Japanese which laid down the general rule that such vessels should remain in neutral ports for twenty-four hours only save in exceptional circumstances[5]. By way of compromise Count Tornielli suggested the rule in the form of the present Article. The right of the neutral Power to fix the length of stay is affirmed, but in case it shall not have exercised the right, the period is fixed at 24 hours. This was accepted by the delegates of Great Britain and Japan but opposed by Germany and Russia. The German delegate proposed to distinguish according as the neutral ports were more or less distant from the theatre of war, allowing a definite period to be fixed for the former but not for the

Duration of stay of belligerents in neutral ports.

---

[1] *Parl. Papers*, Misc. No. 4 (1908), pp. 240–1 ; *La Deux. Confér.* T. i. p. 305.

[2] L. Oppenheim, *op. cit.* Vol. ii. § 353.

[3] *Parl. Papers*, Misc. No. 4 (1908), pp. 241–3 ; *La Deux. Confér.* T. i. pp. 306–9.

[4] *Ibid.* T. iii. p. 702.

[5] *Ibid.* p. 696 (British Articles 11 and 12), p. 701 (Spanish Article 8), p. 700 (Japanese Article 2).

latter. This was opposed by Sir Ernest Satow and M. Tsudzuki, chiefly on the ground of the difficulty in defining the expression "theatre of war." Different states, said Sir Ernest Satow, would interpret the expression in different ways; furthermore, under modern circumstances the theatre of war would be quickly changed, less than a week enabling a fleet to pass from European to American waters; it would be a great responsibility for neutral Powers to have to modify their regulations from time to time according to the varying changes of the war[1]. The Dutch delegate also opposed the German amendment which was ultimately rejected by 7 to 4, with 3 abstentions[2]. The German delegate then moved the suppression of the whole Article but only received the support of one Power, Russia.

The twenty-four hours rule of stay has therefore been accepted as the general rule in the absence of any special regulations to the contrary.

This Article cannot be said to settle the question, but it is something to have the twenty-four hours rule of stay recognised as the normal period allowed: it affords support to a weak neutral state desirous of asserting its neutrality. The twenty-four hours rule of stay though adopted by Great Britain, the United States and other naval Powers, has never been accepted by France, Germany and Russia. The alleged abuse of the hospitality of neutral waters by Russian ships during the Russo-Japanese war called forth protests from Japan, "but the Instructions of the French Minister of Marine expressly stated that 'the duration of sojourn in French ports of belligerents unaccompanied by a prize has not been limited by any special provision[3].'" The twenty-four hours rule of stay will in future apply in the absence of "any special provision to the contrary," and by Article 27 the contracting Powers undertake to notify to the Netherland Government for communication to the other contracting Powers any orders and enactments regulating the situation of belligerent war-ships in their ports and waters. The power of a neutral state to accommodate its friends is not taken away but the neutral will, in order to avoid the application of the twenty-four hours rule of stay, have to make another rule which may one day tell against it, unless it is conceived in extremely wide terms. The object of placing a limitation on the sojourn of belligerent ships in neutral waters is chiefly to prevent such places from being made

---

[1] *La Deux. Confér.* T. III. pp. 627–8.

[2] The following states voted *against*, Great Britain, the United States of America, Spain, Italy, Japan, Holland and Turkey; *for*, Germany, Brazil, France and Russia; *abstained*, Denmark, Norway and Sweden (*Ibid.* T. I. p. 808; T. III. p. 629).

[3] A. S. Hershey, *op. cit.* p. 189. In the Spanish-American war, 1898, France made no specific limit to the length of stay of a belligerent war-ship, unless accompanied by prizes, when the twenty-four hours rule was applied. E. J. Benton, *op. cit.* p. 187.

the base of belligerent operations. Nothing is said in this Article of the reasons for the stay of belligerent war-ships; it makes no distinction between entry to escape the perils of the sea or the enemy, or to take on board stores; these matters are referred to subsequently.

Article 13 is closely connected with the preceding Article, the provisions of which are to apply to belligerent war-ships which happen to be in neutral ports on the outbreak of hostilities. It must be read in connection with Article 24. The proposal to differentiate as regards ports in proximity to the theatre of war was again made by the German delegate in connection with this Article but, after the failure of the attempt in regard to Article 12, it was withdrawn[1]. A case similar to that contemplated by this Article occurred at the commencement of the Russo-Japanese war. The Russian gun-boat *Manjur* was lying in the neutral harbour of Shanghai when war broke out. The Japanese Consul drew the attention of the Chinese Government to the position of the ship, and the Tao-tai of Shanghai ordered the commander of the *Manjur* to leave as soon as possible. He refused; a Japanese cruiser was lying off the mouth of the river. Further parleying ensued, and the Chinese Government again ordered him to leave within 24 hours. The weakness of the neutral Government caused a further delay, and Japan refrained from taking extreme measures, but continued to protest against the presence of the Russian gun-boat in port. Negotiations were carried on between Russia and China on the one hand, and China and Japan on the other, from the middle of February, 1904, until the end of March when the gun-boat was dismantled to the satisfaction of the commander of the Japanese cruiser *Akitsushima*[2].

Whether the duration of stay is fixed at 24 hours or longer, it is recognised that exceptional circumstances permit a prolonga-

Lengthened stay of belligerent war-ships in special cases.

tion of the specified time. Article 14 deals with these cases. The proposals for exemption from the general rule were as follows: "stress of weather" (Japanese draft, Article 2), "damage, stress of weather or other *force majeure*" (Spanish draft, Article 3), "stress of weather, the absence of provisions or damage preventing ships from taking the sea" (Russian draft, Article 5). All three agreed in the exemption due to stress of weather; the question as to the extent of the damage for which a belligerent war-ship should be entitled to exceed the regular period of stay was raised

---

[1] *La Deux. Conför.* T. I. p. 311.

[2] S. Takahashi, *op. cit.* pp. 418–429; T. J. Lawrence, *War and Neutrality*, pp. 187–9; A. S. Hershey, *op. cit.* p. 188.

by the Japanese delegate who desired a definite time to be fixed; this was rejected and the question remains open. The length of time will vary with the condition of the ship and the facilities for repair afforded by the port.

The second paragraph of this Article is in accordance with the spirit of 10 H. C. 1907, Article 1, and 11 H. C. 1907, Article 4, and occasioned no discussion.

The Japanese draft (Article 3) proposed that not more than three belligerent ships belonging to the same state or its allies should anchor at the same time in the same port or waters of the same neutral state[1]. This was supported by the British delegate. The number was taken as being that usually allowed in time of peace. The German delegate remarked that some states had probably not fixed any number for visits in time of peace and suggested that the number should be left to the determination of the neutral. The question was re-opened at the meeting of the Committee on the 28th September[2], when the Russian delegate pointed out that a first-class battle-ship was nearly always accompanied by other smaller ships, and suggested that, while the principle was maintained, the neutral should be allowed to give special permission to more than three. This was objected to as increasing a neutral's difficulties; ultimately the compromise suggested by the Swedish delegate was adopted which now forms Article 15, and fixes the maximum number of one belligerent's war-ships in a neutral port or roadsteads at one time at three *in default of special provisions to the contrary*[3].

Number of belligerent war-ships in a neutral port.

Article 16 settles the order of departure from a neutral port when ships of the two belligerents are both there simultaneously. This Article unlike the foregoing takes into account the presence of belligerent *merchant-ships* in a neutral port. The twenty-four hours rule of departure which was recognised as established by custom is adopted in the first paragraph. The order of departure occasioned some discussion. Four proposals were made: (*a*) that the order should be settled by the neutral, (*b*) that priority of demand should be taken into consideration, (*c*) that the weakest ship should leave first, (*d*) that the order of arrival should determine the order of departure. The last was finally adopted, except where the ship which arrives first is entitled to an extension of its stay[4]. The twenty-four hours interval was also adopted in the third paragraph of this Article where a belligerent war-ship

Order of departure from neutral ports.

---

[1] *La Deux. Confér.* T. III. p. 700.
[3] *La Deux. Confér.* T. I. p. 812; T. III. pp. 648–9.
[2] *Ibid.* p. 648.
[4] *Ibid.* T. I. p. 818.

and a merchant-ship of its enemy are in the same neutral port simultaneously; the former may not leave until twenty-four hours after the latter, but the converse does not hold good. The merchant-ship may, if it desires, leave within less than twenty-four hours after a war-ship of the other belligerent.

The rule of the twenty-four hours interval is probably a hundred years older than the rule of the twenty-four hours stay[1]. It was adopted to prevent a belligerent ship from using neutral waters as a "trap for an enemy of inferior strength[2]." The possibility of evasion of the rule was shown in December, 1861, when the United States corvette *Tuscarora* for several weeks prevented the Confederate cruiser *Nashville* from leaving Southampton[3]. The British Government thereupon in January, 1862, laid down the twenty-four hours rule of stay. The "Institut de Droit International" in 1898 proposed to extend the twenty-four hours interval to the case of a belligerent merchant-ship and an enemy man-of-war, and also "in accordance," as Dr Westlake states, "as may be believed with general practice" proposed that the order of arrival of the vessels should determine the order of departure, unless the first to arrive did not wish to exercise the right of departing first[4]. Article 16 now lays down a general rule of twenty-four hours interval, and settles the order of departure without any saving clause "in default of special provisions to the contrary."

Article 17 is closely connected with Article 15 and provides that only

Repairs in neutral ports and roadsteads. such repairs as are absolutely necessary to render belligerent ships seaworthy may be executed in neutral ports, and that no increase may be made to their fighting force. These provisions were contained in both the British and Japanese drafts and are statements of the generally recognised law on this matter. The neutral decides what repairs are necessary and these must be executed as quickly as possible. The British draft (Art. 19) proposed that a neutral should not knowingly permit a war-ship to repair damage caused in battle[5], and a Portuguese amendment was to the same effect. This was, however, abandoned as there was a feeling that it would sometimes be difficult to decide on the cause of damage[6]. It is not difficult for the neutral to fix

---

[1] It is referred to as a rule of the law of nations in a letter from a French Captain to the Governor of Cadiz in 1759 (J. Westlake, *War*, p. 207). The rule of the 24 hours stay was first introduced by Great Britain in the *Neutrality Regulations* of 1862.

[2] W. E. Hall, *op. cit.* p. 627.

[3] W. E. Hall, *op. cit.* p. 628; T. J. Lawrence, *Inter. Law*, p. 510.

[4] J. Westlake, *War*, p. 207; *Annuaire*, Vol. XVII. p. 286.

[5] *La Deux. Confér.* T. III. p. 697.

[6] *Parl. Papers*, Misc. No. 4 (1908), p. 248; *La Deux. Confér.* T. I. p. 315.

the amount of repairs necessary to enable a ship to keep the seas, but no addition may be made to her armament. To put a ship in a condition to undertake offensive operations is clearly to aid her country in its war. "The principle," says Hall, "is obvious, its application is susceptible of much variation; and in the treatment of ships, as in all other matters in which the neutral holds the delicate scales between two belligerents, a tendency towards the enforcement of a harsher rule becomes more defined with each successive war[1]." Cases which occurred during the Russo-Japanese war afford striking evidence of this. Several Russian ships took refuge in the German harbour of Tsing-tau near Kiao-chau Bay after the battle of the 10th August, 1904. The *Czarewitch* and some destroyers being in an unseaworthy condition were not allowed to repair, but, together with their crews, were kept until the termination of the war. Similar treatment was accorded to the *Diana* in the French harbour of Saigon. The Russian cruisers *Askold* and *Grosovoi* which put into Shanghai in a damaged condition were ultimately dismantled and their crews interned by the Chinese authorities. The *Lena* put into San Francisco on the 11th September, 1904, in need of repairs; the United States authorities estimated they would take six weeks to execute in order to make her seaworthy, and on the request of the commander the United States authorities disarmed her and interned her crew. After the great naval engagement in the Straits of Korea on the 27th May, 1905, three Russian cruisers the *Aurora, Oleg* and *Zamtchug (Jemtchug)* put into Manilla in a damaged condition with wounded men on board. The Russian admiral asked for permission to repair, but this was ultimately refused and the ships were ordered to leave within 24 hours or to be interned, on the ground that time cannot be given for the repair of injuries received in battle[2].

These cases are of unequal value as precedents. In the case of the ships taking refuge within "the theatre of war," their internment was probably no disadvantage to Russia, as had repairs been allowed, all or most of the ships must have been captured or sunk by the Japanese who had secured complete command of the sea. The Russian Government does not appear to have made representations to any of the interning Powers, and in the case of the *Lena*, the commander asked for internment,

---

[1] *Inter. Law*, p. 627.

[2] See on this subject A. S. Hershey, *op. cit.* pp. 204–210; S. Takahashi, *op. cit.* p. 447 (war-ships at Kiao-chau), p. 455 (*Diana*), p. 429 (*Askold* and *Grosovoi*), p. 452 (war-ships at Manilla), p. 455 (*Lena*), p. 457 (*Terek*). The latter ship was interned at Batavia, as under the Dutch neutrality regulations the amount of coal she was able to take on board within the 24 hours was insufficient for her requirements. See also J. B. Moore, *op. cit.* Vol. VII. § 1316.

while in the case of the ships in Manilla and Batavia the Russian Government chose internment as an alternative to quitting. The distinction said to have been drawn by the American Secretary of War between the disablement of a vessel caused by a storm or by an explosion or other accident on board, on the one hand, and the damage suffered in battle, on the other[1], was the distinction proposed to be made by the British draft. There is nothing in Article 17 to prevent a neutral state from making such a distinction if it allows a belligerent to execute repairs in its ports or roadsteads.

It will also be noticed that this Article does not refer to repairs in territorial waters, only in ports and roadsteads; the reason given by Count Tornielli being that it is probably difficult for ships to effect repairs in the former, and further that the control of neutrals over repairs executed under such conditions would not be possible[2].

Article 18 enacts the substance of the second half of the second Rule
Increase of armament in neutral waters. of the Treaty of Washington of 1871, the first half having been already embodied in Article 5. The addition of the words "territorial waters" to the Rule was moved by Sir Ernest Satow and is justified by the reason that the Rule of the Treaty of Washington spoke of neutral duties, whereas this Article is a prohibition to belligerents[3].

Article 19 deals with a question, which together with that of the
Supply of provisions and fuel to belligerent war-ships in neutral ports. period of stay of belligerent war-ships occasioned the chief difficulties. What amount of provisions and fuel may be taken on board by belligerent war-ships in neutral ports? The first paragraph allows belligerent war-ships to re-victual in neutral ports or roadsteads only to complete their supplies up to the amount usual in time of peace. This occasioned no difficulty. The British rule as laid down in the Instructions of 1904 is that a belligerent war-ship may take in "provisions and such other things as may be necessary for the subsistence of her crew." The amount will be in the discretion of the neutral.

The second paragraph deals with the supply of fuel and gave rise to lengthy discussions. The British proposal (Article 17) said that the quantity of provisions or fuel (*munitions, vivres ou combustibles*) taken on board in neutral jurisdiction should in no case exceed that which was necessary to enable it to reach the nearest port of its own country; the

---

[1] J. B. Moore, *op. cit.* Vol. VII. p. 995.
[2] *La Deux. Confér.* T. III. p. 631.
[3] *Parl. Papers,* Misc. No. 4 (1908), p. 248; *La Deux. Confér.* T. I. p. 315; T. III. p. 632.

Japanese proposal added " or some nearer neutral destination[1]"; the Spanish proposal was to the same effect. On the other hand it was contended by Germany, France and Russia that belligerents should be allowed to take in enough fuel to complete their normal supply in time of peace. These two alternatives were considered by the Examining Committee on the 11th and 12th September, 1907[2], and again at the full meeting of the Third Committee on the 4th October, 1907[3]. Admiral Siegel (Germany) contended that there was a great difficulty in arriving at the quantity of fuel necessary to take a ship to its nearest home port. It was necessary to ascertain what was the nearest port, what was its distance, the most economical speed, which would necessarily vary with the quality of the coal supplied, the state of the boilers, etc., the condition of the weather and a consequent lengthening of the voyage. These were burdens which should not be placed on neutrals[4]. In support of the British proposal, Sir Ernest Satow argued that a neutral had no right to give assistance to a belligerent to reach his adversary; that the only reason why coal should be given to a belligerent ship was to prevent it from becoming a helpless derelict on the ocean; sufficient should therefore be given to enable it to preserve its existence, and this was the origin of the rule of the nearest home port, a rule which had been accepted by nearly all states which had issued rules on the subject[5]. The Japanese delegate preferred the suppression of the provisions relating to coal in the Article to the acceptance of the German proposal but this was rejected by 10 to 4. The Russian proposal combined both tests as alternatives as stated in the second paragraph and this was carried in the Examining Committee by 11 votes, with 3 abstentions[6].

The third paragraph of the original draft stated that "re-victualling and coaling do not give a right to prolong the legal length of stay (*la durée légale du séjour*)." The German delegate objected to the last words as impliedly recognising the twenty-four hours rule and at the full meeting of the Third Committee on the 4th October the Russian delegate proposed its suppression, but was opposed by the Japanese delegate[7] on the ground that its suppression would introduce an element of uncertainty into Article 12 so as to completely change its nature: that Article was a compromise. Neutrals would have to resort to severe measures of surveillance to see that belligerents did not make use of the re-victualling permission unduly to prolong their stay. Sir Ernest Satow supported M. Tsudzuki's

---

[1] This proposal was in accordance with the British regulation of 1904.
[2] *La Deux. Confér.* T. III. pp. 682–6.   [3] *Ibid.* pp. 478–481.   [4] *Ibid.* p. 683.
[5] *Ibid.* p. 683.   [6] *Ibid.* p. 685.   [7] *Ibid.* p. 479.

arguments. The Russian amendment was however carried by 27 to 5 (Great Britain, Japan, China, Spain and Portugal); 9 states (including the United States) abstained from voting[1].

A legitimate extension of stay is recognised in the third paragraph in countries where ships of war are not supplied with coal within 24 hours of their arrival, as is the case in Italy.

This Article completely fails to satisfy the requirements of Powers which set a high standard of neutrality, and desire strictly to maintain the rule that neutrals must abstain from rendering assistance to the belligerents. National interests were in this case the determining factor. Great Britain, with coaling stations all over the world, and therefore in war-time independent to a large extent of neutrals, was unable to get other Powers not so situated to take the same view of neutral obligations. International law is not an abstraction irrespective of politico-geographical considerations; it is the reflection of the life of the society of states. The British and Japanese proposals are logical deductions from admitted principles and have been tested by experience, but the majority of states have not up to the present found it expedient to admit them. In the first serious attempt to reach an agreement on such highly controversial matters as those under consideration, it is not astonishing that unanimity was not reached. The standard set by this Article falls far short of that of Great Britain, the United States and Japan, and this Article has not been accepted by Great Britain and Japan: the United States have not signed the Convention. To permit more fuel and supplies "to be obtained than can, in a reasonably liberal sense of the word, be called necessary for reaching a place of safety is to provide the belligerent with means of aggressive action: and consequently to violate the essential principles of neutrality[2]."

Article 20 is closely connected with the preceding Article. Whichever of the standards laid down therein is adopted, within what length of time may a ship return for another supply of provisions or fuel? The British and Spanish drafts both fixed the time at three months, the one viewing it from the neutral, the other from the belligerent standpoint. This period was fixed by Great Britain during the American Civil War; but as the conditions of navigation have totally changed since then it was urged that time and distance should both be taken into consideration, 1000 miles being suggested by a technical Committee to which this and other questions were referred. No agreement was however reached on this point and the proposal as it

Three months rule.

---

[1] *La Deux. Confér.* T. III. p. 480.   [2] W. E. Hall, *op. cit.* p. 607.

stands in Article 20 was adopted. The Russian delegate returned to this subject at the meeting on the 28th September and quoting from the British Foreign Office Instructions of February, 1904, desired the addition of the words "without special permission" to the rule prohibiting belligerent war-ships from receiving supplies from the same neutral Power within the succeeding three months, but this was rejected and the Article was finally adopted as worded in the Convention[1].

Sir Ernest Satow proposed to insert after Article 20 a provision forbidding a neutral from knowingly allowing a belligerent war-ship to take on board provisions or fuel in order to go forth to encounter the enemy or to undertake operations of war (Art. 16 of British draft). The Japanese draft (Art. 5) contained a similar proposal. Spain was the only other Power which supported this proposal which was defeated by 8 to 3[2].

Articles 21–23 deal with the position of prizes in neutral ports[3].

Belligerent prizes in neutral ports. Some countries entirely exclude them, in others they are placed on the same footing as belligerent war-ships (cp. Article 6 of the Convention of Constantinople, 1888, with regard to the Suez Canal). The rule adopted by Article 21 allows them to be brought in only on account of unseaworthiness, stress of weather or want of fuel or provisions. They must leave as soon as the reason for entry is removed, and failure to comply with the neutral's orders to leave authorises that Power to employ the means at its disposal to release the prize with its officers and crew and to intern the prize crew. Article 21 deals with the case of a prize brought within neutral jurisdiction in a regular manner. Article 22 provides for the case where one has come in under circumstances other than those contemplated in the preceding Article. The neutral Power is to release it with its officers and crew and intern the prize crew.

The object of Article 23 is "to render rarer, or to prevent the destruction of prizes" (M. Renault), and provides that a neutral Power may allow prizes to enter its ports and roadsteads when they are brought in to be sequestrated pending the decision of a Prize Court. The connection of this subject with the destruction of neutral prizes, which was under the consideration of the Fourth Committee, caused the Third and Fourth Committees to hold a joint meeting on the 10th September under the presidency of M. de Martens[4], when Sir Ernest Satow formulated objections

---

[1] *La Deux. Confér.* T. i. p. 319; T. iii. p. 650.

[2] *Ibid.* p. 636. During the Russo-Japanese war the Governor of Malta issued a proclamation refusing hospitality to belligerent ships "proceeding to the seat of war" or proceeding to search for contraband.

[3] See on this subject W. E. Hall, *op. cit.* pp. 609–610.

[4] *La Deux. Confér.* T. iii. pp. 1068–70.

against this Article. He pointed out that it made no distinction between enemy and neutral prizes. International law allowed a belligerent to sink enemy prizes, the capture of which made them the property of the captor, and therefore enabled him to deal with them at his pleasure; to allow a belligerent to take a prize into a neutral port was to accord him the power of making use of the port to his peculiar advantage. The adoption of the Article would imply the abandonment of the British position which was that neutral prizes must either be taken into the captor's ports or released. There was nothing in the Article to ensure the prevention of the destruction of neutral prizes for it was by no means certain that neutrals would allow them to be brought into their ports, and there were often cases where, even if the permission were granted, belligerents could not avail themselves of it. There would, furthermore, be a danger to the neutral in admitting prizes into its ports, a belligerent would not view it with indifference and complications would ensue; the neutral, it was true, had the option of closing his ports, but it might be difficult to exercise it[1]. Sir Ernest Satow's speech failed to convince the Committee and the Article was carried by 9 votes to 2 (Great Britain and Japan) with 5 abstentions. At the meeting of the Examining Committee on the 28th September several Powers which previously voted for this Article spoke against its retention, and at the full meeting of the Third Committee on the 4th October its suppression was moved by the Swedish delegate (M. de Hammarskjöld) on the ground that certain states had only consented to assume the onerous responsibility it imposed on them for the purpose of enabling an agreement to be reached regarding the destruction of neutral prizes; that agreement not having been obtained the *raison d'être* of the Article failed. The Article was however maintained by 29 to 7 (Denmark, Spain, Great Britain, Japan, Norway, Portugal and Sweden) with 6 abstentions (the United States, China, Cuba, Luxemburg, Persia and Switzerland)[2].

The Report points out that neutral states are left free to admit prizes or not. Article 23 only says that their neutrality is not compromised if they do admit them and keep them; they can make such arrangements as regards their conservation as they think fit, and remove them to the port most convenient to themselves. The Prize Court referred to in this Article is the National Prize Court of the captor, not the International Prize Court[3].

Great Britain and Japan who throughout opposed this Article have reserved it on signing the Convention.

[1] *La Deux. Confér.* T. III. p. 1069.   [2] *Ibid.* pp. 481–2.   [3] *Ibid.* T. I. p. 321.

Article 24 enacts a generally recognised rule of international law by providing that if a belligerent war-ship does not leave a neutral port after notification by the neutral Power, such Power is entitled to take such measures as it considers necessary to render it incapable of putting to sea during the continuation of the war, and the commander of the ship is to facilitate the execution of such measures. The Article however is not mandatory in form. The only divergence of opinion was with reference to the treatment of the officers and crew : they are to be detained, not interned ; but a sufficient number must be left on board to look after the vessel. This provision was inserted on the proposition of Count Tornielli, but objected to by Great Britain and Japan who preferred to leave the matter to the neutral[1]. The last paragraph relating to the position of officers is similar to 5 H. C. 1907, Art. 11, par. 3[2].

Refusal of belligerent war-ships to quit neutral ports.

The third Rule of the Treaty of Washington was as follows: "A neutral government is bound :...Thirdly, To exercise due diligence in its own ports and waters and as to all persons within its jurisdiction, to prevent any violation of the foregoing obligations and duties." Article 25 embodies this principle, which met with no opposition. The words "due diligence," the meaning of which occasioned such divergent interpretations, are replaced by "such vigilance as the means at its disposal permit." This formula was suggested by the delegates of Holland and Belgium in the place of "all needful diligence" which the Committee had originally proposed[3]. The change of phrase is happy and will, it is hoped, occasion no difficulty in its interpretation. By this Article the incorporation of the principles of the Three Rules of the Treaty of Washington into a great International Act is completed.

Neutral vigilance.

The Japanese delegate proposed the following: "A neutral state, if it deems it necessary for the better safeguarding of its neutrality, is free to maintain or establish stricter rules than those provided by the present Convention[4]." The Report states that the need for this Article was doubted as the basis of the Convention is the sovereignty of the neutral state. Various Articles reserve the right to the neutral Power to issue more stringent rules, e.g. Articles 9, 12, 15 and 23. The only thing required is that a neutral should accord the same treatment to both belligerents. The proposal was rejected by 10 votes to 3, with

Japanese proposal regarding more stringent neutrality regulations

---

[1] *La Deux. Confér.* T. I. pp. 322–3.
[2] For instances of ships and crews so detained see *ante*, p. 474.
[3] *La Deux. Confér.* T. III. p. 639.   [4] *Ibid.* T. I. p. 323; T. III. pp. 639, 728.

2 abstentions. At the second reading of the Draft Convention the Japanese delegate accepted the withdrawal of his Article, with the reserve that Japan will always deem itself entitled to maintain the interpretation which he had given.

Article 26 embodies a proposal of the Russian delegate stating that the exercise by a neutral Power of the rights laid down in the Convention [including presumedly the right of issuing more stringent regulations than those expressed therein] can under no circumstances be considered as an unfriendly act by either belligerent who has accepted the Articles referring thereto. It is well that this principle should clearly be laid down as it affords assistance to neutrals availing themselves of the provisions of the Convention.

Article 27 which has already been referred to was proposed by the Russian delegate at the termination of the discussion of the Draft Convention. Various Articles refer to regulations, laws, ordinances etc., to be issued by the contracting parties, the advisability of these being brought to the notice of the latter was recognised and this Article was adopted without any opposition.

Communication of neutral regulations.

The Convention is, like the other Conventions, preceded by a preamble, the acceptance of which was not effected till several explanations had been made by the Reporter, which are for the most part embodied in the Report[1]. The third paragraph refers to the impossibility of concerting measures applicable to all circumstances which may arise; this it is pointed out does not leave such cases to the arbitrary will of the parties; account must be taken of the general principles of the law of nations, e.g. the expression "territorial waters" is nowhere defined. In paragraph 5, the desirability of Powers issuing "*prescriptions précises*" is referred to, and in Article 27 the duty of mutual communication of these "*prescriptions*" is enjoined. The word is a general one allowing each Government to make use of the form best suited to its constitutional institutions. The seventh paragraph states that the rules which neutrals have issued should not, in principle, be changed during the war except in cases where experience has shown the necessity of such change for the protection of the Power making it. The presence of belligerent war-ships in certain of its ports may be found to cause inconvenience to the neutral Power, they may be forbidden to enter, or their length of stay shortened. The first draft only provided for the issue by neutrals of *more rigorous measures*; the existing form resulted from an adverse vote. Sir Ernest

The preamble.

---

[1] *Parl. Papers*, Misc. No. 4 (1908), p. 256; *La Deux. Confér.* T. I. p. 825.

Satow stated that he could not conceive cases where it would be necessary to take *less rigorous measures*, but the Russian delegate (M. Tcharykow) thought the eventuality possible. Sir Ernest Satow and M. Tsudzuki, after the vote, asked that it should be mentioned that in their opinion cases could not be conceived where a neutral state would be obliged to take *less rigorous measures* in the course of the war for the preservation of its rights, whilst the English doctrine had always recognised that neutrals had the right, for this purpose, to lay down more rigorous measures[1]. This accords with the Japanese reservation already mentioned.

At the Eighth Plenary Meeting of the Conference on the 9th October, 1907, various reservations were made. Sir Edward Fry for Great Britain made a reservation on the whole Convention, the Greek, Japanese, Spanish and United States delegates did the same. The Persian, Siamese, Turkish, German, Russian and Dominican delegates made reservations on several Articles. Great Britain, the United States, Cuba, Spain, Greece, Japan and Portugal abstained from voting; the states previously mentioned voted with reservations.

The following states have not signed this Convention: the United

Signatory Powers and reservations.
States of America, China, Cuba, Spain and Nicaragua. The following states made reservations on signing:

Germany, Articles 11, 12, 13 and 20.

Dominican Republic, Article 12.

Great Britain, Articles 19 and 23.

Japan, Articles 19 and 23.

Persia, Articles 12, 19 and 21.

Siam, Articles 12, 19 and 23.

Turkey under reserve of the Declaration as regards the Bosphorus and Dardanelles already mentioned.

The foregoing Convention was formulated after a long and laborious

The value of the Convention.
examination of various drafts, and of the rules of neutrality adopted in different countries, rules which were found to be often contradictory. The subject of neutrality was "a welter of *Interessenfragen*," and the attempt to harmonise the conflicting elements was as Count Tornielli stated a "work of an order almost exclusively diplomatic." Compromise is the leading feature of the whole Convention. "The conciliation of interests can only be the result of mutual renunciations obtained by the conviction of acquiring equivalent advantages." The Convention is clearly only the beginning of a Code of

---

[1] *Parl. Papers*, Misc. No. 4 (1908), p. 256; *La Deux. Confér.* T. I. p. 326.

neutrality. "We do not flatter ourselves," said Count Tornielli, "that our work is complete or precise. We leave to our successors the task of revising it[1]." It is, however, of importance that so much was accomplished. The absolute duty of respect for neutral territory has been almost unanimously accepted. The twenty-four hours rule of stay, and the twenty-four hours interval have been generally accepted, but neutrals may increase these periods by special enactment. The adoption of these rules will afford considerable assistance in the future to a weak neutral. The three months interval of taking in supplies and fuel in the same neutral country has also been adopted, and there is no proviso for special regulations to the contrary. A neutral is also strengthened in his duty to dismantle belligerent ships failing to leave his ports after due notice. The Three Rules of the Treaty of Washington with wise modifications have now received almost universal acceptance.

The defects are however striking, viewing the Convention from a scientific standpoint. The rules laid down are nearly all accompanied by provisoes enabling them to be excluded by a neutral strong enough and sufficiently interested to do so. The rights of neutrals are asserted, but their duties are not sufficiently emphasised. A neutral Power may allow belligerents to remain in his ports for an unlimited period, and he may allow prizes to be brought within his ports for the purpose of awaiting the decision of a Prize Court—a provision which in effect may nullify the prohibition to bring them in except on account of unseaworthiness, stress of weather or want of fuel or provisions. A friendly neutral Power in the neighbourhood of a great trade route may thus afford most valuable assistance to a belligerent, by enabling him quickly to disembarrass himself of his captures, leave them in safe keeping, and again sally forth to prey on the commerce of his adversary. A neutral may also allow belligerent ships to take in enough coal to fill their ordinary bunkers, irrespective of the distance they may be from ports of their own country or the objects for which the supply is taken on board[2]. Clearly there will be work for the next Conference to revise the labours of its predecessor in these and other respects.

---

[1] See speech of Count Tornielli at the Meeting of the Third Committee on the 4th Oct. 1907. (*La Deux. Confér.* T. III. pp. 484–5.)

[2] The permission to belligerent vessels *compléter le plein de leurs soutes proprement dites*, is in effect a permission to allow an increase in the defensive power of the ship, as the main belt of the armour of warships is often backed up by the coal bunkers.

LES DÉCLARATIONS DE 1899 ET 1907.

1899

DÉCLARATION I.
Des Projectiles et des Explosifs du Haut de Ballons.

Les soussignés, Plénipotentiaires des Puissances représentées à la Conférence Internationale de la Paix à La Haye, dûment autorisés à cet effet par leurs Gouvernements,

S'inspirant des sentiments qui ont trouvé leur expression dans la Déclaration de Saint-Pétersbourg du 29 novembre (11 décembre), 1868,

Déclarent :

Les Puissances contractantes consentent, pour une durée de cinq ans, à l'interdiction de lancer des projectiles et des explosifs du haut de ballons ou par d'autres modes analogues nouveaux.

La présente Déclaration n'est obligatoire que pour les Puissances contractantes, en cas de guerre entre deux ou plusieurs d'entre elles.

Elle cessera d'être obligatoire du moment où dans une guerre entre des Puissances contractantes, une Puissance non-contractante se joindrait à l'un des belligérants.

1907

XIV. Déclaration relative à l'Interdiction de lancer des Projectiles et des Explosifs du Haut de Ballons.

Les soussignés, Plénipotentiaires des Puissances *conviées* à la *Deuxième* Conférence Internationale de la Paix à La Haye, dûment autorisés à cet effet par leurs Gouvernements,

S'inspirant des sentiments qui ont trouvé leur expression dans la Déclaration de Saint-Pétersbourg du 29 novembre (11 décembre), 1868, *et désirant renouveler la Déclaration de la Haye du 29 juillet, 1899, arrivée à expiration,*

Déclarent :

Les Puissances contractantes consentent, *pour une période allant jusqu'à la fin de la Troisième Conférence de la Paix,* à l'interdiction de lancer des projectiles et des explosifs du haut de ballons ou par d'autres modes analogues nouveaux.

La présente Déclaration n'est obligatoire que pour les Puissances contractantes, en cas de guerre entre deux ou plusieurs d'entre elles.

Elle cessera d'être obligatoire du moment où, dans une guerre entre des Puissances contractantes, une Puissance non-contractante se joindrait à l'un des belligérants.

The Declarations of 1899 and 1907.

1899

Declaration I.
Projectiles and Explosives from Balloons.

The Undersigned, Plenipotentiaries of the Powers represented at the International Peace Conference at The Hague, duly authorized to that effect by their Governments,

Inspired by the sentiments which found expression in the Declaration of St Petersburg of the 29th November (11th December), 1868,

Declare :

The Contracting Powers agree to prohibit, for a term of five years, the discharge of projectiles and explosives from balloons or by other new methods of a similar nature.

The present Declaration is only binding on the Contracting Powers in case of war between two or more of them.

It shall cease to be binding from the time when, in a war between the Contracting Powers, one of the belligerents is joined by a non-Contracting Power.

1907

XIV. Declaration prohibiting the Discharge of Projectiles and Explosives from Balloons.

The Undersigned, Plenipotentiaries of the Powers *invited* to the *Second* International Peace Conference at The Hague, duly authorized to that effect by their Governments,

Inspired by the sentiments which found expression in the Declaration of St Petersburg of the 29th November (11th December), 1868, *and being desirous of renewing the Declaration of The Hague of the 29th July, 1899, which has now expired,*

Declare :

The Contracting Powers agree to prohibit, *for a period extending to the close of the Third Peace Conference,* the discharge of projectiles and explosives from balloons or by other new methods of a similar nature.

The present Declaration is only binding on the Contracting Powers in case of war between two or more of them.

It shall cease to be binding from the time when, in a war between the Contracting Powers, one of the belligerents is joined by a non-Contracting Power.

1899	1907
La présente Déclaration sera ratifiée dans le plus bref délai possible.	La présente Déclaration sera ratifiée dans le plus bref délai possible.
Les ratifications seront déposées à La Haye.	Les ratifications seront déposées à La Haye.
Il sera dressé du dépôt de chaque ratification un procès-verbal, dont une copie, certifiée conforme, sera remise par la voie diplomatique à toutes les Puissances contractantes.	Il sera dressé du dépôt des ratifications un procès-verbal, dont une copie, certifiée conforme, sera remise par la voie diplomatique à toutes les Puissances contractantes.
Les Puissances non-signataires pourront adhérer à la présente Déclaration. Elles auront, à cet effet, à faire connaître leur adhésion aux Puissances contractantes, au moyen d'une notification écrite, adressée au Gouvernement des Pays-Bas et communiquée par celui-ci à toutes les autres Puissances contractantes.	Les Puissances non-signataires pourront adhérer à la présente Déclaration. Elles auront, à cet effet, à faire connaître leur adhésion aux Puissances contractantes, au moyen d'une notification écrite, adressée au Gouvernement des Pays-Bas et communiquée par celui-ci à toutes les autres Puissances contractantes.
S'il arrivait qu'une des Hautes Parties contractantes dénonçât la présente Déclaration, cette dénonciation ne produirait ses effets qu'un an après la notification faite par écrit au Gouvernement des Pays-Bas et communiquée immédiatement par celui-ci à toutes les autres Puissances contractantes.	S'il arrivait qu'une des Hautes Parties contractantes dénonçât la présente Déclaration, cette dénonciation ne produirait ses effets qu'un an après la notification faite par écrit au Gouvernement des Pays-Bas et communiquée immédiatement par celui-ci à toutes les autres Puissances contractantes.
Cette dénonciation ne produira ses effets qu'à l'égard de la Puissance qui l'aura notifiée.	Cette dénonciation ne produira ses effets qu'à l'égard de la Puissance qui l'aura notifiée.
En foi de quoi, les Plénipotentiaires ont signé la présente Déclaration et l'ont revêtu de leurs cachets.	En foi de quoi, les Plénipotentiaires ont revêtu la présente Déclaration de leurs signatures.
Fait à La Haye, le 29 Juillet, 1899, en un seul exemplaire, qui restera déposé dans les archives du Gouvernement des Pays-Bas et dont des copies, certifiées conformes, seront remises par la voie diplomatique aux Puissances contractantes.	Fait à La Haye, le *18 Octobre, 1907*, en un seul exemplaire, qui restera déposé dans les archives du Gouvernement des Pays-Bas et dont des copies, certifiées conformes, seront remises par la voie diplomatique aux Puissances contractantes.

1899	1907

The present Declaration shall be ratified as soon as possible.

The ratifications shall be deposited at The Hague.

A *procès-verbal* shall be drawn up on the receipt of each ratification, of which a duly certified copy shall be sent through the diplomatic channel to all the Contracting Powers.

Non-Signatory Powers may accede to the present Declaration. For this purpose they must make known their accession to the Contracting Powers by means of a written notification addressed to the Netherland Government, and communicated by it to all the other Contracting Powers.

In the event of one of the High Contracting Parties denouncing the present Declaration, such denunciation shall not take effect until a year after the notification made in writing to the Netherland Government, and forthwith communicated by it to all the other Contracting Powers.

This denunciation shall only affect the notifying Power.

In faith whereof the Plenipotentiaries have signed the present Declaration, and affixed their seals thereto.

Done at The Hague the 29th July, 1899, in a single copy, which shall remain deposited in the archives of the Netherland Government, and of which duly certified copies shall be sent through the diplomatic channel to the Contracting Powers.

The present Declaration shall be ratified as soon as possible.

The ratifications shall be deposited at The Hague.

A *procès-verbal* shall be drawn up on the receipt of each ratification, of which a duly certified copy shall be sent through the diplomatic channel to all the Contracting Powers.

Non-Signatory Powers may accede to the present Declaration. For this purpose they must make known their accession to the Contracting Powers by means of a written notification, addressed to the Netherland Government, and communicated by it to all the other Contracting Powers.

In the event of one of the High Contracting Parties denouncing the present Declaration, such denunciation shall not take effect until a year after the notification made in writing to the Netherland Government, and forthwith communicated by it to all the other Contracting Powers.

This denunciation shall only affect the notifying Power.

In faith whereof the Plenipotentiaries have signed the present Declaration.

Done at The Hague, the *18th October, 1907*, in a single copy, which shall remain deposited in the archives of the Netherland Government, and of which duly certified copies shall be sent, through the diplomatic channel, to the Contracting Powers.

I.   Declaration prohibiting the discharge of projectiles and explosives from balloons[1].

The Circular of Count Mouravieff of the 11th June, 1899, suggested as one of the topics for the consideration of the First Peace Conference "the restriction of the explosives already existing, and the prohibition of the discharge of projectiles or explosives of any kind from balloons or by any similar means[2]." The subject was taken into consideration by the First Committee under the presidency of M. Beernaert and the foregoing Declaration was adopted.   Notwithstanding the strenuous attempt of Captain Crozier, the United States delegate, to make the Declaration one of a permanent character, it was only accepted for a period of five years, which expired on the 4th September, 1905.   Count Benckendorff's Circular suggested the reconsideration of the matter by the Second Peace Conference and the Belgian delegate introduced the topic by moving the renewal of the Declaration in the same terms as in 1899[3].   The subject was considered by the Second Committee over which M. Beernaert presided, when amendments were introduced by the Russian and Italian delegates.

The Russian amendment was "to replace the general and temporary prohibition by a permanent restriction prohibiting the discharge from balloons of projectiles or explosives against undefended towns, villages, houses or buildings[4]."   The Italian amendment was to the same effect as the Russian and was with a view of rendering the Declaration permanent, whereas the Belgian proposal was to renew the Declaration for a further period of five years; it further required that a balloon to be employed in operations of war should be "*dirigeable et monté par un équipage militaire.*"

The object of the Russian amendment was ultimately attained by the insertion in Article 25 of the Regulations for the law of war on land of the prohibition to attack or bombard undefended towns, villages etc., *by any means whatever*[5].

[1] *Conférence internationale de la Paix*, 1899, Part II. First Committee, p. 49; De Martens, *Nouveau Recueil de Traités* (2nd series), Vol. XXVI. p. 994; *La Deux. Confér.* T. I. pp. 87, 104; T. III. pp. 15, 148–159, 252; *Parl. Papers*, Misc. No. 4 (1908), pp. 25, 106–8; *Livre Jaune*, p. 77; *Weissbuch*, p. 7; Bonfils-Fauchille, *Le Droit international*, pp. 859–863 (with bibliography on the subject of *La guerre aérienne*); G. B. Davis, *The amelioration of the rules of war on land*, *Amer. Journ. of Inter. Law*, Vol. II. p. 74; Idem, *The launching of projectiles from balloons*, Vol. II. p. 528; Idem, *Elements of International Law* (3rd ed.), pp. 547–550; E. Lémonon, *La seconde Conférence de la Paix*, pp. 382–394; J. Westlake, *War*, p. 274; R. P. Hearne, *Aerial warfare*; T. E. Holland, *The laws of war on land*, pp. 41, 81, 123; J. D. Scott, *The Hague Peace Conferences*, Vol. I. p. 649.

[2] See *ante*, p. 40.

[3] See *La Deux. Confér.* T. III. p. 252.   [4] *Ibid.* T. I. p. 104; T. III. p. 15.

[5] See *ante*, p. 269; see also *La Deux. Confér.* T. III. p. 16.

The discussion on the various projects took place at the meeting of the First Sub-Committee of the Second Committee on the 7th August, 1907[1]. The developments in the science of aerostatics since 1899 caused several states which had supported the Declaration in 1899 either to refrain from voting or to oppose the proposal. The French delegate (M. Renault) pointed out that it was an unlawful act to bombard churches, hospitals etc. in whatever way the explosives were fired, but that it was perfectly lawful to endeavour to destroy arsenals, barracks etc., whether the explosives were discharged from cannon or balloon. The problem of aerial navigation was progressing so rapidly that he was not prepared to forego the advantage of profiting by new discoveries which did not in any way tend to make the conduct of war less humane[2].

The Belgian delegate urged the renewal of the Declaration to show the humanitarian spirit of the Congress by giving the lie to those who affirmed that it had only been accepted in 1899 because at the time the science of aerostatics was so little advanced that there was then no chance of balloons being used for the purpose of discharging explosives[3].

Lord Reay asked if it was not enough to have two elements in which nations might give free course to their animosities and settle their quarrels, without adding a third. Anticipating the subject of the limitation of expenditure on armaments he urged that a beginning might be made with regard to instruments of aerial warfare. Nations were already groaning under the increasing burdens of naval and military armaments, let the Conference act, he said, while there was yet time and thus prohibit a new scourge more terrible in its effect than the instruments of war whose field of action they were endeavouring to limit[4].

The Belgian proposal was carried in Committee by 28 votes (2 of these, Germany and Roumania, being conditional on unanimity) to 6 (the Argentine Republic, Spain, France, Montenegro, Persia and Russia); 10 countries not being represented.

The question was then raised as to whether the Russian proposal should be put, but on Count Tornielli moving the Italian proposal, M. Tcharykow accepted its principle. This proposal consisted of two Articles: (1) It is forbidden to discharge projectiles and explosives from balloons which are not dirigible and sent up by a military force. (2) The bombardment

---

[1] *La Deux. Confér.* T. III. pp. 150–9.   [2] *Ibid.* p. 152.

[3] *Ibid.* p. 153. See the remarks of M. de Lapradelle on this subject in *La Revue générale de Droit international public*, 1899, p. 691.

[4] *La Deux. Confér.* p. 153.

by military balloons is subject to the same restrictions accepted for land and sea warfare in so far as this is compatible with the new method of fighting[1]. The German delegate pointed out that the Italian proposal dealt with two distinct matters and asked that a division should be taken on each. He said that as regards the first it was possible to discharge projectiles from balloons which were not dirigible, and further there was no connection between the power to direct balloons and that of discharging projectiles from them[2]. The 1st Article of the Italian amendment was carried by 21 votes to 8 with 6 abstentions, Article 2 was also carried by 31 votes to 1 with 3 abstentions[3].

The matter came before the full meeting of the Second Committee on the 14th August, when the French proposal for the addition of the words " *by any means whatever* " was made to Article 25 of the " Regulations " of 4 H. C. 1907, and the Declaration in the form proposed by the Belgian delegate was recommended to the Conference[4].

The Report was considered at the Fourth Plenary Meeting of the Conference on the 17th August, when Sir Edward Fry moved to replace the words " for a period of five years," recommended by the Commission, by the words "until the termination of the Third Peace Conference." This was carried by 28 to 8 with 8 abstentions[5]; but the renewal of the Declaration for a period of five years was also carried by 29 to 8 with 7 abstentions. In presenting his Report on the drafting of the Final Act at the Tenth Plenary Meeting of the Conference on the 17th October, 1907, M. Renault recalled the fact that the Declaration was voted by 29 for, 8 against and 7 abstentions. It may be asked, he said, why it should appear in the Final Act, as it was not accepted unanimously. The answer was that the Drafting Committee had, before inserting it in the Final Act, ascertained that the states voting against it raised no objection to this proceeding[6]. Nothing is said in the Report regarding the fact that the Belgian form of the Declaration received a larger number of votes than the British, but the Declaration stands in the form proposed by Sir Edward Fry, and in this form it has been signed.

---

[1] *La Deux. Confér.* T. III. p. 155.   [2] *Ibid.* p. 157.   [3] *Ibid.* pp. 158–9.

[4] *Ibid.* p. 16. See *ante*, pp. 269–270. The first paragraph of Article 1 of 9 H. C. 1907, which forbids the bombardment by naval forces of undefended ports, towns, villages, dwellings or buildings, does not contain the words " by any means whatever." From the discussions in the Sub-Committee it would appear that the members considered that the discharge of projectiles from balloons whether by a military or naval force was governed by the same rules. (See Article 2 of the Italian proposal.)

[5] *Ibid.* T. I. pp. 87–8.   [6] *Ibid.* T. I. p. 583.

The Declaration has been signed by 27 states out of the 44 present at
the Conference. The following have not signed: Germany, **Signatory** **Powers.** Chili, Denmark, Spain, France, Guatemala, Italy, Japan, Mexico, Montenegro, Nicaragua, Paraguay, Roumania, Russia, Servia, Sweden and Venezuela.

With the exception of Austria-Hungary, all the great European military Powers have refused to agree to the prohibition contained in this Declaration. A great opportunity of making a beginning in the restriction of expenditure on armaments has thus been lost, and the allegations of those to whom the Belgian delegate referred have not been answered. The bombardment of undefended towns etc. by projectiles from balloons is not a legitimate act of warfare, but 17 states retain the right to make use of this method of warfare against such places as do not come under that undefined description.

DECLARATION II (1899).

Des Gaz Asphyxiants ou Délétères.

Les soussignés, Plénipotentiaires des Puissances représentées à la Conférence Internationale de la Paix à La Haye, dûment autorisés à cet effet par leurs Gouvernements,

S'inspirant des sentiments qui ont trouvé leur expression dans la Déclaration de Saint-Pétersbourg du 29 novembre (11 décembre), 1868,

Déclarent:

Les Puissances contractantes s'interdisent l'emploi de projectiles qui ont pour but unique de répandre des gaz asphyxiants ou délétères.

La présente Déclaration n'est obligatoire que pour les Puissances contractantes, en cas de guerre entre deux ou plusieurs d'entre elles.

Elle cessera d'être obligatoire du moment où, dans une guerre entre des Puissances contractantes, une Puis-

Asphyxiating or Deleterious Gases.

The Undersigned, Plenipotentiaries of the Powers represented at the International Peace Conference at the Hague duly authorized to that effect by their Governments,

Inspired by the sentiments which found expression in the Declaration of St Petersburg of the 29th November (11th December), 1868,

Declare:

The Contracting Powers agree to abstain from the use of projectiles the sole object of which is the diffusion of asphyxiating or deleterious gases.

The present Declaration is only binding on the Contracting Powers in the case of a war between two or more of them.

It shall cease to be binding from the time when, in a war between the Contracting Powers, one of the belli-

sance non-contractante se joindrait à l'un des belligérants.

La présente Déclaration sera ratifiée dans le plus bref délai possible.

Les ratifications seront déposées à La Haye.

Il sera dressé du dépôt de chaque ratification un procès-verbal, dont une copie, certifiée conforme, sera remise par la voie diplomatique à toutes les Puissances contractantes.

Les Puissances non-signataires pourront adhérer à la présente Déclaration. Elles auront, à cet effet, à faire connaître leur adhésion aux Puissances contractantes, au moyen d'une notification écrite, adressée au Gouvernement des Pays-Bas et communiquée par celui-ci à toutes les autres Puissances contractantes.

S'il arrivait qu'une des Hautes Parties contractantes dénonçât la présente Déclaration, cette dénonciation ne produirait ses effets qu'un an après la notification faite par écrit au Gouvernement des Pays-Bas et communiquée immédiatement par celui-ci à toutes les autres Puissances contractantes.

Cette dénonciation ne produira ses effets qu'à l'égard de la Puissance qui l'aura notifiée.

En foi de quoi, les Plénipotentiaires ont signé la présente Déclaration et l'ont revêtu de leurs cachets.

Fait à La Haye, le 29 Juillet, 1899, en un seul exemplaire, qui restera déposé dans les archives du Gouvernement des Pays-Bas et dont des copies, certifiées conformes, seront remises par la voie diplomatique aux Puissances contractantes.

gerents shall be joined by a non-Contracting Power.

The present Declaration shall be ratified as soon as possible.

The ratifications shall be deposited at the Hague.

A *procès-verbal* shall be drawn up on the receipt of each ratification, of which a duly certified copy shall be sent through the diplomatic channel to all the Contracting Powers.

Non-Signatory Powers can accede to the present Declaration. For this purpose they must make their accession known to the Contracting Powers by means of a written notification addressed to the Netherland Government, and by it communicated to all the other Contracting Powers.

In the event of one of the High Contracting Parties denouncing the present Declaration, such denunciation shall not take effect until a year after the notification made in writing to the Government of the Netherlands, and forthwith communicated by it to all the other Contracting Powers.

This denunciation shall only affect the notifying Power.

In faith of which the Plenipotentiaries have signed the present Declaration, and affixed their seals thereto.

Done at the Hague, the 29th July, 1899, in a single copy, which shall be kept in the archives of the Netherland Government, and copies of which, duly certified, shall be sent by the diplomatic channel to the Contracting Powers.

II. DECLARATION PROHIBITING THE USE OF ASPHYXIATING OR DELETERIOUS GASES[1].

The question of the prohibition of new kinds of explosives was considered by the First Committee of the Conference of 1899, and the Russian delegate expressed the opinion that the use of asphyxiating gases was barbarous and on the same footing as the poisoning of a river. Captain Mahan, the United States naval delegate, opposed this view and gave the following reasons for voting against the prohibition: "(1) That no shell emitting such gases is as yet in practical use or has undergone adequate experiment; consequently, a vote taken now would be taken in ignorance of the facts as to whether the results would be of a decisive character, or whether injury in excess of that necessary to attain the end of warfare, of immediately disabling the enemy, would be inflicted. (2) That the reproach addressed against those supposed shells was equally uttered formerly against firearms and torpedoes, although each is now employed without scruple. Until we know the effects of such asphyxiating shells, there was no saying whether they would be more or less merciful than missiles now permitted. (3) That it was illogical and not demonstrably humane to be tender about asphyxiating men with gas, when all were prepared to admit that it was allowable to blow the bottom out of an ironclad at midnight, throwing four or five hundred men into the sea to be asphyxiated by water, with barely the remotest chance of escape. If, and when, a shell emitting asphyxiating gases has been successfully produced, then and not before, will men be able to vote intelligently on the subject[2]."

The British naval delegate (Admiral Sir John Fisher) supported the prohibition on the understanding that the vote was unanimous. When the question was reconsidered Captain Mahan declined to withdraw his negative vote and Sir Julian Pauncefote voted with him[3].

This Declaration remained unsigned by both Great Britain and the United States until the commencement of the Second Peace Conference, when Sir Edward Fry was instructed to sign it on behalf of the British Government[4], but the United States have not signed. It has been signed by all the other Powers represented at the First Peace Conference but not by those which were represented only at the Second.

[1] De Martens, *Recueil Nouveau de Traités* (2nd series), Vol. xxvi. p. 998; *Parl. Papers*, Misc. No. 1 (1899), pp. 81, 181; F. W. Holls, *The Peace Conference at the Hague*, p. 118.

[2] *Parl. Papers*, Misc. No. 1 (1899), p. 81; F. W. Holls, *op. cit.* p. 119.

[3] *Parl. Papers*, Misc. No. 1 (1899), pp. 181–2.

[4] *Parl. Papers*, Misc. No. 1 (1907), p. 26; *La Deux. Confér.* T. i. p. 89.

DECLARATION III (1899).

Des Balles à Enveloppe Dure etc.

Les soussignés, Plénipotentiaires des Puissances représentées à la Conférence Internationale de la Paix à La Haye, dûment autorisés à cet effet par leurs Gouvernements,

S'inspirant des sentiments qui ont trouvé leur expression dans la Déclaration de Saint-Pétersbourg du 29 novembre (11 décembre), 1868,

Déclarent :

Les Puissances contractantes s'interdisent l'emploi de balles qui s'épanouissent ou s'aplatissent facilement dans le corps humain, telles que les balles à enveloppe dure dont l'enveloppe ne couvrirait pas entièrement le noyau ou serait pourvue d'incisions.

La présente Déclaration n'est obligatoire que pour les Puissances contractantes, en cas de guerre entre deux ou plusieurs d'entre elles.

Elle cessera d'être obligatoire du moment où, dans une guerre entre des Puissances contractantes, une Puissance non-contractante se joindrait à l'un des belligérants.

La présente Déclaration sera ratifiée dans le plus bref délai possible.

Les ratifications seront déposées à La Haye.

Il sera dressé du dépôt de chaque ratification un procès-verbal, dont une copie, certifiée conforme, sera remise par la voie diplomatique à toutes les Puissances contractantes.

Les Puissances non-signataires pourront adhérer à la présente Déclaration. Elles auront, à cet effet, à faire connaître leur adhésion aux Puissances

Bullets with a Hard Envelope etc.

The Undersigned, Plenipotentiaries of the Powers represented at the International Peace Conference at the Hague, duly authorized to that effect by their Governments,

Inspired by the sentiments which found expression in the Declaration of St Petersburg of the 29th November (11th December), 1868,

Declare :

The Contracting Parties agree to abstain from the use of bullets which expand or flatten easily in the human body, such as bullets with a hard envelope which does not entirely cover the core, or is pierced with incisions.

The present Declaration is only binding for the Contracting Powers in the case of a war between two or more of them.

It shall cease to be binding from the time when, in a war between the Contracting Powers, one of the belligerents is joined by a non-Contracting Power.

The present Declaration shall be ratified as soon as possible.

The ratifications shall be deposited at the Hague.

A *procès-verbal* shall be drawn up on the receipt of each ratification, a copy of which, duly certified, shall be sent through the diplomatic channel to all the Contracting Powers.

Non-Signatory Powers may accede to the present Declaration. For this purpose they must make their accession known to the Contracting

contractantes, au moyen d'une notification écrite, adressée au Gouvernement des Pays-Bas et communiquée
par celui-ci à toutes les autres Puissances contractantes.

S'il arrivait qu'une des Hautes
Parties contractantes dénonçât la présente Déclaration, cette dénonciation
ne produirait ses effets qu'un an après
la notification faite par écrit au
Gouvernement des Pays-Bas et communiquée immédiatement par celui-ci
à toutes les autres Puissances contractantes.

Cette dénonciation ne produira ses
effets qu'à l'égard de la Puissance qui
l'aura notifiée.

En foi de quoi, les Plénipotentiaires
ont signé la présente Déclaration et
l'ont revêtu de leurs cachets.

Fait à La Haye, le 29 Juillet, 1899,
en un seul exemplaire, qui restera
déposé dans les archives du Gouvernement des Pays-Bas et dont des copies,
certifiées conformes, seront remises par
la voie diplomatique aux Puissances
contractantes.

Powers by means of a written notification addressed to the Netherland
Government, and by it communicated
to all the other Contracting Powers.

In the event of one of the High
Contracting Parties denouncing the
present Declaration, such denunciation
shall not take effect until a year after
the notification made in writing to the
Netherland Government, and forthwith communicated by it to all the
other Contracting Powers.

This denunciation shall only affect
the notifying Power.

In faith of which the Plenipotentiaries have signed the present Declaration, and have affixed their seals
thereto.

Done at the Hague the 29th July,
1899, in a single copy, which shall be
kept in the archives of the Netherland
Government, and of which copies, duly
certified, shall be sent through the
diplomatic channel to the Contracting
Powers.

III. DECLARATION PROHIBITING THE USE OF EXPANDING BULLETS[1].

The discussions leading to the adoption of this Declaration at the First
Peace Conference showed considerable difference of opinion among the
delegates. The chief opponents were the British and United States
delegates. It was recognised by the delegates of both Powers that the
use of bullets inflicting unnecessarily severe wounds should be prohibited,

---

[1] De Martens, *Nouveau Recueil de Traités* (2nd series), Vol. XXVI. p. 1002; *Parl. Papers*,
Misc. No. 1 (1899), pp. 62, 88, 118, 169, 179, 182–5, 192–4, 218, 260; T. E. Holland, *The
laws of war on land*, p. 42; F. W. Holls, *op. cit.* pp. 99–117; G. B. Davis, *International Law*,
p. 547; E. Lémonon, *La seconde Conférence*, p. 387.

and Captain Crozier (United States) moved an amendment to this effect, but his only supporter was the British delegate[1]. The British view was expressed in a letter from the War Office to Lord Salisbury which the latter communicated to Sir Julian Pauncefote, and in which it was pointed out that experience in the Chitral campaign had demonstrated that a bullet with a hard covering had not sufficient stopping power, and the British Government was not prepared to give up the use of the bullet known as the " Mark iv " pattern as it possessed the minimum of destructive effect and did not inflict unnecessary suffering. For this reason the Indian Government had adopted the Dum-dum[2] bullet, in which a very small portion of the head of the leaden bullet is not covered by a hard metal envelope[3]. It was clear that this bullet was the one at which the prohibition was aimed, though no direct evidence was adduced that it was of the nature indicated by the Declaration.

On the outbreak of the Boer war " Mark iv " bullets were not served out to the British troops, and the occasional use of expanding bullets by the Boers led to energetic protests on the part of the British Commanders.

Until the opening of the Second Conference neither Great Britain, the United States nor Portugal had signed this Declaration, but at the Fourth Plenary Meeting on the 17th August, 1907, the delegates of Great Britain and Portugal intimated their accession[4].

At the meeting of the First Sub-Committee of the Second Committee the President stated that none of the signatory Powers had asked for revision, and therefore any discussion on the subject was out of order. The United States Delegation had however filed a proposal in the following terms : " *The use of bullets which inflict unnecessarily cruel wounds, such as explosive bullets, and in general every kind of bullet which exceeds the limit necessary for placing a man immediately* hors de combat, *should be forbidden*[5]." These were the terms of the United States amendment in 1899 which, owing to the curious method of procedure at the Conference, was never put to the vote. General G. B. Davis (United States) at the meeting of the Second Committee on the 14th August, 1907, drew attention to this proposal, and also to the ruling of the President at the meeting of the Sub-Committee in which he stated that as the modification or restriction of the Declaration did not appear in the programme of the Conference a

---

[1] *Parl. Papers*, Misc. No. 1 (1899), p. 183.
[2] So called from the Arsenal near Calcutta where the bullet was first made.
[3] See *Parl. Papers*, Misc. No. 1 (1899), p. 118.
[4] *La Deux. Confér.* T. i. p. 26; *Parl. Papers*, Misc. No. 4 (1907), p. 26.
[5] *Ibid.* T. iii. p. 251.

restrictive proposal of the United States was not connected with it[1]. He pointed out that his Delegation found it difficult to understand "that no one had asked for a revision of the Declaration[2]." No discussion of the subject was allowed by the Chairman.

The Declaration has been signed by all the states represented at the First Peace Conference except the United States: it has not been signed by those states which were represented only at the Second Peace Conference.

---

[1] *La Deux. Confér.* T. III. p. 159.

[2] *Ibid.* p. 17. General Davis in an Article on *The Declarations of* 1899, in the *Amer. Journ. of Inter. Law* (Vol. II. p. 76), discusses the proposition which he was not allowed to make at the Conference.

ANNEXE AU PREMIER VŒU ÉMIS PAR LA DEUXIÈME CONFÉRENCE DE LA PAIX[1].

Projét d'une Convention relative à l'Établissement d'une Cour de Justice Arbitrale.

Titre I.

Organisation de la Cour de justice arbitrale.

ART. 1.

Dans le but de faire progresser la cause de l'arbitrage, les Puissances contractantes conviennent d'organiser, sans porter atteinte à la Cour permanente d'arbitrage, une Cour de justice arbitrale, d'un accès libre et facile, réunissant des juges représentant les divers systèmes juridiques du monde, et capable d'assurer la continuité de la jurisprudence arbitrale.

ART. 2.

La Cour de Justice arbitrale se compose de juges et de juges suppléants choisis parmi les personnes jouissant de la plus haute considération morale et qui tous devront remplir les conditions requises, dans leurs pays respectifs, pour l'admission dans la haute magistrature, ou être des jurisconsultes d'une compétence notoire en matière de droit international.

[1] See *ante*, p. 66.

ANNEX TO THE FIRST WISH EXPRESSED BY THE SECOND PEACE CONFERENCE[2].

Draft Convention relative to the Creation of a Judicial Arbitration Court.

Part I.

Constitution of the Judicial Arbitration Court.

ART. 1.

With the view of promoting the cause of arbitration, the Contracting Powers agree to constitute, without derogation to the Permanent Court of Arbitration, a Judicial Arbitration Court, freely and easily accessible, composed of Judges representing the various juridical systems of the world, and capable of insuring continuity in arbitral jurisprudence.

ART. 2.

The Judicial Arbitration Court is composed of Judges and Deputy Judges chosen from persons of the highest moral reputation, and all fulfilling conditions qualifying them, in their respective countries, to occupy high legal posts, or be jurists of recognized competence in matters of international law.

[2] See *ante*, p. 67.

Les juges et les juges suppléants de la Cour sont choisis, autant que possible, parmi les membres de la Cour permanente d'arbitrage. Le choix sera fait dans les six mois qui suivront la ratification de la présente Convention.

The Judges and Deputy Judges of the Court are appointed, as far as possible, from the members of the Permanent Court of Arbitration. The appointment shall be made within the six months after the ratification of the present Convention.

Art. 3.

Les juges et les juges suppléants sont nommés pour une période de douze ans à compter de la date où la nomination aura été notifiée au Conseil administratif institué par la Convention pour le règlement pacifique des conflits internationaux. Leur mandat peut être renouvelé.

En cas de décès ou de démission d'un juge ou d'un juge suppléant, il est pourvu à son remplacement selon le mode fixé pour sa nomination. Dans ce cas, la nomination est faite pour une nouvelle période de douze ans.

Art. 3.

The Judges and Deputy Judges are appointed for a period of twelve years, reckoned from the date on which the appointment is notified to the Administrative Council created by the Convention for the Pacific Settlement of International Disputes. Their appointments can be renewed.

Should one of the Judges, or Deputy Judges, die or resign, the same procedure is followed in filling the vacancy as was followed in appointing him. In this case, the appointment is made for a fresh period of twelve years.

Art. 4.

Les juges de la Cour de justice arbitrale sont égaux entre eux et prennent rang d'après la date de la notification de leur nomination. La préséance appartient au plus âgé, au cas où la date est la même.

Les juges suppléants sont, dans l'exercice de leurs fonctions, assimilés aux juges titulaires. Toutefois, ils prennent rang après ceux-ci.

Art. 4.

The Judges of the Judicial Arbitration Court are equal amongst themselves, and rank according to the date of the notification of their appointment. The Judge who is senior in point of age takes precedence when the date of notification is the same.

The Deputy Judges are assimilated in the exercise of their functions to the Judges. They rank, however, after the latter.

Art. 5.

Les juges jouissent des privilèges et immunités diplomatiques dans l'exercice de leurs fonctions et en dehors de leurs pays.

Art. 5.

The Judges enjoy diplomatic privileges and immunities in the performance of their duties, and when outside their own country.

Avant de prendre possession de leur siège, les juges et les juges suppléants doivent, devant le Conseil administratif, prêter serment ou faire une affirmation solennelle d'exercer leurs fonctions avec impartialité et en toute conscience.

Before taking their seat, the Judges and Deputy Judges must take an oath, or make a solemn affirmation before the Administrative Council, to discharge their duties impartially and conscientiously.

Art. 6.

La Cour désigne annuellement trois juges qui forment une Délégation spéciale et trois autres destinés à les remplacer en cas d'empêchement. Ils peuvent être réélus. L'élection se fait au scrutin de liste. Sont considérés comme élus ceux qui réunissent le plus grand nombre de voix. La Délégation élit elle-même son Président, qui, à défaut d'une majorité, est désigné par le sort.

Un membre de la Délégation ne peut exercer ses fonctions quand la Puissance qui l'a nommé, ou dont il est le national, est une des Parties.

Les membres de la Délégation terminent les affaires qui leur ont été soumises, même au cas où la période pour laquelle ils ont été nommés juges serait expirée.

Art. 6.

The Court annually nominates three Judges to form a special Delegation and three more to replace them if the former are unable to act. They are eligible for re-election. The election is by ballot. The persons who secure the largest number of votes are considered elected. The Delegation itself elects its own President, who, in default of a majority, is appointed by lot.

A member of the Delegation cannot act when the Power which appointed him, or to which he belongs, is one of the parties.

The members of the Delegation are to conclude matters which have been submitted to them, even if the period for which they have been appointed Judges has expired.

Art. 7.

L'exercice des fonctions judiciaires est interdit au juge dans les affaires au sujet desquelles il aura, à un titre quelconque, concouru à la décision d'un Tribunal national, d'un Tribunal d'arbitrage, ou d'une Commission d'enquête, ou figuré dans l'instance comme conseil ou avocat d'une partie.

Aucun juge ne peut intervenir comme agent ou comme avocat devant la Cour de justice arbitrale ou la Cour permanente d'arbitrage, devant un

Art. 7.

A Judge may not exercise his judicial functions in any case in which he has, in any way whatever, taken part in the decision of a National Tribunal, of a Tribunal of Arbitration, or of a Commission of Inquiry, or has figured in the suit as counsel or advocate for one of the parties.

No Judge can act as agent or advocate before the Judicial Arbitration Court or the Permanent Court of Arbitration, before a Special Tribunal

Tribunal spécial d'arbitrage ou une Commission d'enquête, ni y agir pour une Partie en quelque qualité que ce soit, pendant toute la durée de son mandat.

of Arbitration or a Commission of Inquiry, nor act therein for one of the parties in any capacity whatsoever so long as his appointment lasts.

ART. 8.

La Cour élit son Président et son Vice-Président à la majorité absolue des suffrages exprimés. Après deux tours de scrutin, l'élection se fait à la majorité relative et, en cas de partage des voix, le sort décide.

ART. 8.

The Court elects its President and Vice-President by an absolute majority of the votes cast. After two ballots, the election is made by a bare majority and, in case the votes are equal, by lot.

ART. 9.

Les juges de la Cour de justice arbitrale reçoivent une indemnité annuelle de 6,000 florins néerlandais. Cette indemnité est payée à l'expiration de chaque semestre à dater du jour de la première réunion de la Cour.

Pendant l'exercice de leurs fonctions au cours des sessions ou dans les cas spéciaux prévus par la présente Convention, ils touchent une somme de 100 florins par jour. Il leur est alloué, en outre, une indemnité de voyage fixée d'après les règlements de leur pays. Les dispositions du présent alinéa s'appliquent aussi aux juges suppléants remplaçant les juges.

Ces allocations, comprises dans les frais généraux de la Cour, prévus par l'article 31, sont versées par l'entremise du Bureau international institué par la Convention pour le règlement pacifique des conflits internationaux.

ART. 9.

The Judges of the Judicial Arbitration Court receive an annual salary of 6,000 Netherland florins. This salary is paid at the end of each half-year, reckoned from the date on which the Court meets for the first time.

In the exercise of their duties during the sessions or in the special cases covered by the present Convention, they receive the sum of 100 florins per diem. They are further entitled to receive a travelling allowance fixed in accordance with the regulations existing in their own country. The provisions of the present paragraph are applicable also to Deputy Judges when acting for Judges.

These emoluments are included in the general expenses of the Court dealt with in Article 31, and are paid through the International Bureau created by the Convention for the Pacific Settlement of International Disputes.

ART. 10.

Les Juges ne peuvent recevoir de leur propre Gouvernement ou de celui d'une autre Puissance aucune rémuné-

ART. 10.

The Judges may not accept from their own Government or from that of any other Power any remuneration

ration pour des services rentrant dans leurs devoirs comme membres de la Cour.

for services connected with their duties as members of the Court.

ART. 11.

La Cour de justice arbitrale a son siège à La Haye et ne peut, sauf le cas de force majeure, le transporter ailleurs.

La Délégation peut, avec l'assentiment des Parties, choisir un autre lieu pour ses réunions si des circonstances particulières l'exigent.

ART. 11.

The seat of the Judicial Arbitration Court is at The Hague, and cannot except in the case of *force majeure* be transferred elsewhere.

The Delegation may choose, with the assent of the parties concerned, another place for its meetings, if special circumstances render such a step necessary.

ART. 12.

Le Conseil administratif remplit à l'égard de la Cour de justice arbitrale les fonctions qu'il remplit à l'égard de la Cour permanente d'arbitrage.

ART. 12.

The Administrative Council fulfils the same functions with regard to the Judicial Arbitration Court as with regard to the Permanent Court of Arbitration.

ART. 13.

Le Bureau international sert de greffe à la Cour de justice arbitrale et doit mettre ses locaux et son organisation à la disposition de la Cour. Il a la garde des archives et la gestion des affaires administratives.

Le Secrétaire-général du Bureau remplit les fonctions de greffier.

Les Secrétaires adjoints au greffier, les traducteurs, et les sténographes nécessaires sont désignés et assermentés par la Cour.

ART. 13.

The International Bureau acts as registry to the Judicial Arbitration Court, and shall place its offices and staff at the disposal of the Court. It has the custody of the archives and carries out the administrative work.

The Secretary-General of the Bureau acts as Registrar.

The necessary secretaries to assist the Registrar, translators and shorthand writers are appointed and sworn in by the Court.

ART. 14.

La Cour se réunit en session une fois par an. La session commence le troisième mercredi de juin et dure tant que l'ordre du jour n'aura pas été épuisé.

La Cour ne se réunit pas en session, si la Délégation estime que cette réunion n'est pas nécessaire. Toutefois, si une Puissance est partie à un litige

ART. 14.

· The Court meets in session once a year. The session opens on the third Wednesday in June and lasts until all the business on the agenda has been transacted.

The Court does not meet in session if the Delegation considers that such meeting is unnecessary. However, when a Power is party in a case

actuellement pendant devant la Cour et dont l'instruction est terminée ou va être terminée, elle a le droit d'exiger que la session ait lieu.

En cas de nécessité, la Délégation peut convoquer la Cour en session extraordinaire.

Art. 15.

Un compte rendu des travaux de la Cour sera dressé chaque année par la Délégation. Ce compte rendu sera transmis aux Puissances contractantes par l'intermédiaire du Bureau international. Il sera communiqué aussi à tous les juges et juges suppléants de la Cour.

Art. 16.

Les juges et les juges suppléants, membres de la Cour de justice arbitrale, peuvent aussi être nommés aux fonctions de juge et de juge suppléant dans la Cour internationale des prises.

Titre II.

Compétence et Procédure.

Art. 17.

La Cour de justice arbitrale est compétente pour tous les cas qui sont portés devant elle, en vertu d'une stipulation générale d'arbitrage ou d'un accord spécial.

Art. 18.

La Délégation est compétente :—

1. Pour juger les cas d'arbitrage visés à l'article précédent, si les parties sont d'accord pour réclamer l'application de la procédure sommaire, réglée au titre IV., chapitre iv., de la Convention pour le règlement pacifique des conflits internationaux ;

---

actually pending before the Court, the pleadings in which are closed, or about to be closed, it may insist that the session be held.

When necessary, the Delegation may summon the Court in extraordinary session.

Art. 15.

A Report of the work of the Court shall be drawn up every year by the Delegation. This Report shall be forwarded to the Contracting Powers through the International Bureau. It shall also be communicated to the Judges and Deputy Judges of the Court.

Art. 16.

The Judges and Deputy Judges of the Judicial Arbitration Court can also be appointed Judges and Deputy Judges in the International Prize Court.

Part II.

Jurisdiction and Procedure.

Art. 17.

The Judicial Arbitration Court is competent to deal with all cases submitted to it, in virtue either of a general undertaking to have recourse to arbitration or of a special agreement.

Art. 18.

The Delegation is competent :—

1. To decide the cases of arbitration referred to in the preceding Article, if the parties agree upon the application of the summary procedure, laid down in Part IV., Chapter iv., of the Convention for the Pacific Settlement of International Disputes ;

2. Pour procéder à une enquête en vertu et en conformité du titre III. de la dite Convention en tant que la Délégation en est chargée par les Parties agissant d'un commun accord. Avec l'assentiment des Parties et par dérogation à l'article 7, alinéa 1, les membres de la Délégation ayant pris part à l'enquête peuvent siéger comme juges, si le litige est soumis à l'arbitrage de la Cour ou de la Délégation elle-même.

ART. 19.

La Délégation est, en outre, compétente pour l'établissement du compromis visé par l'article 52 de la Convention pour le règlement pacifique des conflits internationaux, si les Parties sont d'accord pour s'en remettre à la Cour.

Elle est également compétente, même si la demande est faite seulement par l'une des Parties, après qu'un accord par la voie diplomatique a été vainement essayé, quand il s'agit :—

1. D'un différend rentrant dans un traité d'arbitrage général conclu ou renouvelé après la mise en vigueur de cette Convention et qui prévoit pour chaque différend un compromis, et n'exclut pour l'établissement de ce dernier ni explicitement ni implicitement la compétence de la Délégation. Toutefois, le recours à la Cour n'a pas lieu si l'autre Partie déclare qu'à son avis le différend n'appartient pas à la catégorie des questions à soumettre à un arbitrage obligatoire, à moins que le traité d'arbitrage ne confère au tribunal arbitral le pouvoir de décider cette question préalable.

2. To hold an inquiry under and in accordance with Part III. of the said Convention, in so far as such an inquiry is intrusted to the Delegation by the joint accord of the parties. With the assent of the parties, and as an exception to Article 7, paragraph 1, the members of the Delegation who have taken part in the inquiry may sit as Judges, if the case in dispute is submitted to the arbitration of the Court or of the Delegation itself.

ART. 19.

The Delegation is also competent to settle the *Compromis* referred to in Article 52 of the Convention for the Pacific Settlement of International Disputes if the parties are agreed to leave it to the Court.

It is equally competent to do so, even if the request is only made by one of the parties, when all attempts to reach an understanding through the diplomatic channel have failed, in the case of :—

1. A dispute covered by a general Treaty of Arbitration concluded or renewed after the present Convention has come into force, providing for a *Compromis* in all disputes, and not either explicitly or implicitly excluding the settlement of the *Compromis* from the competence of the Delegation. Recourse cannot, however, be had to the Court if the other party declares that in its opinion the dispute does not belong to the category of questions which can be submitted to obligatory arbitration, unless the Treaty of Arbitration confers upon the Arbitration Tribunal the power of deciding this preliminary question.

2. D'un différend provenant de dettes contractuelles réclamées à une Puissance par une autre Puissance comme dues à ses nationaux, et pour la solution duquel l'offre d'arbitrage a été acceptée. Cette disposition n'est pas applicable si l'acceptation a été subordonnée à la condition que le compromis soit établi selon un autre mode.

ART. 20.

Chacune des Parties a le droit de désigner un juge de la Cour pour prendre part, avec voix délibérative, à l'examen de l'affaire soumise à la Délégation.

Si la Délégation fonctionne en qualité de Commission d'enquête, ce mandat peut être confié à des personnes prises en dehors des juges de la Cour. Les frais de déplacement et la rétribution à allouer aux dites personnes sont fixés et supportés par les Puissances qui les ont nommés.

ART. 21.

L'accès de la Cour de justice arbitrale, instituée par la présente Convention, n'est ouvert qu'aux Puissances contractantes.

ART. 22.

La Cour de justice arbitrale suit les règles de procédure édictées par la Convention pour le règlement pacifique des conflits internationaux, sauf ce qui est prescrit par la présente Convention.

ART. 23.

La Cour décide du choix de la langue dont elle fera usage et des langues dont l'emploi sera autorisé devant elle.

2. A dispute arising from contract debts claimed from one Power by another Power as due to its nationals, and for the settlement of which the offer of arbitration has been accepted. This provision is not applicable if the acceptance is subject to the condition that the *Compromis* should be settled in some other way.

ART. 20.

Each of the parties concerned has the right to nominate a Judge of the Court to take part, with power to vote, in the examination of the case submitted to the Delegation.

If the Delegation acts as a Commission of Inquiry, this task may be intrusted to persons other than the Judges of the Court. The travelling expenses and remuneration to be given to the said persons are fixed and borne by the Powers appointing them.

ART. 21.

The Contracting Powers only may have access to the Judicial Arbitration Court set up by the present Convention.

ART. 22.

The Judicial Arbitration Court follows the rules of procedure laid down in the Convention for the Pacific Settlement of International Disputes, except in so far as the procedure is prescribed by the present Convention.

ART. 23.

The Court determines what language it will itself use and what languages may be used before it.

ART. 24.

Le Bureau international sert d'inter-médiaire pour toutes les communica-tions à faire aux juges au cours de l'instruction prévue à l'article 63, alinéa 2, de la Convention pour le règlement pacifique des conflits in-ternationaux.

ART. 25.

Pour toutes les notifications à faire, notamment aux Parties, aux témoins, et aux experts, la Cour peut s'adresser directement au Gouvernement de la Puissance sur le territoire de laquelle la notification doit être effectuée. Il en est de même s'il s'agit de faire procéder à l'établissement de tout moyen de preuve.

Les requêtes adressées à cet effet ne peuvent être refusées que si la Puis-sance requise les juge de nature à porter atteinte à sa souveraineté ou à sa sécurité. S'il est donné suite à la requête, les frais ne comprennent que les dépenses d'exécution réellement effectuées.

La Cour a également la faculté de recourir à l'intermédiaire de la Puis-sance sur le territoire de laquelle elle a son siège.

Les notifications à faire aux Parties dans le lieu où siège la Cour peuvent être exécutées par le Bureau inter-national.

ART. 26.

Les débats sont dirigés par le Président ou le Vice-Président et, en cas d'absence ou d'empêchement de l'un et de l'autre, par le plus ancien des juges présents.

Le juge nommé par une des parties ne peut siéger comme Président.

ART. 24.

The International Bureau serves as channel for all communications to be made to the Judges during the inter-change of pleadings provided for in Article 63, paragraph 2, of the Con-vention for the Pacific Settlement of International Disputes.

ART. 25.

For all notices to be served, in particular on the parties, witnesses, or experts, the Court may apply direct to the Government of the State on whose territory the service is to be carried out. The same rule applies in the case of steps being taken to procure evidence.

Requests for this purpose can only be rejected when the Power applied to considers them calculated to impair its sovereign rights or its safety. If the request is complied with, the fees charged must only comprise the ex-penses actually incurred.

The Court is equally entitled to act through the Power on whose territory it sits.

Notices to be given to parties in the place where the Court sits may be served through the International Bureau.

ART. 26.

The discussions are under the control of the President or Vice-President, or, in case they are both absent or cannot act, of the senior Judge present.

The Judge appointed by one of the parties cannot preside.

ART. 27.

Les délibérations de la Cour ont lieu à huis clos et restent secrètes.

Toute décision est prise à la majorité des juges présents. Si la Cour siège en nombre pair et qu'il y ait partage des voix, la voix du dernier des juges, dans l'ordre de préséance établi d'après l'article 4, alinéa 1, ne sera pas comptée.

ART. 28.

Les arrêts de la Cour doivent être motivés. Ils mentionnent les noms des juges qui y ont participé ; ils sont signés par le Président et par le greffier.

ART. 29.

Chaque Partie supporte ses propres frais et une part égale des frais spéciaux de l'instance.

ART. 30.

Les dispositions des articles 21 à 29 sont appliquées par analogie dans la procédure devant la Délégation.

Lorsque le droit d'adjoindre un membre à la Délégation n'a été exercé que par une seule Partie, la voix du membre adjoint n'est pas comptée s'il y a partage de voix.

ART. 31.

Les frais généraux de la Cour sont supportés par les Puissances contractantes.

Le Conseil administratif s'adresse aux Puissances pour obtenir les fonds nécessaires au fonctionnement de la Cour.

ART. 27.

The Court considers its decisions in private, and the proceedings remain secret.

All questions are decided by a majority of the Judges present. If the number of Judges is even and equally divided, the vote of the junior Judge, in the order of precedence laid down in Article 4, paragraph 1, is not counted.

ART. 28.

The judgments of the Court must state the reasons on which they are based. They contain the names of the Judges taking part in them ; they are signed by the President and by the Registrar.

ART. 29.

Each party pays its own costs and an equal share of the costs of the trial.

ART. 30.

The provisions of Articles 21 to 29 are applicable so far as may be to the procedure before the Delegation.

When the right of adding a member to the Delegation has been exercised by one of the parties only, the vote of the additional member is not recorded if the votes are equally divided.

ART. 31.

The general expenses of the Court are borne by the Contracting Powers.

The Administrative Council applies to the Powers to obtain the funds requisite for the working of the Court.

Art. 32.

La Cour fait elle-même son règlement d'ordre intérieur, qui doit être communiqué aux Puissances contractantes.

Après la ratification de la présente Convention, la Cour se réunira aussitôt que possible, pour élaborer ce règlement, pour élire le Président et le Vice-Président, ainsi que pour désigner les membres de la Délégation.

Art. 33.

La Cour peut proposer des modifications à apporter aux dispositions de la présente Convention qui concernent la procédure. Ces propositions sont communiquées par l'intermédiaire du Gouvernement des Pays-Bas aux Puissances contractantes, qui se concerteront sur la suite à y donner.

Titre III.

Dispositions Finales.

Art. 34.

La présente Convention sera ratifiée dans le plus bref délai possible.

Les ratifications seront déposées à La Haye.

Il sera dressé du dépôt de chaque ratification un procès-verbal, dont une copie, certifiée conforme, sera remise par la voie diplomatique à toutes les Puissances signataires.

Art. 35.

La Convention entrera en vigueur six mois après sa ratification.

Elle aura une durée de douze ans, et sera renouvelée tacitement de douze ans en douze ans, sauf dénonciation.

Art. 32.

The Court itself draws up its own rules of procedure, which must be communicated to the Contracting Powers.

After the ratification of the present Convention, the Court shall meet as early as possible in order to draw up these rules, to elect the President and Vice-President, and to appoint the members of the delegation.

Art. 33.

The Court may propose modifications in the provisions of the present Convention concerning procedure. These proposals are communicated through the Netherland Government to the Contracting Powers, which will confer together as to the measures to be taken thereon.

Part III.

Final Provisions.

Art. 34.

The present Convention shall be ratified as soon as possible.

The ratifications shall be deposited at The Hague.

A *procès-verbal* of the deposit of each ratification shall be drawn up, of which a duly certified copy shall be sent through the diplomatic channel to all the Signatory Powers.

Art. 35.

The Convention shall come into force six months after its ratification.

It shall remain in force for twelve years, and shall be tacitly renewed for periods of twelve years, unless denounced.

La dénonciation devra être notifiée, au moins deux ans avant l'expiration de chaque période, au Gouvernement des Pays-Bas, qui en donnera connaissance aux autres Puissances.

La dénonciation ne produira effet qu'à l'égard de la Puissance qui l'aura notifiée. La Convention restera exécutoire dans les rapports entre les autres Puissances.

The denunciation must be notified, at least two years before the expiry of each period, to the Netherland Government, which will inform the other Powers.

The denunciation shall only have effect in respect of the notifying Power. The Convention shall continue in force as far as the other Powers are concerned.

THE DRAFT CONVENTION RELATIVE TO THE CREATION OF
A JUDICIAL ARBITRATION COURT[1].

The genesis of this Draft Convention which is annexed to the *Vœu*
Origin of
the Draft
Convention. already recorded in the Final Act[2] cannot be understood without some reference to the Permanent Court of Arbitration created in 1899 and amended in 1907. It proposes to create another Court, called in order to distinguish it from the body brought into existence by the Conventions of 1899 and 1907, a "Court of Arbitral Justice" or a "Judicial Arbitration Court" intended to sit alongside and supplement the so-called Permanent Court, but of a far more permanent character than the already existing body.

The Permanent Court was called into being in consequence of the recognition by the Conference of 1899 that arbitration is the most effective and most equitable method of settling disputes which diplomacy has failed to settle in questions of a legal nature and especially in the interpretation or application of international conventions (1 H. C. 1899, Art. 16). By Article 20 of the 1 H. C. 1899 the contracting Powers undertook to organise a Permanent Court accessible at all times and working, unless otherwise agreed on by the parties, under the procedure laid down in the Convention. The parties, as is the rule in international arbitrations, choose

---

[1] See *ante*, pp. 66–9, 85; *Parl. Papers*, pp. 59–61, 257–301; *La Deux. Confér.* T. I. pp. 332–5, 847–898; T. II. pp. 144–161, 309–325, 331–351, 596–630, 1031–70; A. Ernst, *L'œuvre de la deuxième Conférence de la Paix*, pp. 14–17; A. H. Fried, *Die zweite Haager Konferenz*, pp. 98–119; E. Lémonon, *La seconde Conférence de la Paix*, pp. 220–279; T. J. Lawrence, *International problems and Hague Conferences*, pp. 73–5; J. Westlake, *Quarterly Review*, January, 1908, p. 284; J. B. Scott, *The proposed Court of Arbitral Justice*, Amer. *Journ. of Inter. Law*, Vol. II. pp. 772–810; Idem, *The Hague Peace Conferences of 1899 and 1907*, Vol. I. pp. 421–466.

[2] See *ante*, pp. 67, 85.

their own judge and Article 17 provides that the Arbitration Convention is concluded for questions already existing or for questions which may eventually arise: it may embrace any dispute or only disputes of a certain category.

From Articles 16, 17 and 20 it is clear that questions of a judicial order were then deemed peculiarly susceptible of arbitration, and it was hoped by means of the erection of a permanent Court that such questions would be frequently arbitrated and decided on the basis of respect for law. It thus seemed that the Convention had laid the foundations of a Court in the strictly juridical sense of the word, save that instead of judges, there would be arbitrators nominated by the free choice of the parties.

By Article 21 the Permanent Court was declared to be competent for all arbitration cases, unless the parties agreed to institute a special tribunal; it is therefore evident that the framers of the Convention considered that it was possible to submit to the Court problems other than those of an exclusively judicial nature. There was thus created a single institution competent to decide purely legal questions on the basis of respect for law, and wider problems of an extra-judicial character, either or both of which were to be decided by judges, or rather arbitrators, chosen by the parties to the dispute.

The Report of the Sub-Committee of the First Committee in 1907, prepared by Mr J. B. Scott[1] (from which the foregoing is taken), goes on to observe that in private litigation parties do not choose their own judges, but, as M. Bourgeois pointed out during the discussion, no nation in matters involving political interest will consent to go before a Court of arbitration unless it takes an active part in the appointment of the members composing it. In matters of a purely legal nature, he said, it is not the same, for everyone realises that a real Court composed of jurists may be considered as the most competent instrument for dealing with controversies of this nature and giving decisions on pure questions of law[2].

The intention of the framers of the Draft Convention was to organise a Court competent primarily for controversies of a legal nature, but at the same time not prohibited from dealing, if the parties so desire, with cases of a different character. The Permanent Court established in 1899 is not strictly speaking permanent, for it requires to be organised each time resort is had to it, the panel of judges from which the litigants choose the

---

[1] The subject was discussed by the First Sub-Committee of the First Committee and subsequently by an Examining Committee called *Comité d'Examen*, B.

[2] *La Deux. Confér.* T. i. p. 348; T. ii. pp. 347-8.

arbitrators is, together with the Administrative Bureau, the only permanent part of the system. Another defect of the system, as has already been pointed out, is its expense[1], which, said Mr Choate, was probably one of the reasons why certain nations had failed to appear before it. " It should be one element of reform," he continued, "that the expense of the Court itself, including the salaries of the judges, shall be borne at common expense of all the signatory Powers, so as to furnish to the suitors a Court, at least, free of expense to them, as is the case with suitors of all nations in their national courts. The fact that there was nothing permanent, or continuous, or connected in the sessions of the Court or in the adjudication of the cases submitted to it has been an obvious source of weakness and want of prestige in the Tribunal. Each trial it had before it has been wholly independent of every other, and its occasional utterances, widely distant in point of time and disconnected in subject-matter, have not gone far towards constituting a consistent body of international law or of valuable contributions to international law, which ought to emanate from an international tribunal representing the power and might of all the nations.... Let us then seek to develope out of it a permanent court which shall hold regular and continuous sessions, which shall consist of the same judges, which shall pay due heed to its own decisions, which shall speak with the authority of the united voice of the nations and gradually build up a system of international law, definite and precise, which shall command the approval and regulate the conduct of the nations. By such a step in advance, we shall justify the confidence which has been placed in us and shall make the work of this Second Conference worthy of comparison with that of the Conference of 1899[2]."

Two proposals were before the First Sub-Committee of the First Committee at its meeting on the 1st August, namely a Russian draft[3] and a United States draft[4]. The Russian draft was in the nature of an extension of the work of the existing Permanent Court, the members of which were to assemble every year in full session for the following purposes : (1) to select by ballot three members from the list of arbitrators who must be ready at any time to constitute the Permanent Court: (2) to consider the annual report of the Administrative Council and of the International Bureau : (3) to express the opinion of the Permanent Court upon the questions which have arisen during the course of the

The Russian draft.

---

[1] See *ante*, p. 177.

[2] *La Deux. Confér.* T. II. p. 828; Mr Choate's speech in introducing the subject for discussion before the First Sub-Committee of the First Committee on the 1st August, 1907, is set out in English on pp. 327–330.

[3] *La Deux. Confér.* T. II. p. 1030.   [4] *Ibid.* p. 1031.

procedure of an Arbitration Court as well as on the acts of the Administrative Council and the International Bureau: (4) to exchange ideas on the progress of international arbitration in general.

Under this scheme there would have been an annual meeting of the whole panel of judges of the Arbitration Court for the business set forth; three of their number were to be chosen, and these, as Mr Scott suggests, would, when selected, probably reside at the Hague and devote their time to cases presented for their decision [1]. The whole of the Russian scheme, which consisted of four Articles, was intended for incorporation into Convention No. 1 as Chapter ii., Articles 24–27. It was not discussed by the Examining Committee, though both it and the United States scheme were referred to that Committee after a discussion of the general principles of the two schemes by the First Sub-Committee on the 1st and 3rd August.

The United States draft proposed that a permanent Court of Arbitration should be established at the Hague to consist of 15 judges, the mode of choice to be left to the Conference, " but they shall be so chosen from the different countries that the various systems of law and procedure and the principal languages shall be suitably represented in the personnel of the Court " (Art. 1). The Court should meet annually at the Hague and remain in session as long as necessary; the judges were to receive a sufficient salary to enable them to devote their time to the consideration of the matters brought before them (Art. 2). No judge was to take part in the consideration of any case when his nation was a party thereto (unless with the express consent of the parties) (Art. 3). The cases which might come before the Court were set forth in Article 4. The judges were to act on Commissions of Enquiry or Special Arbitration Tribunals (Art. 5). The present Permanent Court of Arbitration might, as far as possible, constitute the basis of the Court, care being taken that the Powers which recently signed the Convention of 1899 are represented on it (Art. 6)[2].

The only important opposition to the general scheme of a really permanent Court as outlined by the United States draft came from M. Beernaert, who contended that the comparative failure of the Permanent Court established in 1899 was due not to inherent defects but to the timidity of Governments to make trial of a new institution; the Permanent Court was preferable to that proposed by the United States plan, which he proceeded to criticise in detail, especially dwelling on the fact that permanent judges were imposed on the parties to the dispute who would thus be

The United States draft.

---

[1] *The Hague Peace Conferences*, Vol. i. p. 438.

[2] *La Deux. Confér.* T. ii. p. 1031; J. B. Scott, *The Hague Peace Conferences*, p. 821.

deprived of the right of choice which was essential to the idea of arbitration[1].

M. Léon Bourgeois, in his capacity of French delegate, replied to the various speeches, particularly emphasising the fact that the proposed Court was not to take the place of the Permanent Court established in 1899, but that each would have its own separate sphere and that it was in no sense obligatory on the contracting parties to take cases before it[2]. Before the vote was taken several delegates enquired as to the manner in which the judges who should compose the new Court would be chosen, and no reply being forthcoming they decided to abstain from voting. The United States proposal was put to the vote and carried by 28 votes, with 12 abstentions[3].

In the Examining Committee (*Comité d'Examen, B*) the United States draft was taken as a basis, but it was subsequently withdrawn in favour of a common draft prepared by the American, British and German delegates[4]. During the course of the discussions M. Ruy Barbosa (Brazil), on the 20th August, presented a draft based on the principle of the equality of states in their representation on the Court to be established, and the abolition of the existing Court. He supported his proposal in lengthy, detailed and somewhat heated speeches[5]. His draft was not discussed by the Examining Committee and was subsequently withdrawn. Amendments were also presented by the Bulgarian, Haitian and Uruguayan delegates regarding the composition of the Court, the latter dealing with the question of obligatory arbitration[6].

Proceedings in the Examining Committee.

The Examining Committee held 8 meetings between the 13th August and the 16th September but their labours did not result in their being able to lay before the Conference a draft Convention for its acceptance. The rock which so nearly proved fatal to the Prize Court Convention, viz. the mode of appointment of the judges, wrecked the scheme.

It is not necessary to enter into a detailed explanation of the draft Convention, it will be sufficient to summarise its contents. It proposes the creation of a really permanent Court which shall meet at the Hague once a year for the hearing of such cases as shall be set down for it. The Court is to be freely and easily

The draft Convention.

---

[1] *La Deux. Confér.* T. II. pp. 331–4.   [2] *La Deux. Confér.* T. II. pp. 347–9.

[3] *Ibid.* T. II. p. 550. The states abstaining from voting were: Austria-Hungary, Belgium, Denmark, Spain, Greece, Norway, Roumania, Servia, Siam, Sweden, Switzerland and Turkey.

[4] *La Deux. Confér.* T. II. p. 1035.

[5] *Ibid.* pp. 618–622, 624–7; see *post*, p. 515.   [6] *Ibid.* pp. 1033, 1034, 915.

accessible, composed of judges representing the various judicial systems of the world and capable of insuring continuity in arbitral jurisprudence (Art. 1). It is to be composed of judges and deputy-judges of the highest qualification, appointed for a period of twelve years and taken as far as possible from the members of the Permanent Court of Arbitration (Arts. 2 and 3). The Court is annually to nominate three judges to form a special Delegation and three more to replace them should the necessity arise (Art. 6). No judge is to exercise his functions in any case in which he has taken part in the decision of a national tribunal, or in which he has acted as counsel or advocate; a judge cannot act in the latter capacity before the Judicial Arbitration Court, the Permanent Court of Arbitration, a Special Tribunal of Arbitration or a Commission of Inquiry (Art. 7).

The judges are to receive an annual salary of 6000 Netherland florins (about £480) per annum, together with a further allowance of 100 florins per diem when exercising their functions, and travelling expenses fixed in accordance with the regulations in their own country. These emoluments are included in the general expenses of the Court and are paid through the International Bureau created by 1 H. C. 1899 (Art. 9). The judges may not accept any remuneration from their own or any other Government for services connected with their duties in their capacity of members of the Court (Art. 10).

The Delegation is competent (1) to decide arbitrations, if the parties are agreed that the summary procedure laid down in Part IV. Chapter iv. 1 H. C. 1907 is to be applied: (2) to hold an inquiry under Part III. of that Convention. With the assent of the parties, and as an exception to the rule laid down in Article 7, the members of the Delegation who have taken part in the inquiry may sit as judges if the case in dispute is submitted to the arbitration of the Court or of the Delegation itself (Art. 18). The Delegation is also competent to settle the *Compromis* under Article 53 of 1 H. C. 1907.

It will thus be seen that the draft follows the general principles of the United States scheme with the addition of the small Committee as suggested by the Russian proposal, but nothing is said of the number of judges who shall compose the Court or the mode in which they are to be chosen. This subject occupied the attention of the Examining Committee for a considerable time but all attempts to produce a scheme which would meet with general acceptance failed. At the meeting on the 5th September Mr Choate reviewed the various suggestions made on this important subject[1].

---

[1] *La Deux. Confér.* T. II. pp. 689-693, where Mr Choate's speech is given in English. The *résumé* of these various schemes is taken from Mr Choate's speech and Mr J. B. Scott's *Hague Peace Conferences,* pp. 457-460.

The Sub-Committee which had charge of the preparation of the draft

Proposed methods of choosing Judges. had attempted to devise a scheme which should serve as a basis of discussion. It recognised the equal sovereignty of nations and took account at the same time of the differences that existed between them in population, in territory, in commerce, in language, in system of law and other respects. A Court of seventeen judges was proposed to be organised for a period of twelve years. The eight great Powers would each nominate a judge for the full period of twelve years, other states for smaller periods varying in proportion to their population, territorial extent, commerce etc.[1] These periods ranged from ten years to one.

M. Barbosa had presented a counter-scheme[2] "based upon the alleged equality, not only in sovereignty, but in all other respects of all the states. It proposed to abolish the existing Court, and for a new Court to be constituted consisting of forty-five judges, one to be appointed by each state, and these to be divided into groups, in alphabetical order, of fifteen each, which were to sit for alternate periods of three years....Two objections to it were suggested—first, that an allotment of periods by alphabetical order was really the creation of a court by chance, and second, that it deprived each nation of any hand or voice in the Court for six years out of the nine for which it was proposed to establish it, whereas the first scheme had given every nation a seat in the Court by a permanent judge for a fixed period, besides the right to have a judge of its own appointment upon the Court whenever it had a case before it for decision[3]." This system was not considered by the Examining Committee. M. Barbosa subsequently withdrew the draft. Although it had been put forward as a counter proposal, the Brazilian delegate was not dissatisfied with the existing Court, and had introduced the alternative scheme merely "to illustrate by a concrete example the kind of Court consistent with the unimpaired equality of nations, and the exercise of sovereignty[4]," which he was prepared to accept.

Another proposal was that seventeen nations including the eight great Powers, and nine others which together should represent all parts of the world, languages, legal systems, interests etc., "should be selected by the Conference with a power to each to appoint a judge for the whole term of the Court, thus recognising the principle of equality of sovereignty to be exercised in the power of creating the Court and selecting the judges[5]."

[1] See Table set out in *La Deux. Confér.* T. ii. pp. 609-612.

[2] *Ibid.* pp. 1045-8 ; see also pp. 618-622.   [3] *Ibid.* p. 690.

[4] J. B. Scott, *The Hague Peace Conferences*, Vol. i. p. 459.

[5] *La Deux. Confér.* T. ii. p. 690.

According to another proposal four judges should be assigned to America as a unit, the selection to be left to the States of the American Continent, while the other nations should elect thirteen judges among themselves.

All these schemes having failed, Mr Choate then proposed the following : " The plan would be for an election, each state casting one vote for a prescribed number of judges, which should be deemed suitable for the temporary and provisional organisation of the Court, to hold office, either until the next Conference, or for a specified number of years, or until the Powers, by a diplomatic interchange of views, should adopt some different method as a permanency[1]."

A final effort was made to secure an acceptable result by sending all

Final efforts.

the various proposals to a Sub-Committee of 8 delegates consisting of Baron Marschall von Bieberstein, Count Tornielli, Sir Edward Fry, MM. Nélidow, Bourgeois, Choate, Barbosa and Mérey de Kapos-Mère, but this endeavour failed also, and the Examining Committee met for the last time on the 18th September when Mr Choate made a final effort which he said he hoped would meet all the objections raised to the other schemes. Each state was to nominate a judge and deputy-judge and to send their names to the International Bureau. The Bureau was then to make a list of the names submitted and of countries nominating them and to send the list to the signatory Powers. Each would then vote for 15 judges and 15 deputy-judges taken from the list, and return their votes to the Bureau who would notify the names of those receiving the greatest number of votes; in case of equality of votes the decision to be by lot. The project, said Mr Choate, was simplicity itself. If only 15 nations accepted it, a beginning would be made and accessions would soon follow[2]. M. Ruy Barbosa was inflexible in his opposition, and when it was put to the vote Mr Choate's proposal was rejected by 9 to 5. Sir Edward Fry then moved to accept the draft, leaving out all the provisions relating to the nomination of the judges or the rotation to be established, and recommending that it be brought into force as soon as an agreement had been reached respecting the selection of the judges and the constitution of the Court. The draft was accepted by 8 votes to 5 with 2 abstentions, and Sir Edward Fry's proposal by the same numbers[3].

The First Committee adopted the motion of Sir Edward Fry as a *Declaration* (the name was changed to *Vœu* in the Final Act) at their meeting on the 10th October, and the Conference at its Ninth Plenary

---

[1] *La Deux. Confér.* T. ɪɪ. p. 691.   [2] *Ibid.* pp. 697-9.
[3] *Ibid.* pp. 704-8.

Meeting on the 16th October also adopted it by 36 votes with 6 abstentions.

Reservations. The following states made reservations chiefly in the sense of accepting the Court providing that the principle of the legal equality of states be recognised in the composition of the Court: Mexico, Brazil, Colombia, San Salvador, Persia, Guatemala, Hayti, Venezuela, Paraguay, San Domingo, Panama, Ecuador, China, Bolivia and Nicaragua[1]. On signing the Final Act Switzerland made a reservation of this *Vœu*, the Swiss Federal Council having declined to accept it.

The labour of weeks spent in discussing the various projects for the composition of the proposed Court of Arbitral Justice was frustrated, and rendered fruitless for the present by the opposition of the smaller Powers, headed by the Brazilian delegate, M. Ruy Barbosa. To them the doctrine of the equality of states was a dogma accepted in its crudest meaning. Equality before the law, and equality in influence are two very different things. The "primacy of the great Powers" is a fact, if it is not a legal principle, and if these Powers should be able in the future to agree upon a method for the appointment of the judges for the Court, the lesser Powers will in course of time gradually be found desirous of taking their part in an institution which would contain the germs of the most important judicial body ever known to the world. But are these Powers really in earnest in their desire to establish such an institution? The international *Palais de Justice* has been built, furnished and decorated, and is ready for the judges to take their seats; it is for the Powers to open the doors and send them in[2].

---

[1] *La Deux. Confér.* T. I. pp. 383–5.   [2] *Ibid.* p. 391.

THE RESULTS OF THE SECOND PEACE CONFERENCE.

The Second Peace Conference held its First Plenary Meeting on the 15th June, 1907, and its last on the 18th October[1]. The members of the Conference at their Final Meeting expressed profound appreciation of the humanitarian worth of the Conference, and condemned the pessimism of those who viewed the ideal of peace as a dangerous illusion. But outside the walls of the Palace where the delegates had sat for four tedious months, a different note was at once apparent. The humanitarian sentiments were derided. Peace, it was said, was neither more nor less secure after the Conference than before; the assembly had been actuated not by equitable principles but by political considerations. The failures of the Conference as embodied in its *Vœux* and Resolutions were emphasised; the noble sentiments, and high principles enunciated in the speeches at the Final Meeting were contrasted with the achievements of the representatives of forty-four sovereign Powers after four months of unintermitted labour; the "law of facts" had prevailed, the Conference was a failure, a "fiasco," its one value was to afford a warning against the besetting sin of the hour—"against the moral and intellectual dishonesty of pandering to sentiment merely because it was popular, without regard to the inevitable results[2]." The world had in fact become wearied by the complicated reports of the long drawn out proceedings of the Conference, and bored by the reiteration of the arguments of the delegates based on political self-interest; the enthusiasm which had greeted the commencement of the Conference had been turned to disgust at its apparently small results.

Judgments passed under such circumstances are apt to be coloured by the feelings of the moment, the failures are magnified, the positive and permanent results are neglected or belittled. There is a truth in

---

[1] The official record of the Conference, *La Deuxième Conférence Internationale de la Paix*, consists of 3 folio volumes, containing over 3000 pages, and these do not represent the whole of the printed matter officially supplied to the delegates. The Special Correspondent of *The Times* estimated that the total number of documents which were printed for circulation was close on 850, and as 600 copies of each were sent out the total number of copies approximated to 510,000 (see *The Times* for 19th Oct. 1907).

[2] See leading Article on "The Hague Fiasco" in *The Times*, 19th Oct. 1907.

the adverse criticisms which were expressed so freely at the conclusion of the Conference, but it is by no means the whole truth.

The foregoing pages show the actual results obtained by the Second Peace Conference, and the processes by which they were framed; the Conventions have been examined and their ambiguities and omissions noted. All legislation which is the result of compromise contains much that is open to criticism, international agreements no less than national statutes. A brief summary of work of the Second Conference will serve to assist in forming a judgment on its permanent value.

The Convention for the Pacific Settlement of International Disputes prepared in 1899 was amended and enlarged, especially as regards Commissions of Inquiry, and a new chapter was added for facilitating appeal to arbitration by summary procedure. Already one important case has been decided under the terms of the new and still unratified Convention—the Casablanca Arbitration Case between France and Germany[1]—and another, the dispute between Great Britain and the United States regarding the Atlantic fishery question, has been set down for trial, the *Protocole de Compromis* in the latter case expressly providing for the application of the new summary procedure in the determination of questions arising under the award.

The second Convention provides for a case of compulsory arbitration in regard to contract debts, but its value is weakened by the abstentions from signature, and the reservations of many of the Powers in whose interest the Convention was proposed.

By the third Convention the signatory Powers recognise that war ought to be preceded by a declaration.

By the fourth Convention an important addition is made to the Convention relating to the laws and customs of land warfare of 1899 by the provision of a sanction for the breach of the Regulations adopted. Several alterations and additions are made to the Regulations themselves, though some of these are equivocal.

In the fifth Convention a commencement is made of a Code relating to neutrals in land warfare.

The sixth Convention registers a concession in favour of enemy private property at sea, by exempting from capture merchant-ships in port at the outbreak of war, as well as those on the high seas ignorant of its existence; but here again there is evidence of compromise, and the *desirability* of allowing days of grace to ships in enemy ports is all that

---

[1] For the Award in the Casablanca Arbitration see *Amer. Journ. of Inter. Law*, Vol. III. pp. 698, 755.

the Convention provides, while the important qualification regarding ships whose build indicates that they are intended for conversion into war-ships may raise difficult questions in the application of the Convention.

The seventh Convention lays down the conditions to which merchant-ships converted into war-ships must conform in order to comply with the rule abolishing privateering; they are simple and straightforward, but the really difficult questions connected with the place and duration of the conversion are left unsolved.

The eighth Convention relating to submarine mines is a very unsatisfactory document. The endeavours of Great Britain to safeguard neutral commerce by strictly limiting the localities in which mines may be laid, and of Germany to prohibit floating mines altogether for a period of five years were unfortunately unsuccessful, and the Convention fails to prohibit the use of these deadly weapons under circumstances which would render their employment disastrous to innocent neutrals; the absence of a prohibition is, however, not to be mistaken for a tacit permission.

The bombardment of undefended coast towns is prohibited by the ninth Convention, except in case of the non-provision of supplies for the enemy fleet demanding them. The prohibition to bombard such towns for non-payment of a ransom is now recognised as a definite rule of international law.

By the tenth Convention important changes are introduced into the Convention of 1899 applying to naval warfare the principles of the Geneva Convention, and the Conference is to be congratulated on the execution of a highly humane piece of work. Several problems connected with this subject left outstanding from the first Conference were found capable of solution by the second.

The eleventh Convention is a valuable contribution towards the laws of naval warfare; small coasting fishing boats, a class of vessels which had in practice been left unmolested for a considerable time, are exempted from capture, and this exemption is extended to small boats engaged in petty local navigation. Enemy merchant seamen are also exempt from capture as prisoners of war. None of the topics in this Convention were mentioned in Count Benckendorff's Circular.

The twelfth Convention establishing an International Prize Court (an-other subject which was not mentioned in the Russian programme) is the greatest achievement of the Conference. At the Tenth Plenary Meeting of the Conference on the 17th October, 1907, Sir Edward Fry spoke as follows of this Convention: "I have no intention to pass in review the

labours of this Conference, I shall confine myself to saying that of all the projects we have adopted, the most remarkable in my opinion is that of the Prize Court, because it is the first time in the history of the world that there has been organised a Court truly international. International law of to-day is not much more than a chaos of opinions which are often contradictory, and of decisions based on national laws. We hope to see little by little formed in the future, around this Court, a system of laws truly international which will owe its existence only to principles of justice and equity, and which consequently will command not only the admiration of the world, but the respect and obedience of civilised nations[1]." The obstacles to be overcome before the International Prize Court is an accomplished fact are great, but some of these have been removed by the Declaration of London of 1909, which however, like the Prize Court Convention (and all the Conventions of the Second Peace Conference), still remains unratified. It would be a striking testimony to the value of international gatherings, and the growth of the power of law, should both of these important Acts be ratified, even though some reservation were made by the ratifying Powers.

The thirteenth Convention regarding the rights and duties of neutrals in naval war is of too complex a character wholly to praise or blame; its weakness in regard to the enunciation of neutral *duties* has already been noticed. In none of the discussions was the influence of political considerations greater than in those on this subject.

The Declaration of 1899 prohibiting the discharge of projectiles and explosives from balloons, which had expired in 1905, was renewed until the termination of the next Peace Conference. It has not however been signed by such important Powers as Germany, France, and Russia. Several of the Powers which signed and ratified the Declaration in 1899 have clearly manifested their intention to remain unfettered in their use of what may in the future prove a most important factor in warfare both by land and sea, and in view of the abstention from signature of several important states it would appear unlikely that the Declaration will be ratified by many of the signatory Powers.

Such were the positive results of the Second Peace Conference; the failures which were many have already been discussed; the net results, though considerable, "are less than might have been hoped for, but perhaps as great as could reasonably be expected when all the circumstances are considered[2]."

---

[1] *Parl. Papers*, Misc. No. 4 (1908), p. 79; *La Deux. Confér.* T. I. p. 592.

[2] Report of Sir Edward Fry to Sir Edward Grey, *Parl. Papers*, Misc. No. 1 (1908), p. 19.

The most important work of the Second Peace Conference, apart from the amendments to the Conventions of the First, is to be found in the Conventions relating to maritime international law. Except in regard to the treatment of sick, wounded and shipwrecked persons in naval warfare, no attempt had been made since 1856 to enter into any international agreement on the subject, and many of the rules had, owing to modern changes, become obsolete or unworkable. The difficulties which the Conference had to face in dealing with this topic have already been referred to[1]; that they were not entirely overcome at the first attempt is no cause for surprise. Conventions 7 to 13 all deal with naval warfare, and although the solutions provided for the difficult problems with which they deal are frequently of a tentative character, the results of the London Naval Conference afford reason to believe that many of the Conventions of 1907 will be elucidated and strengthened by the Conference of 1915.

In comparing the work of the Second Peace Conference with the First, it is necessary to recall the fact that the First Conference did not commence its labours on an arid plain, the soil had already been tilled, the seed sown and watered, and two of the three Conventions adopted by it were the fruits of previous international gatherings, subsequent discussions and international practice.

The Second Conference also was able to reap the results of the labours of the First, and like it to enter new fields and sow seeds for its successors; the bulk of its work, indeed, was of the latter character, and the fruits will appear in due time. These are, in fact, already becoming apparent. The Convention of the 20th December, 1907, between the five Central American States of Costa Rica, Guatemala, Honduras, Nicaragua and San Salvador, whereby the signatory Powers agreed to submit to the decision of a permanent Arbitration Court all disputes (without any exceptions) which may arise between them, may be indirectly attributed to the discussion at the Hague. Already two cases have come before the Court sitting at Cartago (Costa Rica). An important step towards the preparation of regulations relative to the laws and customs of Naval Warfare has been taken by the London Naval Conference of 1909. The delegates, in preparing the Declaration of London, were able to avail themselves of the experience gained in the lengthy discussions on blockade, contraband, etc. at the Hague in 1907. The Second Conference, no less than the First, must be judged, not merely by the results of the moment, but by its subsequent influence.

The expectations of the immediate results of the Second Conference

---

[1] See *ante*, pp. 87–98.

were not fully realised, too much had been anticipated from it, more might have been forthcoming but for the following circumstances.

The Second Conference was overpowered by numbers, the Committees were too large. It was also hampered at every turn by the effects of the legal doctrine that all the states represented were equal, and for this reason the Conference has been described as a "sham" which brought forth a progeny of shams[1]. Dr Westlake makes use of the same expression when he says "in a word the voting was a sham, and of shams we ought to have no more[2]." "The claim of many of the smaller States to equality," writes Sir Edward Fry, "as regards not only their independence, but their share in all international institutions waived by most of them in the case of the Prize Court, but successfully asserted in the case of the proposed new Arbitral Court, is one which may produce great difficulties, and may perhaps drive the greater Powers to act in many cases by themselves[3]." As a consequence of this principle (in the support of which the smaller Powers received encouragement from several of the greater who were desirous of obtaining their votes), and of the regulation adopted by the Conference that no Convention should be recommended for acceptance unless there was unanimity, proposals affecting maritime international law were placed at the mercy of purely inland states such as Luxemburg, Switzerland, and Servia, which ranked for the purpose of voting on a level with Great Britain, the United States, and Germany. The Prize Court Convention was nearly wrecked by the opposition of the smaller states, and the creation of an Arbitration Tribunal of a truly permanent character was frustrated by the same Powers.

Sir Edward Fry's hint that the greater Powers might be driven to act by themselves bore fruit in the Naval Conference of London, when problems relating to contraband and blockade which were found insoluble in 1907 were adjusted by the representatives of a small number of the greater Powers. The Third Conference will, if it desires to avoid the excessive waste of time of the Second, be compelled either to abandon the principle of requiring unanimous votes, or to abandon entirely the principle of voting.

Another reason why no results were reached on several of the subjects introduced was the absence of preparation on the part of many of the Delegations. The soil must be tilled before the seed can be successfully sown. The German Delegation appears to have come fully prepared with

---

[1] See *The Times*, 19th October, 1907.

[2] *Quarterly Review*, January, 1908, p. 230.

[3] *Parl. Papers*, Misc. No. 1 (1908), p. 21. See *ante*, p. 517.

drafts on all or nearly all the subjects enumerated in the Russian Circular, and the British, the United States, French and other Delegations had prepared drafts on matters in which they were specially interested. A careful examination, however, of the *procès-verbal* of the Committees, Sub-Committees and Examining Committees reveals the fact that delay was frequently occasioned by absence of instructions on the part of many of the Delegations. Owing to the wide latitude given by the Chairman to the introduction of new topics, and the fact that the discussions were not confined within due limits, new points were raised and proposals made which often left even the best instructed Delegations unprepared to take any definite line. Some questions of the greatest importance such as the British proposal for the abolition of contraband were publicly discussed for the first time, without the valuable assistance which the Conference derived in most of the other subjects from the previous careful and scientific examination by text-writers, or the body of experts composing the " Institut de Droit International." The Conference felt these drawbacks and re-solved that two years before the summoning of the next Conference by a careful preparation of drafts, and preliminary discussions of various topics it should be ascertained what subjects were ripe for embodiment in an international regulation, and a programme should then be prepared[1]. A useful precedent will be found in the various memoranda sent in to the British Government before the meeting of the London Naval Conference, as by means of these the views of the Governments summoned to the Conference were made known, and bases for discussion prepared before the delegates assembled.

The defects in the rules of procedure were striking and in many points fatal to progress. The President at the commencement of the Conference expressed the hope that speeches should be limited to ten minutes; this hope was unrealised. Frequently the same delegate addressed a Committee at inordinate length, and several times in the course of one meeting. "The least hopeful proposals were, under the pseudo-parliamentary procedure, allowed to be put through an indefinite number of stages without any likelihood of their ultimate decision[2]." Amendments and contradictory resolutions were passed only to be sent on to another Committee where the same procedure not infrequently occurred.

Some of these causes of want of greater success are capable of remedy by a future Conference, but the more fundamental and permanent cause was political. Each Delegation had the primary duty to discharge of

---

[1] See *ante*, p. 94.

[2] *Edinburgh Review*, January, 1908, p. 224.

defending its state's national interests: the Conference was not composed merely of lawyers intent on framing a scientific code of international law; it was a battlefield of diplomatists. In questions where political considerations were supreme, compromise was often impossible. Each delegate "did his best to advance his nation's interests, but inasmuch as nations differ in status and power, proposals made by one nation would not commend themselves to another, and heated arguments would follow moving the whole assembly to excitement, each representative insisting on his nation's sovereign rights, and declining to submit to coercion, with the result that proposals would be dropped half-way or suspended in a void of empty theories[1]."

Notwithstanding all these circumstances the Conference was not a failure; it was disappointing but it is not discouraging. War will not be banished from the world by Peace Conferences; nevertheless such gatherings, by removing doubts in international rules, and bringing into greater prominence the solidarity of the interests of mankind, may do much to encourage arbitration and to remove the causes of war. The Second Peace Conference no less than the First produced solid results in these directions, and by establishing an International Prize Court it has provided the means for a pacific solution of the questions which may arise in construing its Conventions.

The work of future Conferences will be greatly assisted if more careful preparation is previously made of the questions to be brought forward; these must be chosen by the Powers themselves, and only those should be introduced on which bases of discussion can be first framed. The Permanent Administrative Council established at the Hague under the provisions of the Convention for the Pacific Settlement of International Disputes might form a truly International Bureau for the preparatory work of future Conferences. Rules of procedure must be carefully drafted to avoid lengthy and futile discussions: voting should be abolished, and the sense of the Conference taken not by merely counting states, but by taking into account their differences in territory, wealth, population, armed forces, conceptions of right, and experience of the topics under consideration. States should be free to enter into Conventions among themselves as the results of such discussions. It should be possible for one state whose proposals have received the support of a substantial number of other states to ignore the dissentients, and to negotiate a Convention with those who have supported its proposals, without incurring the censure of the Conference or being accused of attempting to frustrate its labours.

[1] Report of the Chinese Minister Lu-Cheng-Hsiang to the Emperor (*The Times*, 20th February, 1908).

Tsars have deserved well of posterity for their initiative in the summoning of International Conferences, but it is now time that such gatherings should meet freed from the patronage of any one monarch.

The appeal to the sentiment of the world which is made by the name of the "Peace Conference" has not been without its effect, but those objects which were the very basis of the invitation issued for the First Conference, "the maintenance of the general peace, and a possible reduction of the excessive armaments which were burdening all nations," were absent from the programme sketched out for the Second[1]. Every International Conference which makes for the growth of international law, and a fuller acceptance of its rules is, however, a real "Peace" Conference, and is of value in maintaining "the general peace," even though its work should consist in the preparation of laws of war.

There is much work in store for many years for future Conferences in settling and codifying the rules of international law, rules which govern the relations of states both in peace and war. The road to be travelled before the goal is reached will doubtless be long and tedious, and often there will apparently only be movement in a circle. No one who has studied the history of the attempts to codify national law will lightly estimate the labour involved, or be discouraged by the slowness of the rate of progress. Every addition to accepted rules, every solution of a disputed point is an advance towards the reign of law among states, and to this end the Second Peace Conference contributed in no small measure.

---

[1] See *ante*, p. 75.

TABLE OF THE DEPOSITS

of acts of ratification and accessions to the Conventions and Declarations signed the 29th July, 1899, at the FIRST PEACE CONFERENCE.

	I. Convention for the pacific settlement of International disputes.	II. Convention respecting the laws and customs of war on land.	III. Convention for the adaptation of the principles of the Geneva Convention of the 22nd Aug. 1864 to maritime war, excluding Art. 10.	IV (1). Declaration prohibiting the discharge of projectiles and explosives from balloons.	IV (2). Declaration prohibiting the use of projectiles whose sole object is the diffusion of asphyxiating or deleterious gases.	IV (3). Declaration prohibiting the use of bullets which expand or flatten easily in the human body, etc.
Germany	S.	S.	S.	S.	S.	S.
Argentina	A.	A.	A.	...	...	...
Austria-Hungary ...	S.	S.	S.	S.	S.	S.
Belgium	S.	S.	S.	S.	S.	S.
Bolivia	A.	A.	A.	...	...	...
Brazil	A.	A.	A.	...	...	...
Bulgaria	S.	S.	S.	S.	S.	S.
Chile	A.	A.	A.	...	...	...
China	S.	A.	S.	S.	S.	S.
Colombia	A.	A.	A.	...	...	...
Corea	...	A.	A.	...	...	...
Cuba	A.	A.	A.	...	...	...
Denmark	S.	S.	S.	S.	S.	S.
Dominican Republic ...	A.	A.	A.	...	...	...
Ecuador	A.	A.	A.		S.	...
Spain	S.	S.	S.	S.	S.	S.
United States of America	S. R.	S.	S.			
France	S.	S.	S.	S.	S.	S.
Great Britain	S.	S.	S.	S.	A.	A.
Greece	S.	S.	S.	S.	S.	S.
Guatemala	A.	A.	A.		...	...
Hayti	A.	A.	A.		...	...
Honduras	...	A.	A.		...	...
Italy	S.	S.	S.	S.	S.	S.
Japan	S.	S.	S.	S.	S.	S.
Luxemburg	S.	S.	S.	S.	S.	S.
Mexico	S.	S.	S.	S.	S.	S.
Montenegro	S.	S.	S.	S.	S.	S.
Nicaragua	A.	A.	A.	...	...	...
Norway	S.	S.	S.	S.	S.	S.
Panama	A.	A.	A.	...	...	...
Paraguay	A.	A.	A.	...	...	...
Netherlands	S.	S.	S.	S.	S.	S.
Peru	A.	A.	A.	...	...	...
Persia	S.	S.	S.	...	S.	S.
Portugal	S.	S.	S.	...	S.	A.
Roumania	S. R.	S.	S.	...	S.	S.
Russia	S.	S.	S.	S.	S.	S.
Salvador	A.	A.	A.		...	...
Servia	S. R.	S.	S.	S.	S.	S.
Siam	S.	S.	S.	S.	S.	S.
Sweden	S.	S.	S.	S.	S.	S.
Switzerland	S.	A.	S.	S.	S.	S.
Turkey	S. R.	S.	S.	S.	S.	S.
Uruguay	A.	A.	A.	...	...	...
Venezuela	A.	A.	A.	...	...	...

(Note in column IV (1): "Lapsed after the 4th September, 1905.")

S. = Signed and Ratified.   A. = Acceded.   R. = Reservation.

RÉSERVES.

I. États-Unis d'Amérique   Rien de ce qui est contenu dans cette Convention ne peut être interprété de façon à obliger les États-Unis d'Amérique à se départir de leur politique traditionnelle, en vertu de laquelle ils s'abstiennent d'intervenir, de s'ingérer, ou de s'immiscer dans les questions politiques ou dans la politique ou dans l'administration intérieure d'aucun État étranger. Il est bien entendu également que rien dans la Convention ne pourra être interprété comme impliquant un abandon par les États-Unis d'Amérique de leur attitude traditionnelle à l'égard des questions purement Américaines[1].

Roumanie   Le Gouvernement Royal de Roumanie, complètement acquis au principe de l'arbitrage facultatif, dont il apprécie toute l'importance dans les relations internationales, n'entend cependant pas prendre, par l'article 15, un engagement d'accepter un arbitrage dans tous les cas qui y sont prévus, et il croit devoir formuler des réserves expresses à cet égard.

Il ne peut donc voter cet article que sous cette réserve.

Le Gouvernement Royal de Roumanie déclare qu'il ne peut adhérer à l'article 16 qu'avec la réserve expresse, consignée au procès-verbal, qu'il est décidé à ne pas accepter, en aucun cas, un arbitrage international pour des contestations ou litiges antérieurs à la conclusion de la présente Convention.

Le Gouvernement Royal de Roumanie déclare qu'en adhérant à l'article 18 de la Convention, il n'entend prendre aucun engagement en matière d'arbitrage obligatoire[2].

Serbie   Au nom du Gouvernement Royal de Serbie, nous avons l'honneur de déclarer que l'adoption par nous du principe de bons offices et de la médiation n'implique pas une reconnaissance du droit pour les États tiers d'user de ces moyens autrement qu'avec la réserve extrême qu'exige la nature délicate de ces démarches.

Nous n'admettrons les bons offices et la médiation qu'à condition de leur conserver pleinement et intégralement leur caractère de conseil purement amical et nous ne saurions jamais les accepter dans des formes et des circonstances telles qu'elles pourraient leur imprimer le caractère d'une intervention[3].

Turquie   La Délégation Ottomane, considérant que ce travail de la Conférence a été une œuvre de haute loyauté et d'humanité destinée uniquement à raffermir la paix générale en sauvegardant les intérêts et les droits de chacun, déclare au nom de son Gouvernement adhérer à l'ensemble du projet qui vient d'être adopté, aux conditions suivantes :

1. Il est formellement entendu que le recours aux bons offices, à la médiation, aux Commissions d'Enquête et à l'arbitrage est purement facultatif et ne saurait en aucun cas revêtir un caractère obligatoire ou dégénérer en intervention.

2. Le Gouvernement Impérial aura à juger lui-même des cas où ses intérêts lui permettraient d'admettre ces moyens, sans que son abstention ou son refus d'y avoir recours puissent être considérés par les États Signataires comme un procédé peu amical.

Il va de soi qu'en aucun cas les moyens dont il s'agit ne sauraient s'appliquer à des questions d'ordre intérieur[4].

[1] De Martens, *Nouveau Recueil, etc.* (2nd series), Vol. XXVI. p. 172.
[2] *Ibid.* p. 702.   [3] *Ibid.* p. 702.   [4] *Ibid.* p. 172.

RESERVATIONS.

United States

Nothing contained in this Convention shall be so construed as to require the United States of America to depart from its traditional policy of not intruding upon, interfering with, or entangling itself in the political questions or policy or internal administration of any foreign state; nor shall anything contained in the said convention be construed to imply a relinquishment by the United States of America of its traditional attitude towards purely American questions.

Roumania

The Royal Government of Roumania, being completely in favour of the principle of facultative arbitration, of which it appreciates the great importance in international relations, nevertheless, does not intend to undertake, by article 15, an engagement to accept arbitration in every case there provided for, and it believes it ought to form express reservations in that respect.

It cannot therefore vote for this article, except under that reservation.

The Royal Government of Roumania declares that it cannot adhere to article 16 except with the express reservation, entered in the *procès-verbal*, that it has decided not to accept, in any case, an international arbitration for disagreements or disputes previous to the conclusion of the present Convention.

The Royal Government of Roumania declares that in adhering to article 18 of the Convention, it makes no engagement in regard to obligatory arbitration.

Servia

In the name of the Royal Government of Servia, we have the honour to declare that our adoption of the principle of good offices and mediation does not imply a recognition of the right of third states to use these means except with the extreme reserve which proceedings of this delicate nature require.

We shall not admit good offices and mediation except on condition that their character of purely friendly counsel is fully and completely maintained, and we could never accept them in forms and circumstances such as to impress upon them the character of intervention.

Turkey

The Turkish Delegation, considering that the work of this Conference has been a work of high loyalty and humanity, destined solely to assure general peace by safeguarding the interests and the rights of each one, declares, in the name of its Government, that it adheres to the project just adopted, on the following conditions:

1. It is formally understood that recourse to good offices and mediation, to commissions of inquiry and arbitration is purely facultative and could not in any case assume an obligatory character or degenerate into intervention.

2. The Imperial Government itself will be the judge of the cases where its interests would permit it to admit these methods, without its abstention or refusal to have recourse to them being considered by the signatory states as an unfriendly act.

It goes without saying that in no case should such methods be applied to questions of internal order.

Table of the States represented at the Second International Peace

Signatures affixed and reservations made up to June 30, 1908, when, by virtue of the
the exception however of

	I. Convention for the Pacific Settlement of International Disputes.	II. Convention respecting the Limitation of the Employment of Force for the Recovery of Contract Debts.	III. Convention relative to the Opening of Hostilities.	IV. Convention concerning the Laws and Customs of War on Land.	V. Convention respecting the Rights and Duties of Neutral Powers and Persons in War on Land.	VI. Convention relative to the Status of Enemy Merchant-ships at the Outbreak of Hostilities.	VII. Convention relative to the Conversion of Merchant-ships into War-ships.
Germany	S.*	S.	S.	S. R.	S.	S. R.	S.
America (United States of)	S. R.	S.	S.	S.	S.	...	...
Argentina	S.	S. R.	S.	S.	S. R.	S.	S.
Austria-Hungary	S.	S.	S.	S. R.	S.	S.	S.
Belgium	S.	...	S.	S.	S.	S.	S.
Bolivia	S.	S. R.	S.	S.	S.	S.	S.
Brazil	S. R.	...	S.	S.	S.	S.	S.
Bulgaria	S.	S.	S.	S.	S.	S.	S.
Chile	S. R.	S.	S.	S.	S.	S.	S.
China	S.	...	...	...	...	...	...
Colombia	S.	S. R.	S.	S.	S.	S.	S.
Cuba	S.	S.	S.	S.	S.	S.	S.
Denmark	S.	S.	S.	S.	S.	S.	S.
Dominican Republic	S.	S. R.	S.	S.	S.	S.	...
Ecuador	S.	S. R.	S.	S.	S.	S.	S.
Spain	S.	S.	S.	...	S.	S.	S.
France	S.	S.	S.	S.	S.	S.	S.
Great Britain	S.	S.	S.	S.	S. R.	S.	S.
Greece	S. R.	S. R.	S.	S.	S.	S.	S.
Guatemala	S.	S. R.	S.	S.	S.	S.	S.
Hayti	S.	S.	S.	S.	S.	S.	S.
Italy	S.	S.	S.	S.	S.	S.	S.
Japan	S. R.	S.	S.	S. R.	S.	S.	S.
Luxemburg	S.	...	S.	S.	S.	S.	S.
Mexico	S.	S.	S.	S.	S.	S.	S.
Montenegro	S.	S.	S.	S. R.	S.	S.	S.
Nicaragua	...	...	...	...	...	...	...
Norway	S.	S.	S.	S.	S.	S.	S.
Panama	S.	S.	S.	S.	S.	S.	S.
Paraguay	S.	S..	S.	S.	S.	S.	S.
Netherlands	S.	S.	S.	S.	S.	S.	S.
Peru	S.	S. R.	S.	S.	S.	S.	S.
Persia	S.	S.	S.	S.	S.	S.	S.
Portugal	S.	S.	S.	S.	S.	S.	S.
Roumania	S. R.	...	S.	S.	S.	S.	S.
Russia	S.	S.	S.	S. R.	S.	S. R.	S.
Salvador	S.	S. R.	S.	S.	S.	S.	S.
Servia	S.	S.	S.	S.	S.	S.	S.
Siam	S.	...	S.	S.	S.	S.	S.
Sweden	S.	...	S.	S.	S.	S.	S.
Switzerland	S. R.	...	S.	S.	S.	S.	S.
Turkey	S. R.	S.	S.	S. R.	S.	S.	S. R.
Uruguay	S.	S. R.	S.	S.	S.	S.	...
Venezuela	S.	...	S.	S.	S.	S.	S.

* S. = Signed. R. = Reservation.

SIGNATURES.

Conference which signed the Conventions, Declaration, and Final Act.

Final Act, the period within which the above instruments must be signed expires, with Convention XII (see Article 53).

VIII. Convention relative to the Laying of Automatic Submarine Contact Mines.	IX. Convention respecting Bombardments by Naval Forces in Time of War.	X. Convention for the Adaptation of the Principles of the Geneva Convention to Maritime War.	XI. Convention relative to certain Restrictions in the Exercise of the Right of Capture in Maritime War.	XII. Convention relative to the Establishment of an International Prize Court.	XIII. Convention respecting the Rights and Duties of Neutral Powers in Maritime War.	XIV. Declaration prohibiting the Discharge of Projectiles and Explosives from Balloons.	XV. Final Act of the Second International Peace Conference.
S. R.	S. R.	S.	S.	S.	S. R.	...	S.
S.	S.	S.	S.	S.	...	S.	S.
S.	S.	S.	S.	S.	S.	S.	S.
S.	S.	S.	S.	S.	S.	S.	S.
S.	S.	S.	S.	S.	S.	S.	S.
S.	S.	S.	S.	...	S.	S.	...
S.	S.	S.	S.	S.	S.	S.	S.
S.	S. R.	S.	S.	S. R.	S.	...	S.
...	...	S. R.	...	...	...	S.	S.
S.	S.	S.	S.	S.	S.	S.	S.
S.	S.	S.	S.	S. R	S.	S.	S.
S.	S.	S.	S.	S.	S.	...	S.
S. R.	S.	S.	S.	...	S. R.	S.	S.
S.	S.	...	S.	S. R.	S.	S.	S.
...	...	S.	S.	S.	...	...	S.
S. R.	S. R.	S.	S.	S.	S. R.	...	S.
S. R.	S. R.	S. R.	S.	S.[1]	S. R.	S.	S.
S.	S.	S.	S.	...	S.	S.	S.
S.	S.	S.	S.	S. R.	S.	...	S.
S.	S.	S.	S.	S. R.	S.	...	S.
S.	S.	S.	S.	S.	S.	...	S.
S.	S. R.	S.	S.	S.[1]	S. R.	S.	S.
S.	S.	S.	S.	...	S.	...	S.
S.	S.	S.	S.	...	S.	...	S.
...	S.	S.	...	...	S.	...	S.
...	...	...	...	...	...	...	S.
S.	S.	S.	S.	S.	S.	S.	S.
S.	S.	S.	S.	S.	S.	S.	S.
S.	S.	S.	S.	S.	S.	...	S.
S.	S.	S.	S.	S.	S.	...	S.
S.	S.	S. R.	S.	S. R.	S. R.	S.	S.
...	S.	S.	S.	S.	S.	S.	S.
S.	S.	S.	S.	...	S.	...	S.
...	S.	S.	...	...	S.	...	S.
S.	S.	S.	S.	S. R.	S.	S.	S.
S.	S.	S.	S.	...	S.	...	S.
S. R.	S.	S.	S.	S. R.	S. R.	S.	S.
...	S.	S.	S.	S.	S.	...	S. R.
S. R.	S.	S. R.	S.	S. R.	S. R.	S.	S.
S.	S.	S.	S.	S. R.	S.	...	S.
S.	S.	S.	S.	...	S.	...	S.

[1] Signed after June 30, 1908.

Réserves.

I.	Amérique	Sous réserve de la Déclaration faite dans la séance plénière de la Conférence du 16 Octobre, 1907.
	Brésil	Avec réserve sur l'Article 53, alinéas 2, 3, et 4.
	Chili	Sous la réserve de la Déclaration, formulée à propos de l'Article 39 dans la septième séance du 7 Octobre de la Première Commission.
	Grèce	Avec la réserve de l'alinéa 2 de l'Article 53.
	Japon	Avec réserve des alinéas 3 et 4 de l'Article 48, de l'alinéa 2 de l'Article 53 et de l'Article 54.
	Roumanie	Avec les mêmes réserves formulées par les Plénipotentiaires Roumains à la signature de la Convention pour le règlement pacifique des conflits internationaux du 29 Juillet, 1899.
	Suisse	Sous réserve de l'Article 53, chiffre 2.
	Turquie	Sous réserve des Déclarations portées au procès-verbal de la neuvième séance plénière de la Conférence du 16 Octobre, 1907.

II.	Argentine	La République Argentine fait les réserves suivantes :—

1. En ce qui concerne les dettes provenant de contrats ordinaires entre le ressortissant d'une nation et un Gouvernement étranger, on n'aura recours à l'arbitrage que dans le cas spécifique de déni de justice par les juridictions du pays du contrat, qui doivent être préalablement épuisées.

2. Les emprunts publics, avec émission de bons, constituant la dette nationale, ne pourront donner lieu, en aucun cas, à l'agression militaire ni à l'occupation matérielle du sol des nations Américaines.

	Bolivie	Sous la réserve exprimée à la Première Commission.
	Colombie	La Colombie fait les réserves suivantes :—

Elle n'accepte pas en aucun cas l'emploi de la force pour le recouvrement de dettes quelle que soit leur nature. Elle n'accepte pas l'arbitrage qu'après décision définitive des Tribunaux des pays débiteurs.

	Rép. Dominicaine	Avec la réserve faite dans la séance plénière du 16 Octobre, 1907.
	Equateur	Avec la réserve faite dans la séance plénière du 16 Octobre, 1907.
	Grèce	Avec la réserve faite dans la séance plénière du 16 Octobre, 1907.
	Guatémala	

1. En ce qui concerne les dettes provenant de contrats ordinaires entre les ressortissants d'une nation et un Gouvernement étranger on n'aura recours à l'arbitrage que dans le cas de dénégation de justice par les juridictions du pays du contrat, qui doivent être préalablement épuisées.

2. Les emprunts publics avec émission de bons constituant des dettes nationales ne pourront donner lieu, en aucun cas, à l'agression militaire ni à l'occupation matérielle du sol des nations Américaines.

RESERVATIONS.

I. America

Under reservation of the Declaration made at the plenary meeting of the Conference held on October 16, 1907. (See *ante*, p. 179r)

Brazil

With reservation in regard to Article 53, paragraphs 2, 3, and 4.

Chile

Under reservation of the Declaration made respecting Article 39 at the seventh meeting of the First Commission held on October 7.

Greece

With the reservation of paragraph 2 of Article 53.

Japan

With reservation of paragraphs 3 and 4 of Article 48, of paragraph 2 of Article 53, and Article 54.

Roumania

With the same reservations made by the Roumanian Plenipotentiaries on signing the Convention for the pacific settlement of international disputes on July 29, 1899. (See *ante*, p. 529.)

Switzerland

Under reservation of Article 53, No. 2.

Turkey

Under reservation of the Declarations recorded in the Minutes of the proceedings of the ninth plenary meeting of the Conference, held on October 16, 1907. (See *ante*, p. 179.)

II. Argentina

The Argentine Republic makes the following reservations :—

1. In regard to debts arising from ordinary contracts between the subject or citizen of a State and a foreign Government, recourse shall not be had to arbitration except in the specific case of denial of justice by the Tribunals of the country which made the contract ; the legal remedies must first be exhausted.

2. Public loans, with issue of bonds, constituting the national debt, cannot in any circumstances give rise to military aggression nor to the effective occupation of the territory of any American State.

Bolivia

Under the reservation made to the First Commission.

Colombia

Colombia makes the following reservations :—

It does not in any circumstances admit the employment of force for the recovery of debts whatever their nature may be. It does not accept arbitration until the Tribunals of the debtor States have pronounced their final sentence.

Dominican Republic

With the reservation made at the plenary meeting of October 16, 1907. (See *ante*, p. 191.)

Ecuador

With the reservation made at the plenary meeting of October 16, 1907. (See *ante*, p. 191.)

Greece

With the reservation made at the plenary meeting of October 16, 1907. (See *ante*, p. 191.)

Guatemala

1. In regard to debts arising from ordinary contracts between the subjects or citizens of a State and a foreign Government, recourse shall not be had to arbitration except in the case of denial of justice by the Tribunals of the country which made the contract; the legal remedies must first be exhausted.

2. Public loans, with issue of bonds, constituting national debts, cannot in any circumstances give rise to military aggression nor to the effective occupation of the territory of any American State.

	Pérou	Sous la réserve que les principes établis dans cette Convention ne pourront pas s'appliquer à des réclamations ou différends provenant de contrats passés par un pays avec des sujets étrangers lorsque dans ces contrats il aura été expressément stipulé que les réclamations ou différends devront être soumis aux Juges et Tribunaux du pays.
	Salvador	Nous faisons les mêmes réserves que la République Argentine ci-dessus.
	Uruguay	Sous réserve du second alinéa de l'Article 1er, parce que la Délégation considère que le refus de l'arbitrage pourra se faire toujours de plein droit si la loi fondamentale du pays débiteur, antérieure au contrat qui a originé les doutes ou contestations, ou ce contrat même, a établi que ces doutes ou contestations seront décidés par les Tribunaux du dit pays.
IV.	Allemagne	Sous réserve de l'Article 44 du Règlement annexé.
	Autriche-Hongrie	Sous réserve de la Déclaration faite dans la séance plénière de la Conférence du 17 Août, 1907.
	Japon	Avec réserve de l'Article 44.
	Monténégro	Sous réserves formulées à l'Article 44 du Règlement annexé à la présente Convention et consignées au procès-verbal de la quatrième séance plénière du 17 Août, 1907.
	Russie	Sous réserves formulées à l'Article 44 du Règlement annexé à la présente Convention et consignées au procès-verbal de la quatrième séance plénière du 17 Août, 1907.
	Turquie	Sous réserve de l'Article 3.
V.	Argentine	La République Argentine fait réserve de l'Article 19.
	Grande-Bretagne	Sous réserve des Articles 16, 17, et 18.
VI.	Allemagne	Sous réserve de l'Article 3 et de l'Article 4, alinéa 2.
	Russie	Sous réserves formulées à l'Article 3 et à l'Article 4, alinéa 2, de la présente Convention, et consignées au procès-verbal de la septième séance plénière du 27 Septembre, 1907.
VII.	Turquie	Sous réserve de la Déclaration faite à la huitième séance plénière de la Conférence du 9 Octobre, 1907.
VIII.	Allemagne	Sous réserve de l'Article 2.
	Rép. Dominicaine	Avec réserve sur l'alinéa 1er de l'Article 1er.
	France	Sous réserve de l'Article 2.
	Grande-Bretagne	Sous réserve de la Déclaration suivante :— En apposant leurs signatures à cette Convention les Plénipotentiaires Britanniques déclarent que le simple fait que la dite Convention ne défend pas tel acte ou tel procédé ne doit pas être considéré comme privant le Gouvernement de Sa Majesté Britannique du droit de contester la légalité du dit acte ou procédé.
	Siam	Sous réserve de l'Article 1er, alinéa 1er.
	Turquie	Sous réserve des Déclarations consignées au procès-verbal de la huitième séance plénière de la Conférence du 9 Octobre, 1907.

Peru	Under the reservation that the principles laid down in this Convention cannot apply to claims or differences arising from contracts entered into by a State with the subjects of a foreign State when it is expressly stipulated in the said contracts that the claims or differences must be submitted to the Judges and Tribunals of the country.
Salvador	We make the same reservations as the Argentine Republic above.
Uruguay	Under reservation of the second paragraph of Article 1, be- cause the Delegation considers that refusal to submit to arbitration can always be legitimately made if the fundamental law of the debtor State, prior to the contract, which gave rise to the misunderstandings or disputes, or the said contract itself, has laid down that such misunderstandings or disputes shall be decided by the Tribunals of the said country.

IV.

Germany	Under reservation of Article 44 of the annexed Regulations.
Austria-Hungary	Under reservation of the Declaration made at the plenary meeting of the Conference held on August 17, 1907.
Japan	With the reservation of Article 44.
Montenegro	Under reservations made about Article 44 of the Regulations annexed to the present Convention, and recorded in the Minutes of the proceedings of the fourth plenary meeting held on August 17, 1907.
Russia	Under reservations made about Article 44 of the Regulations annexed to the present Convention, and recorded in the Minutes of the proceedings of the fourth plenary meeting held on August 17, 1907.
Turkey	Under reservation of Article 3.

V.

Argentina	The Argentine Republic reserves Article 19.
Great Britain	Under reservation of Articles 16, 17, and 18.

VI.

Germany	Under reservation of Article 3 and Article 4, paragraph 2.
Russia	Under reservations made about Article 3 and Article 4, paragraph 2, of the present Convention, and recorded in the Minutes of the proceedings of the seventh plenary meeting held on September 27, 1907. (See *ante*, pp. 304–5.)

VII.

Turkey	With reservation of the Declaration made at the eighth plenary meeting of the Conference held on October 9, 1907. (See *ante*, p. 320.)

VIII.

Germany	Under reservation of Article 2.
Dominican Republic	With reservation in regard to paragraph 1 of Article 1.
France	Under reservation of Article 2.
Great Britain	Under reservation of the following Declaration:—
	In affixing their signatures to the above Convention, the British Plenipotentiaries declare that the mere fact that this Convention does not prohibit a particular act or proceeding must not be held as debarring His Britannic Majesty's Government from contesting its legitimacy. (See *ante*, p. 341.)
Siam	Under reservation of Article 1, paragraph 1.
Turkey	Under reservation of the Declarations recorded in the Minutes of the proceedings of the eighth plenary meeting of the Conference held on October 9, 1907. (See *ante*, p. 343.)

IX.	Allemagne	Sous réserve de l'Article 1er, alinéa 2.
	Chili	Sous la réserve de l'Article 3 formulée dans la quatrième séance plénière du 17 Août.
	France	Sous réserve de l'alinéa 2 de l'Article 1er.
	Grande-Bretagne	Sous réserve de l'alinéa 2 de l'Article 1er.
	Japon	Avec réserve de l'alinéa 2 de l'Article 1er.
X.	Chine	Sous réserve de l'Article 21.
	Grande-Bretagne	Sous réserve des Articles 6 et 21 et de la Déclaration suivante :—
		En apposant leurs signatures à cette Convention les Plénipotentiaires Britanniques déclarent que le Gouvernement de Sa Majesté entend que l'application de l'Article 12 se borne au seul cas des combattants recueillis pendant ou après un combat naval auquel ils auront pris part.
	Perse	Sous réserve du droit reconnu par la Conférence de l'emploi du Lion et du Soleil Rouge au lieu et à la place de la Croix Rouge.
	Turquie	Sous réserve du droit reconnu par la Conférence de la Paix de l'emploi du Croissant Rouge.
XII.	Chili	Sous la réserve de l'Article 15 formulée à la sixième séance plénière du 21 Septembre.
	Cuba	Sous réserve de l'Article 15.
	Equateur	Sous réserve de l'Article 15.
	Guatémala	Sous les réserves formulées concernant l'Article 15.
	Haïti	Avec la réserve relative à l'Article 15.
	Perse	Sous réserve de l'Article 15.
	Salvador	Sous réserve de l'Article 15.
	Siam	Sous réserve de l'Article 15.
	Turquie	Sous réserve de l'Article 15.
	Uruguay	Sous réserve de l'Article 15.
XIII.	Allemagne	Sous réserve des Articles 11, 12, 13, et 20.
	Rép. Dominicaine	Avec réserve sur l'Article 12.
	Grande-Bretagne	Sous réserve des Articles 19 et 23.
	Japon	Avec réserve des Articles 19 et 23.
	Perse	Sous réserve des Articles 12, 19, et 21.
	Siam	Sous réserve des Articles 12, 19, et 23.
	Turquie	Sous réserve de la Déclaration concernant l'Article 10 portée au procès-verbal de la huitième séance plénière de la Conférence du 9 Octobre, 1907.
XV.	Suisse	Sous réserve du Vœu No. 1, que le Conseil Fédéral Suisse n'accepte pas.

IX.	Germany	Under reservation of Article 1, paragraph 2.
	Chile	Under the reservation of Article 3 made at the fourth plenary meeting held on August 17.
	France	Under reservation of paragraph 2 of Article 1.
	Great Britain	Under reservation of paragraph 2 of Article 1.
	Japan	With reservation of paragraph 2 of Article 1.
X.	China	Under reservation of Article 21.
	Great Britain	Under reservation of Articles 6 and 21, and of the following Declaration :—
		In affixing their signatures to this Convention, the British Plenipotentiaries declare that His Majesty's Government understand Article 12 to apply only to the case of combatants rescued during or after a naval engagement in which they have taken part.
	Persia	Under reservation of the right admitted by the Conference to employ the Lion and the Red Sun, instead of and in the place of the Red Cross.
	Turkey	Under reservation of the right admitted by the Peace Conference to employ the Red Crescent.
XII.	Chile	Under the reservation of Article 15 made at the sixth plenary meeting held on September 21. (See *ante*, p. 441.)
	Cuba	Under reservation of Article 15.
	Ecuador	Under reservation of Article 15.
	Guatemala	Under the reservations made in regard to Article 15.
	Hayti	With the reservation relative to Article 15.
	Persia	Under reservation of Article 15.
	Salvador	Under reservation of Article 15.
	Siam	Under reservation of Article 15.
	Turkey	Under reservation of Article 15.
	Uruguay	Under reservation of Article 15.
XIII.	Germany	Under reservation of Articles 11, 12, 13, and 20.
	Dominican Republic	With reservation as to Article 12.
	Great Britain	Under reservation of Articles 19 and 23.
	Japan	With reservation of Articles 19 and 23.
	Persia	Under reservation of Articles 12, 19, and 21.
	Siam	Under reservation of Articles 12, 19, and 23.
	Turkey	Under reservation of the Declaration respecting Article 10 recorded in the Minutes of the proceedings of the eighth plenary meeting of the Conference held on October 9, 1907. (See *ante*, p. 468.)
XV.	Switzerland	Under reservation of Wish No. 1, which the Swiss Federal Council does not accept.

Final Protocol of the London Naval Conference.

Protocole de Clôture.

La Conférence Navale de Londres, convoquée par le Gouvernement de Sa Majesté Britannique, s'est réunie, le 4 décembre 1908, au Ministère des Affaires Étrangères, à l'effet de déterminer les principes généralement reconnus du droit international dans le sens de l'article 7 de la Convention signée à La Haye le 18 octobre 1907, pour l'établissement d'une Cour internationale des prises.

Les Puissances, dont l'énumération suit, ont pris part à cette Conférence, pour laquelle elles avaient désigné les Délégués nommés ci-après :—

[*Dénomination des Plénipotentiaires.*]

Dans une série de réunions, tenues du 4 décembre 1908 au 26 février 1909, la Conférence a arrêté, pour être soumis à la signature des Plénipotentiaires, la *Déclaration relative au droit de la guerre maritime*, dont le texte est annexé au présent Protocole.

En outre, le vœu suivant a été adopté par les Délégués des Puissances qui ont signé ou qui ont exprimé l'intention de signer la Convention de La Haye en date du 18 octobre 1907 pour l'établissement d'une Cour internationale des prises :—

Les Délégués des Puissances représentées à la Conférence Navale et qui ont signé ou qui ont exprimé l'intention

Final Protocol.

The London Naval Conference, called together by His Britannic Majesty's Government, assembled at the Foreign Office on the 4th December, 1908, with the object of laying down the generally-recognised principles of international law in accordance with Article 7 of the Convention signed at The Hague on the 18th October, 1907, for the establishment of an International Prize Court.

The Powers enumerated below took part in this Conference, at which they appointed as their Representatives the following Delegates[1] :—

[*Names of Plenipotentiaries.*]

In a series of sittings held from the 4th December, 1908, to the 26th February, 1909, the Conference has drawn up for signature by the Plenipotentiaries the *Declaration concerning the laws of naval war*, the text of which is annexed to the present Protocol.

Furthermore, the following wish has been recorded by the Delegates of those Powers which have signed or expressed the intention of signing the Convention of The Hague of the 18th October, 1907, for the establishment of an International Prize Court:—

The Delegates of the Powers represented at the Naval Conference which have signed or expressed the intention

---

[1] For names of Powers see *post*, p. 540.

de signer la Convention de La Haye en date du 18 octobre 1907 pour l'établissement d'une Cour internationale des prises, considérant les difficultés d'ordre constitutionnel qui, pour certains États, s'opposent à la ratification, sous sa forme actuelle, de cette Convention, sont d'accord pour signaler à leurs Gouvernements respectifs l'avantage que présenterait la conclusion d'un arrangement en vertu duquel lesdits États auraient, lors du dépôt de leurs ratifications, la faculté d'y joindre une réserve portant que le droit de recourir à la Cour internationale des prises, à propos des décisions de leurs tribunaux nationaux, se présentera comme une action directe en indemnité, pourvu toutefois que l'effet de cette réserve ne soit pas de nature à porter atteinte aux droits garantis par ladite Convention, soit aux particuliers, soit à leurs Gouvernements, et que les termes de la réserve forment l'objet d'une entente ultérieure entre les Puissances Signataires de la même Convention.

En foi de quoi les Plénipotentiaires et les Délégués remplaçant les Plénipotentiaires qui ont déjà dû quitter Londres ont signé le présent Protocole.

Fait à Londres le vingt-six février mil neuf cent neuf, en un seul exemplaire, qui sera déposé dans les archives du Gouvernement Britannique et dont des copies, certifiées conformes, seront remises par la voie diplomatique aux Puissances représentées à la Conférence Navale.

[*Suivent les Signatures.*]

of signing the Convention of The Hague of the 18th October, 1907, for the establishment of an International Prize Court, having regard to the difficulties of a constitutional nature which, in some States, stand in the way of the ratification of that Convention in its present form, agree to call the attention of their respective Governments to the advantage of concluding an arrangement under which such States would have the power, at the time of depositing their ratifications, to add thereto a reservation to the effect that resort to the International Prize Court in respect of decisions of their National Tribunals shall take the form of a direct claim for compensation, provided always that the effect of this reservation shall not be such as to impair the rights secured under the said Convention either to individuals or to their Governments, and that the terms of the reservation shall form the subject of a subsequent understanding between the Powers signatory of that Convention[1].

In faith whereof the Plenipotentiaries and the Delegates representing those Plenipotentiaries who have already left London have signed the present Protocol.

Done at London the twenty-sixth day of February, one thousand nine hundred and nine, in a single original, which shall be deposited in the archives of the British Government and of which duly certified copies shall be sent through the diplomatic channel to the Powers represented at the Naval Conference.

[*Here follow the Signatures.*]

[1] See *ante*, p. 443.

THE DECLARATION OF LONDON, 1909

Déclaration relative au Droit de la Guerre Maritime.	Declaration concerning the Laws of Naval War[1].

Sa Majesté l'Empereur d'Allemagne, Roi de Prusse; le Président des États-Unis d'Amérique; Sa Majesté l'Empereur d'Autriche, Roi de Bohême, &c., et Roi Apostolique de Hongrie; Sa Majesté le Roi d'Espagne; le Président de la République Française; Sa Majesté le Roi du Royaume-Uni de Grande-Bretagne et d'Irlande et des Territoires Britanniques au delà des Mers, Empereur des Indes; Sa Majesté le Roi d'Italie; Sa Majesté l'Empereur du Japon; Sa Majesté la Reine des Pays-Bas; Sa Majesté l'Empereur de Toutes les Russies;

Considérant l'invitation par laquelle le Gouvernement Britannique a proposé à diverses Puissances de se réunir en Conférence afin de déterminer en commun ce que comportent les règles généralement reconnues du droit international au sens de l'article 7 de la

His Majesty the German Emperor, King of Prussia; the President of the United States of America; His Majesty the Emperor of Austria, King of Bohemia, &c., and Apostolic King of Hungary; His Majesty the King of Spain; the President of the French Republic; His Majesty the King of the United Kingdom of Great Britain and Ireland and of the British Dominions beyond the Seas, Emperor of India; His Majesty the King of Italy; His Majesty the Emperor of Japan; Her Majesty the Queen of the Netherlands; His Majesty the Emperor of All the Russias;

Having regard to the terms in which the British Government invited various Powers to meet in conference in order to arrive at an agreement as to what are the generally recognized rules of international law within the meaning of Article 7 of the Convention of the 18th

---

[1] For Report on this Declaration see *post*, p. 567. See also as regards the Conference and this Declaration *Parl. Papers*, Misc. Nos. 4 and 5 (1909), especially No. 5 (1909), pp. 93–104, which contains the Report of the British Delegates to Sir Edward Grey; T. G. Bowles, *The Declaration of London, The Nineteenth Century*, Vol. LXV. p. 744; *The Edinburgh Review*, July, 1909, p. 162; E. Lémonon, *La Conférence navale de Londres, Revue de Droit International* (2nd series), pp. 239, 485; C. H. Stockton, *The International Naval Conference of London, Am. Journ. of Int. Law*, Vol. III. p. 596; E. A. Whittuck, *International Documents*, p. 254.

Convention du 18 octobre 1907, relative à l'établissement d'une Cour internationale des prises ;

Reconnaissant tous les avantages que, dans le cas malheureux d'une guerre maritime, la détermination desdites règles présente, soit pour le commerce pacifique, soit pour les belligérants et pour leurs relations politiques avec les Gouvernements neutres ;

Considérant que les principes généraux du droit international sont souvent, dans leur application pratique, l'objet de méthodes divergentes ;

Animés du désir d'assurer dorénavant une plus grande uniformité à cet égard ;

Espérant qu'une œuvre d'un intérêt commun aussi important rencontrera l'approbation générale ;

Ont nommé pour Leurs Plénipotentiaires, savoir :

[*Dénomination des Plénipotentiaires*[1].]

Lesquels, après s'être communiqué leurs pleins pouvoirs, trouvés en bonne et due forme, sont convenus de faire la présente Déclaration :

October, 1907, relative to the establishment of an International Prize Court ;

Recognizing all the advantages which an agreement as to the said rules would present in the unfortunate event of a naval war, both as regards peaceful commerce, and as regards the belligerents and their diplomatic relations with neutral Governments ;

Having regard to the divergence often found in the methods by which it is sought to apply in practice the general principles of international law ;

Animated by the desire to insure henceforward a greater measure of uniformity in this respect ;

Hoping that a work so important to the common welfare will meet with general approval ;

Have appointed as their Plenipotentiaries, that is to say :

[*Names of Plenipotentiaries*[1].]

Who, after having communicated their full powers, found to be in good and due form, have agreed to make the present Declaration :—

Disposition préliminaire.

Les Puissances Signataires sont d'accord pour constater que les règles contenues dans les Chapitres suivants répondent, en substance, aux principes généralement reconnus du droit international.

Preliminary Provision.

The Signatory Powers are agreed that the rules contained in the following Chapters correspond in substance with the generally recognized principles of international law.

---

[1] Great Britain was represented by the Earl of Desart, K.C.B., King's Proctor; the United States of America by Rear-Admiral Charles H. Stockton, retired, and Mr George Grafton Wilson, Professor at Brown University, and Lecturer on International Law at the Naval War College and at Harvard University. For text of British Instructions see *Parl. Papers*, Misc. No. 4 (1909), pp. 20–32.

Chapitre Premier.	Chapter I.
Du blocus en temps de guerre.	Blockade in time of War.

ART. 1.

Le blocus doit être limité aux ports et aux côtes de l'ennemi ou occupés par lui.

ART. 1.

A blockade must not extend beyond the ports and coasts belonging to or occupied by the enemy.

ART. 2.

Conformément à la Déclaration de Paris de 1856, le blocus, pour être obligatoire, doit être effectif, c'est-à-dire maintenu par une force suffisante pour interdire réellement l'accès du littoral ennemi.

ART. 2.

In accordance with the Declaration of Paris of 1856, a blockade, in order to be binding, must be effective—that is to say, it must be maintained by a force sufficient really to prevent access to the enemy coastline[1].

ART. 3.

La question de savoir si le blocus est effectif est une question de fait.

ART. 3.

The question whether a blockade is effective is a question of fact.

ART. 4.

Le blocus n'est pas considéré comme levé si, par suite du mauvais temps, les forces bloquantes se sont momentanément éloignées.

ART. 4.

A blockade is not regarded as raised if the blockading force is temporarily withdrawn in consequence of stress of weather.

ART. 5.

Le blocus doit être impartialement appliqué aux divers pavillons.

ART. 5.

A blockade must be applied impartially to the ships of all nations.

ART. 6.

Le commandant de la force bloquante peut accorder à des navires de guerre la permission d'entrer dans le port bloqué et d'en sortir ultérieurement.

ART. 6.

The commander of a blockading force may give permission to a warship to enter, and subsequently to leave, a blockaded port.

ART. 7.

Un navire neutre, en cas de détresse constatée par une autorité des forces bloquantes, peut pénétrer dans la localité bloquée et en sortir ultérieurement à la condition de n'y avoir laissé ni pris aucun chargement.

ART. 7.

In circumstances of distress, acknowledged by an authority of the blockading force, a neutral vessel may enter a place under blockade and subsequently leave it, provided that she has neither discharged nor shipped any cargo there.

---

[1] See *ante*, p. 2.

ART. 8.

Le blocus, pour être obligatoire, doit être déclaré conformément à l'article 9 et notifié conformément aux articles 11 et 16.

ART. 9.

La déclaration de blocus est faite, soit par la Puissance bloquante, soit par les autorités navales agissant en son nom.

Elle précise :

1°. La date du commencement du blocus ;

2°. Les limites géographiques du littoral bloqué ;

3°. Le délai de sortie à accorder aux navires neutres.

ART. 10.

Si la Puissance bloquante ou les autorités navales agissant en son nom ne se conforment pas aux mentions, qu'en exécution de l'article 9—1° et 2°, elles ont dû inscrire dans la déclaration de blocus, cette déclaration est nulle, et une nouvelle déclaration est nécessaire pour que le blocus produise ses effets.

ART. 11.

La déclaration de blocus est notifiée :

1°. Aux Puissances neutres, par la Puissance bloquante, au moyen d'une communication adressée aux Gouvernements eux-mêmes ou à leurs représentants accrédités auprès d'elle ;

2°. Aux autorités locales, par le commandant de la force bloquante. Ces autorités, de leur côté, en informeront, aussitôt que possible, les consuls étrangers qui exercent leurs fonctions dans le port ou sur le littoral bloqués.

ART. 8.

A blockade, in order to be binding, must be declared in accordance with Article 9, and notified in accordance with Articles 11 and 16.

ART. 9.

A declaration of blockade is made either by the blockading Power or by the naval authorities acting in its name.

It specifies—

(1) The date when the blockade begins ;

(2) The geographical limits of the coastline under blockade ;

(3) The period within which neutral vessels may come out.

ART. 10.

If the operations of the blockading Power, or of the naval authorities acting in its name, do not tally with the particulars, which, in accordance with Article 9 (1) and (2), must be inserted in the declaration of blockade, the declaration is void, and a new declaration is necessary in order to make the blockade operative.

ART. 11.

A declaration of blockade is notified—

(1) To neutral Powers, by the blockading Power by means of a communication addressed to the Governments direct, or to their representatives accredited to it ;

(2) To the local authorities, by the officer commanding the blockading force. The local authorities will, in turn, inform the foreign consular officers at the port or on the coastline under blockade as soon as possible.

ART. 12.

Les règles relatives à la déclaration et à la notification de blocus sont applicables dans le cas où le blocus serait étendu ou viendrait à être repris après avoir été levé.

ART. 13.

La levée volontaire du blocus, ainsi que toute restriction qui y serait apportée, doit être notifiée dans la forme prescrite par l'article 11.

ART. 14.

La saisissabilité d'un navire neutre pour violation de blocus est subordonnée à la connaissance réelle ou présumée du blocus.

ART. 15.

La connaissance du blocus est, sauf preuve contraire, présumée, lorsque le navire a quitté un port neutre postérieurement à la notification, en temps utile, du blocus à la Puissance dont relève ce port.

ART. 16.

Si le navire qui approche du port bloqué n'a pas. connu ou ne peut être présumé avoir connu l'existence du blocus, la notification doit être faite au navire même par un officier de l'un des bâtiments de la force bloquante. Cette notification doit être portée sur le livre de bord avec indication de la date et de l'heure, ainsi que de la position géographique du navire à ce moment.

Le navire neutre qui sort du port bloqué, alors que, par la négligence du commandant de la force bloquante, aucune déclaration de blocus n'a été

ART. 12.

The rules as to declaration and notification of blockade apply to cases where the limits of a blockade are extended, or where a blockade is re-established after having been raised.

ART. 13.

The voluntary raising of a blockade, as also any restriction in the limits of a blockade, must be notified in the manner prescribed by Article 11.

ART. 14.

The liability of a neutral vessel to capture for breach of blockade is contingent on her knowledge, actual or presumptive, of the blockade.

ART. 15.

Failing proof to the contrary, knowledge of the blockade is presumed if the vessel left a neutral port subsequently to the notification of the blockade to the Power to which such port belongs, provided that such notification was made in sufficient time.

ART. 16.

If a vessel approaching a blockaded port has no knowledge, actual or presumptive, of the blockade, the notification must be made to the vessel itself by an officer of one of the ships of the blockading force. This notification should be entered in the vessel's logbook, and must state the day and hour, and the geographical position of the vessel at the time.

If through the negligence of the officer commanding the blockading force no declaration of blockade has been notified to the local authorities,

notifiée aux autorités locales ou qu'un délai n'a pas été indiqué dans la déclaration notifiée, doit être laissé libre de passer.

or, if in the declaration, as notified, no period has been mentioned within which neutral vessels may come out, a neutral vessel coming out of the blockaded port must be allowed to pass free.

ART. 17.

La saisie des navires neutres pour violation de blocus ne peut être effectuée que dans le rayon d'action des bâtiments de guerre chargés d'assurer l'effectivité du blocus.

ART. 17.

Neutral vessels may not be captured for breach of blockade except within the area of operations of the warships detailed to render the blockade effective.

ART. 18.

Les forces bloquantes ne doivent pas barrer l'accès aux ports et aux côtes neutres.

ART. 18.

The blockading forces must not bar access to neutral ports or coasts.

ART. 19.

La violation du blocus est insuffi‑ ment caractérisée pour autoriser la saisie du navire, lorsque celui-ci est actuellement dirigé vers un port non bloqué, quelle que soit la destination ultérieure du navire ou de son chargement.

ART. 19.

Whatever may be the ulterior destination of a vessel or of her cargo, she cannot be captured for breach of blockade, if, at the moment, she is on her way to a non-blockaded port.

ART. 20.

Le navire qui, en violation du blocus, est sorti du port bloqué ou a tenté d'y entrer, reste saisissable tant qu'il est poursuivi par un bâtiment de la force bloquante. Si la chasse en est abandonnée ou si le blocus est levé, la saisie n'en peut plus être pratiquée.

ART. 20.

A vessel which has broken blockade outwards, or which has attempted to break blockade inwards, is liable to capture so long as she is pursued by a ship of the blockading force. If the pursuit is abandoned, or if the blockade is raised, her capture can no longer be effected.

ART. 21.

Le navire reconnu coupable de violation de blocus est confisqué. Le chargement est également confisqué, à moins qu'il soit prouvé qu'au moment où la marchandise a été embarquée, le chargeur n'a ni connu ni pu connaître l'intention de violer le blocus.

ART. 21.

A vessel found guilty of breach of blockade is condemned. The cargo is also condemned, unless it is proved that at the time of the shipment of the goods the shipper neither knew nor could have known of the intention to break the blockade.

H.

Chapitre II.

De la contrebande de guerre.

Art. 22.

Sont de plein droit considérés comme contrebande de guerre les objets et matériaux suivants, compris sous le nom de contrebande absolue, savoir:

1°. Les armes de toute nature, y compris les armes de chasse, et les pièces détachées caractérisées.

2°. Les projectiles, gargousses et cartouches de toute nature, et les pièces détachées caractérisées.

3°. Les poudres et les explosifs spécialement affectés à la guerre.

4°. Les affûts, caissons, avant-trains, fourgons, forges de campagne, et les pièces détachées caractérisées.

5°. Les effets d'habillement et d'équipement militaires caractérisés.

6°. Les harnachements militaires caractérisés de toute nature.

7°. Les animaux de selle, de trait et de bât, utilisables pour la guerre.

8°. Le matériel de campement et les pièces détachées caractérisées.

9°. Les plaques de blindage.

10°. Les bâtiments et embarcations de guerre et les pièces détachées spécialement caractérisées comme ne pouvant être utilisées que sur un navire de guerre.

11°. Les instruments et appareils exclusivement faits pour la fabrication des munitions de guerre, pour la fabrication et la réparation des armes et du matériel militaire, terrestre ou naval.

Chapter II.

Contraband of War[1].

Art. 22.

The following articles may, without notice[2], be treated as contraband of war, under the name of absolute contraband :—

(1) Arms of all kinds, including arms for sporting purposes, and their distinctive component parts.

(2) Projectiles, charges, and cartridges of all kinds, and their distinctive component parts.

(3) Powder and explosives specially prepared for use in war.

(4) Gun-mountings, limber boxes, limbers, military waggons, field forges, and their distinctive component parts.

(5) Clothing and equipment of a distinctively military character.

(6) All kinds of harness of a distinctively military character.

(7) Saddle, draught, and pack animals suitable for use in war.

(8) Articles of camp equipment, and their distinctive component parts.

(9) Armour plates.

(10) Warships, including boats, and their distinctive component parts of such a nature that they can only be used on a vessel of war.

(11) Implements and apparatus designed exclusively for the manufacture of munitions of war, for the manufacture or repair of arms, or war material for use on land or sea.

---

[1] See *ante,* p. 4.

[2] See note, p. 583, *post.*

Art. 23.

Les objets et matériaux qui sont exclusivement employés à la guerre peuvent être ajoutés à la liste de contrebande absolue au moyen d'une déclaration notifiée.

La notification est adressée aux Gouvernements des autres Puissances ou à leurs représentants accrédités auprès de la Puissance qui fait la déclaration. La notification faite après l'ouverture des hostilités n'est adressée qu'aux Puissances neutres.

Art. 24.

Sont de plein droit considérés comme contrebande de guerre les objets et matériaux susceptibles de servir aux usages de la guerre comme à des usages pacifiques, et compris sous le nom de contrebande conditionnelle, savoir :

1°. Les vivres.

2°. Les fourrages et les graines propres à la nourriture des animaux.

3°. Les vêtements et les tissus d'habillement, les chaussures, propres à des usages militaires.

4°. L'or et l'argent monnayés et en lingots, les papiers représentatifs de la monnaie.

5°. Les véhicules de toute nature pouvant servir à la guerre, ainsi que les pièces détachées.

6°. Les navires, bateaux et embarcations de tout genre, les docks flottants, parties de bassins, ainsi que les pièces détachées.

7°. Le matériel fixe ou roulant des chemins de fer, le matériel des télégraphes, radiotélégraphes et téléphones.

Art. 23.

Articles exclusively used for war may be added to the list of absolute contraband by a declaration, which must be notified.

Such notification must be addressed to the Governments of other Powers, or to their representatives accredited to the Power making the declaration. A notification made after the outbreak of hostilities is addressed only to neutral Powers.

Art. 24.

The following articles, susceptible of use in war as well as for purposes of peace, may, without notice[1], be treated as contraband of war, under the name of conditional contraband :—

(1) Foodstuffs.

(2) Forage and grain, suitable for feeding animals.

(3) Clothing, fabrics for clothing, and boots and shoes, suitable for use in war.

(4) Gold and silver in coin or bullion ; paper money.

(5) Vehicles of all kinds available for use in war, and their component parts.

(6) Vessels, craft, and boats of all kinds ; floating docks, parts of docks and their component parts.

(7) Railway material, both fixed and rolling-stock, and material for telegraphs, wireless telegraphs, and telephones.

---

[1] See note, p. 583, *post*.

8°. Les aérostats et les appareils d'aviation, les pièces détachées caractérisées ainsi que les accessoires, objets et matériaux caractérisés comme devant servir à l'aérostation ou à l'aviation.

9°. Les combustibles ; les matières lubréfiantes.

10°. Les poudres et les explosifs qui ne sont pas spécialement affectés à la guerre.

11°. Les fils de fer barbelés, ainsi que les instruments servant à les fixer ou à les couper.

12°. Les fers à cheval et le matériel de maréchalerie.

13°. Les objets de harnachement et de sellerie.

14°. Les jumelles, les télescopes, les chronomètres et les divers instruments nautiques.

(8) Balloons and flying machines and their distinctive component parts, together with accessories and articles recognizable as intended for use in connection with balloons and flying machines.

(9) Fuel ; lubricants.

(10) Powder and explosives not specially prepared for use in war.

(11) Barbed wire and implements for fixing and cutting the same.

(12) Horseshoes and shoeing materials.

(13) Harness and saddlery.

(14) Field glasses, telescopes, chronometers, and all kinds of nautical instruments.

Art. 25.

Les objets et matériaux susceptibles de servir aux usages de la guerre comme à des usages pacifiques, et autres que ceux visés aux articles 22 et 24, peuvent être ajoutés à la liste de contrebande conditionnelle au moyen d'une déclaration qui sera notifiée de la manière prévue à l'article 23, deuxième alinéa.

Art. 25.

Articles susceptible of use in war as well as for purposes of peace, other than those enumerated in Articles 22 and 24, may be added to the list of conditional contraband by a declaration, which must be notified in the manner provided for in the second paragraph of Article 23.

Art. 26.

Si une Puissance renonce, en ce qui la concerne, à considérer comme contrebande de guerre des objets et matériaux qui rentrent dans une des catégories énumérées aux articles 22 et 24, elle fera connaître son intention par une déclaration notifiée de la manière prévue à l'article 23, deuxième alinéa.

Art. 26.

If a Power waives, so far as it is concerned, the right to treat as contraband of war an article comprised in any of the classes enumerated in Articles 22 and 24, such intention shall be announced by a declaration, which must be notified in the manner provided for in the second paragraph of Article 23.

ART. 27.

Les objets et matériaux, qui ne sont pas susceptibles de servir aux usages de la guerre, ne peuvent pas être déclarés contrebande de guerre.

ART. 28.

Ne peuvent pas être déclarés contrebande de guerre les articles suivants, savoir :

1°. Le coton brut, les laines, soies, jutes, lins, chanvres bruts, et les autres matières premières des industries textiles, ainsi que leurs filés.

2°. Les noix et graines oléagineuses ; le coprah.

3°. Les caoutchoucs, résines, gommes et laques ; le houblon.

4°. Les peaux brutes, les cornes, os et ivoires.

5°. Les engrais naturels et artificiels, y compris les nitrates et phosphates pouvant servir à l'agriculture.

6°. Les minerais.

7°. Les terres, les argiles, la chaux, la craie, les pierres y compris les marbres, les briques, ardoises et tuiles.

8°. Les porcelaines et verreries.

9°. Le papier et les matières préparées pour sa fabrication.

10°. Les savons, couleurs, y compris les matières exclusivement destinées à les produire, et les vernis.

11°. L'hypochlorite de chaux, les cendres de soude, la soude caustique, le sulfate de soude en pains, l'ammoniaque, le sulfate d'ammoniaque et le sulfate de cuivre.

12°. Les machines servant à l'agriculture, aux mines, aux industries textiles et à l'imprimerie.

13°. Les pierres précieuses, les pierres fines, les perles, la nacre et les coraux.

ART. 27.

Articles which are not susceptible of use in war may not be declared contraband of war.

ART. 28.

The following may not be declared contraband of war :—

(1) Raw cotton, wool, silk, jute, flax, hemp, and other raw materials of the textile industries, and yarns of the same.

(2) Oil seeds and nuts ; copra.

(3) Rubber, resins, gums, and lacs ; hops.

(4) Raw hides, horns, bones, and ivory.

(5) Natural and artificial manures, including nitrates and phosphates for agricultural purposes.

(6) Metallic ores.

(7) Earths, clays, lime, chalk, stone, including marble, bricks, slates, and tiles.

(8) Chinaware and glass.

(9) Paper and paper-making materials.

(10) Soap, paint and colours, including articles exclusively used in their manufacture, and varnish.

(11) Bleaching powder, soda ash, caustic soda, salt cake, ammonia, sulphate of ammonia, and sulphate of copper.

(12) Agricultural, mining, textile, and printing machinery.

(13) Precious and semi-precious stones, pearls, mother-of-pearl, and coral.

14°. Les horloges, pendules, et montres autres que les chronomètres.

15°. Les articles de mode et les objets de fantaisie.

16°. Les plumes de tout genre, les crins et soies.

17°. Les objets d'ameublement ou d'ornement; les meubles et accessoires de bureau.

(14) Clocks and watches, other than chronometers.

(15) Fashion and fancy goods.

(16) Feathers of all kinds, hairs, and bristles.

(17) Articles of household furniture and decoration; office furniture and requisites.

Art. 29.

Ne peuvent non plus être considérés comme contrebande de guerre :

1°. Les objets et matériaux servant exclusivement à soigner les malades et les blessés. Toutefois, ils peuvent, en cas de nécessité militaire importante, être réquisitionnés, moyennant une indemnité, lorsqu'ils ont la destination prévue à l'article 30.

2°. Les objets et matériaux destinés à l'usage du navire où ils sont trouvés, ainsi qu'à l'usage de l'équipage et des passagers de ce navire pendant la traversée.

Art. 29.

Likewise the following may not be treated as contraband of war :—

(1) Articles serving exclusively to aid the sick and wounded. They can, however, in case of urgent military necessity and subject to the payment of compensation, be requisitioned, if their destination is that specified in Article 30.

(2) Articles intended for the use of the vessel in which they are found, as well as those intended for the use of her crew and passengers during the voyage.

Art. 30.

Les articles de contrebande absolue sont saisissables, s'il est établi qu'ils sont destinés au territoire de l'ennemi ou à un territoire occupé par lui ou à ses forces armées. Peu importe que le transport de ces objets se fasse directement ou exige, soit un transbordement, soit un trajet par terre.

Art. 30.

Absolute contraband is liable to capture if it is shown to be destined to territory belonging to or occupied by the enemy, or to the armed forces of the enemy. It is immaterial whether the carriage of the goods is direct or entails transhipment or a subsequent transport by land.

Art. 31.

La destination prévue à l'article 30 est définitivement prouvée dans les cas suivants :

1°. Lorsque la marchandise est documentée pour être débarquée dans un port de l'ennemi ou pour être livrée à ses forces armées.

Art. 31.

Proof of the destination specified in Article 30 is complete in the following cases :—

(1) When the goods are documented for discharge in an enemy port, or for delivery to the armed forces of the enemy.

2°. Lorsque le navire ne doit aborder qu'à des ports ennemis, ou lorsqu'il doit toucher à un port de l'ennemi ou rejoindre ses forces armées, avant-d'arriver au port neutre pour lequel la marchandise est documentée.

(2) When the vessel is to call at enemy ports only, or when she is to touch at an enemy port or meet the armed forces of the enemy before reaching the neutral port for which the goods in question are documented.

ART. 32.

Les papiers de bord font preuve complète de l'itinéraire du navire transportant de la contrebande absolue, à moins que le navire soit rencontré ayant manifestement dévié de la route qu'il devrait suivre d'après ses papiers de bord et sans pouvoir justifier d'une cause suffisante de cette déviation.

ART. 32.

Where a vessel is carrying absolute contraband, her papers are conclusive proof as to the voyage on which she is engaged, unless she is found clearly out of the course indicated by her papers and unable to give adequate reasons to justify such deviation.

ART. 33.

Les articles de contrebande conditionnelle sont saisissables, s'il est établi qu'ils sont destinés à l'usage des forces armées ou des administrations de l'État ennemi, à moins, dans ce dernier cas, que les circonstances établissent qu'en fait ces articles ne peuvent être utilisés pour la guerre en cours ; cette dernière réserve ne s'applique pas aux envois visés par l'article 24—4°.

ART. 33.

Conditional contraband is liable to capture if it is shown to be destined for the use of the armed forces or of a government department of the enemy State, unless in this latter case the circumstances show that the goods cannot in fact be used for the purposes of the war in progress. This latter exception does not apply to a consignment coming under Article 24 (4).

ART. 34.

Il y a présomption de la destination prévue à l'article 33, si l'envoi est adressé aux autorités ennemies, ou à un commerçant établi en pays ennemi et lorsqu'il est notoire que ce commerçant fournit à l'ennemi des objets et matériaux de cette nature. Il en

ART. 34.

The destination referred to in Article 33 is presumed to exist if the goods are consigned to enemy authorities, or to a contractor established in the enemy country who, as a matter of common knowledge, supplies articles of this kind to the enemy[1]. A similar

---

[1] Considerable discussion took place in the Press, and several questions were asked in the House of Commons with reference to this Article, both with regard to the translation of *commerçant* by "contractor," and as to whether *ennemi* meant enemy government. The Report (see *post*, p. 588) in discussing the destination of conditional contraband says, "It may be an enemy authority or a trader established in an enemy country who as a matter of common

est de même si l'envoi est à destination d'une place fortifiée ennemie, ou d'une autre place servant de base aux forces armées ennemies ; toutefois, cette présomption ne s'applique pas au navire de commerce lui-même faisant route vers une de ces places et dont on entend établir le caractère de contrebande.

A défaut des présomptions ci-dessus, la destination est présumée innocente.

Les présomptions établies dans le présent article admettent la preuve contraire.

presumption arises if the goods are consigned to a fortified place belonging to the enemy, or other place serving as a base for the armed forces of the enemy. No such presumption, however, arises in the case of a merchant vessel bound for one of these places if it is sought to prove that she herself is contraband.

In cases where the above presumptions do not arise, the destination is presumed to be innocent.

The presumptions set up by this Article may be rebutted.

ART. 35.

Les articles de contrebande conditionnelle ne sont saisissables que sur le navire qui fait route vers le territoire de l'ennemi ou vers un territoire occupé par lui ou vers ses forces armées et qui ne doit pas les décharger dans un port intermédiaire neutre.

Les papiers de bord font preuve complète de l'itinéraire du navire ainsi que du lieu de déchargement des

ART. 35.

Conditional contraband is not liable to capture, except when found on board a vessel bound for territory belonging to or occupied by the enemy, or for the armed forces of the enemy, and when it is not to be discharged in an intervening neutral port.

The ship's papers are conclusive proof[1] both as to the voyage on which the vessel is engaged and as to the

---

knowledge, supplies the enemy *Government* with articles of the kind in question." The Under-Secretary for Foreign Affairs (Mr Mackinnon Wood) stated in the House of Commons on the 29th March, 1909, that the word *commerçant* in this Article "cannot possibly apply to a mere merchant who supplies goods to the general public," and the Secretary of State for Foreign Affairs (Sir Edward Grey) on the 5th April, 1909, in answer to a question on the divergence between the terms of Article 34 and the General Report, replied as follows : " For the reasons already given, I cannot admit that there is any ambiguity as to the meaning of Article 34. It is made clear, both by Article 33, on which Article 34 is dependent, and by the general official report of the Conference, that the word *ennemi* in Article 34 can only mean the enemy government. It is evident, however, that if the point had been raised at the time it would have been made perfectly clear in the drafting, and we therefore propose to make a declaration, at the time of the ratification, that the word *ennemi* in Article 34 means the government of the enemy." (See *The Times*, 6th April, 1909.)

[1] The General Report qualifies this by the statement, "It must not be too literally interpreted, for that would make all frauds easy...the ship's papers are proof, unless facts show their evidence to be false." (See *post*, p. 589. See also letter of Mr Arthur Cohen, K.C., in *The Times*, 6th April, 1909.) On " ship's papers " see T. E. Holland, *Manual of Naval Prize Law*, pp. 3, 43, 45–59.

marchandises, à moins que ce navire soit rencontré ayant manifestement dévié de la route qu'il devrait suivre d'après ses papiers de bord et sans pouvoir justifier d'une cause suffisante de cette déviation.

port of discharge of the goods, unless she is found clearly out of the course indicated by her papers, and unable to give adequate reasons to justify such deviation.

ART. 36.

Par dérogation à l'article 35, si le territoire de l'ennemi n'a pas de frontière maritime, les articles de contrebande conditionnelle sont saisissables, lorsqu'il est établi qu'ils ont la destination prévue à l'article 33.

ART. 36.

Notwithstanding the provisions of Article 35, conditional contraband, if shown to have the destination referred to in Article 33, is liable to capture in cases where the enemy country has no seaboard.

ART. 37.

Le navire transportant des articles, qui sont saisissables comme contrebande absolue ou conditionnelle, peut être saisi, en haute mer ou dans les eaux des belligérants, pendant tout le cours de son voyage, même s'il a l'intention de toucher à un port d'escale avant d'atteindre la destination ennemie.

ART. 37.

A vessel carrying goods liable to capture as absolute or conditional contraband may be captured on the high seas or in the territorial waters of the belligerents throughout the whole of her voyage, even if she is to touch at a port of call before reaching the hostile destination.

ART. 38.

Une saisie ne peut être pratiquée en raison d'un transport de contrebande antérieurement effectué et actuellement achevé.

ART. 38.

A vessel may not be captured on the ground that she has carried contraband on a previous occasion if such carriage is in point of fact at an end.

ART. 39.

Les articles de contrebande sont sujets à confiscation.

ART. 39.

Contraband goods are liable to condemnation.

ART. 40.

La confiscation du navire transportant de la contrebande est permise, si cette contrebande forme, soit par sa valeur, soit par son poids, soit par son volume, soit par son fret, plus de la moitié de la cargaison.

ART. 40.

A vessel carrying contraband may be condemned if the contraband, reckoned either by value, weight, volume, or freight, forms more than half the cargo.

ART. 41.

Si le navire transportant de la contrebande est relâché, les frais occasionnés au capteur par la procédure devant la juridiction nationale des prises ainsi que par la conservation du navire et de sa cargaison pendant l'instruction sont à la charge du navire.

ART. 41.

If a vessel carrying contraband is released, the costs and expenses incurred by the captor in respect of the proceedings in the national prize court and the custody of the ship and cargo during the proceedings are to be borne by the ship.

ART. 42.

Les marchandises qui appartiennent au propriétaire de la contrebande et qui se trouvent à bord du même navire sont sujettes à confiscation.

ART. 42.

Goods which belong to the owner of the contraband and are on board the same vessel are liable to condemnation.

ART. 43.

Si un navire est rencontré en mer naviguant dans l'ignorance des hostilités ou de la déclaration de contrebande applicable à son chargement, les articles de contrebande ne peuvent être confisqués que moyennant indemnité ; le navire et le surplus de la cargaison sont exempts de la confiscation et des frais prévus par l'article 41. Il en est de même si le capitaine, après avoir eu connaissance de l'ouverture des hostilités ou de la déclaration de contrebande, n'a pu encore décharger les articles de contrebande.

Le navire est réputé connaître l'état de guerre ou la déclaration de contrebande, lorsqu'il a quitté un port neutre, après que la notification de l'ouverture des hostilités ou de la déclaration de contrebande a été faite en temps utile à la Puissance dont relève ce port. L'état de guerre est, en outre, réputé connu par le navire lorsqu'il a quitté un port ennemi après l'ouverture des hostilités.

ART. 43.

If a vessel is encountered at sea while unaware of the outbreak of hostilities or of the declaration of contraband which applies to her cargo, the contraband cannot be condemned except on payment of compensation ; the vessel herself and the remainder of the cargo are not liable to condemnation or to the costs and expenses referred to in Article 41. The same rule applies if the master, after becoming aware of the outbreak of hostilities, or of the declaration of contraband, has had no opportunity of discharging the contraband.

A vessel is deemed to be aware of the existence of a state of war, or of a declaration of contraband, if she left a neutral port subsequently to the notification to the Power to which such port belongs of the outbreak of hostilities or of the declaration of contraband respectively, provided that such notification was made in sufficient time. A vessel is also deemed to be aware of the existence of a state of

war if she left an enemy port after the outbreak of hostilities.

Art. 44.

Le navire arrêté pour cause de contrebande et non susceptible de confiscation à raison de la proportion de la contrebande peut être autorisé, suivant les circonstances, à continuer sa route, si le capitaine est prêt à livrer la contrebande au bâtiment belligérant.

La remise de la contrebande est mentionnée par le capteur sur le livre de bord du navire arrêté, et le capitaine de ce navire doit remettre au capteur copie certifiée conforme de tous papiers utiles.

Le capteur a la faculté de détruire la contrebande qui lui est ainsi livrée.

Art. 44.

A vessel which has been stopped on the ground that she is carrying contraband, and which is not liable to condemnation on account of the proportion of contraband on board, may, when the circumstances permit, be allowed to continue her voyage if the master is willing to hand over the contraband to the belligerent warship.

The delivery of the contraband must be entered by the captor on the logbook of the vessel stopped, and the master must give the captor duly certified copies of all relevant papers.

The captor is at liberty to destroy the contraband that has been handed over to him under these conditions.

Chapitre III.
De l'assistance hostile.

Chapter III.
Unneutral Service.

Art. 45.

Un navire neutre est confisqué et, d'une manière générale, passible du traitement que subirait un navire neutre sujet à confiscation pour contrebande de guerre :

1°. Lorsqu'il voyage spécialement en vue du transport de passagers individuels incorporés dans la force armée de l'ennemi, ou en vue de la transmission de nouvelles dans l'intérêt de l'ennemi.

2°. Lorsqu'à la connaissance soit du propriétaire, soit de celui qui a affrété le navire en totalité, soit du

Art. 45.

A neutral vessel will be condemned and will, in a general way, receive the same treatment as a neutral vessel liable to condemnation for carriage of contraband :—

(1) If she is on a voyage specially undertaken with a view to the transport of individual passengers who are embodied in the armed forces of the enemy, or with a view to the transmission of intelligence in the interest of the enemy.

(2) If, to the knowledge of either the owner, the charterer, or the master, she is transporting a military detach-

capitaine, il transporte un détachement militaire de l'ennemi ou une ou plusieurs personnes qui, pendant le voyage, prêtent une assistance directe aux opérations de l'ennemi.

Dans les cas visés aux numéros précédents, les marchandises appartenant au propriétaire du navire sont également sujettes à confiscation.

Les dispositions du présent article ne s'appliquent pas si, lorsque le navire est rencontré en mer, il ignore les hostilités ou si le capitaine, après avoir appris l'ouverture des hostilités, n'a pu encore débarquer les personnes transportées. Le navire est réputé connaître l'état de guerre, lorsqu'il a quitté un port ennemi après l'ouverture des hostilités ou un port neutre postérieurement à la notification en temps utile de l'ouverture des hostilités à la Puissance dont relève ce port.

ment of the enemy, or one or more persons who, in the course of the voyage, directly assist the operations of the enemy.

In the cases specified under the above heads, goods belonging to the owner of the vessel are likewise liable to condemnation.

The provisions of the present Article do not apply if the vessel is encountered at sea while unaware of the outbreak of hostilities, or if the master, after becoming aware of the outbreak of hostilities, has had no opportunity of disembarking the passengers. The vessel is deemed to be aware of the existence of a state of war if she left an enemy port subsequently to the outbreak of hostilities, or a neutral port subsequently to the notification of the outbreak of hostilities to the Power to which such port belongs, provided that such notification was made in sufficient time.

ART. 46.

Un navire neutre est confisqué et, d'une manière générale, passible du traitement qu'il subirait s'il était un navire de commerce ennemi :

1°. Lorsqu'il prend une part directe aux hostilités.

2°. Lorsqu'il se trouve sous les ordres ou sous le contrôle d'un agent placé à bord par le Gouvernement ennemi.

3°. Lorsqu'il est affrété en totalité par le Gouvernement ennemi.

4°. Lorsqu'il est actuellement et exclusivement affecté, soit au transport de troupes ennemies, soit à la

ART. 46.

A neutral vessel will be condemned and, in a general way, receive the same treatment as would be applicable to her if she were an enemy merchant vessel :

(1) If she takes a direct part in the hostilities ;

(2) If she is under the orders or control of an agent placed on board by the enemy Government ;

(3) If she is in the exclusive employment of the enemy Government ;

(4) If she is at the time exclusively devoted either to the transport of enemy troops or to the transmission

transmission de nouvelles dans l'intérêt de l'ennemi.

Dans les cas visés par le présent article, les marchandises appartenant au propriétaire du navire sont également sujettes à confiscation.

of intelligence in the interest of the enemy.

In the cases covered by the present Article, goods belonging to the owner of the vessel are likewise liable to condemnation.

ART. 47.

Tout individu incorporé dans la force armée de l'ennemi, et qui sera trouvé à bord d'un navire de commerce neutre, pourra être fait prisonnier de guerre, quand même il n'y aurait pas lieu de saisir ce navire.

ART. 47.

Any individual embodied in the armed forces of the enemy who is found on board a neutral merchant vessel, may be made a prisoner of war, even though there be no ground for the capture of the vessel.

Chapitre IV.

De la destruction des prises neutres.

Chapter IV.

Destruction of Neutral Prizes[1].

ART. 48.

Un navire neutre saisi ne peut être détruit par le capteur, mais il doit être conduit dans tel port qu'il appartiendra pour y être statué ce que de droit sur la validité de la capture.

ART. 48.

A neutral vessel which has been captured may not be destroyed by the captor; she must be taken into such port as is proper for the determination there of all questions concerning the validity of the capture[2].

ART. 49.

Par exception, un navire neutre, saisi par un bâtiment belligérant et qui serait sujet à confiscation, peut être détruit, si l'observation de l'article 48 peut compromettre la sécurité[3] du bâtiment de guerre ou le succès des opérations dans lesquelles celui-ci est actuellement engagé.

ART. 49.

As an exception, a neutral vessel which has been captured by a belligerent warship, and which would be liable to condemnation, may be destroyed if the observance of Article 48 would involve danger[3] to the safety of the warship or to the success of the operations in which she is engaged at the time

---

[1] See *ante*, pp. 88—92.
[2] As to prizes taken into *neutral* ports, see 13 H. C. 1907, Art. 23 (*ante*, pp. 452, 478).
[3] See *post*, p. 598.

ART. 50.

Avant la destruction, les personnes qui se trouvent à bord devront être mises en sûreté, et tous les papiers de bord et autres pièces, que les intéressés estimeront utiles pour le jugement sur la validité de la capture, devront être transbordés sur le bâtiment de guerre.

ART. 51.

Le capteur qui a détruit un navire neutre doit, préalablement à tout jugement sur la validité de la capture, justifier en fait n'avoir agi qu'en présence d'une nécessité exceptionnelle, comme elle est prévue à l'article 49. Faute par lui de ce faire, il est tenu à indemnité vis-à-vis des intéressés, sans qu'il y ait à rechercher si la capture était valable ou non.

ART. 52.

Si la capture d'un navire neutre, dont la destruction a été justifiée, est ensuite déclarée nulle, le capteur doit indemniser les intéressés en remplacement de la restitution à laquelle ils auraient droit.

ART. 53.

Si des marchandises neutres qui n'étaient pas susceptibles de confiscation ont été détruites avec le navire, le propriétaire de ces marchandises a droit à une indemnité.

ART. 54.

Le capteur a la faculté d'exiger la remise ou de procéder à la destruction des marchandises confiscables trouvées

ART. 50.

Before the vessel is destroyed all persons on board must be placed in safety, and all the ship's papers and other documents which the parties interested consider relevant for the purpose of deciding on the validity of the capture must be taken on board the warship.

ART. 51.

A captor who has destroyed a neutral vessel must, prior to any decision respecting the validity of the prize, establish that he only acted in the face of an exceptional necessity of the nature contemplated in Article 49. If he fails to do this, he must compensate the parties interested and no examination shall be made of the question whether the capture was valid or not.

ART. 52.

If the capture of a neutral vessel is subsequently held to be invalid, though the act of destruction has been held to have been justifiable, the captor must pay compensation to the parties interested, in place of the restitution to which they would have been entitled.

ART. 53.

If neutral goods not liable to condemnation have been destroyed with the vessel, the owner of such goods is entitled to compensation.

ART. 54.

The captor has the right to demand the handing over, or to proceed himself to the destruction of, any goods

à bord d'un navire qui lui-même n'est pas sujet à confiscation, lorsque les circonstances sont telles que, d'après l'article 49, elles justifieraient la destruction d'un navire passible de confiscation. Il mentionne les objets livrés ou détruits sur le livre de bord du navire arrêté et se fait remettre par le capitaine copie certifiée conforme de tous papiers utiles. Lorsque la remise ou la destruction a été effectuée et que les formalités ont été remplies, le capitaine doit être autorisé à continuer sa route.

Les dispositions des articles 51 et 52 concernant la responsabilité du capteur qui a détruit un navire neutre sont applicables.

Chapitre V.

Du transfert de pavillon.

ART. 55.

Le transfert sous pavillon neutre d'un navire ennemi, effectué avant l'ouverture des hostilités, est valable à moins qu'il soit établi que ce transfert a été effectué en vue d'éluder les conséquences qu'entraîne le caractère de navire ennemi. Il y a néanmoins présomption de nullité si l'acte de transfert ne se trouve pas à bord, alors que le navire a perdu la nationalité belligérante moins de soixante jours avant l'ouverture des hostilités ; la preuve contraire est admise.

Il y a présomption absolue de validité d'un transfert effectué plus de trente jours avant l'ouverture des hostilités, s'il est absolu, complet, conforme à la législation des pays intéressés, et

liable to condemnation found on board a vessel not herself liable to condemnation, provided that the circumstances are such as would, under Article 49, justify the destruction of a vessel herself liable to condemnation. The captor must enter the goods surrendered or destroyed in the logbook of the vessel stopped, and must obtain duly certified copies of all relevant papers. When the goods have been handed over or destroyed, and the formalities duly carried out, the master must be allowed to continue his voyage.

The provisions of Articles 51 and 52 respecting the obligations of a captor who has destroyed a neutral vessel are applicable.

Chapter V.

Transfer to a Neutral Flag.

ART. 55.

The transfer of an enemy vessel to a neutral flag, effected before the outbreak of hostilities, is valid, unless it is proved that such transfer was made in order to evade the consequences to which an enemy vessel, as such, is exposed. There is, however, a presumption, if the bill of sale is not on board a vessel which has lost her belligerent nationality less than sixty days before the outbreak of hostilities, that the transfer is void. This presumption may be rebutted.

Where the transfer was effected more than thirty days before the outbreak of hostilities, there is an absolute presumption that it is valid if it is unconditional, complete, and in

s'il a cet effet que le contrôle du navire et le bénéfice de son emploi ne restent pas entre les mêmes mains qu'avant le transfert. Toutefois, si le navire a perdu la nationalité belligérante moins de soixante jours avant l'ouverture des hostilités et si l'acte de transfert ne se trouve pas à bord, la saisie du navire ne pourra donner lieu à des dommages et intérêts.

conformity with the laws of the countries concerned, and if its effect is such that neither the control of, nor the profits arising from the employment of, the vessel remain in the same hands as before the transfer. If, however, the vessel lost her belligerent nationality less than sixty days before the outbreak of hostilities and if the bill of sale is not on board, the capture of the vessel gives no right to damages.

Art. 56.

Le transfert sous pavillon neutre d'un navire ennemi, effectué après l'ouverture des hostilités, est nul, à moins qu'il soit établi que ce transfert n'a pas été effectué en vue d'éluder les conséquences qu'entraîne le caractère de navire ennemi.

Toutefois, il y a présomption absolue de nullité :

1°. Si le transfert a été effectué pendant que le navire est en voyage ou dans un port bloqué.

2°. S'il y a faculté de réméré ou de retour.

3°. Si les conditions, auxquelles est soumis le droit de pavillon d'après la législation du pavillon arboré, n'ont pas été observées.

Art. 56.

The transfer of an enemy vessel to a neutral flag, effected after the outbreak of hostilities, is void unless it is proved that such transfer was not made in order to evade the consequences to which an enemy vessel, as such, is exposed.

There is, however, an absolute presumption that a transfer is void—

(1) If the transfer has been made during a voyage or in a blockaded port.

(2) If a right to repurchase or recover the vessel is reserved to the vendor.

(3) If the requirements of the municipal law governing the right to fly the flag under which the vessel is sailing, have not been fulfilled.

Chapitre VI.

Du caractère ennemi.

Art. 57.

Sous réserve des dispositions relatives au transfert de pavillon, le caractère neutre ou ennemi du navire est déterminé par le pavillon qu'il a le droit de porter.

Chapter VI.

Enemy Character.

Art. 57.

Subject to the provisions respecting transfer to another flag, the neutral or enemy character of a vessel is determined by the flag which she is entitled to fly.

Le cas où le navire neutre se livre à une navigation réservée en temps de paix reste hors de cause et n'est nullement visé par cette règle.

The case where a neutral vessel is engaged in a trade which is closed in time of peace, remains outside the scope of, and is in no wise affected by, this rule[1].

ART. 58.

Le caractère neutre ou ennemi des marchandises trouvées à bord d'un navire ennemi est déterminé par le caractère neutre ou ennemi de leur propriétaire.

ART. 58.

The neutral or enemy character of goods found on board an enemy vessel is determined by the neutral or enemy character of the owner[2].

ART. 59.

Si le caractère neutre de la marchandise trouvée à bord d'un navire ennemi n'est pas établi, la marchandise est présumée ennemie.

ART. 59.

In the absence of proof of the neutral character of goods found on board an enemy vessel, they are presumed to be enemy goods.

ART. 60.

Le caractère ennemi de la marchandise chargée à bord d'un navire ennemi subsiste jusqu'à l'arrivée à destination, nonobstant un transfert intervenu pendant le cours de l'expédition, après l'ouverture des hostilités.

Toutefois, si, antérieurement à la capture, un précédent propriétaire neutre exerce, en cas de faillite du propriétaire ennemi actuel, un droit de revendication légale sur la marchandise, celle-ci reprend le caractère neutre.

ART. 60.

Enemy goods on board an enemy vessel retain their enemy character until they reach their destination, notwithstanding any transfer effected after the outbreak of hostilities while the goods are being forwarded.

If, however, prior to the capture, a former neutral owner exercises, on the bankruptcy of an existing enemy owner, a recognized legal right to recover the goods, they regain their neutral character.

Chapitre VII.
Du convoi.
ART. 61.

Les navires neutres soùs convoi de leur pavillon sont exempts de visite. Le commandant du convoi donne par

Chapter VII.
Convoy.
ART. 61.

Neutral vessels under convoy of warships of their own nationality are exempt from search. The commander

---

[1] For "the Rule of war of 1756," to which this paragraph has reference, see Wheaton's *Elements of International Law*, § 508 ; see also *post*, pp. 596, 604.

[2] The Conference was unable to agree on rules for the determination of the neutral or enemy character of the owner (see *post*, p. 571).

H.   36

écrit, à la demande du commandant d'un bâtiment de guerre belligérant, sur le caractère des navires et sur leur chargement, toutes informations que la visite servirait à obtenir.

of a convoy gives, in writing, at the request of the commander of a belligerent warship, all information as to the character of the vessels and their cargoes, which could be obtained by search.

ART. 62.

Si le commandant du bâtiment de guerre belligérant a lieu de soupçonner que la religion du commandant du convoi a été surprise, il lui communique ses soupçons. C'est au commandant du convoi seul qu'il appartient en ce cas de procéder à une vérification. Il doit constater le résultat de cette vérification par un procès-verbal dont une copie est remise à l'officier du bâtiment de guerre. Si des faits ainsi constatés justifient, dans l'opinion du commandant du convoi, la saisie d'un ou de plusieurs navires, la protection du convoi doit leur être retirée.

ART. 62.

If the commander of the belligerent warship has reason to suspect that the confidence of the commander of the convoy has been abused, he communicates his suspicions to him. In such a case it is for the commander of the convoy alone to investigate the matter. He must record the result of such investigation in a report, of which a copy is handed to the officer of the warship. If, in the opinion of the commander of the convoy, the facts shown in the report justify the capture of one or more vessels, the protection of the convoy must be withdrawn from such vessels.

Chapitre VIII.

De la résistance à la visite.

ART. 63.

La résistance opposée par la force à l'exercice légitime du droit d'arrêt, de visite et de saisie entraîne, dans tous les cas, la confiscation du navire. Le chargement est passible du même traitement que subirait le chargement d'un navire ennemi ; les marchandises appartenant au capitaine ou au propriétaire du navire sont considérées comme marchandises ennemies.

Chapter VIII.

Resistance to Search.

ART. 63.

Forcible resistance to the legitimate exercise of the right of stoppage, search, and capture, involves in all cases the condemnation of the vessel. The cargo is liable to the same treatment as the cargo of an enemy vessel. Goods belonging to the master or owner of the vessel are treated as enemy goods.

Chapitre IX.	**Chapter IX.**
Des dommages et intérêts.	**Compensation.**

Art. 64.	Art. 64.

Si la saisie du navire ou des marchandises n'est pas validée par la juridiction des prises ou si, sans qu'il y ait eu de mise en jugement, la saisie n'est pas maintenue, les intéressés ont droit à des dommages et intérêts, à moins qu'il y ait eu des motifs suffisants de saisir le navire ou les marchandises.

If the capture of a vessel or of goods is not upheld by the prize court, or if the prize is released without any judgment being given, the parties interested have the right to compensation, unless there were good reasons for capturing the vessel or goods.

DISPOSITIONS FINALES.	**FINAL PROVISIONS.**
Art. 65.	Art. 65.

Les dispositions de la présente Déclaration forment un ensemble indivisible.

The provisions of the present Declaration must be treated as a whole, and cannot be separated.

Art. 66.	Art. 66.

Les Puissances Signataires s'engagent à s'assurer, dans le cas d'une guerre où les belligérants seraient tous parties à la présente Déclaration, l'observation réciproque des règles contenues dans cette Déclaration. Elles donneront, en conséquence, à leurs autorités et à leurs forces armées les instructions nécessaires et prendront les mesures qu'il conviendra pour en garantir l'application par leurs tribunaux, spécialement par leurs tribunaux de prises.

The Signatory Powers undertake to insure in any war in which all the belligerents are parties to the present Declaration the mutual observance of the rules contained herein. They will therefore issue the necessary instructions to their authorities and to their armed forces, and will take such measures as may be required in order to insure that it will be applied by their courts, and more particularly by their prize courts.

Art. 67.	Art. 67.

La présente Déclaration sera ratifiée aussitôt que possible.

Les ratifications seront déposées à Londres.

Le premier dépôt de ratifications sera constaté par un procès-verbal

The present Declaration shall be ratified as soon as possible.

The ratifications shall be deposited in London.

The first deposit of ratifications shall be recorded in a Protocol signed

36—2

signé par les Représentants des Puissances qui y prennent part, et par le Principal Secrétaire d'État de Sa Majesté Britannique au Département des Affaires Étrangères.

Les dépôts ultérieurs de ratifications se feront au moyen d'une notification écrite adressée au Gouvernement Britannique et accompagnée de l'instrument de ratification.

Copie certifiée conforme du procès-verbal relatif au premier dépôt de ratifications, des notifications mentionnées à l'alinéa précédent, ainsi que de instruments de ratification qui les accompagnent, sera immédiatement, par les soins du Gouvernement Britannique et par la voie diplomatique, remise aux Puissances Signataires. Dans les cas visés par l'alinéa précédent, ledit Gouvernement leur fera connaître en même temps la date à laquelle il a reçu la notification.

by the Representatives of the Powers taking part therein, and by His Britannic Majesty's Principal Secretary of State for Foreign Affairs.

The subsequent deposits of ratifications shall be made by means of a written notification addressed to the British Government, and accompanied by the instrument of ratification.

A duly certified copy of the Protocol relating to the first deposit of ratifications, and of the notifications mentioned in the preceding paragraph as well as of the instruments of ratification which accompany them, shall be immediately sent by the British Government, through the diplomatic channel, to the Signatory Powers. The said Government shall, in the cases contemplated in the preceding paragraph, inform them at the same time of the date on which it received the notification.

ART. 68.

La présente Déclaration produira effet, pour les Puissances qui auront participé au premier dépôt de ratifications, soixante jours après la date du procès-verbal de ce dépôt et, pour les Puissances qui ratifieront ultérieurement, soixante jours après que la notification de leur ratification aura été reçue par le Gouvernement Britannique.

ART. 68.

The present Declaration shall take effect, in the case of the Powers which were parties to the first deposit of ratifications, sixty days after the date of the Protocol recording such deposit, and, in the case of the Powers which shall ratify subsequently, sixty days after the notification of their ratification shall have been received by the British Government.

ART. 69.

S'il arrivait qu'une des Puissances Signataires voulût dénoncer la présente Déclaration, elle ne pourra le faire que pour la fin d'une période de douze ans

ART. 69.

In the event of one of the Signatory Powers wishing to denounce the present Declaration, such denunciation can only be made to take effect at

commençant à courir soixante jours après le premier dépôt de ratifications et, ensuite, pour la fin de périodes successives de six ans, dont la première commencera à l'expiration de la période de douze ans.

La dénonciation devra être, au moins un an à l'avance, notifiée par écrit au Gouvernement Britannique, qui en donnera connaissance à toutes les autres Puissances.

Elle ne produira ses effets qu'à l'égard de la Puissance qui l'aura notifiée.

ART. 70.

Les Puissances représentées à la Conférence Navale de Londres, attachant un prix particulier à la reconnaissance générale des règles adoptées par elles, expriment l'espoir que les Puissances qui n'y étaient pas représentées adhèreront à la présente Déclaration. Elles prient le Gouvernement Britannique de vouloir bien les inviter à le faire.

La Puissance qui désire adhérer notifie par écrit son intention au Gouvernement Britannique, en lui transmettant l'acte d'adhésion, qui sera déposé dans les archives dudit Gouvernement.

Ce Gouvernement transmettra immédiatement à toutes les autres Puissances copie certifiée conforme de la notification, ainsi que de l'acte d'adhésion, en indiquant la date à laquelle il a reçu la notification. L'adhésion produira effet soixante jours après cette date.

the end of a period of twelve years, beginning sixty days after the first deposit of ratifications, and, after that time, at the end of successive periods of six years, of which the first will begin at the end of the period of twelve years[1].

Such denunciation must be notified in writing, at least one year in advance, to the British Government, which shall inform all the other Powers.

It will only operate in respect of the denouncing Power.

ART. 70.

The Powers represented at the London Naval Conference attach particular importance to the general recognition of the rules which they have adopted, and therefore express the hope that the Powers which were not represented there will accede to the present Declaration. They request the British Government to invite them to do so.

A Power which desires to accede shall notify its intention in writing to the British Government, and transmit simultaneously the act of accession, which will be deposited in the archives of the said Government.

The said Government shall forthwith transmit to all the other Powers a duly certified copy of the notification, together with the act of accession, and communicate the date on which such notification was received. The accession takes effect sixty days after such date.

---

[1] Cp. 12 H. C. 1907, Art. 55 (1) and (2), *ante*, p. 427.

La situation des Puissances adhérentes sera, en tout ce qui concerne cette Déclaration, assimilée à la situation des Puissances Signataires.

In respect of all matters concerning this Declaration, acceding Powers shall be on the same footing as the Signatory Powers.

ART. 71.

La présente Déclaration, qui portera la date du 26 février 1909, pourra être signée à Londres jusqu'au 30 juin 1909, par les Plénipotentiaires des Puissances représentées à la Conférence Navale.

En foi de quoi, les Plénipotentiaires ont revêtu la présente Déclaration de leurs signatures et y ont apposé leurs cachets.

Fait à Londres, le vingt-six février mil neuf cent neuf, en un seul exemplaire, qui restera déposé dans les archives du Gouvernement Britannique et dont des copies, certifiées conformes, seront remise par la voie diplomatique aux Puissances représentées à la Conférence Navale.

[*Suivent les Signatures.*]

ART. 71.

The present Declaration, which bears the date of the 26th February, 1909, may be signed in London up till the 30th June, 1909, by the Plenipotentiaries of the Powers represented at the Naval Conference.

In faith whereof the Plenipotentiaries have signed the present Declaration, and have thereto affixed their seals.

Done at London, the twenty-sixth day of February, one thousand nine hundred and nine, in a single original, which shall remain deposited in the archives of the British Government, and of which duly certified copies shall be sent through the diplomatic channel to the Powers represented at the Naval Conference.

[*Here follow the Signatures*[1].]

---

[1] The Declaration has been signed by all the Powers represented at the Conference.

GENERAL REPORT ON THE DECLARATION PRESENTED TO THE NAVAL
CONFERENCE ON BEHALF OF ITS DRAFTING COMMITTEE[1].

(Translation[2].)

On the 27th February, 1908, the British Government addressed a
Origin of   circular to various Powers[3] inviting them to meet at a Con-
Conference.   ference with the object of reaching an agreement as to the
definition of the generally recognized principles of international law in the

[1] This Committee consists of Messrs Kriege (*Germany*), Wilson (*United States of America*), Dumba (*Austria-Hungary*), Estrada (*Spain*), Renault (*France*) (Reporter), Hurst (*Great Britain*), Ricci-Busatti (*Italy*), Sakamoto (*Japan*), Ruyssenaers (*Netherlands*), Baron Taube (*Russia*).

"The work of the Conference was materially facilitated by the preliminary exchange of views between the several Governments which had agreed to send Delegates. This entitled His Majesty's Government, with the valuable assistance of the eminent French jurist, M. Fromageot, whose services had been placed at their disposal by the courtesy of the French Government, to present to the Conference as bases for its discussion a set of draft articles dealing with the questions comprised in the programme, and laying down a number of generally recognised rules of international law which it was found possible to deduce from the statements furnished by the different Powers....Under the courteous and efficient chairmanship of M. Renault, the distinguished French Plenipotentiary, whose unfailing tact, unrivalled knowledge, and wide experience materially contributed to the smooth progress of the discussions, the main lines of the general agreement which was subsequently embodied in the terms of the final Declaration, were laid down in this Grand Committee. A more restricted number of members was then selected to constitute an Examining Committee, which proceeded to work out in greater detail the questions presenting special difficulties, whilst the duty of preparing the final text of the rules agreed upon was assigned to a Drafting Committee. A small Legal Committee was also appointed to consider the very technical questions involved in the problem of how to determine what constitutes enemy property. Over the Legal Committee, M. Fromageot presided, whilst M. Renault acted as chairman and reporter of the other committees. The proceedings of the Conference in plenary meetings are recorded in the minutes, and short summaries were made of the discussions in Grand Committee. Attached to these minutes is, among other papers, the General Report to the Conference prepared by M. Renault. We desire to call your particular attention to this document, which contains a most lucid explanatory and critical commentary on the provisions of the Declaration. It should be borne in mind that, in accordance with the principles and practice of continental jurisprudence, such a report is considered an authoritative statement of the meaning and intention of the instrument which it explains, and that consequently foreign Governments and Courts, and, no doubt also, the International Prize Court, will construe and interpret the provisions of the Declaration by the light of the commentary given in the report." (Extract from Report of British Delegates to Sir Edward Grey, *Parl. Papers*, Misc. No. 4 (1909), pp. 93, 94.)

[2] For original French text of the Report see *Parl. Papers*, Misc. No. 5 (1000), pp. 542–577; and for the translation, *Parl. Papers*, Misc. No. 4 (1909), p. 33. The original Report and the translation contain the text of the various Articles; these are here omitted, but referred to in the side-notes of which there are none in the original or in the translation. The translation of the Report contains only two footnotes, viz. the names of the members of the Committee, and the note on "de plein droit" (Article 23).

[3] The Powers are those enumerated in the Declaration (*ante*, p. 511).

sense of Article 7, paragraph 2, of the Convention signed at The Hague on the 18th October, 1907, for the establishment of an International Prize Court. This agreement appeared necessary to the British Government on account of certain divergences of view which had become apparent at the second Peace Conference in connection with the settlement of various important questions of international maritime law in time of war. The existence of these divergent views might, it seemed, render difficult the acceptance of the International Prize Court, as the power of this Court would be the more extended in proportion as the rules to be applied by it were more uncertain.

The British Government suggested that the following questions might form the programme of the proposed Conference, and invited the Powers to express their views regarding them in preparatory Memoranda[1]:

Programme suggested by British Government.

(a) *Contraband, including the circumstances under which particular articles can be considered as contraband; the penalties for their carriage; the immunity of a ship from search when under convoy; and the rules with regard to compensation where vessels have been seized but have been found in fact only to be carrying innocent cargo;*

(b) *Blockade, including the questions as to the locality where seizure can be effected, and the notice that is necessary before a ship can be seized;*

(c) *The doctrine of continuous voyage in respect both of contraband and of blockade;*

(d) *The legality of the destruction of neutral vessels prior to their condemnation by a prize court;*

(e) *The rules as to neutral ships or persons rendering "unneutral service" ("assistance hostile");*

(f) *The legality of the conversion of a merchant-vessel into a warship on the high seas;*

(g) *The rules as to the transfer of merchant-vessels from a belligerent to a neutral flag during or in contemplation of hostilities;*

(h) *The question whether the nationality or the domicile of the owner should be adopted as the dominant factor in deciding whether property is enemy property.*

The invitations were accepted, and the Conference met on the 4th December last. The British Government had been so good as to assist its deliberations by presenting a collection of papers which quickly became known among us by the name

Bases of discussion at Conference.

---

[1] For texts of the Memoranda of the Powers see *Parl. Papers*, Misc. No. 5 (1909), pp. 2–56. The British Memorandum in English is to be found in No. 4 (1909), pp. 8–11.

of *the Red Book,* and which, after a short introduction, contains a "State-ment of the views expressed by the Powers in their Memoranda, and observations intended to serve as a basis for the deliberations of the Conference." These are the "bases of discussion" which served as a starting-point for the examination of the chief questions of existing inter-national maritime law. The Conference could not but express its gratitude for this valuable preparatory work, which was of great assistance to it. It made it possible to observe, in the first place, that the divergences in the practices and doctrines of the different countries were perhaps less wide than was generally believed, that the essential ideas were often the same in all countries, and that the methods of application alone varied with traditions or prejudices, with permanent or accidental interests. It was, therefore, possible to extract a common element which it could be agreed to recommend for uniform application. This is the end to which the efforts of the different Delegations tended, and they vied with one another in their zeal in the search for the grounds of a common understanding. Their efforts were strenuous, as is shown by the prolonged discussions of the Conference, the Grand Committee, and the Examining Committees, and by the numerous proposals which were presented. Sailors, diplo-matists, and jurists cordially co-operated in a work the description of which, rather than a final estimate of its essential value, is the object of this Report, as our impartiality might naturally be suspected.

The body of rules contained in the *Declaration,* which is the result of the deliberations of the Naval Conference, and which is to be entitled *Declaration concerning the laws of naval war,* answers well to the desire expressed by the British Government in its invitation of February 1908. The questions in the pro-gramme are all settled except two, with regard to which explanations will be given later. The solutions have been extracted from the various views or practices which prevail and represent what may be called the *media sententia.* They are not always in absolute agreement with the views peculiar to each country, but they shock the essential ideas of none. They must not be examined separately, but as a whole, otherwise there is a risk of the most serious misunderstandings. In fact, if one or more isolated rules are examined either from the belligerent or the neutral point of view, the reader may find that the interests with which he is especially concerned are jeopardized by the adoption of these rules. But they have another side. The work is one of compromise and mutual concessions. Is it, as a whole, a good one?

We confidently hope that those who study it seriously will answer that

it is.   The Declaration puts uniformity and certainty in the place of the diversity and obscurity from which international relations have too long suffered.   The Conference has tried to reconcile in an equitable and practical way the rights of belligerents with those of neutral commerce ; it consists of Powers whose conditions, from the political, economic, and geographical points of view, vary considerably.   There is therefore reason to suppose that the rules on which these Powers have agreed take sufficient account of the different interests involved, and hence may be accepted without objection by all the others.

The Preamble of the Declaration summarizes the general ideas just set forth.

The Preamble.   *Having regard to the terms in which the British Government invited various Powers to meet in conference in order to arrive at an agreement as to what are the generally recognized rules of international law within the meaning of Article 7 of the Convention of the 18th October, 1907, relative to the establishment of an International Prize Court ;*

Recognizing all the advantages which an agreement as to the said rules would present in the unfortunate event of a naval war, both as regards peaceful commerce, and as regards the belligerents and their diplomatic relations with neutral Governments ;

Having regard to the divergence often found in the methods by which it is sought to apply in practice the general principles of international law ;

Animated by the desire to insure henceforward a greater measure of uniformity in this respect ;

Hoping that a work so important to the common welfare will meet with general approval ;

What is the scope of application of the rules thus laid down ?   They must be observed in the relations between the signatory parties, since those parties acknowledge them as principles of recognized international law and, besides, expressly bind themselves to secure the benefit of them for one another.   The Signatory Powers who are or will be parties to the Convention establishing the International Prize Court will have, besides, an opportunity of having these rules applied to disputes in which they are concerned, whether the Court regards them as generally recognized rules, or takes account of the pledge given to observe them.   It is moreover to be hoped that these rules will before long be accepted by the majority of States, who will recognize the advantage of substituting exact provisions for more or less indefinite usages which tend to give rise to controversy.

It has been said above that two points in the programme of the Conference were not decided.

1. The programme mentions under head (*f*): *the legality of the conversion of a merchant vessel into a warship on the high seas.* The conflicting views on this subject which became apparent at the Conference of The Hague in 1907, have recurred at the present Conference. It may be concluded, both from the statements in the Memoranda and from the discussion, that there is no generally accepted rule on this point, nor do there appear to be any precedents which can be adduced. Though the two opposite opinions were defended with great warmth, a lively desire for an understanding was expressed on all sides; everybody was at least agreed that it would be a great advantage to put an end to uncertainty. Serious efforts were made to do justice to the interests espoused by both sides, but these unfortunately failed. A subsidiary question dependent on the previous one, on which, at one moment, it appeared possible to come to an agreement, is that of *reconversion.* According to one proposal, it was to be laid down that "merchant vessels converted into warships cannot be reconverted into merchant vessels during the whole course of the war." The rule was absolute and made no distinction as regards the place where reconversion could be effected; it was dictated by the idea that such conversion would always have disadvantages, would be productive of surprises, and lead to actual frauds. As unanimity in favour of this proposal was not forthcoming, a subsidiary one was brought forward, viz., "the conversion of a warship into a merchant vessel on the high seas is forbidden during the war." The case had in view was that of a warship (generally a recently converted merchant vessel) doffing its character so as to be able freely to revictual or refit in a neutral port without being bound by the restrictions imposed on warships. Will not the position of the neutral State between two belligerents be delicate, and will not such State expose itself to reproach whether it treats the newly converted ship as a merchant vessel or as a warship? Agreement might perhaps have been reached on this proposal, but it seemed very difficult to deal with this secondary aspect of a question which there was no hope of settling as a whole. This was the decisive reason for the rejection of all proposals.

The question of conversion on the high seas and that of reconversion therefore remain open.

2. Under head (*h*), the British Programme mentions: *the question whether the nationality or the domicile of the owner should be adopted as the dominant factor in deciding whether property is enemy property.* This question was subjected to a search-

Marginal notes:

Unsolved problems: (1) Conversion of merchant vessels into warships[1].

(2) Enemy character of property.

---

[1] See *ante*, pp. 308–321, also *Parl. Papers*, Misc. No. 5 (1909), pp. 263–8 for various Memoranda on the subject.

ing examination by a special Committee, which had to acknowledge the uncertainty of actual practice; it was proposed to put an end to this by the following provisions:—

"The neutral or enemy character of goods found on board an enemy vessel is determined by the neutral or enemy nationality of their owner, or, if he is of no nationality or of double nationality (*i.e.* both neutral and enemy), by his domicile in a neutral or enemy country;

"Provided that goods belonging to a limited liability or joint stock company are considered as neutral or enemy according as the company has its headquarters in a neutral or enemy country."

Unanimity not being forthcoming, these provisions remained without effect.

We now reach the explanation of the Declaration itself, on which we shall try, by summarizing the Reports already approved by the Conference, to give an exact and uncontroversial commentary; this, when it has become an official commentary by receiving the approval of the Conference, may serve as a guide to the different authorities—administrative, military, and judicial—who may be called on to apply it.

PRELIMINARY PROVISION.

The Signatory Powers are agreed that the rules contained in the following Chapters correspond in substance with the generally recognized principles of international law.

This provision dominates all the rules which follow. Its spirit has been indicated in the general remarks to be found at the beginning of this Report. The purpose of the Conference has, above all, been to note, to define, and, where needful, to complete what might be considered as customary law.

Chapter I.

BLOCKADE IN TIME OF WAR[1].

Blockade is here regarded solely as an operation of war, and there is no intention of touching in any way on what is called *pacific blockade*.

Blockade, as an operation of war, can be directed by a belligerent only against his adversary. This very simple rule is laid down at the start, but its full scope is apparent only when it is read in connexion with Article 18.

Article 1.
(See *ante*, p. 542.)

---

[1] For British rules on this subject see *Parl. Papers*, Misc. No. 4 (1909), pp. 5–7; for Instructions to British Delegation, *Ibid.* p. 25.

The first condition necessary to render a blockade binding is that it should be effective. There has been universal agreement on this subject for a long time. As for the definition of an effective blockade, we thought that we had only to adopt the one to be found in the Declaration of Paris of the 16th April, 1856, which, conventionally, binds a great number of States, and is in fact accepted by the rest.

Article 2.
(See *ante*, p. 542.)

It is easily to be understood that difficulties often arise on the question whether a blockade is effective or not; opposing interests are at stake. The blockading belligerent wishes to economize his efforts, and neutrals desire their trade to be as little hampered as possible. Diplomatic protests have sometimes been made on this subject. The point may be a delicate one, because no absolute rule can be laid down as to the number and position of the blockading ships. All depends on matters of fact and geographical conditions. In one case a single ship will suffice to blockade a port as effectively as possible, whereas in another a whole fleet may not be enough really to prevent access to one or more ports declared to be blockaded. It is therefore essentially a *question of fact*, to be decided on the merits of each case, and not according to a formula drawn up beforehand. Who shall decide it? The judicial authority. This will be, in the first place, the national tribunal which is called on to pronounce as to the validity of the prize and which the vessel captured for breach of blockade can ask to declare the capture void, because the blockade, not being effective, was not binding. This resort has always existed; it may not always have given satisfaction to the Powers concerned, because they may have thought that the national tribunal was rather naturally led to consider effective the blockade declared to be so by its Government. But when the International Prize Court Convention comes into force, there will be an absolutely impartial tribunal, to which neutrals may apply, and which will decide whether, in a given case, the blockade was effective or not. The possibility of this resort, besides allowing certain injustices to be redressed, will most likely have a preventive effect, in that a Government will take care to establish its blockades in such a way that their effect cannot be annulled by decisions which would inflict on it a heavy loss. The full scope of Article 3 is thus seen when it is understood that the question with which it deals must be settled by a Court. The foregoing explanation is inserted in the Report at the request of the Committee, in order to remove all possibility of misunderstanding.

Article 3.
(See *ante*, p. 542.)

It is not enough for a blockade to be established: it must be maintained.

If it is raised it may be re-established, but this requires the observance
of the same formalities as though it were established for
the first time. By tradition, a blockade is not regarded as
raised when it is in consequence of stress of weather that the
blockading forces are temporarily withdrawn. This is laid down in
Article 4. It must be considered limitative in the sense that stress of
weather is the only form of compulsion which can be alleged. If the
blockading forces were withdrawn for any other reason, the blockade would
be regarded as raised, and, if it were resumed, Articles 12 (last rule) and 13
would apply.

*Article 4.
(See ante,
p. 542.)*

Blockade, as an operation of lawful warfare, must be respected by
neutrals in so far as it really remains an operation of war
which has the object of interrupting all commercial relations
with the blockaded port. It may not be made the means of
allowing a belligerent to favour the vessels of certain nations by letting
them pass. This is the point of Article 5.

*Article 5.
(See ante,
p. 542.)*

Does the prohibition which applies to all merchant vessels apply also to
warships? No definite reply can be given. The commander
of the blockading forces may think it useful to cut off all
communication with the blockaded place, and refuse access to
neutral warships; no rule is imposed on him. If he lets them in, it is as a
matter of courtesy. If a rule has been drawn up merely to lay down this,
it is in order that it may not be claimed that a blockade has ceased to be
effective on account of leave granted to such and such neutral warships.

*Article 6.
(See ante,
p. 542.)*

The blockading commander must act impartially, as stated in Article 5.
Nevertheless, the mere fact that he has let a warship pass does not oblige
him to let pass all neutral warships which may come. It is a question of
judgment. The presence of a neutral warship in a blockaded port may not
have the same consequences at all stages of the blockade, and the commander
must be left free to judge whether he can be courteous without
making any sacrifice of his military interests.

Distress can explain the entrance of a neutral vessel into a blockaded
place, for instance, if she is in want of food or water, or needs
immediate repairs. As soon as her distress is acknowledged
by an authority of the blockading force, she *may* cross the
line of blockade; it is not a favour which she has to ask of the humanity
or courtesy of the blockading authority. The latter may deny the state of
distress, but when once it is proved to exist, the consequence follows of
itself. The vessel which has thus entered the blockaded port will not be
obliged to remain there for the whole duration of the blockade; she may

*Article 7.
(See ante,
p. 542.)*

leave as soon as she is fit to do so, when she has obtained the food or water which she needs, or when she has been repaired. But the leave granted to her must not be made an excuse for commercial transactions; therefore she is forbidden to discharge or ship any cargo.

It is needless to say that a blockading squadron which insisted on preventing a vessel in distress from passing, might do so if she afforded her the help which she needed.

Independently of the condition prescribed by the Declaration of Paris **Article 8.** that it must be effective, a blockade, to be binding, must be (See *ante*, *declared* and *notified*. Article 8 confines itself to laying p. 543.) down the principle which is applied by the following Articles.

To remove all possibility of misunderstanding it is enough to define clearly the meaning of these two expressions, which will frequently be used. The *declaration of·blockade* is the act of the competent authority (a Government or commander of a squadron) stating that a blockade is, or is about to be, established under conditions to be specified (Article 9). The *notification* is the fact of bringing the declaration of blockade to the knowledge of the neutral Powers or of certain authorities (Article 11).

These two things—declaration and notification—will in most cases be done previously to the enforcement of the rules of blockade, that is to say, to the real prohibition of passage. Nevertheless, as we shall see later, it is sometimes possible for passage to be forbidden by the very fact of the blockade which is brought to the knowledge of a vessel approaching a blockaded port by means of a *notification* which is *special*, whereas the notification which has just been defined, and which is spoken of in Article 11, is of a general character.

The declaration of blockade in most cases emanates from the bellige-**Article 9.** rent Government itself. That Government may have left the (See *ante*, commander of its naval forces free himself to declare a p. 543.) blockade according to the circumstances. There will not, perhaps, be as much reason as formerly to give this discretion, because of the ease and rapidity of communication. This, being merely an internal question, matters little.

The declaration of blockade must specify certain points which it is in the interest of neutrals to know, in order to be aware of the extent of their obligations. The moment from which it is forbidden to communicate with the blockaded place must be exactly known. It is important, as affecting the obligations both of the blockading Power and of neutrals, that there should be no uncertainty as to the places

really blockaded. Finally, the custom has long been established of allowing neutral vessels which are in a blockaded port to leave it. This custom is here confirmed, in the sense that the blockading Power *must allow* a period within which vessels may leave; the length of this period is not fixed, because it clearly depends on very varying circumstances, but it is understood that the period should be *reasonable*.

The object of this article is to insure the observance of Article 9.

Article 10.
(See *ante*, p. 543.)
Supposing the declaration of blockade contains statements which do not tally with the actual facts; it states that the blockade began, or will begin, on such a day, whereas, in fact, it only began several days later. Its geographical limits are inaccurately given; they are wider than those within which the blockading forces are operating. What shall be the sanction? The nullity of the declaration of blockade, which prevents it from being operative. If then, in such a case, a neutral vessel is captured for breach of blockade, she can refer to the nullity of the declaration of blockade as a plea for the nullity of the capture; if her plea is rejected by the national tribunal, she can appeal to the International Court.

To avoid misunderstandings, the significance of this provision must be noticed. The declaration states that the blockade begins on the 1st February, it really only begins on the 8th. It is needless to say that the declaration had no effect from the 1st to the 8th, because at that time there was no blockade at all; the declaration states a fact, but does not take the place of one. The rule goes further: the declaration shall not even be operative from the 8th onwards; it is definitely void, and another must be made.

There is no question here of cases where Article 9 is disregarded by neglect to allow neutral vessels in the blockaded port time to leave it. The sanction could not be the same. There is no reason to annul the declaration as regards neutral vessels wishing to enter the blockaded port. A special sanction is needed in that case, and it is provided by Article 16, paragraph 2.

A declaration of blockade is not valid unless notified. The observance

Article 11.
(See *ante*, p. 543.)
of a rule can only be required by those who have the opportunity of knowing it.

Two notifications must be made :—

1. The first is addressed to neutral Powers by the belligerent Power, which communicates it to the Governments themselves or to their representatives accredited to it. The communication to the Governments will in most cases be made through the diplomatic agents; it might happen

that a belligerent had no diplomatic relations with a neutral country; he will then address himself, ordinarily by telegraph, directly to the Government of that country. It is the duty of the neutral Governments advised of the declaration of blockade to take the necessary measures to dispatch the news to the different parts of their territory, especially their ports.

2. The second notification is made by the commander of the blockading force to the local authorities. These must inform, as soon as possible, the foreign Consuls residing at the blockaded place or on the blockaded coastline. These authorities would be responsible for the neglect of this obligation. Neutrals might suffer loss from the fact of not having been informed of the blockade in sufficient time.

Supposing a blockade is extended beyond its original limits: as regards the new part, it is a new blockade and, in consequence, the rules as to declaration and notification must be applied to it. The same is true in cases where a blockade is re-established after having been raised; the fact that a blockade has already existed in the same locality must not be taken into account.

Article 12. (See *ante*, p. 544.)

If it is indispensable to know of the establishment of a blockade, it would at least be useful for the public to be told of its raising, since it puts an end to the restrictions imposed on the relations of neutrals with the blockaded port. It has therefore been thought fit to ask the Power which raises a blockade to make known the fact in the form in which it has notified the establishment of the blockade (Article 11). Only it must be observed that the sanction could not be the same in the two cases. To ensure the notification of the declaration of blockade there is a direct and adequate sanction: an unnotified blockade is not binding. In the case of the raising there can be no parallel to this. The public will really gain by the raising, even without being told of it officially. The blockading Power which did not notify the raising would expose itself to diplomatic remonstrances on the ground of the nonfulfilment of an international duty. This nonfulfilment will have more or less serious consequences, according to circumstances. Sometimes the raising of the blockade will really have become known at once, and official notification would add nothing to this effective publicity.

Article 13. (See *ante*, p. 544.)

It is needless to add that only the *voluntary* raising of a blockade is here in question; if the blockading force has been driven off by the arrival of enemy forces, it cannot be held bound to make known its defeat, which its adversary will undertake to do without delay. Instead of raising a blockade, a belligerent may confine himself to restricting it; he only

H.   37

blockades one port instead of two. As regards the port which ceases to be included in the blockade, it is a case of voluntary raising, and consequently the same rule applies.

For a vessel to be liable to capture for breach of blockade, the first

Article 14.
(See *ante,*
p. 544.)

condition is that she must be aware of the blockade, because it is not just to punish some one for breaking a rule which he does not know. Nevertheless, there are circumstances in which, even in the absence of proof of actual knowledge, knowledge may be presumed, the right of rebutting this presumption being always reserved to the party concerned. (Article 15.)

A vessel has left a neutral port subsequently to the notification of the

Article 15.
(See *ante,*
p. 544.)

blockade made to the Powers to which the port belongs. Was this notification made in sufficient time, that is to say, so as to reach the port in question, where it had to be published by the port authorities? That is a question of fact to be examined. If it is settled affirmatively, it is natural to suppose that the vessel was aware of the blockade at the time of her departure. This presumption is not however absolute, and the right to adduce proof to the contrary is reserved. It is for the incriminated vessel to furnish it, by showing that circumstances existed which explain her ignorance.

A vessel is supposed to be approaching a blockaded port without its

Article 16.
(See *ante,*
p. 544.)

being possible to tell whether she knows or is presumed to know of the existence of the blockade; no notification in the sense of Article 11 has reached her. In that case a special notification is necessary in order that the vessel may be duly informed of the fact of the blockade. This notification is made to the vessel herself by an officer of one of the warships of the blockading force, and is entered on the vessel's logbook. It may be made to the vessels of a convoyed fleet by a neutral warship through the commander of the convoy, who acknowledges receipt of it and takes the necessary measures to have the notification entered on the logbook of each vessel. The entry notes the time and place where it is made, and the names of the blockaded places. The vessel is prevented from passing, and the blockade is thus made *binding* for her, though not *previously* notified; this adverb is therefore omitted in Article 8. It cannot be admitted that a merchant vessel should claim to disregard a real blockade, and to break it for the sole reason that she was not personally aware of it. But, though she may be prevented from passing, she may only be captured when she tries to break blockade after receiving the notification. This special notification is seen

to play a very small part, and must not be confused with the special notification absolutely insisted on by the practice of certain navies[1].

What has just been said refers to the vessel coming in. The vessel leaving the blockaded port must also be considered. If a regular notification of the blockade has been made to the local authorities (Article 11 (2)), the position is simple : the vessel is, or is presumed to be, aware of the blockade, and is therefore liable to capture in case she has not kept to the period for leaving allowed by the blockading Power. But it may happen that no declaration of blockade has been notified to the local authorities, or that that declaration has contained no mention of the period allowed for leaving, in spite of the rule prescribed by Article 9 (3). The sanction of the blockading Power's offence is that the vessel must be allowed to go free. It is a strong sanction, which corresponds exactly with the nature of the offence committed, and will be the best means of preventing its commission.

It is needless to say that this provision only concerns vessels to which the period allowed for leaving would have been of use—that is to say, neutral vessels which were in the port at the time when the blockade was established; it has nothing to do with vessels which are in the port after having broken blockade.

The commander of the blockading squadron may always repair his omission or mistake, make a notification of the blockade to the local authorities, or complete that which he has already made.

As is seen from these explanations, the most ordinary case is assumed —that in which the absence of notification implies negligence on the part of the commander of the blockading forces. The situation is clearly altogether changed if the commander has done all in his power to make the notification, but has been prevented from doing so by lack of goodwill on the part of the local authorities, who have intercepted all communications from outside. In that case he cannot be forced to let pass vessels which wish to leave, and which, in the absence of the prescribed notification and of presumptive knowledge of the blockade, are in a position similar to that contemplated in Article 16, paragraph 1.

The other condition of the liability of a vessel to capture is that she

Article 17. should be found within the area of operations of the war-
(See *ante*, ships detailed to make the blockade effective; it is not
p. 545.) enough that she should be on her way to the blockaded port.

As for what constitutes the *area of operations*, an explanation has been

---

[1] The first paragraph of this Article is based on a proposition of the Italian Delegation (*Parl. Papers*, Misc. No. 5 (1909), p. 161).

given which has been universally accepted, and is quoted here as furnishing the best commentary on the rule laid down by Article 17 :—

"When a Government decides to undertake blockading operations against some part of the enemy coast it details a certain number of warships to take part in the blockade, and entrusts the command to an officer whose duty is to use them for the purpose of making the blockade effective. The commander of the naval force thus formed posts the ships at his disposal according to the line of the coast and the geographical position of the blockaded places, and instructs each ship as to the part which she has to play, and especially as to the zone which she is to watch. All the zones watched taken together, and so organized as to make the blockade effective, form the area of operations of the blockading naval force.

"The area of operations so constituted is intimately connected with the effectiveness of the blockade, and also with the number of ships employed on it.

"Cases may occur in which a single ship will be enough to keep a blockade effective,—for instance, at the entrance of a port, or at the mouth of a river with a small estuary, so long as circumstances allow the blockading ship to stay near enough to the entrance. In that case the area of operations is itself near the coast. But, on the other hand, if circumstances force her to remain far off, one ship may not be enough to secure effectiveness, and to maintain this she will then have to be supported by others. From this cause the area of operations becomes wider, and extends further from the coast. It may therefore vary with circumstances, and with the number of blockading ships, but it will always be limited by the condition that effectiveness must be assured.

"It does not seem possible to fix the limits of the area of operations in definite figures, any more than to fix beforehand and definitely the number of ships necessary to assure the effectiveness of any blockade. These points must be settled according to circumstances in each particular case of a blockade. This might perhaps be done at the time of making the declaration.

"It is clear that a blockade will not be established in the same way on a defenceless coast as on one possessing all modern means of defence. In the latter case there could be no question of enforcing a rule such as that which formerly required that ships should be stationary and sufficiently close to the blockaded places ; the position would be too dangerous for the ships of the blockading force which, besides, now possess more powerful means of watching effectively a much wider zone than formerly.

"The area of operations of a blockading naval force may be rather wide, but as it depends on the number of ships contributing to the effectiveness of the blockade, and is always limited by the condition that it should be effective, it will never reach distant seas where merchant vessels sail which are, perhaps, making for the blockaded ports, but whose destination is contingent on the changes which circumstances may produce in the blockade during their voyage. To sum up, the idea of the area of operations joined with that of effectiveness, as we have tried to define it, that is to say, including the zone of operations of the blockading forces, allows the belligerent effectively to exercise the right of blockade which he admittedly possesses and, on the other hand, saves neutrals from exposure to the drawbacks of blockade at a great distance, while it leaves them free to run the risk which they knowingly incur by approaching points to which access is forbidden by the belligerent[1]."

This rule has been thought necessary the better to protect the com-

Article 18. (See *ante*, p. 545.) mercial interests of neutral countries; it completes Article 1, according to which a blockade must not extend beyond the ports and coasts of the enemy, which implies that, as it is an operation of war, it must not be directed against a neutral port, in spite of the importance to a belligerent of the part played by that neutral port in supplying his adversary.

It is the true destination of the vessel which must be considered when

Article 19. (See *ante*, p. 545.) a breach of blockade is in question, and not the ulterior destination of the cargo. Proof or presumption of the latter is therefore not enough to justify the capture, for breach of blockade, of a ship actually bound for an unblockaded port. But the cruiser might always prove that this destination to an unblockaded port is only apparent, and that in reality the immediate destination of the vessel is the blockaded port.

A vessel has left the blockaded port or has tried to enter it. Shall she

Article 20. (See *ante*, p. 545.) remain indefinitely liable to capture? To reply by an absolute affirmative would be to go too far. This vessel must remain liable to capture so long as she is pursued by a ship of the blockading force; it would not be enough for her to be encountered by a cruiser of the blockading enemy which did not belong to the blockading squadron[2]. The question whether or not the pursuit is abandoned is

---

[1] Exposé par M. le Contre-Amiral de Bris (French Naval Delegate), *Parl. Papers*, Misc. No. 5 (1909), p. 955 (annexe, 67).

[2] As regards the question whether the continuous pursuit of a vessel guilty of breach of blockade must be undertaken by the same cruiser or can be taken up by others in the various lines of the blockade, see the following Memorandum of the United States Delegation: "As

one of fact; it is not enough that the vessel should take refuge in a neutral port. The ship which is pursuing her can wait till she leaves it, so that the pursuit is necessarily suspended, but not abandoned. Capture is no longer possible when the blockade has been raised.

The vessel is condemned in all cases. The cargo is also condemned on

Article 21.
(See *ante*,
p. 545.)

principle, but the interested party is allowed to oppose a plea of good faith, that is to say, to prove that, when the goods were shipped, the shipper did not know and could not have known of the intention to break the blockade.

Chapter II.

CONTRABAND OF WAR[1].

This chapter is one of the most, if not the most important, of the Declaration. It deals with a matter which has sometimes given rise to serious disputes between belligerents and neutrals. Therefore regulations to establish exactly the rights and duties of each have often been urgently called for. Peaceful trade may be grateful for the precision with which a subject of the highest importance to its interests is now for the first time treated.

The notion of contraband of war connotes two elements: it concerns objects of a certain kind and with a certain destination. Cannons, for instance, are carried in a neutral vessel. Are they contraband? That depends: if they are destined for a neutral Government,—no; if they are destined for an enemy Government,—yes. The trade in certain articles is by no means generally forbidden during war; it is the trade with the enemy in these articles which is illicit, and against which the belligerent to whose detriment it is carried on may protect himself by the measures allowed by international law.

Articles 22 and 24 enumerate the articles which may be contraband of war, and which are so in fact when they have a certain destination laid

regards Article 25 [of the *Bases de discussion*] the Delegation, while believing that this Article could be combined with Article 24 with advantage, so as to deal with the whole question together, accepts the article, under the reservation that a pursuit is considered as continued and not abandoned within the meaning of the article, even if it is abandoned by one line of the blockading force to be resumed after an interval by a ship of the second line, until the limit of the area of operations is reached. In certain conditions there might be several lines, each having its respective zone of pursuit." (Annexe, No. 69, *Parl. Papers*, Misc. No. 5 (1909), p. 256. See also p. 175 for explanations of this memorandum. See also Article by Admiral C. H. Stockton, *Am. Journ. of Int. Law*, Vol. III. p. 604.)

[1] For British rules on this subject see *Parl. Papers*, Misc. No. 4 (1909), pp. 3–5, and Instructions to British Delegation, *Ibid.* p. 23.

down in Articles 30 and 33. The traditional distinction between *absolute* and *conditional* contraband is maintained: Articles 22 and 30 refer to the former, and Articles 24 and 33 to the latter.

This list is that drawn up at the second Peace Conference by the Com-
Article 22. mittee charged with the special study of the question of con-
(See *ante*, traband[1]. It was the result of mutual concessions, and it has
p. 546.) not seemed wise to reopen discussion on this subject for the
purpose either of cutting out or of adding articles.

The words *de plein droit* (without notice)[2] imply that the provision becomes operative by the mere fact of the war, and that no declaration by the belligerents is necessary. Trade is already warned in time of peace.

Certain discoveries or inventions might make the list in Article 22
Article 23. insufficient. An addition may be made to it on condition
(See *ante*, that it concerns articles *exclusively used for war*. This
p. 547.) addition must be notified to the other Powers, which will
take the necessary measures to inform their subjects of it. In theory the notification may be made in time of peace or of war. The former case will doubtless rarely occur, because a State which made such a notification might be suspected of meditating a war; it would, nevertheless, have the advantage of informing trade beforehand. There was no reason for making it impossible.

The right given to a Power to make an addition to the list by a mere declaration has been thought too wide. It should be noticed that this right does not involve the dangers supposed. In the first place, it is under-stood that the declaration is only operative for the Power which makes it, in the sense that the article added will only be contraband for it, as a belligerent; other States may, of course, also make a similar declaration. The addition may only refer to articles *exclusively used for war*; at pre-sent, it would be hard to mention any such articles which are not included in the list. The future is left free. If a Power claimed to add to the list of absolute contraband articles not exclusively used for war, it might expose itself to diplomatic remonstrances, because it would be disregard-ing an accepted rule. Besides, there would be an eventual resort to the International Prize Court. Suppose that the Court holds that the article mentioned in the declaration of absolute contraband is wrongly placed

---

[1] See *La Deux. Confér.* T. III. pp. 1108–14.

[2] The following note is appended to the translation of "De plein droit" in *Parl. Papers*, Misc. No. 4 (1909), p. 49: "In view of the difficulty of finding an exact equivalent in English for the expression 'de plein droit,' it has been decided to translate it by the words 'without notice,' which represents the meaning attached to it by the draftsman of the present General Report."

there because it is not exclusively used for war, but that it might have been included in a declaration of conditional contraband. Confiscation may then be justified if the capture was made in the conditions laid down for this kind of contraband (Articles 33—35) which differ from those enforced for absolute contraband (Article 30).

It had been suggested that, in the interest of neutral trade, a period should elapse between the notification and its enforcement. But that would be very damaging to the belligerent, whose object is precisely to protect himself, since, during that period, the trade in articles which he thinks dangerous would be free and the effect of his measure a failure. Account has been taken, in another form, of the considerations of equity which have been adduced (see Article 43).

On the expression *de plein droit* (without notice) the same remark

Article 24.
(See *ante*, p. 547.)

must be made with regard to Article 22[1]. The articles enumerated are only conditional contraband if they have the destination specified in Article 33.

Foodstuffs include products necessary or useful for sustaining man, whether solid or liquid.

Paper money only includes inconvertible paper money, *i.e.* banknotes which may or not be legal tender. Bills of exchange and cheques are excluded.

Engines and boilers are included in (6).

Railway material includes fixtures (such as rails, sleepers, turntables, parts of bridges), and rolling stock (such as locomotives, carriages, and trucks).

Article 25.
(See *ante*, p. 548.)

This provision corresponds, as regards conditional contraband, to that in Article 23 as regards absolute contraband.

A belligerent may not wish to use the right to treat as contraband of

Article 26.
(See *ante*, p. 548.)

war all the articles included in the above lists. It may suit him to add to conditional contraband an article included in absolute contraband or to declare free, so far as he is concerned, the trade in some article included in one class or the other. It is desirable that he should make known his intention on this subject, and he will probably do so in order to have the credit of the measure. If he does not do so, but confines himself to giving instructions to his cruisers, the vessels searched will be agreeably surprised if the searcher does not reproach them with carrying what they themselves consider contraband. Nothing can prevent a Power from making such a declaration in time of peace. See what is said as regards Article 23.

---

[1] See note 2, p. 583, *ante*.

The existence of a so-called *free* list (Article 28) makes it useful thus
to put on record that articles which cannot be used for purposes of war may not be declared contraband of war. It might have been thought that articles not included in that list might at least be declared conditional contraband.

Article 27.
(See *ante*,
p. 549.)

To lessen the drawbacks of war as regards neutral trade it has been thought useful to draw up this so-called *free list*, but this does not mean, as has been explained above, that all articles outside it might be declared contraband of war.

Article 28.
(See *ante*,
p. 549.)

The *ores* here referred to are the product of mines from which metals are derived.

There was a demand that *dyestuffs* should be included in (10), but this seemed too general, for there are materials from which colours are derived, such as coal, which also have other uses. Products only used for making colours enjoy the exemption.

" Articles de Paris," an expression the meaning of which is universally understood, come under (15).

(16) refers to the hair of certain animals, such as pigs and wild boars.

Carpets and mats come under household furniture and ornaments (17).

The articles enumerated in Article 29 are also excluded from treatment as contraband, but for reasons different from those which have led to the inclusion of the list in Article 28.

Article 29.
(See *ante*,
p. 550.)

Motives of humanity have exempted articles exclusively used to aid the sick and wounded, which, of course, include drugs and different medicines. This does not refer to hospital-ships, which enjoy special immunity under the convention of The Hague of the 18th October, 1907, but to ordinary merchant vessels, whose cargo includes articles of the kind mentioned. The cruiser has, however, the right, in case of urgent necessity, to requisition such articles for the needs of her crew or of the fleet to which she belongs, but they can only be requisitioned on payment of compensation. It must, however, be observed that this right of requisition may not be exercised in all cases. The articles in question must have the destination specified in Article 30, that is to say, an enemy destination. Otherwise, the ordinary law regains its sway ; a belligerent could not have the right of requisition as regards neutral vessels on the high seas.

Articles intended for the use of the vessel, which might in themselves and by their nature, be contraband of war, may not be so treated,—for instance, arms intended for the defence of the vessel against pirates or for making signals. The same is true of articles intended for the use of the crew and passengers during the voyage ; the crew here include all persons in the service of the vessel in general.

Destination of Contraband.—As has been said, the second element in the notion of contraband is *destination.* Great difficulties have arisen on this subject, which find expression in the *theory of continuous voyage,* so often attacked or adduced without a clear comprehension of its exact meaning[1]. Cases must simply be considered on their merits so as to see how they can be settled without unnecessarily annoying neutrals or sacrificing the legitimate rights of belligerents.

In order to effect a compromise between conflicting theories and practices, absolute and conditional contraband have been differently treated in this connection.

Articles 30 to 32 refer to absolute, and Articles 33 to 36 to conditional, contraband.

The articles included in the list in Article 22 are absolute contraband when they are destined for territory belonging to or occupied by the enemy, or for his armed military or naval forces. These articles are liable to capture as soon as a final destination of this kind can be shown by the captor to exist. It is not, therefore, the destination of the vessel which is decisive, but that of the goods. It makes no difference if these goods are on board a vessel which is to discharge them in a neutral port; as soon as the captor is able to show that they are to be forwarded from there by land or sea to an enemy country, it is enough to justify the capture and subsequent condemnation of the cargo. The very principle of continuous voyage, as regards absolute contraband, is established by Article 30. The journey made by the goods is regarded as a whole.

Article 30.
(See ante,
p. 550.)

As has been said, the obligation of proving that the contraband goods really have the destination specified in Article 30 rests with the captor. In certain cases proof of the destination specified in Article 31 is *conclusive,* that is to say, the proof may not be rebutted.

Article 31.
(See ante,
p. 550.)

First Case.—The goods are *documented* for discharge in an enemy port, that is to say, according to the ship's papers referring to those goods, they are to be discharged there. In this case there is a real admission of enemy destination on the part of the interested parties themselves.

Second Case.—The vessel is to touch at enemy ports only; or she is to touch at an enemy port before reaching the neutral port for which the

---

[1] "When an adventure includes the carriage of goods to a neutral port, and thence to an ulterior destination, the doctrine of 'continuous voyage' consists in treating for certain purposes the whole journey as one transportation, with the consequences which would have attached had there been no interposition of the neutral port." (See British Memorandum, *Parl. Papers,* Misc. No. 4 (1909), pp. 7-9.)

goods are documented, so that although these goods, according to the papers referring to them, are to be discharged in a neutral port, the vessel carrying them is to touch at an enemy port before reaching that neutral port. They will be liable to capture, and the possibility of proving that their neutral destination is real and in accordance with the intentions of the parties interested is not admitted. The fact that, before reaching that destination, the vessel will touch at an enemy port, would occasion too great a risk for the belligerent whose cruiser searches the vessel. Even without assuming that there is intentional fraud, there might be a strong temptation for the master of the merchant vessel to discharge the contraband, for which he would get a good price, and for the local authorities to requisition the goods.

The same case arises where the vessel, before reaching the neutral port, is to join the armed forces of the enemy.

For the sake of simplicity, the provision only speaks of an *enemy port*, but it is understood that a *port occupied by the enemy* must be regarded as an enemy port, as follows from the general rule in Article 30.

The papers, therefore, are conclusive proof of the course of the vessel

Article 32.
(See *ante*, p. 551.)
unless she is encountered in circumstances which show that their statements are not to be trusted. See also the explanations given as regards Article 35.

The rules for conditional contraband differ from those laid down for

Article 33.
(See *ante*, p. 551.)
absolute contraband in two respects : (1) there is no question of destination for the enemy in general, but of destination for the use of his armed forces or government departments ; (2) the doctrine of continuous voyage is excluded. Articles 33 and 34 refer to the first, and Article 35 to the second principle.

The articles included in the list of conditional contraband may serve for peaceful uses as well as for hostile purposes. If, from the circumstances, the peaceful purpose is clear, their capture is not justified ; it is otherwise if a hostile purpose is to be assumed, as, for instance, in the case of foodstuffs destined for an enemy army or fleet, or of coal destined for an enemy fleet. In such a case there is clearly no room for doubt. But what is the solution when the articles are destined for the civil government departments of the enemy State ? It may be money sent to a government department, for use in the payment of its official salaries, or rails sent to a department of public works. In those cases there is *enemy destination* which renders the goods liable in the first place to capture, and in the second to condemnation. The reasons for this are at once legal and practical. The State is one, although it necessarily acts

through different departments. If a civil department may freely receive foodstuffs or money, that department is not the only gainer, but the entire State, including its military administration, gains also, since the general resources of the State are thereby increased. Further, the receipts of a civil department may be considered of greater use to the military administration and directly assigned to the latter. Money or foodstuffs really destined for a civil department may thus come to be used directly for the needs of the army. This possibility, which is always present, shows why destination for the departments of the enemy State is assimilated to that for its armed forces.

It is the *departments of the State* which are dependent on the central power that are in question, and not all the departments which may exist in the enemy State; local and municipal bodies, for instance, are not included, and articles destined for their use would not be contraband.

War may be waged in such circumstances that destination for the use of a civil department cannot be suspect, and consequently cannot make goods contraband. For instance, there is a war in Europe, and the colonies of the belligerent countries are not, in fact, affected by it. Foodstuffs or other articles in the list of conditional contraband destined for the use of the civil government of a colony would not be held to be contraband of war, because the considerations adduced above do not apply to their case; the resources of the civil government cannot be drawn on for the needs of the war. Gold, silver, or paper money are exceptions, because a sum of money can easily be sent from one end of the world to the other.

Contraband articles will not usually be directly addressed to the military authorities or to the government departments of the enemy State. Their true destination will be more or less concealed, and the captor must prove it in order to justify their capture. But it has been thought reasonable to set up presumptions based on the nature of the person to whom, or place for which, the articles are destined. It may be an enemy authority or a trader established in an enemy country who, as a matter of common knowledge, supplies the enemy Government with articles of the kind in question. It may be a fortified place belonging to the enemy or a place used as a base, whether of operations or of supply, for the armed forces of the enemy.

Article 34.
(See *ante*,
p. 551.)

This general presumption may not be applied to the merchant vessel herself on her way to a fortified place, though she may in herself be conditional contraband, but only if her destination for the use of the armed forces or government departments of the enemy State is directly proved.

In the absence of the above presumptions, the destination is presumed

to be innocent. That is the ordinary law, according to which the captor must prove the illicit character of the goods which he claims to capture.

Finally, all the presumptions thus set up in the interest of the captor or against him may be rebutted. The national tribunals, in the first place, and, in the second, the International Court, will exercise their judgment.

As has been said above, the doctrine of continuous voyage is excluded **Article 35.** for conditional contraband, which is only liable to capture **(See** *ante,* when it is to be discharged in an enemy port. As soon as the **p. 552.)** goods are documented for discharge in a neutral port they can no longer be contraband, and no examination will be made as to whether they are to be forwarded to the enemy by sea or land from that neutral port. It is here that the case of absolute contraband is essentially different.

The ship's papers furnish complete proof as to the voyage on which the vessel is engaged and as to the place where the cargo is to be discharged; but this would not be so if the vessel were encountered clearly out of the course which she should follow according to her papers, and unable to give adequate reasons to justify such deviation.

This rule as to the proof furnished by the ship's papers is intended to prevent claims frivolously raised by a cruiser and giving rise to unjustifiable captures. It must not be too literally interpreted, for that would make all frauds easy. Thus it does not hold good when the vessel is encountered at sea clearly out of the course which she ought to have followed, and unable to justify such deviation. The ship's papers are then in contradiction with the true facts and lose all value as evidence; the cruiser will be free to decide according to the merits of the case. In the same way, a search of the vessel may reveal facts which irrefutably prove that her destination or the place where the goods are to be discharged is incorrectly entered in the ship's papers. The commander of the cruiser is then free to judge of the circumstances and capture the vessel or not according to his judgment. To resume, the ship's papers are proof, unless facts show their evidence to be false[1]. This qualification of the value of the ship's papers as proof seems self-evident and unworthy of special mention. The aim has been not to appear to weaken the force of the general rule, which forms a safe-guard for neutral trade.

It does not follow that, because a single entry in the ship's papers is shown to be false, their evidence loses its value as a whole. The entries which cannot be proved false retain their value.

---

[1] See note on Article 35, *ante*, p. 552.

The case contemplated is certainly rare, but has nevertheless arisen in

Article 36.
(See *ante*,
p. 553.)

recent wars. In the case of absolute contraband, there is no difficulty, since destination for the enemy may always be proved, whatever the route by which the goods are sent (Article 30). For conditional contraband the case is different, and an exception must be made to the general rule laid down in Article 35, paragraph 1, so as to allow the captor to prove that the suspected goods really have the special destination referred to in Article 33 without the possibility of being confronted by the objection that they were to be discharged in a neutral port.

The vessel may be captured for contraband during the whole of her

Article 37.
(See *ante*,
p. 553.)

voyage, provided that she is in waters where an act of war is lawful. The fact that she intends to touch at a port of call before reaching the enemy destination does not prevent capture, provided that destination in her particular case is proved in conformity with the rules laid down in Article 30 to 32 for absolute, and in Articles 33 to 35 for conditional contraband, subject to the exception

Article 38.
(See *ante*,
p. 553.)

provided for in Article 36.

A vessel is liable to capture for carrying contraband, but not for having done so.

Article 39.
(See *ante*,
p. 553.)

This presents no difficulty.

It was universally admitted that in certain cases the condemnation of

Article 40.
(See *ante*,
p. 553.)

the contraband is not enough, and that the vessel herself should also be condemned, but opinions differed as to what these cases were. It was decided that the contraband must bear a certain proportion to the total cargo. But the question divides itself into two parts : (1) What shall be the proportion ? The solution adopted is the mean between those proposed, which varied from a quarter to three quarters. (2) How shall this proportion be reckoned ? Must the contraband form more than half the cargo in volume, weight, value, or freight ? The adoption of a single fixed standard gives rise to theoretical objections, and also to practices intended to avoid condemnation of the vessel in spite of the importance of the cargo. If the standard of volume or weight is adopted, the master will ship innocent goods occupying space, or of weight, sufficient to exceed the contraband. A similar remark may be made as regards the standard of value or freight. The consequence is that, in order to justify condemnation, it is enough that the contraband should form more than half the cargo by any one of the above standards.

This may seem harsh; but, on the one hand, any other system would make fraudulent calculations easy, and, on the other, the condemnation of the vessel may be said to be justified when the carriage of contraband formed an important part of her venture—a statement which applies to all the cases specified.

It is not just that, on the one hand, the carriage of more than a certain
Article 41. proportion of contraband should involve the condemnation of
(See *ante,* the vessel, while if the contraband forms less than this pro-
p. 554.) portion, it alone is confiscated. This often involves no loss
for the master, the freight of this contraband having been paid in advance. Does this not encourage trade in contraband, and ought not a certain penalty to be imposed for the carriage of a proportion of contraband less than that required to entail condemnation? A kind of fine was proposed which should bear a relation to the value of the contraband articles. Objections of various sorts were brought forward against this proposal, although the principle of the infliction of some kind of pecuniary loss for the carriage of contraband seemed justified. The same object was attained in another way by providing that the costs and expenses incurred by the captor in respect of the proceedings in the national prize court and of the custody of the vessel and of her cargo during the proceedings are to be paid by the vessel. The expenses of the custody of the vessel include in this case the keep of the captured vessel's crew. It should be added that the loss to a vessel by being taken to a prize port and kept there is the most serious deterrent as regards the carriage of contraband.

The owner of the contraband is punished in the first place by the
Article 42. condemnation of his contraband property; and in the second
(See *ante,* by that of the goods, even if innocent, which he may possess
p. 554.) on board the same vessel.

This provision is intended to spare neutrals who might in fact be
Article 43. carrying contraband, but against whom no charge could be
(See *ante,* made. This may arise in two cases. The first is that in
p. 554.) which they are unaware of the outbreak of hostilities; the
second is that in which, though aware of this, they do not know of the declaration of contraband made by a belligerent, in accordance with Articles 23 and 25, which is, as it happens, the one applicable to the whole or a part of the cargo. It would be unjust to capture the ship and condemn the contraband; on the other hand, the cruiser cannot be obliged to let go on to the enemy goods suitable for use in the war of which he may stand in urgent need. These opposing interests are reconciled by making condemnation conditional on the payment of compensation (see

the convention of the 18th October, 1907, on the rules for enemy merchant vessels on the outbreak of hostilities, which expresses a similar idea[1].

A neutral vessel is stopped for carrying contraband. She is not liable to condemnation, because the contraband does not reach the proportion specified in Article 40. She can nevertheless be taken to a prize port for judgment to be passed on the contraband. This right of the captor appears too wide in certain cases, if the importance of the contraband, possibly slight (for instance, a case of guns or revolvers), is compared with the heavy loss incurred by the vessel by being thus turned out of her course and detained during the time taken up by the proceedings. The question has, therefore, been asked whether the right of the neutral vessel to continue her voyage might not be admitted if the contraband articles were handed over to the captor, who, on his part, might only refuse to receive them for sufficient reasons, for instance, the rough state of the sea, which would make transhipment difficult or impossible, well-founded suspicions as to the amount of contraband which the merchant vessel is really carrying, the difficulty of stowing the articles on board the warship, &c. This proposal did not gain sufficient support. It was alleged to be impossible to impose such an obligation on the cruiser, for which this handing over of goods would almost always have drawbacks. If, by chance, it has none, the cruiser will not refuse it, because she herself will gain by not being turned out of her course by having to take the vessel to a port. The idea of an obligation having thus been excluded, it was decided to provide for the voluntarily handing over of the contraband, which, it is hoped, will be carried out whenever possible, to the great advantage of both parties. The formalities provided for are very simple and need no explanation.

Article 44.
(See *ante*, p. 555.)

There must be a judgment of a prize court as regards the goods thus handed over. For this purpose the captor must be furnished with the necessary papers. It may be supposed that there might be doubt as to the character of certain articles which the cruiser claims as contraband; the master of the merchant vessel contests this claim, but prefers to deliver them up so as to be at liberty to continue his voyage. This is merely a capture which has to be confirmed by the prize court.

The contraband delivered up by the merchant vessel may hamper the cruiser, which must be left free to destroy it at the moment of handing over or later.

---

[1] See *ante*, pp. 296-7 (Articles 2, 3 and 4).

Chapter III.

Unneutral service[1].

In a general way, it may be said that the merchant vessel which violates neutrality, whether by carrying contraband of war or by breaking blockade, affords aid to the enemy, and it is on this ground that the belligerent whom she injures by her acts is justified in inflicting on her certain losses. But there are cases where such unneutral service bears a particularly distinctive character, and for such cases it has been thought necessary to make special provision. They have been divided into two classes according to the gravity of the act of which the neutral vessel is accused.

In the cases included in the first class (Article 45), the vessel is condemned, and receives the treatment of a vessel subject to condemnation for carrying contraband. This means that the vessel does not lose her neutral character and has a full claim to the rights enjoyed by neutral vessels ; for instance, she may not be destroyed by the captor except under the conditions laid down for neutral vessels (Articles 48 *et seqq.*) ; the rule that *the flag covers the goods* applies to goods she carries on board.

In the more serious cases which belong to the second class (Article 46), the vessel is, again, condemned ; but further, she is treated not only as a vessel subject to condemnation for carrying contraband, but as an enemy merchant vessel, which treatment entails certain consequences. The rule governing the destruction of neutral prizes does not apply to the vessel, and, as she has become an enemy vessel, it is no longer the second but the third rule of the Declaration of Paris which is applicable. The goods on board will be presumed to be enemy goods ; neutrals will have the right to claim their property on establishing their neutrality (Article 59). It would, however, be going too far to say that the original neutral character of the vessel is completely lost, so that she should be treated as though she had always been an enemy vessel. The vessel may plead that the allegation made against her has no foundation in fact, that the act of which she is accused has not the character of unneutral service. She has, therefore, the right of appeal to the International Court in virtue of the provisions which protect neutral property.

---

[1] For British rules on this subject see *Parl. Papers*, Misc. No. 4 (1909), p. 9 ; for Instructions to British Delegation, *Ibid.* p. 30.

The first case supposes passengers travelling *as individuals*; the case of a *military detachment* is dealt with hereafter. The case is that of individuals *embodied* in the armed military or naval forces of the enemy. There was some doubt as to the meaning of this word. Does it include those individuals only who are summoned to serve in virtue of the law of their country and who have really joined the corps to which they are to belong? Or does it also include such individuals from the moment when they are summoned, and before they join that corps? The question is of great practical importance. Supposing the case is one of individuals who are natives of a continental European country and are settled in America; these individuals have military obligations towards their country of origin; they have, for instance, to belong to the reserve of the active army of that country. Their country is at war and they sail to perform their service. Shall they be considered as *embodied* in the sense of the provision which we are discussing? If we judged by the municipal law of certain countries, we might argue that they should be so considered. But, apart from reasons of pure law, the contrary opinion has seemed more in accordance with practical necessity and has been accepted by all in a spirit of conciliation. It would be difficult, perhaps even impossible, without having recourse to vexatious measures to which neutral Governments would not submit, to pick out among the passengers in a vessel, those who are bound to perform military service and are on their way to do so.

Article 45.
(See ante, p. 555.)

The transmission of intelligence in the interest of the enemy is to be treated in the same way as the carriage of passengers embodied in his armed force. The reference to a vessel *especially* undertaking a voyage is intended to show that her usual service is not meant. She has been turned from her course; she has touched at a port which she does not ordinarily visit in order to embark the passengers in question. She need not be *exclusively* devoted to the service of the enemy; that case would come into the second class (Article 56 (4)).

In the two cases just mentioned the vessel has performed but a single service; she has been employed to carry certain people, or transmit certain intelligence; she is not continuously in the service of the enemy. In consequence she may be captured during the voyage on which she is performing the service which she has to render. Once that voyage is finished, all is over, in the sense that she may not be captured for having rendered the service in question. The principle is the same as that recognized in the case of contraband (Article 38).

The second case also falls under two heads.

There is, first, the carriage of a military detachment of the enemy, or that of one or more persons who during the voyage directly assist his operations, for instance, by signalling. If these people are soldiers or sailors in uniform there is no difficulty, the vessel is clearly liable to condemnation. If they are soldiers or sailors in mufti who might be mistaken for ordinary passengers, knowledge on the part of the master or owner is required, the charterer being assimilated to the latter. The rule is the same in the case of persons directly assisting the enemy during the voyage.

In these cases, if the vessel is condemned for unneutral service, the goods belonging to her owner are also liable to condemnation.

These provisions assume that the state of war was known to the vessel engaged in the operations specified; such knowledge is the reason and justification of her condemnation. The position is altogether different when the vessel is unaware of the outbreak of hostilities, so that she undertakes the service in ordinary circumstances. She may have learnt of the outbreak of hostilities while at sea, but have had no chance of landing the persons whom she was carrying. Condemnation would then be unjust, and the equitable rule adopted is in accordance with the provisions already accepted in other matters. If a vessel has left an enemy port subsequently to the outbreak of hostilities, or a neutral port after that outbreak has been notified to the Power to whom such port belongs, her knowledge of the existence of a state of war will be presumed.

The question here is merely one of preventing the condemnation of the vessel. The persons found on board her who belong to the armed forces of the enemy may be made prisoners of war by the cruiser.

Article 46.
(See *ante*,
p. 557.)
The cases here contemplated[1] are more serious than those in Article 45, which justifies the severer treatment inflicted on the vessel, as explained above.

First Case.—The vessel takes a direct part in the hostilities. This may take different forms. It is needless to say that, in an armed conflict, the vessel takes all the risks incidental thereto. We suppose her to have fallen into the power of the enemy whom she was fighting, and who is entitled to treat her as an enemy merchant vessel.

Second Case.—The vessel is under the orders or control of an agent placed on board by the enemy Government. His presence marks the relation in which she stands to the enemy In other circumstances the

---

[1] For further explanations of the cases dealt with in this Article see *Parl. Papers*, Misc. No. 5 (1909), pp. 191–3. Articles 45, 46 and 47 are based on a German draft (see Annexe, No. 55, *Ibid.* p. 247).

vessel may also have relations with the enemy, but to be subject to condemnation she must come under the third head.

Third Case.—The whole vessel is chartered by the enemy Government, and is therefore entirely at its disposal; it can use her for different purposes more or less directly connected with the war, notably, as a transport; such is the position of colliers which accompany a belligerent fleet. There will often be a charter-party between the belligerent Government and the owner or master of the vessel, but all that is required is proof, and the fact that the whole vessel has in fact been chartered is enough, in whatever way it may be established.

Fourth Case.—The vessel is at the time exclusively devoted to the carriage of enemy troops or to the transmission of intelligence in the enemy's interest. The case is different from those dealt with by Article 45, and the question is one of a service to which the ship is permanently devoted. The decision accordingly is that, so long as such service lasts, the vessel is liable to capture, even if, at the moment when an enemy cruiser searches her, she is engaged neither in the transport of troops nor in the transmission of intelligence.

As in the cases in Article 45 and for the same reasons, goods found on board belonging to the owner of the vessel are also liable to condemnation.

It was proposed to treat as an enemy merchant vessel a neutral vessel making, at the time, and with the sanction of the enemy Government, a voyage which she has only been permitted to make subsequently to the outbreak of hostilities or during the two preceding months[1]. This rule would be enforced notably on neutral merchant vessels admitted by a belligerent to a service reserved in time of peace to the national marine of that belligerent—for instance, to the coasting trade. Several Delegations formally rejected this proposal, so that the question thus raised remains an open one[2].

Individuals embodied in the armed military or naval forces of a belligerent may be on board a neutral merchant vessel when she is searched. If the vessel is subject to condemnation, the cruiser will capture her and take her to one of her own ports with the persons on board. Clearly the soldiers or sailors of the enemy State will not be set free, but will be treated as prisoners of war. Perhaps the case will not be one for the capture of the ship—for instance, because the master was unaware of the status of an individual who had come on

Article 47.
(See *ante*,
p. 557.)

---

[1] See Article 2 (4) of German proposition, *Parl. Papers*, Misc. No. 5 (1909), p. 247, and Exposé by M. Kriege, p. 279.

[2] See Article 57, par. 2, and *post*, p. 602.

board as an ordinary passenger. Must the soldier or soldiers on board the vessel be set free? That does not appear admissible. The belligerent cruiser cannot be compelled to set free active enemies who are physically in her power and are more dangerous than this or that contraband article. She must naturally proceed with great discretion, and must act on her own responsibility in requiring the surrender of these individuals, but the right to do so is hers; it has therefore been thought necessary to explain the point.

Chapter IV.

DESTRUCTION OF NEUTRAL PRIZES[1].

The destruction of neutral prizes was a subject comprised in the programme of the second Peace Conference, and on that occasion no settlement was reached. It reappeared in the programme of the present Conference, and this time agreement has been found possible. Such a result, which bears witness to the sincere desire of all parties to arrive at an understanding, is a matter for congratulation. It has been shown once more that conflicting hard-and-fast rules do not always correspond to things as they are, and that if there be readiness to descend to particulars, and to arrive at the precise way in which the rules have been applied, it will often be found that the actual practice is very much the same, although the doctrines professed appear to be entirely in conflict. To enable two parties to agree, it is first of all necessary that they should understand each other, and this frequently is not the case. Thus it has been found that those who declared for the right to destroy neutral prizes never claimed to use this right wantonly or at every opportunity, but only by way of exception; while, on the other hand, those who maintained the principle that destruction is forbidden, admitted that the principle must give way in certain exceptional cases. It therefore became a question of reaching an understanding with regard to those exceptional cases to which, according to both views, the right to destroy should be confined. But this

---

[1] See *ante*, pp. 88–92. The rule laid down in the British Memorandum on the subject is as follows : "The duty of a belligerent captor is to bring in, for adjudication by a Prize Court, any merchant-ship which he has seized. Where this is impossible, she may, if she is an enemy ship, be destroyed after removal of the crew and papers; if the nationality of a ship is neutral, or if there is any doubt as to the nationality, she should be dismissed, for her destruction cannot be justified as between the neutral owner and the captor by any necessity on the part of a belligerent" (*Parl. Papers*, Misc. No. 4 (1909), p. 9). The British delegate was instructed that an agreement "might perhaps be found by proceeding on the lines of an affirmation of the general principle that neutral prizes must not be destroyed before adjudication, followed by a precise statement of the conditions on which alone a departure from the principle would be allowed in exceptional circumstances" (*Ibid.* p. 28).

was not all: there was need for some guarantee against abuse in the exercise of this right; the possibility of arbitrary action in determining these exceptional cases must be limited by throwing some real responsibility upon the captor. It was at this stage that a new idea was introduced into the discussion, thanks to which it was possible to arrive at an agreement. The possibility of intervention by a court of justice will make the captor reflect before he acts, and at the same time secure reparation in cases where there was no reason for the destruction.

Such is the general spirit of the provisions of this chapter.

The general principle is very simple. A neutral vessel which has been **Article 48.** seized may not be destroyed by the captor; so much may be **(See** *ante,* admitted by every one, whatever view is taken as to the effect **p. 557.)** produced by the capture. The vessel must be taken into a port for the determination there as to the validity of the prize. A prize crew will be put on board or not, according to circumstances.

The first condition necessary to justify the destruction of the captured **Article 49.** vessel is that she should be liable to condemnation upon the **(See** *ante,* facts of the case. If the captor cannot even hope to obtain **p. 557.)** the condemnation of the vessel, how can he lay claim to the right to destroy her?

The second condition is that the observance of the general principle would involve danger to the safety of the warship or to the success of the operations in which she is engaged at the time. This is what was finally agreed upon after various solutions had been tried. It was understood that the phrase *compromettre la sécurité* was synonymous with *mettre en danger le navire*, and might be translated into English by: *involve danger.* It is, of course, the situation at the moment when the destruction takes place which must be considered in order to decide whether the conditions are or are not fulfilled. For a danger which did not exist at the actual moment of the capture may have appeared some time afterwards.

Article 50. This provision lays down the precautions to be taken in **(See** *ante,* the interests of the persons on board and of the administra- **p. 558.)** tion of justice.

This claim gives a guarantee against the arbitrary destruction of prizes **Article 51.** by throwing a real responsibility upon the captor who has **(See** *ante,* carried out the destruction. The result is that before any **p. 558.)** decision is given respecting the validity of the prize, the captor must prove that the situation he was in was really one which fell under the head of the exceptional cases contemplated. This must be proved in proceedings to which the neutral is a party, and if the latter is not satisfied with the decision of the national prize court he may take his

case to the International Court. Proof to the above effect is, therefore, a condition precedent which the captor must fulfil. If he fails to do this, he must compensate the parties interested in the vessel and the cargo, and the question whether the capture was valid or not will not be gone into. In this way a real sanction is provided in respect of the obligation not to destroy a prize except in particular cases, the sanction taking the form of a fine inflicted on the captor. If, on the other hand, this proof is given, the prize procedure follows the usual course; if the prize is declared valid, no compensation is due; if it is declared void, the parties interested have a right to be compensated. Resort to the International Court can only be made after the decision of the prize court has been given on the whole matter, and not immediately after the preliminary question has been decided.

Supposing a vessel which has been destroyed carried neutral goods **Articles 52 and 53. (See *ante*, p. 558.)** not liable to condemnation : the owner of such goods has, in every case, a right to compensation, that is, without there being occasion to distinguish between cases where the destruction was or was not justified. This is equitable and a further guarantee against arbitrary destruction.

A cruiser encounters a neutral merchant vessel carrying contraband in **Article 54. (See *ante*, p. 558.)** a proportion less than that specified in Article 40. The captain may put a prize crew on board the vessel and take her into a port for adjudication. He may, in conformity with the provisions of Article 44, agree to the handing over of the contraband if offered by the vessel stopped. But what is to happen if neither of these solutions is reached ? The vessel stopped does not offer to hand over the contraband, and the cruiser is not in a position to take the vessel into a national port. Is the cruiser obliged to let the neutral vessel go with the contraband on board? To require this seemed going too far, at least in certain exceptional circumstances. These circumstances are in fact the same as would have justified the destruction of the vessel, had she been liable to condemnation. In such a case, the cruiser may demand the handing over, or proceed to the destruction, of the goods liable to condemnation. The reasons for which the right to destroy the vessel has been recognized may justify the destruction of the contraband goods, the more so as the considerations of humanity which can be adduced against the destruction of a vessel do not in this case apply. Against arbitrary demands by the cruiser there are the same guarantees as those which made it possible to recognize the right to destroy the vessel. The captor must, as a preliminary, prove that he was really faced by the exceptional circum-

stances specified ; failing this, he is condemned to pay the value of the goods handed over or destroyed, and the question whether they were contraband or not will not be gone into.

The Article prescribes certain formalities which are necessary to establish the facts of the case and to enable the prize court to adjudicate.

Of course, when once the goods have been handed over or destroyed, and the formalities carried out, the vessel which has been stopped must be left free to continue her voyage.

Chapter V.

TRANSFER TO A NEUTRAL FLAG[1].

An enemy merchant vessel is liable to capture, whereas a neutral merchant vessel is immune. It can therefore be readily understood that a belligerent cruiser encountering a merchant vessel which lays claim to neutral nationality has to inquire whether such nationality has been acquired legitimately or merely in order to shield the vessel from the risks to which she would have been exposed had she retained her former nationality. This question naturally arises when the transfer has taken place a comparatively short time before the moment at which the ship is searched, whether the actual date be before, or after, the outbreak of hostilities. The answer will be different according as the question is looked at from the point of view of commercial or belligerent interests. Fortunately, rules have been agreed upon which conciliate both these interests as far as possible and which at the same time tell belligerents and neutral commerce what their position is.

The general rule laid down in the first paragraph is that the transfer

Article 55.
(See *ante*,
p. 559.)

of an enemy vessel to a neutral flag is valid, assuming, of course, that the ordinary requirements of the law have been fulfilled. It is upon the captor, if he wishes to have the transfer annulled, that the onus lies of proving that its object was to evade the consequences entailed by the war in prospect. There is one case which is treated as suspicious, that, namely, in which the bill of sale is not on board when the ship has changed her nationality less than sixty days before the outbreak of hostilities. The presumption of validity which has been set up by the first paragraph in favour of the vessel is then replaced by a presumption in favour of the captor. It is presumed that the transfer is void, but the presumption may be rebutted. With a view to such

---

[1] For British rules see *Parl. Papers*, Misc. No. 4 (1909), p. 10 ; for Instructions to British Delegation, *Ibid.* p. 81.

rebuttal, proof may be given that the transfer was not effected in order to evade the consequences of the war; it is unnecessary to add that the ordinary requirements of the law must have been fulfilled.

It was thought desirable to give to commerce a guarantee that the right of treating a transfer as void on the ground that it was effected in order to evade the consequences of war should not extend too far, and should not cover too long a period. Consequently, if the transfer has been effected more than thirty days before the outbreak of hostilities, it cannot be impeached on that ground alone, and it is regarded as unquestionably valid if it has been made under conditions which show that it is genuine and final; these conditions are as follows: the transfer must be unconditional, complete, and in conformity with the laws of the countries concerned, and its effect must be such that both the control of, and the profits earned by, the vessel pass into other hands. When once these conditions are proved to exist, the captor is not allowed to set up the contention that the vendor foresaw the war in which his country was about to be involved, and wished by the sale to shield himself from the risks to which a state of war would have exposed him in respect of the vessels he was transferring. Even in this case, however, when a vessel is encountered by a cruiser and her bill of sale is not on board, she may be captured if a change of nationality has taken place less than sixty days before the outbreak of hostilities; that circumstance has made her suspect. But if before the prize court the proof required by the second paragraph is adduced, she must be released, though she cannot claim compensation, inasmuch as there was good reason for capturing her.

The rule respecting *transfers made after the outbreak of hostilities* is more simple. Such a transfer is only valid if it is proved that its object was not to evade the consequences to which an enemy vessel, as such, is exposed. The rule accepted in respect of transfers made before the outbreak of hostilities is inverted. In that case there is a presumption that the transfer is valid; in the present, that it is void—provided always that proof to the contrary may be given. For instance, it might be proved that the transfer had taken place by inheritance.

Article 56 recites cases in which the presumption that the transfer is void is absolute, for reasons which can be readily understood: in the first case, the connection between the transfer and the war risk run by the vessel is evident; in the second, the transferee is a mere man of straw, who is to be treated as owner during a dangerous period, after which the vendor will recover possession of his vessel; lastly, the third case might

Article 56.
(See *ante*,
p. 560.)

strictly be regarded as already provided for, since a vessel which lays claim to neutral nationality must naturally prove that she has a right to it.

At one time provision was made in this Article for the case of a vessel which was retained, after the transfer, in the trade in which she had previously been engaged[1]. Such a circumstance is in the highest degree suspicious ; the transfer has a fictitious appearance, inasmuch as nothing has changed in regard to the vessel's trade. This would apply, for instance, if a vessel were running on the same line before and after the transfer. It was, however, objected, that to set up an absolute presumption would sometimes be too severe, and that certain kinds of vessels, as, for example, tank-ships[2], could, on account of their build, engage only in a certain definite trade. To meet this objection, the word "*route*" was then added, so that it would have been necessary that the vessel should be engaged *in the same trade and on the same route*; it was thought that in this way the above contention would have been satisfactorily met. However, the suppression of this case from the list being insisted on, it was agreed to eliminate it. Consequently a transfer of this character now falls within the general rule ; it is certainly presumed to be void, but the presumption may be rebutted.

Chapter VI.

ENEMY CHARACTER[3].

The rule in the Declaration of Paris, that "the neutral flag covers enemy goods, with the exception of contraband of war," corresponds so closely with the advance of civilization, and has taken so firm a hold on the public mind that it is impossible, in the face of so extensive an application, to avoid seeing in that rule the embodiment of a principle of the common law of nations which can no longer be disputed. The determination of the neutral or enemy character of merchant vessels accordingly decides not only the question of the validity of their capture, but also the fate of the non-contraband goods on board. A similar general observation may be made with reference to the neutral or enemy character of goods. No one thinks of contesting to-day the principle according to which "neutral goods, with the exception of contraband of war, are not liable to capture on board an enemy ship." It is, therefore, only in respect of goods found on

---

[1] See British proposition, *Parl. Papers*, Misc. No. 5 (1909), pp. 180, 212, 244, 252.

[2] *les navires pétroliers.*

[3] For British rules as to enemy property see *Ibid.* No. 4 (1909), p. 11 ; for British Instructions, *Ibid.* p. 32. For discussions on this subject see *Ibid.* No. 5 (1909), pp. 167, 181, 188, 191, 206, 209.

board an enemy ship that the question whether they are neutral or enemy property arises.

The determination of what constitutes neutral or enemy character thus appears as a development of the two principles laid down in 1856, or rather as a means of securing their just application in practice.

The advantage of deducing from the practices of different countries some clear and simple rules on this subject may be said to need no demonstration. The uncertainty as to the risks of capture, if it does not put an end to trade, is at least the most serious of hindrances to its continuance. A trader ought to know the risks which he runs in putting his goods on board this or that ship, while the underwriter, if he does not know the extent of those risks, is obliged to charge war premiums which are often either excessive or else inadequate.

The rules which form this chapter are, unfortunately, incomplete; certain important points had to be laid aside, as has been already observed in the introductory explanations, and as will be further explained below.

The principle, therefore, is that *the neutral or enemy character of a*
Article 57. *vessel is determined by the flag which she is entitled to fly.* It
(See *ante*, is a simple rule which appears satisfactorily to meet the
p. 560.) special case of ships, as distinguished from that of other
movable property, and notably of the cargo. From more than one point of view, ships may be said to possess an individuality; notably they have a nationality, a national *character*. This attribute of nationality finds visible expression in the right to fly a flag; it has the effect of placing ships under the protection and control of the State to which they belong; it makes them amenable to the sovereignty and to the laws of that State, and liable to requisition, should the occasion arise. Here is the surest test of whether a vessel is really a unit in the merchant marine of a country, and here therefore the best test by which to decide whether her character is neutral or enemy. It is, moreover, preferable to rely exclusively upon this test, and to discard all considerations connected with the personal status of the owner.

The text makes use of the words "the flag which the vessel is entitled to fly"; that expression means, of course, the flag under which, whether she is actually flying it or not, the vessel is entitled to sail according to the municipal laws which govern that right.

Article 57 safeguards the provisions respecting transfer to another flag, as to which it is sufficient to refer to Articles 55 and 56; a vessel may very well have the right to fly a neutral flag, as far as the law of the

country to which she claims to belong is concerned, but may be treated as an enemy vessel by a belligerent, because the transfer in virtue of which she has hoisted the neutral flag is annulled by Article 55 or Article 56.

Lastly, the question was raised whether a vessel loses her neutral character when she is engaged in a trade which the enemy, prior to the war, reserved exclusively for his national vessels; but as has been observed above in connection with the subject of *Unneutral service*, no agreement was reached, and the question remains an open one, as the second paragraph of Article 57 is careful to explain.

Unlike ships, goods have no individuality of their own; their neutral or enemy character is made to depend upon the personal status of their owner. This opinion prevailed after an exhaustive study of different views, which inclined towards reliance on the country of origin of the goods, the status of the person at whose risk they are, of the consignee, or of the consignor. The test adopted in Article 58 appears, moreover, to be in conformity with the terms of the Declaration of Paris, as also with those of the convention of The Hague of the 18th October, 1907, relative to the establishment of an International Prize Court, where the expression *neutral or enemy property* is used (Articles 1, 3, 4, 8)[1].

Article 58.
(See *ante*, p. 561.)

But it cannot be concealed that Article 58 solves no more than a part of the problem, and that the easier part; it is the neutral or enemy character of the owner which determines the character of the goods, but what is to determine the neutral or enemy character of the owner? On this point nothing is said, because it was found impossible to arrive at an agreement. Opinions were divided between *domicile* and *nationality*; no useful purpose will be served by reproducing here the arguments adduced to support the two positions. It was hoped that a compromise might have been reached on the basis of a clause to the following effect:—

"The neutral or enemy character of goods found on board an enemy vessel is determined by the neutral or enemy nationality of their owner, or, if he is of no nationality or of double nationality (*i.e.*, both neutral and enemy), by his domicile in a neutral or enemy country;

"Provided that goods belonging to a limited liability or joint stock company are considered as neutral or enemy according as the company has its headquarters in a neutral or enemy country[2]."

But there was no unanimity.

[1] See *ante*, pp. 408, 409, 411.
[2] For discussions see *Parl. Papers*, Misc. No. 5 (1909), pp. 279, 380.

Article 59 gives expression to the traditional rule according to which

Article 59.
(See *ante*, p. 561.)

goods found on board an enemy vessel are, failing proof to the contrary, presumed to be enemy goods; this is merely a simple presumption, which leaves to the claimant the right, but at the same time the onus, of proving his title.

This provision contemplates the case where goods which were enemy

Article 60.
(See *ante*, p. 561.)

property at the time of dispatch have been the subject of a sale or transfer during the course of the voyage. The ease with which enemy goods might secure protection from the exercise of the right of capture by means of a sale which is made subject to a reconveyance of the property on arrival has always led to a refusal to recognise such transfers. The enemy character subsists.

With regard to the moment from which goods must be considered to acquire and retain the enemy character of their owner, the text has been inspired by the same spirit of equity as governed the convention of The Hague, relative to the status of merchant vessels on the outbreak of hostilities, and by the same desire to protect mercantile operations undertaken in the security of a time of peace. It is only when the transfer takes place after the outbreak of hostilities that it is, so far as the loss of enemy character is concerned, inoperative until the arrival of the goods in question. The date which is taken into consideration here is that of the transfer, and not of the departure of the vessel. For, while the vessel which started before the war began, and remains, perhaps, unaware of the outbreak of hostilities, may enjoy on this account some degree of exemption, the goods may nevertheless possess enemy character; the enemy owner of these goods is in a position to be aware of the state of war, and it is for that very reason that he is likely to seek to evade its consequences.

It was, however, thought right to add what is, if not a limitation, at least a complement agreed to be necessary. In a great number of countries an unpaid vendor has, in the event of the bankruptcy of the buyer, a recognised legal right to recover the goods which have already become the property of the buyer but not yet reached him (*stoppage in transitu*). In such a case the sale is cancelled, and, in consequence of the recovery, the vendor obtains the goods again and is not deemed ever to have ceased to be the owner. This right gives to neutral commerce, in the case of a genuine bankruptcy, a protection too valuable to be sacrificed, and the second paragraph of Article 60 is intended to preserve it.

Chapter VII.

CONVOY[1].

The practice of convoy has, in the past, occasionally given rise to grave difficulties and even to conflict. It is, therefore, satisfactory to be able to record the agreement which has been reached upon this subject.

The principle laid down is simple: a neutral vessel under the convoy

Article 61.
(See *ante*, p. 561.)

of a warship of her own nationality is exempt from search. The reason for this rule is that the belligerent cruiser ought to be able to find in the assurances of the commander of the convoy as good a guarantee as would be afforded by the exercise of the right of search itself; in fact, she cannot call in question the assurances given by the official representative of a neutral Government, without displaying a lack of international courtesy. If neutral Governments allow belligerents to search vessels sailing under their flag, it is because they do not wish to be responsible for the supervision of such vessels, and therefore allow belligerents to protect themselves. The situation is altered when a neutral Government consents to undertake that responsibility; the right of search has no longer the same importance.

But it follows from the explanation of the rule respecting convoy that the neutral Government undertakes to afford the belligerents every guarantee that the vessels convoyed shall not take advantage of the protection accorded to them in order to do anything inconsistent with their neutrality, as, for example, to carry contraband, render unneutral service to the belligerent, or attempt to break blockade. There is need, therefore, that a genuine supervision should be exercised from the outset over the vessels which are to be convoyed; and that supervision must be continued throughout the voyage. The Government must act with vigilance so as to prevent all abuse of the right of convoy, and must give to the officer who is put in command of a convoy precise instructions to this effect.

---

[1] "A neutral vessel is not entitled to resist the exercise of the right of search by a belligerent war-ship on the ground that she is under the convoy of a war-ship of her own nationality." This was the British rule as stated in the Memorandum, but, as was pointed out in the "Instructions," this doctrine has not been enforced in recent wars. Germany was the only other Power maintaining the same view as Great Britain. The British Delegation was instructed that the specific abandonment of the British rule "would effect no substantial alteration in the actual situation, and may very well be admitted to be little more than the formal acknowledgment of a now generally accepted rule." (See *Parl. Papers*, Misc. No. 4 (1909), pp. 4, 25.)

A belligerent cruiser encounters a convoy; she communicates with the commander of the convoy, who must, at her request, give in writing all relevant information about the vessels under his protection. A written declaration is required, because it prevents all ambiguities and misunderstandings, and because it pledges to a greater extent the responsibility of the commander. The object of such a declaration is to make search unnecessary by the mere fact of giving to the cruiser the information which the search itself would have supplied.

In the majority of cases the cruiser will be satisfied with the declaration which the commander of the convoy will have given to her, but she may have serious grounds for believing that the confidence of the commander has been abused, as for example, that a ship under convoy of which the papers are apparently in order and exhibit nothing suspicious is, in fact, carrying contraband cleverly concealed. The cruiser may, in such a case, communicate her suspicions to the commander of the convoy, and an investigation may be considered necessary. If so, it will be made by the commander of the convoy, since it is he alone who exercises authority over the vessels placed under his protection. It appeared, nevertheless, that much difficulty might often be avoided if the belligerent were allowed to be present at this investigation; otherwise he might still suspect, if not the good faith, at least the vigilance and perspicacity of the person who conducted the search. But it was not thought that an obligation to allow the officer of the cruiser to be present at the investigation should be imposed upon the commander of the convoy. He must act as he thinks best; if he agrees to the presence of an officer of the cruiser, it will be as an act of courtesy or good policy. He must in every case draw up a report of the investigation and give a copy to the officer of the cruiser.

Differences of opinion may occur between the two officers, particularly in relation to conditional contraband. The character of a port to which a cargo of corn is destined may be disputed. Is it an ordinary commercial port? or is it a port which serves as a base of supply for the armed forces? The situation which arises out of the mere fact of the convoy must in such a case be respected. The officer of the cruiser can do no more than make his protest, and the difficulty must be settled through the diplomatic channel.

The situation is altogether different if a vessel under convoy is found beyond the possibility of dispute to be carrying contraband. The vessel has no longer a right to protection, since the condition upon which such protection was granted has not been fulfilled. Besides deceiving her own

Government, she has tried to deceive the belligerent. She must therefore be treated as a neutral merchant vessel encountered in the ordinary way and searched by a belligerent cruiser. She cannot complain at being exposed to such rigorous treatment, since there is in her case an aggravation of the offence committed by a carrier of contraband.

Chapter VIII.

RESISTANCE TO SEARCH.

The subject treated in this chapter was not mentioned in the programme submitted by the British Government in February 1908, but it is intimately connected with several of the questions in that programme, and thus attracted the attention of the Conference in the course of its deliberations; and it was thought necessary to frame a rule upon it, the drafting of which presented little difficulty[1].

Article 63.
(See *ante*,
p. 562.)

A belligerent cruiser encounters a merchant vessel and summons her to stop in order that she may be searched. The vessel summoned does not stop, but tries to avoid the search by flight. The cruiser may employ force to stop her, and the merchant vessel, if she is damaged or sunk, has no right to complain, seeing that she has failed to comply with an obligation imposed upon her by the law of nations.

If the vessel is stopped, and it is shown that it was only in order to escape the inconvenience of being searched that recourse was had to flight, and that beyond this she had done nothing contrary to neutrality, she will not be punished for her attempt at flight. If, on the other hand, it is established that the vessel has contraband on board, or that she has in some way or other failed to comply with her duty as a neutral, she will suffer the consequences of her infraction of neutrality, but in this case as in the last, she will not undergo any punishment for her attempt at flight. Expression was given to the contrary view, namely, that a ship should be punished for an obvious attempt at flight as much as for forcible resistance. It was suggested that the prospect of having the escaping vessel condemned as good prize would influence the captain of the cruiser to do his best to spare her. But in the end this view did not prevail.

The situation is different if forcible resistance is made to any legitimate action by the cruiser. The vessel commits an act of hostility and must, from that moment, be treated as an enemy vessel; she will therefore

---

[1] The subject was first introduced by the German delegate at the Second Plenary Meeting on the 7th Dec., 1908, in connection with contraband. (*Parl. Papers*, Misc. No. 5 (1909), p. 140.)

be subject to condemnation, although the search may not have shown that anything contrary to neutrality had been done. So far no difficulty seems to arise.

What must be decided with regard to the cargo? The rule which appeared to be the best is that according to which the cargo will be treated like the cargo on board an enemy vessel. This assimilation involves the following consequences: a neutral vessel which has offered resistance becomes an enemy vessel and the goods on board are presumed to be enemy goods. Neutrals who are interested may claim their property, in accordance with Article 3 of the Declaration of Paris, but enemy goods will be condemned, since the rule that *the flag covers the goods* cannot be adduced, because the captured vessel on board which they are found is considered to be an enemy vessel. It will be noticed that the right to claim the goods is open to all neutrals, even to those whose nationality is that of the captured vessel; it would seem to be an excess of severity to make such persons suffer for the action of the master. There is, however, an exception as regards the goods which belong to the owner of the vessel; it seems natural that he should bear the consequences of the acts of his agent. His property on board the vessel is therefore treated as enemy goods. *A fortiori* the same rule applies to the goods belonging to the master.

Chapter IX.

COMPENSATION.

This chapter is of very general application, inasmuch as the provisions which it contains are operative in all the numerous cases in which a cruiser may capture a vessel or goods.

A cruiser has captured a neutral vessel, on the ground, for example, of

Article 64.
(See *ante*,
p. 569.)

carriage of contraband or breach of blockade. The prize court releases the vessel declaring the capture to be void. This decision alone is evidently not enough to indemnify the parties interested for the loss incurred in consequence of the capture, and this loss may have been considerable, since the vessel has been during a period, which may often be a very long one, prevented from engaging in her ordinary trade. May these parties claim to be compensated for this injury? Reason requires that the affirmative answer should be given, if the injury has been undeserved, that is to say, if the capture was not brought about by some fault of the parties. It may, indeed, happen that there was good reason for the capture, because the master of the vessel searched did not produce evidence which ought in the ordinary course to

have been available, and which was only furnished at a later stage. In such a case it would be unjust that compensation should be awarded. On the other hand, if the cruiser has really been at fault, if the vessel has been captured when there were not good reasons for doing so, it is just that compensation should be granted.

It may also happen that a vessel which has been captured and taken into a port is released by the action of the executive without the intervention of a prize court. The existing practice, under such circumstances, is not uniform. In some countries the prize court has no jurisdiction unless there is a question of validating a capture, and cannot adjudicate on a claim for compensation based upon the ground that the capture would have been held unjustifiable; in other countries the prize court would have jurisdiction to entertain a claim of this kind. On this point, therefore, there is a difference which is not altogether equitable, and it is desirable to lay down a rule which will produce the same result in all countries. It is reasonable that every capture effected without good reasons should give to the parties interested a right to compensation, without its being necessary to draw any distinction between the cases in which the capture has or has not been followed by a decision of a prize court; and this argument is all the more forcible when the capture may have so little justification that the vessel is released by the action of the executive. A provision in general terms has therefore been adopted, which is capable of covering all cases of capture.

It should be observed that in the text no reference is made to the question whether the national tribunals are competent to adjudicate on a claim for compensation. In cases where proceedings are taken against the property captured, no doubt upon this point can be entertained. In the course of the proceedings taken to determine the validity of a capture the parties interested have the opportunity of making good their right to compensation, and, if the national tribunal does not give them satisfaction, they can apply to the International Prize Court. If, on the other hand, the action of the belligerent has been confined to the capture, it is the law of the belligerent captor which decides whether there are tribunals competent to entertain a demand for compensation, and, if so, what are those tribunals; the International Court has not, according to the convention of The Hague, any jurisdiction in such a case. From an international point of view, the diplomatic channel is the only one available for making good such a claim, whether the cause for complaint is founded on a decision actually delivered, or on the absence of any tribunal having jurisdiction to entertain it.

The question was raised as to whether it was necessary to draw a distinction between the direct and the indirect losses suffered by vessel or goods[1]. The best course appeared to be to leave the prize court free to estimate the amount of compensation due, which will vary according to the circumstances and cannot be laid down in advance in rules going into minute details.

For the sake of simplicity, mention has only been made of the vessel, but what has been said applies of course to cargo captured and afterwards released. Innocent goods on board a vessel which has been captured suffer, in the same way, all the inconvenience which attends the capture of the vessel; but if there was good cause for capturing the vessel, whether the capture has subsequently been held to be valid or not, the owners of the cargo have no right to compensation.

It is perhaps useful to indicate certain cases in which the capture of a vessel would be justified, whatever might be the ultimate decision of the prize court. Notably, there is the case where some or all of the ship's papers have been thrown overboard, suppressed, or intentionally destroyed on the initiative of the master or one of the crew or passengers. There is in such a case an element which will justify any suspicion and afford an excuse for capturing the vessel, subject to the master's ability to account for his actions before the prize court. Even if the court should accept the explanation given and should not find any reason for condemnation, the parties interested cannot hope to recover compensation.

An analogous case would be that in which there were found on board two sets of papers, or false or forged papers, if this irregularity were connected with circumstances calculated to contribute to the capture of the vessel.

It appeared sufficient that these cases in which there would be a reasonable excuse for the capture should be mentioned in the present Report, and should not be made the object of express provisions, since, otherwise, the mention of these two particular cases might have led to the supposition that they were the only cases in which a capture could be justified.

Such then are the principles of international law to which the Naval Conference has sought to give recognition as being fitted to regulate in practice the intercourse of nations on certain important questions in regard to which precise rules have hitherto been wanting. The Conference has thus taken up the work of codification begun by the Declaration of Paris

---

[1] See views expressed in Memorandum of Austria-Hungary, *Parl. Papers*, Misc. No. 5 (1909), p. 75.

of 1856. It has worked in the same spirit as the second Peace Conference and, taking advantage of the labours accomplished at The Hague, it has been able to solve some of the problems which, owing to the lack of time, that Conference was compelled to leave unsolved. Let us hope that it may be possible to say that those who have drawn up the Declaration of London of 1909 are not altogether unworthy of their predecessors of 1856 and 1907.

FINAL PROVISIONS.

These provisions have reference to various questions relating to the effect of the Declaration, its ratification, its coming into force, its denunciation, and the accession of unrepresented Powers.

Article 65.
(See *ante*, p. 563.)
This Article is of great importance, and is in conformity with that which was adopted in the Declaration of Paris.

The rules contained in the present Declaration relate to matters of great importance and great diversity. They have not all been accepted with the same degree of eagerness by all the Delegations. Concessions have been made on one point in consideration of concessions obtained on another. The whole, all things considered, has been recognised as satisfactory, and a legitimate expectation would be falsified if one Power might make reservations on a rule to which another Power attached importance.

Article 66.
(See *ante*, p. 563.)
According to the engagement resulting from this Article, the Declaration applies to the relations between the Signatory Powers when the belligerents are likewise parties to the Declaration.

It will be the duty of each Power to take the measures necessary to insure the observance of the Declaration. These measures may vary in different countries, and may or may not involve the intervention of the legislature. The matter is one of national legal requirements.

It should be observed that neutral Powers also may find themselves in a position of having to give instructions to their authorities, notably to the commanders of convoys as previously explained.

Article 67.
(See *ante*, p. 563.)
This provision, of a purely formal character, needs no explanation. The wording adopted at The Hague by the second Peace Conference has been borrowed.

Articles 68 and 69. (See *ante*, p. 564.)
It follows implicitly from Article 69 that the Declaration is of indefinite duration. The periods after which denunciation is allowed have been fixed on the analogy of the convention for the establishment of an International Prize Court.

The Declaration of Paris also contained an invitation to the Powers which were not represented to accede to the Declaration. The official invitation in this case, instead of being made individually by each of the Powers represented at the Conference, may more conveniently be made by Great Britain acting in the name of all the Powers.

Article 70.
(See *ante*,
p. 565.)

The procedure for accession is very simple. The fact that the acceding Powers are placed on the same footing in every respect as the signatory Powers of course involves compliance by the former with Article 65. A Power cannot accede to a part of the Declaration, but only to the whole.

As at The Hague, account has been taken of the situation of certain Powers the Representatives of which may not be in a position to sign the Declaration at once, but which desire nevertheless to be considered as signatory, and not as acceding, Powers.

Article 71.
(See *ante*,
p. 566.)

It is scarcely necessary to say that the *Plenipotentiaries of the Powers* referred to in Article 71 are not necessarily those who were, as such, delegates at the Naval Conference.

APPENDIX.

INSTRUCTIONS TO BRITISH DELEGATION AT THE SECOND PEACE CONFERENCE.

Sir Edward Grey to Sir Edward Fry[1].

Foreign Office, June 12, 1907.

Sir,

1. In my despatch of the 19th April last I informed you that the King had been graciously pleased to appoint you to be His Majesty's First Plenipotentiary to represent this country at the Second Peace Conference, which will assemble at The Hague on the 15th instant, in conjunction with the Right Honourable Sir Ernest Mason Satow, G.C.M.G., the Right Honourable Lord Reay, G.C.S.I., G.C.I.E., and Sir Henry Howard, K.C.M.G., C.B., His Majesty's Minister at the Hague. Lieut. General Sir Edmond Roche Elles, G.C.I.E., K.C.B., and Captain Charles Langdale Ottley, M.V.O., R.N., Director of Naval Intelligence, have been appointed as Expert Delegates to assist you and your colleagues in the discussion of the military and naval questions which will come before the Conference.

2. You are aware from the correspondence that has been furnished to you from time to time that the proposal for this Conference, like that which was held at The Hague in 1899, emanated from His Majesty the Emperor of Russia, who in the spring of last year addressed an invitation to His Majesty's Government to be represented at it. A similar invitation was at the same time sent to some forty-seven other States. The note conveying this invitation also indicated certain topics which it was thought might usefully be discussed at the Conference and which may be summarized as follows :

(I) Improvements to be made in the provisions of the Convention respecting the pacific settlement of international disputes regarding both the Court of Arbitration and the International Commissions of Inquiry.

(II) Additions to be made to the provisions of the Convention of 1899 respecting the Laws and Practices of Land Warfare, among others the opening of hostilities, the rights of neutrals on land, &c., consideration of the Declarations of 1899 and the question of the renewal of the one that has lapsed.

[1] *Parl. Papers*, Misc. No. 1 (1908), p. 11.

(III)   Elaboration of a Convention respecting the Laws and Practices of Naval Warfare concerning—

(A)   The special operations of naval warfare, such as the bombardment of ports, towns, and villages by a naval force, the laying of mines, &c.

(B)   The transformation of commercial vessels into war-ships.

(C)   The private property of belligerents at sea.

(D)   The period to be accorded to commercial vessels in leaving neutral ports or those of the enemy after the outbreak of hostilities.

(E)   The rights and duties of neutrals at sea, among other questions that of contraband, the treatment to which the ships of belligerents should be subjected in neutral ports, destruction by *force majeure* of neutral ships of commerce as prizes.

(F)   Arrangements relative to land warfare which should be made equally applicable to naval warfare.

(IV)   Additions to be made to the Convention of 1899 for the adaptation to naval warfare of the principles of the Geneva Convention of 1864.

3.   In accepting this invitation, His Majesty's Government expressed the opinion that the subjects above indicated might, as a whole, be freely discussed with advantage, but they thought it desirable to reserve generally the right to abstain from taking part in the discussion at the Conference of any of the questions mentioned in the programme, should the discussion take a form unlikely, in their opinion, to lead to any useful result.   Several other Powers have, as you are aware, made a similar reservation.

4.   His Majesty's Government further reserved to themselves the right of suggesting the discussion of other cognate questions of international interest not specifically mentioned in the programme.   Foremost among such questions is that of expenditure on armaments, which His Majesty's Government have from the first been desirous of seeing discussed at the Conference.   They felt it was better to have a discussion, even if it did not lead to a satisfactory conclusion.   Discussion without result would, at any rate, have kept the door open for continuing negotiations on the subject.   Whereas, to put the question aside would seem like an admission that it was hopeless, and had receded since the first Conference, of which it was the prime object.   They felt that, this being a question on which perhaps there must be many discussions, and even failures, before progress is made, even a failure to secure a definite result was better than no discussion at all.

5.   His Majesty's Government have accordingly reserved their right to bring this question forward at the Conference, and have told the United States' Government, who have made a similar reservation, that they would support them in promoting a discussion.   If, therefore, the United States' Delegates bring the subject forward, it will be your duty to support them.   But, after the apparently final declaration of the German Government that under no

circumstances would they take any part in such a discussion, it is doubtful how far it would be expedient to proceed with it. The position of Germany both as a military and a naval Power is such that it is difficult to regard as serious any discussion in which she does not take part. His Majesty's Government would be most reluctant that anything should take place at The Hague Conference, summoned, as it is, in the interests of peace, that would be of a nature to cause friction or ill-feeling. You will therefore consult closely with your United States' colleagues, and ascertain what instructions they have, and consider with them what line it is best to take.

6. The Spanish Government have also made a similar reservation on this question, and their Delegates should also be consulted; and it is possible that the Italian Delegates may also have some instructions as to the procedure to be adopted.

7. Should it be decided that the subject shall be discussed and a practical. proposal be invited, you are authorized to say that His Majesty's Government would agree to a proposal that the Great Powers should communicate to each other in advance their programmes of new naval construction. If this were done, they might be led to realize how closely in some cases the naval construction of one Power is dependent upon that of another; and an opportunity would be given for negotiations with the object of reducing the programmes, before the Governments of the Great Powers were finally committed to them by announcing them to their respective Parliaments. His Majesty's Government are aware that this would not necessarily lead directly to any reduction in expenditure, but they are hopeful that the mere fact of communication between the Powers would provide opportunities for negotiation that do not now exist, and would tend to alleviate the burden of expenditure or retard its increase. Though, however, they consider that this or some other proposal put forward by another Power would be useful for the sake of the discussion to which it would give rise, even if it were not eventually accepted you should not put forward any proposal unless there be a general decision and a strong desire that a discussion should take place, and unless it is made clear that such a course will be taken in good part.

8. I now pass to the consideration of the various heads of the programme in the order in which they are set out in the invitation :

I. *Improvements to be made in the Provisions of the Convention of 1899 respecting the Pacific Settlement of International Disputes.*

9. I am not aware of any proposals that will be made by other Powers for amending the provisions of this Convention, but I believe that Professor de Martens will, with the concurrence of the Government of the Czar, suggest certain amendments for increasing the utility of the " Commission d'Enquête " provided for in Articles IX—XIV of the Convention. The nature of the

proposals is not at present known, but as at present advised, I see no reason for thinking it likely that His Majesty's Government will be unable to agree to them, if you and your colleagues report that you consider that they may be introduced into the Convention with advantage.

10. His Majesty's Government, however, are anxious to secure the adaptation of the machinery of the existing Tribunal, which was created by the Convention, to the purposes of an International Tribunal of Appeal from the decisions of belligerent Prize Courts affecting neutrals. The judgments of the Tribunal in such cases would probably prove the most rapid and efficient means which can, under existing conditions, be devised for giving form and authority to the canons of international law in matters of prize. It would no doubt be necessary that the procedure of the Court should be formulated, and its powers precisely defined, and that the Powers should bind themselves to employ the executive of their Governments to enforce its decrees against their own subjects or citizens. The advantages would far outweigh any difficulty that might arise from the fact that some alterations in the municipal laws of this Country, and probably also of other States, would be required. His Majesty's Government consider that if The Hague Conference accomplishes no other object than the constitution of such a Tribunal, it will render an inestimable service to civilization and mankind.

11. It is not improbable that the question of the choice of languages to be used by and before the Permanent Court of Arbitration may be raised under the present head. By Articles XXX and XXXVIII of the Convention it is for the Tribunal itself to decide this point, unless the parties have themselves settled the language question in advance. His Majesty's Government are aware that in some cases which have come before the Court this rule has been found to involve practical difficulties, but, after careful consideration, they have come to the conclusion that the existing arrangement is the best that can hope to meet with general consent. You should accordingly not support any suggestion which may be made at the Conference for altering the rules as to the choice of languages.

II. *Additions to be made to the Provisions of the Convention of* 1899, *respecting the Laws and Practices of Land Warfare, &c.*

12. The Russian Government have mentioned the opening of hostilities and the rights of neutrals on land as matters which might be treated in additional stipulations. But beyond this indication, no intimation has reached His Majesty's Government as to the precise measures or principles which are to be brought forward for adoption. As at present advised they are not aware that the necessity or advisability of any such additions to the Convention has made itself felt in this country, and they have had no material before them enabling them to foreshadow the direction which a discussion on the points briefly

mentioned in the Russian programme might take at the Conference. They therefore feel unable to lay down any specific directions for your guidance in the matter, and can only at this stage express their readiness to give any definite proposals which may eventually be made the earnest and impartial consideration which the important nature of the subject deserves.

13. The declarations referred to in the Russian note were the agreements to abstain from (1) the use of projectiles diffusing noxious gases ; (2) the use of expanding bullets; and (3) the use of projectiles and explosives from balloons for a term of five years, that were signed by a majority of the Powers at the last Hague Conference, Great Britain, Germany, the United States, &c., dissenting. Should these questions be raised at the Conference, His Majesty's Government think, as regards (1), that it is unnecessary for you to take the initiative in proposing such a prohibition, although you should not dissent from it if there should be a general consensus of the other Powers in its favour; with respect to (2), that the restriction may be supported so far as warfare between the High Contracting Powers is concerned; and with regard to (3), you should support any proposal for the renewal of this prohibition.

III. *Elaboration of a Convention respecting the Laws and Practices of Naval Warfare concerning—*

(A) *The Special Operations of Naval Warfare, such as the Bombardment of Ports, Towns, and Villages, by a Naval Force, the laying of Mines, &c.*

14. His Majesty's Government consider that the objection, on humanitarian grounds, to the bombardment of unfortified towns is too strong to justify a resort to that measure, even though it may be permissible under the abstract doctrines of international law. They wish it, however, to be clearly understood that any general prohibition of such practice must not be held to apply to such operations as the bombardment of towns or places used as bases or storehouses of naval or military equipment and supply, or ports containing fighting ships, and that the landing of troops, or anything partaking of the character of a naval or military operation, is also not covered.

15. His Majesty's Government would view with satisfaction the abandonment of the employment of automatic mines in naval warfare altogether. Failing the acceptance of such a total prohibition they earnestly hope that the employment of these engines of war will only be sanctioned under the strictest limitations. They would advocate an arrangement by which the use of automatic mines should be limited to territorial waters, and, if possible, to such portions of territorial waters as adjoin naval bases or fortified ports. All mines thus employed should be effectively anchored, and so constructed that, in the event of their breaking adrift, they would either automatically become harmless or sink, and that in any case their active life should not exceed a limited period of, say, six months.

(B) *The Transformation of Commercial Vessels into War-ships.*

16. As the best and surest means to meet the many difficulties arising in connection with the question of the status, or belligerent character, of ships engaged in naval operations, His Majesty's Government would like to see the Powers agree upon some precise definition of a "war-ship." Having given their attentive consideration to the problem in its many various aspects, they are of opinion that if such definition is to cover all vessels which may be directly associated with the warlike operations of a fleet, it should establish and comprise two categories of ships, viz.: (A) fighting ships, and (B) fleet auxiliaries. For these two classes of vessels, you might propose for acceptance some such definition as the following:—

(A) "Any vessel under a recognised naval flag, officered and manned by regular commission, and armed for the purpose of attacking an enemy, no vessel being allowed to assume this status unless before leaving a national port, or to surrender it except after arrival at one."

(B) "A vessel under the mercantile flag of either a belligerent or neutral State which is engaged in transporting troops or on duties bringing her into direct communication with the belligerent fighting ships for the purpose of assisting their operations, either by the conveyance of seamen, munitions of war, fuel, provisions, water, or any kind of naval stores, or by executing repairs, or by carrying despatches or information, and whether such ship sails in company with the fighting ships or only meets them from time to time."

17. The general acceptance of definition (A), as supplemented by definition (B), coupled with a general undertaking that no vessel was to perform fighting services unless qualified under definition (A), would, it is believed, prove sufficient to prevent the issue by any Power of letters of marque (whether such Power were a party to the Declaration of Paris or not), as none but regularly commissioned men-of-war would have the status of "fighting ships." You might with advantage ascertain the views of your United States' colleagues on this subject, to which particular importance is likely to be attached by their Government, special regard being had to the fact that, although conditionally refusing to sign the Declaration of Paris, the United States intimated their intention of observing it during the war with Spain in 1898.

(C) *The Private Property of Belligerents at Sea.*

18. It is probable that a proposal will be brought before The Hague Conference to sanction the principle of the immunity of enemies' merchant ships and private property from capture at sea in time of war. His Majesty's Government have given careful consideration to this question, and the arguments on both sides have been fully set out in the various papers which have been at your disposal. They cannot disregard the weighty arguments which have been

put forward in favour of immunity. Anything which restrains acts of war is in itself a step towards the abolition of all war, and by diminishing the apprehension of the evils which war would cause, removes one incentive to expenditure upon armaments. It is also possible to imagine cases in which the interests of Great Britain might benefit by the adoption of this principle of immunity from capture.

19. But, on the other hand, it must be remembered that the principle, if carried to its logical conclusion, must entail the abolition of the right of commercial blockade. Unless commercial blockade is discontinued there will be constant interference with an enemy's ships, and constant disputes as to what constitutes an effective blockade. And when such disputes have once arisen between belligerent Powers it is obvious that the one which considers itself aggrieved by the application of commercial blockade to any of its ports would cease to respect the immunity of the merchant ships and private property of its enemy, wherever they were to be found. It seems to them, therefore, that it is impossible to separate this question of immunity from capture from that of commercial blockade; and that the question to which His Majesty's Government have to apply themselves is whether they should agree to a proposal which would deprive the British navy in time of war of the right of interfering with an enemy's merchant ships or property, and of the power of commercial blockade.

20. The British navy is the only offensive weapon which Great Britain has against Continental Powers. The latter have a double means of offence: they have their navies and they have their powerful armies. During recent years, the proportion between the British army and the great Continental armies has come to be such that the British army operating alone could not be regarded as a means of offence against the mainland of a great Continental Power. For her ability to bring pressure to bear upon her enemies in war Great Britain has, therefore, to rely on the navy alone. His Majesty's Government cannot therefore authorize you to agree to any Resolution which would diminish the effective means which the navy has of bringing pressure to bear upon an enemy.

21. You should, however, raise no objection to the discussion of this question of immunity from capture at the Conference, nor should you refuse to participate in it, nor need you necessarily take the initiative in opposing a Resolution if brought forward. If at some future date the great Continental armies were to be diminished, and other changes favourable to the diminution of armaments were to take place, the British Government might be able to reconsider the question. If, for instance, nations generally were willing to diminish their armaments, naval and military, to an extent which would materially relieve them from the apprehension of the consequences of war, and by rendering aggression difficult would make war itself improbable; and if it became apparent that such a change could be brought about by an

agreement to secure this immunity from capture at sea under all circumstances, and was dependent upon it, the British Government might feel that the risks they would run by adhering to such an agreement and the objections in principle now to be urged against it, would be outweighed by the general gain and relief which such a change would bring. But at the present time they are unable to assent to a Resolution which might, under existing conditions, so limit the prospective liability of war as to remove some of the considerations which now restrain public opinion from contemplating it, and might, after the outbreak of war, tend to prolong it.

(D) *The Period to be accorded to Commercial Vessels in leaving Neutral Ports or those of the Enemy after the Outbreak of Hostilities.*

22. It has been customary on the outbreak of hostilities for belligerents to grant certain days of grace to enemy and neutral ships. In the view of His Majesty's Government the allowance of such an interval before the strict rules of hostilities are enforced should, as indeed the term "days of grace" implies, be treated purely as a matter of grace and favour, and not as one of right, and they are of opinion that any fixed rule on the point would be undesirable, as the circumstances of each case must necessarily differ. It will be to the general interest of this country to maintain the utmost liberty of action in this particular.

(E) *The Rights and Duties of Neutrals at Sea: among other Questions that of Contraband; the Treatment to which the Ships of Belligerents should be subjected in Neutral Ports; Destruction by* force majeure *of Neutral Ships of Commerce as Prizes.*

23. Many questions in regard to neutrality obligations may be raised at the coming Conference as a result of the experience of the late war between Russia and Japan. On the general principles involved nations are agreed, but in the application of these principles great divergence in the standard of obligations adopted by different Powers is sure to arise. Rules based on the following principles would, His Majesty's Government consider, help to clear the situation:—

(a) Neutrals shall not allow their territorial waters to be used for purposes which will directly assist a belligerent in operations of war.

(b) Neutrals shall not allow fighting ships, or ships built or equipped, wholly or partly, for fighting purposes to leave their ports or territorial waters after the outbreak of war with the intention of assisting either of the belligerents.

(c) The customary maritime facilities known as "hospitality" shall not be withheld.

(*d*) A neutral State is not called upon to enforce the observance of the restrictions imposed upon trade by a belligerent by declarations of contraband, but must not assist in their violation.

(*e*) A neutral shall not allow the entrance of prizes into its harbours unless the prize is in want of fuel or supplies, or in actual danger on account of bad weather or unseaworthiness.

24. Great Britain as a belligerent is not likely, in any conditions which can at present be foreseen as probable, to have to depend on the assistance of neutrals in the direct carrying out of operations of war. Her interests as a neutral require uniformity of practice on the part of neutrals generally, and it would be desirable that the rules which obtain in this country as regards the obligations of neutrality should, if possible, obtain international sanction at the Conference.

25. With regard to contraband, many most difficult questions arose during the late war. These cases were sufficient to show that the rules with regard to contraband that were developed at the end of the eighteenth and the beginning of the nineteenth centuries are no longer satisfactory for the changed conditions under which both commerce and war are now carried on. His Majesty's Government recognize to the full the desirability of freeing neutral commerce to the utmost extent possible from interference by belligerent Powers, and they are ready and willing for their part, in lieu of endeavouring to frame new and more satisfactory rules for the prevention of contraband trade in the future, to abandon the principle of contraband of war altogether, thus allowing the oversea trade in neutral vessels between belligerents on the one hand and neutrals on the other, to continue during war without any restriction, subject only to its exclusion by blockade from an enemy's port. They are convinced that not only the interest of Great Britain, but the common interest of all nations will be found, on an unbiassed examination of the subject, to be served by the adoption of the course suggested.

26. In the event of the proposal not being favourably received, an endeavour should be made to frame a list of the articles that are to be regarded as contraband. Your efforts should then be directed to restricting that definition within the narrowest possible limits and upon lines which have the point of practical extinction as their ultimate aim.

27. If a definite list of contraband cannot be secured, you should support and, if necessary, propose regulations intended to insure that nations shall publish during peace the lists of articles they will regard as contraband during war, and that no change shall be made in the list on the outbreak of or during hostilities.

28. A list might be prepared and submitted for adoption by the Conference, specifying the articles which in no event shall fall within the enumeration of contraband, *e.g.*, mails, food-stuffs destined for places other than beleaguered

fortresses, and any raw materials required for the purposes of peaceful industry. It is essential to the interest of Great Britain that every effective measure necessary to protect the importation of food supplies and raw materials for peaceful industries should be accompanied by all the sanctions which the law of nations can supply.

29. His Majesty's Government would further be glad to see the right of search limited in every practicable way, *e.g.*, by the adoption of a system of Consular certificates declaring the absence of contraband from the cargo, and by the exemption of passenger and mail steamers upon defined routes, &c.

30. If an arrangement can be made for the abolition of contraband His Majesty's Government would be willing, for their part, that it should also extend to what are technically known as the "analogues of contraband," viz., the carriage of belligerent despatches and of persons in the naval and military services of a belligerent in cases where the rendering of such services by the neutral was not of such a kind or so great in extent as to identify the neutral vessel with the belligerent forces, and bring her within the definition of war-ship which His Majesty's Government are anxious to secure.

31. The object which His Majesty's Government have in view, as you are aware, is to limit, so far as may be, the restrictions that war entails upon legitimate neutral trade, and they feel that the extent to which this is possible in connection with the "analogues of contraband" is a matter that must be worked out in detail at the Conference.

32. Upon one point, however, they do desire to lay particular stress. The question of the carriage of enemy despatches cannot be entirely separated from that of mails in general, and they would welcome, and wish you to do all you can to secure, an arrangement under which mail packets or bags in transit on board a neutral ship, in accordance with the provisions of the Postal Conventions, should be inviolable, even though such mails should contain despatches for a belligerent, and the neutral vessel carrying such mails should not be subjected to any interference for so doing except in the case of her endeavouring to violate a blockade.

33. The subject of the treatment of interned belligerent vessels appears to be included in the Russian programme under the heading, "Régime auquel seraient soumis les bâtiments des belligérants dans les ports neutres." His Majesty's Government hold that while the war-ship of a belligerent taking refuge in a neutral port must, failing her departure within twenty-four hours, be interned, the question of her ultimate disposal is one which it would be best to leave to be dealt with under the terms of the Treaty of Peace. You will no doubt remember that one of the conditions of peace put forward by the Japanese Plenipotentiaries at the negotiations at Portsmouth, U.S.A., but afterwards abandoned, was the surrender to Japan of the Russian war-ships which had taken refuge at Kiao-chau, Shanghae, and Saigon, and which had there been interned.

34. As regards the sinking of neutral prizes, which gave rise to so much feeling in this country during the Russo-Japanese war, Great Britain has always maintained that the right to destroy is confined to enemy vessels only, and this view is favoured by other Powers. Concerning the right to destroy captured neutral vessels, the view hitherto taken by the greater Naval Powers has been that, in the event of it being impossible to bring in a vessel for adjudication, she must be released. You should urge the maintenance of the doctrine upon this subject which British prize courts have, for at least 200 years, held to be the law.

IV. *Additions to be made to the Convention of* 1899 *for the Adaptation to Naval Warfare of the Principles of the Geneva Convention of* 1864.

35. A Convention of fourteen articles, applying the principles of the Geneva Convention of 1864 to maritime warfare, was signed by the Powers represented at The Hague Conference of 1899, Article X (respecting the landing of the shipwrecked, wounded, or sick of a belligerent Power at a neutral port) being excluded at the time of ratification both by this country and the other Signatory Powers. The Russian programme contemplates supplementary provisions to the Convention, which are to deal only with the treatment of shipwrecked, wounded, or sick men, and with vessels employed for these purposes, and His Majesty's Government see no reason why they should withhold their consent to such provisions, if proposed at the Conference, provided that misuse of the privileges involved can be prevented.

36. In addition to the subjects mentioned in the Russian programme, His Majesty's Government believe that a discussion will be initiated by the Government of the United States on the question of the employment of armed force for the collection of ordinary contract debts due to the subjects or citizens of a Power by other Governments. This practice is viewed with great disfavour on the American Continent, and the objections to it have become embodied in a principle known as the "Drago Doctrine." His Majesty's Government consider that you may express a general adherence to the "Drago Doctrine," subject to the limitations mentioned in section 4 of the "Instructions to the United States' Delegates to the Third International Conference of American States," a copy of which was communicated to my predecessor by the American Ambassador on the 7th November, 1906. That is to say that, as a general principle, the debts of a State to the private subjects of another State are not to be collected by the employment of coercive measures in the nature of war, although occasions may, and do, occur when the non-payment of public debts is accompanied by such circumstances of fraud and injustice or violation of Treaty obligations as to justify the resort to force as a means of compelling payment. Each case, as it arises, must be considered on its merits, and the Government of the injured individual must decide in each case whether the

general rule has or has not been overstepped to a degree sufficient to justify or demand interference.

37. Another matter which may be raised at the Conference is the extension of the 3-mile limit as the normal boundary of territorial waters. His Majesty's Government are opposed to the extension of the 3-mile limit. It is now accepted by practically every country, and to enlarge such limit on account of the longer range of modern artillery or other cause would introduce uncertainty into what is now defined and settled, and would only increase the area over which the preservation of neutrality is obligatory upon a neutral Power, thus tending to diminish the sphere of action of the strongest navy, and to add to the difficulties of the weaker Powers.

38. The foregoing observations and directions will place you in possession generally of the views of His Majesty's Government on the various points set out in the Russian programme. More precise instructions will, if necessary, be furnished to you from time to time as occasion may require.

39. I inclose a Full Power under the Royal sign manual, which will enable you and your co-Plenipotentiaries to sign with or without reservations, and subject to ultimate ratification by the King, any Convention which may result as the outcome of your labours, and I request you to keep me fully and constantly informed of the proceedings of the Conference, which His Majesty's Government will watch with the greatest interest.

I am, &c.

(Signed) E. GREY.

ADDENDA AND ERRATA.

P. 79, line 16, for "American" read "United States" and so elsewhere on pages 79 and 80.

P. 112, Art. 19, 1907, and throughout references in the French text, for "*Voyez*" read "*Voir.*"

P. 164, note 1, add *La Deux. Confér.* T. II. pp. 34, 89, 121–135, 210–369, 377–404, 440–2, 572–589, 711–771.

P. 170, last line, for "M. de Mérey" read "M. Mérey de Kapos-Mère."

P. 184, note 1, add *La Deux. Confér.* T. II. pp. 130–144, 548–553, 916–925.

P. 199, line 1, for "should" read "must."

P. 202, note 1, add *La Deux. Confér.* T. III. pp. 163–179, 253–5.

P. 245, Art. 44, 1907, insert "by a belligerent" after "any compulsion."

P. 247, Art. 49, 1899, for "military necessities" read "the needs of the army."

P. 256, note 1, add *La Deux. Confér.* T. III. pp. 8–15, 101–148, 233–248.

P. 290, note 1, add *La Deux. Confér.* T. III. pp. 34–45, 51–98, 179–232, 256–288.

P. 294, last line, for "18" read "19."

P. 306, last line but one, for "these" read "they."

P. 315, note 1, second line, cancel "of this work."

P. 403, note 2, line 9, for "universal trading" read "universally binding."

P. 540, note 2, for "especially No. 5" read "especially No. 4."

INDEX

Arbitration, Compulsory, xii, 82
Arbitration, International, 170
  (See also under Pacific Settlement of
    International Disputes)
Arbitration, Permanent Court of
  (See under Permanent)
Arbitration, Summary, 155, 177
Armaments, limitation of, 75
Asphyxiating Gas, Declaration prohibiting
  use of, 493
Austrian proposals on
  Obligatory arbitration, 83
  Laws of land warfare, 266
  Conversion of merchant-ships, 319
  Local coasting boats, 403
Automatic Submarine Contact Mines, Con-
    vention regarding use of, 322
  First draft Convention, 333
  Discussion of, 334-7
  Second draft Convention, 337
  Colombian amendment, 337-8
  Defects of, 343-4, 520
  Difficulties of Examining Committee,
    332-3
  Mines in Straits, 340
  Proposals of Committee, 329-32
  Sir E. Satow's declaration, 340-1
  Signatories and reservations, 342
  Text of Convention, 322-7
  Time limit, 335, 339

Balloons, discharge of projectiles and explo-
  sives from, Declaration on, 488-91, 521
  Signatories to, 491
Beaumont, Admiral Sir L. A., 168
Belgian proposals on
  Capture of private property at sea, 80
  Opening of hostilities, 204
  Immunity of fishing boats, 403
  Immunity from capture of merchant
    seamen, 405
  Discharge of projectiles from balloons, 488
Belligerents, legal rights of, 263-5
Benckendorff, Count
  Circular of, 53-5, 76, 166, 184, 290, 328,
    352, 432, 457, 488
Bieberstein, Baron Marschall von
  (See under Marschall)
Blockade
  Anglo-American view on, 4
  Area of, 580-1

Blockade (cont.)
  Breach of, 581-2
  Commercial, 79
  defined by Conference of London, 572-4
  Notification of, 575-7
  Raising of, 577
Blockaded port, entrance into by neutral
  vessel, 574
Bombardment by Naval Forces in Time of
  War
  Authorities on, 352 (note)
  Discussions at the Hague, 354-6
  Signatories and reservations, 357
  Text of Convention, 346-52
  Undefended towns not to be bombarded,
    347, 354, 490, 520
Brazilian proposals on
  Capture of private property at sea, 80
  Submarine mines, 331
  International Prize Court, 441
  Neutral duties in maritime war, 465
  Judicial Arbitration Court, 513, 515
British proposals on
  Contraband, 4
  Limitation of armaments, 75
  Obligatory arbitration, 82
  Destruction of neutral prizes, 90
  Commissions of Inquiry, 169
  Days of grace, 303, 305
  Definition of ships of war, 316
  Conversion of merchant-ships, 317
  Submarine mines, 329
  Immunity from capture of merchant
    seamen, 405
  International Prize Court, 433
  Neutral duties in maritime war, 458, 461,
    462, 463, 464, 467, 469, 472, 475,
    477
Brussels Draft Declaration, 257-8, 278-80
Bullets, Declaration on expanding, 495-7
  Signatories to, 497
  Explosive (See Declaration of St Peters-
    burg), 5

Capture, Restrictions on, in Maritime War
  Text of Convention, 395, 401-6
  Authorities on, 401 (note)
  Postal correspondence, 401
  Fishing boats, etc., 402
  Scientific expeditions, 405
  Crews of merchant-ships, 405, 431

Casablanca affair, 175
Chinese conundrums, 205
Choate, Mr, 79, 167, 434, 435, 516
Coal, supply of to belligerents, 475
Coast Warfare, 352–3
  Rules for, 353
  (See also under Bombardment)
Colombian proposals on
  Submarine mines, 337
Commencement of Hostilities
  Authorities on, 202 (note)
  Period of notice rejected, 204
  Report of Second Committee on, 202–5
  Signatory Powers, 205
  Text of Convention on, 198–201
Commissions of Inquiry, International, 107, 167
  North Sea Commission, 167–70
Compensation
  Declaration of London on, 609–12
Conferences
  at Brussels, 1874, 257
  Geneva, 1864, 12
  1906, 34
  Hague Peace, 1899 and 1907, 39–59
  Hague—on Hospital Ships, 392
  London, Naval, 320, 523, 567
  at St Petersburg, 7
Continuous voyage, 586, 587
Contraband of war, 4
  Articles enumerated as, 546, 582–6
  Articles exempted, 550, 585
  defined, 582
  Destination of, 586–90
  on neutral vessels, 592
  Proportion of cargo condemned, 591, 599
Contract Debts, recovery of
  Argentine reservation to Convention, 192–3
  Compulsory arbitration for, 196, 519
  Events leading to, 184–197
  Meaning of "dettes contractuelles," 193–5
  Signatory states, 190–2
  Text of Convention respecting the limitation of Employment of Force for, 180–3
  (See also under Drago doctrine)
Conventions
  Final Acts of International Peace Conferences, Text of, 60–71
  Geneva, Text of Convention of 1864, 8–12
  Additional Articles, 14–17
  Text of Convention of 1906, 18–35
Conventions, draft
  Proposed Judicial Arbitration Court, Text, 498–509
Conventions of the Hague Conferences of 1899 and 1907
  I. Convention for the Pacific Settlement of International Disputes, Text, 96–164

II. Recovery of Contract Debts, Text, 180–3
III. Relative to the Commencement of Hostilities, Text, 198–201
IV. Concerning the Laws and Customs of War on Land, Text, 206–55
V. Concerning Neutral Powers and Persons in Land Warfare, Text, 281–9
VI. Concerning Enemy Merchant-ships at the Outbreak of Hostilities, Text, 295–9
VII. Concerning Conversion of Merchant-ships into Warships, Text, 308–12
VIII. Concerning Automatic Submarine Contact Mines, Text, 322–7
IX. Concerning Bombardment by Naval Forces in Time of War, Text, 346–52
X. The Geneva Convention and Maritime Warfare, Text, 358–81
XI. Concerning Restrictions on the Exercise of the Right of Capture in Maritime War, Text, 393–40
XII. Concerning the Establishment of an International Prize Court, Text, 407–29
XIII. Concerning Neutral Rights and Duties in Maritime War, Text, 445–56
Conventions on
  Hospital Ships, 392–4
Conversion of merchant vessels into warships
  (See under Merchant-ships)
Convoy
  Declaration of London on, 561, 606–8
Corea, foreign relations of, 35–6
  (See also under Geneva Convention, 1906)
Crews of captured enemy merchantmen, immunity of, 405
Cuban proposals on
  Laws of land warfare, 26

Danish proposals on
  Submarine Cables, 271
Days of grace (See under Merchant-ships)
Declaration
  of London, 1909, Text, 540–66
  Report on, 567–613
  of Paris, 1856, 1–2
  of St Petersburg, 1868, 5–7
Declarations
  Brussels Draft, 273–80
Declarations of the Hague Conferences of 1899 and 1907
  I. Declaration prohibiting the Discharge of Projectiles and Explosives from Balloons, Text, 484–7
  II. On Asphyxiating or Deleterious Gases, Text, 491–2
  III. Prohibiting use of Expanding Bullets, Text, 494–5
"Dettes contractuelles," meaning of, 193

Disarmament proposals, 75
Dogger Bank affair, 44, 167–8
Drago doctrine, connection with Recovery of
    Contract Debts, 184, 187
    Connection with Monroe doctrine, 173,
        197
    distinguished from Calvo doctrine, 186
    United States proposition, 188
Dunant, H. and G. Moynier, 12
Dutch proposals on
    Capture of private property at sea, 80
    Declaration of war, 204
    Days of grace, 302
    Submarine mines, 331, 340

Enemy character, 571
    Declaration of London on, 602–6

Fisher, Admiral Sir John, 493
Fishing boats exempt from capture, 402–6,
    520
Forced guides, 266–9
Foreign Enlistment Act, 1870, 466
French proposals on
    Capture of private property at sea, 80
    Commissions of Inquiry, 169
    Summary arbitration, 177
    Declaration of war, 203
    Bombardments, 270
    Neutral powers in land warfare, 290
    Days of grace, 302
Fry, Sir Edward, 45, 57, 77, 169, 170, 176,
    385, 389, 432, 434, 435, 516
    on International Prize Court, 521, 523
Fuel, supply of to belligerent ships of war,
    475

Geneva Conference
    (See under Conferences)
Geneva Convention, 1864, Text of, 8
    States signing or adhering to, 12
    Conference of 1906 to revise, 13, 36
Geneva Convention, 1906, Text of, 18
    British reservations, 36, 38
    Corea, position of, 35–6
    Sick and wounded, provision for, 37, 522
    States ratifying, 35
Geneva Convention and Maritime Warfare
    Abuse of hospital ships, 385
    Application of Convention, 391
    Assistance by merchant-ships, 386
    British reservation on Art. 12, 389
    Conventions of 1899, 1907, 382
    Inviolability of hospital staff, 387
    Inviolability of sick and wounded, 387
    Rescue by neutral war-vessel, 390
    Rules for hospital ships, 383–5
    Search for shipwrecked and wounded,
        391
    Sick bays on warships, 385
    Signatories, 391
    Surrender to warship of sick and wounded
        (Art. 12), 387
    Text of Convention, 358–81

German proposals on
    Neutrals in belligerent territory, 85, 293,
        294
    Laws of land warfare, 261, 263, 265
    Submarine mines, 331, 336
    Geneva Convention and maritime war-
        fare, 382, 386
    Postal correspondence, 401
    International Prize Court, 430
    Neutral duties in maritime war, 469

Hague Conference,
    Work of future Conferences, 93, 525–6
Hague Conferences, Final Acts of, 72
    Accession of non-signatory Powers, 73
    Signatory Powers of, 74
Hague Peace Conference, 1899
    British Delegation, 42 (note)
    Declarations of, 50
    Initiative of Russia, 39
    Final Act of, 41–2, 72
    Powers represented at, 40, 42
    Results of, 42, 50, 164–6
    Subjects for discussion by, 40
    United States Delegation, 42 (note)
    Vœux of, 50, 75, 78
Hague Peace Conference, 1907
    Authorities on, 51
    British Delegation, 57, instructions to,
        614–24
    Committees, work of, 58
    Count Benckendorff's Circular, 53
    Difficulties of, 523–5
    Powers represented at, 74
    Procedure, 174–7, 524
    Proposed by President Roosevelt, 51
    Results of, 518
    Summary of work of, 518–22
    United States Delegation, 57
    Vœux of, 75, 82, 85
Hospital ships, 383–6
    Distinguishing marks of, 384
    Exemption from port dues, 392–4
    Flags of neutral, 383
    Lights on, 384
    not contraband, 585
    (See also under Geneva Convention and
        Maritime Warfare)

Immunity of enemy private property at sea, 78
    Proposal of United States for, 79
    Other proposals, 80
    Result of discussion at the Hague in
        1907, 81
Institut de Droit International, proposals on
    Declaration of war, 203
    Submarine mines, 332, 344
    International Prize Court, 432
    Right of innocent passage, 467
    Destruction of prizes at sea, 90
    Submarine cables, 271
    Laws of war on land, 258
    Bombardment of coast towns, 353
    Departure from neutral ports, 473

Instructions to British Delegation, 615
International Disputes, Pacific Settlement of
    Authorities on, 164 (note)
    Reservation to Convention, 179
    Signatories to, 178-9
    Text of Convention, 33-164
Italian proposals on
    Obligatory arbitration, 83
    Conversion of merchant-ships, 318
    Submarine mines, 330
    Immunity of ships engaged on scientific
        missions, 403
    Discharge of projectiles from balloons,
        488-9
    Contraband, 4

Japanese leases, case of the, 48
Japanese proposals on
    Laws of land warfare, 262
    Internment of wounded on neutral terri-
        tory, 292
    Submarine mines, 331
    Neutral duties in maritime war, 459, 463,
        469, 472, 480
Judicial Arbitration Court, proposed, 85
    Composition of, 514
    Draft Convention
        discussed, 513
        Origin of, 509
        Text of, 498-509
        Russian draft, 511
        United States draft, 512
    Judges, proposed method of choosing, 515
    Opposition of Brazilian delegate, 516-7
    Partial acceptance of, 516
    Proceedings in Examining Committee, 513
    Reservations, 517

Letters of Marque, 3
Lieber, Dr F., prepares Instructions for U.S.
    Army, 256
    Value of Instructions, 257-8
Limitation of armaments, 75-8
London, Naval Conference of, 4, 320, 522, 523
    Bases of discussion at, 568-9
    Declaration concerning laws of naval
        warfare, 569
    Origin of, 567-8
    Preamble of Declaration, 570
    Programme suggested, 568
London, Naval Conference of, on
    Conversion of merchant- into warships,
        320, 571
    Enemy character of property, 571

Mahan, Captain A. T., 42, 387
    on asphyxiating gas, 493
"Marcy Amendment," 3
Marschall von Bieberstein, Baron, attitude
    on exemption from capture of private
        property at sea, 79
    on compulsory arbitration, 83
    on submarine mines, 335, 342
    on International Prize Court, 432

Martens, M. de, 169, 193, 258-9, 315
Merchant-ships, conversion of, into warships,
    Authorities on, 312 (note)
    Conference of London on, 320, 571
    Italian compromise, 318
    Problems for the Conference, 315-6
    Problems unsolved, 316-20
    Seizure of cargo, 305
    Seizure of merchant-ships constructed for
        conversion into warships, 305, 520
    Signatory Powers and reservations, 307
    Terms of Convention, 315-6
    Text of Convention, 308-12
Merchant-ships of Enemy at Outbreak of
    Hostilities
    Days of grace, development of practice,
        300-4, 519
    Ships on high seas, 304-6, 519
    Text of Convention, 295-9
Military necessities, xii
Milutine, General, his attitude towards ex-
    plosive bullets, 7
Mines, Submarine
    considered by Institut de Droit Inter-
        national, 344-5
    dangerous to neutrals, 328
    in straits, 340
    Kinds of, 328
    (See also under Automatic Submarine
        Contact Mines)
Monroe doctrine, 173, 193, 197
Mouravieff, Count, Circular of
    summoning Hague Conference, 39, 40,
        75, 258, 488
"Muscat Dhows" case, 48, 172

Naval Warfare, Code of
    Beginnings of, made by Second Hague
        Conference, 92
Naval Warfare, Laws and Customs of
    Discussion of at Second Peace Conference,
        87
Neutral flag, Transfer to
    Declaration of London on, 600-2
Neutrality
    Neutral Powers and Persons in land
        warfare, 85-6
    Authorities on, 290 (note)
    Signatory Powers, 294
    Text of Convention on, 281-9
Neutrality Regulations of Gt Britain, 458,
    476 (note)
Neutral jurisdiction, fitting out or arming of
    ships in, 465-6
Neutral Persons in land warfare, 293-4
Neutral Ports and Waters
    Belligerent prizes in, 478-9
    Duration of stay of belligerents in, 469-72
    Number of belligerent warships in, 472
    Order of departure from, 472
    Refusal to quit, 480
    Repairs in, 473-5
    Supply of provisions and fuel in, 475-7
    Three months' rule, 477

Neutral Powers in land warfare
  Position of " occupied " territory, 291
  Rights and duties of, 290–4
Neutral prizes, Destruction of, 4, 89, 478
  Discussion at Second Peace Conference, 89
  Declaration of London, 557, 597
Neutral property on enemy ships, 3
Neutral Rights and Duties in Maritime War
  Authorities on, 457
  Communication of neutral regulations, 481
  Convention, preamble to, 481
  Development of law of, 457
  Governing principle of, 461
  Impartiality of treatment, 466
  Increase of armament in neutral waters, 475
  Japanese proposals, 480
  Neutral pilots, 469
  Neutral vigilance, 480
  Passage of belligerent ships through territorial waters, 467–8
  Proposals at Hague Conference, 458
  Questionnaire, 458–61
  Signatories and reservations, 482
  Value of Convention, 482
  Violations of neutrality, 461, 464–80
  (See also under Neutral Ports)
Neutral states, export of arms from, 464
Neutral territory
  as base of belligerent operations, 464
  Belligerents interned and wounded tended in, 292
  Prize Courts on, 463
  Railway material in, 294
  (See also under Wireless telegraphy)
Neutral war-vessels, rescue by, 390
Neutrals, supply of instruments of warfare by, 464

Ottley, Captain, 57, 302, 303, 330, 337 (note), 354, 356
Owner's property on captured vessels, 609

Pacific Settlement of International Disputes
  Arbitration procedure, 174
  Arbitration system of, 170
  Authorities on, 164 (note)
  First Conference, work of, 164
  Good offices and mediation, 167
  Second Conference, object of, 166
  Summary arbitration, 177
  Text of Convention, 33–164
  Value of Convention, 43
Pan-American Conference, Third resolution regarding collection of public debts, 187
Paris, Declaration of, 1
Passage, right of innocent, 340, 467
Pauncefote, Sir Julian, 41 (note), 42 (note), 50, 164
Permanent Court of Arbitration at the Hague, cases before, 44–8

Permanent Court of Arbitration at the Hague (*cont.*)
  Choice of language used before, 174
  Cost of, 177, 511
  Established by Convention for Pacific Settlement of International Disputes, 43
  Judges acting as advocates before, 175
  Members of, 171 and note, 170–4
  Objections to, 177, 512
  Proceedings of, 174–7
  Regulations of Convention concerning, 170–4
" Peterburg and Smolensk " incident, 314
" Pious Funds " case, 44–6, 171, 172, 177
Port dues, exemption of hospital ships from, Convention on, 392–4
Porter, General, 57, 188, 190, 193, 331
Portuguese proposals on
  Immunity of fishing boats, 403
  Obligatory arbitration, 82
Postal correspondence, protection of in war, 401–2
Prisoners of war, Bureau for information relative to, 43 and note, 262
Prisoners, internment of, 261–3
  Payment of for work done, 262
Privateering, Declaration of Paris on, 2, 312
  Prussian proposals on, 313
Private property, immunity from capture at sea
  Discussion at Second Peace Conference, 78
  United States proposal, 79
  Other proposals, 80
  Result of discussions, 81
Prize Court, International
  Appeals to from National, 436–7
  Competence of, 436
  Constitution of, 439
  Constitutional difficulties regarding establishment of, 443
  Convention on, 435
  Draft proposals for, 432–5
  Importance of, 521
  Law to be administered by, 437
  Need of, 431
  Questionnaire, 433
  Signatories, 442
Prize courts on neutral territory, 463
Prizes in neutral ports, 478
Projectiles and explosives, Discharge of from balloons (See under Balloons)
Public opinion and international law, xiii

Reay, Lord, 316, 317, 489
" Red Cross," when used, 36
  has no religious significance, 37
Renault, M., 10, 72, 302, 302, 318, 321 (note), 382, 387, 388, 389
Rescue of shipwrecked by neutral warships, 390
Rescue of shipwrecked by neutral merchant-ships, 387

Reservations of the Powers on signing the Conventions of the Peace Conferences
First Conference, 528-31
Second Conference, 532-7
Resistance to search, Declaration of London on, 608
Bojdestvensky, Admiral, 169
Roosevelt, President, 51, 53, 184
Russian proposals on
Explosive bullets, 7
Limitation of armaments, 75
Destruction of neutral prizes, 89
Commissions of Inquiry, 169
Laws of land warfare, 267
Days of grace, 302
Submarine mines, 332
Neutral duties in maritime warfare, 458, 463, 469, 476, 480
Discharge of projectiles from balloons, 488
Judicial Arbitration Court, 511

Satow, Sir Ernest, 4, 90, 335, 336, 337, 339, 340-1, 405, 475
Scientific missions, ships engaged in, 405
Search, resistance to, 562, 608
Sick and wounded, provisions of Geneva Convention for, 37, 387-8, 522
"Smolensk and Peterburg" incident, 314
Spanish proposals on
Submarine mines, 331
Neutral duties in maritime war, 458, 477
St Petersburg, Conference at on projectiles, 7
Declaration of, 5
Straits, right of passage, 340, 467-8
Submarine cables, 271-2
Swedish proposals on Days of grace, 302

Three months' rule, 477

Tornielli, Count, 458, 462, 475, 480
Triana, M., 337, 338
Twenty-four hours' rule, 469, 470, 471, 473

United States, Instructions for army, 256
Neutrality Acts, 466
United States proposals on
Summons of Second Peace Conference, 51
Immunity of enemy private property at sea, 78
Recovery of contract debts, 188
Submarine mines, 331
Judicial Arbitration Court, 512, 516
Unneutral Service, Declaration of London on, 593-7

Venezuela, blockaded for recovery of debt, 46-7, 184-5
Voluntary Aid Societies, 13, 36
Volunteer Navies, 312-15

War, declaration of
Convention regulating, 198
Modern practice regarding, 202-3
War on Land, Laws and Customs of
Authorities on, 256 (note)
Codification of Laws on, 13, 256 and note
Signatory Powers to Convention, 272
Texts of Conventions on, 206-55
Discussion of by Hague Conference, 258, 259
Conventions on, 259
Changes in Convention in 1907, 260
Changes in Regulations in 1907, 261-8
Washington, Treaty of, 306, 464, 465, 475, 480, 483
Wireless telegraphy stations, 291-2

COSIMO

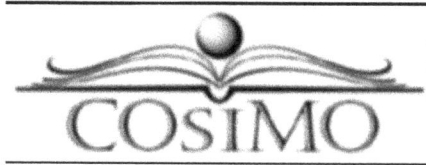

COSIMO is a specialty publisher of books and publications that inspire, inform, and engage readers. Our mission is to offer unique books to niche audiences around the world.

COSIMO BOOKS publishes books and publications for innovative authors, nonprofit organizations, and businesses. **COSIMO BOOKS** specializes in bringing books back into print, publishing new books quickly and effectively, and making these publications available to readers around the world.

COSIMO CLASSICS offers a collection of distinctive titles by the great authors and thinkers throughout the ages. At **COSIMO CLASSICS** timeless works find new life as affordable books, covering a variety of subjects including: Business, Economics, History, Personal Development, Philosophy, Religion & Spirituality, and much more!

COSIMO REPORTS publishes public reports that affect your world, from global trends to the economy, and from health to geopolitics.

FOR MORE INFORMATION CONTACT US AT
INFO@COSIMOBOOKS.COM

➤ if you are a book lover interested in our current catalog of books

➤ if you represent a bookstore, book club, or anyone else interested in special discounts for bulk purchases

➤ if you are an author who wants to get published

➤ if you represent an organization or business seeking to publish books and other publications for your members, donors, or customers.

COSIMO BOOKS ARE ALWAYS
AVAILABLE AT ONLINE BOOKSTORES

VISIT COSIMOBOOKS.COM
BE INSPIRED, BE INFORMED

Lightning Source UK Ltd.
Milton Keynes UK
UKHW010733290920
370728UK00001B/7